CW00430548

BEASTS IN THE CELLAR
THE EXPLOITATION FILM CAREER OF TONY TENSER

First edition published by FAB Press, June 2005

FAB Press
7 Farleigh
Ramsden Road
Godalming
Surrey
GU7 1QE
England, U.K.

www.fabpress.com

Text copyright © 2005 John Hamilton.
The moral rights of the author have been asserted.

Edited and Designed by Harvey Fenton,
with thanks to Francis Brewster for production assistance.

This Volume copyright © FAB Press 2005.

World Rights Reserved.

No part of this book may be reproduced or transmitted in any form or by any means, electronic or mechanical,
including photocopying, recording, or by any information storage and retrieval system, without the prior written
permission of the Publisher.

Copyright of the promotional artwork reproduced in these pages is the property of the companies concerned.
These illustrations are reproduced here in the spirit of publicity, and with the gracious permission of Tony Tenser.

Cover illustration (hardback edition)
Adapted from the British quad poster artwork used to promote the theatrical re-release of **Repulsion**.

Front cover illustration (paperback edition)
Adapted from the Italian poster artwork used to promote the theatrical release of **Witchfinder General**.

Back cover illustrations (paperback edition)
top: Promotional artwork for **Primitive London**.
centre: Barbara Steele, resplendent as the mistress of Satanic ceremonies, in **Curse of the Crimson Altar**.
bottom: Peter Cushing as mad scientist Emmanuel Hildern in **The Creeping Flesh**.

Frontispiece illustration
Nita Lorraine wearing an astonishing costume in this publicity photograph for **Curse of the Crimson Altar**.

A CIP catalogue record for this book is available from the British Library.

hardback:
ISBN 1903254264
paperback:
ISBN 1903254272

A FAB PRESS PUBLICATION

BEASTS
in the
CELLAR

The
Exploitation
Film Career
of
TONY
TENSER

John Hamilton

Author's Acknowledgements

No book can be written without the assistance and generosity of a number of individuals and organisations, and this is certainly no exception. I would like to express my gratitude to the research facilities and support provided by the British Film Institute library in Stephen Street, London, and in particular Julian Grainger. Similarly, my research was aided by David Barrett at the British Board of Film Classification in Soho Square, London, and the staff at the BBC Written Archive Centre in Reading. My thanks also are due to the Manchester Festival of Fantastic Films for allowing me access to their video tapes, to Marc Morris, Peter Nicolson, Gary Parfitt, Carl Daft at Blue Underground, and Richard Dacre of Flashbacks, all of whom contributed towards the selection of stills, and to Jonathan Sothcott, who provided many of the contacts I needed. After seeing an early draft of the manuscript, Allan Bryce has enthusiastically supported this book in the pages of 'The Dark Side' magazine, providing us with a great deal of advance publicity. The work you currently have in your hands would not exist at all if it were not for Harvey Fenton at FAB Press, who is largely responsible for fostering my interest in the genre over the years, and whose remarkable editorial and design efforts pulled this book together. I must also highlight the work of Francis Brewster at FAB Press, whose commitment and attention to detail is truly inspiring. I would like to acknowledge the editors and journalists of the trade papers 'CinemaTV Today' and 'Kine Weekly', without which any serious study of sixties British cinema is incomplete, and I would also like to pay tribute to Denis Meikle, author of 'A History of Horrors', by far the best book ever written on a British Film company, and the man who inspired me to research the subject that led to this book. I have endeavoured as much as possible to ensure recognition is given to all sources; my humble apologies to anyone I may have inadvertently neglected to mention.

I am extremely grateful to everyone who offered help and encouragement throughout the long writing process, in particular all the industry luminaries who allowed me free access to their time and records, and shared their memories about their work. I would like to single out the following for special thanks: Patrick Allen, Michael Armstrong, John Bown, Nicola Bown, Julie Ege, Freddie Francis, Sally Geeson, Renee Glynn, Richard Gordon, Pamela Green, Piers Haggard, Nicky Henson, Bernard Kay, Sybilla Kay, Christopher Lee, Stanley Long, Christopher Neame, Ian Ogilvy, Gerry O'Hara, John Scott, George Sewell, Graham Stark, Stephen Weeks, Graham and Pat Whitworth, Anneke Wills, Barbara Windsor and Norman Wisdom. I am particularly indebted to Spike Milligan, Michael Ripper and Vernon Sewell, all of whom have since passed on, but their generosity and energy made me regret not getting to know them sooner.

Finally I would like to acknowledge the contribution of two people without whom this book would not have been possible. My wife Alison, whose unswerving support sustained me through long nights at the laptop, and Tony Tenser, who was a never-ending source of detail, anecdotes and humour. Neither of them ever lost faith that it would come together.

I would like to dedicate this book to my own little 'horrors', Alec, Emma and Amy.

Author's Note:
Tenser's career is notable for a number of reasons, not least of which is the preponderance of titles by which many of his films are known. Wherever possible the titles and dates quoted relate to the film's British release, unless otherwise stated. Original titles - by which I mean those titles that relate to the UK release - are shown in italics. Thus in cases such as *Curse of the Crimson Altar*, which was known variously as 'Dreams in the Witch House' and 'The Crimson Cult' during production, only the British release title is identified by italics. In the debate over which title is appropriate for *Witchfinder General*, 'The Witchfinder General' or indeed 'Matthew Hopkins Witchfinder General,' I have taken the obvious option of referring to the original script, production material and publicity material, all of which refer to the film only as *Witchfinder General*, as indeed does correspondence and writings from the cast and crew.

Contents

'When, nearly fifty years ago, I started out as a cinema manager and later a distributor and producer, the film industry was experiencing some of the greatest changes in its history. Every aspect of the film business and everyone working in it was affected by the rise of television, widespread use of colour film, the later relaxation in censorship and so on. John Hamilton's book captures in considerable detail the ups and downs of the industry during a very challenging and exciting time. For my part I consider myself extremely fortunate to have been involved in an industry I loved during this period. I was always happy in the background and I never for one moment considered I was making films for anything other than profit, certainly not for posterity and I wouldn't say I played a greater role than many, many others. I now find myself humbled to be the subject of these chronicles.'

Tony Tenser, June 2005

Celluloid Goldmine

Exploitation: *cash in on, develop, make capital out of, make use of, profit by, profit from, trade on, use, utilise, work on* - Oxford University Press.

In 1960, London's Soho was the recognised centre of the British film industry; all the Hollywood majors and those few British production companies which survived the Fifties jostled for space amongst the strip clubs and cafes in and around Wardour Street. As American dollars flooded into the capital, the back streets and alleyways of W1 became occupied by the offices of independent producers, most of whom were armed with little more than a desk and some lurid posters. These entrepreneurs were the foundation of the much-maligned British exploitation industry; their movies were cheaply made, nearly always contained gratuitous sex or horror, and frequently the only creative thing they had going for them was the poster. The term 'exploitation' derives from the need for the films to focus attention on particular elements to the exclusion of everything else; typically a monster, a faded star or a well-endowed leading lady. Frequently all three! These films were sold indiscriminately and forgotten. Hardly the environment for the faint-hearted, and not too many producers lasted the course. However, one man not only survived but positively thrived. That man was of course Tony Tenser.

Tenser was singled out by Robert Murphy in the British Film Institute study 'Sixties British Cinema' as, 'the most imaginative of the exploitation producers.' Despite providing a platform for directors of the calibre of Michael Reeves, Roman Polanski and Robert Hartford-Davis, Tenser was never interested in the 'craft' of filmmaking; rather his skill lay in setting up and selling films. Michael Armstrong, one of many young directors who got their break under Tenser recognised this: 'Tony's great love was the press conferences, the publicity and the selling side. He loved the publicity side, to him that was the film industry.'

Throughout his remarkable career Tenser consistently demonstrated an inherent understanding of what the public would or wouldn't pay to go and see, or in some cases how films could be made to look like what the public would pay to go and see. Confident in his ability to market films, Tenser could drive a project from an idea on a page to a film on general release in a matter of months, and while these films may have been thrown together on the cheap they were always on the right side of respectability, just. 'I didn't make sex films,' Tenser stresses, 'You can see more in the newspapers than you ever saw

left:
This British advertising campaign book for **Curse of the Crimson Altar** is typical of the brash, confident style employed by Tenser's companies throughout his filmmaking career.

opposite:
Master showman Tony Tenser, photographed in 1970.

WATCH IT!

IT'S A TIGON

They're strange creatures.
They disappear and
make films. Then
suddenly they're upon
you! Look what's in
the Tigon's lair—

" THE SORCERERS "
" BLOOD BEAST FROM HELL "
" WITCHFINDER GENERAL "

TIGON PICTURES LTD.
205 WARDOUR STREET,
LONDON, W.1
Tel. 01-734 9514
Cables: TIGONPIX LONDON, W.1

above:
A typical Tenser press
advert from 1968.

below:
Tony Tenser relaxing
during the filming of
Witchfinder General.

in my films. I didn't make sleaze, I was never a so-called 'sleaze merchant' - I made exploitation films.'

Unlike most of his contemporaries, Tenser never hesitated to plough his own money back into the company; he needed to be successful to ensure that he could make the next film. Again and again as one looks through Tenser's back catalogue it is easy to understand his own simple assessment of his work; 'I'd rather be ashamed of a film that was making money than proud of one that wasn't.'

In choosing to study the films of a producer rather than those of a director or a writer, this book isn't really about subjects, styles or even genres; the movies are too diverse to be categorised that easily. The accumulated filmography of Tony Tenser contains some significant films by important filmmakers but it certainly doesn't reflect the development of British cinema. There is no common theme or style to Tony Tenser movies - they weren't even all low budget. An out and out 'nudie' flick, *Naked - As Nature Intended*, cost £5,000. A decade later Tenser made *Hannie Caulder* for over £600,000! Tenser's filmography includes comedies, sex films, science-fiction, westerns and even a children's film, *Black Beauty* - though true to form the critics lambasted it for being too violent -

and of course, he made horror movies. Tony Tenser and his company, Tigon, remain synonymous with some of the most imaginative of the British horror movies, in particular those of Michael Reeves: *The Sorcerers* and *Witchfinder General*. But while Tenser was a fan of the genre and in particular Boris Karloff, he had never considered himself a horror filmmaker. It isn't even true to claim that Tenser's motivation was always money, *Miss Julie* for example, a filmed adaptation of the Royal Shakespeare Company's Strindberg play was only one of the curious films to bear the Tigon marque.

'Beasts in the Cellar' is about films which were shamelessly commercial and frequently promoted and sold with more imagination than went into making them. These films have only one thing in common - they were produced by a remarkable man. In his definitive study of the British sex industry, 'Doing Rude Things', David McGillivray, a leading contributor to exploitation movies in his own right, made the statement; 'The reason that that the British industry is in the state that it is in today is because it has no-one like Tony Tenser to kick it up the backside.' By the time you finish reading this book hopefully you will understand why McGillivray chose to single out Tenser for such attention.

Chapter One

'The Greatest, Nudest Film of All!'

- (Original British Press Release, *Naked - As Nature Intended*)

When Samuel Anthony Tenser was just a small child, he vividly remembers sitting in the old Gable cinema, in the heart of London's East End, watching Bela Lugosi lighting up the screen as the immortal Count Dracula. 'I spent half the film under the seat, I was terrified!' he recalls. 'That was when I first got interested in this type of film, but as children we only had cinema and I went to see everything. I loved all films, especially Westerns.'

Tony Tenser was born in London, one of seven children, on the 10th of August 1920. His parents were Lithuanian immigrants struggling to make a living in the East End rag trade during the depression of the inter-war years. Taking a job even on the lowest rung of the British film industry was way beyond the reach of a working class family like the Tensers. Tony was an extremely bright child, and he overcame the poverty of his background to win a charitable scholarship to grammar school. The family's circumstances were however such that whatever ambitions he had for himself took second place. He left school at the age of sixteen and helped to support his family by taking uninspiring employment as a labourer in a lumberyard in Bethnal Green.

With admirable commitment and ambition he worked his way up to manager by the outbreak of the Second World War. After serving as a repair technician in the RAF, Tenser returned to civilian life looking for a job. By then he was 25 years old. An uncle - also in the family's tailoring trade - made uniforms for the ABC cinema chain and pointed out that they were recruiting cinema managers. Tenser applied and was duly employed as a trainee.

These were the days when each individual cinema manager was in the driving seat as far as his own territory was concerned, and the success or failure of a film could hinge on his ability to create interest in the product at a local level. Tenser had that ability, and swiftly became one of ABC's brightest stars. In fact his gift for knowing what would catch the public's attention won him the title of Cinema Manager of the Year for 1949.

Tenser's natural instinct for selling and showmanship, mixed with driving ambition and an inherent work ethic made it inevitable that he would outgrow cinema management very quickly. He was soon thinking about the jump from exhibition into distribution. In the early 50s he took a job in the publicity department of a small company called International Film Distributors, travelling the country helping local managers to maximise the publicity potential of their movies. He was soon running the department.

Tenser's next move was another natural progression into the job of head of publicity for Miracle Films, an independent distributor specialising in European features. Their biggest success was with the early Brigitte Bardot movies, and Tenser was given a free hand when it came to selling the French starlet to the great British public. 'We had a film called *The Light Across the Street* [*La lumière d'en face* (1955)] and I saw the film, went through the stills blurbs and came up with the phrase, "sex kitten." That really took off!' If he had achieved nothing else in his lifetime, Tenser would have been guaranteed immortality as the man who coined the sex kitten tag and launched a million tabloid headlines.[1]

Promoting these films was natural for Tenser, who had found the perfect outlet for his creativity. 'We had another film called *...And God Created Woman* [*Et Dieu... créa la femme (1956)*], and I added the punch line, "but the Devil shaped Bardot." The film did very well but then receipts started to fall. I went to see a chap called Michael Klinger who ran the Gargoyle Club, one of the many strip clubs in London in those days. We had a chat and I asked if I could borrow some of his girls to do a demonstration through the West End of London at Friday lunchtime,

below:
Michael Klinger, Tenser's business partner and joint founder of the Compton Cinema Club.

above:
London's first and most successful private cinema, the Compton Cinema Club, as seen during the early Sixties.

below:
Trade ad for the Compton Club. Note Tenser's distinctive tagline for **Paris Playgirls**.

┌COMPTON┐
CINEMA
Tel.: GER 1522
OLD COMPTON STREET
W.1.

TOP FEATURE FILMS
COMPLETELY UNABRIDGED

at present showing
BELINDA LEE in
"The WILD and the
WANTON"
coming shortly
3 Swedish girls in Paris,
Blonde Angels . Fierce Brunet-
tes... bursting with the torrent:
of a gay and impetuous love.
they become...
"PARIS PLAYGIRLS"
Members only

COMPTON CINEMA
60/62 Old Compton Street, W.1
I desire to become a member of the
COMPTON CINEMA CLUB, subject to
its rules and byelaws. I am over 21.
10/- enclosed.
Name ....
Address ....
....
Signature ....
Age .... Date ....
CFR

protesting against Bardot putting strippers out of business! That's what we did, eight girls and two Afghan hounds!' The police were bemused, the press loved it and receipts went through the roof. It also marked the beginning of a close association between Tenser and Klinger.

By a curious coincidence Michael Klinger, the son of an immigrant Pole, also came from the East End of London. Unlike Tenser however, young Klinger had a trade - not that he got much opportunity to practice it though. He had qualified at the Brixton School of Building as a mechanical engineer, but would go through a dizzying list of occupations before finding himself in the world of London's Soho clubs.

Large, affable, and a very shrewd businessman, Klinger was a man with great ambition and energy. Tony remembers him with a great deal of affection. 'Klinger was a Machiavellian character, a smaller version of Lew Grade. Like myself, he was Jewish but unlike me he never lost his East End accent. I remember he called everybody "son." He called his own father son! We would be walking through the back streets of Soho. His father's name was Gerswin and he had a flat above one of the shops. Michael would shout out, "Gerswin! How are you, son?" He was full of fun and was a good partner.'

Klinger's clubs - he ran the Nell Gwynn as well as the Gargoyle - were in the centre of what passed for the British film industry in those days, and it was frequently used for promotional events. The Miss Cinema

competition was held in the Gargoyle annually, as well as informal parties and more formal film get-togethers. Movers and shakers like Hammer's James Carreras were regular patrons, and it was inevitable that the glamour of the film business would rub off on the proprietor.

At Miracle, Tenser would use the club and its seemingly endless supply of publicity-hungry young ladies for his various promotional stunts, and the two men soon struck up a rapport on the subject they were both passionate about: films. Klinger made no secret of the fact that he wanted a way out of the club scene and into the film business. He had plenty of contacts but lacked the experience or the capital.

At that time the British film industry was still struggling to emerge from one of its interminable recessions. Film production had all but been wiped out in 1955 when even relatively lean and efficient companies like Hammer shelved practically their whole production schedules and/or moved over to television. On the distribution side things were a little better, in so far as there was always Hollywood product to rely on, but the market was showing itself to be extremely vulnerable to the social impact of television. In 1946 there were 1,635 million cinema tickets sold in the United Kingdom, but by 1963 the tally had dropped to a mere 357 million! Of course such a radical decline forced a 'rationalisation' in the number of cinemas, and closures were widespread.

It was against this background that Tenser sat down with Klinger to discuss merging their talents to form a film-related business. Self-confidence had never been in short supply for either man, but it was immediately obvious that a move straight into the highly competitive arenas of either film production or distribution would be a considerable risk, quite apart from the amount of capital required to get such a venture off the ground.

It was Tenser who suggested the idea of a private cinema, a "members only" club. Freed from the restrictions of censorship imposed by the industry under the auspices of the British Board of Film Censors, a private club could show its clientelle whatever films they liked. The investment would be relatively small and they would, Tenser reasoned, have a guaranteed market for their product. A suitable site was scouted out at 60-62 Old Compton Street, a nondescript office block in the heart of the West End, which had the advantage of possessing a huge basement area. Out of loyalty, Tenser offered his employers, Miracle Films, first refusal as his business partner. Undeterred by the flat "no," Tenser resigned from Miracle to devote himself entirely to the new venture and the two men set up in partnership as Compton Cinema Ltd., with their prime asset being The

Compton Cinema Club. Membership cost 10 shillings, and only persons over the age of 21 years could join.

Klinger continued to run his clubs, and The Gargoyle proved extremely useful as a base from which to promote the new cinema club. After extensive renovation the cinema opened its doors at the end of October 1960. The first film on the bill was Leslie Stevens's *Private Property (1960)*. A controversial film about a wife treated as a possession by her brutish husband, it featured Warren Oates among others, and had been banned outright by the Censors earlier that year.

For the princely sum of ten shillings a year, members gained access to a purpose-built cinema, housed in the building's basement, with back projection - a first for those days - and slightly fewer than two hundred comfortable seats. Films started at 12.00 daily, seven days a week, with seat prices ranging from 7/6 to 12/6. The Compton also offered its members the relative novelty of central heating and air conditioning, as well as a private bar selling alcohol and coffee.

Up until then the adult market meant 'sexploitation'; 8mm films churned out by small photographic studios around the country and generally sold by mail order. The films screened at The Compton were certainly 'adult' but hardly pornography. Naturist documentaries were shown alongside the stronger 'arthouse' films from Europe and banned movies from the States. There was no obligation for The Compton's films to carry a BBFC certificate. Indeed, given the nature of the club it was a positive advantage if they didn't!

'I knew quite a lot of films didn't get a certificate, or else they were heavily cut, not because of sex or violence, but for political or religious reasons,' Tenser explains. 'We knew we could establish our legitimacy by showing those films.' Movies like Brando's *The Wild One (1953)* - which had been banned outright by the censors - proved a big hit with The Compton's clientelle, and with prominent members like John Trevelyan, the secretary of the BBFC, and filmmakers like Bryan Forbes, the club very quickly had a profile far beyond its sexploitation roots.

above:
An early Club double bill for the imported films **Assassinos** and **Ein Toter Hing im Netz**.

above:
1961 advert for Compton's mainstream releases, all of which required BBFC certificates.

left:
'For Adults Only'; using sex to sell cinema club tickets.

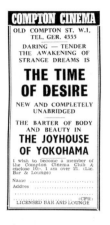

COMPTON CINEMA

OLD COMPTON ST. W.1.
TEL. GER. 4555

DARING — TENDER
THE AWAKENING OF
STRANGE DREAMS IS

**THE TIME
OF DESIRE**

NEW AND COMPLETELY
UNABRIDGED

THE BARTER OF BODY
AND BEAUTY IN

**THE JOYHOUSE
OF YOKOHAMA**

I wish to become a member of
the Compton Cinema Club &
enclose 10/-. I am over 21. (Lic.
Bar & Lounge)

Name ....

Addres ....

(CFR)
LICENSED BAR AND LOUNGE

above:
An example of Tenser importing exploitation films from the Far East.

right:
An early advert for Compton Club. Note the membership fee. Members also had to pay at the door.

below:
'The name for continentals'. In this case that meant Yugoslavia, Sweden, Italy and France.

COMPTON-CAMEO FILMS LTD.
60/62 OLD COMPTON STREET
LONDON W.1 TEL. GER 7066

The name for Continentals!

A True Story of Love Life & Death

THE **9th.** CIRCLE

BEST FILM 1960

DUSICA ZEGERAC

Blonde Angels-
Fierce Brunettes
as

PARIS PLAYGIRLS x

Delicious JEANNE VALERIE
in BOLOGNINI's

A DAY OF SIN x

From the sizzling story by
ALBERTO two WOMEN MORAVIA

TEENAGE SEX!
TEENAGE SAVAGERY! in

THE **DAMNED** AND THE **DARING** x

WATCH OUT FOR THESE
SENSATIONAL COMPTON -
CAMEO FILMS AT YOUR
CINEMA

COMPTON CINEMA

OLD COMPTON ST. W.1.
TEL. 4555

France's Most Fascinating
Females

**AGNES LAURENT
DORA DOLL
VERA VALMONT**

Provoke and Excite in

**"STRIPTEASE
DE PARIS"**

Also

Beauty, Naked and So
Care Free

"TRAVELLING LIGHT"

Members only

— — — — — — — — — —

COMPTON CINEMA
60/62 Old Compton Street, W.1

I desire to become a member of the
COMPTON CINEMA CLUB, subject to
its rules and byelaws. I am over 21.
10/- enclosed.

Name ....
Address ....

Signature ....
Age .... Date ....

CFR

The success of the Compton Group, both in respect of the cinema club and later with its film distribution and production activities, was rooted deeply in the way that films, particularly the cheaper or imported variety, were exhibited during the late 1950s and early 60s. Film exhibition was at that time divided into two sectors: the majors and the independents.

Strictly in terms of revenue, the market was dominated by two main players, Rank and ABC, the so-called majors. These were the days before the multiplexes, so one cinema meant one screen, and although on paper only around 25% of all cinemas were in the hands of these two companies, they were generally located in more lucrative inner cities locations so between them the majors accounted for nearly half of the British domestic gross. Understandably the inclination of the majors was towards glossy Hollywood movies with well-established (i.e. American) stars. However, the Quota Laws that operated in the UK required that 30% of the playing time per year be devoted to British, or at least nominally British movies.

Both Rank and ABC would supplement their mainstream movies with documentaries or 'B' features, frequently shown late at night or early in the morning. These features would be commissioned or made 'in house' for this specific purpose, and neither company had any real interest in producing or promoting independently made British movies. Foreign language features could be acquired relatively cheaply but didn't count towards the quota limits and, without

leading names, were thought to be unattractive to a mainstream audience, and were therefore largely avoided by Rank and ABC.

The remaining screens in Britain - the vast majority - were in the hands of the so-called independents. Located in rural areas or less profitable city sites, the independents competed for the Hollywood blockbusters but their bread and butter soon became the low-budget British movies or dubbed action movies with fading American stars and big, spectacular effects. As a group, the independents appeared to represent considerable buying power, but there were simply too many small companies looking out for too many vested interests for them to ever bond into a force, and outside of Rank and ABC film exhibition remained piecemeal.

Gradually, smaller-scale production and distribution sprung up, dealing with movies that catered specifically to the independent market. By the end of the 1950s a host of small distributors, including Butchers, Gala, and Regal, targeted these cinemas with the often risqué foreign language films. In fact the Bardot movies promoted by Tony Tenser at Miracle started this trend. The films were tame even by the standards of the day, with nothing more daring than the occasional flash of bosom, but creatively exploitative and teasing posters made them seem far more shocking than their English-language counterparts and therefore not suitable for the majority of the paying public. For anyone interested in more explicit material there was simply nothing available.

The Compton Cinema Club tapped into a market not yet exploited by either the majors or the independents, showing films that were adult in both subject matter and presentation. Operating on the very fringe of respectability, Compton still needed to stay one step ahead of the independents, who were hungry to move into any growing market. As an extremely small player they were soon having difficulties acquiring product to meet the growing demand. Larger distributors, which at this time meant practically everyone, were reluctant to co-operate with the interloper. 'We found we couldn't get enough new films,' recalls Tenser, 'or when we put the censored bits back in, the big distributors wouldn't allow them to be shown in a private club.'

From the outset it had been the intention of the two partners to move Compton into the film industry proper as soon as possible. Always more inclined towards the distribution side of the business, Tenser was all too aware that the real money lay in exhibiting films throughout the country rather than in a solitary cinema. The partners felt it was time to move into the independent market, as Tenser recalls: 'I had a chat with Klinger and suggested we form a distribution company, to show films, firstly uncut in our own cinema and then with the cuts made, throughout the country.'

Compton Film Distributors was formed, with former British Lion employee Graham Whitworth joining as Director of Publicity. Whitworth, like Tenser, came from a background as a cinema manager and together they were responsible for much of the publicity-driven success Compton was to enjoy over the next five years.

Applying the lessons learned during Tenser's reign at Miracle, imaginative publicity stunts were an immediate feature of the Compton launches. Whitworth vividly remembers the *modus operandi* of selling a Compton film: 'I would get the materials, the stills and what-have-you, and select the ones we wanted to go out to the press and the ones we could use for the artwork. I would then sit down with Michael and Tony and talk about what we were going to call it. We came up with some wild titles. Then we would bounce around ideas on how to get it into the papers. We knew if we could get the attention of the national press, or even the London boys since everybody fed off of them, we would have a real winner.'

Compton Film Distributors aimed their product at the independent cinemas and, operating with a small capital base, launched themselves into the market with a modest slate of imported films, including such titles as *The Adventures of Remi*, *A Taste of Love* and *Tower of Lust*. All of the films were either subtitled or dubbed. They relied heavily on eye-catching posters and catchpenny titles to find their audience, and needless to say they proved exceptionally popular.

The Club turned out to be a cash cow for Compton, and with the initial success of their distribution arm exceeding their admittedly modest aims, Compton once again found itself struggling to get sufficient product to meet demand. The impetus grew to move their control one stage back along the process and enter into film production.

Once again Tenser and Klinger were content to temper their ambitions with a dose of reality. The average budget for a British film in 1960 was between £180,000 and £200,000, far out of reach for Compton, especially when a successful independent release averaged a domestic gross of around £100,000! There was no question of a Compton movie breaking into the circuits of the majors, and they simply could not afford to risk their capital on a domestic mainstream movie without a guarantee of national release, or even international sales. So they opted to stay close to their roots. The cinema club represented a guaranteed outlet for as long as they wanted it, and all they needed was product that met the requirements of their chosen market. Tenser was in no doubt about what would sell.

In 1960 full frontal nudity had still not been seen in British films, though continental imports had played nationally (handled by the smaller distributors) for some time. The censor, John Trevelyan, made it quite clear that he would not permit naked flesh to be shown in mainstream films.[2] But foreign-language films weren't considered exploitation - they were subtitled and therefore art. Even with censorial trimming, the continental films remained somewhat racier than their domestic competition, and proved very popular with an audience of flesh-fanciers who would otherwise not be seen dead at a legitimate arthouse movie.

British sexploitation producers didn't have the option to dress their films as art, and denied access to the national circuit they were squeezed into making 8mm stag movies. Compared with a cinema release, this was as financially unrewarding as it was creatively restrictive. However, enterprising producers soon found that if the nudity was centred around the "naturist" movement then the film would be treated as a documentary and they could show as much bare flesh as they liked - at least up to a point.

Nat Miller, who appears later in the Compton story, had made the first British nudist camp film, *Nudist Paradise*, in 1958. This tame little romp started what was to become, in the fullness of time, the British porn industry, but the film was no more than relatively innocent smut dressed up as an educational movie. It was quickly followed by the likes of *The Nudist Story* (1959), *Nudist Memories* (1959) and *Some Like It Cool* (1960) - the latter directed by a young Michael Winner.

The stars of these films were primarily ladies, who were only allowed to display naked bottoms and breasts. All of the films that followed continued the theme. These were not much more than home movies, with no physical contact between the sexes shown. It was the ideal product for a private cinema club, and while the censor adopted a view of paternal bemusement, queues formed round the block. Tenser reasoned that a "nudie" film, shot quickly with an unknown cast, would not only represent minimal financial risk, but would also be perfect for the type of market that Compton had in mind. And Michael Klinger knew just the man to make it for them.

Some years earlier, while Klinger was promoting the Gargoyle Club, he had used George Harrison Marks to take pictures of the girls.[3] Marks worked out of Soho, naturally. He ran a studio and small gallery just around the corner from Compton, and had a nice sideline as the editor and publisher of a series of A5 (small format) "candid photography" magazines, usually featuring his girlfriend and partner, Pamela Green.[4] The couple soon expanded into

THE COMPTON CINEMA
60/62 OLD COMPTON ST.
LONDON W.1.

★ TOP FEATURE FILMS COMPLETELY UNABRIDGED SHOWN FOR THE FIRST TIME
★ LICENSED BAR & MEMBERS LOUNGE
★ ANNUAL MEMBERSHIP FEE 10/-

GRAND OPENING
PROGRAMME
"PRIVATE PROPERTY"
Starring KAT MANX

You must be a member for 48 HOURS to be admitted

JOIN NOW!
And be amongst the first to see this Sensational Programme

GALA PREMIERE
TUESDAY NOV. 15th.
all seats bookable

Complete this form and send 10/- to the
COMPTON CINEMA
60/62 Old Compton St., W.1.
I desire to become a member of the COMPTON CINEMA, subject to its rules and bye-laws. I am over 18.

Name ....
(Block capitals)

Address ....

Signature ....

Age ...... Date ....

above:
The first ever press advertisement for The Compton Cinema Club.

right:
Bridget Leonard,
Pamela Green, Jackie
Salt and Petrina Forsyth
protect their modesty in
**Naked - As Nature
Intended**.

below:
Another early Compton
Cinema Club bill, this
one including an early
Russ Meyer nudie film,
**Wild Gals of the
Naked West**.

8mm films, sold by mail order and mainly featuring Green herself in a variety of contrived story lines where she invariably ended up naked.

Always restless and anxious to push the boundaries of acceptability further and further, Marks was extremely receptive when Michael Klinger invited him to discuss a film project. Compton imposed some conditions: the film had to be a minimum of 55 minutes long, it had to star Pamela Green and feature a naturist camp, and of course it had to be cheap.

On the 4th of September 1960, George Harrison Marks set out with his cast and small crew to make the film that would eventually be called *Naked - As Nature Intended*. He was armed with no more than a rough shooting script bearing the title *Cornish Holiday*, chronicling the adventures of five girls as they made their way towards a nudist beach in Cornwall. It was Marks's job to film them in various states of undress against exotic backgrounds. All nudity would be shot within the confines of the Spielplatz Sun Club in Cornwall and the beaches at Bedruthan.

To save money, the plan was to shoot the rest of the film largely on location at various sites, all of which had to meet three basic requirements. They had to be accessible, recognisable and free. A provisional itinerary was drawn up, consisting mainly of familiar tourist attractions scouted by Marks during the height of the tourist season. The summer months were also spent casting the movie. Pamela Green had been included as a prerequisite of the deal, as Compton felt she was enough of a celebrity to guarantee interest among the club members and attract the attention of the press.

Klinger and Tenser retained final approval of the rest of the cast, but in all other regards Marks was given a free hand. Acting ability was not a major consideration, and as Pamela Green remembers, Marks was also required to set aside his predilection for fuller figures: 'They really weren't the type of girl he liked. They had no shape because they were going to be running about a beach. They couldn't have large breasts or they would be bouncing about all over the place!'

Followers of Marks's photography magazines would have spotted some familiar figures among a cast that included Petrina Forsyth, Angela Jones, Bridget Leonard and Jackie Salt. They were all professional models, and although none of them had acted before, but they had no problems with nudity. Stuart Samuels, a friend of Marks, was to be the only male in the cast, offering some "comic relief" in a recurring cameo role. Compton installed John Brason as production manager in order to keep an eye on the fledgling producer/director, and experienced cameraman Roy Pointer was brought in to handle the 35mm equipment. Douglas Webb, a professional photographer and close friend of both Marks and Green, was engaged as stills photographer.

Altogether, the cast and crew amounted to no more than twenty people. To avoid dealing with professional sound equipment on location, the film was shot with only a guide track for the dialogue - none of which was scripted - and this was later dropped in favour of off-screen narration. Marks and his crew set out with high hopes of a quick and trouble-free shoot, but almost immediately ran into trouble when he discovered that beaches that had appeared to be photogenic in the height of summer now looked cold and barren. As location after location proved unusable the crew simply moved on to the next on their agenda.

Shooting so late in the season did mean however that there were fewer locals and tourists with prying eyes to get in the way, and the Compton management had been concerned about filming the nudity on ostensibly public beaches. Pamela Green, a regular nude bather herself, doesn't recall any difficulties; in fact she says it was quite the opposite. 'Small crowds always gathered whenever we shot but they were more curious than anything. No-one hurried their children away or anything like that.'

In the interests of cutting costs, the car featured throughout the film actually belonged to Marks himself. Between set-ups it was used to help transport the crew between locations. Compton felt the script was innocuous enough to meet the censor's requirements but they nevertheless insisted that the film should be seen to be endorsed by the naturist movement. Tenser did a deal with the aging president of the Spielplatz Club, Charles Macaskie, who was duly wheeled out of his heated caravan for the briefest of cameo appearances. Mrs Macaskie, somewhat more active than her husband, also features briefly in the film. The other nudists who appear in these sequences were all genuine guests of the club.

Despite the fact that Spielplatz was a common location for this type of film - *Nudist Memories* had been filmed there and Pamela Green had been using it to touch up her suntan for some years - it proved to be a disappointment for the filmmakers. Far from being an exotic backdrop, the worn-out tennis courts, dingy chalets and murky swimming pool created a rather seedy aura, and of course the ever-present 'real' nudists raised the threat of exposed pubic hair!

John Trevelyan at the BBFC had adopted a fairly lenient outlook on this type of innocent behaviour, but the sight of pubic hair was forbidden in Britain at the time, even in magazines, and models were either shaved or had their genital area airbrushed. The presence of so many non-models provided a major headache for Pointer, who was rapidly running out of ways to keep nether regions casually covered. Towels, bags, balls; all seemed to attach themselves to the actors.

In his autobiography, 'What The Censor Saw', Trevelyan remembered the difficulties this type of production raised. 'Normally the more genuine the film the more problems it gave us. When real nudist gatherings were filmed, we carefully removed all sight of genitals, if necessary going through the film several times to make sure we had not missed any.'

In fact Trevelyan did have some objections to the staged sequences, and demanded cuts to two scenes. The first scene to suffer showed Pamela emerging from a shower in the flat she shares with Petrina Forsyth, who reclines in her babydoll nightdress. Trevelyan apparently thought this suggested a lesbian relationship and removed it, although stills from this scene were widely used by Whitworth's team to publicise the film.

COMPTON THEATRES
PRESENT
COMPTON
CINEMA CLUB · SOHO · GER 4555
MEMBERSHIP 10/- JOIN NOW
* TOP FEATURE FILMS COMPLETELY UNABRIDGED SHOWN FOR THE FIRST TIME
* LICENSED BAR AND MEMBERS' LOUNGE
NOW SHOWING
A Daring Revealing Story of Life after Dark!
TAKE ME WHEN YOUNG
TONIGHT FOR SURE
EASTMAN COLOUR

COMING SHORTLY
Incredibly SENSUAL...
LORNA
too much for one man
Starring LORNA MAITLAND incredible vulgar...
THE BEST THING IN SIGHT...
EROTICA
48-24-36 and we mean it!
Also
"WILD GALS OF THE NAKED WEST"
and
"SURFTIDE 77"
To: COMPTON CINEMA
Old Compton Street, London W.1.
I wish to become a member of the Compton Cinema Club and enclose. 10/- Membership Fee. I am over 21
NAME
ADDRESS
CFR
ALL ENQUIRIES
REGENT 7521 9-30am -10-30pm

above:
More early Russ Meyer films - **Lorna** and **Erotica** - are included on the bill at The Compton Cinema Club.

left:
Writer/Director/Producer George Harrison Marks and the models of **Naked - As Nature Intended**. Pamela Green is bottom left.

above:

The statuesque Pamela Green in a scene from **Naked - As Nature Intended** that caused problems for Britain's head censor, John Trevelyan.

The second lost sequence also hints at lesbianism, as Pamela Green recalls: 'Jackie was supposed to fall into the Channel, which she did with great enthusiasm. We hauled her back in, soaking wet and then came the instructions from George, "Rub her down, all of you." Innocent enough you would have thought, but the prospect of girls rubbing each other down was too much for the BBFC!' The whole sequence was cut and we now see Jackie standing on the side of the boat and then inexplicably appearing soaking wet.

Other scenes listed in the script - an underwater swim for example - were never shot due to technical difficulties or prevailing weather conditions. Despite the relative simplicity of the film, Marks's inexperience at handling actors and crews caused increasing problems as shooting progressed. The girls were supposed to supply their own wardrobe, but no-one had thought to check before leaving London that what had been brought along was appropriate for the film. In most cases it wasn't, and Pamela Green was duly installed as the production's unofficial wardrobe mistress, supplying her dresses to the other girls.

Further delays were caused when Petrina Forsyth balked at the thought of full frontal nudity, although it had been agreed

from the outset. She received a stern rebuke from the increasingly impatient Pamela Green. 'Petrina became very coy, saying everyone would see her "biscuit". I'd had enough by then and told her to take her hands away from her "biscuit", and threw her a beach ball to give her something to do with her hands. She proceeded to run around with her legs clamped together!'

Not only was the recorded dialogue unusable, but with scenes arbitrarily cut or added as the locations were changed, work finished with insufficient footage to make up the required running time. Behind schedule, and already a little over the meagre £3000 budget, shooting moved to a small studio in Dean Street usually reserved for television commercials. These sequences, consisting of some rather obvious studio/beach shots, couldn't hope to match up with the footage already shot on location, and stood out noticeably in the final print.

Unable to resist the temptation to visit a film set, both Klinger and Tenser made the trip from London to observe some of the location work, but other than these goodwill visits they largely left Marks and Brason to their own devices. Naturally there was some concern at Compton over the budget, but relatively speaking the sums involved were so insignificant that they had a degree of comfort. By the time the film was finally delivered, the title had changed to *As Nature Intended*, and later, at the suggestion of Michael Klinger, it became *Naked - As Nature Intended*.

Compton felt they had closed off the censorship question before filming had even begun, but when the final cut was submitted to the BBFC for certification they fell foul of one the great vagaries of the British rating system. The British Board of Film Censors had no written constitution, and unlike the system in force in the USA, where a detailed production code governed the ground rules of film censorship, the BBFC had no such code - at least not one it cared to publish. Despite the team's best efforts to remove all hints of lesbianism, and the token endorsement by the naturist movement, Trevelyan, who had by then realised that the naturist movie was now the preserve of more exploitative filmmakers, felt the film showed too much nudity, and promptly banned it outright. Tenser was hoping for an 'A' certificate, in common with most of the nudies of the time, which would at least allow Compton to secure a national release for the film. He felt, paradoxically, that an outright ban was still better than an 'X', which almost certainly would have restricted the bookings. A ban would, at worst, create the type of 'forbidden fruit' image upon which the Club thrived, but Tenser had not finished with the BBFC yet.

Compton invoked another curious anomaly of the British ratings system, the right of veto by local licensing authorities.

Individual local authorities had the option to accept or reject the BBFC's certificate, ask for additional cuts or even impose their own certificate. Tenser and Klinger duly showed *Naked - As Nature Intended* to the Greater London Council, who could see no real difference in content to the host of other "naturist" movies that played in the capital, and with only slight reservations they passed the film.

NAKED - AS NATURE INTENDED

*'Queen of the Pin-Ups and Britain's
Top Figure Model'*
- UK Press release -

Synopsis

Three young girls escape their humdrum lives by going on a motoring holiday to Cornwall. Petrina is a secretary, Jackie works in a shoe shop and Pamela is a dancer. None of the girls had ever considered sunbathing nude before. Two other girls, Bridget and Angela, are also going on holiday to Cornwall. Both are experienced nudists, intent on a hiking holiday culminating with a visit to a Nudist Camp where both are members. After visiting a number of tourist attractions the two groups meet on a beach - and Pamela, Petrina and Jackie discover they have inadvertently wandered into a nudist colony...

Critique

'The film is put together with much more style and originality than most nudist capers. Pamela Green and the other whistle-worthy ladies put a lot of energy into all the waving, leaping, laughing and running that seems to keep nudists pretty well occupied.'
- The Daily Cinema, 15/11/61.

'...the film is a waste of time for all but docile viewers who still feel there's something naughty in eyeing the unclad female form.'
- Monthly Film Bulletin, November 1961.

Despite the fact that most of the film's running time comprised of "comic" incidents staged around familiar tourist sites, Tenser and Klinger were immediately aware of the commercial potential of their first movie. The poverty of the budget, Harrison Marks's crude direction and the amateurish acting seemed to pale into insignificance when the girls finally stripped off. The now-laughable off-screen narration was littered with gems like: 'That reminds me of that definition - even a girl that can't add up can certainly distract.'

Compton were impressed enough with their first film to seek out a partner who could ensure *Naked - As Nature Intended* achieved wider distribution. They

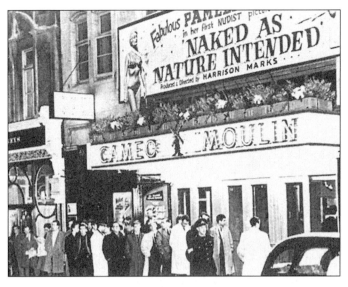

approached Basil Clavering and Charles H. V. Brown, owners of the Cameo Cinemas - a small independent concern, specialising in potboilers and exploitation films. The Compton-Cameo partnership was formed with the primary intention of buying these smaller films, premiering them at the cinema club and, if they were successful, giving them a wider release on the Cameo circuit. The two directors of Cameo took a back seat and left the selection of the movies to Klinger and Tenser.

The fledgling partnership had exactly the right eye-catching movie to launch their new venture. The world premiere of *Naked - As Nature Intended* was hastily arranged for the 30th of November 1961, when it became the debut feature at the newly refurbished Cameo-Moulin in Windmill Street. All of the directors of the new company were present, along with Graham Whitworth, Marks and the girls and, much to the delight of the assembled photographers, the photogenic Pamela Green, who cut an inaugural ribbon and was presented with a huge bouquet of flowers.

Green was central to Compton's publicity campaign. As well as being the central image on the poster, she was touted heavily as, 'the fabulous Pamela Green in her first nudist picture.' Compton's publicity team re-christened Marks as the 'renowned photographer on the portrayal of feminine beauty.' By the time the first - rather poor - notices were in, the queues had already started forming around the block.

above:
The Cameo-Moulin, in Windmill Street, London during 1961.

left:
Queues of raincoat-clad men gather for a screening of **Naked - As Nature Intended**.

above:
Trade ad for the national circuit release of **Naked - As Nature Intended**, directed by 'Harrison Marks'.

A West End run was secured for *Naked - As Nature Intended*, but Compton first had to cope with the demands of the local authorities. 'We went to the local council and they agreed to allow us to show the film subject to some conditions,' Tenser explains. 'Basically they wanted no front-of-house pictures, no stills, and only silhouettes on the poster. I got insert cards made up for outside the cinema saying, "We regret we are unable to show you scenes from this film, but they are available in the foyer." Everyone flocked inside!'

Tenser's tactic of going straight to the London boroughs and ignoring the BBFC ruling had left the Board in the potentially embarrassing position of watching helplessly as Compton hawked a nominally banned film round every local authority one by one. Outmanoeuvred, the censors backed down a week before the official premiere and agreed to reclassify the film for national release in exchange for some token cuts. The press covering the premiere had the unexpected novelty of photographing a beaming Tony Tenser and George Harrison Marks standing in front of the film's poster proudly displaying its 'A' certificate.[5]

Compton's problems weren't over though. When *Naked - As Nature Intended* went on general release with Anita Ekberg's *The Call Girl Business*, they found that the local authority loop-hole could also work in reverse. Birmingham City Council decided to take the unusual step of banning a film which now carried a BBFC certificate, and once again the Compton sales team were forced to come up with a creative solution.

'Birmingham local council wouldn't pass the film,' recalls Tenser, 'but Walsall, which is near Birmingham - only a bus ride away - did. So we took out adverts on the panels of the Walsall buses saying "The film you can only see in Walsall!" The manager of the cinema in Walsall originally booked a three-day run and it stayed there for six or seven weeks!'[6] The coffers were swelled further when the tiny independent distributor Crown International later picked up the film for North American release.

Even as the tills were ringing for *Naked - As Nature Intended*, Tenser dismissed suggestions that he was a sexploitation filmmaker and, for all his background in the strip clubs of Soho, so did Michael Klinger. 'These films were harmless. You would see more in a newspaper today,' Tenser remarks. Both men were looking to break into the mainstream of cinema however, and felt that financing another "nudie" would be a backwards step, so they began to look for more suitable properties.

The writing was already on the wall for the nudist fad. There were too many films exploiting a short-lived novelty. By the time nudity surfaced for the first time in a mainstream British feature, *A Kind Of Loving (1962)*, the nudist film was a quaint memory. Soho's exploitation filmmakers were already moving on, either (in the case of Harrison Marks) to more explicit porn, or (as with Compton) gradually away from sex. In the meantime there was still a demand to be met and Compton would be associated, albeit briefly, with two other successful nudie films.

My Bare Lady was filmed in England by American filmmakers Arthur Knight and Phineas Lonestar Jr. They had noted the success of the British naturist movies and sought to reproduce that success with an American audience. It was really no more than an American spin on the usual voyeurism, now even more blatantly dressed as propaganda for the naturist movement. The prim and proper leading lady, Tina (Julie Martin) finds herself in a nudist camp by accident and subsequently becomes convinced of the merits of naturism. Filmed on location in the UK and France, it offered slightly warmer-looking locations, and amongst the obligatory bouncing breasts and wobbly bottoms the occasional American accent could be heard. Generally though, the nudists' frolics remained interchangeable amongst the dozens of lesser-known films in the genre. Compton did not become involved in financing production, but agreed to take the British rights. It was Tenser who

above:
George Harrison Marks
and Angela Jones on
location for **Naked - As
Nature Intended.**

suggested the title, a pun on the popular West End musical. Compton then earmarked *My Bare Lady* as a suitable release for the cinema club.

Tenser received his first writing credit - for the voice-over narration - on what was to be his last involvement in the naturist movie genre. Tenser took a German naturist film and renamed it *The Nude Ones*, taking inspiration from the Cliff Richard film *The Young Ones*, which was generating a lot of publicity at the time. The original German-language soundtrack was removed in favour of a monologue written by Tenser himself and spoken, once more, by Guy Kingsley Poynter.

The film itself is surprisingly similar to *Naked - As Nature Intended*; a prolonged travelogue with three friends exploring a holiday island and stumbling on, surprise, surprise, nudists. Appropriately enough, the dialogue is of the same ilk as the earlier film: when horses are led into the sea, Poynter cries out enthusiastically: 'Look, sea horse!' The movie played as support feature to *My Bare Lady* on a double bill that ran for a total of 128 minutes, which must have exhausted the stamina of even the most enthusiastic patron. By the time these films surfaced at the cinema club in December 1962, Compton was already planning on making their first mainstream feature film.

Footnotes

1. The promotional materials for these Bardot movies became minor works of sexploitation in their own right. The ads for *...And God Created Woman* included this delightfully florid effort: 'A young bride, innocent yet radiating passion from every inch... the husband she loves who must not share her bed... how each glance, each gesture incites in him that which must not be... and then she walks, the travelling eye is transfixed and the husband's feelings become your feelings...'

2. Rather than being forced to deal with an official organ of the British government, the BBFC was created by the film industry in 1912 to pre-empt legislative interference. At the time cinema was being heavily criticised by a handful of outspoken and self-appointed moral guardians. The BBFC's unique status meant in effect that it had a dual role of protecting the public from filmmakers and protecting filmmakers from the public.

3. One of the original innovators of the British soft porn industry in the 1950s and '60s, George Harrison Marks was a former stand-up comic turned professional photographer - specialising in pictures of cats! Together with live-in girlfriend Pamela Green, he edited and published the softest of softcore magazines with titles like 'Solo' and 'Kamera'. Ostensibly these were photography journals, consisting exclusively of naked pictures of busty, and of course shaven, models, amongst them the statuesque Marie Devereux and of course Pamela herself, in various guises. Marks

COMPTON-CAMEO FILMS LTD.

60-62 Old Compton Street, London, W.1.   GER 1522 (5 lines)

PAMELA GREEN — *Lovely Star of "Naked - as Nature Intended"*

TASTE OF LOVE	LOLA	PAVEMENTS OF PARIS
THE CAPTIVE	THE TENEMENT	DAMNED AND THE DARING
ADVENTURES OF REMI	PARIS PLAYGIRLS	THE CALL GIRL BUSINESS
ASSASSINS IN THE SUN	FIRES ON THE PLAIN	LAST YEAR AT MARIENBAD
	GHOST OF DRAG STRIP HOLLOW — MISSILE TO THE MOON	

COUNT ON COMPTON-CAMEO FOR 1962

December (1961)	JANUARY			1962			February (1962)
	SUN	MON	TUE	WED	THU	FRI	SAT	

above:
Compton-Cameo's official calendar for 1962, complete with a typically elegant study of Pamela Green by George Harrison Marks.

had a low attention span for this type of stuff and soon he was making and selling short films; featuring token storylines they were generally no more than filmed versions of the magazines. He split with Green soon after making *Naked - As Nature Intended* and moved further down the road towards increasingly explicit material, trading on his by then somewhat tawdry reputation with such big screen efforts as *The Nine Ages Of Nakedness (1969)*. His biggest hit was also the most successful British sex film ever made, *Come Play with Me*, which mixed the seaside postcard humour of *Naked - As Nature Intended* with porn starlet Mary Millington dropping her knickers. Marks survived the demise of the porn industry in the '70s, despite two much-publicised visits to the Old Bailey and a battle with alcoholism. He emerged in his element with the '80s home video boom, running Kane magazine and making movies like *The Spanking Academy of Dr. Blunt* (1992). By the time of his death in 1997 he could lay claim to a filmography with over 500 titles!

4. Pamela Green was born in Kingston, London, the daughter of a former merchant seaman and an amateur artist. Pamela herself seemed set for a very respectable career as an artist/designer, but while studying at St.Martin's School of Art, she took up nude modelling in order to supplement her income. This led in turn to appearances as a dancer in the legitimate theatre, appearing with amongst others the likes of Norman Wisdom. She met struggling journalist/photographer Marks in 1953 when she was appearing in *Paris to Piccadilly*, a version of the Folies Bergere, and went into partnership with him both professionally and personally, posing for his pictures under various names and disguises including that of the infamous redhead Rita Landre. It was as Rita that she attracted the attention of filmmaker Michael Powell, who cast her as a model/prostitute in his landmark horror film *Peeping Tom (1960)*, Pamela's only significant mainstream credit. Powell also reproduced, with appropriate concessions to modesty, many of Pamela's costumes and much of the original set design from her work with Marks. More modelling followed, along with the odd film role, including *The Day the Earth Caught Fire (1961)*, and *The Naked World of Harrison Marks (1965)*. Green stayed with Marks for eight years, after which she moved in with stills photographer Douglas Webb. She devoted herself to posing for Webb and assisting him in his work in various films like *Legend of the Werewolf (1974)* - in which she had a small unbilled role as a tart. She also popped up in various popular TV shows, including *The Sweeney*. Webb had a stroke in 1985 and the couple subsequently retired to the Isle of Wight, where Pamela continued to model right up to Webb's death in 1997. Although she was generally regarded as the business brains behind the partnership with Marks, and certainly was responsible for much of the set and costume design, Green never really capitalised on her popularity as a model, and mainstream success eluded her. Cult fame seems to have assured Pamela of immortality as a "British Betty Page" and she has a cottage industry selling her photographs and videos. She didn't film again for Compton but her association with the company didn't end with *Naked - As Nature Intended*. A year after she made the film her picture - taken by Marks - was used on the company's calendar.

5. *Naked - As Nature Intended* was certificated as an 'A'-rated film (defined as 'passed as more suitable for adult audiences') on 24 November 1961. It is a curious inconsistency with the British rating system that when it received its video release in the mid-Eighties, long after the so-called 'permissive age', in an era when topless bathing and nudity in the papers and on television were everyday occurances, it carried a '15' certificate.

6. Tenser had the same problem seven years later when Tigon released the double-bill of *Witchfinder General* and *The Blood Beast Terror*. Having already played in nearly three hundred cinemas without any difficulty, the bill was banned outright in Sale, near Manchester. Failing to persuade the local authority to lift their ban, Tigon simply quoted it in their publicity for screenings elsewhere.

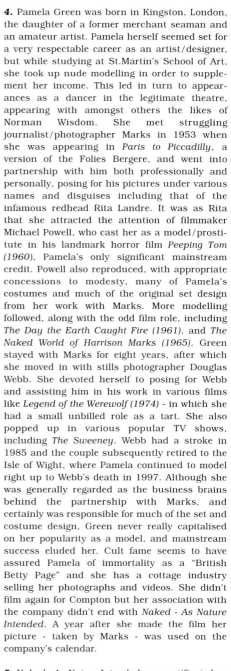

Chapter Two

'A Slice of Life in the Raw'

- (UK Press release, *Saturday Night Out*)

Tony Tenser and Michael Klinger may have been slow to get into film production - *Naked - As Nature Intended* trailed Nat Miller's *Nudist Paradise* by three years - but they quickly recognised that the limited market for the beach ball and bums movies was already drying up. By the end of 1962 the audience demographics had changed; there were estimated to be more than five million teenagers in Britain, 60% of whom were going to the cinema once a week. These teenagers didn't want their films bland or coy, they wanted films exploring issues, provocatively and intelligently; they wanted that 'something different.' Compton duly set out to deliver it.

For their first venture into the world of mainstream cinema Tenser and Klinger formed a new company, Tekli - the name was composed of the first letters of their surnames - and engaged the services of Robert Hartford-Davis, an ambitious former technician with MGM.[1] Hartford-Davis had obtained an outline called *That Kind of Girl* by Jan Read, a respected writer whose CV included the likes of *The Blue Lamp (1949)* and *Grip of the Strangler (1958)*.

Read's story focused on a not-so-innocent au pair in London and her encounters with a number of men, all of whom naturally enough had one thing on their mind. The writer expanded his script to play on the contemporary vogue for kitchen-sink realism and, encouraged by Tenser, added some distinctly exploitative elements: promiscuity, rape, venereal disease and, for good measure, political unrest. Tenser was in no doubt about the attraction of the script: '...quite a melodrama, but these were hot subjects then and we knew the film would make quite a bit of money. Venereal disease in particular might mean nothing now but then it was a terrible thing, and unheard of in movies.'

Hartford-Davis originally pencilled himself in as the director but Compton, with their future filmmaking ambitions resting on the success or failure of this project, was less than keen. Klinger and Tenser wanted someone with more experience of handling a cast and crew, but the budget of £23,000 was hardly conducive to hiring a 'name' director. Hartford-Davis, who was a well-known figure in Soho's café society, thought he had an ideal candidate in Gerry O'Hara, so he set up a meeting between him and Tenser. O'Hara not only fitted the bill as far as price was concerned, but he was also a

very experienced assistant director and, like Hartford-Davis, very keen to step up to full directing.[2] O'Hara's previous directing experience was limited to just three days shooting on *Third Man on the Mountain (1959)*, when the director, Ken Annakin, fell ill but his manner convinced Compton, and, as O'Hara later said; 'If you spend your working life with the likes of Carol Reed and Otto Preminger, some of it has to rub off.'

Hiring O'Hara presented Compton with one minor problem; he was already working for Tony Richardson on *Tom Jones (1963)*. Klinger took the lead on some delicate negotiations, with Richardson finally agreeing to release O'Hara three weeks early; contracts were signed at Old Compton Street giving O'Hara the princely sum of £400 for what was a planned fifteen-day shoot (in the event he actually worked for seventeen days). To placate Hartford-Davis, O'Hara was given only the directing duties; the hiring of cast and crew, as well as decisions regarding the

below:
Venereal disease had been hinted at in movies before but **That Kind of Girl** was the first British film to use it so blatantly as the main plot device.

above:
Margaret-Rose Keil is attacked by Elliot (Peter Burton) in **That Kind of Girl**. Interestingly, Keil is abused throughout the film by the men she encounters but is nevertheless presented as the instigator of all the trouble.

final cut of the film would be left to Hartford-Davis. Klinger and Tenser of course maintained control over the major casting and the marketing of the picture, but other than that they would not be too closely involved on a day-to-day basis.

As soon as shooting began Hartford-Davis made it obvious that he was going to be a very active presence on the studio floor, much to O'Hara's frustration. 'Bob badly wanted to direct and when they wouldn't let him he tried to direct through me. He wanted to direct by proxy!', O'Hara recalls. 'Of course he was making suggestions and comments from the first day. This continued until I had to say, 'Bob you will have to stop. I'm not going to have it. If you want to direct it go ahead but it's you or me - it's not both of us'. He knew I was quite prepared to walk off the picture and backed off after that.'

In his capacity as producer, Hartford-Davis employed his friend Peter Newbrook as director of photography, a role he was to fill in many of Hartford-Davis's later movies. Like O'Hara, Newbrook was more familiar with large budgets, having worked on the likes of *Lawrence of Arabia (1962)*, and he would go on to make his own directional debut with the dreary horror film *The Asphyx (1972)*. Lending the production team some much-needed experience was the ubiquitous Nat Miller, an experienced producer in his own right. As production controller he would act as the linkman between Compton and the filmmakers.

Hartford-Davis was particularly concerned with casting and *That Kind of Girl* shows his flair for selecting actors. His skill in this regard would continue to be a notable asset throughout his career. In particular two performers catch the eye. Linda Marlowe was given a support role here but she later starred as 'Dirty' Harriet Zapper in the *'Big Zapper'* movies for exploitation maverick Lindsay Shonteff. Marlowe also went on to achieve recognition as a stage actress for, amongst others, the Royal Shakespeare Company and as a leading lady for controversial playwright Steven Berkoff. Surpassing Marlowe in terms of stage success but only glimpsed here as a doctor at a VD clinic is RSC regular John Wood; he would lend his considerable talent to films like *The Madness of King George (1994)* and *Richard III (1995)*. The remainder of the supporting cast were all familiar to watchers of television and provincial theatre; competent and professional but largely unknown to the cinema going public.

For the title role as 'that kind of girl' Hartford-Davis opted for Margaret-Rose Keil, a twenty-year old German actress in her first English language role. Best known at the time as a topless model, Graham Whitworth's publicity team made much of her appearances in a handful of forgettable Italian movies. Pretty and blonde, Keil was a big hit with the British press, and her casting was as much to do with her willingness to pose for promotional pictures as her acting ability. Whitworth ensured the press had a steady stream of photos featuring Ms Keil, scantily clad in various glamorous poses, which somewhat undermined the impression Compton were trying to create. Tenser at the time made a point of reassuring the press, 'It's a strong subject but treated with taste.' Continuing, to the assembled journalists' disappointment, 'We could have made it for half the price and three times as dirty, but that's not the way to do it.' Sadly Keil's only other involvement with British cinema was a brief association with the film *Night of the Big Heat (1967)*, but she was dropped before any scenes were shot.

Long before O'Hara and his crew assembled for the first day of shooting John Trevelyan's office had cast an eye over the

script and suggested a number of 'refinements' to a receptive Compton. It was a common practice of Trevelyan's to review scripts and advise on what would or would not be passed, thereby giving the producers the opportunity to save money by not shooting scenes that wouldn't make it to the screen. Tenser was particularly concerned about his subject matter and there was a lurking suspicion at Compton that the film might have been heading for an outright ban. Tenser concedes that Compton had Trevelyan at the forefront of their thinking going into the project. 'In those days you just didn't see films about VD in a cinema and we had to make sure we could get [agreement on] the censorship before the film started. We needed to get the censor on our side, so I went to see John Trevelyan with a copy of the script and we had a long chat and made changes. Getting a certificate was the main consideration.' Trevelyan's approach was never adversarial; he thought of himself as a partner in the creative process; Tenser would go on to send all his scripts to Trevelyan and later, as the personal relationship developed, he was not above calling the censor during shooting to ask for advice on how to approach certain scenes.

With Trevelyan's approval Compton sought to deflect any criticism from the media by having the film endorsed by 'experts', in this case the Royal Medical Association, which branded the film's anti-Venereal Disease theme as, 'compulsory viewing for adolescents.' The RMA even went so far as to make their facilities available to the filmmakers. O'Hara remembers the offer was too good to refuse: 'The reason it was extended to a seventeen day shoot rather than fifteen was we had access to the VD Clinic at St. Thomas' Hospital and they

would only let us shoot there at weekends when they were closed. Tony saved on the sets but had the overtime to deal with!' The filming finished on time and on budget and Klinger and Tenser even found the money to buy drinks for the cast and crew at the local pub! With no role to play in the post production process, O'Hara took a job immediately after the film wrapped, as assistant to Otto Preminger on the lavishly budgeted *The Cardinal (1963)*. Assembling and editing the final cut of *That Kind of Girl* was left to Derek York under the close supervision, of course, of Robert Hartford-Davis.

While the finishing touches were still being applied to the *That Kind of Girl*, Compton began to gear up for the film's release. Hartford-Davis had been using his contacts for some time to talk up the film and Graham Whitworth's sensational headlines had stimulated quite a bit of interest in the tabloids during shooting. With taglines like *'Why was she 'easy?' Why couldn't she say, 'no'?*, Compton found their film was almost selling itself.

above:
Margaret-Rose Keil learns the awful truth in **That Kind of Girl**.

opposite bottom left:
Former model Margaret-Rose Keil was hired more for her looks than ability, and Compton's Head of Publicity Graham Whitworth ensured the press were kept supplied with suitable pictures.

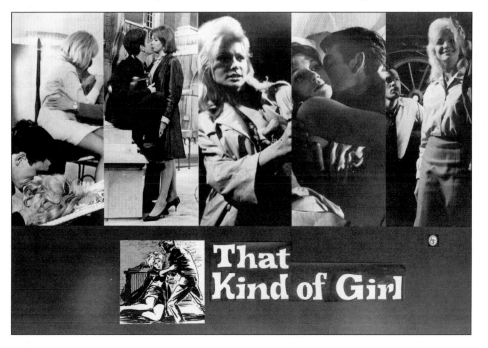

left:
An early example of the lurid style of advertising that was to become a feature of Compton marketing campaigns. Note the hand-drawn logo and primitive cut-and-paste layout work.

right:
Margaret-Rose Keil's character is comforted after being raped. The fact that she contracts VD from the assault is used by the filmmakers to suggest that she should be more careful in the future!

COMPTON—CAMEO FILMS PRESENT A TEKLI Film Production
That Kind of Girl x *the SHOCK FILM of the Year!*
MARGARET-ROSE KEIL · DAVID WESTON · LINDA MARLOWE · PETER BURTON · FRANK JARVIS

THAT KIND OF GIRL

'She Quenched His Burning Desires…
But the Passion Brought Misery'
- British Press Release -

Synopsis

Eva, an eighteen-year old au pair living with the Millar family, has two men in her life. Max, an earnest but dull student who invites her on anti-nuclear protest marches, and Elliot, with his smooth charm and sports car. She sleeps with Elliot but rebuffs the crude advances of Max. Later she meets and falls for Keith, who has had a row with his fiancée over sex before marriage. Eva does not need much encouragement to sleep with Keith, but when Elliot sees them together he is enraged. He follows Eva home, then attacks and rapes her. Later at the police station a medical examination reveals Eva has contracted VD from her attacker. As the word of her condition spreads, the people she has known reflect on their misfortune at meeting 'that kind of girl.'

Critique

'There is so much padding and surplus material before the film arrives at its main theme - the dangers through ignorance of VD …the story is sheer melodrama, running the weird gamut of anti-nuclear demonstrations, striptease, pre-marital intercourse, rape and the improper use of the phone - scarcely a digestible mixture.'
- Monthly Film Bulletin, 05/63

'…the worthiness of the cautionary theme must be held to over ride the banalities of the story and acting.'
- Daily Telegraph, 31/05/63

'Grisly but fairly sober-minded warning of the dangers of casual promiscuity: plot unstable but staging and acting efficient.'
- The Daily Cinema. 29/03/63

Beneath the exploitation headlines - and there was a veritable shopping list of those to choose from - *That Kind of Girl* has a middle-class, middle-aged morality about it. The horror of Eva's situation doesn't come from the fact that she was used and abused

below:
British front of house still for Gerry O'Hara's **That Kind of Girl**.

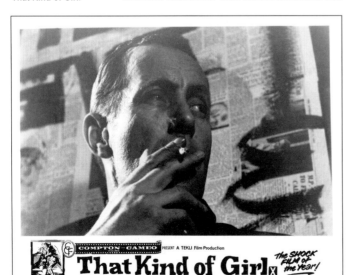

COMPTON—CAMEO FILMS PRESENT A TEKLI Film Production
That Kind of Girl x *the SHOCK FILM of the Year!*
MARGARET-ROSE KEIL · DAVID WESTON · LINDA MARLOWE · PETER BURTON · FRANK JARVIS

by the men she meets, but rather that she should get herself in those situations without taking precautions! When he learns that his would-be girlfriend has contracted VD from her rapist the reaction from Max is: 'She has taught me one thing, no mucking around from now on. The next girl I go with is going to be steady and when I marry she's got to be a virgin!' Read's simplistic approach has all men as sex-hungry opportunists who do whatever is necessary to get their leg over, while all women are either nice girls who don't or bad girls who do. Graham Whitworth seized on this as the main thrust of Compton's advertising, urging local newspapers to run an article under the title 'Can 'That Kind of Girl' exist here?', before suggesting that they 'perform a tremendous local social service to the whole community... by confronting them with the perils of a great and ever-increasing social menace.' Paradoxically the script seems to suggest that Eva is providing something of a 'social service' by taking the pressure off the 'nice girls.'

Well acted throughout, the cast add considerable credibility to the heady cocktail with only Margaret-Rose Keil struggling. Keil was simply too attractive to play a girl who needs to lower her moral standards to attract men; she clearly had no need to associate with the losers in the film. Sadly the au pair's obvious nymphomania is suggested but not explored. Gerry O'Hara handles his task with some confidence and manages to keep the action going at a pace that overcomes the weaknesses in the script. Peter Newbrook's excellent black and white photography was a considerable bonus. If Keil let the side down in front of the camera, she more than made up for it by exciting the attention of the press; the pattern for Compton movies was set - saturation press coverage, eye-catching headlines followed by mixed, usually negative reviews and the inevitable queues round the block. *That Kind of Girl* repeated its British success during a later release in North America under the more provocative title of 'Teenage Tramp'.

* * * *

As the finishing touches were being put to *That Kind of Girl,* Tony Tenser identified a suitable subject for Tekli's second feature. 'The Yellow Teddybears was based on real life,' he recalls. 'From a story I got from a newspaper about an all girl's school, where if a girl lost her virginity she would wear a yellow golliwog.' When the outline, titled 'The Yellow Golliwog', was submitted to the BBFC, Tenser found himself summoned to Trevelyan's office for one of his 'friendly chats.' 'Trevelyan was a nice guy and we got on very well but he said he was not happy with the title,' Tenser concedes. 'He thought it could be racist, and he didn't want it to

COMPTON-CAMEO FILMS presents

REAP YOUR REWARDS WITH THESE RELEASES

British Quota!
'THAT KIND OF GIRL' (X)
Starring Margaret-Rose Keil

Thrills Galore!
'SAMSON' (U)
with BRAD HARRIS
SUPERTOTALSCOPE
Eastman Colour

Adventure!
CAMERON MITCHELL
'Fury of The Vikings' (A)
TOTALSCOPE
Eastman Colour

Excitement!
'GOLIATH AGAINST THE GIANTS' (U)
SUPERTOTALSCOPE
Eastman Colour

The Independent Line-Up with Pulling-Power Plus!!

COMPTON-CAMEO FILMS LTD
60-62 OLD COMPTON STREET, LONDON, W.1.   Telephone : REGent 7521 (10 lines)
BRANCHES THROUGHOUT THE UNITED KINGDOM

above:
Contemporary advert for Compton releases. The taglines - "Thrills, Adventure, Excitement" and... "British Quota" shows that it was aimed at exhibitors rather than the general public.

have an association with the school. So I said what if we change it to *The Yellow Teddybears,* which is even better than Golliwogs anyway, and he said that was fine. We also changed the name of the school.'

Hartford-Davis was still overseeing the final cut of *That Kind of Girl,* but his competent handling of the production chores impressed Compton enough for them to install him as producer/director on *The Yellow Teddybears.* Serious work on the script started in late February 1963. In early March, Hartford-Davis was given some time off to accompany Klinger on the company's first sales trip to Hollywood. Klinger hoped he could attract a buyer for *That Kind of Girl* and also generate some interest in forthcoming projects. Tenser remained in London running the day-to-day business and overseeing pre-production on *The Yellow Teddybears.* The trip wasn't entirely successful; Klinger signed some agreements in principle on the distribution front but no financial commitment was forthcoming; Compton still had to bear full financial responsibility for *The Yellow Teddybears.* Nevertheless, contacts were made which would prove to be important in later years, when trips across the Atlantic would become commonplace for both Tenser and Klinger. Immediately on his return to the UK, Hartford-Davis started work on *The Yellow Teddybears,* and on the 18th of March 1963 he went onto the floor at Shepperton Studios.

The Ford brothers, Derek and Donald, both of whom were close friends of Hartford-Davis, had been commissioned to write a script from Tenser's promising outline. Individually and as a partnership the Fords had considerable experience in the industry but were at first a little disturbed by the explosive subject matter, as Derek remembers; 'I was very adverse to it because in those days you couldn't have anything to do with schoolgirls and sex. But... it was turned into a sociological documentary; it's all very well to teach sex, but how do you teach morality?'[3] Working under Tenser's guidance the Fords fashioned a script that

above:
Annette Whiteley squeezed into a school girl outfit, and Jacqueline Ellis as her teacher in **The Yellow Teddybears**.

combined such morsels as underage sex, prostitution, abortion, child neglect, and teenage rebellion. The titular 'teddybear girls' all display the sort of behaviour one would expect from girls so willing to part with their virginity. The Fords used the reliable old plot device of contrasting a good girl with a bad girl and following their respective stories; needless to say the 'bad girl', Linda, ends up on the game and pregnant. Appropriate parental and authority figures were included in the narrative to reflect society's moral prejudices but apart from the salacious subject matter the script was rather staid and altogether more moralistic than the film's title and publicity suggested. Tenser was nevertheless convinced the film would sell itself and Hartford-Davis was handed a budget only marginally larger than the one given to O'Hara, after which the Compton management took a back seat on the hiring of cast and crew.

For the crucial role of Linda, Hartford-Davis tested a number of drama school graduates before settling on Annette Whiteley, whose buxom appearance belied her seventeen years but created exactly the sort of look that Compton liked. Whiteley had already made one film, *Girl on Approval* (1961), as well as making a number of television appearances including a part in 'Emergency Ward 10'. The remaining parts were filled by experienced but not necessarily better-known names such as Jill Adams, who had appeared in the comedy *Carry On Constable (1960)*, and had worked with Hartford-Davis before, in his 1961 feature *Crosstrap*. Jacqueline Ellis and John Bonney were cast as teachers whose wholesome love affair was meant to contrast with the school-girls' casual flings. Veteran Raymond Huntley, who played in Hammer's *The Mummy (1959)*, brought gravitas to the film as Chairman of the school's Board of Governors. Huntley could count the unique distinction of being the first stage Dracula amongst his many credits. Another

interesting casting choice was Caron Gardner, who had supplemented her modelling for Harrison Marks by working as a receptionist at The Gargoyle Club, and was suggested for the role by her employer Michael Klinger. She would later decorate horror films such as *The Evil of Frankenstein (1964)* and *Burke and Hare (1971)*.

To lend the film a much-needed air of respectability, Hartford-Davis engaged the Wimbledon Girls Choir, who were commissioned to deliver the suitably austere 'A Lover and His Lass' for the soundtrack, and to ensure that all markets were catered for the pop group The Embers were brought in to perform the film's title track. All too aware that his future career as a director depended on his ability to bring *The Yellow Teddybears* in on time and on budget, Hartford-Davis surrounded himself with his regular collaborators; Peter Newbrook was back, as was Malcolm Mitchell who had provided the score for *That Kind of Girl*. Of course Compton employed Nat Miller once again as production controller.

Shooting proceeded without complication. Tenser and Klinger were both impressed by their director's speed and efficiency, and the quality of his work. The assembled footage was rushed through the editing process and, despite the last-minute inclusion of a shower sequence, the film was awarded an 'X' certificate by Trevelyan - meaning that no-one under the age of sixteen was permitted to see it. A release date was set for early summer, which would mean *The Yellow Teddybears* opening less than four months after shooting started - something of an achievement by anyone's standards.

By late June, Klinger and Tenser decided they had outgrown the little Cameo circuits and wanted their own productions to break out and achieve wider national release. They bought Clavering and Brown out of the partnership, retaining the name Compton-Cameo for the distribution arm, but decided that their movies should compete on the main independent circuits. *The Yellow Teddybears*, the first film to be released under the new arrangement, was

right:
Linda (Annette Whiteley) and boyfriend Kinky (Iain Gregory), the lead singer in a beat group. **The Yellow Teddybears** was an early attempt by Hartford-Davis to work a pop band into the narrative of one of his films.

an absolute gift to a company with limited resources looking to make a big impact. The interest being generated prior to release was constant, but after it opened the publicity was immense. The world premiere took place on the 13th of July at the Cinephone, a Jacey cinema on Oxford Street. The Embers played in the foyer while the ebullient Tenser, along with colleagues Klinger and Robert Hartford-Davis, rubbed shoulders with the likes of Hollywood star Robert Mitchum and the Earl of Kimberley, a non-executive director of Compton.

THE YELLOW TEDDYBEARS

'Why Did They Wear the Yellow Teddybears?'
- British press ads -

Synopsis

A private club has started up amongst the girls of the Sixth Form at Peterbridge New Town Grammar with only one entrance requirement: no virgins. The girls flaunt their promiscuity by wearing a yellow teddybear on the lapel of their school uniforms. Linda is the leader of the group and the most forward; she boasts about her older boyfriend, Kinky, and openly defies her strict parents George and Muriel. When Linda finds out that she is pregnant she rejects Kinky's home-made cures in favour of a back street abortion arranged by June, a local prostitute. When George finds out what has been going on he reacts angrily, denouncing the school and attacking Linda for ruining his 'political career'. His ranting has serious implications, both for Linda and the teachers who tried to help her.

Critique

'A film that sets out to be daring but is curiously old fashioned.'
- Daily Worker, 13/07/63

'...an embarrassingly inept attempt to investigate the mind and mores of sexually promiscuous teenagers.'
- Daily Herald, 13/07/63

'...a likely contender for the year's funniest British film...'
- Kine Weekly, 07/63

'Amateur performances, cliché ridden dialogue, stock characters, halting direction and a sententious 'sociological' message is tagged on to a story one suspects will be exploited sensationally.'
- Evening News, 11/07/63

Hartford-Davis's approach could be described as stately rather than exploita- tive; despite plenty of material to get his

teeth into, there is actually far more talking than doing. The old-fashioned moral tone of *That Kind of Girl* was retained; 'least I expected was you to bring up my daughter properly,' barks the thoroughly unpleasant George. The holier-than-thou veneer is paper-thin of course, and as a whole the film is simplistic, as all the middle-class characters are seen as reactionary and out of touch while the younger teachers have an open-minded and progressive attitude.

The Fords were certainly guilty of padding out their script - the interminable swimming gala being a particularly noteworthy example - and some of their 'hip' dialogue is cringe-making: 'she travels with me, she swings.' But none of this worried Compton too much, and Tenser was delighted at the way his original idea had transferred to the screen retaining its most saleable element of course, the schoolgirls themselves, although Annette Whiteley in particular was too unsettlingly mature to squeeze into her school uniform.

The Yellow Teddybears was released rather incongruously teamed-up with the necrophilia horror classic *The Terror of Dr. Hichcock (1962)*, starring Barbara Steele and Robert Flemyng. This program was a dream double-bill for the publicity men, and it duly caused a bit of a stir in the West End, taking considerable box-office. The publicity team incidentally provided *Hichcock* with one of the all time great ad lines, 'The candle of his lust burnt brightest in the shadow of the grave!' That film also gave Tenser his first sight of two performers, Steele and Flemyng, who would go on to feature prominently in his later movies.

Compton followed the example set by *That Kind of Girl*, and sought to diffuse criticism by seizing the moral high-ground, this time by using endorsements from the local City Education Authorities. In Birmingham, Graham Whitworth hosted a preview of the film followed by a debate with local head teachers, doctors, clergymen and marriage guidance counsellors, as well as

above:
The emphasis is on the schoolgirls in the British artwork for **The Yellow Teddybears**. Intriguingly, the fact that the film is based on a true life story was played down by Compton at the time at the time of its release.

MICHAEL KLINGER and TONY TENSER present

The Yellow Teddybears

A TEKLI FILMS PRODUCTION

GUEST STARS
JILL ADAMS   RAYMOND HUNTLEY
HARRIETTE JOHNS   JOHN GLYN JONES

PRODUCED AND DIRECTED BY
ROBERT HARTFORD-DAVIS

starring
JACQUELINE ELLIS
ANNETTE WHITELEY
IAIN GREGORY
DOUG SHELDON
GEORGINA PATTERSON

A COMPTON CAMEO FILMS RELEASE

above:
Schoolgirls and showers - Jacqueline Ellis in the foreground fails to distract attention from Compton exploitation at its most obvious.

below:
British admat.

local schoolchildren. The assembled members of the public were then asked to vote as to whether they thought it suitable for a general audience - which they did. That stunt grabbed the headlines: Birmingham Post - 'Schoolgirls have X-film lesson on Life!'; News of the World - 'Shocked? Not us! say Girls.'; Daily Mail - 'The Girls Who Took an X-Lesson at the Cinema Yesterday.' The story also merited coverage on the BBC and local radio. John Trevelyan, always happy to see public debate on the merits of films, was required by the conventions of the time to award the film an 'X' certificate, effectively undermining the Education Authorities' argument by depriving anyone under the age of sixteen from seeing it! Always the realist, Trevelyan went on the record, saying '*The Yellow Teddybears* deals with the special difficulties of sex which young people - especially girls - are faced with today. Any performance which stimulates discussion with adults and helps the understanding of the problem, is to be encouraged.' This of course was exactly the sort of publicity that Tenser and the Compton publicity team wanted; by now the box-office receipts from *That Kind of Girl* were pouring in and it looked very much like *The Yellow Teddybears* would be following a similar pattern.

*   *   *   *   *

The Compton Group now considered itself established as a production and finance house - at least for low-budget films. 'Every day the post bag seemed to contain scripts or ideas,' Tenser remembers. 'We also had a lot of people dropping by the office, some of them we knew, a lot of them had heard about us from our films or from people in the industry. After *The Yellow Teddybears* we started getting a lot of attention in the trade press.' Faced with a small army of would-be film producers, the different approaches of Michael Klinger and Tony Tenser soon surfaced; 'In personalities and stature, we were completely the opposite,' Tenser comments. 'I was more of a 'hatchet man.' Michael was a very sweet chap, and was always happy and laughing and joking. When somebody wanted to talk us into a deal, they would go to Michael. He wasn't a fool, but when he would half agree to a deal he would say 'You had better talk to Tony.' I would look at it, and if it wasn't right I would chop it.' This didn't always sit well with filmmakers, as Tenser accepts: 'Michael cared what people thought of him but I didn't mind if they disliked me.'

Tenser had always considered the cinema club to be a stepping stone into the film industry proper; even so, the club remained a source of considerable cash income. 'That Kind of Girl was made very economically and earned quite a bit of money. That gave us the bug,' Tenser explains. 'The club side of the business became the tail of the dog, production and distribution became the dog itself.' An upbeat press statement from Tenser reflected the company's strategy, promising that future releases would 'contain the necessary ingredients of action, colour and thrills with high commercial value.' Having made a series of overseas deals to distribute the two finished features, Compton had also established a number of provisional agreements over future productions, so Tenser was confident enough to green-light preparation of a new project for their director of choice Robert Hartford-Davis. Under the subsidiary Tekli Film Productions, Michael Klinger had optioned a treatment by the Fords called 'Theirs Is the Kingdom,' a war movie centring on the Battle of the Somme. Hartford-Davis was particularly keen to get away from exploitation, and persuaded a more reluctant Tenser that the forthcoming Fiftieth anniversary of the outbreak of The Great War presented an excellent opportunity. Television and newspapers had already picked up on the memorial theme and public interest was obviously piqued, but Tenser had some pragmatic objections. Working from a rough draft of the script, Klinger, Tenser and Hartford-Davis 'guesstimated' the potential budget. Almost immediately the film was put aside and the director was invited to suggest cheaper alternatives. 'Theirs Is the Kingdom' remained dear to the hearts of Klinger and Hartford-Davis, and would resurface several times over the coming years as Compton explored various alternative finance options.

In the meantime the ever-resourceful Fords came up with a more suitable proposal - a comedy about a bunch of sailors on shore leave with money in their pockets and time on their hands. This was hardly an original concept, but within the scope of the tried and proved Compton treatment it was a potential box-office winner. Hartford-Davis jumped at the chance of making a comedy, and as the Fords put the finishing touches to their script he started to assemble his crew. It was pretty much the old team again: Hartford-Davis at the helm with Peter Newbrook handling the photography. Robert Sterne, who would later become a close friend and colleague of Michael Klinger on movies like Get Carter (1971) and Shout at the Devil (1976), came on board as Associate Producer.

Hartford-Davis again assembled one of his impressive casts, including the distinguished character actor Bernard Lee ('M' in

the Bond series), and Nigel Green who was just beginning to make an impact in films such as Jason and the Argonauts (1963).[4] With Erika Remberg filling in as the mandatory imported starlet, Hartford-Davis made the decision to hire two of the most impressive young actresses to emerge in British films in recent years. Heather Sears, who took top billing, was a minor star who had for a short time in the late Fifties been regarded as a major talent.[5] By contrast, eighteen-year old Francesca Annis was then merely a promising young actress, glimpsed in Cleopatra (1963) as a handmaiden to Elizabeth Taylor, signed up for her first significant role.[6] The cast was again fleshed-out with reliable performers,

above:
Barbara Roscoe, as a Soho tart, flirts with a client while David Burke's club manager looks on.

below:
Nigel Green and David Lodge share a scene in **Saturday Night Out**.

above:
Heather Sears relaxing off-set; she was at the time considered a catch for Compton and her pictures were used heavily by Graham Whitworth to promote the film.

right:
Inigo Jackson, Bernard Lee (back to camera) John Bonney and Robert Hartford-Davis shooting the opening scenes of **Saturday Night Out**.

below:
Heather Sears patiently waits for the set-up on **Saturday Night Out**.

including John Bonney, who had impressed in *The Yellow Teddybears*, Vera Day, the Hammer starlet who enlivened *Quatermass 2 (1957)* and *Grip of the Strangler (1958)*, the veteran actress Patricia Hayes, and David Lodge, soon to be a regular member of the Hartford-Davis repertory company.[7] There were also a couple of noteworthy actresses who took minor roles: Margaret Nolan, a former stripper and Harrison Marks model who would later achieve immortality as a Bond girl, and Martine Beswick (who appeared in the title sequence of *Dr. No* and

went on to something like immortality as Hammer's *Sister Hyde*) can be glimpsed as a barmaid in her first featured role.

The Fords' humorous script and the film's cast were both intended to appeal to a more mature audience, but Hartford-Davis again covered all bases by hiring a pop group to liven-up the soundtrack. Two songs, including the title track, were performed by The Searchers, a 'beat combo' who happened to be both cheap and available at the time. It has been claimed that one of the groups considered by Hartford-Davis were The Beatles, who were apparently suggested by their manager Brian Epstein. The budget that had been allocated to Hartford-Davis allegedly wouldn't stretch to food and lodgings for the band, so he went for the local alternative instead! Hartford-Davis assembled his crew on the 16th of September 1963 to start shooting *Saturday Night Out*, boasting to the press that he was making a 'large budget film with an all star cast.'

Saturday Night Out represented something of a gamble for Compton as, although the film contained some exploitable elements, it was by no stretch of the imagination an exploitation film. Despite appearances to the contrary Hartford-Davis showed most interest in the humour and characters involved; sex featured of course, but for once as a backdrop rather than the *raison d'être*. Tenser and Klinger were keen to ensure that *Saturday Night Out* was seen by the industry and media to be a step up from their 'usual fare', and arranged for a spectacular premiere at the Rialto cinema in late February 1964.

SATURDAY NIGHT OUT

'A Slice of Life in the Raw'
- British trade Ads -

Synopsis

Five sailors and one passenger leave a newly-docked ship determined to make the most of their one night in London. The passenger, George, finds himself at the centre of a blackmail attempt, though he succeeds in turning the tables on the blackmailers. One of the sailors literally has a wife in every port and spends his whole leave in bed; another is on his way to a classical concert when he is distracted by a would-be suicide. Two others, Jamey and Harry, leave their friend Paddy to his drinking and go off intent on a night of love, even if they have to pay for it!

Critique

'Both script and direction, though striving hard to inject a flavouring of sex and wit, are colourless, but the acting is generally rather better than anything else in the film.'
- Monthly Film Bulletin, 05/64

'Entertaining collection of sexual, comic and poignant anecdotes involving a group of seamen on the loose: competently staged, briskly paced and brightly acted.'
- The Daily Cinema, 04/03/64

'Hartford-Davis has done a routine but uninspired job as director and producer. Perhaps the greatest disappointment in the film is the appearance of Miss Sears, after a longish layoff, in a role which gives poor scope for her talent.'
- Variety, 18/03/64

'Rather squalid bunch of stories about seamen on a night ashore in London. The script aims at a 'slice of life' effect but turns out to be a lump of pud.'
- Daily Worker, 17/03/64

'Behind the peep-show facade of life in the raw, there is a warmth, a vitality and an astringency that turns cliché into comedy.'
- Daily Herald, 06/03/64

'Heather Sears, Bernard Lee, Erika Remberg and Francesca Annis are all excellent, but dragged down into the unsavoury depth.'
- Evening News, 05/03/64

above:
Inside the 'Garden of Eden' strip club, Barbara Roscoe fails to impress her boss David Burke. Given Klinger's background and the proximity of Compton's offices to the heart of Soho, one has to assume it was a accurate recreation.

above:
Heather Sears in **Saturday Night Out**.

left:
Colin Campbell and Inigo Jackson consider the charms of the local barmaid (Patsy Fagan). Future Bond and Hammer star Martine Beswick also featured in the pub sequences, but for once Compton missed a trick as she wasn't used to promote the film.

above:
Caroline Mortimer as the duplicitous tart in **Saturday Night Out**.

above:
Robert Hartford-Davis directs Heather Sears.

right:
Harry (Inigo Jackson) tries to pick up Margaret (Toni Gilpin) while Jamey (Colin Campbell) and Paddy (Nigel Green) look unimpressed.

Partnered by an Italian horror flick called *The Spectre* (Riccardo Freda's follow-up to the previous year's *The Terror of Dr. Hichcock*), most critics thought of *Saturday Night Out* as being more of the same low-budget exploitation; the budget may have been marginally bigger but the film had enough sleaze to identify it as Compton product. Tenser took the view that for the first time he had made a film that 'started with a story not a headline.'

It would be nice to report that Hartford-Davis's first attempt at a mature film was an unmitigated success, but sadly it wasn't. The cast certainly looked good on paper, and Bernard Lee and John Bonney are both outstanding, overcoming the inadequacies of Hartford-Davis's direction. Perhaps it is not much of a surprise that it is the seedier elements that work best, the director wringing some truth from the seedy night-clubs and duplicitous tarts, but he is much less comfortable with the love stories and the humour doesn't work. Heather Sears makes a particularly irritating 'beat chick.' Some of the dialogue sparkles, indicating the growing maturity of the Fords' writing: 'It's not for the tourists' says a barman recommending a stay at Casa Louis, adding salaciously, 'Louis can fix anything, make a short stay quite memorable.' But for the most part the writers can come up with nothing more original than the usual randy sailors, self-serving floosies and land-ladies with hearts of gold. The nice girl orphan with a hard-luck story segment is particularly irritating. Robert Richards's score is mostly unobtrusive, but The Searchers are quite clearly included for their commercial appeal rather than any story-line requirement.

Graham Whitworth pulled out all the stops with one of his most comprehensive marketing campaigns yet. The premiere took place at the Rialto, with Whitworth orchestrating the arrivals of the cast and crew as well as luminaries such as the celebrated illustrator and artist Feliks Topolski and Baron Adam Konopka, the headline-grabbing big-game hunter. The Searchers were there playing for the crowds but it was starlet Francesca Annis, returning tanned and beautiful from filming *Flipper's New Adventure (1964)* in the Bahamas who stole the show. 'We knew then that she was something special,'

Graham Whitworth recalls, 'and the press knew it too. There were lots of actresses who looked good in photographs and not so good on the screen, but Francesca always looked beautiful and was a very talented actress. She was a real find for us.' The gentlemen of the press, always alert to a pretty face, were captivated, and Annis had the dubious pleasure of seeing her picture in all the tabloids the next day. A star, as they say, was born. Tenser and Klinger may have rubbed their hands at the saturation coverage but ultimately the domestic returns on *Saturday Night Out* didn't quite match those of their predecessors. It hardly mattered though, as the brains at Compton were already thinking beyond the limited domestic circuits.

*   *   *   *   *

While *Saturday Night Out* was still shooting Tony Tenser was proclaiming Compton-Cameo to be 'a major force in the distribution of the finest screen product.' The company had launched a major sales push, establishing representative offices in Rome, Paris, Tokyo and New York. Tenser boldly predicted that they would be releasing as many as forty films during 1964, with more in 1965. At that point Compton-Cameo boasted the likes of *The Sword of El Cid*, *The Shadow of Zorro*, *Jason and the Golden Fleece* and *Invasion of the Normans* on general release. These were dubbed films carrying 'U' certificates and relying on action and spectacle rather than plot. Such stars as they had were usually well past their prime and happy to slum it for a few dollars. As Tenser remembers it wasn't just the acting that was a little out of sync: 'We had a few of these, what we called 'dustbin lid films' - Spartacus type stuff. Italian films dubbed into American accents, with a fellow talking gibberish, and the words come out as 'goodbye'. Good fun, family films.' Compton maximised their income by releasing these films as double-bills, a practice enthusiastically endorsed by Tenser throughout his career. 'This may appear to affect the gross value of the individual film,' he explains, 'but we found where two films are coupled together, the result in effect is far in excess of many solo bookings.' By using their new network of contacts throughout the world Compton could be first in the queue for UK distribution rights to films still in production; a Christopher Lee horror movie, *The Virgin of Nuremberg (1963)* (later re-titled *The Castle of Terror*), and the aforementioned *The Spectre* (with Barbara Steele) were acquired in this way.

Film production was also becoming increasingly important for the Group; it was the ideal way to raise their profile as well as securing maximum revenue. Two recently acquired properties signalled the company's

growing confidence. 'Torment' was a period-piece thriller - a genre they had previously given a wide berth - and 'I Would Rather Stay Poor' was based on the novel by James Hadley Chase (René Brabazon Raymond), another first for Compton, as the company had never previously purchased a well-known subject for adaptation. Tenser was predicting a minimum of four Tekli films a year, and amongst those on the slate were a big budget special effects feast ('The Loch Ness Monster') and the Somme epic, which now bore the title 'The Great Offensive - Somme 1916.' Both projects had been provisionally assigned to Robert Hartford-Davis, now very much the director/producer in residence.

That Kind of Girl and *Saturday Night Out* had both dealt with universal themes but been unashamedly English in execution, and as such it was unsurprising that returns from overseas markets were adequate but hardly spectacular. Just around the corner

above:
British thesp Robert Flemyng as the titular doctor with horror star Barbara Steele in the necrophilia classic **The Terror of Dr. Hichcock** (L'orribile segreto del Dr. Hichcock).

below:
Compton's bread and butter remained the dubbed action movies churned out by the Italian studios with interchangeable plots, characters and stars. This time round it is Brad Harris as Samson (Sansone) directed by Gianfranco Parolini.

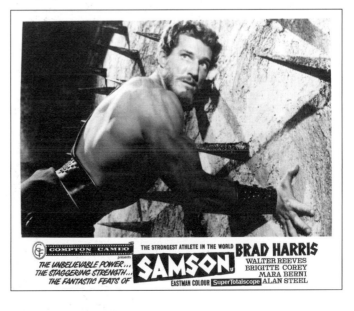

right:
Annette Whiteley,
Robert Hartford-Davis
and John Turner pose
on set of **The Black
Torment**.

below:
British trade artwork for
The Black Torment.
Compton was aiming for
Gainsborough style
melodrama with their
advertising.

opposite top:
Heather Sears looks
rather worried as Robert
Hartford-Davis sets up
the next shot during
filming of **The Black
Torment**.

below:
Heather Sears, John
Turner share a joke with
director Robert Hartford-
Davis on the set of **The
Black Torment**.

from Compton's Soho base was the head office of a company that was making movies for very similar amounts of money, but finding no difficulty in getting their products accepted throughout the world. From the American mid-West to the Asian sub-continent, Hammer Films found ready markets for their particular brand of eroticism and horror. Until the mid-1950s, Hammer had thrived on a diet of low-budget comedies and lame thrillers which were usually adapted from television or radio subjects. They started to broaden their appeal with *The Quatermass Xperiment (1955)*, then under the direction of the enterprising James Carreras they more or less stumbled into the Gothic horror movie genre with *The Curse of Frankenstein (1957)* starring Peter Cushing and Christopher Lee,

quickly followed by *Dracula (1958)*. Both films are now accepted as classics of the form, prompting a box-office roll that was to last for well over a decade. By 1964 the best years were behind them in terms of quality, but Tenser watched with growing interest as Hammer continued to churn out period-piece horrors and contemporary thrillers more or less to order. 'We decided we had done the sex or rather the nudie side,' he says, 'and I thought the next thing for us was of course horror films. Like nudie films there is always a good audience for horror movies, always. I don't mean just on a general circuit release but there is a good audience in other countries in the world, because they are more graphic than anything else.' The 'Torment' script, by Derek and Donald Ford was an exhilarating mix of both sex and horror, and hence seemed ideal. Hartford-Davis - still tinkering with his Somme movie - accepted the commission and enthusiasti-cally threw himself into pre-production. Originally announced as 'Torment', then 'Bed of Torment', Compton's first costume drama went before the cameras in February 1964 as *The Black Torment*. It was to be Compton's most difficult shoot to date, with the normally reliable Hartford-Davis clashing with his management over the budget and general interference.

Hartford-Davis again surrounded himself with familiar faces: Peter Newbrook was director of photography, Robert Sterne acted as production manager, and Robert Richards was recalled to write the score. The Fords' script was packed full of reliable standbys such as arrogant aristocrats, muttering peasants, ghostly apparitions and cowering wenches in low-cut frocks.

The casting was as meticulous as ever. Peter Arne, who had been a swarthy villain in British movies for over a decade, made an excellent, if obvious, 'heavy' in a role almost identical to the one he had played in an earlier movie, *The Hellfire Club (1960)*.[8] Opposite Arne was John Turner, playing the unfortunate Sir Richard Fordyke, who finds himself victim to the ghost of his first wife. Turner's previous experience was largely confined to the stage, though he had appeared in *Petticoat Pirates (1961)* and the Italian import *Ten Desperate Men (1963)*. Heather Sears retained her star billing in the role of Fordyke's new wife, and was joined at the manor house by Annette Whiteley, a schoolgirl no longer, who appeared briefly as the buxom maid. Ann Lynn made a fetching support and the remainder of the cast was filled out with prominent character actors of the calibre of Francis De Wolff, Joseph Tomelty, and Patrick Troughton, TV's second Doctor Who. Catching the eye as the pretty first victim is Edina Ronay, the daughter of gourmet Egon Ronay, and best remembered for her later scantily-clad contributions to Michael Carreras's *Slave Girls (1966)* and Lindsay Shonteff's *Zapper's Blade of Vengeance (1974)*. Although her screen time was limited to the opening sequence, Ronay was to feature heavily in the publicity, a decorous function she was called on to repeat in a later Compton film, *A Study in Terror (1965)*.

Tenser may have been inspired by Hammer's financial success but Hartford-Davis was influenced more by the dark, brooding look of the Italian Gothic dramas –

maybe in part because the releases of both *Saturday Night Out* and *The Yellow Teddybears* had been accompanied by two fine examples of the genre by Riccardo Freda. There was to be none of the trademark humour, highly stylised 'Kensington Gore', and garish colours of Hammer; instead shadows and languorous blues dominated the screen. Hartford-Davis, who never felt entirely comfortable with Compton's kitchen sink melodramas,

below:
Line-reading rehearsal for **The Black Torment**. Heather Sears, Norman Bird, Annette Whiteley, Robert Hartford-Davis, Peter Arne and John Turner (back to camera) seem to be enjoying the moment.

above:
Annette Whiteley, no longer a school girl, in **The Black Torment**.

relished the prospect of a costume drama. As Derek Ford recalled when interviewed for Shivers magazine thirty years later, subtlety wasn't really a consideration for Hartford-Davis: 'He lived at a fever pitch. Somebody screaming, someone dying, a throat-slit - that was a great picture to him.'

The Black Torment was an important film for Tenser and Klinger - it not only marked an increase in their usual budget, but the pair also hoped it would mark a new direction for the company. Both men wanted to be more actively involved in film production, particularly Michael Klinger

who was harbouring ambitions to line-produce his own movies, and even before shooting started the Compton management were re-shaping the final product. To accommodate Tenser's requirement for low-cut dresses and heaving bosoms, the Fords reluctantly re-wrote their script, transporting the action from the original choice of the early nineteenth century further back to the 1780's. It was the first indication that the management were going to be far more hands-on than in previous projects, but if Hartford-Davis recognised the signs he ignored them.

above:
Heather Sears taking a cigarette break on the set of **The Black Torment**.

right:
John Turner, Peter Arne, Heather Sears and Robert Hartford-Davis during the filming of **The Black Torment**.

In all his previous films for Compton, Hartford-Davis had directed at a rapid pace, frequently at the expense of style and content, but on *The Black Torment* he was behind schedule almost from the outset. With commitments already made on a number of projects, money was tighter than ever at Compton, and Tenser was immediately alarmed by Hartford-Davis's slippage. Derek Ford was witness to an impromptu set visit from the front office: 'Bob was getting so carried away with having this magnificent set and all of these wonderful costumes that he was indulging himself and we were running behind schedule. Tony and Michael came down in the second week and said, 'what's happening? How many pages are you behind?' Bob said, 'about ten, I suppose', and... Tony picked up the script and ripped ten pages out and said, 'there you are, you're back on schedule.' Hartford-Davis remained tight-lipped, but privately he seethed. It was only due to the intervention of his friends that he was persuaded not to quit at the end of that day's shooting. Tenser acknowledges the friction with the director but regards the suggestion of interference slightly differently. 'People who worked for us, like Robert Hartford-Davis, were made aware of the economics of it, as we did with any director at that stage of our career - because you can let it soon run away. I think that Klinger used to get himself more involved in the technicalities of the film, and if they want to call that interference, I don't. He's the producer, along with me, and we are putting the money up and employing everyone - you can't say the boss is interfering with my work.'

While Hartford-Davis struggled through the shooting of *The Black Torment*, Tenser was entertaining two men who would prove influential to the development of the company. The ex-patriot Pole Roman Polanski was in London trying to drum up interest in a script called 'When Katelbach Comes.' The director had returned from Hollywood after losing out on the Best Foreign Language Film academy award for his remarkable thriller *Knife in the Water (1962)*. US film companies showed vague interest, but considered the Pole to be a director of art-house films, and no-one was prepared to commit. Polanski was living in Paris at the time but his friend, would-be producer Gene Gutowski, persuaded him that he would find a more receptive audience in London, and offered him room and board while they searched for a business partner. Starting with the London bases of the US majors, the pair trawled the West End attending meeting after meeting with indifferent studio executives. Polanski wasn't considered 'bankable' and his script - a dense black comedy - did little to dispel that myth. Low on funds, Gutowski became increasingly desperate as his letter to James Carreras at Hammer Films illustrated: 'The

above:
Lady Elizabeth (Heather Sears) comes face to face with the horrors of **The Black Torment**.

only thing I beg you, now having tied up with Roman Polanski, is a quick yes or a no. He has become my financial responsibility and it is essential he make a film immediately.' Like their American counterparts, the British had no difficulty in providing a prompt 'no.'

Attracted initially by the prestigious-sounding name and impressive letterhead, the pair turned up uninvited at the Compton Group's Old Compton Street office where, receptive as ever, Tenser invited them in for coffee. 'Klinger was on a six-week sabbatical with his wife, a second honeymoon. Whilst he was away I was running the firm on my own,' Tenser claims. 'My secretary phoned upstairs to say there is a Mr Gutowski and a Mr Polanski here to see me. I had heard of Polanski because he made *Knife in the Water*, which had got excellent critical reviews. What it had done at the box office I don't know. I guessed that if they were coming to me then they had gone to everybody else. But Polanski was a name, he is a director that draws the press, a brilliant director but a difficult personality to understand.'

below:
Catherine Deneuve through the lens of Roman Polanski on the set of **Repulsion**.

above:
Admat from the US campaign book for **The Black Torment**.

below:
Boys night out: Roman Polanski flanked by Michael Klinger and Tony Tenser. The relationship between the three men was seldom as harmonious as this informal picture suggests.

Tenser and Klinger had already discussed expanding Compton's productions into more mainstream movies, but that still meant the films had to be cheap and they had to be commercial. 'When Katelbach Comes' was rejected out of hand as neither.[9] Tenser had high hopes for the period pot-boiler *The Black Torment*, and he told Polanski that Compton would be in the market for another, preferably contemporary, horror movie. By this time Polanski and Gutowski were in the right frame of mind to compromise, and since Tenser's offer was all there was, the pair reluctantly agreed to produce a script specifically geared towards Tenser's requirements. Returning to Paris, Polanski sat down with his regular writing partner, Gérard Brach, and in just seventeen days they fashioned a treatment about a beautiful but disturbed virgin slowly descending into homicidal madness. With no requirement for star names, limited sets and a strong sexual undercurrent, it was exactly what Compton were looking for.

Polanski returned to Old Compton Street with what he regarded as a satisfactory, albeit workmanlike story. Again, it was Tenser who entertained the diminutive director. 'Up they came and they didn't have a script but they had a synopsis, probably about sixteen pages, in French, of a film called *Lovelihead*. I said I would read it - my French isn't very good but I got the bare bones of it - and I thought it sounded very good. So I said yes, if Roman directs it. Gutowski wanted to be the line producer and Klinger and I would be executive producers.'

When the first draft of the full script was delivered, Polanski and Gutowski estimated the budget to be in the region of £90,000, which was considerably higher than Compton's normal range of between £40,000 and £60,000, but low compared with similar projects elsewhere. Negotiations with Polanski and Gutowski over cuts and trims to lower the cost took until May to resolve, and the contracts for the film, now renamed *Repulsion*, weren't signed until June. In return for producing, directing and writing the film, Polanski, Brach and Gutowksi shared the princely sum of £5,000 between them, plus a small percentage of the net profits. Compton also agreed to alleviate Gutowski's financial situation by advancing Polanski his living expenses, allowing the director to move into an apartment in Eaton Mews. Interestingly such minor considerations as final cut didn't enter into the negotiations at all, as neither Tenser nor Klinger had any pretensions towards artistic creativity - within agreed financial constraints the director was free to create his vision. The extensive trimming forced the budget down to a more palatable £45,000. Compton regarded the figure as an absolute ceiling, but they soon discovered that their director regarded it as a mere guideline.

With the problems of *The Black Torment* at the forefront of their minds, Klinger and Tenser were watching the box-office performance of one Italian import that Compton had missed out on, *Mondo Cane (1962)*, which had just opened in London and was causing a minor sensation. The film was, nominally at least, a documentary directed by Gualtiero Jacopetti and Franco E. Prosperi, highlighting some of the more bizarre aspects of daily life. Mixing carefully staged set-pieces with actual documentary footage, it features such treats as bullfighting complete with ritual slaughter, orgies, cannibalism, shark attacks, and even an Asian restaurant serving dog! 'Mondo Cane was an amazing film, extremely well-made though quite shocking in parts,' Tenser reflects, 'and of course it was showing a lot of stuff that you couldn't see anywhere else; quite an eye-opener in its way.' The film swings wildly from the mundane to the repulsive, and it attracted a great deal of mixed notices when it was released in Britain. Needless to say it was a huge hit. The marginal cost of the film in comparison to the profits reaped was not wasted on two filmmakers, Stanley Long and Arnold Louis Miller, who were responsible for a number of 8mm softcore flicks in the late Fifties. The two men had formed a partnership in order to make more mainstream films and, after a series of routine documentaries, they had branched out into the lucrative territory of nudie flicks with the likes of *Nudes of the World (1961)* and *Take Your Clothes Off and Live! (1963)*. The former had the distinction of a narration by Blue Peter's Valerie Singleton. Long and Miller had actually pre-empted Jacopetti and Prosperi when they made *West End Jungle* in 1961, featuring amongst other delights, prostitution and an exposé on the lives of au pair girls. The film caused some controversy, not least because some of the 'factual' scenes, actually staged for the cameras, were a little too much for the censor to take. As a result it was banned outright.

Stanley Long had worked with Derek Ford on a number of documentaries, and it was Ford who suggested that Compton may be interested in a reworking of *Mondo Cane* within a British setting. It was the exposure of the corrupt underbelly of civilised society that had made the Italian film compulsive viewing, and Long pitched the idea of finding similar material in and around the centre of London. The film would be shot under the banner of their Searchlight Films, with Stanley Long handling the camera work and Arnold Miller producing. Best of all, Long insisted that the film must be made by shooting on the hoof with a minimal crew, meaning that by editing the film quickly, Compton could get the finished product into the cinemas while *Mondo Cane* was still on general release. Needless to say Compton jumped at the chance and *London in the Raw* was duly commissioned.

above:
Stanley Long orchestrates his bunny girls for **London in the Raw**.

With his own roots in cinema management, Tenser ensured that as the distribution book expanded, Compton's sales team worked hard to foster a feeling of partnership, both with the press and the local exhibitors. This philosophy was summed up by Tenser in a speech to Compton's sales managers during the summer of 1964: 'We need to bring back a touch of really old-fashioned showmanship and bang the drum hard,' he declared. 'Publicists are just as important as salesmen.' At the same conference Graham Whitworth noted that, 'Compton is creating a publicity department that is going to make a big name for itself and would be talked about throughout the industry. We have lots of new ideas and we will go out of our way to get to know the exhibitors personally to find out the best way in which we can help them.' The Compton premieres already had a reputation for glamour and saucy sensationalism, and the press loved every minute of them. The regional sales managers for Compton were already distributing press handouts for the company's own slate of productions as well as a whole raft of films that they had purchased for release. For the first time, Tenser found himself getting enquiries from cinema owners around the country asking when certain Compton films were going to be available in their area.

By the time that Hartford-Davis retreated to the editing suite to assemble *The Black Torment*, *London in the Raw* was ready to open. Graham Whitworth remembers the premiere particularly well: 'It was not the best film we ever made but as always I had to get the press's attention. Tony came up with this idea of getting these girls, the Mitchell sisters, Valerie and Marion, to come into the theatre wearing just a long shawl, nothing underneath. There were the usual crowds and photographers outside and when the girls came into the cinema, they dropped their shawls and there it was, 'London in the Raw!' Supported by pictures of scantily clad girls, the press happily ran stories with headlines like, 'London in the Raw: The Bare Facts!'

below:
British admat for **London in the Raw**.

above:
British front of house still for **London in the Raw**.

'*...An attempt to branch into 'isn't life beastly' Mondo Cane territory doesn't really achieve the right jaded cynical air. Despite the polish of the production it's a bit of a hodge-podge.*'
- The Daily Cinema, 10/07/64

Purporting to be 24 hours in the life of the capital, *London in the Raw* certainly lived up to its claim as 'new insight into the city's seedier side.' With its Soho prostitutes and gambling dens, dancing girls and winos, it was as cynical a piece of voyeurism and exploitation as Compton had produced, right down to the mock moralising tone of the narration. Predictably the actual flesh on show is kept to a minimum, though you wouldn't know it from Graham Whitworth's posters – 'The World's Greatest City LAID BARE!' Long's uncompromising camera work almost overcame the low production values but the film never really shakes off its feeling of tackiness; the rapid turnaround time in the shooting and editing is all too obvious on the screen. That's not to say that *London in the Raw* wasn't worth the price of a ticket. With the graphic sequence of an actual (and bloody) hair transplant, Long can lay claim to shooting one of the most sickening scenes in British exploitation, one that manages to out-do even *Mondo Cane* for grossness.

London in Raw opened to good business in London, where one might have expected the locals to have a certain curiosity about themselves, Graham Whitworth and his team worked overtime to raise the interest of provincial audiences. Stories were sent to the press about people who were fainting or leaving the theatre in need of medical attention. The Evening News reported that twenty people, all men, needed treatment at the Plaza in Leeds

LONDON IN THE RAW

'*Lifting the façade of London's neon bright easy money jungle*'
- British Press Releases -

Synopsis

A dizzying parade of behind the scenes and informal shots of strip clubs, the jazz cellars, and arty restaurants, held together by a narration from TV personality David Gell.

Critique

'*What we have here is something of a Mondo Cane of London Town with a distinct bias towards the unpleasant, murky or sordid.*'
- Monthly Film Bulletin, 08/64

above:
A familiar scene for both Tenser and Klinger, inside a London club.

right:
Both Stanley Long and Michael Klinger were closely associated with the early Sixties club scene in London, and it was to feature in a number of the movies they made.

when *London in the Raw* opened, and a further two had to be taken to hospital. In the Sixties it was common for discretely-dressed St John's Ambulance staff to be on duty at theatres, but certainly not cinemas. It didn't take Compton long to realise that for a suitable donation to their coffers, the first-aid workers could be on duty, in full uniform, in the foyers of all the significant openings. Where the publicity budget of local cinemas couldn't stretch to professionals, usherettes and other cinema staff were encouraged to don uniforms and pose prominently in the foyers. The reaction took everybody at Compton by surprise - even the man who orchestrated it: 'It took off like wild fire. The press loved it and couldn't get enough of these stories.' Whitworth confesses. 'I would get a phone call everyday saying, 'Hello Graham, how many people fainted last night then?'

Tenser had raised the question of a follow-up with Searchlight before *London in the Raw* had opened, and with the grosses coming in from around the country, Stanley Long and Arnold Louis Miller signed on the dotted line for a sequel. With the public still recovering, announcements appeared that Compton were preparing 'London in the Raw 2.'

*   *   *   *   *

At a press conference in the summer of 1964 Tony Tenser and Michael Klinger announced pre-production work on a horror story, 'The Teenage Terror', a sexy comedy, 'The Pleasure Girls' and the perennial favourite, 'The Loch Ness Monster.' After the difficulties on *The Black Torment*, Hartford-Davis had made it clear that he would not be working with Compton again in the foreseeable future, and his name had become 'unattached' from the Nessie project, which Tenser was claiming would be the 'biggest science fiction film ever attempted in this country.' This would be followed by 'I Would Rather Stay Poor' - the Hadley Chase book bought and paid for some years earlier - and another science fiction movie, 'The Day the Earth Caved In'. Press conferences were always good opportunities to stretch the truth a little, and Compton were past masters at hyperbole, Tenser without any sign of tongue in cheek assuring the press that Compton movies would be 'major, mainstream movies with big name casts'.

The departure of Hartford-Davis from the fold certainly forced a rethink, and out went several projects that had been lined-up for their star director, including 'The Somme 1916' - now formally binned. Nevertheless, Tenser continued to announce new projects at a furious pace throughout the summer. 'The Pleasure Girls', 'The Face of Terror' and 'The Shattered Room' joined the growing list, but

pride of place was still reserved for 'Nessie', which by the autumn found itself in the nurturing hand of famed fantasy director George Pal. Ultimately only *The Pleasure Girls* would ever make it to the screen, but several films not mentioned at the press conferences had slipped into pre-production almost unnoticed: Polanski's *Repulsion*, 'London in the Raw 2', and a new Sherlock Holmes script which had been written by the Ford brothers.

Despite making the effort to suggest that Compton was moving into the big league in terms of film production, neither Tenser nor Klinger ever made any attempt to hide or disguise their exploitation background. The budgets may have increased significantly since Harrison Marks had packed his crew and equipment into his own car, but Compton were still firmly in control of the financing of their films, as well as overseeing the aspects of their scripts that they considered to be essential to selling the movie. Indeed, as the costs increased the pressure to exploit the saleable elements also increased. This was to prove particularly problematical for writer/director Gerry O'Hara, lining up to make his second film for the Group.

The Pleasure Girls was to be sold as a piece of exploitation cinema - the American tagline was 'Kept in a Plush Pad for His Desires... She Played the Game and Paid the Price' - but director Gerry O'Hara had actually conceived it as something very different. O'Hara had wanted to start directing his second feature as soon as possible after *That Kind of Girl* but found himself working as assistant director on Preminger's *The Cardinal (1963)*, and by the time he was free the impetus was lost. Seeking to kick-start his directorial career, O'Hara wrote a script called 'A Time and a Place' as one of several commissions for British producer Raymond Stross. The concept was drawn heavily from O'Hara's own experiences: 'I lived on the King's Road during the Profumo period and I knew Rachman the notorious property dealer,

above:
Press still from the Birmingham opening of **London in the Raw**.

below:
The power of the press. Compton buys the front pages of trade paper Kine Weekly to promote **The Pleasure Girls**, in the process highlighting their starlet Suzanna Leigh; unknown when she was signed, both she and co-star Francesca Annis were well on their way to stardom by the time the film opened.

right:
Mark Eden as Prinny takes a beating in **The Pleasure Girls**. The film's writer/director Gerry O'Hara based the whole gambling subplot on actual events, if anything playing down the violence for the screen.

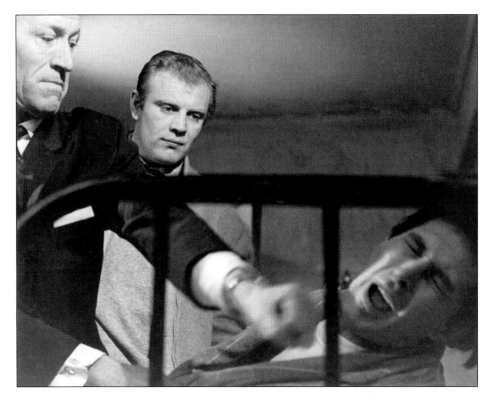

Christine Keeler, and Mandy Rice-Davies. I also knew about the illegal gambling. I knew about a guy caught up in it all who was hung out of a window for his troubles. That actually happened, only in real in life they also wasted him and took off the front of his mouth.' O'Hara's story revolved round a town house in London and the lifestyle of the 'swinging birds.' The focus was the arrival of a new girl in the house, and the complicated love lives of the others are seen through her eyes.

Stross liked the film, which he saw as a vehicle for his wife, the actress Anne Heywood, but he had a number of projects he intended to make first. O'Hara was impatient to start, and persuaded Stross to sell the rights back to him. Touting his script around London, O'Hara found himself back at the Old Compton Street offices of Klinger and Tenser. After some initial hesitation, Klinger agreed to take on the project, with the finances subject to Tenser's approval. After some negotiation a budget of £30,000 was agreed, including a payment of £1,300 as O'Hara's fee. Tenser was, however, insistent that a line producer of Compton's choice was attached to run the production. Harry Fine, an experienced producer, was engaged and immediately given the responsibility of casting the film.[10] It was Fine who handed the highly distinctive Klaus Kinski the role of the Rachman-like manipulator. The often volatile maverick European actor was on a stopover in London, and as always found himself short of cash; he committed himself to the project sight unseen in return for a £900 fee.[11]

Both Klinger and Tenser were delighted, thinking that they had landed the perfect hook for the European market, but O'Hara was less impressed. Kinski had a reputation for being difficult on set and he was presenting Gerry O'Hara with problems even before shooting had started: 'He turned out to be a nice guy but his English was appalling. He had a kind of lisp and simply couldn't get round some words. What I used to do was re-write the lines and simplify the words. If he couldn't roll his 'r's I took out all the 'r' words.' In fact Kinski didn't pose any major problems for the director once shooting started. 'He was aloof and didn't exactly mix with everyone else,' O'Hara says, 'but he was fine. He did his stuff and left, I don't think he cared enough about it to cause problems.'

below:
Euro-star Klaus Kinski making a rare appearance in a British film. The actor was on stopover in London at the time and took the job because he had found himself short of money.

They made love their way...
ANY WAY!!!

The **Pleasure Girls**

IAN McSHANE   FRANCESCA ANNIS   ROSEMARY NICOLS   A TIMES FILM RELEASE

Irene Lamb had been engaged as casting director and was sending a number of starlets along to Old Compton Street for Fine's approval, but Klinger had already decided on his leading lady - Francesca Annis, who had been so effective in *Saturday Night Out*. By conceding the point to Klinger, Fine and O'Hara found that they had a free hand with the rest of the cast, pulling together an impressive ensemble. Ian McShane, who took the role of the beatnik Keith, had made only one film previously, the forgettable *The Wild and the Willing (1962)*. He would go on to carve a film career in films such as *Battle of Britain (1969)* and *Villain (1971)*. Always a talented actor, he has since enjoyed massive success in television with shows like *Dallas* and *Lovejoy*. Mark Eden was cast in the role of 'Prinny', up to his neck in debt and still looking out for number one. Eden would appear in a run of conventional leading roles before appearing on television as Alan Bradley in *Coronation Street*. He would work for Tenser again at Tigon, on *Curse of the Crimson Altar*. Co-incidentally, further down the cast list for *The Pleasure Girls* was Anneke Wills, who soon after shooting wrapped married Michael Gough, another star of *Curse of the Crimson Altar*. Wills had some success on television as a 'companion' for the BBC's 'Doctor Who', but she eventually drifted out of acting into interior design. Rosemary Nicols was likewise destined for short-lived success on TV, in *Department S*, before becoming a television producer. Undoubtedly the most eye-catching amongst the young cast was former debutante

SUZANNA LEIGH   TONY TANNER in
THE PLEASURE GIRLS
co-starring Ian McShane · Francesca Annis · Rosemary Nicols · Mark Eden   A Times Film Presentation

above:
Colleen Fitzpatrick, Francesca Annis and Suzanna Leigh posing for a publicity picture for **The Pleasure Girls**.

Suzanna Leigh, the archetypal Sixties starlet, who brought the film valuable column inches in Britain's tabloid press. Leigh, who had been at school with Francesca Annis, was being hailed in some newspapers as the 'next Grace Kelly.'[12] Leigh's rising star and prominent socialite status might have won Compton some headlines, but it caused a headache for Harry Fine when, in the first week of production, she was approached by Hollywood producer Hal Wallis to test for *Boeing Boeing*. Fine later had to accommodate the actress with a six-day break so she could travel to Rabat, the capital city of Morocco, in order to attend the wedding of Princess Neza.

left:
Gerry O'Hara, left, issues instructions to Ian McShane and Francesca Annis.

above:
A still taken from the party scene of **The Pleasure Girls** and released to the press to suggest an orgy ensues. In fact this still featuring two uncredited actors is about as raunchy as it gets.

below:
Suzanna Leigh and Klaus Kinski in **The Pleasure Girls**.

To make maximum use of the film's limited budget, shooting took place over four and a half weeks in an actual townhouse in Kensington, and although this created some sound and lighting problems, which showed on the film print, the cost benefits were considerable. The cost of renting a house for a week worked out at about 1% of the equivalent studio time! The contrast in technical quality between *The Pleasure Girls* and *Repulsion*, where an interior set was built on a sound stage, is obvious but so was the difference in their budgets. The decision to shoot on site also meant that the exteriors would be limited to the back streets around Kensington and Chelsea, within easy reach of the house. Such studio shooting that was required was done at Twickenham.

Tenser and Klinger had signed off the script at an early stage, but as the dailies came in they realised that O'Hara was shooting a far less explicit film than they had thought they would be getting. O'Hara was oblivious to any problems, and soon found himself under pressure from his own producer: 'Harry was my arch enemy because he was firing the bullets for Tony and Michael. One day he came on set while

Rosemary Nicols was wearing a dressing gown, just a white towelling thing. He saw what was going on, went to C & A or wherever and came back with a see-through nightie. I said it was ridiculous; crass and tatty, and a Chelsea girl wouldn't wear that. He said never mind what she wouldn't wear, shoot it!' O'Hara stood his ground and refused point blank to shoot the scene. Faced with a rebellion, Fine had no choice but to back down.

O'Hara didn't object to lovemaking but he wasn't going to load the film with nudity and sex. It wasn't long before the cast knew that there was a problem. Anneke Wills remembers a number of imposed changes: 'It wasn't supposed to be that sort of movie but when the producers saw the rushes they realised they wouldn't be able to sell it. So out came all the normal stuff like talking in telephone boxes and in came all the bedroom scenes.' Even then, Wills recalls that there was more humour than tension about the whole thing: 'Gerry said I wasn't well enough endowed to be seen nude from the front, so I was only filmed from behind!' O'Hara thought he had done enough to resolve the sex issue, only to find it coming back to haunt him after filming wrapped.

The next battle was over the film's title song, 'The Pleasure Girls', performed by The Three Quarters. O'Hara considered the song to be jarring and out of context with the film he was making. Fine took his lead from the earlier Compton films, and wanted to ensure that the film was clearly pitched at the trendy set. Tenser and Klinger backed the producer and Gerry O'Hara pragmatically backed down: 'There is no point in getting out of your pram on these movies. If something didn't suit, you did what you could to get it changed but at the end of the day, you got on with it.' When *The Pleasure Girls* wrapped without further incident the director assumed that would be that.

*   *   *   *   *

When he was first introduced to the Compton Group, Roman Polanski remarked that the grand-sounding name belied the fact that they were simply a 'small scale producer and distributor of low budget programmers.' All of that was about to change. Tony Tenser was already putting the finishing touches to the partners' most ambitious venture; a site had been acquired in Birmingham, and Compton was investing around £100,000 in a purpose-built cinema, the Superama. At a time when cinemas up and down the country were closing or being converted into bingo halls, Tenser and Klinger were proclaiming that the Superama would be the first in a chain of modern, state of the art cinemas that would win the public back to the silver screen. To ensure maximum exposure for their grand schemes, Tenser proposed that the long overdue official announcement should coincide with the premiere of their latest epic, so Graham Whitworth was instructed to pull out all the stops for *The Black Torment*.

THE BLACK TORMENT

'You're Just a Carriage Ride Away
from Terror'
- British Trade Ads -

Synopsis

Sir Richard returns to his ancestral home, Fordyke House, with his new bride Lady Elizabeth, to find his tenants openly hostile. When he learns that a local girl was raped and murdered he dismisses the suggestion that her dying words implicated him. Fordyke House is soon plagued with mysterious incidents, sightings of Sir Richard's dead first wife, and windows opening on their own. When Sir Richard's father is found brutally murdered the militia intervene, determined to bring matters to a head.

Critique

'Twenty years ago this film would have had Margaret Lockwood and James Mason... but the recipe still works, and now it's in colour.'
- Daily Express, 15/10/64

'One of the uneasy period chillers which provokes rather too many unintentional giggles... Quite well made and directed, this grisly little item will create a few clammy hands but it is much too far fetched to be taken too seriously by anyone but the gallant cast.'
- Daily Mirror, 15/10/64

'A ludicrous horror film made with no style or flair, a ploddingly explicit script that signals every move far in advance, and a positive genius for putting the camera in all the wrong

left:
Tenser's idea of 18th Century dress, as modelled by Edina Ronay in **The Black Torment**.

above:
The climatic battle between Sir Richard (John Turner) and Seymour (Peter Arne) in **The Black Torment**.

places at the wrong time. It is directed by Mr. Robert Hartford-Davis, who makes Mr. Terence Fisher look like Eisenstein and Feuillade rolled into one.'
- The Times, 15/10/64

'...a creditable attempt at the elusive style of Gothic romance. It is told with considerable narrative drive and acted in a manner to provide more thrills than laughs.'
- The Daily Telegraph, 16/10/64

'One of those ludicrous British horror films which produce more squeals of amusement than of terror. Badly directed, badly acted and even more badly photographed.'
- The Sunday Times, 18/10/64

From the moment Edina Ronay's off-screen panting opens *The Black Torment*, you realise that Compton have moved into new territory, high melodrama replacing social issues. Unfortunately the teasingly daring opening sequence sets a standard that the Fords' script struggles to maintain, the dramatic possibilities offered by a deranged aristocrat raping and torturing the locals go largely unrealised. Indeed, aside from the murder of Annette Whiteley's busty wench, which is never attributed to him, Sir Richard is merely guilty of disturbing the peasants' sleep and ordering goods he doesn't pay for. Hartford-Davis settles instead for a conventional but nonetheless entertaining gothic thriller.

Setting aside the off-set problems, Hartford-Davis certainly seems to be having fun, and keeps the narrative galloping along at such a pace you hardly notice the plot inconstancies. Not all of Hartford-Davis's tricks work; the point of view shots from Sir Giles's perspective are embarrassingly inept, and the speeded-up photography in the chase sequences undermines the impact. Most of the action takes place at night, and Peter Newbrook's fine colour cinematography cloaks the day-for-night shots in the eerily blue gloom of moonlight -

below:
Robert Hartford-Davis on the set of **The Black Torment**. This was the director's last collaboration with Compton after the producers' interference on set almost led to him walking away from the job.

right:
John Turner and Heather Sears pose on set of **The Black Torment** as Raymond Huntley looks on.

reinforced by the blue motif carried through carpets, wall hangings and clothes. Newbrook also shrouds Fordyke House - or rather the handful of studio sets - in effective, creeping shadows, though the attempt to mould the house into a central character in the narrative (à la *Mandalay*) gets a little lost in all the gruesome action.

From an acting point of view Turner gives a bravura performance as Sir Richard, blasting out every line with so much gusto that he seems totally insane even in his 'quieter' moments - which are few. Heather Sears's coquettish Elizabeth is almost overwhelmed by the sheer physical force of Turner's acting, but manages to salvage some fragile vulnerability. Peter Arne is of course so sneeringly nasty that you know he is the villain from the word go, and Joseph Tomelty acts with such a tortured expression that it is painful to watch him go through his motions. The remainder of the cast are straight from Hammer's 'muttering yokels' drama school, and it's a shame that both Annette Whiteley and Edina Ronay are given little to do.

If you are not too demanding, then *The Black Torment* is a thoroughly entertaining movie and it's a real shame that Compton didn't get to have another stab at the genre.

The premiere of *The Black Torment* took place at the Rialto on the 15th of October 1964. Eight of the dancers from the nearby Windmill Theatre, bedecked in their rhinestone and glitter costumes, had come along to the Rialto to welcome the guests. The semi-naked girls provided a colourful distraction for the press, and champagne flowed freely amongst the likes of Annette Whiteley and Peter Arne, and Gerry O'Hara and Francesca Annis, now a couple. There was, however one noticeable absentee; soon after he handed over his cut, Robert Hartford-Davis had cleared out his desk and turned his back on Compton once and for all. 'Robert Hartford-Davis didn't make great films but they were still solid pictures,' Tenser reflects. 'He was very competent and knew what he was doing.'[13]

Footnotes

1. Hartford-Davis had left school at the age of fifteen, and worked as a film technician until he was nearly forty, learning the craft from the likes of John Huston, King Vidor and Basil Dearden. After a spell in Hollywood, taking a degree at the University of California, Hartford-Davis returned to Britain to make his feature directorial debut with *Crosstrap (1961)*. His film career benefited enormously from the contacts he made during his early days in Soho, forming close working associations with not only Klinger and Tenser, but also the likes of Stanley Long, Peter Newbrook and the Ford Brothers.

2. Gerry O'Hara gained experience as assistant director on large-scale movies like *Anastasia (1956)* and *Exodus (1960)*, working with directors of the status of Carol Reed, Otto Preminger and Tony Richardson. He would continue to turn out for them in assistant duties long after he had started to write and direct his own films. O'Hara didn't flourish as a director despite some interesting projects, including *All the Right Noises (1969)*, *The Brute (1977)*, and of course Compton's *The Pleasure Girls*. The critical reaction to his films seemed to swing from one extreme to another, with *Maroc 7 (1966)* and *The Bitch (1979)* attracting reviews that were as virulent as the notices for *All the Right Noises* were complimentary. He enjoyed success on the television action shows *The Avengers* and *The Professionals*, before falling under the spell of exploitation king Harry Alan Towers, for whom he wrote or directed straight to video efforts like *Fanny Hill (1983)*. His last film as a director was the lamentable *The Mummy Lives (1993)*.

3. Born in Tilbury, Essex in 1932, Derek Ford was a softly-spoken, intelligent man with an extensive background in radio, television and mainstream cinema. After National Service he joined Martin Leas as a clapper boy working on commercials, before making his debut as a writer - working with his brother Donald - on the BBC's Children's Hour. His work life centred on Soho from 1961, when he renewed his writing partnership with Donald. Apart from his work for Tenser, Ford became a very successful writer/director working almost exclusively in the exploitation field, making films such as *Corruption (1967)*, again with Robert Hartford-Davis (and frequently misidentified as a Tigon film), and *What's Up Nurse? (1977)*. After retiring from filmmaking Derek took up writing novels with some success. Donald Ford, the older brother by seven years, has served as a Juvenile Court Magistrate as well as writing such worthy books as 'The Delinquent Child' and 'The Deprived Child'.

4. South African-born Green was a huge strapping man, ideal for the military types he played in many movies. He was heroic in *The Masque of the Red Death (1964)*, made an excellent Nayland Smith in *The Face of Fu Manchu (1965)*, and also appeared in *The Skull (1965)* for Freddie Francis, Hammer's *Countess Dracula (1970)*, and Stephen Weeks's *Gawain and The Green Knight (1972)*, his last film. Tragically, Green killed himself at his Brighton home on the 15th of May 1972, reportedly depressed with the state of his career. He was only 48.

above:
Sir Richard learns the truth in this scene depicted on a British front of house still for **The Black Torment**.

5. Born in London in 1935, Sears won a British Academy Award and Variety Club Best Actress Award for only her third film, playing Joan Crawford's daughter in *The Story of Esther Costello (1957)*. The same year Sears was voted Top Actress by British Moviegoers but her popularity was short lived; after good roles in *Room at the Top (1958)* and *Sons and Lovers (1960)* her career lost momentum. Hammer's *The Phantom of the Opera (1962)* and her work for Compton were the only films she completed in the Sixties. She died in 1994 after a long battle with cancer.

6. Brazilian-born Annis was the daughter of the English actor and director Anthony Annis, who had made a career out of doubling for Laurence Olivier. Influenced more by her mother, a Brazilian shipping heiress and strict Roman Catholic, young Annis spent much of her early life aspiring to be a Carmelite nun. Attending the Corona Stage School initially to study ballet, she soon caught the acting bug and after a series of minor British movies made her international film debut at the age of 16 as a serving maid to Elizabeth Taylor in *Cleopatra (1963)*. British movies could not find a way to accommodate her fragile beauty, and her film career never really took off - not that one would have known it due to the amount of press attention she received. Whether it was her plastic surgery (on her nose) in 1966, or her four year affair with Jon Finch, Annis was never out of the tabloids but she seemed unable or unwilling to get career capital out of the attention. She made a somewhat gentle Lady Macbeth for Polanski opposite Finch, but annoyed the film's backers, Playboy Productions, by refusing to pose nude to promote the film, so they went ahead and used nude stills of her lifted straight from the movie. She continued to work in movies like *Krull (1983)* and *Dune (1984)* but she found her niche on the small screen with series like *Lillie*, *Between the Lines* and *Headhunters*, and one-off TV movies like *Why Didn't They Ask Evans?* and *Onassis: The Richest Man in the World*. Her affair with actor Ralph Fiennes, twenty years her junior and her co-star on stage in Hamlet (Annis played his mother!), ensured she continued her love/hate relationship with the tabloids.

below:
Annette Whiteley enjoying a brief respite from the horrors of **The Black Torment**.

above:
Edina Ronay in a posed publicity shot for **The Black Torment**. Despite enjoying only the briefest of appearances the starlet was to be the focal point for Compton's publicity machine.

below:
The Black Torment had a typically colourful premiere in London's West End. Election night crowds packing Coventry Street were treated to the spectacle of eight Windmill girls arriving at the Rialto in their brief costumes and eye-catching head-dresses. They were welcomed by Michael Klinger and Tony Tenser, seen here in the centre as a champagne toast is drunk to their acquisition of the Windmill theatre.

7. Lodge, born in 1921, went on to work for Hartford-Davis on *The Sandwich Man (1966)*, *Corruption (1967)*, *Incense for the Damned (1970)*, *The Fiend (1971)* and *Nobody Ordered Love (1971)*. Hartford-Davis went so far as to rewrite the script of *Corruption* so the middle-aged Lodge could appear as part of an otherwise all teenage gang. Lodge himself was a capable if uninspiring support actor, who worked frequently in television, memorably appearing on Spike Milligan's *Q* series, where he gently mocked his tough guy image. In cinema he took roles in cult classics like *I'm All Right Jack (1959)* and *Scream and Scream Again (1969)* as well as working on the *Carry On* and *Pink Panther* films.

8. Malaysian Peter Arne seemed perpetually cast as a smirking villain, a role he essayed with great aplomb for three decades. He made his debut in 1944, but was best known for his roles in films like *Ice Cold in Alex (1958)*, *The Pirates of Blood River (1961)*, and *The Oblong Box (1969)*. He provided excellent support in big-budget non-genre movies like *Khartoum (1966)*, *Return of the Pink Panther (1975)*, and *Agatha (1979)*. An extremely charming and courteous man, his death was as wasteful as it was tragic when in 1983 he was murdered by his homosexual lover, who later committed suicide.

9. Polanski originally conceived 'When Katelbach Comes' as a project for himself and his ex-wife Barbara Kwiatkowska, who had acted for him already under the name of Barbara Lass, and was by then married to the actor Karlheinz Böhm. Kwiatkowska was to play the lead - a Polish rather than French student in the first drafts - with Polanski acting opposite her as the weakling husband. If the film had progressed beyond planning and into production it seems certain that Böhm would have refused to allow his wife to work with Polanski in such an overtly sexual film.

10. Fine moved from television to films in the early Sixties, but he had worked in the industry for twenty years prior to that. After *The Pleasure Girls* he worked for Michael Klinger on the likes of *The Penthouse (1967)* before meeting up with Michael Style and Tudor Gates to form Fantale Films, the company who re-invented Hammer horror with *The Vampire Lovers (1970)*, *Lust for a Vampire (1970)* and *Twins of Evil (1971)*.

11. Born Nikolaus Günther Nakszynski in Poland in 1926, and a stage actor of some reputation and controversy in post-war Europe, Kinski discovered a lucrative market for support roles in European flicks, including a short spell in forgettable British movies. He worked constantly throughout his career, often on horror or exploitation movies, and in the process he achieved considerable cult status, but little critical credit. A long-cherished directional debut, *Paganini (1989)*, was heavily edited by its producers and opened to such a critical savaging that a bitter Kinski retired to his California home and devoted his remaining years to his family. He died in 1991 of natural causes. His work with Werner Herzog on films like *Aguirre, Wrath of God (1972)*, *Nosferatu the Vampyre (1979)*, and *Fitzcarraldo (1982)* gives him a permanent footnote in film history. His CV can also boast the likes of Lindsay Shonteff's *Sumuru (1967)*, and Jess Franco's *Venus in Furs (1969)* and *Jack the Ripper (1976)*.

12. Convent-educated Suzanna Leigh was born in Reading but so personifies the Belgravia spirit that it is not a surprise to find she spent most of her life there. In the mid-Sixties she had a high profile in London's smartest set and, for a short period, was touted as a major star find by American Hal Wallis, producer of the Elvis movies. In 1966 he flew Leigh, in a blaze of publicity, to Hollywood for a seven-year non-exclusive contract, earning £10,000 a day and appearing in *Boeing Boeing (1965)* with Tony Curtis and Jerry Lewis, and the Elvis movie *Paradise, Hawaiian Style (1966)*. The tabloids made much of her trysts with the likes of Steve McQueen, Tony Curtis, Kirk Douglas, and The Earl of Litchfield but after problems with American Equity her Hollywood career fizzled out. She was soon back in Britain labouring in routine stuff like *The Deadly Bees (1966)*, *The Lost Continent (1968)*, and Hartford-Davis's *The Fiend (1971)*. Leigh kept the headline writers busy with her marriage to the financier Tim Hue-Williams and the subsequent acrimonious and very public divorce. By the mid-Nineties the bubble had well and truly burst and in July 1997 the Daily Express - quick to spot a 'how the mighty have fallen story' - reminded everyone who she was and took pious delight in telling its readers that Leigh was now bankrupt (she reputedly lost over £1m in bad investments) and living on income support on a housing estate in Northolt.

13. After quitting Compton, Hartford-Davis formed Titan International Films with Peter Newbrook, and produced a handful of diverse, interesting and largely neglected movies, including the disastrous *Gonks Go Beat (1965)* and the more visceral *Corruption (1967)*. All of Hartford-Davis's films display an imagination and elegance lacking in the work of many of his peer group. His particular trademark was a highly mobile camera making persuasive use of zooms, tracking shots etc... basically anything to keep the camera going. He made several British genre movies, notably *Incense for the Damned (1970)* and *The Fiend (1971)*, before moving to the US. Initially Hartford-Davis enjoyed some success in Hollywood - he was voted Best Action Director of 1973-74 by European critics - before spending the last years of his life working on second rate films and television.

Chapter Three

'The Nightmare World of a Virgin's Dreams'

- (British publicity slogan for *Repulsion*)

With filmmaking established as a profitable side-line for Compton and distribution, under the Compton-Cameo banner, proving increasingly successful, the obvious way for Klinger and Tenser to expand was by moving into exhibition. The company had been founded to provide a purpose-built cinema supplying entertaining product in a comfortable and relaxing environment. Tenser was convinced he could apply the same ethos to a chain of mainstream cinemas and do something to help reverse the decline that had gripped the industry for well over a decade. Klinger was more inclined towards film production, but accepted the appeal of large-scale showcase cinemas, and also reasoned that the acquisition of bricks and mortar would add considerable weight to the company's balance sheet. As work started on the Superama in Birmingham, planning permission was already being sought for two sister theatres in Derby and Southport. Then in October 1964 the legendary Windmill Theatre came to Compton's acquisitive attention.[1]

Located on Windmill Street, only a stones throw from the Compton offices, the Windmill was one of the best known of London's more risqué theatres, but despite its reputation for Parisian decadence, it had found itself increasingly left behind by the 'Swinging Sixties.' At the time Compton's finances were fully committed elsewhere and the opportunity to acquire the place came completely out of the blue. Tenser takes up the story: 'I had a phone call from a friend of mine in the film business who was connected to Sheila Van Damm, owner of the Windmill Theatre. The Windmill used to have shows, just dancing shows really but the dancing girls wore brief costumes - very brief! The real attraction I suppose were the girls who stood at the back showing their breasts, but they weren't allowed to move, they had to stand still! Van Damm said they were thinking of selling the Windmill, would I like to buy it? So I asked how much they wanted, they quoted a figure and I said that sounded reasonable for the freehold. So I got hold of Klinger and he said, 'we'll find the money.' We hunted round and eventually found a guy in the City who was in the property business; his name was Laurie Marsh.' The figure in question was £250,000, and Tenser's plan was to turn the Windmill into a 'super cinema', with a preview theatre and three floors of offices.

Laurie Marsh, a thirty two-year old self-made millionaire with significant property holdings, was amenable to providing the finance in exchange for a share of the freehold. Marsh had little interest in the film industry in any capacity at that point, though he was later to play a significant role in shaping the Tigon Group. The acquisition and redevelopment of the Windmill, a prime location off Shaftesbury Avenue in the heart of the West End, was perfectly in line with Marsh's policy of buying property for development and/or resale, and provided Compton with a flagship for their burgeoning empire. The office space available above the auditorium

below:
Self-promotion: Michael Klinger and Tony Tenser buy the front page of the November 19th, 1964 edition of trade paper Kine Weekly. The partners would continue to use the trade papers to raise their personal profiles as well as to promote their films throughout the lifetime of Compton.

above:
Pauline Collins, second from right, making her feature film debut in **Secrets of a Windmill Girl**. To her credit the popular actress has never denied her early work within the world of exploitation movies.

meant that the Group's ever-expanding publicity department could relocate just round the corner from the main office.

The famous revues, proudly hailed as the 'shows that Hitler's bombs couldn't stop', would end, and of course the girls would have to go, but Compton never missed a trick. The last few shows were captured on celluloid by Stanley Long and Arnold Miller, still thought of as documentary filmmakers (albeit of exploitative subjects), who were called in at short notice to do the filming under the auspices of their Searchlight Films. At the time of filming no-one had a clear idea of what to do with the footage, and it was filed away under the title 'The Windmill Girls Story', but as always with Compton it didn't go to waste. It took a couple of years - an unheard of delay in Compton terms, where turnaround time was seldom more than a few months - but in 1966 a use was found for the Searchlight footage, as it formed the basis of *Secrets of a Windmill Girl*. In the meantime Messrs Long and Miller had taken their cameras back on to the mean streets of London, and with *London in the Raw* still playing to good crowds in the West End, the imaginatively titled sequel *London in the Raw 2* started shooting.

*   *   *   *   *

Book-keeping records for the Compton Cinema Club for the last quarter of 1964 show that membership had swollen to almost 35,000 paying members, or around 175 times the number fire regulations would allow in the auditorium at any one sitting! Respectability was harder to come by than success however, and the Club had never really lost its slightly seedy, tawdry image. Klinger and Tenser remained more determined than ever to position the Compton Group as a major player in the UK film industry.

With workmen rushing to meet the scheduled November opening date for the Superama and refurbishment plans signed off for the Windmill, solid box-office hits from their own films and a sales force that spanned the globe, the Compton partners launched their latest charm offensive. 'We are ambitious, industrious and greedy for the good things in life,' Klinger told Kine Weekly. 'We have worked very hard indeed for our success. We have ceased to undersell the company; we have got rid of the 'poor cousin' image; we have built our business in a straightforward and honourable way and are now in a major position as both producers and importers of top quality feature films.' Surprisingly, from the very early days both Tenser and Klinger drew only modest salaries; a key factor in Compton's continuing growth was the way that profits were always pumped straight back into the business. The new ventures, whether in bricks and mortar or film production, represented much more to Klinger and Tenser than speculative investments - this was their future.

Compton's ambitions peaked when Michael Klinger confirmed that the Group was to make a bid for the ailing production giant British Lion.

British Lion's close association with Alexander Korda had yielded some of the classics of the British cinema, including

left:
A Windmill Girl fixes
her make-up.

below:
Laurie Marsh, property
tycoon, self-made
millionaire and partner
in The Compton Group.

Anna Karenina (1948) starring Vivien Leigh, and Carol Reed's *The Third Man (1949)* but for years it had been dependant on state hand-outs from an increasingly reluctant Government. Years of indifferent management and a succession of poor films had gradually eroded the company's position, leading to it being placed on the market with an asking price in the region of £1.6m. This sum seemed to limit the prospective bidders to industry heavyweights such as Leslie Grade, brother of Lew, Sam Spiegel the American producer of *Lawrence of Arabia*, and Sydney Box the veteran British film mogul.

The press seemed bemused and unsure about whether the Compton bid was just a publicity stunt, but Klinger took it seriously enough; he was genuinely keen to take on all comers and emerge with not only a massive back catalogue but also the company's sprawling Shepperton base. Tenser was more cautious, but took a pragmatic approach - the backlot alone was in excess of 60 acres and the freedom to dispose of such a prime slice of real estate would be the cornerstone of the Group's fundraising activities. Compton rounded up a number of potential investors for a meeting at their offices, chaired by Klinger, during which plans were made to table an initial offer. The intention at that point was to retain the production facilities but considerably slim down the surplus backlot.

The flurry of activity alerted Wardour Street's finest, who foresaw the upstarts at Compton asset-stripping the already beleaguered industry. As a result the Secretary of Industry, Edward Heath, was subjected to some intensive canvassing. When the Government announced the conditions of sale shortly afterwards, they imposed upon the deal the right to veto any future development of the site. The film industry's power brokers breathed a sigh of relief, and Klinger saw interest amongst his prospective backers rapidly evaporate. 'It brought us to the attention of some people who maybe hadn't heard of us before,' Tenser remarks ruefully, 'I am sure they took it seriously so maybe it got us a little more respect in the industry.' In the end British Lion was sold to to a consortium run by Sir Michael Balcon that included the likes of the Boulting brothers, John Schlesinger and Brian Epstein. It staggered on for a few more years before finally being gobbled up by EMI.

below:
April Wilding and
Pauline Collins pose in
the centre of London's
Piccadilly Circus for a
publicity shot to promote
**Secrets of a Windmill
Girl**. Given the film's
subject matter, this was
a rather demure attempt
to generate publicity.

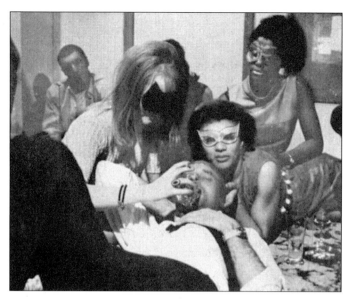

above:
Swinging London, Compton-style.

below:
British front of house still for **Primitive London**. The film was shot in colour, but at the time promotional stills were produced in black and white only.

Undeterred, Klinger and Tenser barely paused for breath. In November 1964 they were in Birmingham as the Superama prepared for its grand opening. Hailed as the country's most modern and comfortable cinema experience, the Superama was a bright and spacious 650 seater, combining the very best acoustic design and sound systems with the biggest screen in Britain, relative to auditorium size. The Compton publicity team again applied their considerable skills to produce an opening night

extravaganza in the presence of the Lord Mayor of Birmingham, which included the band of the Royal Warwickshire Fusiliers and guest appearances by actors Oliver Reed, Francesca Annis and Sylvia Syms. The female cast members of *The Black Torment* were wheeled in for good measure, along with personalities such as radio disc jockey Pete Murray. Among the more curious exhibits in the foyer was a selection of wild Australian flowers picked over eighteen months earlier, and preserved in huge cones of ice! Michael Klinger took the spotlight and promised that Compton's feature presentations would make the audience 'laugh, cry and think.' The Lord Mayor then extended his official welcome to the city, recalling in his speech that one of Compton's predecessors had opened a cinema in Birmingham with similar high principals but 'all we have seen since it opened was a lot of bosoms and a lot of bottoms!' The irony of that statement plainly escaped him!

To emphasise the quality of the screen and the new sound system, Compton started proceedings with clips from the 70mm epics *El Cid*, *King of Kings* and *Lawrence of Arabia*. For Graham Whitworth, acting as master of ceremonies for the VIP guests, the opening represented a personal triumph and the pinnacle of his career at Compton, but it also provided one or two nervous moments for him. 'Oliver Reed was wild in those days, though perhaps not as

PRIMITIVE LONDON X EASTMAN COLOUR

Directed by ARNOLD LOUIS MILLER Photography by STANLEY A. LONG   Executive Producers MICHAEL KLINGER and TONY TENSER

wild as he later became. After the show, he and Pete decided to go on a tour of the city nightlife - on the roof of a car!'

In deference to the mixed audience Tenser opted for the highly-regarded *Lord of the Flies (1963)* rather than one of Compton's more risqué offerings, but controversy was never far away. Graham Whitworth found himself on the receiving end of unexpected headlines when the opening show was inadvertently scheduled for a Sunday evening - strictly forbidden by local bylaws at the time. 'That was a genuine oversight,' Whitworth claims, 'But you know what they say, all publicity is good publicity.' Gracious host that he was, the Right Worshipful Gentleman didn't comment on the show being screened on a holy day but he was reportedly disappointed by a reference in the film to a male member!

*   *   *   *   *

By March 1965, *London in the Raw 2*, now re-titled *Primitive London*, was cut-together and ready to give the public another sight of the capital's underbelly.

PRIMITIVE LONDON

'They turned London inside out...
and filmed it!'
- UK Press Release -

Synopsis

A 'true life' documentary featuring such delights as child birth, Mods, Rockers and Beatniks, and such 'violent' sports as judo, kendo and indoor bowling! Guaranteed crowd-pullers such as strippers and wife swapping parties are also a feature, alongside a piece on the killing and packing of battery hens. There are some staged recreations (a Jack the Ripper murder for example), which are intermixed with appearances from pop stars Billy J Kramer and MacDonald Hobley.

Critique

'It isn't easy to take the film's sociological pretensions...David Gell's commentary suggests bland disgust while at the same time pandering to the film's air of titillation.'
- Daily Cinema, 03/65

'The colour perhaps appropriately is hideous. The tedium has no bounds.'
- Monthly Film Bulletin, 05/65

'Untidy documentary which hardly justifies its catchpenny title. Editing is shaky, Eastman colour is variable and the commentary overgabby, and stuffed with verbal wind.'
- Variety, 21/04/65

Messrs Miller and Long promised that they would show us 'The Jungle Behind the Bright Lights,' but *Primitive London* amounts to little more than a re-working of the previous film, and it's clear that the makers had very little interest in finding anything new. The opening childbirth scene is typical of their inventiveness, with David Gell's trite throwaway that the child will soon be cast adrift in an 'easy come, easy go city in which he must find his own identity.' As with its predecessor the film juxtaposes bland and bizarre vignettes, undermined by an increasingly bored Gell stumbling through the narration. The titillation, care of the girls from The Churchill Club, comes too late to salvage the film.

The newly refurbished Windmill theatre was now available, so Compton engaged the TV compere, Ray Martine, who made an appearance in the film, to act as master of ceremonies for the World Premiere of *Primitive London* on the 25th of March. With the 'Windmill Girls' consigned

above:
The infamous poultry scene from **Primitive London**.

left:
Just in case anyone didn't get the joke, Compton's Kine Weekly cover juxtaposed fresh meat with 'beautiful chicks'!

right:
British artwork for
Primitive London.
The leopard skins
became Compton's
motif for promoting the
film.

to history Michael Klinger hired some of the 'exotic dancers' from the nearby Churchill Club for the night, including Vicki Grey, regarded at the time as one of the best dancers in Soho, and particularly eye-catching in £1,000-worth of (borrowed) leopard-skin bikini and fur coat. In a publicity stunt that recalled the best of Tenser's Miracle tricks, Ms. Grey toured the West End dressed in her leopard skins accompanied by a 'pet' cheetah called Kinna. The ultimate matching accessory would have been a leopard on a leash, but a suitable animal wasn't available, so Graham Whitworth convinced Colchester Zoo to lend him their three-year-old cheetah instead.

Despite the lack of new ideas the opening proved very successful for Compton, if nothing else proving that you can fool some of the people some of the time. The Windmill Theatre, which six months earlier had been playing half-empty, now saw the 'house full' boards being dusted down again; with only 300 seats in the theatre *Primitive London*, supported by *Runaway Killer*, took a very respectable £2,300 in its first week. By way of comparison *The Ipcress File*, opening in massive West End cinemas under a barrage of publicity, took some £7,900 during the same week. However, when *Primitive London* went out on circuit release a month

later, with *Naked - As Nature Intended* hauled out of the vaults as support, the returns were no better than average. It was obvious to Klinger and Tenser that the public's appetite for such things had started to wane.

* * * * *

Associating with a director of Roman Polanski's calibre brought Klinger and Tenser some immediate benefits in terms of their company's profile within the industry. Conveniently forgetting that Polanski and his begging bowl had been turned away from every office in Wardour Street, the trade press now crowed that such an acclaimed director working in Britain was evidence of the importance of the British film industry. Polanski's arrival at the Twickenham studios to start shooting was trumpeted loudly in both the trade and national press.

Tenser and Klinger could afford to be smug. The film getting all this attention was budgeted no differently from their other films, and they didn't anticipate that Polanski, despite his new-found status, would to be treated any differently from the other directors who passed through the Compton St. offices. After working with first-time directors like Harrison Marks and Gerry O'Hara, the making of *The Black Torment* had given Klinger and Tenser their first experience of a head-on confrontation with their director. Now there was a new challenge for Compton - a director with a strong artistic vision. The first skirmish was over the casting: for the leading role, Klinger proposed a selection of Compton's 'starlets de jour', amongst them Francesca Annis and Suzanna Leigh. To placate Klinger, Polanski agreed to test Annis, though he had already decided that she was physically unsuitable; the test was shot and the actress duly rejected. Polanski then proposed his own choice, Catherine Deneuve, a beautiful French actress who was practically unknown in the UK at the time.[2] Tenser and Klinger were outraged when her agent immediately made her pay requirements known – the amount being demanded was considerably higher than the sum the local talent would happily accept. Polanski held out and the Compton partners backed down, though not before they had reminded Polanski and Gutowski of the carefully-considered budget. Deneuve was cast against type as the repressed Carol; withdrawn and alone she haunts the rooms of her dingy apartment tormented by twisted visions and hallucinations. Of course, with a French actress in the lead, Polanski needed another French actress to take the role of Carol's sexually active sister. Yvonne Furneaux, the British-based French actress, best known from Hammer's *The Mummy (1959)*, was tested and promptly cast.[3]

below:
British front of house
still for **Primitive
London**.

Unusually, the men in *Repulsion* are limited to supporting roles. Unfamiliar with British actors, Polanski sketched rough portraits of how he imagined his characters looking, then sat down and scoured The Spotlight - the actor's directory - to find suitable candidates. The resulting selections: John Fraser, Ian Hendry and Patrick Wymark, were all excellent choices, but they were also relatively expensive. Klinger cannily succeeded in convincing each in turn that they should accept less than their usual rates in return for the privilege of working with a hot young director.

Polanski and Gutowski were also largely unfamiliar with the names being suggested for the crew. They did however insist on Gil Taylor, who had worked for Kubrick on *Dr. Strangelove* (1964), as director of photography. Taylor was widely regarded as one of the best cameramen in the industry and his price reflected his status. Compton were once again persuaded to dig deep, but in return they impressed on Gutowski the impact on both the budget and more significantly the schedule - Taylor was already committed to start his next film, *The Bedford Incident*, for Columbia, so *Repulsion* would have to start and finish on time. Having got his own way on Deneuve and Taylor, Polanski was willing to compromise on the remainder of the

crew; Alastair McIntyre from *The Black Torment* came on as editor, Ted Sturgis was installed as assistant director and Seamus Flannery was hired as the film's art director. To help safeguard their interests, Compton installed the amenable and reliable Bob Sterne as production manager.

Uneasy about the way that costs had increased before a single frame had been shot, Klinger and Tenser jumped at the offer from Sam Waynberg's Berlin-based Planet Films GmbH to buy the German rights, sight unseen. Waynberg, an admirer of Polanski's earlier work, was later to prove instrumental in getting *Repulsion* selected for the Berlin Film Festival, and lobbied tirelessly for its recognition by the official jury.

With minimal exterior filming at locations in the West End of London (including Polanski's friend Vidal Sassoon's beauty salon), *Repulsion* was set predominately in a single location, a flat. Unlike Gerry O'Hara, Polanski saw the apartment as more than a backdrop; it was central to his story and the entire set was therefore constructed on the soundstages at Twickenham. The walls and ceilings were all designed to be moveable, so that the effect could be created, in camera, of the apartment's dimensions distorting - corridors seeming to lengthen, and ceilings to get lower.

above:
Low angle shot of Catherine Deneuve in **Repulsion**. Note the ceiling - a relative novelty for studio-shot movies at the time, as only walls are usually constructed on set.

below:
Catherine Deneuve posing for the press in a shot taken outside her London hotel.

Filming began in June 1965 and almost immediately Polanski started to impress; word of mouth on the rushes as well as the relentless self-promotion of the director created a real buzz in London. Riding the crest of the wave Tenser announced, much to Polanski's surprise, that Compton were considering three more movies from the same team! This outward show of solidarity wasn't in evidence on set however, where Polanski's meticulous shooting style was causing severe over-runs. Management visits to Twickenham inevitably created friction, as Tenser and Klinger were forced to witness retake after retake of apparently perfect shots. Klinger in particular would openly question the approach of their director. 'Any difficulties we had, would be around shooting things that we felt wouldn't be used in the film,' Tenser explains. 'For example if you think about the scene where all the hands are coming out of the wall. To do that, we had to specially cut holes in the wall and different kinds of people, ethnic and non-ethnic, children and adults, had to put their hands through. They were put in with latex and Polanski started shooting, then they had to stop because someone needed a pee or wanted to scratch his nose, whatever. They had to be cut out, went to the toilet and then had to be refitted. This took time and was costing a lot of money. Klinger, I think, said 'look, why so many hands?' Polanski wouldn't answer. 'Could we lose some here and there?' He said nothing, he refused to answer.' Faced with an obstinate director, Tenser remembers being totally reliant on Gene Gutowski: 'We had an excellent relationship with Gene. When we had difficulties with the directing of the film, Gutowski would act as a go-between to get it right. Sometimes it worked in our favour but more often it worked in Polanski's.'

above:
Forced to listen to her sister's noisy love-making, Carol starts to retreat into her secluded world.

The delays soon threatened the availability of Gil Taylor, but any pressure to increase his work-rate was stubbornly resisted by Polanski. Unusually for a foreigner working on his first British movie Polanski enjoyed the support of his crew, who would work unpaid overtime to finish shots - something unheard of in the strict union structure of the British film industry. One of Polanski's staunchest supporters was none other than Bob Sterne; doing what he could to speed-up the shooting without impeding the director, he found himself in court when he allowed a scene involving a car crash to go ahead without waiting for police permission. Tenser had no choice but to remain pragmatic: 'It was his film, his baby, and that's the way he wanted to make it. At the end of the day you have to say he was right but then we were right too.' Without a special effects team, the crew had to work out ad hoc solutions on set, which also slowed progress.

Polanski also refused to pander to cinematic niceties in his handling of the cast, in particular Deneuve; he insisted his leading lady was filmed in close-up, without make-up and in extremely unflattering wide-angle shots, over-riding the objections of Taylor who, initially at least, regarded this as sacrilege. Polanski's relationship with Deneuve was becoming somewhat fraught on other counts. It was widely reported that he refused her permission to take time off to visit her boyfriend in Paris, allegedly to maintain an air of sexual frustration. Rumours continued to spread about friction between the director and his leading lady, and matters inevitably came to a head when Deneuve refused to be filmed nude under the diaphanous night-gown she had been told to wear, insisting on protecting her modesty, first with knickers and then a body stocking. Polanski agreed to compromise, but when he showed Deneuve the results she conceded the effect was far from satisfactory, and reluctantly agreed to strip off.[4]

opposite:
Character study of Catherine Deneuve. The stark but effective lighting was by Gil Taylor.

left:
Catherine Deneuve caught between shots during the filming of **Repulsion**'s street scene.

above:
Carol (Catherine Deneuve) starts to daydream in the early scenes of **Repulsion**, which were shot on location at Vidal Sassoon's London salon.

below:
Cut throat razor in hand, Carol (Catherine Deneuve) is about to defend herself from unwanted sexual advances.

As the schedule slipped further, Gil Taylor departed to be replaced for the last three weeks of principal photography by Stanley Long. Pressure mounted on Polanski to get the job finished and at one point the Pole threatened to resign. Even Stanley Long thought Polanski took his quest for perfection too far: 'I remember we needed a close-up of a clock and Roman insisted on going back to the pub and shooting the same clock we had seen earlier. It was a second or two but he wanted the same clock. I think by then he had been through so much with Tony and Michael that there was an element of, 'right now I'll show them.' Klinger's temper finally boiled over whilst watching the seemingly interminable set-up process for what he felt was a straight-forward shot of Deneuve handling an open razor, which had been treated with silver foil to accentuate the light. A blazing row erupted in front of the cast and crew before Klinger stormed off the set. Again Gutowski intervened, promising to encourage the director to speed up. Crisis meetings

followed and eventually compromise took precedent over art, the special effects required for the remaining interior shots were rushed through quickly and a reluctant Polanski picked up his tempo. By the end of shooting Compton had sunk some £95,000 into the movie, surprisingly close to Polanski's original assessment, and well outside Klinger and Tenser's comfort zone. The two men now felt distinctly nervous about their previous pronouncements of future Polanski collaborations.

At the end of shooting on *That Kind of Girl*, Compton's first feature film production, the cast and crew had adjourned for a pint in the local pub. In sharp contrast the wrap party for *Repulsion* took place at the ultra-trendy Ad Lib Club in London. As well as the cast and crew from *Repulsion*, starlets Francesca Annis, Christiane Maybach, Suzanna Leigh and Edina Ronay were all in attendance. At that time the capital was the heartbeat of the swinging Sixties, and there was a feeling, certainly in the popular press, that London itself was revolving around the ex-patriot Pole. The tabloids covered Polanski's every move, his romantic trysts and his partying, and his inner circle revelled in the publicity. The likes of Michael Caine, Charlotte Rampling and John Barry, along with a host of lesser names, hurried to share Polanski's spotlight at the Ad Lib Club that night.

After a short break the star director and his editor, Alastair McIntyre, locked themselves into the studio to do the serious work of cutting a film out of the mountain of footage that been had shot. For McIntyre it was obvious that they were making something special, as he told Ivan Butler: 'There are few occasions when I've been conscious all the time I was working on a bloody good film, and *Repulsion* was one of them.' Stanley Long agrees: 'Polanski is a brilliant film director but his real genius, if you like, is as an editor - that's where his films are made.' At Compton, the frayed nerves were easing slightly as they saw the footage; Polanski was still well over budget but the Compton publicity team now had something they could get their teeth into. Starting with a series of teaser covers on the trade papers, followed by the release of tantalising press stills and leaked stories, Compton slowly built up the anticipation for the release of *Repulsion*.

With some trepidation, the director screened his rough cut of *Repulsion* for the Compton management and sales directors, who gathered in the smoky atmosphere of the Cinema Club. He needn't have worried about their reaction. 'Electrifying,' was how Tony Tenser described it to the press, but Polanski wasn't satisfied. The director ignored the protestations of Compton and started to rework some of the key sequences. He also dumped the soundtrack and had it completely redone.[5]

While Polanski tinkered with Compton's prize asset, Tenser began to map out his release strategy for *Repulsion*; this would be the first Compton film to be treated as something other than a commodity. Such was the level of media attention commanded by Polanski that Compton wanted to unveil *Repulsion* at the Cannes Film Festival in May, where it could assume pride of place on the company's sales desk. Cannes at the time was still very much a buyers and sellers market rather than a festival proper, but the name itself epitomised glamour for the film industry and it would give Klinger and Tenser the opportunity to promote their wares to those territories that remained unsigned. Despite strenuous overtures, *Repulsion* wasn't accepted as the official British entry in the formal competition itself. Denied the profile and prestige that official endorsement would have endowed, Compton were nevertheless content to show their prize possession out of competition, and while the screenings were not open to the public the UK media were sufficiently well represented to ensure good coverage at home. Klinger and Tenser agreed that if the film was well received at Cannes, they would allow Waynberg to enter the film into the Berlin Film Festival. This seemed a minor risk; if *Repulsion* won over the Germans then the Berlin Film Festival sounded sufficiently prestigious to impress the critics and public throughout the world; if however *Repulsion* was ignored, then Berlin was far enough away to make little impact. As it turned out, Compton could not have orchestrated a more positive reception at Cannes if they had tried, and the world's press ran out of superlatives describing *Repulsion*. Tenser and the sales team holding court at the Carlton Hotel found themselves under siege from would-be buyers. Buoyed by the reception at Cannes and beyond, Compton decided that they would open *Repulsion* in London in early June, but hold back general release until after Berlin later the same month.

Before opening in the UK, the print had to be submitted to the BBFC for classification; the script had already been submitted and approved in the time-honoured fashion of course, ahead of production. Tenser, by now an old hand at second-guessing the censor, felt that Polanski could probably get away with the violence but worried that the scene in which Deneuve's character eavesdrops on the noisy lovemaking of her sister in the next room would have to be toned down. For once he was proved wrong as John Trevelyan, accepting that *Repulsion* was an important work by an important filmmaker, pronounced himself satisfied with it as it was and awarded the film an 'X' certificate without asking for cuts. Trevelyan in fact was less concerned about the sex than the

disturbing behaviour of the central character; he went so far as to consult Dr. Steven Blake, a psychiatrist attached to the BBFC, who pronounced the film a realistic portrayal of schizophrenia.

*   *   *   *   *

The summer was going to be extremely busy for Compton. On the 27th of May they had their first big premiere of the season, *The Pleasure Girls*, at the Cinephone in Oxford Street. As far as Gerry O'Hara was aware Compton had been satisfied with the film he had delivered; certainly no-one had indicated that there was any problem. At Compton however they felt that the film didn't really hit the mark as a comedy and that the whole approach was too restrained for it to be considered a sex film. The decision to radically change the film came as something of an unpleasant surprise for its director: 'I assume that Tony and Michael thought that they needed the sex scenes that I had refused to do. Compton

above:
Yvonne Furneaux as Helen explains to Carol that she will be spending the weekend with her lover, played by Ian Hendry.

below:
Carol starts to feel her world closing in around her, but Helen seems oblivious to her sister's growing detachment from reality.

THE PLEASURE GIRLS

'Some Go Far, Some Go Too Far'
- UK Trade Ads -

Synopsis

One Friday afternoon, Sally leaves a comfortable middle class family home to live with in London with four friends, Dee, Marion, Angela and Cobber. Sally spends the weekend exploring swinging London before she starts her career as a model. She meets and falls for a young beatnik, Keith, at a party and the two spend some time together. At the same party she is introduced to Nikko, Dee's boyfriend, a married property speculator involved with some unsavoury characters. One of the girls, Marion, is pregnant, and her boyfriend Prinny has arranged a back-street abortion but his gambling is out of control and they can't raise the necessary money. Prinny falls victim to loan sharks and their ruthless methods. Before the weekend is over Sally will have learned a great deal about life in the city.

Critique

'Although the story plods down familiar tracks, and it is not without its ludicrous moments, the film is very much better than its synopsis suggests. Gerry O'Hara has an excellent ear for dialogue and a nice quiet way with his camera, so that much of the film is both engaging and exact... and there are fine performances from Ian McShane, Francesca Annis, Tony Tanner and Rosemary Nicols.'
- Monthly Film Bulletin, 07/65

'In spite of the film's idiocies it is more accurate and more acceptable than say 'The Party's Over'... And it features a nice actor Ian McShane, whose throwaway approach is good to watch and leaves one wanting to see him more often'
- The Sun, 26/05/65

'It is better than it sounds.'
- The Sunday Times, 06/06/65

'...just a routine, slick and morally orthodox addition to the vast and swelling repository of films about innocent girls who come up to London and fight for their chastity'
- Daily Telegraph, 28/05/65

'..amazingly, director-writer Gerry O'Hara has found something true and wise in all this. What could have so easily been just a leery - and no doubt immensely profitable - peepshow becomes in part at least a valid picture of modern youth'
- The Sunday Telegraph, 30/05/65

To promote the launch of *The Pleasure Girls*, Compton hired the usual glamorous models to tour the West End - this time rather bizarrely in a traction engine -

above:
The party sequence from **The Pleasure Girls**. Rosemary Nicols and Mark Eden can be glimpsed far left.

below:
Francesca Annis at the premiere of **The Pleasure Girls**. Annis captivated the press and stole much of the attention away from the film itself.

had hired a scratch crew and shot nude scenes that weren't in the script. One of the guys they hired phoned me one night and said, 'I have been working on your film, shooting screwing scenes!' A disgruntled O'Hara sat through a private screening of the new footage in the company of Harry Fine, who had overseen the shooting of these inserts. O'Hara complained vociferously, but privately accepted that his hands were tied: 'Technically there wasn't anything I could do. They had the right to cut it any way they liked, add anything or take anything out for that matter.'

There was one route open to O'Hara, though hardly an official one; he went to see the Secretary of the British Board of Film Censors, and as always Trevelyan was receptive to the young filmmaker. 'I don't suppose really there was much that John could do either,' O'Hara concedes, 'except maybe have conversations with Fine or someone at Compton. I don't know if he did or not, but I guess they must have had second thoughts about all the people they were upsetting.' None of the new footage was ever used in the end, but of course that didn't stop Compton using sex to sell the film. Graham Whitworth's central promotional image for the film was Klaus Kinski studying a topless Suzanna Leigh who, we are told, is 'Kept in a plush pad for his desires... She played the game and paid the price!' In case that didn't have the desired effect, the film's trailers and stills would concentrate heavily on the film's more salacious moments. With the wrangling over the final cut of *The Pleasure Girls* behind them, the producers and director were all smiles together for the premiere at the Cinephone.

handing out leaflets. For reasons best known to Graham Whitworth and Tony Tenser they also set up a ten pin bowling alley in the foyer of the Cinephone, and encouraged both cast members and guest celebrities to try their hand. Not that the film really needed gimmicks to sell itself; by far the most polished of Compton's exploitation movies, *The Pleasure Girls* is also the most enjoyable.

Rattling along at a cracking pace from the moment The Three Quarters pound out the opening bars of 'Hey, hey the pleasure girls!', the energy levels rarely drop right through to the end of the last reel. O'Hara had grown considerably as a director since *That Kind of Girl*, and working for the first time from his own script he managed to get a considerable result from very little substance, pulling the various threads together with great skill. The script itself is weak, the girls are all interchangeable (there is one Australian, but that's the extent of her character development) and they all burble phrases like 'super hats', 'super men', 'oh its super', or 'he's smashing.'

Compton's hook had been the prospect of five teenage girls sharing a house in 'swinging London' but by far the best subplot involves Mark Eden's Prinny and his insurmountable gambling/ abortion problems. Prinny's increasingly frantic ducking and diving gives the film a real edge, and Eden, perhaps not an actor with the greatest range, successfully creates an arrogant, callous character who neverthe-less retains sympathy. Opposite Eden, Rosemary Nicols's Marion is suitably

MICHAEL KLINGER and TONY TENSER present

THE PLEASURE GIRLS.

Co-starring
MARK EDEN TONY TANNER
SUZANNA LEIGH
and introducing
ROSEMARY NICOLS

haunted and desperate. Much of the publicity hype centred on Francesca Annis, now on her way to becoming a star, and Ian McShane; both were hailed as 'overnight successes', though in fact they are lumbered with the least interesting story and the least engaging characters. Despite his considerable charm McShane struggles badly with lines like 'I could love you so much. Please don't make it easy for me', and 'Sex is like a drug. I can't kick it that easy'.

The Rachman-esque Klaus Kinski is really just an obvious plot device, his love affair with the debutante Dee is far less interesting than it could have been, and the audience barely glimpses the seedy world he inhabits. Kinski's disinterest with the film shows in his manner and delivery - he

above:
Francesca Annis, as Sally, meets Paddy (Tony Tanner) on her arrival in Chelsea.

They made love their way...
ANY WAY!!!

The Pleasure Girls

IAN McSHANE FRANCESCA ANNIS ROSEMARY NICOLS

directed by GERRY O'HARA
produced by HARRY FINE

A TIMES FILM
RELEASE

above:
Leslie Elliot, assistant managing director of The Compton Group, pictured at the premiere of **The Pleasure Girls**.

left:
A mirror captures Mark Eden's post coital distress; Rosemary Nicols looks on.

right:
Part of the cinema trade teaser campaign for **Repulsion**. By 1965 Compton were masters at using the trade papers to create word of mouth on their movies, in the process testing possible taglines and artwork in anticipation of national release.

below:
Helen (Yvonne Furneaux) arrives home too late to save Carol.

mumbles with the conviction of the speaking clock but fortunately his screen-time is kept to a minimum. Playing opposite Kinski, Suzanna Leigh makes Dee as vivacious and flirty as you suspect the actress was in real life, and it's easy to see why she was soon attracting the attention of Hollywood producers. Of particular interest was the way in which O'Hara incorporates the character of Paddy, Dee's homosexual brother (played by theatre actor Tony Tanner). For once, an openly gay character isn't played as a mincing carica-ture or a psychotic villain. At a time when homosexuality was still illegal in the UK, O'Hara gives us a character that in all respects is a perfectly normal person who just happens to be gay.

The reviews were so good that O'Hara used most of his salary to place adverts in the trades, promoting his services by using cuttings from the papers. The response of the public reaction for once mirrored that of the critics and the combination of exploita-tion and a quality product ensured *The Pleasure Girls* was Compton's most successful film to date.

* * * * *

Despite *Repulsion*'s rapturous reception at Cannes, the Compton Group was still regarded as an interloper by the rest of the industry. It was a position that Tenser accepted, albeit grudgingly: 'No matter how good we were, it remained the same,' Tenser reflects. 'If we failed they said 'we told you so'; if we succeeded they said 'look at those bastards'. It's like somebody who lives in a small town, and he is driving a posh car. They say, 'look at that guy. Why has he got that car, why haven't I got one?' Somebody else is driving the same car, he won it on the pools - 'he is so lucky, that could have been us.' Two guys, same car; one earned it the hard way, one has won it. One is hated, one is loved. That's how it was with Compton.' The Group's success, in monetary terms, was obvious. Klinger, talking to The Daily Cinema, noted with obvious pride that 'if somebody had invested £10 in our company four years ago it would be worth something like £3,500 today!' The investment in cinemas continued with the purchase and redevelopment of the Circlorama in Piccadilly, followed by the Panama Club in Windmill Street - opposite the Windmill Club. Tenser then sought to recreate the success of the Compton Cinema Club with a new basement cinema in Oxford Street. With *Repulsion* waiting in the wings, Klinger and Tenser rightly regarded Compton as a major player, all they needed now was the film that would bring them international success.

left:
As a former cinema manager, Tenser was only too aware of the need to continue to exploit a film even after initial opening. These Kine Weeklies are aimed specifically at exhibitors, who were then still responsible for the booking and local promotion of films.

REPULSION

'Violence and Sensuality in an Unawakened Girl'
- UK Trade ads -

Synopsis

Carol stays with her sister, Helen, in a flat in the West End of London; a beautiful but repressed girl, Carol shrugs off the attentions of men she passes in the street, as well as her boyfriend Colin. Carol's tenuous grasp of reality starts to slip, and when Helen leaves on holiday with her married lover Michael it breaks completely. In a series of increasingly violent and disturbing hallucinations Carol retreats totally within her own world. When the real world, in the shape of Colin and her landlord, threaten to intrude she reacts with shocking brutality. When Helen and Michael return they find the apartment in a shambles, and a prostrate Carol hiding beneath the bed. Under the piercing gaze of her neighbours, Carol is led out of the apartment to an uncertain fate.

Critique

'It is too ruthless, too utterly relentless in its depiction of a girl going mad, committing mindless murders and finishing up beyond sanity and even out of sympathy. Repulsion may not be the stuff of entertainment but it is the stuff of which films are made.'
- The Evening Standard, 10/06/65

'A film easier to admire than to actually like...'
- The Times, 11/06/65

'It would be a really vicious film if it was not so desperately silly and boring. What a come

down for the director once one of Poland's brightest hopes'
- The Daily Worker, 12/06/65

'Serious horror, yes. But not horror without argument. Not horror for horror's sake.'
- Dylis Powell, The Sunday Times, 13/06/65

'...brilliantly executed, stark and absorbing, and also occasionally ugly if not downright revolting... a remarkable shocker of a film.'
- Saturday Review, 16/10/65

below:
Dressed and posed by Polanski to suggest a child-like vulnerability, Carol is left exposed mentally and physically when her landlord calls to discuss the rent.

MICHAEL KLINGER and TONY TENSER present
ROMAN POLANSKI'S **REPULSION** x
Starring
CATHERINE DENEUVE IAN HENDRY   JOHN FRASER PATRICK WYMARK   Guest Star YVONNE FURNEAUX

Original screenplay by
ROMAN POLANSKI and GERARD BRACH
Directed by ROMAN POLANSKI
Produced by GENE GUTOWSKI

above:
British front of house still captures Patrick Wymark moments before his violent death.

below:
Patrick Wymark, misreading the signs, is about to make sexual advances on Catherine Deneuve.

Repulsion is indeed a remarkable film, all the more so because it came from Compton at that time. Whatever the shortcomings of the budget Polanski's careful plotting and the deliberately slow build-up underpin extremely effective visual images, and the set-pieces - two violent murders - are genuinely powerful and shocking. The screenplay may have been written to order but it is a stunning piece of work, effectively capturing the hopelessness of Carol's mental disintegration in a series of increasingly disturbed fantasies involving subjugation and brutal rape by a stranger.

For once in a Compton film, sexuality is used as something other than a publicity tool; Carol's sexual frustration is contrasted with the openness of everybody else in the film, all of whom appear to be sexually active. Sex is discussed in a casual manner, from the salon where desiccated harridans tell Carol to make 'men beg for it', to the street and the pub, where Carol is categorised as fair game but 'still keeping her legs crossed.' Even in the 'safety' of her apartment itself, Carol is confronted with the noisy rutting of her sister next door, the unwanted attention of her boyfriend and the attempted rape by her landlord.

Some of Polanski's images are a little clumsy, such as the flat which becomes a metaphor for Carol's disintegrating mind, but the hands-through-the-wall scene remains disturbing and powerful to this day. The secondary theme of society's failure to recognise or deal with mental illness is nicely underplayed. The photography throughout is superb - it's impossible to tell where Gil Taylor's work ends and Stanley Long's takes over - and the acting is exceptional. The closing sequence, with its studied close-up of the photograph, and in particular the look of absolute hatred passing between the young Carol and her father, is profoundly chilling.

When *Repulsion* opened, London belonged to Polanski. The premiere at the Rialto in Coventry Street was the 'must have' ticket of the summer and amongst those turning out in the sunshine to get their picture taken, were golden couples Michael Caine and Luciana Palucci, and Warren Beatty and Leslie Caron. The broadly-grinning Tenser and Klinger were both there along with most of the cast members from Compton's recent productions. The guest of honour was of course Catherine Deneuve, who took a break from filming in Paris to pose demurely on Tenser's arm and smile sweetly for the hoardes of British pressmen.

The film was a spectacular success, breaking house records at the Rialto in its first week, followed quickly by a slot at the Windmill on an indefinite booking and a simultaneous run at the Cinephone. A week later Tenser and Klinger were in Germany to see 'their' film pick up the Special Jury Award Silver Bear and the International Critics Grand Prize at the Berlin Film Festival. Indeed word of mouth had been so strong overseas that even before the film had opened nationally in the UK, Compton had re-cooped their costs thanks to advance sales to Germany, Japan and South America. *Repulsion* went on to repeat its critical and financial success in every overseas market. A worldwide release plan saw Polanski and either Klinger or Tenser as guests of honour at premieres in such diverse places as Stockholm, Paris, Munich, New York and Rio de Janeiro.

When Michael Klinger and Robert Hartford-Davis travelled to Hollywood soon after finishing *That Kind of Girl*, they found their American counterparts friendly but not particularly forthcoming; *Repulsion* changed that. Not only was Roman Polanski seen for the first time as a bankable director but also the profile of the whole Compton Group increased massively. Klinger and Tenser wanted to exploit some of that goodwill and arranged a return visit to Hollywood as soon as was practical.

Operating from their base in the Beverly Hills Hilton, Klinger set out in search of American finance for future projects and to work at generating interest in a number of projects in pre-production, while Tenser called on Hollywood majors including Columbia and MGM to negotiate a deal on *Repulsion*. Tenser found that not only were the doors now wide open, but the movie capital's top executives were actually very keen to speak to him: 'I had no problems at all, they were falling over themselves to be nice to me. I can remember Martin Ransohoff at MGM was extremely interested in Polanski, 'would he come to the States? Would he do this, would he do that? I said I really didn't know but you could ask him. Martin was very keen to meet Polanski. I am sure he was thinking of

above:
Despite the tension, Catherine Deneuve can still find something to smile about during a quiet moment on the set of **Repulsion**.

working with him even then.' Columbia were the highest bidders in the end, but Polanski gained an important admirer in Martin Ransohoff at MGM.[6]

Klinger was equally successful, and the two partners returned from the States having secured financing in principle to produce a slate of nine new movies. Amongst the most interesting were 'Embryo', the story of a scientist growing a woman outside of the womb, and 'Alice in Wonderland', a big budget musical with actors and puppets, which was to feature the Bolshoi Ballet. Compton also optioned a 'Repulsion-esque' story of a sane girl incarcerated in an asylum called 'The Outcast', along with 'Blood Moon', a rather straightforward thriller-cum-horror film from the pen of a then-unknown young man called Michael Reeves. There were also a couple of curiosities: a sci-fi western called 'Way Station Outer Space', and 'The Magnificent Spy', a female James Bond-style adventure set to star the Olympic long jump champion Mary Rand. (As intriguing as these plans were, Compton never actually managed to get any of these films made, though 'Embryo' survived long after the option lapsed to become a vehicle for Rock Hudson and Barbara Carrera in 1976.)

Prominent amongst Compton's future plans was, of course, a new project from Polanski. *Repulsion*'s reception at Cannes had been enough to bring Klinger to the

right:
Better known at the time for 'Carry On' movies, Barbara Windsor gets a rare dramatic role as Annie Chapman, seen here in a French front of house still for **A Study in Terror**.

negotiating table, more than willing to forget about the past differences of opinion. Polanski felt that *Repulsion*, however good the final film, was simply a means to end, put together to meet the requirements of low-budget filmmakers.[7] The film he really wanted to make was 'When Katelbach Comes', the script that had been rejected by producers in both America and the UK, including Tony Tenser. Even before *Repulsion*'s staggering success, Gutowski and Polanski knew they had done enough to land the project they really wanted to make, and they found Michael Klinger extremely accommodating when they suggested that their next film for Compton should be 'Katelbach'. 'We were all very impressed with Polanski, especially Michael Klinger,' Tenser recalls. 'Even though they had rows, they formed a very good relationship. Katelbach is the name of a gangster in the story, it's a name like 'Dinglepooh' - you are supposed to laugh it. The whole film is supposed to have a comic feel about it but it really hasn't, it wasn't very comic at all and I was convinced that it wouldn't make a good film. Klinger disagreed and we agreed to differ. The film got made but we didn't touch the script at all.' In the same that week an ebullient Michael Klinger bounded onto a stage in Berlin to lift the Silver Bear, Polanski started shooting under the abridged title of 'Katelbach'. The film later became *Cul-de-Sac*.

*   *   *   *   *

In 1960 there had been nearly 3500 cinemas in Britain but by 1965, with the main distribution circuits in the hands of two major players, Rank and ABC, this had fallen by one third. Even discounting the disastrous low of 1960, when cinema admissions in the UK had dropped by over 50% in a single year, the number of cinema tickets sold in the years up to 1965 continued to fall on average by a crippling

50 million a year. Compton however was defying the market by growing rapidly year on year. The success was rooted firmly in the energy and ambition of Klinger and Tenser, but equally important was their firm understanding of how the distribution and exhibition market worked. As a relatively small player Compton was totally dependant on the willingness of the individual cinema manager to sell their product, something former cinema managers Tony Tenser and Graham Whitworth never lost sight of. The imaginative and colourful promotions orchestrated by the Compton promotion team had always played a significant part in the success of the films. From the outset the company's pressbooks and campaign sheets had invited the cinema managers to 'formulate a publicity campaign and submit full written details for possible agreement that the costs above normal theatre advertising can be shared on a 50/50 basis.' A surprising number took up the challenge and the box-office returns followed. In less than five years Compton's publicity team had refined the promotion and exploitation of movies into a fine art, from the high-profile, headline-grabbing premieres, to the day to day 'hands on' support given to local cinema managers. Whitworth himself, as Director of Publicity, was the main point of contact: 'I was either always on the phone or else running all over the country speaking to these guys, I knew all the cinema managers by their first names. I also knew all the press boys in the big cities and they knew they could call me any time and get what they wanted.'

below:
John Neville, Donald Houston, Tony Tenser, Mrs Henry Lester and Michael Klinger gather at the Sherlock Holmes pub in London for the pre-production launch of **A Study in Terror**.

Soon after *The Pleasure Girls* went into the national circuits, Graham Whitworth, feeling that he gone about as far as he could with Compton, resigned to set up his own independent publicity and promotional company, Arrow Publicity. Compton's network of contacts continued to serve Whitworth as he went from strength to strength as an independent. Twelve months later the same network provided Tenser with the basis to build an even bigger and more successful company in a shorter period of time.

*　　*　　*　　*　　*

Graham Whitworth was succeeded at Compton by the Publicity Controller Ron Shin. By the time Shin came on board the company already had their second period piece in the can, though it was very different from *The Black Torment*. During the shooting of *Repulsion*, Herman Cohen, the American producer of such films as *Horrors of the Black Museum* and *Black Zoo* visited Polanski's set as a guest of Tenser.[8] 'Herman, who I knew very well, brought a chap called Henry Lester with him, a middle-European who spoke immaculate English,' Tenser explains. 'They wanted to know if I would be interested in doing a Sherlock Holmes movie.' Lester was introduced as the managing director of Sir Nigel Films, a company named after a character in Conan Doyle's 'The White Company', and formed by the author's estate to administer the film and television rights of Doyle's work. The Chairman of Sir Nigel Films was Adrian Conan Doyle, the late author's son, and together with Lester they had been trying to get a Sherlock Holmes project off the ground for some time.

Lester and Conan Doyle's original plan was to produce a Broadway musical called 'Baker Street', which they hoped would star the prominent British thespian John Neville. When that generated little interest, Lester came to London and convinced Herman Cohen that a Holmes film project was viable, and Cohen in turn suggested they approach Tony Tenser. The prospect of another period thriller was certainly appealing and Cohen's access to American money was an added sweetener for what was sure to be an expensive project. Tenser still had some reservations though: 'I liked Herman a lot, he was a very shrewd man and I liked the idea of making a Holmes movie but I didn't want to make one of the old stories, they have all been done to death. I told him yes and I would think about how we could do it.' Derek and Donald Ford were summoned to Old Compton Street and asked if they could do a 'Black Torment' on Conan Doyle. Tenser even had a basic concept in mind: 'I said that the fictitious Sherlock Holmes was at the same period as the real Jack the Ripper and in the same

area - the East End. So why not have Sherlock Holmes discovering who Jack the Ripper was?' The Fords drew up a brief outline, which saw the detective called in by a baffled Scotland Yard to assist in the capture of the Whitechapel killer. The two-page synopsis was accepted by Lester, Cohen and Adrian Conan Doyle, and the Fords were duly commissioned to write a full script under the working title of 'Sherlock Holmes and the Vice Murders.' Herman Cohen signed on for the North American rights through Columbia, and with Sir Nigel Films, put up half the budget, which gave Compton the confidence to set a budget of around £160,000. Jim O'Connolly, a former television director who had helmed a couple of low-budget British programmers, was chosen to direct.

Casting the leading role was going to be critical to the success of the movie and Lester had already decided to move away from the traditional approach, telling the press at the time: 'According to Conan Doyle, they were in their early thirties and very virile. Holmes was a good boxer and fencer.' He went on to reassure the Conan Doyle faithful, saying, 'As one of the 'protectors' of the characters of Holmes and Watson, I am naturally very closely involved. Complete authenticity is assured.' Lester's preferred choice was John Neville ,who was finally convinced to take the role but not without some resistance. 'As the script took shape it became more tempting all the time,' Neville said at the time. 'I'd only hesitated because of my commitment to the Nottingham Playhouse and my work there as actor manager.'[9] Since he was central to the film, the shooting schedule had to be planned to allow the actor to return to Nottingham in time for his evening performances as well as the weekly matinees.

The casting of such a distinguished leading man set the tone for the rest of the movie. Compton starlet Edina Ronay was put forward for one of the minor parts, but the remainder of casting was left to the line

above:
Veteran filmmaker James Hill, better known for his television work including **The Avengers** and **The Saint**, was brought in to **A Study in Terror** as a replacement for Jim O'Connolly.

below:
Angela (Adrienne Corrie) and Max Steiner (Peter Carsten) are trapped in the inferno at the climax of **A Study in Terror**.

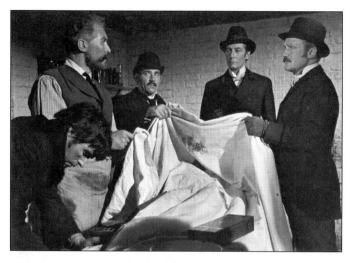

above:
Reviewing the Ripper's handiwork are, from left to right: John Cairney, Anthony Quayle, Frank Finlay, John Neville and Donald Houston.

below:
Crowds gather for the opening night of **A Study in Terror**.

treated as a bumbling, doddering idiot; while he couldn't match Holmes' brilliance he was certainly no fool.'

The script also exploited the widely-held belief that the Ripper was a highly-placed member of the aristocracy, though as Tenser teasingly suggests the Fords could have gone much further. 'They really got into it,' Tenser reveals, 'There were still a lot of documents around at that time and they did a lot of first-hand research on the murders and uncovered a lot of stuff that we couldn't use in the film. I remember Derek put together his own theory on who the Ripper actually was; his evidence was very convincing and I really couldn't fault his thought processes. Of course we definitely couldn't use that, it was far to close to people who were still alive.[12]

The team was ready to begin filming at the end of May 1965, by which time John Fraser had been added to the cast and Jim O'Connolly replaced by James Hill. "We wanted it directed by a director who's more accustomed to making big movies,' Tenser explained. 'O'Connolly didn't really fit that bill. Then James Hill's agent came into the office and said, 'Jimmy's looking for a project and I showed him the script and he said that he would do it.' Hill had been in the industry since the 1940s and had written and directed a number of films, but he was best known for his work on the early *Avengers* series.

By the time the crew was assembling at Shepperton studios, the film also had a new title, 'Fog', as suggested by Herman Cohen, and a new script (or a least an amended one), again at Cohen's instigation. Harry Craig, the noted Hollywood 'script doctor' was brought in to write a final draft of the Fords' script, with a view to broadening the appeal to an international audience.[13] Elsewhere, art director Alex Vetchinsky, who had worked on many of Rank's better films, such as *A Night to Remember (1958)* and *North West Frontier (1959)*, was brought in to add lustre to the

producers and Maude Spector, Compton's regular casting director. Amongst the notables lined up were the likes of Robert Morley, playing Mycroft Holmes, Sherlock's 'smarter brother', as well as actors of the quality of Anthony Quayle, Frank Finlay, and Donald Houston as Dr. Watson.[10] Glamour was a strong attribute of the supporting cast, with the addition of Christiane Maybach, Barbara Windsor and a somewhat incongruously young Judi Dench.[11] The project was officially unveiled to the press at a publicity junket attended by Neville, Houston, and Anna Conan Doyle, wife of Adrian. The event was staged, appropriately enough, at the Sherlock Holmes Pub in London's Northumberland Avenue.

The Fords' finished script, now called 'Sherlock Holmes and the House of Ill Repute', aimed to continue the revisionist view of Watson, started by André Morell in *The Hound of Baskervilles (1959)*, as an equal or near equal to the great detective, an approach endorsed by Houston: 'Sherlock Holmes' genius would dwarf any normal intelligence,' he maintained in the film's press releases, 'but that is no reason for imagining that Watson should always be

look of the film, and the theatrical costumers, Motley, dressed the actors with considerable skill. For the important role of Director of Cinematography Cohen turned to regular collaborator Desmond Dickinson, who forged a career out of making low-budget horror movies look far better than they should; amongst his best were *City of the Dead (1960)* and *Tower of Evil (1971).*

Perhaps Cohen's most inspired recruiting decision of all was the hiring of musician John Scott to write the soundtrack. Scott, a noted jazz musician and music arranger, had little previous experience at scoring movies, a fact he freely admits: 'I was absolutely terrified. I can remember that some time before I had seen and was impressed with *Horrors of the Black Museum*, with a score by Gerard Schurmann. I saw as many of these type of films as I could and I suppose tried to get by with something similar.'[14]

Plans were made to undertake location shooting at the Osterley Estate and around the docklands area of East London, with the interiors built at Shepperton, where Herman Cohen maintained his production office. Initially things went well, but James Hill soon started to cause problems, as Herman Cohen later related to the magazine 'Scarlet Street': 'Jim Hill had a habit of disappearing. He was a nice guy but strange. Nobody could get close to him and he was always fidgety and nervous. So the assistant director had a tough time keeping tabs on him.' Hill's 'disappearances' resulted in one piece of impromptu action by the producer: 'We had this big fire scene upstairs in the pub, and we were all set up for it. The spfx were ready, the fire department was standing by and everything else and we had to be out of there that night. That's when the AD came up to me and said, 'Herm, I can't find Jim Hill!' For chrissakes, its 4.30pm and the AD said, 'well he's disappeared.' I said, 'Okay, I'll direct the scene.' So we put the red light on, locked the doors and I did the scene in one take - the whole bloody thing. Jim came back in and said, 'I'm ready to – hey what happened?', I said, 'We've already done the scene. Where the hell have you been?' Well believe me, he never left after that.'

Despite his faults, Hill still encouraged a sense of fun and informality around the set; actors Jeremy Lloyd and Corin Redgrave - both friends of Neville - even called in and picked up unbilled cameos. As Barbara Windsor recalls, Hill was happy to improvise to get a reaction: 'When we were filming my big death scene, I had to walk down an alley, I knew where the killer was going to jump out and I was expecting it. They shot it again and again and I was always looking for him to jump out. We took a break, started again and when I was looking for him, he only jumped out the other side. Scared the life out me!'

above:
The final moments of Annie Chapman, by Compton's standards a rather restrained murder sequence.

John Scott was also based at Shepperton, where recording the film's lush soundtrack on one of the sound stages was presenting some problems. 'These stages used to do a good job for films,' he remembers, 'but of course the sound in films is very different from the sound on records, particularly in those days with optical sound tracks. You could only get so much on the track and they would filter out things that would not go onto the track. The sound for us was awful. I was never really happy with it.'[15] Scott's modesty disguises a remarkable achievement for a first-time composer - his themes underpin the action and add considerable texture to the overall film.

By the time the director's cut had been pulled together Klinger and Tenser were extremely satisfied with the result and were quick to hail this as the type of film that Compton would be making from this point onward. Curiously enough however, neither

below:
Two theatrical heavyweights of the English stage, Robert Morley and John Neville as Mycroft and Sherlock Holmes respectively.

above:
John Neville tangles
with the Ripper, who for
some reason seems to
have abandoned his
trademark scalpel.

titles, all films do, but none of them really fitted. I had to make it sound like a Sherlock Holmes film, so I took a little bit of poetic license with one of Conan Doyle's books, which was called 'A Study in Scarlet' and we called it *A Study in Terror.*'

At Columbia, head of publicity Robert Ferguson was only too aware of the poor track record of all recent Holmes movies. He liked the title but wanted a far more modern, 'with it' theme and drew his inspiration, rather bizarrely, from the phenomenally successful *Batman* television series. The US marketing campaign created a comic book image for the most literary of heroes, complete with ad lines like 'Here Comes the Original Caped Crusader.'

In the UK, Compton retained a more traditional approach but Tenser was careful to distance his film from its predecessors, telling the press: 'No longer is Sherlock Holmes the old fuddy duddy which the public tended to classify him in the past. He's now way out and with it!' Certainly the World Premiere in Leicester Square would reflect Compton's faith in their latest project. Apart from the obligatory appearances by cast and crew, arriving by Hansom cab, the high profile launch also featured the City of London Signals Unit marching in full Sherlock Holmes costumes! A gigantic marquee above the cinema featured the barrel of a smoking revolver, with real smoke. The celebrities then posed for their pictures with two very sullen-looking bloodhounds. Amongst those smiling for the massed ranks of the worlds press were Christopher Lee (a former Sherlock Holmes himself), actresses Tracey Crisp and Suzanna Leigh, director Val Guest, Adrian Conan Doyle, and The Duke and Duchess of Bedford. John Neville, who was still committed to his job in Nottingham, missed the premiere but flew down after the play to make an appearance at the post launch party, held again at the Sherlock Holmes pub.

man felt the need to have their names listed prominently on the credits. 'The film was very well made, excellent in fact,' Tenser asserts, 'but Michael and I weren't ones to push ourselves; we pushed the product. We could have been credited as executive producers along with Herman but we didn't feel that was necessary. We originated the film, we owned it when it was made, that was enough for us.' Compton immediately announced plans for a sequel, 'Sherlock Holmes and the Trunk Murders', and speculated on the possibility of extending this into an ongoing series.

*   *   *   *   *

On the surface all was well at Compton. Polanski was beavering away on his new opus, hopes were high for the Sherlock Holmes film, and the company was attracting more fresh proposals than they could possibly cope with. In the midst of this activity contracts were signed with the New York-based film producer Richard Gordon to finance and distribute his latest venture, *The Projected Man*, a science fiction/horror film being readied to start shooting at the tiny Merton Park studios. First though Tenser had to deal with the sticky problem of a title for 'Fog'; 'We had a number of working

A STUDY IN TERROR

'Spell it with Excitement...
The Name is Sherlock Holmes!'
- UK trade ads -

Synopsis

London 1888, and Jack the Ripper is terrorising the East End, slaughtering prostitutes on a seemingly random basis. Much to the relief of Inspector Lestrade, Sherlock Holmes is drawn into the case when he receives a case of surgical instruments through the post - complete except for a missing scalpel. Holmes's investigations take him from the estate of the aristocratic Osborne family to the medical mission of Dr Murray, in the heart of

Whitechapel. Slowly unravelling the puzzle, Holmes and Watson are drawn into a family feud, a tale of blackmail and revenge set against the ongoing slaughter in the East End. After finally confronting the killer Holmes chooses to keep his identity to himself.

Critique

'Tense and thoroughly deserving of its 'X' certificate at times, the film is discreet with its shocks and with its wit.'
- The Sun, 03/11/65

'John Neville... aquiline, arrogant, deer-stalker hatted, violin scraping and elegantly cab-drawn, has the true Baker Street air.'
- The Daily Mail, 03/11/65

'...most credit is due to director James Hill, who recreates the atmosphere of Victorian London with uncanny success, so that not only does every Whitechapel scene look like the nuisance slum it undoubtedly was, but also seems to smell of gin and perfume. Most of the doomed girls (particularly that super trooper Barbara Windsor) go to their deaths with a flaunt of their hips and a laugh on their lips.'
- The Daily Express, 04/11/65

'Mr Neville looks right and has the necessary strength but the script denies him that touch of mystery, authority and towering intellectualism which the character demands.'
- The Evening News, 04/11/65

'Holmes is merely a caricature, for all the care and skill of John Neville's performance.'
- The Daily Telegraph, 05/11/65

'The gruesome ripping up of bodies isn't exactly Holmes' cup of blood. But the two approaches to crime are entertainingly married in Study, which is more in fun than in deadly earnest. John Neville makes the best screen Holmes to date.'
- The Daily Worker, 06/11/65

'...John Neville and Donald Houston uncomfortably mouth their lines as if suspecting that nobody will listen. The plot is agreeably tangled, and there are two good marginal performances (Peter Carsten and Adrienne Corri): but the film's only real saving graces are Alex Vetchinsky's charmingly period sets and the pleasantly muted colour.'
- Monthly Film Bulletin, 12/65

With buxom doxies cooing, 'Hello darlin', like a bit of fun?', musical cockneys and muttering locals, Compton signalled that their Holmes was set well and truly in the comfortably recognisable 'filmland' that never was the Victorian East End, and Hill's film makes no pretence of striving to provide anything other than entertainment. That said, the film looks remarkably handsome, and taking the lead from his work on *The Avengers*, Hill does not allow the pace to slacken. He is helped enormously by uniformly good performances - even that of Donald Houston, who despite his pronouncements to the contrary insisted on playing Watson as something of an intellectual lightweight.

Plot inconsistencies aside, the narrative is credible enough to hold the attention even if it doesn't bear too much close examination - surely Lord Carfax can recognise his own brother – he had after all been subjected to a severe beating, not extensive plastic surgery! John Scott's soundtrack adds to the film's considerable

above:
James Hill watches an exchange between Donald Houston and John Neville. All the interior scenes were shot at Shepperton studios.

left:
Edina Ronay once again in seductive mood as Mary Kelly; the actress this time was given a little more to do than in **The Black Torment**.

right::
This spread, from the 11th of November 1965 edition of Kine Weekly, is a record of the star-studded premiere of **A Study in Terror**. Clockwise from top left: Michael Klinger, Christiane Maybach and Tony Tenser, Michael Klinger, Mr. Snellinger, Edina Ronay and Tony Tenser, Michael Klinger with Suzannna Leigh, Rosemary Chalmers and Herman Cohen, The Duke and Duchess of Bedford, Edina Ronay arriving in a hansom cab, Alan Kean, James Hill, Mrs. Cynthia Reed, Henry E. Lester and Eric Reed, Norma Foster, Yvonne Furneaux and Tony Tenser.

polish, managing to be both modern and in keeping with the mood of the film. Neville looks the part as Holmes but really doesn't act much like him - far too dapper, energetic and even upbeat. However contrived they sound, his deductions still carry the necessary air of authority though. There are enough 'Holmesian' touches, from deerstalkers to impenetrable disguise and intriguing plot twists, to keep everyone happy. Even so one can't help but think that Holmes gets an enormous head start, with an unsolicited parcel (coyly postmarked Nottingham) handing him the name of his prime suspect.

The film's launch proved to be something of a triumph for Compton, who received an enormous amount of attention in both the trade and general press.[16] The Daily Cinema was impressed enough to note: 'It is plentifully evident that Michael and Tony are now pretty well established in the respect (and affections) of many in our industry - and beyond it!' Despite all the publicity, Compton for once misjudged its audience; released through the Rank circuit, A Study in Terror took a respectable but hardly spectacular £5,166 in its opening week, dropping to £3,668 in the third week. In its own right this should be considered a significant achievement for what was after all a relatively low-budget movie with no major stars, but it was hardly in keeping with Compton's ambitions. By comparison the same week saw the British opening of two mainstream Hollywood films, The Cincinnati Kid and The Sons of Katie Elder, both taking in over £10,000 each. When A Study in Terror opened nationally the returns from the provinces continued to be at best steady. In the US, where Columbia pitched the film well and truly at the juvenile market, A Study in Terror was seen as old-fashioned and quickly sank. Tenser remained philosophical: 'I am not sure what the film did in the States, certainly Herman never complained so I would say it did alright. Over here some of the press slated it but they slated it because it was Compton that made it - they would do that anyway. Critics always slate films, then they put in a little good word here and there to show they don't hate you.' The plans for a sequel were quietly shelved.

Footnotes

1. The Windmill Theatre was built in 1910, originally as a small cinema called the Palais de Lux. It was redeveloped as a conventional theatre and struggled along as such until 1932 when it was bought by the entrepreneur Vivian Van Damm for the express purpose of running non-stop variety acts running from 2.30pm until 11.00pm daily. The theatre soon became infamous for its (almost) nude girls, who were required by law to remain almost motionless. During World War 2 the management made much of the fact that The Windmill was the only London theatre to remain open during the blitz, and the slogan 'We Never Closed' is still displayed in the foyer to this day. After the War, Harry Secombe, Jimmy Edwards and Tony Hancock were amongst the young comedians competing with the girls for attention, but interest in this innocuous titillation began to wane with the growth of Soho's more traditional strip clubs. Van Damm died in 1960 and was succeeded by his daughter who in turn sold the building to Messrs Tenser and Klinger in 1964. They turned it into a cinema, which is how it remained under several owners until 1973, when porn king Paul Raymond bought the building and turned it back into a venue for revues, with the emphasis this time on the girls rather than the comedy.

2. Whilst enormously popular in her native France, Deneuve's reputation abroad is based largely on her beauty and talent rather than her box-office appeal. She came to work for Polanski after having won the French Academy's Grand Prize for 'Best Actress of 1964' for her part in *The Umbrellas of Cherbourg*, and was considered, in Europe at least, to be a major signing for a relatively low-budget movie. Despite the film's success she preferred to continue working mainly in French language films, and her cool sexual allure was never used to better effect than in her signature movie *Belle de jour (1967)*, by Luis Buñuel. David Lewin of the Daily Mail was sufficiently taken with her to coo, 'Catherine Deneuve, a 24 year old French actress, is the most beautiful woman in the world' (12/10/68). In her private life she gave birth to children fathered by both Roger Vadim and Marcello Mastroianni, and in 1965 she married flavour-of-the-month photographer David Bailey. She hit the headlines again in the Eighties when she was elevated officially to national institution by replacing Brigitte Bardot as the model for Marianne, the symbol of the French Republic, and her likeness now adorns public buildings.

3. Yvonne Furneaux was born in Lille, France, and obtained a B.A. in French at Oxford before going to RADA. Amongst her earlier credits were Olivier's *The Beggar's Opera (1953)* and Errol Flynn's *The Master of Ballantrae (1953)*. She worked on movies all over the world but never really achieved the recognition her beauty and intelligence deserved. Apart from the Hammer work her best-known film was Fellini's *La dolce vita (1960)*, and the nadir of her career the truly awful *Frankenstein's Great Aunt Tillie (1985)*.

4. Deneuve was anything but a prude. Polanski, using his friendship with Playboy's London chief Victor Lowndes, arranged to have the actress flown back from Paris for an exclusive pictorial for the gentleman's magazine. The photographs, all taken by another member of Polanski's circle and later husband to Deneuve, David Bailey, covered 4 colour pages and continued to crop up from time to time over the following thirty years. Apart from the fact that the photos were in colour, and *Repulsion* was in black and white, the shoot was of very little interest; Deneuve is either topless or semi-nude and looks generally uncomfortable with the experience. She went on record later as 'bitterly regretting' the decision to pose. Bailey's photos show none of the flair that distinguishes his later work.

5. In the first version there were three murders, not two. After retreating into the shadows of the flat, Deneuve is visited by Ian Hendry's enraged wife, introduced earlier by way of a telephone call, who is duly despatched by Deneuve in the bath. Polanski felt that this murder was out of tune with the psychology of his central character - the only two victims seen on the screen are male, and both in their own way threaten Carol.

6. Although he missed out on *Repulsion*, Martin Ransohoff later bought the North American rights to *Cul-de-Sac*, after seeing only a rough cut. Encouraged by the world-wide receipts from *Repulsion*, Filmways then bankrolled *The Fearless Vampire Killers* at a budget of almost £2m.

7. In his autobiography Polanski is blunt about *Repulsion*, and in particular the difficulties caused by the budget: 'As a result, *Repulsion* became an artistic compromise that never achieved the quality I sought... Out of all my films *Repulsion* is the shoddiest - technically well below the standard I try to achieve.'

8. Detroit-born Herman Cohen was one of the shrewdest and most creative of all the horror film producers operating in the UK during the Sixties and Seventies. His films were always low-budget and generally quite silly, but never less than thoroughly entertaining, and include such titles as *Berserk (1967)*, *Trog (1970)* and *Craze (1973)*, featuring stars of the calibre of Joan Crawford, Telly Savalas and Jack Palance. He began his career working as a cinema usher in his home town, working his way up to manager of the massive Fox Theatre, then graduating to sales manager for the Detroit branch of Columbia Pictures before moving to Hollywood to seek a job in films. He won his spurs as assistant producer on *Bride of the Gorilla (1951)*, before proceeding to write, produce and occasionally appear in his own films for over two decades. (Cohen features fleetingly in a crowd sequence during *A Study in Terror*.) Prior to basing his production company in the UK - he also had an office in the States - Cohen had laboured for AIP on a number of number of drive-in horrors like *I Was a Teenage Werewolf* and *I Was a Teenage Frankenstein*, both made in 1957. A life-long film fan, he stopped producing films in the mid-Seventies but never stopped working. In 1981 he formed Cobra Media, a small film distributor handling movies in North America. He died of throat cancer on the 2nd of June 2002 at the age of seventy-six.

9. A major star on the West End stage, Neville had by 1959 played 22 Shakespearean roles. At the Old Vic his stage rivalry with Richard Burton

above:
Compton again exploiting the power of the press, using the reviews to attract cinema bookings after the film had opened.

above:
Typical Tenser fare.
Exactly what Polanski
thought about
Repulsion being
associated with
Compton's exploitation
movies hasn't been
recorded.

was legendary and proved to be a major crowd puller, with groups of fans booing and cheering for their respective idols during the performances. Attempts by the actor to diversify from Shakespeare proved none too successful, though in the early Sixties he did appear in a notable production of 'Once More with Feeling', directed by his *A Study in Terror* co-star Robert Morley. Frustrated by the opportunities being offered in England he moved to Canada where he actively discouraged film offers, devoting himself to running his own company at The National Arts Centre in Ottawa. Neville saw himself as the archetypal actor/manager, and such film work as he did undertake had to be accommodated around his stage commitments. Despite this predilection for the stage, he has created some memorable film work over the years, including roles in *The Adventures of Baron Munchausen (1988)* and *The Road to Welville (1994)*. In the late Nineties he enjoyed a featured role in the cult TV series *The X-Files*. In addition to *A Study in Terror*, Neville flirted once more with the role of Holmes in an unsuccessful stage production of 'Crucifer of Blood' in New York in 1975, a part originally offered to Peter Cushing.

10. The acting pedigree on display was quite remarkable: Robert Morley had been at the Old Vic in the late Thirties, and also appeared in a number of classic movies such as *The African Queen (1951)* and *Theatre of Blood (1973)*. Like Neville, Morley was also heavily committed to the stage at the time and agreed to his cameo as Mycroft Holmes, shot over five days, only if it could be slotted-in between theatrical engagements. Anthony Quayle started at the Old Vic in 1932 and of course had a long and distinguished career, culminating with his knighthood in 1985. Both Adrienne Corri and Donald Houston were in rep at the Old Vic in the early Sixties. Corri in fact represented another coup for Compton: a bit of a *cause célèbre* in the Fifties as an outspoken unmarried mother, she featured in such cult movies as *Devil Girl from Mars (1954)* and *The Hellfire Club (1960)*. She is best remembered for her role in Kubrick's controversial *A Clockwork Orange (1971)*, where she became one of the first mainstream British actresses to do full frontal nudity. Mixing with the professional thespians was the former World Middleweight Champion Terry Downes (as the appropriated named 'Chunky'), who had retired from the ring in 1964 after holding the title twice, in 1961 and 1962. Interestingly both Frank Finlay and Anthony Quayle would feature in *Murder By Decree (1979)*, Bob Clark's star-filled retelling of the same story.

11. Neville himself recommended Judi Dench for the part. She has gone on to enjoy nearly four decades as one of the most respected ladies of the English stage. As a teenager Dench enjoyed considerable success when she played Ophelia to Neville's 'Hamlet' in 1957, and she went on to create a minor stir as the original Sally Bowles in 'Cabaret'. Later to become Dame Judi, she enjoyed enormous stage success in productions like 'Romeo and Juliet' and 'Cleopatra' at the Royal National Theatre and then with The Sir Peter Hall Company. On the small screen she worked in sitcoms with her actor husband Michael Williams before finally breaking through into mainstream cinema with

movies like the Oscar-nominated *Mrs. Brown (1997)* and her featured role as 'M' in Brosnan's Bond movies.

12. The film pays scant attention to a number of historical details, the most glaring of which is the depiction of the Ripper's victims as young and desirable, rather than middle-aged drunks. The Fords' script also played with some of the less significant details: Barbara Windsor's Annie Chapman for example has just bought a new bonnet; in real life it was Polly Nichols who had spent her ill-gotten gains this way. The cinematic Annie also tries to spend the night with a local butcher wearing a leather apron. In 1888, when a piece of a leather apron commonly used by butchers was discovered next to Chapman's body in real life, it sent the authorities off on a fruitless tangent. The Fords then have Polly Nichols submerged in a trough, a nod to the real Ripper using a trough to wash the blood from his hands, and a reference to one victim, Cathy Eddowes, who was permitted to survive. The murder of the last victim, Mary Kelly, deviates from real life quite substantially; the youngest and prettiest of the Ripper victims, Kelly was brutalised by her killer and quite literally ripped apart in her grubby, ground-floor room. The cinematic Kelly, played by Edina Ronay, entices the killer back to her first floor boudoir and after stripping down to her underwear is dispatched quickly and cleanly.

13. Differences between the initial drafts of the script and what was finally seen on the screen mainly revolve around dialogue rather than events. There remain some minor inconsistencies in the narrative, which result from the rewrites; for example Holmes exclaims at the end of one scene, 'Now Whitechapel!' without actually leaving his apartment.

14. Scott had played as a session musician for Chico Hamilton on *Repulsion*. He was also musical arranger for such diverse talents as Tom Jones, Matt Monro and Rolf Harris. Linking up with Cohen, he wrote the soundtracks for the likes of *Trog (1970)* and *Craze (1973)* before going to Hollywood to compose highly-acclaimed soundtracks for movies such as *The Final Countdown (1980)* and *Greystoke: The Legend of Tarzan Lord of the Apes (1984)*. Despite international success as a composer and conductor Scott remains true to his love of the horror/fantasy genre; his closest friend is horrormeister Norman J. Warren, for whom he has written *Satan's Slave* and *Inseminoid* amongst others.

15. John Scott revisited the theme for *A Study in Terror* in 2002, re-recording the whole soundtrack with the Hollywood Symphony Orchestra and releasing the very impressive album on his own label, complete with sleeve notes from Herman Cohen.

16. Amongst the marketing gimmicks for *A Study in Terror* was a paperback tie-in by Ellery Queen (the pen name of Frederick Dannay and Manfred Lee). Nominally based on the Fords' script, it contrives to deliver a completely different murderer! Compton also released a soundtrack album of John Scott's score, as well as a single, 'The Lover's Theme', recorded by Don Costa and Kathy Keegan.

Chapter Four

'Horror of Horrors'

- (UK Trade ads for *The Projected Man*)

The success of *Repulsion* had placed Roman Polanski and Gene Gutowski in a very strong bargaining position, even though the negotiations for a follow-up had started long before the box-office tills started ringing. Michael Klinger was more determined than ever to get them to commit to Compton. Cadre Films Ltd, the company formed by Polanski and Gutowski to look after their business interests, secured a budget of £120,000 for 'When Katelbach Comes', including an increase in the director's salary to £10,000. Tenser, opposed to the subject from the outset and still smarting over the budget problems on *Repulsion*, insisted on a completion bond through Film Finances Ltd., which effectively made Cadre Films solely responsible for any cost over-runs. Sam Waynberg once again confirmed his personal faith in Polanski by purchasing the German rights up front.

To help ease the budgetary concerns, Klinger suggested shooting on location in Yugoslavia in order to take advantage of tax incentives and greatly reduced production costs, but was unaware that it might not even be possible to find suitable locations there. Polanski was duly despatched to scout the area only to return, predictably, having found nothing suitable. He immediately embarked on a survey of the UK's coastline in a single-engined Beagle piloted by the ever-resourceful Stanley Long. Polanski finally settled on the remote and windswept Holy Island, situated off the Northumberland Coast.[1]

The increased budget brought the benefit of a professional casting director, the highly inventive Maude Spector, who, using Polanski's distinctive character sketches, began to interview potential candidates. Donald Houston was an early choice for the role of the hen-pecked George, one of the two inhabitants of the island playing unwilling host to thugs. Polanski favoured the intense character actor Donald Pleasence, who was readily agreeable and considered something of a coup for the filmmakers.[2] Jacqueline Bisset and Charlotte Rampling, both up-and-coming actresses, were touted for the role of George's wife, the sexually predatory Teresa, but Polanski felt neither had the qualities he wanted so French-Canadian actress Alexandra Stewart was cast. Stewart had been a leading actress in continental movies since the late Fifties but despite

some work on British television (*The Saint*, *Danger Man*, etc.) she was largely unknown in the UK. Casting the pair of gangsters, Richard and Albert, was more difficult. Maude Spector suggested veteran theatre actor Jack MacGowran - perfect for the slight, bookish Albert - but his partner, a large bullying bear of a man, was harder to find. Polanski envisaged Rod Steiger or Jackie Gleason but the budget wouldn't stretch to importing an American star. By chance the filmmakers happened to catch a television interview with 58 year-old Bronx-born Lionel Stander, who seemed to embody the required physical attributes of the character. Stander, living in Europe, was duly tested and cast.[3]

This time round Compton had no objections to Gil Taylor as cameraman, with the likes of production manager Bob Sterne, assistant director Ted Sturgis, and editor Alastair McIntyre all returning from *Repulsion*. Though she didn't get the lead, Polanski did take a bit of a shine to Jackie Bisset and a small role was found for her.[4] Maude Spector brought in professionals like William Franklyn and Renée Houston for the supporting roles, while Polanski himself found a part for his close friend Iain Quarrier, who had little prior experience as an actor.

Filming of what was now called *Cul-de-Sac* commenced at Twickenham Studios on the 20th of June 1965, and almost immediately there was a problem which left Polanski without a leading lady; two days into shooting Alexandra Stewart left the

below:
Donald Pleasance as George, in **Cul-de-Sac**. The actor shaved his head shortly before filming began, a move which enraged Polanski.

above:
Actors Donald Pleasence and Iain Quarrier clown on set with Tony Tenser (centre). In contrast to **Repulsion**, the remote location ensured that set visits by Tenser and Klinger were kept to a minimum.

The island itself proved to be a less than ideal environment. Like its cinematic counterpart, Holy Island is largely inaccessible for large parts of the day and such facilities that existed were geared to cater for the day trippers who descended on the island whenever weather permitted. To the cast and crew, more used to the luxury of studio sets and their own beds in the evening, the attraction of the island's six pubs unrestrained by licensing hours quickly evaporated. The islanders themselves didn't help boost the morale of the crew either; after the initial novelty wore off they began to resent the intrusion of outsiders and adopted an attitude of surly indifference. Soon the bland food, waves of insect infestation and overall tedium took its toll on morale, and arguments broke out on and off the set.

Initially it was Donald Pleasence who caused dissent amongst the cast. Pleasence first incurred his director's wrath by turning up on the Twickenham set having completely shaved his head without prior discussion. As shooting continued it was obvious that he was determined to upstage his colleagues and would resort to a variety of tricks, forcing Polanski into the position of dealing with complaints from the other actors that he was stealing every scene.

By the time the production had shifted to the Holy Island location, Stander had eclipsed Pleasence in terms of unpopularity with his seemingly incessant bragging and constant whinging; on more than one occasion he came close to physical blows with members of the crew. Stander also dented his popularity when he produced a doctor's certificate attesting to heart problems - a fact he had neglected to mention to the film's insurers - and announced he could work no more than six hours a day!

Ever the hard task-master, Polanski pushed his actors to their physical limits. Despite only being shown in long shot, the director insisted on retakes of Dorléac's

production by 'mutual agreement'.[5] A brief flurry of activity led to a meeting at London's Connaught Hotel between Polanski, Gutowski, and French actress Françoise Dorléac, the elder sister of Catherine Deneuve. With Compton's approval she was duly cast.[6]

Tenser expressed concern about Polanski's schedule whilst the crew was still at Twickenham. When they departed for location work on Holy Island, Klinger agreed that he would keep the director on a tight rein but Polanski, who was already behind schedule following the departure of Stewart, now faced added delays due to the weather. Although they were shooting at the height of summer, sudden storms and strong winds played havoc with continuity as the colour of the sky or cloud formations changed unpredictably. True to form, Polanski refused to compromise his art and insisted on re-shooting whole scenes.

right:
Polanski directing Lionel Stander as Richard, and Donald Pleasence in drag as George. Curiously, Polanski had originally intended to play the role of George himself.

nude romp in the freezing North Sea. The actress fainted after the third take, and Donald Pleasence found himself leading a formal protest and threatening a strike. Much to Compton's relief Dorléac recovered sufficiently after only a short break and finished filming.

Deprived of the option of simply dropping in on the shoot, Klinger had to content himself with barracking the London-based Gutowski with enquiries, but even Polanski's producer had no clearer idea of what was happening on the island. Before long a deluge of telegrams started to arrive at the location with requests, instructions and demands. With constant delays and re-scheduled scenes rapidly eating away the budget, Klinger and Tenser soon took it upon themselves to pay their director a personal visit. The sun was shining, the crew was smiling, and Polanski's demeanour was equally welcoming as the Compton management arrived on Holy Island. After a brief meeting with the director, Tenser and Klinger were treated to lunch with the cast, after which they silently watched the afternoon set-ups. Before leaving they extracted a promise from Polanski that he would get the film back on track, but as soon as their car disappeared into the distance Polanski continued exactly where he had left off.

Gutowski could do little to influence his stubborn director, and with time running out the old arguments about unnecessary retakes flared up, with Michael Klinger threatening to halt production completely unless Polanski wrapped quickly. Gutowski and Polanski attempted to buy time by pledging their share of *Repulsion*'s projected box-office against the budget overspends, but even that proved inadequate as the

director slipped further and further behind. Frustrated by Polanski's apparent indifference, Klinger eventually flew to the island and closed down the location shoot. The few remaining scenes were shot in the relative calm of Twickenham under Compton's watchful gaze.[7]

Tenser has always maintained that he was making commercial films, not art, and concedes that the difficulties with Polanski all stemmed from a difference in perspective: 'He had no idea about money at all; it was a means to an end for him. All our problems came over the budget. We used Polanski's own producer, Gutowksi, as the go-between and that may have been a source of friction. We had no quarrel with Gene of course but he had to stick up for his partner and we simply didn't want to go over budget. We couldn't afford it, we didn't have

above:
A shot of George (Donald Pleasence), which offers a splendid panorama of the causeway linking Holy Island with the British mainland.

below:
Roman Polanski on location with Françoise Dorléac, studying the script, which was originally written in French as 'When Katelbach Comes'.

above:
Tony Tenser and
Michael Klinger were
outwardly friendly on the
set but the partners
disagreed over **Cul-de-
Sac**, and Tenser left the
company soon after the
film opened.

below:
Compton cashed in on
the Sixties craze for
spaghetti westerns.

explains. 'The film itself wasn't much of a story but we thought we could rely on the director to put some pep into it. By the time we saw the finished copy I knew that we had made a mistake. I don't think Klinger agreed; he thought he had another winner.' Klinger had assured Tenser that whatever the qualities of the movie, the strength of Polanski's name was enough to sell *Cul-de-Sac*; MGM-Filmways had started negotiations for North American rights and the pre-sales alone had already pushed the film out of the red. Despite his reservations, Tenser remained pragmatic: 'He made good films and if he came to us with another one we would have looked it.'

*   *   *   *   *

The production of *Cul-de-Sac* brought tensions between Klinger and Tenser to the surface, and during the course of 1965 the company continued to grow. Michael Klinger wanted to associate with mainstream filmmakers and make expensive, higher-profile projects; when they added the big budget adventure movie 'Beau Brigand' to their slate of projects, Klinger made it clear this was the direction he envisaged for the company. Set to star Patrick Allen and Peter Cushing, 'Beau Brigand' was a foreign legion romp to be filmed entirely on location in Tunisia, and partly financed by sources in that country. Klinger was a natural showman who was aiming high. Tony Tenser on the other hand wanted to continue producing the type of films that had established Compton in the first place – low-budget exploitation.

While Klinger was meeting potential investors for his 'Alice in Wonderland' project, Tenser was signing a deal with Michael Reeves to produce a number of low-budget thrillers. Reeves, whose previous credit had been the Italian horror movie *La sorella di Satana* (aka *Revenge of the Blood Beast*) had called into Old Compton Street shortly after Christmas 1965, and during 1966 Compton would take titles such as 'Blood Moon', 'Crescendo' and 'The Devil's Discord' to various stages of pre-production. Compton's approach to film-making was becoming increasingly schizophrenic, and burdened by a production slate busy with unlikely titles.

Though film production hadn't reached the level of six or seven features a year predicted by Tenser and Klinger, Compton had nevertheless consolidated their position as the UK's largest independent distributor. The diversity of the product they made available was quite staggering, from the 'dustbin lid' films like *Hercules Attacks* and *Goliath, King of the Slaves* (both starring Gordon Scott), to westerns like *Gunfight at High Noon* and *Duel at Rio Bravo*, and thrillers such as *The Case of 44's*. Amongst the stars unleashed on the British public by Compton in a series of dubbed epics were

the money.' Compton was still a very tight ship, and every expense was questioned, checked and then rechecked. Tenser summed it up neatly when he says, 'Polanski had his own methods of working and we tried to leave him to it. But, because of the nature of our company and the limitations of our finances, we had to handle him very carefully.'

Polanski had been nursing *Cul-de-Sac* for too long to allow vulgar financial considerations to corrupt his vision. Isolated in London, Gutowski was ineffective at insulating his temperamental director from the more intrusive demands of Compton, while at the same time doing his best to appease and reassure Klinger and Tenser that they had another *Repulsion* on their hands. Even before he entered the cutting rooms with Alastair McIntyre, Polanski knew his relationship with his English backers was irreparably damaged. Exhausted by the shoot, Polanski had postponed the start of editing in order to take a skiing holiday with Gutowski, without first consulting Klinger or Tenser. Enraged at this cavalier attitude, Michael Klinger threatened to withhold their wages; the matter was only resolved when Polanski threatened legal action

There were disagreements over *Cul-de-Sac* within Compton too. Tenser still had reservations about its viability. 'Polanski sold Klinger on *Cul-de-Sac* and I went along with it because I thought it was okay,' he

cult favourites like Rossana Podesta, Scilla Gabel and Barbara Steele along with better known figures such as Steve Reeves and Christopher Lee. Klinger's film production ambitions for Compton were dependent on the company's distribution and sales apparatus maintaining a healthy turnover on their acquired titles. What's more, they simply weren't getting the opportunities to produce good quality mainstream movies, so despite lofty ambitions Compton was unable to resist a good low-budget offer when it came along. When the producers of *The Projected Man* presented themselves at Old Compton Street looking for finance, Tenser readily agreed to meet.

Hollywood writer Frank Quattrocchi had originally written *The Projected Man* as an American science fiction thriller in the late Fifties. He touted the story around Hollywood for a while before it ended up on the desk of Alex Gordon, then employed to find new properties for the US exploitation giants AIP. Gordon liked the basic concept, so when AIP passed on the option he sent it to his brother Richard, a New York-based independent producer.[8]

Richard Gordon had built his reputation by making low-budget movies, predominately horror/sci-fi, and always filmed in his native England with imported American leads. Gordon hoped to make an anglicised version of *The Projected Man* in partnership with Gerry Fernback, with a script by Peter Bryan, and with 'B' movie veteran Francis Searle scheduled to direct. A decade earlier Searle had been director in residence at Hammer, where he established a reputation for shooting second features quickly and without going over budget. Unfortunately the finance fell through and the project languished in Gordon's office until it was revived in 1965, this time under Gordon and Fernback's Protelco Films banner. Gordon had a production agreement with Planet Films in the UK to make *Island of Terror*, a horror/sci-fi movie starring Peter Cushing, and to sweeten the deal for US distribution he intended to add a suitable support feature.

Creating a packaged double-bill was a common strategy for Gordon at the time: 'I had a very good experience with releasing *The Haunted Strangler (1958)* and *Fiend Without a Face (1958)* as a double-bill. I felt that we could get a much better deal out of the distribution of the films if we put them together. *The Projected Man* was, if you like, made to order.' Gordon intended to raise the money for *The Projected Man* by selling off the UK rights to a third party, and armed with a revised script by 'John C. Cooper' [actually John Croydon] and Gerry Fernback, he approached Compton. 'I knew Michael Klinger quite well,' Gordon remembers, 'Tony Tenser less so but I knew the type of films that they were making and I thought that this would be of interest.'

A deal was struck on *The Projected Man* (*Island of Terror* wasn't part of the agreement), with Compton retaining approval over the key cast and crew. The budget was set at £100,000, a little higher than the usual Compton allocation for this type of film, but they had the comfort of splitting the cost equally with Protelco. Gordon remembers that even at £100,000 *The Projected Man* was offering good value for money: 'I already had a leading man in mind but the main expense would be on the special effects. They needed to look good, there was no point in trying to save money there, it just wouldn't work.' Tenser approved the script without changes and Compton took the UK rights and some territories in the Eastern Hemisphere. Protelco retained the Western Hemisphere. 'Our interest in *The Projected Man* was largely financial,' Tenser confirms. 'We got to approve the script and of course the cast but we knew Richard Gordon and knew we could rely on him. This was a good type of picture for us to get involved with so we put money in it and in return took a credit as executive producers. I wanted the credit so I could ensure the film had the right ingredients that would sell, but other than that we were not too involved.'

Protelco brought in John Croydon, the experienced line producer who had earlier worked for Gordon on *Corridors of Blood (1958)* and *Grip of the Strangler (1958)*. Croydon was in no doubt as to where the appeal of this film lay: 'Horror films have always been a dead cert,' he told The Daily Cinema. 'I feel it's because horror is always visual and visuals have no boundaries. The audience reaction in London to a science fiction-horror movie would be repeated in Bangkok.' It was Croydon who suggested Ian Curteis as director, a curious choice for a film requiring such careful handling. Curteis had never made a feature film before, though he had made some interesting television

above:
Two more of Compton's 'value for money' double bills, using quantity to make up for what they lacked in quality.

below:
Inset: Bryant Haliday and **Crossroads** star Ronald Allen.
Main picture: A terrific shot of Flo Nordhoff's make-up design as Haliday carries off Tracey Crisp. Nordhoff had previously designed the aliens for the cult classic **Fiend Without a Face**.

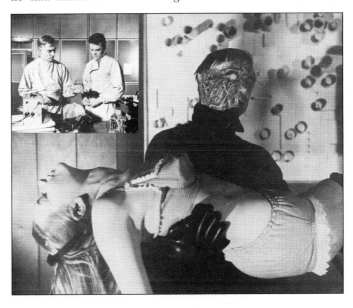

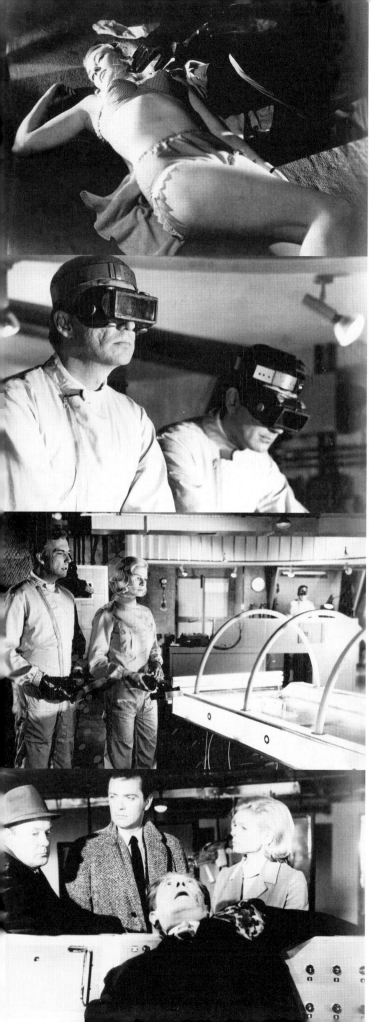

work, in fact *The Projected Man* was to be his only foray into cinema; he later returned to television where he enjoyed considerable success as a writer.

Casting the movie proved very straight-forward. The original script for *The Projected Man* had its hero, called Ruder, cast in the mould of Claude Rains's invisible man, a ruthless scientist transformed into a cold-blooded killer. Gordon, with his love for the old Karloff 'mad scientist' movies, softened the approach and transformed the lead, now named Steiner, into a victim of unscrupulous villains; if Steiner is guilty of anything it is purely scientific zeal. For this role, Gordon wanted Bryant Haliday, the ex-pat American actor who had made something of a name for himself as a minor horror star - indeed Gordon had insisted his casting was built in as a precondition of the deal.**9** Haliday played opposite Mary Peach, a minor star in the UK at the time, as a fellow scientist and former lover.**10** Peach's career had taken a something of a dip and her agents had approached the producers hoping to secure her a starring role. Tenser was particularly keen to employ her and the deal that was struck gave Peach - who had a smaller and less important role than Haliday - top billing in Compton's territories and second billing elsewhere. As for the remainder of the cast, Norman Wooland and Derek Farr were established character actors and dependable performers, and nominal 'hero' Ronald Allen would be familiar to the modern British audience due to his work on the long running soap opera *Crossroads*.**11** Also appearing was Sam Kydd, a veteran bit-part actor specialising in roguish comic relief; he would also appear in Gordon's sister feature *Island of Terror*.**12** One of the 'ingredients' required by Compton was a pretty face for the promotional materials, and former model Tracey Crisp fitted the bill admirably; she was given a minor part as a secretary but had the consolation of featuring prominently in the film's sales campaign.

The success of *The Projected Man* would of course largely rest on the impact of the special effects and, perhaps more significantly, the make-up. The German-based artist Flo Nordhoff, who had worked with Gordon on *Fiend Without a Face*, designed the impressive 'projected man' face. Rather than import Nordhoff from his Munich base or ship Haliday over there, a cast of the star's face was taken and sent out to Germany. Nordhoff was inspired by the idea that Steiner's face had been turned 'inside out' and his final design created that illusion with some success. Some 25% of the film's overall budget was allocated for special effects, and Mike Hope and Robert Hedges were charged with the no less demanding task of creating a host of spectacular laser sequences.

Filming began on the 18th of November 1965 at the tiny Merton Park studios and proceeded smoothly at first.

Additional locations close to the production base were chosen, including a disused building site in London and, for some brief sequences, the area around Battersea Power Station. Once the crew had started shooting the effects sequences it quickly became obvious that Curteis was having difficulties getting the shots he needed. The problem was compounded by the decision to shoot the film in Techniscope; Curteis was simply out of his depth and the schedule started to suffer.

Richard Gordon was supervising *Island of Terror*, which was being shot more or less simultaneously, and was not at first involved with the day to day work at Merton Park. He soon found his attention being diverted back to *The Projected Man* however: '*Island of Terror* was running very smoothly on its own, largely due to Terence Fisher and when *The Projected Man* ran into problems and went over budget, I was more concerned with sorting that out.' Gordon elaborates, 'Special effects in those days were very often a matter of trial and error - you tried something and if it didn't work you did it another way. It wasn't all on computers like it is now. The crew were doing their best but a lot of it wasn't working and needed to be re-done.'

Compton had just dealt with huge cost over-runs on the Polanski movies and wouldn't even consider sanctioning more money. Understandably, the film completion guarantors, National Film Finance Corporation, were beginning to express concern. Gordon was placed in the invidious position of having to remove the director: 'The pressure was a little too much for Ian Curteis and he found himself unable to handle it. Towards the end of the shooting John Croydon and I spoke and we agreed to take him off the picture. John then stepped in and finished the last week or so of filming.'

Having come into the deal late in the process, Tenser hadn't followed his usual practice of submitting the script to the BBFC but neither he or Gordon felt they would have any problems. Unlike many of his contemporaries, Gordon wasn't in the habit of shooting additional footage: 'In virtually all of the films I made we never shot any extra scenes for overseas, what they used to call 'the Japanese market'.' The death of the three burglars however provided a glimpse of what appears to be nudity - care of Norma West laid out on a slab. Richard Gordon states almost apologetically, 'you see what you want to see!' *The Projected Man* was passed without cuts as an 'X' in March 1966.

*   *   *   *   *

Compton now had *Cul-de-Sac* and *The Projected Man* awaiting release, and Arnold Louis Miller had been commissioned to deliver a suitable 'front story' for the old Windmill footage. Significantly, none of these films could be considered 'family

"THE PROJECTED MAN" Starring MARY PEACH · BRYANT HALIDAY · NORMAN WOOLAND · RONALD ALLEN · DEREK FARR · TRACEY CRISP
A MICHAEL KLINGER and TONY TENSER Presentation. Produced by JOHN CROYDON and MAURICE FOSTER. Directed by IAN CURTEIS. Screenplay by JOHN C. COOPER and PETER BRYAN. *Filmed in Eastman Colour and Scloscope*

entertainment'. US television residuals at the time were a lucrative source of revenue and obviously the traditional Compton product was of limited interest to the American networks. Much to Klinger's delight, Tenser agreed on a change of strategy; a number of horror projects were dropped outright as Tenser announced the company planned to, 'get away from the 'X for sex' type of film and find a new image: films for a family audience.'

The first of these new family films, 'Beau Brigand', was now fully financed and with director Jim O'Connolly signed, was slated to start shooting in the summer. Tenser waxed enthusiastically about another film on the same theme, an adaptation of Robert Louis Stevenson's classic 'Treasure Island', and 'The Legend of Loch Ness', now re-written as a kiddie matinee feature, remained on the books to be directed by Hollywood sci-fi veteran George Pal. At the obligatory press conference, Klinger again stated that the Group's aim was to produce up to a dozen films a year; a production slate so big that the two partners were going to radically change the way they worked to accommodate the demand. The proposal was to split Compton's workload evenly, with Tenser and Klinger working on projects independently of each other whilst still retaining the 'Tony Tenser and Michael Klinger present' banner on all Compton films. Michael Klinger proclaimed Compton to be in their strongest financial position to date and, reviving memories of the aborted bid for British Lion, went on to suggest, 'we may even have to take over a studio as a complete entity.'

Klinger's long-cherished aim was to give Compton a permanent production base, taking on a 'minimum of two line producers and to have two or three directors under fixed contracts to write and develop ideas in-house.' This at a time when the cost

above:
British front of house still showing Haliday attacking villain Norman Wooland.

opposite top:
British starlet Tracey Crisp as Steiner's hapless secretary Sheila Anderson in **The Projected Man**.

opposite next to top:
Bryant Haliday and British actor Ronald Allen. The former went on to carve out a niche as a minor horror star in the likes of **Devil Doll** and **Tower of Evil**.

opposite next to bottom:
Hailday and Mary Peach feature in this nice shot of Steiner's laboratory from **The Projected Man**; 25% of the film's budget was allocated for the make-up and special effects. Peach was considered something of a catch for Compton after having starred in a number of mainstream and Hollywood films. She later married Hammer horror writer Jimmy Sangster.

opposite bottom:
Character actor Derek Farr, as Scotland Yard's finest, Inspector Davis, conferring with Ronald Allen and Mary Peach.

above:
One of the many promotional shots from **Secrets of Windmill Girl** to end up in girlie magazines - promoting the impression the film was far more salacious that it actually was.

SECRETS OF A WINDMILL GIRL

'The Thrill, The Excitement, The Despair of a Windmill Girl'
- UK Trade ads -

Synopsis

A man and his girl spill out of a party and climb into their car to speed off into the night, the screeching tyres drowned out by the pounding music behind them. As they embrace, the man loses control and the car crashes. They are both killed outright. A little later, Linda is escorted by the police to a morgue where she identifies the body of her long time friend Pat. Distraught, Linda starts to relate the story of how the girls knew each other at school, then took their first job together in a shoe shop, and ultimately how they auditioned together as dancers at the Windmill Theatre. Linda, demure and quiet, is rejected at first but Pat 'persuades' the stage manager to take her friend on. Pat is soon caught up in a lifestyle that revolves around parties, fast cars and endless men. Linda on the other hand studies hard and ends up falling in love with a steady young man. When the Windmill closes Pat is forced to appear at stag parties and increasingly wild 'rave-ups'.

Critique

'Those enterprising showmen Michael Klinger and Tony Tenser of the Compton Group pay a sincere, lively and thoroughly entertaining post modern cinematic tribute to one of London's most famous landmarks.'
- Jewish Chronicle, 29/04/66

The last of the old-style Compton exploitation films, conceived and filmed on the hoof, sold to the public on the strength of lurid posters and tantalising ad-lines, and actually delivering far less than it promised.

As written and directed by Arnold Louis Miller, *Secrets of a Windmill Girl* has an air of realism; the lifestyle of the girls is portrayed, if not accurately, then at least in the way most of the public perceived it to be. Miller's partner Stanley Long was in fact married to a former Windmill Girl himself, and the two men had been around Soho long enough to ensure the film carried the stamp of authenticity. The film also captures much of the energy of the old Windmill, and the sequences of actual performances enliven the action far more than the fictitious moments.

The girls, Pauline Collins and April Wilding, both acquit themselves admirably though the more salacious scenes are left to professional dancers and models such as Vicky Scott and Deidre O'Dea, both of whom turned out for the premiere in the obligatory skimpy outfits. Amongst the interesting additions to the cast were Dana Gillespie,

and effort involved with maintaining a production studio was considered, in Britain at least, to be a burden that most film companies were actively trying to off-load. To concentrate their capital on film production and raise some much needed cash, Compton decided to sell the Windmill Theatre, purchased only eighteen months earlier and now a newly-renovated 300 hundred seat cinema. The sale, to the Capital and Provincial Cinema Chain, went though in March 1966.

Ironically, only a week after they disposed of the Windmill Theatre, Compton finally released the film that celebrated the club's last days as a night-spot. Appropriately enough Capital and Provincial agreed that the film should open in the cinema that bore its name.

the teenage singer who later decorated films like *The Lost Continent (1968)*, and Harry Fowler, more often associated with comic roles. Fowler was later cut from prints of the film after a dispute with Compton over his fee, though much to the comic's chagrin prints still exist with his contribution intact.

The market for this type of film was fairly well defined and Compton's publicity staff were past masters at getting audiences into cinemas. A front-page advertisement in Cinema Today pitched the film to cinema managers interested in some late night fare, with rentals receiving a boost when Parade magazine agreed to serialise the photo-story in their pages. *Secrets of a Windmill Girl* was never intended to be anything other than a 'programmer' and although it only played at selected cinemas it provided a steady return on Compton's investment.

*　*　*　*　*

In May 1966, Tenser and Klinger once again used the Carlton Hotel in Cannes as the setting for a major press conference, promoting a burgeoning slate of movies including 'Alice in Wonderland', which with a budget of £2m was by far their biggest commitment to a single project. Compton hoped that a Hollywood production partner could be found to provide the necessary backing for their lavish musical. At the same time that the management were on the Croisette, Robert Sterne took a small crew including producer Robert Osborne, director Jim O'Connolly and art director Alex Vetchinsky to scout locations for 'Beau Brigand' in North Africa.

By early summer 1966, Tony Tenser was telling the press: 'We are a young company, with young ideas and young people; we are not afraid to experiment. As a company that sprung from a modest beginning and is now the largest independent group we are justified in saying that experiment pays off.' After a rethink on the new organisation Klinger and Tenser had decided on a more practical restructure and unveiled the changes to the public.

Tony Tenser took over as Managing Director of Exhibition, and resolved specifically to refurbish Derby Picture Hall - a £100,000 investment - and scout out new sites in both the UK and abroad. Harking back to his days as a cinema manager, Tenser called for, '...new ideas - ideas for showmanship, presentation and posters. New everything, from staff uniforms to styles of seats. New style of releases, of competitive trading.' Warming to his theme Tenser told Kine Weekly that most cinemas currently resembled tombs, '...attended by fifteen old people, where a creaky manager and a creaky usherette serve them with warm ice cream and they sit on musty seats.'

As part of their reorganisation the 'Cameo' partnership, which had existed in

name only for several years was finally dropped completely, and Alan Kean, who had joined the Group in May, took charge as Managing Director of Distribution. Michael Klinger continued with the role of Chairman and took personal control of all film production. It was a structure that was supposed to propel Compton forward to become a 'major.'

Just as the new organisation was being unveiled the film that, more than any other, had divided the two partners was about to open. Trade screenings of Polanski's *Cul-de-Sac* had provoked a mixed reaction but the marketing people nevertheless threw themselves into an all-out assault in an effort to drum up business. The campaign started with the same style of 'teaser' advertising that had worked so well for *Repulsion*; by the time movie was released to the public at the end of May 1966, the press was already in a lather.

above:
One of the staged sequences filmed after the Windmill Club itself had been closed and converted into a cinema.

left:
A Compton-style catfight.

above:
George (Donald Pleasence) and Richard (Lionel Stander) at the climax of **Cul-de-Sac**; the two actors spent much of the shoot trying to upstage each other.

below:
Having failed to win the role of Teresa, Jacqueline Bisset was awarded the consolation of a smaller role, and a fling with her director Polanski.

CUL-DE-SAC

'Polanski does it to you again'
- German teaser ads -

Synopsis

Two wounded gangsters, Richard and Albert, find themselves stranded on a causeway between the mainland and a small isolated island. Their only hope of rescue rests with their absent boss, Katelbach. Leaving Albert in the car, Richard takes refuge in an isolated castle, home of George, a retired businessman, and his young wife Teresa. When Richard gate-crashes their home, George and Teresa are in the middle of a bizarre game involving George dressing as a woman and wearing wildly over the top make-up. Dismissing George as a 'queer', Richard has no difficulty in forcing the couple to push his car and Albert up from causeway. He tells George and Teresa that Katelbach will be coming to collect them the next day and in the meantime they are both his prisoners. Later, when Albert dies of his wounds, Teresa and George are forced to dig his grave. The following day some old friends of George visit and Richard is passed off as the gardener and cook. Tensions begin to build as George finds himself being criticised by both his friends and his captor. When he finally gets hold of Richard's gun he gives full vent to the frustrations of the last twelve hours.

Critique

'A superbly executed and conceived character study this, owing more to the actors than the authors, I would say - or else there must be more to build on in the stage directions than the lines.'
- The Daily Telegraph, 03/06/66

'Slow, unreal, arty in the worst most self conscious sense, the film's main interest lies in Mme Dorleac's habit of taking off all her clothes. Fortunately she does this frequently.'
- The Evening News, 02/06/66

'Unfortunately it is not particularly black and not noticeably comic'
- The Times, 02/06/66

'Beyond one very tedious, overlong passage near the start, it is nevertheless a hypnotic experience watching it - principally because of the director's own involvement with it.'
- Alexander Walker, The Evening Standard, 06/06/66

'I found it a crashing bore.'
- The Guardian, 06/06/66

Cul-de-Sac is probably about as personal a project as it's possible to get in mainstream cinema, with little if any compromise to the cinema-going public, and it's easy to understand why Tenser originally rejected the film. It simply wasn't a Compton film. Even Dorléac's predatory Teresa, clearly the stuff that the Compton press releases are made of, doesn't exactly fit into the usual debutante mould.

Cul-de-Sac, relying on a highly personal sense of humour, centres on the bizarre *ménage a trois* that develops between the cuckold George, the coarse and dim gangster and the bored, promiscuous Teresa. The mixed reception given by critics reflects how well each writer related to the three central characters - some did and some didn't. The film was supposed to be funny, and generally viewers simply didn't get the joke. That's not to write the film off completely; there are some interesting performances, notably from Donald Pleasence as the very middle-class business man trying desperately to live a bohemian life and going to ridiculous lengths to please his wife. Stander however is too gruff and obnoxious, and remains nothing more than a bully. Dorléac's Teresa, spoiled and sexually dominant, is potentially the most complex character in the movie and although the actress acquits herself competently she never succeeds in portraying the depth of the character totally convincingly. All the other parts, from the bratish child to the smooth-talking Cecil, are never intended to be anything other than caricatures to decorate the background for the main performers. Jack MacGowran does well though, bringing both humour and pathos to a small part.

Like *Repulsion*, *Cul-de-Sac* is about sex and Polanski has fun with accepted notions of heterosexual and homosexual liaisons, both in and out of the context of 'accepted' relationships. Unlike *Repulsion*, Compton

were given very little to work with. The nudity in the film is purely perfunctory and the sex, such as it is, retains little if any erotic charge. Polanski crafted *Cul-de-Sac* into a highly distinctive and darkly comic character study, admittedly with bizarre twists. At Compton they were crossing their fingers and hoping they had another *Repulsion*.

Whatever reservations were held by Compton, Sam Waynberg's enthusiasm was undimmed; he was as confident as ever that *Cul-de-Sac* would be well received at the Berlin festival and assured Compton that Polanski's new film would be a worldwide success, outperforming *Repulsion*. Joining the dignitaries sent to Germany on behalf of the British industry were Polanski and Gutowski, Lionel Stander and Jacqueline Bisset, and of course Messrs Tenser and Klinger. In contrast to the mixed reception in the UK, the Germans seemed perfectly in tune with Polanski, awarding the movie their

above:
Cul-de-Sac exceeded Tenser's expectations by lifting the Golden Bear at the Berlin Film Festival. The trophy sat in the corner of Michael Klinger's office until he retired from filmmaking in the 1980's.

below:
Character study of Lionel Stander, whose behaviour during the shoot won him no friends in the British film industry. The actor himself was a minor cause célèbre during the McCarthy trials and had been blacklisted by Hollywood studios.

left:
British front of house still boasting about the Golden Bear victory, a sign of just how highly Compton rated the winning of the prize.

above:
French front of house
still featuring Françoise
Dorléac who, twelve
months after **Cul-de-
Sac** opened in the UK,
was killed in a car
crash. She was 25.

For their part, Compton were disappointed by *Cul-de-Sac*'s reception, and Polanski's decision to take his next project to Ransohoff (ultimately *The Fearless Vampire Killers (1967)*), came as something of a relief to Tenser. 'I was given a synopsis of it and in my own opinion the subject matter wouldn't sell many seats. I thought if Polanski directed it would be a good film but it didn't seem to me to be a great premise. Probably his least appealing movie, from my perspective anyway,' he concludes. There was no acrimony from Tenser's perspective: 'There was no split. He didn't come to us with any more films and we didn't have any projects that were suitable. If we had we would have approached either Polanski or Gene Gutowski. He was a brilliant director.' Polanski had simply outgrown Compton - *The Fearless Vampire Killers*, which transported Polanski into the ranks of the Hollywood elite, ended up costing in the region of £2m.[13]

* * * * *

Michael Klinger was firm in his belief that the prestige attached to *Cul-de-Sac* added considerably to the company's reputation as makers of quality films. Polanski's films allowed him to host launch parties and premieres attended by the likes of Warren Beatty and Michael Caine. *Repulsion* and *Cul-de-Sac* also brought awards as well as considerable financial rewards, and represented the first of what Klinger saw as the new Comptons; unfortunately he was having some difficulty finding a project that furthered this vision.

Soon after Jim O'Connolly and his team returned from their scouting expedition in North Africa, Compton's Tunisian backers got cold feet and the finance for 'Beau Brigand' evaporated overnight. The political situation in the Middle East was not considered conducive to persuing such a project at that time. The Compton Group couldn't finance the production alone, so strenuous efforts were made to try and find an alternative partner. Shooting, which had been scheduled to start in June, had already been pushed back as telexes and telephone calls revealed the extent of the nervousness in the region. With Klinger frantically trying to save the situation, shooting was postponed indefinitely.

If there was any pessimism at Compton it wasn't showing; just before he and Tenser had left for Berlin, Klinger had signed a unique co-production deal with SIFA Argentine, one of the leading South American film producers. In return for providing finance Compton would obtain world distribution rights for six new colour films starring Isabel Sarli whose sizzling melodramas, bordering on soft core pornography, were practically unknown to the mainstream audiences but played with

top prize, the Golden Bear, collected on behalf of Compton once again by Michael Klinger. Proving that the Germans did not have a totally unique sense of humour, two months later the film won a Diploma of Merit at the Edinburgh Film Festival. During the same period the UK box-office returns started off slowly and continued the same way.

By now the relationship between Polanski and his English backers had cooled to freezing point. Cadre Films was constantly battling with Compton's accountants over residual payments on the royalties for *Repulsion*, now on general release in such diverse territories as the American mid-West and the Indian subcontinent. Working for Compton meant a running battle with producers who had very different imperatives from those of the filmmakers. Neither Polanski nor Gutowski felt they had the energy to continue this way any longer. Polanski had regarded *Repulsion* as a means to an end - *Cul-de-Sac* - and even as he was putting the final touches to his new film he was looking around for a new source of finance. Martin Ransohoff made Polanski and Gutowski an offer they would find very difficult to refuse: 100% on any film of their choice.

below:
Lionel Stander seems to
be enjoying the interplay
between Françoise
Dorléac and Roman
Polanski. Dorléac
herself was a last
minute addition to the
cast after actress
Alexandra Stewart
withdrew.

huge success at the Compton club. Film production in the UK also looked promising for the Group; to fill the gap left by 'Beau Brigand', Klinger agreed to resurrect 'The Devil's Discord', a contemporary Gothic shocker influenced by Mario Bava's atmospheric horrors. Michael Reeves was to direct from a script by author John Burke, Peter Cushing had been signed to star, and Harry Fine was on board to oversee the production on Compton's behalf. Fledgling American producer Patrick Curtis would share the production credit in exchange for putting in 25% of the budget. To assuage his conscience about investing in a horror movie, Klinger also bought the rights to the critically acclaimed C. Scott Forbes play 'The Meter Man.' A particular favourite of Klinger's, Forbes's hard-hitting screenplay was later reworked and filmed as *The Penthouse (1967)*, directed by Peter Collinson.

With Klinger now in sole charge of film production, *The Projected Man* - the last movie 'green-lighted' by Tenser as Managing Director of the Compton Group - made its bow, on a double-bill with *Passport to Hell*.

THE PROJECTED MAN

'You Must Not See This Film Without Special Eyeshields!'
- British Trade ads -

Synopsis

Dr. Paul Steiner and his young assistant, electronics expert Dr. Chris Mitchel, have invented a means of projecting matter across a room. Steiner has successfully projected a live guinea pig through his system of Light Amplification by Stimulated Emission of Radiation (L.A.S.E.R.) and back into solid form again, though the animal subsequently died. When Dr. Blanchard, a director of the Foundation supporting Steiner's work, announces he is closing the operation down, Steiner calls in his old friend Dr. Patricia G. Hill (nicknamed 'Piggy') to assist with his experiments. Faced with corporate obstinacy and sabotage, Steiner experiments on himself in an effort to save his research. The experiment goes wrong and a horribly scarred and deranged Steiner is let loose as 'the projected man'.

"THE PROJECTED MAN" 'x' Starring MARY PEACH · BRYANT HALIDAY · NORMAN WOOLAND
A MICHAEL KLINGER and TONY TENSER Presentation. RONALD ALLEN · DEREK FARR · TRACEY CRISP
Produced by JOHN CROYDON and MAURICE FOSTER. Directed by IAN CURTEIS. Screenplay by JOHN C. COOPER and PETER BRYAN. Filmed in Eastman Colour and Technicolor.

above:
British front of house still showing Mary Peach billed above Bryant Haliday. This order was reversed for the film's American release.

below:
August 25, 1966 issue of Kine Weekly showing British artwork for **The Projected Man** and its support feature. This was to be the last Compton film for which Tony Tenser was given an on screen credit; he left the company in October 1966.

Critique

'Clever trick photography and the special effects and make-up man have done a good job. It's a pity about the 'X' certificate for there is nothing in the horrors to harm the average, hard-boiled child of today.'
- Kine Weekly, 21/07/66

'An odd mixture, this. It begins well... but... it begins to go gradually downhill.'
- Monthly Film Bulletin, 08/66

'The acting is generally good...no performers stand out but the money saved on names was better invested in the technical areas. Director Ian Curteis fills the screen with compositions inspired by Sidney Furie's Ipcress File style that keep the film visually lively without resorting to outright imitation.'
- Variety, 29/03/67

The Projected Man has a comfortably old-fashioned feel about it, without perhaps the straight-faced moralising of its Forties and Fifties predecessors. The script includes all the usual characters expected in this type of film: a dedicated and honest scientist, granite-jawed lab assistant, beautiful and intelligent female scientist, and of course an interfering and ultimately corrupt bureaucrat. That's not to say The Projected Man doesn't work because, despite the script, it does. The laser is particularly effective and there is no indication of the film's relatively low budget or the difficulties behind the camera. The music is also extremely effective, as indeed are the sound effects throughout, but the Bond-type imagery is misplaced and the film does tend to drag whenever Haliday isn't on the screen. He makes an extraordinarily cultured scientist, his beautiful speaking voice and gentle manner giving the part of Steiner the air of intelligence and worldliness often lacking in this type of role. Haliday of course has all

the best dialogue, dismissing concern for the fate of a laboratory rat with a casual, 'its gone wherever good rats go.'

Haliday makes his job look easy, but Mary Peach really struggles with some dreadful lines like, 'No human being could survive a time transition of that kind. Not without fearful consequences!' Wooland adds considerable depth as the main villain, but neither Peach nor Allen impress as lovers. Tracey Crisp, who sacrifices her clothes and shows a nice line in delicate undies, ends up responsible not only for the initial accident but also for setting fire to Steiner's flat; the less said about her acting the better, but she is admittedly easy on the eyes.[14]

The highlight of the entire film is undoubtedly Nordhoff's make-up. Immediately striking, it works very well both in the shadows and daylight though the producers rely too much on its effect to carry the tension of the film. The final scene with Steiner's haunting, disembodied cries is really quite chilling. Needless to say the villains are excellent and add tremendously to the humour; at one point the mysterious, and uncredited, Blofeld-like cat lover threatens Norman Wooland with, 'Oh no Dr. Blanchard, it's not finished. Don't forget I still have those photographs.'

Richard Gordon had predicted the effects and make-up would sell the film and that's exactly the way that Compton pitched their advertising. The science fiction aspects were played down as the publicity men sold The Projected Man with some success as a 'monster on the loose' film.[15]

*　　*　　*　　*　　*

Unable to refinance 'Beau Brigand', Michael Klinger abandoned the project and the costs were written off. When 'Alice in Wonderland' failed to excite any interest in Hollywood it too was shelved. There was dwindling confidence that 'The Loch Ness Monster' - now budgeted at £500,000 - would be delivered during 1967. It was clear that the new structure wasn't delivering the type of result that either Tenser or Klinger wanted. Gregarious and lively, Klinger thrived on publicity; he loved the spotlight and he loved rubbing shoulders with important creative filmmakers. He needed to be successful, and he needed to be seen to be successful. For Klinger, bigger meant better.

Tony Tenser did not share his partner's outgoing personality and was less ambitious for personal recognition. Now directly responsible for Compton's exhibition interests, Tenser was however still hungry for success as a film producer. He wanted to deliver films that the public wanted to see and that made money. If the film happened to be a hit with critics then so much the better. Compton movies succeeded, Tenser argued, primarily because they were carefully packaged and cheap: '...that didn't mean we did away with quality. British filmmakers would look at Hollywood where money was no object and try to copy them on the same scale. They would waste a lot of money. We tried to cut some of that out and retain the quality.' In a film company with a larger capital base, there may have been room for two opposing views but Compton was still a relatively small operation. On the 13th of October 1966, Tenser announced his resignation as Managing Director. 'There was no animosity,' he recalls. 'We had come to the end of our term. We had come to a time, Klinger and I, when we thought we would be better off each going our own way.' Jack Barlow, who had been Theatrical Controller for Compton, replaced Tenser as Director of Exhibition. Michael Klinger obtained the majority share in the Compton Group and, staying on as Chairman, he would spend the next two years trying to turn Compton into something approaching his vision.[16]

Tenser cashed-in his shares in Compton and immediately started looking for a venture more in tune with the way he wanted to do business.

Footnotes

1. Holy Island, or Lindisfarne, has been inhabited since the sixteenth century, though the population in 1966 was only around three hundred, mainly farmers and fishermen. Five miles off the coast of Northumberland, it is accessible at low tide by a causeway to the mainland.

2. Donald Pleasence (1919-1995) was a short, intense character with beady blue eyes and a round, bald head that meant he was particularly suited to playing the part of nasty, plebeian villains like Blofeld, or any number of Nazis. Quite without the nobility of stars like Christopher Lee or Vincent Price, Pleasence did succeed in avoiding horror movie typecasting for much of his career, attaching himself to a number of art projects. For a brief period he was known for adding class to otherwise worthless movies. Motivated largely by a continuous desire to work, the crud soon outweighed the worthy and, despite the efforts of John Carpenter to single-handedly salvage his career, by the time of his death in 1995 he was largely thought of as a straight-to-video 'B' actor. Amongst his best films: *Sons and Lovers (1960)*, *Dr. Crippen (1962)*, *The Caretaker (1963)*, *Soldier Blue (1970)*, *Death Line (1972)*, and *Halloween (1978)*.

3. The burly American's promising Hollywood career stopped dead in 1948 when his name appeared on the infamous Hollywood blacklist. He drifted into various alternative career paths, which included a stint working on Wall Street, before Tony Richardson cast him in several theatre plays including 'Arturo Ui'. Gradually, he then began to find work in British and European films, developing something of a reputation on the arthouse circuit. Stander finally found mainstream acceptance of sorts as Max the butler in the obnoxious *Hart to Hart* TV series. He enjoyed the

fruits of his belated success to the full but sadly died in 1994 after a long battle against lung cancer, survived by his six daughters.

4. Quite apart from his reputation for pushing his actresses to the limit, Polanski also had a taste for very public affairs; according to his autobiography he exceeded himself on *Cul-de-Sac* by juggling liaisons with Jacqueline Bisset and his then girl friend Jill St. John.

5. Polanski is uncharacteristically vague on why Canadian actress Stewart left the troubled production, saying only that they both felt that it wasn't working out. She went on to have had a very varied if unspectacular career, appearing in films like *Goodbye Emmanuelle (1977)* and *The Uncanny (1977)*.

6. Dorléac had already made over a dozen films in France, as well as international movies like *Genghis Khan (1965)* and *Where the Spies Are (1965)*. Less than a year after *Cul-de-Sac*, having completed work on Ken Russell's *Billion Dollar Brain*, Dorléac was killed in a car accident. She was only 25 years old.

7. After shooting was over, Polanski again convinced his leading lady to pose for his close friend David Bailey, who was by that time dating Catherine Deneuve. This time however the photos appeared in Vogue rather than Playboy. Bailey also provided the stills for the film's press book, designed by the famed Polish artist Jan Lenica.

8. Richard Gordon and brother Alex were both London-born but US-based film producers. Richard first achieved prominence acting as Bela Lugosi's agent during his ill-fated 1951 Dracula tour of England. The chaotic and amateurish production folded when the production company went bust, leaving Bela and his wife stranded and broke in London. Gordon managed to get him a role in *Old Mother Riley Meets the Vampire (1952)* to help him recover some of the money he was owed and allow him to get back to Hollywood. Gordon went on to make two movies in England with Boris Karloff, *Corridors of Blood (1958)* and *Grip of the Strangler (1958)*, which acted as his launch pad into a career producing low-budget international movies which usually featured fading American stars. Among his later movies were *The Cat and the Canary (1979)* and Norman J. Warren's *Inseminoid (1980)*. An intelligent and articulate man, Gordon shrewdly retained the rights to most of his films and continues to work long after retirement age, marketing and promoting his movies with the occasional announcement of a new project.

9. Bryant Haliday is something of a curiosity in the Sixties horror genre. A Harvard Law graduate who taught Latin and Greek, he had spent the first 21 years of his life in a Benedictine monastery preparing for the priesthood. He left to join the legendary New England Brattle Theatre Group, where he learned his craft in over fifty productions, enjoying roles by many of the great writers from Shakespeare to Shaw. Haliday is best known in the industry as the founder of Janus Films, the first company to bring European arthouse films to the campuses of America, introducing teenagers to the delights of Bergman, Fellini, Antonioni and Olmi. By the Sixties he was sufficiently wealthy to look on acting as a hobby, and he began to pop up in

above:
Four Compton logos in the space of one ad! These were the company's 1966 productions, and this particular advert was used as a teaser to excite interest from exhibitors.

below:
The exhibitors played a massively important role in the success of Compton. In the early days Tenser and Graham Whitworth made a point of being on first name terms with as many people in the trade as possible. Even as the company grew they maintained that their partnerships with cinema managers was a cornerstone of the company's strategy.

above:
The French had no problems featuring **Cul-de-Sac**'s brief nude scene with Quarrier and Dorléac in their publicity materials, unlike their British counterparts. By contrast Berlin's Golden Bear doesn't get a mention in the home of the Cannes film festival.

below:
A much less subtle use of nudity, this time from **Secrets of a Windmill Girl**. It's worth nothing that the film's star Pauline Collins appeared in nothing racier than a mini-skirt.

some very odd films: Shonteff's *Devil Doll (1963)* and *Curse of Simba (1965)*, and Richard Gordon's *Tower of Evil (1971)*. By the mid-Seventies he was living comfortably in semi-retirement in France, venturing into the odd theatre or television project. At the time of his death in 1996 Bryant had been away from the screen for so long that he was largely forgotten; the sudden flurry of obituaries and tributes restored some much-merited recognition to him.

10. Mary Peach, later to become Mrs. Jimmy Sangster, had appeared in a number of successful British movies, notably the Rank productions *No Love for Johnnie (1960)* and *A Pair of Briefs (1962)*. International stardom seemed to beckon when she signed a non-exclusive multiple picture contract with Universal and was whisked away to Hollywood to star opposite Rock Hudson in *A Gathering of Eagles (1963)*. For one reason or another it didn't work out, though Ms Peach was to remain in constant demand, working in films as well as TV and stage on both sides of the Atlantic. Sadly she now looks back on *The Projected Man* with something less than enthusiasm, and declined to be interviewed for this book.

11. Born in 1930, Ronald Allen won the John Gielgud scholarship to RADA, which was followed by a successful spell at the Old Vic playing opposite both Burton and Neville during their celebrated runs in the Fifties. Despite a contract with Twentieth Century Fox and parts in *A Night To Remember (1958)* and *Cleopatra (1963)*, film stardom eluded him. He was content to slum it on the most abused of all soaps, *Crossroads*, from 1969 until its demise in the Eighties. Allen had lived all his life under the shadow of homosexual prejudice, so it was a bit of a surprise when he turned up on the 'Comic Strip' spoofs as the homosexual Uncle Quentin, but it did at least allow

him the dignity of going out on a high note. He died in 1991 after a long illness; his former Crossroads co-star Sue Lloyd - his wife of six weeks - was at his side.

12. Interestingly enough Kydd's rough and ready exterior belied a humorous and intelligent man. He wrote a very successful autobiography on his colourful career and equally colourful personal life, and in particular his experiences as a POW in Poland.

13. Klinger had his own views. Speaking ten years later to Sheridan Morley in The Times he said, 'Polanski? Lovely guy, talented monster. Doesn't understand money which is why I will never work with him again; still we did *Repulsion* for £97,000 and *Cul-de-Sac* for £115,000 and since he left me he's never really done anything as good simply because he has never had the discipline of someone leaning on him when he overspends'.

14. Pretty girls were of course a feature of the sales campaigns on all movies of this type; *The Projected Man* differs only in so far as the fact that Tracey Crisp was allowed to completely upstage the nominal star Mary Peach. So much so that over thirty years after the film was made, Ms Peach is still being asked to autograph stills of Ms Crisp.

15. Released in the US nearly a year after its UK release, *The Projected Man* made up the lower half of a double bill with *Island of Terror*, captured some reasonable reviews and did good business.

16. Amongst the first casualties of Tenser's departure was 'The Devil's Discord'; the plug was pulled on the Reeves vehicle only weeks before filming started. Michael Klinger went on to draft extremely ambitious plans for Compton but struggled to get anything into production. 'The Meter Man' (later *The Penthouse*) was the only movie that the company made during this time and it opened to poor box-office. Compton were more successful in exhibition; in April 1967 they opened the Superama in Derby, and ironically Graham Whitworth was called back to supervise the ceremony under the auspices of his own company Arrow Publicity. A month later, with one film already under his belt, Klinger announced Compton would be making twelve to sixteen pictures over the following twelve months. The optimism didn't last - by April 1967, amid boardroom dissent, Klinger petitioned for the winding up of the Compton Group. The petition was opposed by Leslie Elliot, who alleged irregularities in the dealings over the Compton-produced movie *The Penthouse*. After a bitter battle Klinger and his wife resigned their seats on the Board and sold their stock to the existing shareholders. Klinger found life as an independent film producer much more to his liking, going on to produce some of the most successful British movies of the Seventies including the likes of *Get Carter (1971)*, *Shout at the Devil (1976)* and *The Confessions of...* series. The Compton Group, now with no connection to either of its founding partners, was absorbed into Leslie Elliot's Cinecenta who announced his intention of continuing the policy of expansion into exhibition as well as taking over and releasing - under the Compton banner - the slate of 19 films awaiting distribution. Amongst the titles were the likes of Michael Verhoeven's *Danse Macabre* and Joe Massot's *Wonderwall*.

'Leave the Children at Home!'

- (US Trade Ads for *Witchfinder General*, aka *The Conqueror Worm*)

After firmly closing the door on his association with Compton, Tenser threw himself back into the area of the film business he knew best, distribution: 'It never occurred to me to give up. I loved the industry too much. So I decided that I was going to start up on my own again.' Leasing a small office above a shop at 72 Wardour Street, he hired a secretary, bought two second-hand desks and set up 'Tony Tenser Films Ltd' with £10,000 of capital - £5,000 of his own money and £5,000 provided by the Midland Bank. There was no question of competing with the established distribution companies; instead Tony Tenser Films went bargain hunting, obtaining the re-issue rights to older Hollywood movies like *Jack the Giant Killer (1961)*, which could then be repackaged into 'new' double bills.

Tenser's twenty years of experience told him what the exhibitors wanted to see - horror or exploitation movies, preferably with a recognized name. A deal with the UK office of United Artists secured the rights to two Vincent Price movies, *Twice Told Tales (1963)* and *Tower of London (1962)*, neither of which had ever been released nationally, despite having been made some years earlier. Then, recalling his success with the Bardot films, Tenser sought out more interesting foreign language films. 'I had a Japanese film called *Honno (1966)*, which means *Lost Sex*,' he recalls with a broad grin. 'It was a black comedy and it was really quite funny. There was an old boy just lying in a bed and it's all gone, downstairs - if you know what I mean. He is in this hospital ward and a young nurse comes and starts to masturbate him - you don't see anything, just the sheet being moved. Time passes and another nurse would go in and another and days would pass. Eventually, after about a week, there was a cry, everyone cheered and they all came round and congratulated him!'

The UK rights to Tony Tenser Films Ltd's first batch of films were purchased at negligible cost, and Tenser was confident that he could recover a reasonable return by releasing them through the independent circuits. At a time when the film industry in the UK was dependant on word of mouth these releases ensured that the Tenser name remained prominent in the minds of the movers and shakers: 'that was the reason I called the company Tony Tenser Films; I wanted everyone to know who it was.'

While distribution was to be the bread and butter of the new company, Tenser continued to look for production opportunities. He was very soon announcing, with characteristic hyperbole, that his aim was to eventually make up to ten films a year, but conceded, 'until then I will have to be satisfied with five or six!' During the Compton era, the contacts that Tenser and Klinger had established within the industry in general, and in Soho in particular, were absolutely crucial. The Tenser name alone was enough to attract attention and as soon as the Wardour Street office opened, Arnold Louis Miller and a filmmaker called Georges Robin approached Tenser with a proposal to make a sexploitation film called *Mini Weekend*. Robin described the film as a 'mixture of fact and fiction,' coining a new word, 'faction!' However grand that may have sounded, *Mini Weekend* was basically a voyeuristic depiction of a young man's

below:
British artwork for Tenser's release of **Twice Told Tales**, his first film as an independent.

The First of the New Big Ones !!
From **TONY TENSER FILMS**
72 WARDOUR ST., W.I. GER 8284

THE UNDEAD! THE UNEARTHLY! THE UNHOLY!

VINCENT PRICE
in Nathaniel Hawthorne's
"**TWICE TOLD TALES**"

Co-starring Sebastian CABOT Brett HALSEY Beverly GARLAND Richard DENNING and Joyce TAYLOR
Written For The Screen And Produced by Robert E. KENT Directed by Sidney SALKOW **TECHNICOLOR** An Admiral Pictures, Inc. Presentation
A TONY TENSER FILMS RELEASE

sexual fantasies involving a series of different girls, set against the background of a travelogue through London. Miller confirmed that once again he and Stanley Long would be on hand to oversee the shoot, as well as making a financial investment in the picture via their new company, Global Films. Georges Robin had a CV that included some respectable short movies but he had never attempted to make a feature before. Even so, Tenser agreed to underwrite the film's budget with what remained of his start up capital, some £7,000, with Global making up the remainder of the £11,000 budget.

At the time the deal was agreed, *Mini Weekend* existed only as the briefest of outlines, and with a budget that wouldn't stretch to pay for the services of a professional writer, the script was filled out by Tenser himself - his one and only credit for scriptwriting. 'I couldn't claim to have written the greatest script ever, there wasn't much dialogue and we didn't have the money for elaborate scenes. It was okay,' Tenser concedes, 'but it wouldn't win any prizes.'

Working with a roughly-hewn screenplay, an inexperienced director and practically no money, Tenser was dependent on Arnold Miller and Stanley Long to ensure that the film stayed rigidly within budget. Long in fact, with his considerable experience at this zero budget, pseudo-documentary style of shooting offered the best piece of advice: 'If you want to shoot low budget movies you have to use 16mm and if necessary blow it up to 35mm.' Robin was happy to shoot *Mini Weekend* regardless of

above:
Eric Godwin, who joined Tenser in the mid-Sixties as Sales Director and stayed with Tigon until the company ceased distributing movies in the Eighties. Godwin oversaw the distribution of Tigon's biggest ever hit, **Come Play with Me**.

right:
Sultry pose from **Mini Weekend** belies director Georges Robin's rather crude sexploitation approach.

any restrictions, and to Tenser's undying gratitude surplus stock was bought on a generous credit deal from Rank Laboratories: 'If I ever meet that man from Rank again I would shake his hand. He didn't have to do that and without it we couldn't have made the film.' What's more, Robin, Miller and Long all deferred their salary to allow the film to be made; Tenser himself took no payment at all from his contribution.

By necessity, the casting had to reflect the same economy. Leading roles went to Anthony Trent, Liza Rogers and Veronica Lang, none of whom had a great deal of experience; indeed *Mini Weekend* would prove to be the pinnacle of their cinematic careers. The exception was Anna Palk, glimpsed in a small part as the 'girl in the cinema.' Palk went on to minor cult success in horror movies (having already featured in *The Earth Dies Screaming (1964)* and *The Frozen Dead (1966)*), with such delights as *The Nightcomers (1971)* and *Tower of Evil (1971)* still to come. Like the cast, the crew members were all chosen for their cheap but professional attributes, the best known being art director Tony Curtis, later to become resident art designer at Amicus.

Adopting the frantic work ethic of the earlier Long/Miller exposés for Compton, Robin was able shoot the film on the hoof and more or less edit as he went along. The filming of *Mini Weekend* was completed just before Christmas 1966, and it whetted the appetite of Tenser and his newly appointed team, publicity director Frank Law and sales director Eric Godwin, who had worked previously for RKO and Regal Films. At that stage Tony Tenser Films only had a skeleton sales force, who were content to place teaser quotes in the press promising something 'different'. By the time Robin delivered his final print in the last week of April 1967, Godwin had established representative sales offices in Rome, Paris and Stockholm. Extremely satisfied with the first film under his new banner, Tenser was confidently announcing that they, 'had a considerable hit on their hands.'

When the Hyams brothers approached Tenser in late 1966, while *Mini Weekend* was still shooting, he saw the opportunity to expand his tiny distribution business, making film production the core activity for Tony Tenser Films while still maintaining a distribution arm: 'Film production was very attractive at the time,' he recalls, 'there was quite a bit of money coming into London from abroad, America in particular. The distribution side could more or less run itself.'

The Hyams, Phil and Sid, were the elder statesmen of the British film industry; they had built the first Trocadero cinema in London and quickly followed that with the Trocette and then the Troxy. Tenser remembers the arrangement very well: 'They said they had backed someone else, who was very famous in show business, and

above:
More nudity from **Mini Weekend**. This was Tenser's first film as a producer after leaving Compton and it was the inclusion of this sort of fantasy sequence that earned him a credit as co-writer.

they had done extremely well and they now thought that they could back me. I needed money to go on, so I said if they put up £50,000, I wouldn't take it out; it goes straight into the company and they would have a half share. Normally when you sell half your business it's your money. I didn't want it, I wanted it to go into the business, so they agreed.'

With the capital injection from the Hyams, Tenser was once again in a position to play the host to independent filmmakers looking for backing. First through the door was Arnold Louis Miller again, this time accompanied by another acquaintance from the Compton days, American producer Patrick Curtis. Two years earlier Curtis had formed Curtwel Productions with his then girlfriend and later wife, Raquel Welch (Curtis had in fact been acting as her agent at the time); believing that Europe presented better opportunities than Hollywood at the time, he had based himself in London. Curtwel owned the rights to two scripts, 'The Devil's Discord' and 'Crescendo', both of which he wanted Michael Reeves to direct, with the intention being that Compton would produce the films. The restructuring of Compton had left Curtis without a production partner, and finding no interest from the larger outfits he linked up with Global Films. Arnold Miller

opposite top left:
Mini Weekend exploited a degree of nudity that Harrison Marks could only dream about on **Naked - As Nature Intended**; for the first time Tenser could not only show naked breasts but also relate them directly to sexual activity!

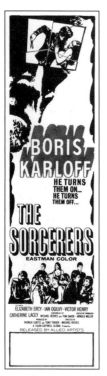

The great Boris Karloff in one of his last decent roles, flanked by Catherine Lacey and a youthful Ian Ogilvy.

below:
Ian Ogilvy as Mike in the night club sequence of **The Sorcerers**. Later commentators were to suggest that Mike Reeves had deliberately made Ogilvy's character semi-autobiographical. and there are certainly a number of superficial similarities.

was confident that he could find the finance and persuaded Curtis that Tony Tenser Films could be trusted to handle the distribution. During this period of uncertainty the two scripts were put on the back burner as Curtis and Reeves developed a new idea, 'The Sorcerer', an original screenplay co-written by Reeves and author Tom Baker.

'The Sorcerer' was a simple story: an ageing hypnotist and his bitter wife gain control of the mind of an impressionable youth and use him to commit a series of crimes. The old couple can experience, vicariously, the sensations and emotions of the younger man. The action would mainly revolve around the activities of the youths in the film - the biggest cinema-going market of course - and Reeves and Baker had

injected enough violence into their script to ensure the film would be readily exploitable. Tenser liked the script immediately and he also liked the young director: 'I had met Mike Reeves at Compton though I didn't know him very well. I knew he had made a film in Italy with Barbara Steele, quite a well made horror film. He impressed me right away, he lived for cinema, he knew absolutely everything about films.'

A budget hadn't been set but Miller proposed that they should film as much as possible on location in London, and use one of the small studios that had sprung up to service the advertising industry rather than the likes of Shepperton or Pinewood. Arnold Miller also wisely chose to shoot the film 'off season', when studios and cutting rooms were quiet, and had negotiated special rates at the tiny Barnes Studios, in West London.

From Tenser's perspective as a distributor the most attractive element of the package however was horror icon Boris Karloff, who had been persuaded by Curtis to take the lead. Unfortunately, even with Karloff attached to the project the modest finance required was proving elusive. Tony Tenser Films initially signed up as the UK distributor of the project and then agreed to put up half the film's budget, which had been set at around the £40,000 mark (the finished film would actually come in at slightly over £50,000). Global provided Stanley Long as cameraman, with Miller and Curtis sharing the producer's chores.[1] Suitable locations in and around London were scouted over the 1966 Christmas holiday period, and in early January 1967 'The Sorcerer' - soon to be re-titled *The Sorcerers* - was ready to start shooting.

Casting the leads was straightforward enough. Karloff and veteran actress Catherine Lacey came as part of the package and Tenser was delighted to approve both.[2] Patrick Curtis, who had been a child actor at Universal when Karloff was their resident ghoul, was particularly keen to work with the old trouper, as was the film buff Tony Tenser: 'Boris was always a boyhood hero of mine and I can't say enough good things about him. He was nearly eighty then but he still remembered all his lines and spoke them perfectly. It was delightful to get the chance to spend time with him.'

Karloff had been approached directly by Michael Reeves when the two men met by chance in Spain. At that point the script had a different emphasis, with the Karloff character being far more manipulative. Tenser later found out that the actor had been unhappy about this and asked for a number of changes: 'Boris was very conscious of his image even at that stage in his career. He didn't want to do anything that put him in a bad light with his fans so he wanted to play a goodie.'

Still relatively inexperienced as a director, Michael Reeves liked to have familiar faces around his set so he cast Ian Ogilvy as the juvenile lead. Ogilvy was a friend of Reeves who had appeared in a number of the director's experimental short films as well as his earlier Italian horror movie. Taking the thankless role of the 'hero's friend' was Victor Henry, who had scored considerable personal success on the stage but had yet to make any impact in the cinema.[3] One of Ogilvy's friends, Nicky Henson, was originally due to take that role but lost out because of the film's scheduling; Henson would get his chance to play second support for Reeves the following year.

Reeves also cast a seventeen-year old Susan George in the role of Audrey, a

above:
Karloff is visited on the set of **The Sorcerers** by his fifth and last wife Evelyn (Evie). The couple had been inseparable since their marriage in 1946.

former girlfriend and victim of Ogilvy. This was in fact George's first mature role, though she had been around for a number of years as a child actress.[4] Producers Miller and Curtis sought to continue the English tradition of importing glamorous European unknowns to add an exotic foreign accent to the proceedings; in this case the colourless Elizabeth Ercy. It was Curtis who suggested the French-born Ercy, who had come to the UK the previous year for a brief role in *Doctor in Clover*, and later appeared in *Fathom (1967)* with Raquel Welch. Tenser remembers that Ms. Welch herself provided the producers with some uncredited assistance: 'Raquel would come in from time to time to see the rushes, a very nice lady. She would help here and there with the costumes and things.'

While he may have been grateful for the help, Miller was very much in his element; tight on money and time, he relied

left:
Tenser clowns around with his boyhood hero Boris Karloff on the set of **The Sorcerers**. Note Karloff's wheelchair, although he hated to be seen using it in photographs and on the screen.

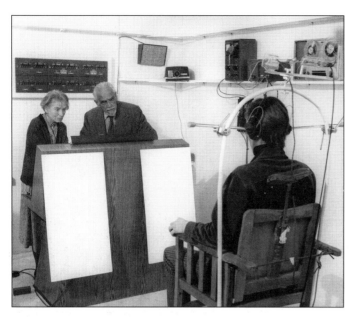

However inventive the production team was, both time and money were rapidly running out. 'Night shooting was a real problem,' Long remembers, 'it's always more expensive anyway, but now it was freezing cold and the crew were getting annoyed because they were being kept waiting around. I think everybody was pretty unhappy about it, so something had to be done.' At a summit meeting at the Gloucester Hotel, Curtis and Reeves met with the representatives of Global and Tony Tenser Films to thrash out a plan to get the film back within budget. Reeves reluctantly revised the script, some additional money was made available, and once again the crew headed out onto the London streets.

Reeves, realising the difficult situation he was facing, reined in his natural enthusiasm and opted for a much more focused and disciplined approach to the remainder of the film. The director's technical expertise was never in doubt - Stanley Long remembers that there was very little he could teach the twenty-three year old about setting up a shot - but the director's discomfort with actors did show. 'I don't think he ever talked to them about their characters or anything,' Long says, 'He kept his distance.' Ian Ogilvy later told Fangoria magazine, 'Michael never directed actors. He always said he didn't know anything about acting and preferred to leave it up to us. The only direction he ever gave was, 'A bit quicker,' or 'a bit slower.' The perception remains that Reeves was aloof and unapproachable, and the complex young man's personality would create considerable friction on his next film for Tenser, but he seems to have had an exceptional rapport with Karloff. 'Boris was old school,' Tenser says, 'Once he agreed he

on his own creativity, an attribute greatly appreciated by Tenser. 'We got to the stage where Arnold came to me and said, there were three or four scenes in which they needed a London taxi. He said if he hired one they needed to have an actor, someone with a Union ticket. So he suggested he could buy an old second-hand one, clean it up so it looks all right and get it licensed only to use in the film. Arnold also said he'd be the taxi driver and we can also use it to do the tracking shots instead of putting rails down or use it to carry the actors about!' Needless to say nothing went to waste; the taxi, complete with cameo by Miller, featured in the film and the vehicle was later sold for a small profit.

The shooting schedule that was drawn up for the production meant that Reeves and his crew had to constantly move from one location to the next. Minor considerations, such as obtaining permission from the police to film, weren't allowed to slow things down; Reeves simply set up his equipment, shot the scene and quickly moved on to the next location. The authorities only caught up with the filmmakers once; when shooting the climactic explosion on a disused building site, concerned locals alerted the police and fire brigade, who arrived in force. The cast and crew disappeared as quickly as possible, leaving Miller with some explaining to do down at the local police station!

Shooting this quickly helped create the film's frantic, almost documentary style, which was exactly the effect that Reeves wanted but it created problems for Stanley Long: 'Michael really wasn't too experienced and it showed, he didn't really know how to plan. He would schedule set-ups spread all over the city, we couldn't possibly get there and then he couldn't understand why we fell behind. He simply wasn't allowing enough time for the set-ups.'

BORIS KARLOFF in
"THE SORCERERS" (X)
CO STARRING CATHERINE LACEY WITH
ELIZABETH ERCY — IAN OGILVY — VICTOR HENRY

TIGON PICTURES LTD. IN EASTMANCOLOUR

above:
British front of house
still from **The Sorcerers**
- note the appearance
of the famous Tigon
logo: half tiger, half lion,
all Tenser.

was going to do something he got on with it, never complained or moaned. He had a lovely nature. Mike seemed to respond to that professionalism, I watched them chatting all the time.'

Shooting interiors at the West London studios proved less problematical than the location work, though the facilities were rather primitive and the acoustics were basic. The closed environment meant that costs could be more tightly controlled, and it also meant more regular visits from the film's backer. Tenser's presence on set didn't pose any problem for Reeves and his crew, which was in marked contrast to many of the Compton films, where the arrival of the executive producer had been treated with dismay. 'Arnold Miller and Patrick Curtis were both very good at their jobs, and I liked them a lot,' Tenser explains. 'Michael Reeves of course knew exactly what he was doing, so there was no need for me to intervene. I never considered myself creative personnel and I didn't want to play any part in that process; I was the distributor and if I could make suggestions on what would or wouldn't help sell the film then I would.'

Working in a studio also allowed Reeves more freedom to explore one of his favourite themes, the juxtaposition of sex and violence. As Stanley Long witnessed, this was particularly evident during the brutal murder of the Susan George character: 'He went right over the top, throwing blood everywhere, up the walls, over the crew - gallons of the stuff. It was an obsession for him.' Reeves, over budget and under pressure, finished the shoot and retired to rented cutting rooms in Wardour Street to assemble the film.

*   *   *   *   *

Tenser now had his first two productions finished and a growing number of releases pending. The company was growing at such a pace that he felt it was time to adopt a different approach. The decision to rename the company seemed a logical one: 'I had partners then and I didn't want to call it 'Tony Tenser Films' anymore. Trading under a personal name wasn't as professional as trading under a company name,' he explained. 'I wanted to keep the 'T' and I wanted to have a mythological figure in it. The cross between a tiger and a lion is normally called a 'Ligon' or a 'Liga'. I called it Tigon, and our motif was a lion with stripes.'

Keen that the new company would be seen as a step forward from Tony Tenser Films, the Tigon Pictures distribution strategy was clearly defined. At a press conference Tenser stated his intention of releasing quality family films aimed at a mainstream audience. Underlining the plan

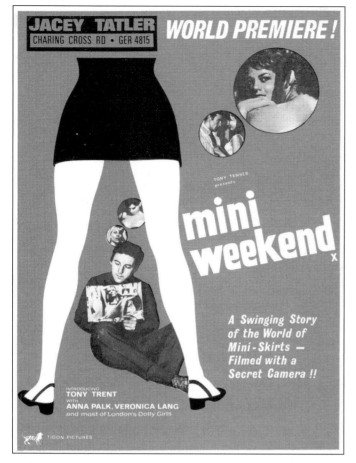

JACEY TATLER
CHARING CROSS RD · GER 4815 **WORLD PREMIERE!**

TONY TENSER
presents

mini
weekend x

*A Swinging Story
of the World of
Mini-Skirts —
Filmed with a
Secret Camera!!*

INTRODUCING
TONY TRENT
WITH
ANNA PALK, VERONICA LANG
and most of London's Dolly Girls

TIGON PICTURES

above:
British trade ad for **Mini Weekend**. The film had started out under the banner of Tony Tenser Films but by the time it was released it became the first Tigon film.

below:
Mini Weekend star Tony Trent making his feature debut as Tom. Incidentally the film's US title **The Tomcat** was a play on this name.

he announced: 'I shall not buy any more dubbed pictures; they are too specialised a market.' The new company's production strategy, under the banner of Tigon British Films, was equally well defined - the aim was to produce sensibly budgeted movies capable of circuit release. A typical Tigon film would be in colour with a budget of around £75,000, based on new scripts generated 'in house'. Taking the lead from *The Sorcerers*, Tigon would save money by scheduling their shoots for off-peak periods such as January/February, when production facilities were traditionally quiet. The company's films would then be distributed

in the UK by Tigon themselves; in the rest of the world they would rely on partnership agreements. The growing importance of US investment, as well as the potential revenues available from US television, would also be major factors in determining projects. 'I think the finance from the export side could be as important as the UK side,' Tenser remarked at the time, stressing that he was not interested in making 'second' or 'B' features but would consider every opportunity on its own merits - before adding, tongue in cheek, 'Of course, if they offered me 50% of *You Only Live Twice*, I'd be in there like a shot!'

Mini Weekend may not have been in quite the same class as Bond, but Frank Law's publicity team was doing its best to build it up. Clearly influenced by Compton, Tigon planned a publicity campaign that kicked off, of course, with a high profile 'world premiere.' The mini-skirt motif of the film was to be the focal point for the film's publicity, with pre-release handouts conveniently diverting attention away from the non-star cast by promising 'lots of dolly girls'. Lacking the financial power of Compton, Law used the London papers to send out an open invitation for as many mini-skirted teenagers as possible to attend the premiere, with the promise of their picture in the tabloids as a reward. Needless to say those members of the general public who dared to turn out were supplemented with the usual round-up of scantily clad models, thus guaranteeing *Mini Weekend* more than its fair share of press attention. And in case anyone missed it, the UK posters trumpeted the main selling point: 'Filmed with a Secret Camera!'

MINI WEEKEND

*'A Swinging Story of the World of
Mini-Skirts'*
- UK press release -

Synopsis

Tom seems to be an ordinary, average young man, living in a small flat with his mother in a suburb of London. To escape the boredom he retreats into a dream world of nubile girls and sexual conquests. Tom's only hobby appears to be leafing though adult magazines, cutting out the pictures of glamorous women and sticking them up on his wall of his bedroom. One weekend he leaves the suburbs for a rare trip to London's Carnaby Street, attracted by the bustle, bright lights and of course the girls in their revealing mini-skirts. Reality and fantasy blur after he attempts and fails to chat up an attractive girl in the street and he lapses into a series of sexual encounters - at a disco, in a boutique and even on a London bus.

Critique

'I shall resist the temptation to make jokes about Mini Weekend... because although it is a poor film as it stands, something good is struggling to come out of it...'
- The Morning Star, 13/05/67

'But the film turns out to be a rather drab, sad account of a young man's day-long search through London... for a bit of sexual excitement. Undoubtedly there is a good film to be made that presents London as a nightmare of erotic temptation... but this is emphatically not it.'
- The Times, 11/05/67

'A flaccid first feature.'
- The New Statesman, 12/05/67

'Screen scripters Tony Tenser and Georges Robin have saddled producer Tenser and director Robin in a Walter Mitty-like sex fantasy theme which rarely gets off the ground.'
- Variety, 07/06/67

'One redeeming feature: a performance of beauty and matter of fact charm by Veronica Lang, a newcomer to watch.'
- The Evening News, 11/05/67

'It is all about as erotic as a plum pudding.'
- The Times, 12/05/67

'Deep down there is a lot of pessimism struggling to get out but the girlie shots, the sexy theme and overall sleaziness success-fully obliterate that. However, it peddles its flesh well enough to make it nicely exploitable.'
- The Daily Cinema, 10/05/67

Mini Weekend was never going to liked by the critics but Robin genuinely hoped it would establish his credentials as a filmmaker, and by introducing a proper narrative Messrs Long and Miller felt they had moved beyond the earlier Searchlight documentaries. The low budget and laboured acting were obstacles to success from the outset, and while the handheld cameras may hint at voyeuristic delights the reality is very much more mundane. Parts of the film worked very well - the scene with a prostitute turning into a hag may be a cliché but it is well staged - whilst others are just tedious. Of course, these issues were of little importance to Tenser, who had achieved considerable returns on lesser products, and Mini Weekend certainly had the right ingredi-ents to sell.

With the American cult classic Carnival of Souls (1962) making up the bill, Mini Weekend became the first film release under the Tigon brand, opening at the Jacey cinema on the 11th of May 1967.

Frank Law's fashion show had the desired effect and *Mini Weekend* enjoyed a good opening. As he prepared to leave for the Cannes Film Festival, Tenser announced that the company was growing at such a rate that he was intending to re-locate to bigger offices in order to accommodate the expanding sales force.

Tenser wanted to press ahead with production of 'The Devil's Discord' as the next Tigon movie so that he could maintain a working relationship with Reeves and Curtis; in fact he had gone so far as to discuss a long-term contract with the talented young director. 'I only had about seven people working for me at the time,' Tenser says, 'it was a tiny company and this was something I'd thought I would never do. We talked about a five year contract, minimum of one film a year and Michael was extremely receptive.' Reeves, who was already under pressure to meet Tenser's deadline for *The Sorcerers*, postponed any decision until he had finished his post production chores.

The last refinement was to be a score by Paul Ferris, another friend of Reeves and a professional musician who had briefly worked with Nicky Henson, during which time the pair had written songs for Cliff Richard. When Henson decided to pursue a career as an actor, Ferris gave up the option of becoming a pop star and decided to concentrate on writing soundtracks instead. *The Sorcerers* was his first commission. The final print, complete with Ferris's score, was prepared for Tenser's trip to Cannes in May and was screened to some enthusiastic overseas distributors, including Allied Artists who snapped up the North American rights. In the UK the censor approved the film with some reservations but no cuts, and a month later *The Sorcerers* was ready for release.

above:
British front of house still for **Mini Weekend**. The budget of only £11,000 prevented the use of a name cast, hence most of the girls featured were models. This meant the publicity materials featured a number of racier than usual stills for the film's promotion.

below:
British admat for **Mini Weekend**.

above:
Captivatingly dramatic British admat for **The Sorcerers**. Despite the relative success of Tenser's releases as an independent, Tigon could not afford to use colour in their artwork, hence the UK poster for this film was produced in black and white.

right:
Karloff and Lacey both picked up prizes for their work on **The Sorcerers**, as did the film itself. However, none of these 'baubles', as Karloff called them, were quoted in the film's publicity - in contrast to **Cul-de-Sac** and **Repulsion**, whose critical achievements were displayed by Tenser with pride.

THE SORCERERS

'He Turned Them On...
He Turned Them Off'
- US Press release -

Synopsis

Retired and discredited hypnotist Professor Marcus Monserrat invents a device which allows the wearer to experience vicariously the senses and pleasures of a selected 'target'. Monserrat hopes this will be his crowning achievement and gain him acceptance in the scientific community but his wife Estelle, after years of hardship, has other ideas. When they persuade a young man, Mike, to take part in the experiment Estelle gains control of their subject and forces him into a series of criminal activities, culminating in bloody murder. Tied up by Estelle, Marcus battles one last time to free Mike from the woman's evil influence.

Critique

'The most intriguing horror idea for ages... Some deft editing puts the sense over quite nicely though inevitably the giggles are built in. But Boris Karloff, limping and lisping still gives off a powerful odour of past gory, glory.'
- The Sunday Telegraph, 18/06/67

'For a straightforward and utterly silly horror yarn you have The Sorcerers. It is a remarkably bad film.'
- The Sun, 16/06/67

'Silly even by contemporary standards.'
- The New Statesman, 30/06/67

'If Michael Reeves's second film is a trifle disappointing after the promise of Revenge of the Blood Beast it is probably because the direction is constantly undercut by the solidly pedestrian camerawork and indifferent colour. All the same Reeves manages to build considerable charge particularly in the second half.'
- Monthly Film Bulletin, 07/67

'Catherine Lacey admirably displays the emergence of the monster from the mouse; Boris Karloff, as he has always tended in horror films, is felt more as a presence than as an actor.'
- The Financial Times, 16/06/67

'A striking debut in the British cinema... directed with quite remarkable intelligence and economy.'
- The Times, 15/06/67

Michael Reeves fashioned a powerful and compelling film out of a script that is in effect a loose conglomeration of clichés. Made in the style of a contemporary thriller,

The Sorcerers owes far more to Don Siegel than Terence Fisher. The energetic camera-work and pulsating soundtrack as well as the unrestrained violence, particularly in the slaughter of the Susan George character, is a million miles removed from the cosy fantasy world of Hammer horror.

Although the poverty of the budget is apparent from time to time - notably in Karloff's laboratory, which is equipped with little more than a slide projector and a tape recorder - the seediness is perfectly suited to the grim world Reeves created. The overwhelming air of pessimism and selfishness is a striking contrast to the inanities of the swinging Sixties.

The Sorcerers could easily have degenerated into a dull and petty film in the hands of a lesser director, so the result is all the more remarkable given Reeves's relative inexperience. The director is helped enormously by his cast, particularly Karloff who could have played the role with his eyes closed, but rises above the inadequacies of the script to deliver a performance of quiet dignity and sadness. The old man's acting style contrasts nicely with that of the casual Ian Ogilvy, looking far more comfortable as the moody and selfish Mike than he was in his later period-piece roles. The real revelation though is Catherine Lacey, hugely entertaining as the bitter Estelle, descending from dotty housewife to cackling psychotic and chewing the scenery for all she is worth.

To the surprise and delight of Tenser, *The Sorcerers* was booked in for a three week West End run at the prestigious Carlton in Haymarket - unheard of in those days for a low-budget horror movie. The film built on this promising start when it opened in the provinces, paired with the Roger Corman movie *Tower of London (1962)*. There was further reason to celebrate in July 1968, when *The Sorcerers* won the 'Grand Prix' at the Sixth Film Festival of Trieste, with Catherine Lacey winning best actress. Boris Karloff was awarded a special medal for 'his great services to horror films.' Sadly neither Lacey nor Karloff were in Trieste to collect their prizes. Lacey had to wait until September, when Tenser treated her to lunch and then presided over an informal ceremony in his Wardour Street office. The Grand Prix was also paraded for the London press at the same time. Karloff, who had no interest in 'baubles' had to wait a little longer for his medal, and again Tenser arranged the honours. 'I got on extremely well with Boris during *The Sorcerers*, and one day we were chatting on set and he said you really must come to tea with Evie and me. Some time later I had to go to Hollywood on business and I knew Boris was working there so I took his medal with me. I found out where he was staying and went up and knocked on his door. Boris was absolutely dumbfounded to see me and

l'ultime création de **Boris Karloff**

GRAND PRIX du FESTIVAL SCIENCE-FICTION TRIESTE

la créature invisible

avec ELISABETH ERCY - IAN OGILVY et CATHERINE LACEY dans le rôle d'"ESTELLE"
mise en scène de MICHAEL REEVES - eastmancolor - TIGON PRODUCTION LONDRES
ETOILE DISTRIBUTION   INTERDIT AUX MOINS DE 13 ANS

asked what I was doing there. 'I've come for that cup of tea,' I said!' Tragically Karloff's medal was stolen, never to be recovered, when his London apartment was broken in to on the 23rd of January 1969; Karloff was terminally ill in hospital at the time.

above:
The French artwork for **The Sorcerers** which, unlike the British promotional artwork, does feature a mention of the film's Grand Prix at Trieste. Tenser incidentally still has the trophy at home.

*   *   *   *   *

Throughout their first months on release the returns for both *The Sorcerers* and *Mini Weekend* were positive but hardly spectacular - neither film though was thought sufficiently big-budget to be of interest to the major circuits, and Tigon was reliant on the more sporadic bookings of the independents. Nevertheless, the return relative to investment was good and, revelling in the success, Tenser made it clear that he regarded his primary loyalty was to those who put money into his films. Speaking to The Daily Cinema he singled out his main backer Phil Hyams: 'I hope to make him rich because I'll also get rich in the process.' Tenser's philosophy had remained largely unchanged since the very early days at Compton: 'The name of the game is to get your money back, because if you lose money no-one will back your next film. The films need to be inexpensive but they need to sell, they need to appeal to an international audience and the one subject that always finds a market is horror. Language doesn't matter, like sex, everyone understands and wants to see a horror film. A film like *The Sorcerers* sold itself really.'

above:
Robert Flemyng as Dr Mallinger. The actor was drafted in as a last minute replacement for Basil Rathbone.

right:
Mallinger and his creature in a posed publicity shot for **The Blood Beast Terror**.

below:
Tony Tenser cuts his birthday cake on the set of **The Blood Beast Terror** while actress Wanda Ventham looks on. Director Vernon Sewell can be seen in the background, wearing sunglasses.

Stanley Long and Arnold Louis Miller were keen to continue their relationship with Tigon, and Tenser proposed an outline he had written for Compton but never developed, 'Trog - The Million Year Old Man'. 'This was an idea I had discussed over lunch one day with the Fords; they told me about humans called troglodytes who lived in caves and I thought why not write a script about these hairy humans and have a prehistoric film. I thought it would make a great love story!' By the time the project was dusted down, fleshed out and a prospective budget drawn up, the figures didn't make sense; it was simply beyond Tigon's modest means. Tenser made a quick profit by selling the title to Herman Cohen, who later turned it into a vehicle for Joan Crawford.

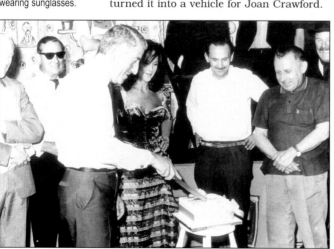

Tenser then cheekily announced that Tigon's next production would be 'The Horrors of Frankenstein', featuring an international star cast. In Hammer House, only a few doors down from Tenser's office, they regarded Frankenstein and Dracula as their private preserve and the press release was met with some consternation. Legally there was nothing Hammer could do, the original subject was long since out of copyright even if the movie versions weren't, but that didn't stop Hammer's boss James Carreras flexing his muscles. Letters were exchanged and an understanding reached; plans to make 'The Horrors of Frankenstein' were quietly dropped as a gesture of goodwill to Carreras.

There was a suspicion at Tigon that Cushing's Baron was actually generating less income than was popularly believed, and even as the memos were circulating Tenser had moved on to what he regarded as a far more viable idea - 'Death's Head Vampire', from a script by Hammer veteran Peter Bryan, who had also been involved in *The Projected Man*.[5] Bryan's treatment could have come straight out of a Hammer crypt; a mad scientist transforms a Death's Head moth into a beautiful young lady and passes her off as his daughter whilst continuing his experiments. The creature kills when sexually aroused and proceeds to decimate the male population of the Home Counties. The look and feel of the production seemed to clearly signpost its inspiration but Tenser dismisses the idea that he was out to mimic Hammer: 'We weren't seeking to get into anyone's territory. We knew that Hammer by then was moving into other markets; James Carreras wanted to take them away from horror movies, so it wasn't an attempt to copy anything they were doing. From our point of view these films could be made cheaply and would be released anywhere in the world.'

Despite Tenser's protests the Hammer influence even extended to their leading man, Peter Cushing, cast in the role of the police inspector hot on the trial of the homicidal creature. At the time, Cushing was considered a bankable name having appeared in a string of low-budget horror movies culminating in the spectacularly nasty *Corruption* by Robert Hartford-Davis. The actor though was growing weary of the typecasting and it was only with some reluctance that he accepted the role, planning to immediately retreat back into television once the job was finished. Restricted by limited resources, Tenser needed the comfort of reliable hands on the tiller; Global were his production partners, with Arnold Louis Miller and Stanley Long coming on board as producer and cameraman respectively. In contrast with the first two Tigon-Global films, Tenser decided not to hire a young director, opting instead for the veteran filmmaker Vernon Sewell. 'Vernon had been making low-budget movies for years and I thought he was very reliable, you don't go far wrong with chaps like Vernon,' Tenser maintains. Sewell himself remembers being attracted to the project by its script: '...it was by a good friend of mine, Peter Bryan, and I

thought it was very clever. I thought it would be good fun. I said to Tony, if Peter Cushing was in it, I'd do it.'

The film received a considerable boost when Basil Rathbone signed on for the role of Professor Mallinger, the meddling scientist. Although Rathbone's status had declined since his peak as the definitive Sherlock Holmes in the Universal series, television re-runs had ensured he remained a household name. Tenser felt that Rathbone still had the marquee value to give 'Death's Head Vampire' the type of international credibility and profile that Karloff had lent to *The Sorcerers*. Rathbone had already made a number of films for American International Pictures, who had made something of a speciality out of

above:
Peter Cushing poised for action as Inspector Quennell. The actor felt that **The Blood Beast Terror** was a low point in his career, a view that bemused its director Vernon Sewell.

above:
A change of pace for starlet Vanessa Howard, better known for making comedies like **Here We Go Round the Mulberry Bush.**

left:
Father and daughter - Peter Cushing and Vanessa Howard as the Quennells in **The Blood Beast Terror.**

above:
Director Vernon Sewell and actor Robert Flemyng explain the finer points of horror cinema pseudo-science to Tony Tenser on the set of **The Blood Beast Terror**.

revitalising the careers of faded stars such as Peter Lorre and Vincent Price. Sadly though, AIP had shoehorned Rathbone into a number of their weaker efforts including *The Comedy of Terrors (1963)* and the humiliating *The Ghost in the Invisible Bikini (1966)*. Rathbone, feeling that a return to period drama, albeit on a low budget, would be more suited to his Shakespearean delivery, signed the contracts with Tigon. With commendable enthusiasm, Rathbone wrote to his producers in early July setting out requirements for his costumes, and expressing his hope that there would not be too many last minute script changes, commenting, 'I like to get a part under my belt and I find it difficult to unlearn.'

Rathbone was scheduled to fly to London on the 4th of August to start work the following Monday, but on the 21st of July he collapsed in New York and died of a massive heart attack. Two weeks before principal photography was due to begin Tigon were without one of their leading actors. Cancelling or postponing the film was discounted; financial commitments had been made and there was simply no question of not going ahead. After a frantic search Robert Flemyng, the English stage and film actor who had starred in an early Compton release, *L'orribile segreto del Dr. Hichcock (1962)*, was drafted in as a last-minute replacement.[6] Filming commenced a week later at the Goldhawk studios, on the stages vacated the previous week by Cliff Richard's *Two a Penny,* and continued over the next six weeks.

Despite the sad loss of Rathbone, Tenser felt that with Cushing topping the bill there was no need to attract any other names to the film. The titular beast was played by Wanda Ventham, with the juvenile lead going to Vanessa Howard, who had appeared in *Corruption (1967)* and later worked for Freddie Francis in *Mumsy,*

Nanny, Sonny and Girly (1969).[7] Comic relief, at the time considered obligatory in this particular brand of British horror, was supplied courtesy of Roy Hudd, better known for his long-running radio shows, who turned up for just a single day of shooting.

Supplementing Messrs Long and Miller was editor Howard Lanning, a friend of Tenser's from the early Sixties, and Paul Ferris whose fine score on *The Sorcerers* earned him a recall. Lanning's brother Dennis did the sound, while Roger Dicken handled the cheap and cheerful special effects. Dicken learned his trade with Hammer and would go on to receive an Oscar nomination for his work on *When Dinosaurs Ruled the Earth (1969)*.

Sewell ensured that the 'Death's Head' shoot proceeded without incident, though he did experience some minor turbulence from an unexpected source. Believing that Cushing was more than capable of performing without his assistance, Sewell left the actor to develop his character more or less on his own, and was somewhat surprised by an approach early in the shoot: 'Peter and I hadn't discussed the film or the script at all, which I hadn't thought unusual; he was a very professional actor. Then after a day Peter came up to me and he obviously wasn't happy. He said, 'I think this is perhaps the worst film I have ever made.' Well I felt quite flattered really.' Tenser recalls that Cushing found his patience tried by Bryan's script. 'He rewrote a lot of his dialogue but that wasn't a problem for us. There was a wonderful line that wasn't in the script when the giant moth is lured into the flames and the sergeant turns and says, 'They will never believe this at the Yard.' Peter's character says, 'They will never believe this anywhere!' Cushing took liberties with much of the script - he even revised Roy Hudd's eyeball-rolling cameo in an effort to inject some more humour.

If the storyline for 'Death's Head Vampire' was very straight-forward, then so much the better from Tenser's perspective: 'I had to choose films that you could watch and not come out with a question mark on your forehead. Everything needed to be there and you didn't have to try and digest it. That was why horror films came to prominence in the first place. Mainly, with some exceptions, they are visual, you know what is going to happen and you are ready for it.' Despite the charges of 'exploitation' often levied against his work, Tenser always stressed the need for some subtlety: 'You don't need to cut people's heads off or show something horrible happening, you can show a woman scream, a man with a knife and then have a thump.' Tigon was about to embark on a film that was to stretch that philosophy to breaking point.

*　　*　　*　　*　　*

While 'Death's Head Vampire' was in development several potential Michael Reeves projects had been proposed and rejected. Impatient to start work on his next film, Patrick Curtis and his Curtwel Productions had proposed taking Reeves elsewhere, but the director was keen to continue the working relationship with Tenser if a suitable project could be found. Out of the blue, Tenser received the galley proofs of a new book by English author Ronald Bassett, called 'Witchfinder General', it was the story of a self-appointed witch hunter named Matthew Hopkins.[8] Bassett portrayed Hopkins as a small-time opportunist who exploited gullible peasants for his own ends, and weaved a Jacobean revenge tale into the historical facts of the real-life Hopkins and the slaughter of Cromwell's Civil War.

The book was still a few months away from publication and it was extremely unusual for Tigon to see a book so early in the process; normally galleys would be sent round the majors first, with independent companies well down the pecking order. As luck would have it, Tenser knew Bassett's agent from his days at Rank twenty years before, and the two had remained on nodding terms ever since. 'The author's agent came to see me and we had a lunch together. I had read the galley proof and said I liked it, and how much do you want? We agreed a deal and I bought the film rights. I phoned up Michael Reeves and I said, I'd like you to read this book. He read the book and I said I have the rights to make a film. Would you like to do it? He said 'I'd love to,' and we went from there.'

Initially, Tenser sought to repeat the success of *The Sorcerers*, engaging the services of Miller and Long through Global, with Tom Baker scripting, Reeves as director, and Boris Karloff in the lead. Long and Miller however had already gone their separate ways. The latter agreed to come on board as a producer but Stanley Long, recalling the frustrating and chaotic night shoots on *The Sorcerers*, declined. Karloff was not physically up to the rigours of such a demanding part, and Baker and Reeves were beavering away on the script, broadening the scope. They envisaged a more epic feel, something of an English western set against panoramic backdrops.

Reeves had earmarked the title role for Donald Pleasence, with Ian Ogilvy as the leading man. The director had already met Pleasence, and discussed using the actor in a proposed adaptation of 'All the Little Animals'. He seemed ideal for Reeves's view of Hopkins; an under-achieving would-be Napoleon. Tenser for his part had been a great admirer of Pleasence ever since *Cul-de-Sac* and would undoubtedly have approved the choice, but for once he was not to have a completely free hand. Tigon's finances were already fully committed to 'Death's Head Vampire,' and Reeves was anxious that *Witchfinder*, which needed a great deal of location work, should start filming before the onset of winter. Arnold Miller was prepared to put up a fair share of the costs but even if Reeves scaled down his vision there would still be a budget shortfall that Tenser couldn't resolve on his own.

above:
Robert Russell as John Stearne and Vincent Price as Matthew Hopkins in **Witchfinder General**.

below:
Tenser's first and most successful adaptation of an existing novel.

above:
Hira Talfrey as a suspected witch is dragged to meet her fate in **Witchfinder General**. Reeves's decision to shoot the torture, maiming and killing sequences in unflinching detail was to cause problems for both Tenser and British censor John Trevelyan.

below:
A study of Vincent Price as Hopkins, a role he hadn't wanted in a film he initially hated.

Reeves encouraged his friend Philip Waddilove to join the production as line producer and take a small stake in the film, but the price tag was still too high. The only solution was to find another partner. Reeves and Miller started pre-production work in earnest, scouting locations with Waddilove in Norfolk and Suffolk, while Tenser assumed responsibility for securing the remaining finance.

At this time, American International Pictures were looking to establish a strong European base. The formidable Louis 'Deke' Heyward had come to London in 1965 to oversee production of the troubled *The City Under the Sea (1965)*, and, recognising the opportunities in the capital, he persuaded AIP's Hollywood heads Jim Nicholson and Sam Arkoff to set up there. In June 1967, Heyward announced his appointment as AIP's Head of European Production, operating out of a sumptuous building in London's Grosvenor Square. One of the first people to visit him at the new offices was Tony Tenser. Heyward was only vaguely aware of Reeves but was impressed with the script for *Witchfinder*; it seemed the ideal opportunity to establish his credentials as a major player in London. Nicholson and Arkoff agreed to contribute around £32,000 of the total £82,000 budget in exchange for the North American rights, and on the understanding that their contract player, Vincent Price, take the title role.

The casting didn't unduly concern Tenser: 'Vincent Price was a good choice, I thought, and I knew they needed a name to sell the film in America. I wouldn't have accepted anybody just for the sake of it but Vinnie was ideal.' To placate Price, who was less than enamoured by the script he received, a large part of AIP's investment - some £12,000 - was set aside to cover Price's renumeration, thus guaranteeing their reluctant star payment in full irrespective what happened to the production. The contract also gave AIP the right to re-edit the film as they saw fit for the American market. Sam Arkoff formally signed the contracts in London on the 9th of September 1967.

Reeves was furious with the thought of Price as the film's star - his vision of Matthew Hopkins certainly wasn't that of a tall, urbane Hollywood actor. A cinema buff, Reeves was also concerned about Price's recent track record, particularly with regard to his AIP films where too often the actor hid behind mannerisms and self-parody. The contracts had been signed though, and Reeves was required to make the most of it.

Given a free hand with the remainder of the cast, Reeves made no concessions at all to Hollywood, opting to cast predominately young and unknown actors. Ian Ogilvy was the lead protagonist, and Nicky Henson joined him as the hero's friend and confidante. Hilary Dwyer accepted the key part of Sara, the unwitting catalyst for most of the violence.[9] Patrick Wymark, a veteran from *Repulsion*, was a late addition to the cast; already committed to a Chekhov play in Bury St. Edmonds, he was persuaded to spend his afternoons off filming a cameo as

Oliver Cromwell. He also contributed the opening narration. Television actor Rupert Davies signed on as Sara's father, John Lowes, a Catholic priest. Davies had been a huge television star in the title role of the popular series *Maigret*, but when the show was cancelled he found himself struggling for work. *Steptoe and Son* actor Wilfrid Brambell won himself special billing for a fleeting cameo, as did Bernard Kay who appeared briefly as a disinterested fisherman. The supporting role of Stearne, Hopkins's boorish sidekick, was taken by the previously unknown Robert Russell, who offered a nice line in plebeian brutality to contrast with Price's more cultured villainy.[10]

Locations included the town of Bury St. Edmonds, the villages of Lavenham and Kersey, and Orford Castle. The moated grange used to 'duck' the witches was found at Kentwell Hall, in Long Melford, Suffolk. The production also made extensive use of an army training range, allowing Reeves to shoot sweeping pans across unspoiled countryside. Interiors were to be shot in two abandoned aircraft hangers in Bury St. Edmonds, hurriedly converted into soundstages with improvised soundproofing in a futile effort to block out the RAF jets that screamed overhead.

First-time cinematographer John Coquillon filled in for Stanley Long as cameraman, helping Reeves to create possibly the most visually striking horror film ever.[11] To underscore the visual beauty, Paul Ferris was recalled to provide a lush, romantic score. The versatile Ferris also makes a cameo appearance in the film under the name of Morris Jar (a tribute to the veteran composer Maurice Jarre.)

Shooting of the film, which had been re-titled from 'The Witchfinder General' to simply *Witchfinder General*, began on the 17th of September 1967. Although Reeves had shot his first British feature film only a few months earlier, his confidence had grown considerably. Nicky Henson recalls, 'Michael was a completely different man on the film set to what he was in every day life. If you met him on the street you would think he was shy, retiring, unsure of himself. I was amazed to see him on my first day, there was this huge authority figure right at the centre of things, totally controlling an elderly unit round him.'

Reeves's continued reluctance to deal with actors caused some friction almost immediately. Still smarting over the enforced casting of Price, Reeves refused to participate in the obligatory photocall at Heathrow airport when the actor arrived. The ever sensitive Price, who had been reluctantly convinced to take the part by the charismatic Heyward, took this as a personal slight.[12] The relationship deteriorated further on Price's first day on the set when the actor, never a confident horseman, was thrown from his mount and

above:
The freezing night shoots at Orford castle were the last scenes Price worked on for the film. He left the location immediately afterwards.

retired to his hotel room, ego bruised but otherwise unhurt. Rather than visit his star, Reeves chose to stay on set and prepare for the next day's work.

Tenser witnessed the tension first hand during a set visit a few days later: 'There was a scene they were shooting where Vincent Price wasn't happy with Michael Reeves - he felt he wasn't saying very much to him. We were all set up, and Vincent says his lines. Michael stops and says, 'Vinnie, please don't shake your head about.' Vincent replies, 'Don't shake my head about. Thank you, young man.' They started again and Vincent keeps his head still but he is projecting his voice too much and waving his arms about. 'Stop. Vinnie please keep the voice down and don't throw your arms about.' 'Don't shake my head, don't throw my arms about. Thank you young man.' They start for a third time and I think he was shuffling his feet, something like that. Michael stops again and says, 'Please Vinnie.' Vincent drew himself up to his full height, looked down on Michael Reeves and said, 'Young man, I have made 92 films, how many have you made?' Michael shouted at him, 'Three good ones!'

below:
Tony Tenser and Samuel Z. Arkoff chat to a stunt woman, Gillian Aldham during the filming of **Witchfinder General**'s witch burning sequences. This was the American's only visit to the film's location.

above:
Price assaulting Hilary Dwyer. The actress would go on to play his wife and his daughter in two subsequent movies, **The Oblong Box** and **Cry of the Banshee** - both for AIP.

right:
Tenser looks worried as Michael Reeves sets fire to a witch. The producer later conceded it was actually the ever-present rain that caused him most concern!

below:
The extras for **Witchfinder General** were recruited locally and from the Territorial Army. The crew also doubled as village folk to make up the numbers.

Concerned about Price's performance, Reeves was attempting, in the only way he knew, to contain the actor's natural inclination to overact. 'I would say that it was a case of the old trouper being told what to do by the young whipper-snapper,' concludes Tenser. 'Vincent was playing around, he was hamming it up to show off.' Whatever his personal feelings for the director, Tenser remembers that Price was never less than professional and cordial throughout: 'He never complained to me once. We would drink and have a chat in the hotel and he would tell me about his real love, hunting for paintings. Never once did he make any comments about Michael. I think there was an element of envy. I also think that Vincent had a crush on Mike and when Mike treated him so indifferently he was hurt.'

Nicky Henson, making his first major film, recalls the happy evenings in a small hotel taken over by the cast and crew: 'Vincent was wonderful with us, we all had an absolute ball. We were young and we were up all night, every night and he would stay up with us, drinking and telling stories right through the night and then he would go to work the next day and be word perfect.' Price's generosity extended to the crew; when a catering truck failed to show up one day, he took it on himself to go to the local town and buy sufficient food to cook a meal for every person on set.

Whatever the impression Price may have given off set, it was clear that he took the role very seriously. 'Hopkins was not just a sadist. Else I would not have been interested in playing him. He was a human being - not a humane one perhaps - but he had all the usual weaknesses, including a fondness for young women,' Price told the press before continuing, 'I saw him as a man who, at first, really believed in the Christian justness of his cause but, when he found he could turn it to profit, degenerated into an ogre whose lust for power and greed ran away with him. He became the complete hypocrite - cowardly as well as demonic.'

Shooting so late in the year afforded John Coquillon the opportunity to create some breathtaking shots of the autumn scenery, but it meant Reeves had to contend with the English weather. 'It rained on and off throughout, very fine rain though you hardly saw it on the screen,' recalls Tenser. 'It did cause concern when we were shooting the witch burning though. We had the whole Territorial Army dressed in costume, all of the houses had been dressed, the cobbles covered in straw, television aerials removed. We had three days to get the shots and of course Vincent Price was there only for a fixed time, after which he was moving on to his next film. We couldn't afford to have any hold-ups. I called the insurance broker and said we needed something in case it rained. 'Pluvius, old boy,' he said. Named after the Roman god of weather, they had a payment you made up front and if it rains you are covered. We took it and of course after that it didn't rain those days!'

Filmed exactly halfway through the shooting schedule, the sequences involving the witch burning proved something of a *cause célèbre* when the BBC's six o'clock news carried a nine-minute feature which included interviews with stunt woman Gillian Aldam, Price and Reeves. The following day national newspapers condemned the broadcast of the sequence and in particular the scene where Aldam is lowered into the flames. No sooner had the media left the location than Philip Waddilove got a telephone call from Tenser announcing that he would be visiting the next day, bringing Sam Arkoff and Deke Heyward with him. As it happened the Americans only stayed for a few hours, chatting mainly to Price and Tenser before watching some filming. Tenser would continue to visit throughout the shoot but it was the only time the Hollywood backers descended on the production.

Even with AIP's money the budget was too tight, forcing Reeves to make compromises. Ian Ogilvy remembers that Reeves wanted to show, 'rotting corpses lying in ditches and us ride by without noticing them. Because that's what the ditches of England were full of at the time.' It was too expensive to set up these shots. Reeves was also placed under a different type of pressure: 'The American producers sent endless little directives by letter or telegram,' Ogilvy recalls. 'In the tavern scene we want lots of naked girls running around. And Mike was saying, you know, we're making a historical movie here.' To placate Heyward, Tigon insisted on casting the likes of Maggie Nolan, a former model and stripper, and Maggie Kimberley, the model wife of John Kimberley (the same Earl of Kimberley who had served on the Compton board). Reeves followed orders and shot the required 'continental scenes', but they did not involve any of the star names, and were never included in the British prints of the film.

The minor inconveniences caused by the producers were easily dealt with, but Reeves had some real technical problems - the soundproofing, or lack of it, in the hangers caused delays, and the shoots in Orford Castle proved to be a nightmare for the crew. The castle was open to tourists during the day so Reeves had to set up his shots at night, when the cellars were

freezing cold. It was not only difficult for Coquillon to light these dingy spaces, but it was also almost impossible to record the sound satisfactorily. However, it was while he concocted these scenes that Reeves created much of *Witchfinder*'s reputation as a *tour de force* of cinematic violence.

The original script called for Ogilvy to attack Price, and as he falls a vat of coals is kicked over, causing the witchfinder to become engulfed in flames. Time constraints forced a rethink and, as Nicky Henson witnessed, provided Reeves with an opportunity to improvise: 'That whole sequence, the most notorious in the film, was made up on the spot! We winged it. We had to shoot the whole of that scene in one night in Orford Castle. Rehearse, shoot, retakes, all in a few hours; the turnaround was quite extraordinary. I did all the stuff running through the castle and I have just shot a guard in one of the corridors. I said to Mike, 'its just dawned on me we have a problem. I have got to shoot Ian.' Mike says, 'Yeah that's the whole point, his best friend shoots him. That's the point of the scene.' I said I'd just used my pistol and he said so what you've got another one. I said, 'but I have got to shoot Vincent. It's not a fucking revolver!' I couldn't shoot him as I hadn't got another gun and the penny dropped and Mike went, 'Ah! Jesus!' So he thinks for a minute, 'I've got it. I'll put you behind that rail so he can't get at you and he will scream 'you took him from me. You took him from me!' Mike moved the camera here and there, thinking it all out in his head on the spur of the moment, and then he put it all together in the editing.'

Curiously, despite the number of technically complex shots in the film, the scene that caused the most concern was one of the simplest; where Ian Ogilvy questions a boatman, Bernard Kay, on the beach about the whereabouts of the fugitive King Charles. 'I remember it was very, very cold,' Kay says. 'I was supposed to be there

above:
Actress/model Maggie Nolan. Even on serious films like **Witchfinder General**, Tigon's publicity department couldn't resist sending out glamour shots to the press.

below:
The infamous Lavenham witch-burning scene. Behind the scenes footage was captured by the BBC for a news programme, but it has subsequently disappeared.

right:
Ian Ogilvy as Richard and the defiled Sara, played by Hilary Dwyer.

middle left:
The Belgian artwork for **Witchfinder General** drew heavy inspiration from the British poster.

middle right:
John Streane brutalizing Sara. It was the shocking juxtaposition of violence and beauty that helped make **Witchfinder General** Michael Reeves's most disturbingly effective and distinctive work.

bottom:
A classic image of the gallows.

VINCENT PRICE

IAN OGILVY · RUPERT DAVIES · WILFRID BRAMBELL

IL GRANDE INQUISITORE

con PATRICK WYMARK · ROBERT RUSSEL e con HILARY DWYER

diretto da: MICHAEL REEVES   prodotto da: TONY TENSER

EASTMANCOLOR

top left:
This Italian locandina poster for **Witchfinder General** suggests a western rather than a horror film.

top right:
Patrick Wymark in his second of three appearances for Tenser, this time as Oliver Cromwell.

above:
An example of the bloodletting that delayed the film's release, causing much debate between Reeves and John Trevelyan.

left:
A witch being dragged to the gallows. A rather modern looking village can be glimpsed in the background!

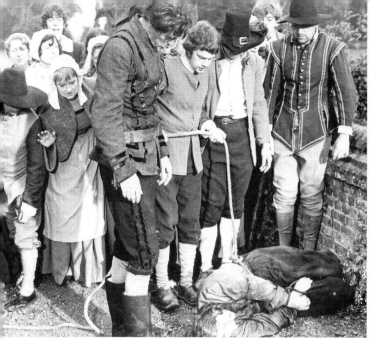

above:
Television star Rupert Davies on the receiving end of the traditional witch-test of ducking. The ducking idea also turns up in the later Tenser film **Blood on Satan's Claw**.

below:
The stunning American artwork for **Witchfinder General** owed more to the skills of AIP than either Poe or Reeves.

for one day, a sort of guest spot, and I looked at the lines and thought we would get through this in a couple of hours. I think it turned out the longest day that I ever worked!' Reeves was adamant that he had to capture just the right shot, which would allow a dissolve from the waves, into the flames of Lavenham. He insisted on take after take while the crew stood around, freezing on the beach.

Back at Tigon the rising costs were causing Tenser some concern: 'Mike was running over schedule and the budget was a worry - we were still a small company then and we had to keep it down. I sat down with Mike and the producers and came to an agreement on the number of rehearsals and the number of retakes. It was very amicable and in the end it came in about £20,000 over, mainly because of the locations and the weather. I didn't ask AIP to pay their half - it wasn't in the contract and I wanted them to see that when they do business with an English company we stick to our responsibilities.'

Finishing his scenes in the last week in October 1967, Vincent Price celebrated with an interview on set for the BBC's 'Town and Around', broadcast as part of a Halloween special. Reeves retired to the cutting studio to pull the film together, and immediately he realised there were two significant weaknesses with the voices of his main performers. Despite his bullish appearance, Robert Russell had a rather soft, lilting accent so Bernard Kay was summoned to provide more earthy tones. More significant was Price's delivery, which was quite obviously too theatrical, necessitating the actor's return to London for re-dubbing, though to his relief Reeves himself didn't supervise either of these sessions.

In the meantime negotiations were going on with censor John Trevelyan over what should and shouldn't be in the final UK print. Tenser was relatively confident that Trevelyan would pass the film without too much difficulty. The censor's office was only a short walk from Tigon's head office and Tenser habitually kept his friend Trevelyan involved throughout the scripting and shooting process on all their movies. As per usual, an early draft of the script had been reworked after a number of comments from Trevelyan. Tenser was also on hand throughout shooting to provide the voice of reason: 'Michael was very much a director who wanted to look realistic. During the last scene where Ian Ogilvy kicks back with his spurs and catches Robert Russell in the eye, you see blood spurting out of the eye. Then there is a vicious fight with an axe. Before they shot I saw the assistant director with a bucket full of blood and he had some string, thick pieces which he was mashing into the blood. He said these were the guts that would come spilling out of Vincent Price when he gets hit with the axe. He also told me they were going to use real pig's guts but the farmer decided at the last minute not to sell them the pig. I pulled Michael Reeves aside and told him that he couldn't do that, the censor wouldn't allow it and he would have shot a whole scene that would have to be cut. I told him I knew Trevelyan very well and I knew how his mind worked. If I were him, I would ban it too and I suggested he shot round it. So reluctantly, very reluctantly he did just that.'

Curiously, it wasn't the depiction of violence that caused Trevelyan difficulties, at least not directly. Viewing a 'work in progress' print with Reeves, Trevelyan indicated he didn't foresee any problems. Elated, Reeves proceeded to fine-tune his soundtrack, supplementing the existing dialogue with blood-curdling screams and bone-crushing sound effects. The impact of these effects was further heightened by the juxtaposition with Ferris's evocative score. After seeing the final cut, Trevelyan decided that he had no choice but to summon

Reeves to his office and hand over a list of required amendments. These included a reduction in the screams of John Lowes, cutting completely a sequence of a woman being strangled in the cells and, predictably, significant cuts to both the witch burning scenes and the mutilation of Hopkins by the demented Richard. Trevelyan had accepted Reeves's assurances that he deplored violence, and went on the record agreeing that the director was seeking to expose the brutality of human nature. He was clear however that in doing so Reeves had overstepped the mark and was in danger of exploiting violence for violence's sake. Tenser supported the censor, for pragmatic reasons: 'Trevelyan knew his job, he also loved films and he would not cut things for the sake of it. The cuts he asked for were because he genuinely thought that they were needed.' Though he felt that it severely undermined the power of his film, Reeves had to comply.[13] His battles with the censor finally over, Reeves assembled a print that satisfied everyone, himself included, and arrangements were made to release what was easily Tigon's most ambitious project.

The finished film was greeted with unrestrained enthusiasm at Tigon. Tenser lavishly praised the work of both director and cast, singling out Rupert Davies in particular: 'As the priest he is terrific. Full of life and bonhomie at the beginning and completely spent, haggard and injured after all he has been through at the end.' Hilary Dwyer was also praised by Tenser at the time and hailed as, 'a new and stronger Vivien Leigh.'

Even as Tigon polished up their publicity materials, the Americans had started tinkering. The director's cut had been finished in early spring 1968 and delivered to Heyward at AIP's London office. Arkoff and Nicholson were also impressed, but sought to exercise their right to final cut. 'Sam Arkoff wasn't a gambler, he made sure that every step he took had a reason. A very shrewd man and very good at putting a film together,' recalls Tenser. 'He wanted to make sure it would be a complete success and thought the title *Witchfinder General* wouldn't appeal to the average American. He knew he could sell it if there was a connotation with Edgar Allan Poe.' For the North American release *Witchfinder General* became *Edgar Allan Poe's The Conqueror Worm*, a title taken from an obscure Poe poem which had little if any relevance to Reeves's movie. Vincent Price was duly summoned back to the sound studio to read the dreary poem as a prologue to the action and to strengthen the connection with the earlier AIP Poe films. AIP press releases even stated that it had been 'filmed on location in Hollywood.' For that piece of ingenuity, and of course his contribution to the tavern scenes, Heyward earned himself an 'additional

material by' alongside the credit 'based on the book by Ronald Bassett and the poem by Edgar Allan Poe.' AIP also dropped the producer credits for both Arnold Miller and Philip Waddilove, replacing them with a single credit for Heyward. Tenser retained his credit as 'executive producer.'

above:
A witch (Gillian Aldham) is hauled into place for Matthew Hopkins's subtle 'improvements' on his witch-burning technique.

WITCHFINDER GENERAL

'They reveled in torture and murder all in the name of justice'
- Australian trade ads -

Synopsis

Matthew Hopkins and his assistant Stearne are engaged by the people of Brandeston to investigate allegations of witchcraft in their village. One of the suspected witches is the local priest, Father John Lowes. Trooper Richard Marshall, Lowes's future son-in-law, returns to Brandeston to find to his horror that Hopkins and Stearne have tortured and murdered Lowes, and raped his fiancée, Sara. While the witchfinders move on to the next village to continue their reign of terror, Marshall swears revenge in the ruins of Lowes's chapel.

Critique

'Peculiarly nauseating.'
- Dylis Powell, The Sunday Times, 12/05/68

'A heavy reliance on the lung power of pretty young women being subjected to pretty awful experiences.'
- The Sun, 10/05/68

'The squeals and blood and Patrick Wymark in a cameo role are the only things which stand out in this crude and savage bit of non-history.'
- The Morning Star, 11/05/68

below:
Vincent Price is Matthew Hopkins, the **Witchfinder General**.

MONDIAL FILM présente

VINCENT PRICE
dans

CHASSEUR
DE SORCIÈRES

LE
GRAND INQUISITEUR

un film de MICHAEL REEVERS

avec IAN OGILVY · HILARY DWYER · RUPERT DAVIES

Eastmancolor · Interdit aux moins de 18 ans

above:
French pressbook for
Witchfinder General.

below:
One of the lasting
images of the film, a
witch at the end of a
rope. The screenplay
muddled fact and fiction
in the interests of film-
making, but the real
Matthew Hopkins's
reign of terror resulted
in the death of up to
200 'witches'.

'Sometimes foolish, rather fun and nicely
coloured.'
- The Daily Telegraph, 10/05/68

'...an exercise in sadistic extravagance all
the more repugnant for being ably directed
by Michael Reeves.'
- The Sunday Telegraph, 12/05/68

'Mr Reeves is no longer merely promising. He
already has real achievements behind him:
not merely good horror films, but good films.
Period.'
- The Times, 11/05/68

'Vincent Price damps down his habitual
villainy as Hopkins... the flaw is a preoccu-
pation with blood and violence.'
- The Evening News, 09/05/68

'...the film is less concerned with narrative
than exploiting every opportunity for gratuitous
sadism, lingering over hangings, protracted
torture sessions, rape and mutilations.'
- The Guardian, 10/05/68

Stripped of his habitual mannerisms,
Price delivered a disturbing performance of sneering evil, arguably a
career best from the veteran. There
were strong performances too from
Rupert Davies and Hilary Dwyer.
Reeves's direction is confident and

uncompromising, and regardless of damage
inflicted by the BBFC, the power of the film
to shock was undiminished. John
Coquillon's stunning photography and Paul
Ferris's rich score helped to counterpoint the
deliberately crude and unrelenting violence.
The film as a whole displayed a maturity and
command of cinema only hinted at in
Reeves's previous work. The film was a
tremendous personal triumph for the
director, the first significant nail in the coffin
of Hammer's stately horrors, and it effectively
redefined the genre for a generation.

If *Witchfinder General* stunned the
public, it also surprised its star. Tenser
remembers talking to an unhappy Price
during the post-production: 'Vincent was
convinced that it wouldn't be any good
because of the relationship he had with
Reeves. I think he was in something of a
sulk. I spoke to him when he came back
over to re-dub his dialogue, and he thought
it was a waste of time. He thought the film
wasn't any good. I'm certainly not a betting
man but I made a wager with him that he
would like the final print when he saw it. I
know it was screened for him by AIP, but I
never found out if he liked it - certainly he
never came back to me for the money!'[14]

Needless to say, the papers were full of
letters of complaint about the film's violent
content, and there were some concerns at
Tigon that the local authorities may move to
ban the film. There was indeed sporadic
resistance in the more reactionary
boroughs, but on the whole the film played
to packed houses without issues
throughout the UK. In the US, the
rebranding of *Witchfinder* as *The Conqueror
Worm* helped it on its way to taking over
$1.5m during its initial run, a considerable
return for AIP's modest outlay.[15]

*   *   *   *   *

Although finished first, 'Death's Head
Vampire', initially retitled 'Blood Beast from
Hell' and later *The Blood Beast Terror*, was
held back while Reeves put the finishing
touches to *Witchfinder*. Even in its edited
form *Witchfinder* made the more traditional
Blood Beast look anaemic, and the last-
minute change of title couldn't convince the
public otherwise. Opening initially in
London on a double bill with the Italian
horror *Castle of the Living Dead (1964)*,
which starred Christopher Lee and co-
incidentally featured some second-unit
footage by Michael Reeves, Sewell's film
fared poorly and was completely eclipsed by
the critical and box-office success of its
cousin. Tenser saved the situation
somewhat when he convinced the giant ABC
chain that *Blood Beast* would make an ideal
partner for *Witchfinder General* on their
national circuit. The pairing ensured that
Tigon had very respectable returns on their
first national release.

left:
Maker, Monster and
Mate: Wanda Ventham
and Robert Flemyng
discuss the fate of the
former's future soul
partner.

THE BLOOD BEAST TERROR

*'No-one Is Safe... from these
DEADLY VAMPIRES!!'*
- US Press Book -

Synopsis

Two brutal and bloody murders have left the police baffled. The only witness is hopelessly insane and the only clue is several petal-like scales that were found scattered around the crime scenes. As the police investigate, Inspector Quennell is drawn to the house of Doctor Mallinger, a local entomologist. A further murder implicates the professor and his mysterious daughter Clare, but before the police can make an arrest they flee. Quennell traces the Mallingers to a tiny fishing village, and posing as a bank manager he moves into the area to track them down.

Critique

'Further adventures in the monsters of 19th century rural England cycle, lamely directed and sloppily scripted. Peter Cushing, Robert Flemyng and Wanda Ventham turn in reliable performances but Vanessa Howard is embarrassingly wooden as the unfortunate Meg.'
- Monthly Film Bulletin, 07/68

'This concoction of horrific nonsense has enough blood and mystery to please the uncritical.'
- Kine Weekly, 24/02/68

The Blood Beast Terror will probably never satisfy anyone apart from the least demanding horror fan. Sewell does what he can, and certainly adds a touch of style and elegance, but his best efforts are undermined from the outset by the paltry budget. A lazy narrative, poorly edited stock footage and the cheapskate special effects destroy the tension, and despite some interesting performances - notably that of the energetic Peter Cushing - the film never stood a chance.

It made for a merely adequate support feature in the UK, but the continued popularity of the 'English Gothic' style ensured that *The Blood Beast Terror* fared better overseas. Tenser successfully

below:
Veteran actor John
Paul, left, helps retrieve
a victim of the Death's
Head Vampire.

TIGON PICTURES PRESENTS

PETER CUSHING
in

THE BLOOD BEAST TERROR x

ROBERT FLEMING   WANDA VENTHAM   Guest Star ROY HUDD
Eastman Colour

above:
Kevin Stoney as Granger, the butler, in **The Blood Beast Terror**, a part that seems to have been written purely so the film could feature a character who looked evil and could torture that falcon.

below:
The US advertising campaign predictably found a way to include Edgar Allan Poe's name.

recovered Tigon's investment when he sold the film for a fixed sum in 1968 to the New York-based distributor Pacemaker who, despite holding release back for a year, confidently predicted that Cushing's name was sufficient to find the film an audience. Further overseas sales were made, including Latin America, pushing the film into healthy profit and proving Tenser's earlier assumption that 'horror films always have a worldwide market.'

Pacemaker re-christened the film *The Vampire-Beast Craves Blood* for the North American market, and released it on a mind-numbing double-bill with *Curse of the Blood Ghouls*. The publicity team managed to concoct an adline that out-did even Tenser: 'A ravishing Psycho-Fiend with diabolical power to turn into a Giant Death Head Vampire, to feast on the blood of her lovers before clawing them to death.' *Blood Beast*'s venerable director Vernon Sewell was horrified: 'I have always made what they called 'B' pictures but it wasn't until I heard that title and read the blurbs that I realised I had made exploitation!'

*   *   *   *   *

Tigon's latest success was celebrated in an editorial in the industry's main trade paper, which was extravagant in its praise of the company's founder. 'The expenditure of energy, both mentally and physically, in this industry has usually been a marked feature of those who survive,' The Daily Cinema

noted. 'But the successful ones have the added qualification of imagination and understanding of what it takes to stay in business.' Reflecting on the relative size of Tigon, still a tiny outfit, the same article went on to ask, 'what Tony's real potential could be with the facilities afforded so many others in production and distribution.' AIP certainly felt that Tigon represented a potentially rich vein for future projects - at a reasonable price of course. 'He gets more out of every pound than anyone we know,' announced Louis 'Deke' Heyward, adding that Tenser, 'gives the director his head and the result is more a creative picture than just a money picture.' Tenser underlined the success of the relationship with AIP saying, 'what I feel benefits me benefits them too.'

Soon after *Witchfinder General* had started shooting, Tenser met with Heyward to discuss future collaborations. Tigon had already optioned 'O'Hooligan's Mob', a gangster story, for Reeves, as well as 'The Amorous Trooper', another adaptation from a novel by Ronald Bassett. Heyward wasn't interested in either of these but offered an old script by Jerry Sohl that had been on the shelf at AIP for some time, H.P. Lovecraft's 'Dreams in the Witch House', which he suggested would make an excellent vehicle for Michael Reeves and Vincent Price. Tenser was less keen: 'The script had been written some years before and was set in America so I suppose Vincent would have been fine but I really didn't think he would want to do another after the problems on *Witchfinder*. I suggested Boris Karloff and Deke seemed to like that.' Heyward was putting the finishing touches to AIP's first European production slate, which included intriguing projects such as: 'I'll Massage You with Diamonds', 'Dante's Inferno', and 'Public Parts, Private Places'. 'Dreams in the Witch House' was duly added to the roster.

The arrangement drawn up with Heyward for 'Dreams in the Witch House' was very similar to that agreed for *Witchfinder General*; AIP would provide 50% of the funding in exchange for North American rights. AIP also retained script approval and final say on 'above the title' casting, while the film production chores would be left entirely to Tigon. The script proved problematical - the action had to be transferred to England and the original draft didn't really reflect the broad appeal that Heyward felt the film needed, so AIP requested some additional scenes. Karloff himself wasn't happy with the draft, and also asked for some amendments. The scripting chores were farmed out to various writers including Mervyn Haisman and Henry Lincoln, and the story moved further and further away from its source material. The over-runs on *Witchfinder General* had effectively ruled out Michael Reeves as director, and Tenser was forced to look elsewhere.

above:
Robert Flemyng and
Peter Cushing in **The
Blood Beast Terror**.

Footnotes

1. A former child actor, Patrick Curtis made his screen debut playing Olivia de Havilland's son in *Gone with the Wind (1939)*, under his own name of Smith, later adopting the surname of Curtis as a tribute to the matinee idol Tony Curtis. Prior to turning to film production, Curtis's main claim to fame was as the winner of the Adohr Milk Company's nationwide Adohrable Baby competition, at the age of two. By the Sixties Curtis had met then-unknown actress Raquel Welch, and convinced the starlet to let him act as her agent. Curtis became her second husband, and is generally credited with creating the phenomenal publicity machine surrounding the actress, and, as her business partner in Curtwel (the first letters of their respective surnames), her producer in a series of European and American movies.

2. Lacey was best known as a stage actress, though she did make a number of films including *The Shadow of the Cat (1961)* for John Gilling and later on Hammer's *The Mummy's Shroud (1967)*. Ian Ogilvy told Fangoria magazine that the actress was less than happy to be making a horror picture: 'Catherine hated her part. It worried and depressed her. She really didn't like doing these things at all.' Amongst her many non-genre movies were the likes of *Whisky Galore! (1949)* and Joseph Losey's *The Servant (1963)*. Her last role was in Billy Wilder's extravagant but flawed *The Private Life of Sherlock Holmes (1970)*.

3. Although not known as a film actor – though he did make one more decent film, *All Neat in Black Stockings (1968)*, with Susan George - Victor Henry created something of a stir through his work in TV and the theatre. He was particularly effective in the Royal Court production of 'Look Back in Anger', and the hugely successful Heathcote Williams production 'AC/DC', which prompted the Daily Mail to describe him as 'one of the greatest actors of his generation.' Tragically, he was involved in a horrific accident in 1972, when on the cusp of stardom; he was hit on the head whilst standing at a bus stop - a bus cornered too quickly and skidded, causing the pole to crash down upon him.

He was hospitalised, where he remained in a vegetative state, without ever regaining consciousness, until his death on the 26th of November 1985. Many newspapers wrongly printed his obituary at the time of his accident. By the time he did die, he was practically unknown.

4. Before making *The Sorcerers*, Susan George had graduated from the Corona Stage School, starred in several Children's Film Foundation movies and worked in the West End on 'The Sound of Music' for over two years. A publicist's dream, she had a natural gift for getting the press hot under the collar and was soon better known for the events of her private life, rather than her work as an actress. One tabloid astounded its readers by putting together a First XI cricket team of her paramours, including the likes of George Best, Rod Stewart, Jimmy Connors, Andy Gibb and Prince Charles. George is obviously a strong-willed and intelligent actress, so it is interesting that Reeves was only the first in a long line of directors to cast her as the victim of unwanted and violent male attention: Pete Walker, Peter Collinson, and most famously Sam Peckinpah, all followed Reeves's lead. In the late Eighties, tiring of the typecasting, she formed Amy Films with husband Simon MacCorkindale and tried her hand, with mixed success, at film production.

5. Peter Bryan was a close friend of Tony Hinds, Hammer's Head of Production, and was commissioned to script many of the studio's better movies during Hinds's tenure, including *The Brides Of Dracula (1960)* and *The Plague Of The Zombies (1966)*. A cameraman by trade, he had worked behind the lens on pre-horror Hammer movies before leaving to form his own documentary company.

6. Liverpool born Flemyng had a long and distinguished stage career before entering the world of filmmaking, working with Gielgud, Olivier and Guinness, and near the end of his life he enjoyed considerable success with two remarkable seasons at the National Theatre. Flemyng's distinguished service in the Royal Medical Corps had earned him the Military Cross in 1941 and an

TIGON
MAKE
EXCITING
PICTURES

TONY TENSER presents
VINCENT PRICE
IAN OGILVY RUPERT DAVIES
WILFRID BRAMBELL

WITCHFINDER
GENERAL X

EASTMAN COLOUR

WITH
PATRICK
WYMARK
AS CROMWELL

ROBERT RUSSELL
NICKY HENSON
AND INTRODUCING
HILARY DWYER

Directed by MICHAEL REEVES
Screenplay by TOM BAKER & MICHAEL REEVES
Photography by JOHNNY COQUILLON Music by PAUL FERRIS
From the book by RONALD BASSETT
Producers ARNOLD MILLER · PHILIP WADDILOVE
LOUIS M HEYWARD
Executive Producer TONY TENSER

RELEASED BY TIGON PICTURES LTD
A TIGON BRITISH—AMERICAN INTERNATIONAL PRODUCTION

PETER CUSHING
THE
BLOOD BEAST
TERROR

EASTMAN
COLOUR

THE
BOX OFFICE
SUCCESS OF
THE YEAR
Have YOU
Booked it yet?

TIGON PICTURES LIMITED
203 Wardour Street · London W1
Tel: 01-734 9743
Cables: TIGONPIX LONDON W1

above:
A trade ad for
Witchfinder General
and **The Blood Beast
Terror**. The latter was
completed first but had
to wait for the release of
the Reeves film before it
was shown to the
public.

OBE in 1944. At the age of 33 he was one of the youngest full Colonels in the British Army. Returning to acting after the War, he specialised in portrayals of troubled men struggling with inner anguish; his film work included *The Guinea Pig (1948)* and *Blackmailed (1950)*. An actor of considerable depth, Flemyng was given less than two weeks notice for *The Blood Beast Terror* and understandably never really got to grips with the role. He certainly appeared to be having more fun with a similar role in the earlier *The Terror of Dr. Hichcock*. An articulate and intelligent man, Flemyng was also extremely active for the Actor's Charitable Trust and despite being nearly crippled by a hip replacement operation that went badly wrong, he continued to work up until his swan-song in the BBC series *The Choir* in 1995.

7. A trained dancer, and professional actress from the age of 15, Howard had appeared in a number of plays and musicals like *The Impossible Years* and *110 in the Shade*. Her film work was sporadic and didn't do her justice; amongst others she appeared in *Here We Go Round the Mulberry Bush (1967)* and Amicus's *What Became of Jack and Jill? (1971)*, in which she took the lead role. Her stage career peaked with a part alongside Frankie Howerd on Broadway, in 'The Wind in the Sassafras Trees'. Howard had her 15 minutes in the limelight as one of the leading candidates for the much-touted role of Candy opposite Marlon Brando in the film of the same name. Other short-listed dollies included Sydne Rome and Ewa Aulin. The whole circus occupied the attention of the press for a while, with the obligatory bikini parades etc., before the part was finally given to Aulin. Curiously, another leading contender, and the hot favourite of the somewhat partisan British tabloids, was *Blood on Satan's Claw* star Linda Hayden. After a couple of lame comedies in the late Sixties, including the lead role in Freddie Francis's *Mumsy, Nanny, Sonny and Girly (1969)*, Howard quietly disappeared.

8. There is not too much recorded information on Matthew Hopkins and his assistant John Stearne. He was a local minister's son, who terrorised East Anglia in 1645-47 when law and order had more or less broken down and the witch trials were at their height. Between them, Hopkins and Stearne were responsible for around 120-200 deaths, most notably that of John Lowes, the 70-year-old vicar of Brandeston. An outspoken catholic unpopular with his parishioners, Lowes was tortured into confessing his 'guilt' using the method of sleep deprivation. Hopkins's motives were never clear, but it seems certain that the idea of a 'Witchfinder General' for the whole of England was a fiction invented by Bassett, and it is most likely that Hopkins was motivated purely by misguided zeal. Hopkins's death is as poorly documented as his life, but it was less dramatic than the demise conjured up for him in the film; most accounts settle for the idea that he passed away in his bed from consumption in 1647. What became of Stearne isn't known.

9. 22 year-old Hilary Dwyer learned her trade at the Webber Douglas Drama School before she progressed through provincial theatre and television shows like *The Prisoner* and *The Avengers*. Too intelligent for the starlet roles required by British studios at the time, *Witchfinder General* would remain her best-known role, but she also featured in Tigon's *The Body Stealers*. AIP's 'Deke' Heyward took a shine to Dwyer and attempted to shoehorn

her into several of his productions without too much success: *The Oblong Box (1969)* and *Cry of the Banshee (1970)* both also featured Vincent Price, and neither was a notable success. Her last film for Heyward was as second lead in *Wuthering Heights (1970)*, which reunited her with Ian Ogilvy but did very little for either of them. Retiring from acting after a period in television, Dwyer set up her own production company under her married name, and proceeded to enjoy a number of successful television and cinema producing credits.

10. Born in London but raised in South Africa, Russell had been a graduate of the Webber Douglas Drama School (as was Hilary Dwyer). He served his time with both the RSC in Stratford and with Olivier at the National Theatre. He was given parts in some films, such as *Bedazzled (1967)* and *Inspector Clouseau (1968)*, but was considered too surly-looking to be a leading man and soon fell back into television character roles.

11. Coquillon went on to do several movies for AIP's British operation under the control of Louis 'Deke' Heyward, before hooking up with Peckinpah on *Straw Dogs (1971)*, *Pat Garrett & Billy The Kid (1973)* and *The Osterman Weekend (1983)*. Canadian by birth, he learned his trade as a documentary filmmaker in Africa and indeed at one stage owned World Safari with Henry Geddes, head of the Children's Film Foundation, specialising in second unit material from Africa. He died in 1987.

12. Price was never ambiguous about his feelings for Reeves. He told Cinefantastique, 'Reeves hated me. He didn't want me at all. I didn't like him either. It was one of the first times in my life that I've been in a picture where the director and I just clashed (Price twisted his hands together) like that! ...Afterwards, I realised what he wanted was a low-key, very laid back performance. He did get it, but I was fighting with him almost every step of the way. Had I known what he wanted I would have co-operated. I think its one of the best performances I've ever given.'

13. Reeves took part in an exchange of letters with The Listener in 1968, defending his film by saying, 'Violence is horrible, degrading and sordid. Insofar as one is going to show it on the screen at all, it should be presented as such - and the more people it shocks into sickening recognition of these facts, the better.'

14. In her definitive study, 'The Complete Films of Vincent Price', Lucy Chase Williams records that Price took the unusual step of writing to Reeves soon after that screening saying, 'Congratulations. The contrasts of the superb scenery, and the brutality, the action the hero forces against the execrable almost inaction of the forces of evil, make for suspense I've rarely experienced. So my dear Michael, in spite of the fact that we didn't get along too well, I do think you have made a very fine picture, and what's more, I liked what you gave me to do.'

15. There was something of a reunion for the Witchfinder crew when on the 6th of January 1968 producer Philip Waddilove married his fiancée Susi Field. Amongst those present were Tenser, Arnold Louis Miller, Michael Reeves, Rupert Davies, Nicky Henson and Ian Ogilvy.

Chapter Six

'The King, Crown Prince and Queen of Suspense'

- (UK Trade ads for *Curse of the Crimson Altar*)

Tenser hired Gerry Levy to take on the production chores for 'Dreams in the Witch House.' The two men had known each other since Levy had owned and run Leap Film Distributors in the early Sixties, a minor rival to Compton specialising in dubbed European films and American re-releases. Levy, in partnership with his brother, Howard Lanning, moved into film production with Ledeck Film Productions, primarily in the role of sponsors. Levy's debut as a feature director (and writer under the name of Peter Marcus) was on the Ledeck film *Where Has Poor Mickey Gone? (1964)*, which Tenser had released through Compton.

Encouraged by the earlier experience of *The Pleasure Girls*, Tenser hoped that by shooting the whole of 'Dreams in the Witch House' in or around one location he could make significant cost savings. During the last weeks of November 1967, Levy had scouted out options for the principal location before settling on Grims Dyke House, the former home of W.S. Gilbert of Gilbert and Sullivan fame, which not only offered the filmmakers a suitably imposing manor house but also extensive woods and a lake.[1]

Levy's script for 'Dreams in the Witch House' revolved around the disappearance of an antiques dealer staying at Craxted Lodge, home to the sinister J.D. Morley and his lovely niece, Eve. When the missing man's brother starts to investigate he finds himself involved in apparent occult happenings. On Tenser's instigation an early draft of the script, still carrying the credit to Lovecraft, was sent to Vernon Sewell, who had completed *The Blood Beast Terror* on time and within budget. Sewell particularly liked the original Lovecraft story and, thinking that the script was a fair adaptation, agreed to take the reins. By then the contracts with Karloff had been signed and the film was scheduled to start shooting in early 1968, by which time the title had evolved, firstly into 'Witch House', then 'The Crimson Altar', and then into its formal shooting title 'The Crimson Cult'. (It wasn't until the 11th of May 1968 that the UK title was changed to *Curse of the Crimson Altar*.)

During a lifeless exchange of dialogue early in the film the heroine exclaims, 'Its like one of these old houses in horror movies,' while the hero dryly retorts, 'Yes

you almost expect Boris Karloff to pop out.' In fact, Karloff's involvement in the film was in doubt right up until the day filming began. When Tenser met up with the actor in London, the extent of his physical frailty was obvious: 'He hadn't been in the best of health during *The Sorcerers*, but in the years since, he had deteriorated quite a lot. It was very sad, he was such a lovely man but the end was obviously in sight.'

There was genuine concern that Karloff wouldn't be able to finish the picture, so at the eleventh hour the decision was taken to drop him completely and find a suitable replacement. Heyward approved the removal of Karloff from the project but insisted that there must be a recognised name above the credits. Once again Vincent Price's name was mentioned but organising this would have caused a further delay. A frustrated Vernon Sewell found his star changing on an almost daily basis: 'Karloff was originally to play the villain but he was in no state and anyway they couldn't get insurance so we dropped Karloff. Someone then telephoned to say that they were going for Vincent Price and then a few days later I was told they had cast Christopher Lee. Then a week before the film started, the studio decided to have Karloff because they had to pay him whether he died or not. Of course we still had Christopher Lee so the whole script had to be re-written to put Karloff back in a week before the start.' Associate Producer Gerry Levy took on the re-writing chores. To satisfy the completion guarantors, he ensured that

below:
Spanish admat for
Curse of the Crimson Altar.

above:
Boris Karloff in his last British film. Neither Tenser nor the US backers AIP thought he would finish the film but he surprised everyone by not only completing the movie but also going to Hollywood to make four more films back to back.

the new Karloff scenes were kept as peripheral as possible to the main action. The shooting schedule was then rearranged so that Karloff's scenes were shot first, over the course of eight days. 'Karloff's legs were giving him trouble, as was his breathing,' Tenser explains. 'We had a contingency of sorts; we got all the shots we needed of Karloff first - those where he had lines or you saw his face. Where there were long shots or you saw him from behind were left till last.'

Karloff's revised part was that of a local occult expert, a suitably eccentric red herring. Of course, shooting any film with an 81-year-old in poor health was going to be difficult, and there was a strong feeling amongst the cast and crew that they were working with Karloff for the last time.[2] To his credit Karloff insisted on delivering 100 percent, which surprised even Vernon Sewell: 'He was dying basically and I felt for him very much. He was in a wheelchair more or less throughout and he came up to me at one point and said, 'look here, Vernon, in this scene do you think I could walk from here to there. I don't want the audience to see me in a wheelchair too much?' So he staggered across the set and when he got there he almost passed out with the effort.' It says a great deal for Karloff's stamina that he not only finished his scenes, which included an exhausting night shoot, but then returned to Hollywood where, incredibly, he had already committed to appearing in four new movies!

Karloff's replacement as the main villain of the piece, and in many ways his heir apparent as the 'king of horror', Christopher Lee was at that time reaching the very height of horror fame and on the cusp of international stardom.[3] Sewell was already familiar with the star: 'I knew Christopher very well, he had been in a film

I made called *Battle of the V-1 (1958)*. He was very good in it and we got on very well. A very good actor - very underrated even then.' Lee's signature on the contract and the renewed participation of Karloff generated some excitement at Tigon, where there was talk of making the film an 'all star' event. Peter Cushing was considered, but Sewell was against rewriting the script again to accommodate Cushing and anyway he felt that that the actor's displeasure regarding *The Blood Beast Terror* would rule out any possibility of his participation. Cushing had in fact returned to television, somewhat disillusioned with the film roles he was being offered. Instead, Tigon recalled Rupert Davies for a cameo, again as a priest, though it was a slightly less strenuous outing this time for the actor, who was struggling to get work and was only too happy to take the odd day's filming.[4] Fleshing out the supporting roles was Michael Gough, a favourite villain of Herman Cohen from films like *Horrors of the Black Museum (1959)* and *Black Zoo (1963)*, who was drafted in as another red herring, Lee's retarded butler.

Tigon completed the cast with something of a coup when they signed Barbara Steele for her first British movie since *Your Money Or Your Wife (1960)*. A former graduate of the Rank Charm School, Steele had starred in a run of successful Euro-horror movies in the early Sixties, several of which had been released by Tenser through both Compton and Tigon. Despite her success on the Continent, Steele remained relatively unknown in her home country. Nevertheless, Tigon press hype couldn't resist referring to her as 'the Queen of Suspense.'[5] The nominal leads went to Mark Eden, who had emerged with considerable credit from *The Pleasure Girls*, and Virginia Wetherell, who had previously enjoyed some television credits and minor film parts. Heyward was particularly impressed with Wetherell, and for a time he hoped to add her to his growing stable of directors and actors pencilled in for future productions: Michael Reeves, Hilary Dwyer and Ian Ogilvy had already been singled out, and others such as Gordon Hessler and Christopher Wicking would follow. Wetherell slipped through the net in the end, though she did work for Hammer a few years later.

Behind the cameras, Levy hired Howard and Dennis Lanning, to carry out editing and sound duties respectively, and much to Vernon Sewell's delight, *Witchfinder General*'s John Coquillon for the cinematography. 'I'd known Johnny for years,' Sewell recalls, 'he was still very young but a very, very good cameraman.' Coquillon was just the man Sewell needed in the cramped conditions of Grims Dyke. 'I suppose using the house meant that we saved about two thirds of the cost of a studio, quite a bit in those days, and it

looked marvellous on film but that was really down to Johnny. He was very creative, he didn't mind trying new things which I always used to like, bouncing lights off the low ceilings and what have you.' Sewell was less pleased when he was informed that the film would require nudity to be added to the already frothy mix of bondage and witchcraft: 'They told me one day I had to have a naked woman in it somewhere, so I just showed a woman

above:
'That's how to treat a producer!' Christopher Lee greets Tony Tenser.

opposite bottom:
Barbara Steele, seen here torturing the hero Mark Eden, was cast in **Curse of the Crimson Altar** purely for her cult status and was given little dialogue, and no scenes with either Lee or Karloff.

left:
A typical Tenser advert playing on a popular contemporary television commercial slogan, in this case an oil company, which at the time was encouraging consumers to 'Put a Tiger in your tank'.

above:
Another example of the Spanish artwork for **Curse of the Crimson Altar**, retaining Karloff and Lee's billing but using an image of Michael Gough that was missing from both the British and American adverts.

top right:
One of ritualistic orgy sequences that featured heavily in the publicity materials but only briefly in the film. The girls are Carol Anne and Jenny Shaw.

below:
Vivienne Carlton on the sacrificial altar in one of **Curse of the Crimson Altar**'s fantasy sequences.

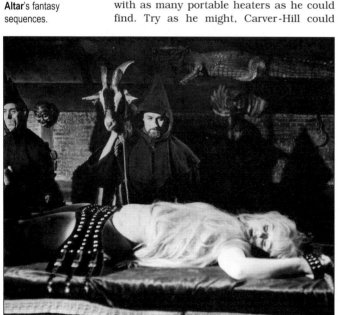

getting in and out of bed, simple as that. I certainly wasn't going to do anything more explicit.' Virginia Wetherell was even less keen, so a body double was used for the fleeting glimpse of flesh.

If lighting the old house proved to be a technical challenge for Coquillon, then heating it became a major problem for everyone. Grims Dyke had been empty for about five years before Tigon moved in, and shooting took place in the depths of winter. Art Directors Derek Barrington and Peter Jaques supervised the re-dressing of the empty rooms, corridors and kitchens with hired furniture, while the production manager Alex Carver-Hill filled the house with as many portable heaters as he could find. Try as he might, Carver-Hill could

make little significant difference to the chill that constantly hung in the air. The crew dressed as if they were working outdoors, while the cast huddled round the fires for warmth between shots.

The stamina of cast and crew was further tested by the night shooting, never a pleasant experience, but especially problematic in the depths of winter. Karloff unsurprisingly suffered more than anyone else, and caused a scare when he caught a cold and had to be hospitalised. 'He had three or four days in a private hospital,' Tenser says, 'I was very worried of course and went to see him one afternoon. I asked for Mr. Karloff and they said, 'who? Nobody here of that name.' It took a little while but we finally found him under his real name - Pratt. He was that modest, didn't want any fuss, he accepted the hospital was a precaution more than anything and he recovered well.'[6]

By this stage in his career Vernon Sewell had accepted the world of low-budget horrors and, realising the understated elegance of his earlier pictures was a thing of the past, he had adopted a more pragmatic approach. He simply made the most of it: 'I liked the two horror pictures I did for Tigon. They may not be much to look at but I thought they were great fun, I enjoyed doing them very much.' As reliable as ever, Sewell finished principal photography on time and within budget and swiftly retired to the cutting rooms to assemble his print.

In the early spring of 1968 Tenser finally managed to secure a new office and moved the whole Tigon operation into the first floor of number 205 Wardour Street. The new premises were also the base of

Tigon's Distribution arm, and the walls were adorned with posters for many of the films both distributed and produced by the company. Tigon had made four horror films one after the other in a little over 12 months, and Tenser felt that there was still some mileage in the genre, but not for the moment on the big screen. A subsidiary company, Tigon Television Ltd, had been formed specifically to develop projects for TV, and one of the ideas being discussed attracted the attention of Christopher Lee. Although it was not yet on general release, Lee had recently worked in Hammer's adaptation of Dennis Wheatley's *The Devil Rides Out (1967)*, and, during the filming of 'The Crimson Cult', the actor had enthused about the film's qualities to the ever receptive Tenser.

Wheatley had written over fifty novels in a variety of genres, but needless to say it was his graphic treatment of Satanism and devil worship that attracted the public, his occult fiction topping the bestseller lists both at home and abroad. Tenser, familiar with the books, considered it a golden opportunity: 'After we had finished shooting, I went to see Christopher Lee about doing some of the Dennis Wheatley black magic stories as a television series. He was very interested and we talked it through with Wheatley, how it could be done and so on. Unfortunately we couldn't get the rights so we didn't to it at that point.' The idea was put on hold, but the box-office failure of the Hammer film later that year killed the proposal dead.

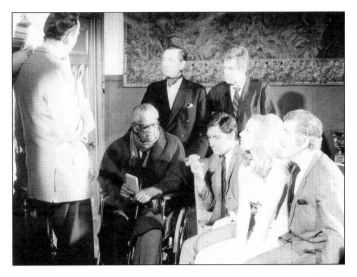

Tenser was then given the opportunity to vary Tigon's output, when he was approached by former Sunday Times journalist Elkan Allan with a project that was curious even by Tigon's standards. Allan was a highly-regarded documentary filmmaker and an innovative broadcaster - he had developed the pop show *Ready Steady Go!*, and won several awards for his television scripts. Allan's plan amounted to little more than an elaborate publicity stunt and a good old-fashioned exploitation film - repackaged for a more permissive age. It was the audacity of the scheme that appealed to Tenser; instead of hiring actors to have sex on the screen why not get real couples to do it for free?

above:
The principal cast - less Barbara Steele - are joined by Vernon Sewell (rear left) and Tony Tenser (front far right).

below:
An example of the nudity that was filmed for proposed export prints. As directed by Sewell, these scenes were all much tamer than they look, and none of the principal actors participated.

above:
British pressbook for **Love in Our Time**, the debut feature from television producer and documentary film maker Elkan Allan.

below:
Nudity from **Love in Our Time**. Despite the claim that only real life couples were used, everyone in the cast was a professional actor or model.

In January 1968, Allan placed a series of advertisements in the The New Statesman, the Evening Standard and significantly The Stage, stating:

<u>Film</u>: *Couples prepared to re-enact their happy or unhappy relationships in documentary film.*

Despite Allan's insistence at the time that his concept was 'outdating *cinéma vérité*, *nouvelle vague* and all that!' the whole thing was a clever scam. The offices of Tigon were inundated with photographs and letters from would-be porn stars, exhibitionists and assorted 'performance artists' willing to bare all in the name of cinema, but they were never really considered serious contenders. Contrary to later claims by the director, sorting through the piles of applicants was a relatively straightforward process, because Tenser simply had no intention of letting his cameras loose on a bunch of amateurs in the countryside, and anyway, Trevelyan would have laughed such an idea out of his office.

It took three months for Allan to piece together his story-lines, all of which seemed to have been culled direct from the Compton catalogue: wife swapping, extra martial affairs, underage sex and so on. Allan would claim later that there were over a thousand applicants that he personally whittled down to 422, all of whom were then interviewed. The truth was far more prosaic: Tigon screen-tested around 50 actors, and from these 9 couples were selected to appear in the final film. Amongst the 'real people in real situations' were the likes of actress Ann Michelle, who later starred in the Tigon release *Virgin Witch* (1971), Bill Cummings, who had appeared in *Thunderball* (1965), and the well-known stunt arranger Eddie Stacey.

Tigon financed the full production, with Tenser acting as the line producer, ably assisted by George Mills, the hugely experi-enced production manager whose CV included the likes of *Corridors of Blood* (1958) for Richard Gordon, and *Gorgo* (1960). The crew also included industry veterans cinematographer William Brayne and composer Reg Tilsley, both of whom would be held over to work for Tenser during the summer.

Allan fashioned a mixture of action and talking heads, linked together by a commentary written and narrated by the director himself. Tenser, always on the lookout for a fresh angle, suggested that Allan should get the film endorsed by a professional, so Dr. Eustace Chesser, LRCP, LRCS, LRFPS, the Edinburgh-born author of such books as 'Love Without Fear' and 'How to Make a Success of Your Marriage', was shown the footage. 'By itself sexual love is genitally motivated and so we tend to see our partners through sex-tinted spectacles. I like this film,' Eustace claimed in tones that revived memories of similar outpour-ings on *That Kind of Girl* and *The Yellow Teddybears*, 'and if it helps to rid ourselves of our inhibitions it will have more than justified itself.'

Love in Our Time was a first for Tigon; shot cheaply and quickly, it was much closer in spirit to the Compton films *London in the Raw* and *Primitive London*. The rushes convinced Tenser that the film had enough exploitable elements to sell on the national circuits and before leaving for the Cannes Film Festival that May, while *Love in Our Time* was still being cut, he announced a follow-up. 'He and She', also by Elkan Allan, was to be a similar 'documentary' on the far more risky subject of male and female homosexuality.

*   *   *   *   *

The 1968 Cannes Film Festival was an important one for Tenser and Tigon; for the first time the company's millionaire sponsor Laurie Marsh stepped out of the background and joined the company's official delegation. The Hyams brothers were still important to Tenser but Marsh, who four years earlier had provided the capital for Compton's purchase of the Windmill Theatre, had emerged as a major influence in the company's affairs. At only thirty-six years of age, Marsh was something of a *cause célèbre* in the property sector; he was the managing director and major shareholder in the property group Star (Great Britain) Holdings Ltd., and had established a reputation as a shrewd and opportunistic businessman. In the past, Marsh had flirted with the entertainment industry through his various leisure and property interests such as cinemas and bingo halls, as well as the Windmill of course. He was now actively working to establish a high-profile foothold in the film industry for himself.

Tenser's company was ideally placed to act as a springboard for the tycoon's ambitions. 'I'd known Laurie Marsh for a number of years and eventually he came into Tigon and he put some more money in but he mainly would get as much finance as we needed without the deals being silly. We split the partnership into three instead of two and everybody was happy with that. He came in but he didn't sit with me at the time, he was still the Managing Director of a large property company himself.'

Cannes was Marsh's first real exposure to the glamour and excitement of films and over the months that followed, he gradually eased himself into a more active position in the film business, accompanying Tenser at home and abroad as they followed up on their sales contacts. The two men set up operations at the Martinez. Tenser, an old hand at the Cannes hustle and bustle, was there promoting *Witchfinder*, *Blood Beast* and 'The Crimson Cult', all of which still had to find buyers for some territories, while Marsh enjoyed the spectacle of the film business elite at play.

Co-incidentally, Israeli filmmaker Menahem Golan was also staying at the Hotel Martinez and, over dinner, he and Marsh discovered that they had a mutual admiration for the English comedian Norman Wisdom.[7] In fact Golan's connection with Wisdom was somewhat stronger; having based himself in Liverpool for some time the Israeli had actually struck up a friendship of sorts with the comic, whose career was going through something of a barren patch. Wisdom had enjoyed stage and film success up until the early Sixties, invariably playing the same clownish character, but when his box-office lustre began to tarnish, he decided to broaden his range.[8] Golan suggested a more sophisticated role in an 'adult' comedy about a middle-aged man experiencing a midlife crisis. Wisdom developed the idea into a full script, *What's Good for the Goose*. Taking his familiar 'little man' persona and turning it on its head, Wisdom gave himself the part of a successful banker who finds himself in amongst the dolly birds and hippies at a beachfront resort.

Golan was in Cannes with the sole purpose of finding a backer for what he intended to be his English-language debut. Marsh was impressed, and agreed then and there on a deal to make the movie, with Golan at the helm. Tenser was less keen: 'I wasn't sure how I would deal with Golan. Menahem Golan was a fervent Israeli who had fought for Israel, so I knew I was dealing with a very tough man. I knew he was a very competent director but I wasn't sure how he was going to handle Norman Wisdom.' Tenser had to be pragmatic though: 'Laurie Marsh had shaken hands on the deal, so we had to do it and it wasn't a bad script. I thought we could get a good movie out of it.'

At the back of his mind, Tenser also knew that he had to push out into other markets: 'I wasn't worried about being seen as a horror film producer, but I was worried about making films that people liked and would go and see and would make a profit. I didn't worry about careers or anything like that.' By the spring of 1968 UK film production was starting to become dominated by projects peddling sex to a mainstream audience, such as *Three Into Two Won't Go*, *30 Is a Dangerous Age, Cynthia*, and *Prudence and the Pill*. Even the stage hit, *The Killing of Sister George*, was being adapted by Robert Aldrich into an adult sex comedy. When Judy Geeson, then an archetypal Sixties media chick, took her clothes off for *Here We Go Round the Mulberry Bush*, the story made the front page of newspapers - a fact that wouldn't be lost on the Tigon casting directors. 'As an independent I had to make sure I stayed close to whatever was popular at the time. It wasn't a case of aping what was fashionable, but knowing what would sell. Just then a comedy, and a sex comedy at that, seemed ideal.' Crucial to the deal was the agreement by Golan and Wisdom that they would deliver two versions - one for a family audience and one intended for a more 'adult' market. The contracts were signed in London in May; Tenser would produce, with Golan directing and Wisdom top-billed. Less than seven weeks later, on the 15th of July, the cast and crew assembled at the Palace Hotel in Southport to start principal photography.

The Palace had been empty for some years while the management struggled to find a buyer. In the meantime the premises, fixtures and fittings had been maintained in a good state of repair.[9] The electricity was still on and the lifts all worked, as did the kitchen equipment, and the bedrooms were all in a fully useable condition. Tenser, who had discovered the hotel some years earlier, had been wanting to film there for some time; its real advantage, apart from the ideal

above:
Norman Wisdom as his fans never dreamed of seeing him, with co-star Sally Geeson in **What's Good for the Goose**.

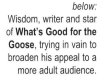

below:
Wisdom, writer and star of **What's Good for the Goose**, trying in vain to broaden his appeal to a more adult audience.

right:
The disco scene in **What's Good for the Goose** sees Wisdom reverting to type as the bumbling idiot.

above:
Teenager Sally Geeson was cast in **What's Good for the Goose** largely because of the success enjoyed by her older sister Judy in similar roles; she was still legally a minor in the UK at the time, so her father had to counter-sign her contract.

below:
British front of house still for Tenser's most dated movie; everything from the dialogue to the fashions and even the cars combine to locate the film firmly in 1968.

seaside location, was the size of the place - the Palace was huge. As well as accommodating all of the interior sets, the hotel could supply room and board for the entire cast and crew. The only downside was the lack of access to 35mm viewing facilities, but Tenser got round this problem by arranging for the rushes to be screened at the local cinema in Southport.

Tenser, who intended to be on set for the duration of filming, brought his production manager George Mills on board, along with William Brayne and Reg Tilsley from *Love in Our Time*. Even so, he had some reason for trepidation about the actual shoot: 'The more I thought about it, the more I didn't think that Menahem Golan and Norman were going to get on. Norman had worked mainly with one or two directors who he could manipulate in his own way. Menahem was not going to be used like that.'

There had been signs of trouble during the casting process when Wisdom, despite 'associate producer' billing, found himself sidelined; although two of his suggestions, David Lodge and Terence Alexander, were used, he was not otherwise involved. Wisdom quietly fumed. Unusually, for Tigon at least, the 'adult' sequences would feature the fiilm's stars, so the casting of the female lead was key to the film, or at least the selling of it. Again Wisdom found himself excluded. Golan met and tested Sally Geeson, the sister of Judy whose earlier strip had so electrified the gentlemen of the press. Two years younger than Judy, Sally seemed unperturbed about stripping off for her feature film debut, although at the age of eighteen she was still technically a minor and therefore legally unable to commit to a contract; at the time of the film's production the age of majority was still set at twenty-one. Careful negotiations were undertaken between Menahem Golan and Sally's father (who was also her agent) before permission was granted for the girl to fleetingly appear naked in the film.

If Wisdom tried to draw comfort from the thought that during shooting he would be an active collaborator, he was sadly mistaken. Golan showed no inclination to listen to his star. 'He had liked the script of course,' Wisdom explains, 'which was fine but when I wanted to bring in new things he wouldn't let me, he insisted on doing things his way. He really didn't want to listen to any of my ideas.' Tenser concedes the point: 'They simply didn't get on. I don't think they fell out or anything like that. It was just a personality thing.' The longer the shoot went on, the more strained the relationship became. 'This was probably my most difficult experience,' Wisdom says, 'It's a shame because I think that if we had worked together better we could have made the film so much better. By the time we were half way through I didn't think it would turn out the way either of us wanted.'

Surprisingly, neither of the leading players had any difficulty with the nudity. Wisdom remembers those scenes with some humour: 'I didn't mind them at all, in fact I rather enjoyed them. I wanted to expand my range and I didn't mind doing it as long as they didn't go over the top.' Geeson was equally unruffled. She told Cinema X: 'There is no point in making a fuss, you've just got to live with it, that's all there is to it. I'll admit I was very frightened at first. I just kept quiet and did exactly what I was told. When the director said, 'Right clothes off!' I did just that. No dithering.'

The so-called 'naughty bits' comprised of three scenes: a brief sequence in the bathroom, Sally and Norman in bed together, and a midnight skinny-dip. To protect the sensibilities of the British audience the actors played these scenes in their undies, though it was felt that we could cope with a mercifully brief shot of Norman's bottom.

There was never any intention of using the stronger scenes in the British prints but that didn't stop Tigon's publicity director, Victor Churchill, exploiting the idea that 'Britain's favourite comedian' was getting into saucy stuff. He took to describing the film variously as 'adult' and 'spicy'. The national press remained largely indifferent and even the trade papers weren't giving it much more than a passing glance; Southport was a long way from Wardour Street and there was no rush to cover the film. Trying to drum up some interest, Churchill herded a gaggle of geese through the lunchtime traffic on Wardour Street. While admiring the man's enthusiasm, the showbusiness reporters demonstrated little in the way of interest. The wags in Soho were already predicting that What's Good for the Goose would challenge even the most creative of selling teams.

Tenser returned to London soon after filming wrapped and signed-off Tigon's financial accounts; in overseas revenues alone Tigon had banked a commendable $300,000, mainly due to the performance of the two Michael Reeves movies. Confident of the current production slate's bankability, Tenser was anticipating that returns in the following financial year would exceed $1m. (To put these figures into perspective, Denis Meikle calculates that during the period from October 1964 to September 1967, Hammer generated some £2.7m in overseas earnings on a production slate of 17 movies including She and One Million Years BC.)

At around this time, the producer pulled off one of his most audacious deals, when he met with David Horne of the independent US distributor National Showmanship Films. Even as What's Good for the Goose was still being edited, they negotiated what Tenser describes, with tongue well in cheek, as 'one of the best deals I ever did,' convincing National Showmanship Films to buy the North American rights for What's Good for the Goose, sight-unseen. As was common practice at the time for British films, Tigon sold the US rights for a flat fee rather than a percentage; occasionally this would mean the production company losing out on a potential gold-mine but it meant that the administrative hassles of recovering the due share of the takings could be avoided. It also meant that the producer wasn't exposed to the vagaries of American box-office returns, and in the case of What's Good for the Goose, it turned out to be a very wise move indeed.

Tenser always maintained that his policy of 'open door and a coffee to anyone and everyone' was a cornerstone of his success, but a curious incident took place during the filming of What's Good for the Goose that stretched his policy well beyond the normal call of duty. A young director by the name of Stephen Weeks arrived unannounced at the Palace Hotel one night, long after shooting had finished for the day. Weeks had with him a script for a short film he had set up, called '1917: The Gap', which was due to start shooting in Wales at eight o'clock the following morning. The cast and crew were already on location and the complex main set was already built but, unfortunately, the financing had fallen through at the eleventh hour and there was not enough money to actually start filming. By the time that Weeks and his agent had tried all the obvious routes to raise cash, time had almost run out and it was literally Tigon or nothing. Weeks takes up the story: 'I finally arrived in Southport and met Tony. I think it was ten o'clock at night. He was in his pyjamas and he read the script while I sat there and said, 'I'll do it! How much do you want to start with?' I said, 'about

above:
Despite appearing in two AIP horror movies, Sally Geeson remains best known as a comedienne from her work in the likes of **Bless This House** and **Carry On Abroad**

below:
Tony Tenser and future wife Diane in Southport, where the majority of **What's Good for the Goose** was filmed.

TIGON MAKE EXCITING PICTURES

We have just finished shooting

'WHAT'S GOOD FOR THE GOOSE'

starring

NORMAN WISDOM

Directed by
MENACHEM GOLAN

Never has a 'crew' laughed so much!!!!

TIGON PICTURES LIMITED
205 Wardour Street · London W1
Tel: 01-734 9743
Cables: TIGONPIX LONDON W1

above:
British trade ad for **What's Good for the Goose**. The fact that the 'crew laughed' does not inspire a great deal of confidence, but it would appear to be the best that the publicity team could come up with; promoting the film's national release proved to be just as challenging.

fifteen hundred quid' and he went off to find the production accountant, who had the key to the safe. They couldn't find him so drastic measures were required - we broke into the safe!'

His cash secured, Weeks made an overnight taxi journey from Southport to Swansea. It was a trip that Weeks wouldn't easily forget: 'The driver went off the road twice, I had to stay awake to keep him awake! I arrived at the location at about 8:45 and all the crew were thinking I had overslept at the hotel!' After this inauspicious start, and with a total budget of £20,000 and a seven day shooting schedule agreed, Stephen Weeks began work on his big screen debut.[10]

Nominally, the script of *1917* is based on a play called 'The Gap' by a 'little known' playwright called Derek Banham. It's about British and German soldiers spinning out the monotony of life in the trenches during the First World War, but in fact no such play existed; Tenser said he needed a film of at least 34 minutes and Weeks, reluctant to tinker with the story, simply added various credit cards at the end as one of his tactics to increase the film's running time. He also felt that laying claim to a theatrical heritage would lend the film an air of legitimacy; Derek Banham was in fact a friend and former advertising colleague of Weeks. The original finance for the film had also been provided by a colleague in the advertising industry, who committed on the strength of a gentleman's agreement and later reneged just as casually when he decided to invest his money elsewhere - hence the nighttime dash across the country to Southport.

Weeks may have stretched the truth with the credits but the basic story, of a soldier establishing a rapport with the enemy by offering food, was based on fact. The director had found the story while researching for a planned documentary on the battlefields of the First World War, which was later filmed in 1979 as *Scars*. The only material change to the real story was the nationality of the soldier - from British to German to avoid the clichéd convention that a German character could only ever be portrayed as a villain.

As it was such a small, home-grown production, Weeks had taken total control of the casting process, though by necessity he could only hire young and therefore largely inexperienced actors. The likes of David Leland would go on to considerable success as the writer of *Mona Lisa (1986)* and director of such films as *Wish You Were Here (1987)* and *The Land Girls (1998)*. Anthony Trent had starred in *Mini Weekend*, whilst Geoffrey Davies later achieved recognition for his role as Dick Stuart-Clark, in TV's *Doctor* series (and co-incidentally ended up back in the trenches in *Oh! What a Lovely War (1969)*). Timothy Bateson was the exception amongst the cast; a

reliable and experienced support or character actor, he could turn his hand to either comedy or drama with aplomb. Bateson had made his first film in 1947 and appeared in such varied films as *Richard III (1955)*, *The Evil of Frankenstein (1964)* and *Les Misérables (1998)*.

The cast and crew were of course in place before the contract with Tenser had been agreed. In fact, Weeks was too young to sign - as a minor he had to have his parents endorse his signature! Tenser had no alternative but to accept the production exactly as it stood when he became involved; there was simply no time to impose any changes. Realising that his young director may need support however, he insisted that George Mills was attached to the project, much to Weeks's relief: 'George was a very nice man. An old-school British type and he was very useful to sort out the problems we had day to day. Up until then it was all being done by the assistant director and myself.'

One problem that needed to be addressed was the provision of authentic looking horse carcasses to litter the battlefield. Shepperton had a mock dead horse made of leather but that was too expensive for the film's meagre budget. Weeks found a solution locally: 'The knackers yard asked how many we wanted and we said two. The price was less than it would have cost even just to drive the leather horse from London.' Weeks ended up getting more than he bargained for. 'Just before lunch one day the van arrives and out come these two horses, coughing and limping. The driver asks where we want them and I rather nervously point. He then leads them across, stands them in the spot and, 'Bang! Bang!' Two dead horses - it was very cheap on lunches that day!'

This commitment to authenticity, albeit unintentional, also surfaced in several other areas. Weeks had found a bleak, desolate landscape in the Swansea valley, but the sense of dereliction was heightened when he transported a dead forest to the location from a site next to a copper works in Port Talbot. A dredging company based at Swansea docks provided huge mounds of mud to dress the set, and the local civil defence staff provided sandbags and equipment. A disused zinc works was also hired, further cheap manpower was provide by the Territorial Army, and unemployed coal miners acted as extras. The set itself was constructed on three sides and set against the stark, desolate landscape of slag heaps. Even with an additional half-day spent shooting pick-ups in a commercial studio in London, the film was delivered within budget. There was one small hiccup when the Censor's office insisted on an 'X' certificate because of the line, 'up to my neck in shit and bullets', which was considered a profanity.

With a running time of fractionally more than the required thirty-four minutes, *1917* qualified as a support feature and was therefore entitled to a percentage share of the main feature's takings. However, Tenser had financed the project without a main feature in mind, and had nothing appropriate at Tigon at the time. Given the small sum involved, he was happy to leave the film on the shelf until a suitable feature could be found.

Tenser was impressed with Weeks though, and offered him a long-term contract. Having agreed to the deal in principle, Weeks started work on 'The Cawnpore Massacre' while the details were worked out. This project was to be a big-budget retelling of the infamous incident during the Indian Mutiny, when British officers and their families surrendered the garrison of Cawnpore after a long and bitterly fought siege, only to be put to the sword by their captors. Tenser liked the idea and pressed the director to sign a formal contract, but Weeks stalled. With his long hair and sandals, the director was very much a product of his age; the idea of freedom and a distrust of the establishment were like a mantra to him and he was happy to let things drift. It soon became apparent that Tenser would be demanding a degree of control over the end product that Weeks was unprepared to surrender so the two men, unable to

resolve their differences over the terms of the contract, parted company amicably. Weeks took 'The Cawnpore Massacre' with him but he was unable to find the finance to make it a reality.

*   *   *   *   *

Tenser remained keen to ensure that all of his financial eggs weren't in one basket - or one genre for that matter. *What's Good for the Goose* had been financed entirely by Tigon, but Tenser's second summer project for 1968, a sci-fi thriller called 'Thin Air', was to be a co-production with a company new to films but with a strong financial pedigree. Sagittarius was, as Tenser explains, 'a film company run by a fellow called Henry White. He was a film producer and he teamed up with a man called Edgar Bronfman. Bronfman was from the Seagram's Whisky family, the biggest whisky firm in the world. They brought this film to me and asked if I would be interested.'

'Thin Air' was a Fifties-style science fiction film written by American actor Mike St. Clair, who had appeared in numerous television shows as well as films like *Our Man Flint (1965)* and *Thoroughly Modern Millie (1967)*. This would be Tenser's first science fiction film since *The Projected Man*, and the plans for it also represent a more significant departure for Tigon; engaging

above:
Tenser on one of his most unusual set visits - to the Welsh location of the short film **1917**. Director Stephen Weeks can be seen standing next to him, holding a megaphone.

below:
This British promotional artwork for **1917** would seem to be adopting a 'less is more' approach to Weeks's film!

above:
Tenser meets up with stars Patrick Allen, George Sanders and director Gerry Levy on the set of **The Body Stealers**.

Gerry Levy to direct, the emphasis would be very much on securing an 'A' certificate for the finished film, making it accessible to the lucrative family audience market.

Levy, under his usual 'nom de plume' Peter Marcus, lightened the mood of the script to make it more appropriate for its intended audience, and oversaw the seamless switching of the setting from the original California, to England. The story now featured a very Sixties never-say-die adventurer, played by lantern-jawed Patrick Allen, investigating a series of mysterious kidnappings of military personnel, and in the process unwittingly stumbling upon an alien invasion in progress. Allen, of course, had been associated with the aborted Compton epic 'Beau Brigand', since which time he had enjoyed notable domestic success in both cinema and television.[11] 'I was always disappointed about Beau Brigand,' Patrick Allen recalls, 'But these things happen in this business, I didn't bear any grudge. When I got the script through my first thought was how much do they pay, not 'oh no its Tigon!'

Many of the supporting parts were given to a number of familiar names, the most prominent of whom was Hollywood star George Sanders, playing a general in the first of two visits to the world of Tigon.[12] Ever the film-buff, Tenser relished the opportunity to meet another of his idols, only to find Sanders's detachment from the film was total: 'He had been a big star but he was gone by then. He had a script under the table and would read from it, he couldn't remember his lines. A very nice man to speak to though.'[13] The meatier part of the

villain of the piece went to the robust character actor Maurice Evans who, despite a number of film roles, was predominantly known for his remarkable theatrical career.[14] The film's billing reflected the high esteem in which the veteran performers were held, with both Sanders and Evans's names above the title. 'The cast was really exceptional for this type of film,' Patrick Allen insists, 'I had seen Maurice Evans on stage and he was a fantastic actor and of course George Sanders had made so many great movies. It was a pleasure to work with people like that.'

Also featured was Robert Flemyng, being repaid for his last-minute commitment to *The Blood Beast Terror* with an underwritten part as a naval officer. Another Tenser veteran, Hilary Dwyer, who had impressed Tenser so much in *Witchfinder General*, was given the female lead as a rather dowdy but efficient doctor. Tenser also landed a nice piece of novelty casting when Neil Connery, brother of Sean (then the biggest star in British cinema), signed on for the second lead, a rather colourless scientist. Connery had flirted with films before, in a Bond spoof *Operation Kid Brother (1967)*, but soon drifted away from acting, finding success as the boss of his own decorating firm in Glasgow.

Even for a film targeting a family audience, Tigon's publicity team required a pretty face to sell to the press. Levy auditioned a bevy of starlets before settling on Lorna Wilde, a tall, leggy former model hoping to break into films. Tenser had final approval over all the cast so, out of courtesy, Wilde was asked to make a formal

above:
Violence breaks out in **The Haunted House of Horror**, with Richard O'Sullivan and Veronica Doran coming between perennial beach boy Frankie Avalon (far left) and prime suspect Julian Barnes.

visit to Tigon's Wardour street base. 'I remember Lorna Wilde very well, she came in to the office and I wasn't too sure but I thought I should take her to lunch. She was a striking girl of course and turned lots of heads everywhere she went. We were walking along Wardour Street and I was feeling very good about being seen with her, then we passed one of the guys from the office and he shouted out, 'how's the wife and kids, Tony?' Back to earth with a bang!' Ms Wilde also made an impression on her leading man: 'Lorna was gorgeous, absolutely lovely,' Patrick Allen recalls, 'Her boyfriend or her husband owned a marina on the south coast somewhere so acting was really just a hobby for her, lucky thing!'

Levy picked a familiar crew to work behind the camera: With Howard Lanning, John Coquillon, and Reg Tilsley all on return duties for Tigon, Levy also brought in horror genre veteran Roy Ashton, formerly of Hammer and now jobbing as an independent, to handle the rather routine make-up chores.[15] Just a week after *What's Good for the Goose* started shooting, 'Thin Air' was also shooting on location, before the crew moved to the sound stages at Shepperton on the 29th of July 1968.

*   *   *   *   *

By the end time summer 1968 was drawing to an close, Tigon were in the enviable position of having two full-length features ready for release, and Tenser felt confident enough to look further afield for finance. Tigon's press releases at the time were promising up to ten new productions a year,

and in late September, Tenser flew to Hollywood for a series of meetings to discuss future projects. Before he undertook what was his first visit to the American movie capital since leaving Compton, he made sure he had talked up their latest movie, 'Thin Air', calling it 'a very commercial picture,' and announcing, 'what we needed was a very commercial title so we changed it to 'Invasion X'.' Tigon's production partners, Sagittarius, remained unconvinced by either the new title or the finished product and held off on Tenser's offer of further collaborations. Bronfman and White's efforts to become major players on both sides of the Atlantic seemed to be taking off when they announced a number of high profile projects independent of Tigon, including the likes of *Jane Eyre (1970)* with George C. Scott.

Unperturbed, Tenser hooked himself up with AIP once again, with a script called 'The Dark', by a promising young screenwriter called Michael Armstrong.[16] 'The Dark' seemed to be custom-made for AIP - a group of horny teenagers conduct a séance in an abandoned house, and discover that one of them is a psychotic killer. Armstrong's original script, written eight years earlier when he was still a teenager himself, was more concerned with the explicit heterosexual and homosexual tensions within the group, rather than the violence inherent in the story, but the American drive-in giants considered the idea to be an easy sell. Sam Arkoff and Jim Nicholson both liked the script, and approved the project. At a press conference announcing the new venture, Tenser

above:
Mark Wynter as Gary, with girlfriend Dorothy (Carol Dilworth). His early death was an attempt by Michael Armstrong to mirror the structure of **Psycho**.

below:
Atmospheric shot from **The Haunted House of Horror**, which was filmed on the same location as **What's Good for the Goose**. British actress Jill Haworth is flanked by Barnes, Avalon and O'Sullivan.

promised that the two companies would continue their close association over a number of un-named forthcoming projects. AIP's man in London, Louis 'Deke' Heyward, waxed lyrical about the Armstrong script, describing it as having, 'all the terror of *Psycho* and yet with a young feel.'

Heyward was the prime mover behind AIP's closer relationship with Tigon; he was on a crusade to consolidate the company's London operation and Tenser had a number of scripts more or less ready to roll. At the Californian end, the Tigon films were seen as being the ideal product to fill the gap in their schedules left by the failing Poe series, and as a bonus, working with Tigon allowed them to take advantage of the cheaper production costs in the UK.

Experimentation wasn't a natural part of the AIP ethos; they may have been keen to explore new avenues but they weren't comfortable in departing too radically from their tried and trusted formula. It would have come as no surprise to Tenser therefore that, as a prerequisite for the deal to make 'The Dark', AIP insisted that Boris Karloff had to headline. Armstrong agreed, reluctantly, to adapt his tightly constructed narrative so that the aging star could be accommodated. Karloff, who owed AIP ten days work on his existing contract, was

given a small role as an investigating police officer. 'The Dark' was scheduled to follow *What's Good for the Goose* into the Palace, and if the atmosphere on Wisdom's film had been somewhat strained it was nothing compared with the difficulties Tigon faced bringing the 'The Dark' to the screen.

Only a few months earlier, Armstrong had been a would-be filmmaker struggling to get projects off the ground. He had a chance meeting with John Trevelyan, who suggested that Tigon were receptive to new talent. Armstrong wisely followed-up on this suggestion, and was staggered when he discovered how accommodating Tenser's set-up was: 'I had dug out this old horror story script and tried to get someone interested; of course no-one wanted to know. Then John Trevelyan phoned Tony for me and arranged for me to go and see him. I went on the Thursday and told him that I had a project and, of course, wanted to direct it. I left the script with him. On the Saturday I got a call at home saying would I go and see him on the Monday. I did, and I signed a contract. It was as simple as that, quite extraordinary!'

Armstrong soon found that Tigon's production partners weren't so easy going. Heyward believed that if it were to appeal to an American audience, the script needed a

number of changes. The murderer, he argued, was too obvious from the begining and what the script needed was a red herring. Heyward's idea was to expand Karloff's screentime and throw the audience off the scent by dropping a number of hints that the policeman was the murderer. Armstrong was appalled: 'The script came back and there were just these lines all the way through and on the back Deke had written all these new scenes. They didn't make sense or fit in with the rest of the film. He had just written all this stuff with the police inspector in a wheelchair, who we are supposed to believe was wheeling around this empty house chopping up teenagers with a kukri knife!'

Karloff, over eighty and confined to a wheelchair, would have made an unlikely policeman even if he was in the best of health, but by the time the film was ready to start shooting the actor was seriously ill. Heyward had also simplified the film's structure into a linear format and cut the running time by simply removing many of the exposition scenes. Armstrong's complex web of subplots was in shreds. By this stage it was clear to the producers that Karloff would be in no condition to undertake his duties, so following a series of frantic telephone calls, the former matinee idol Dennis Price was drafted in as a last-minute replacement. Twenty years earlier Price had been one of the biggest stars in British cinemas, but a gay scandal, attempted suicide and bankruptcy had left the actor broken and penniless, happy to take whatever work he was offered. Bizarrely, Price was simply shoe-horned into the existing role - in the headlong rush to replace Karloff, no-one thought to rewrite the script, leaving Price's shadowy police inspector to stalk his victims in a wheelchair!

After having accommodated Heyward on Karloff, Armstrong was dismayed to be forced to deal with the American's equally strong views on the remainder of the cast: 'I had in mind Ian Ogilvy and Jane Merrow in the leading roles, with featured roles for Scott Walker and David Bowie as the killer.' Armstrong was particularly keen on including the then-obscure singer: 'I'd known Bowie for some time and I had written a couple of cabaret scenes into my first draft specifically for him. I even suggested to Tony that he put David under contract.' AIP took a very different view - they wanted to offer the male lead to Frankie Avalon or Fabian, both contract players with fading careers in need of a boost.[17] Heyward suggested Sue Lyon or Carol Lynley for the female lead, assuring Tenser that both of them would jump at the chance to work with either Fabian or Avalon. As it happened neither was available, so English actress Jill Haworth - at the time widely tipped for future

above:
Robin Stewart as Henry attempts to subdue the hysterical Madge (Veronica Doran) in **The Haunted House of Horror**.

stardom - was drafted in, with Armstrong reluctantly accepting beachboy Avalon as the lesser of two evils.[18]

With leads in place and the £80,000 budget agreed, Heyward finally backed off and gave Armstrong and casting director Jim David the freedom to hire whoever they wanted for the supporting roles. Auditioning a number of lesser-known British actors, Armstrong opted for Robin Stewart and Richard O'Sullivan, both of whom would later achieve small-screen fame in domestic sitcoms. Two other crucial roles went to Julian Barnes and Mark Wynter, the pop singer and minor celebrity star of his own television show, *Call in on Wynter*.

The delays caused by the script rewrite meant that the schedule had slipped but, even with all the roles now filled, the production path was far from smooth. On the eve of shooting, Heyward baffled Armstrong by asking for the parts played by Julian Barnes and Robin Stewart to be swapped over, leaving the inexperienced Barnes to cope with the complex role of the murderer. Armstrong had committed his future to Tigon by signing a contract for five films over a five year period but, depressed and confused by the constant changes on his debut project, he was ready to quit completely. 'Tony called me in, he knew what I was thinking,' Armstrong reflects. 'He assured me it would be all right, he had a plan! We would shoot two versions - one of the original script and one with Deke's revised script. I was told this was done all the time.'

Heyward was also having doubts. Faced with what he considered to be Armstrong's resistance to reasonable requests, he sought to invoke AIP's right of veto over the director - to his mind Armstrong was too inexperienced for such a complicated project. With filming just about to start, Tenser refused to allow a change of

above:
Michael Armstrong, centre, directing the party scene from **The Haunted House of Horror**. Richard O'Sullivan and Veronica Doran are to the left.

director. He did however broker a compromise with AIP. It was agreed that the rushes from the first few days work would be sent to London and if they were not up to scratch then Armstrong would be removed. Gerry Levy was put on notice as a precaution.

Tenser's young director may have been forgiven for thinking that the worst was now behind him, as they now had a script more or less agreed and, if nothing else, Armstrong finally had the opportunity to prove that he could deliver footage to the required standard. The production crew moved in to the Palace during early October, but perversely there were a few problems due to the fact that the hotel had been left in an immaculate condition after the completion of the *What's Good for the Goose* shoot. 'The Palace was basically in too good a condition for what we required.' Armstrong comments. 'So most of the sets were built from scratch inside the Palace, with the hotel's interior only featured very briefly; the cellars, some running down stairs and some shots in the corridors.'

Once again Tenser joined the cast and crew, headed up by George Mills, on site at the Palace - an arrangement that seemed guaranteed to help forge a strong team spirit. 'What can I say?' Armstrong smiles, 'They were all young, good looking and a long way from home. Let's say they got on famously and let it at that!' The director was happy with the way that filming progressed: 'Tony stayed with us throughout and we talked every day about progress. It seemed to be going well and he was very supportive, mercifully Deke never visited the set. The rushes went off to London as promised and nothing was heard, which I assume was an endorsement of some kind. The only problem I had was with one member of the crew who seemed out to make trouble, he looked on me as a kid, still wet behind the ears. Tony asked me if I wanted him to deal with it and I said I would. I took the guy aside and laid it on the line for him. After that I think I had their respect.'

Of course, there remained the question of Heyward's scenes. 'They were shot, or at least some of them were. I think they gave up after the first couple of days,' Armstrong confirms. 'I think Tony directed them himself but I can't say because I left the set. I wanted nothing to do with them.'

As the shoot progressed, Armstrong soon found himself running out of time: 'Realistically we were never going to do it in four weeks and with hindsight I can see that now. There were a lot of scenes wandering around with candles and each candle had to be lit individually so it was a complicated thing to try and rush. We had to undershoot because of the timeframe, so some of the shooting was rushed and we hadn't been able to cover things as well as I would have liked.' Despite early difficulties the director has nothing but praise for his crew: 'We could have done with more time but on the last day of shooting Tony came in and said, 'that's it.' We hadn't shot any of the chase at the end and we needed to have something - so the cast and the whole crew agreed to come in and work on Saturday without overtime, quite extraordinary.'

Tenser did not return to London immediately, choosing instead to stay on in Southport for a little longer. Having shot two films at the Palace, Tenser now wanted to take on the site as a permanent production base for Tigon. 'It was ideal, there was more than enough space for all the facilities you need in a studio and the location was perfect. I went to see the local council with a deal; if they put up half the money we would guarantee sufficient work through Tigon, to ensure that it never lost money. The council turned it down, saying they didn't go into commercial ventures. It was great shame. I think they knocked it down a little after that.'

While Armstrong was in the cutting room with editor Peter Pitt, assembling the first cut of 'The Dark', Tenser reviewed possible future projects for Tigon's new star director. The horror-thriller 'The Maze', from a script by Armstrong himself, was one option; another was the potboiler 'Kill Me Kindly', intended as a vehicle for a major Hollywood star such as Bette Davis or Joan Crawford. 'We had a contract so Tony came up with a number of suggestions and I gave him a number of ideas,' Armstrong explains. 'I didn't really put too much effort into it at the time, I was still editing at the time so that took priority.'

On the 19th of January 1969, Sam Arkoff and Jim Nicholson arrived in London to view screenings of AIP's most recent European projects, *De Sade*, *The Oblong Box* and of course, 'The Dark'. Although he hadn't finished editing the picture yet, Armstrong was confident about screening a reasonably complete 'working copy,' but he was more than a little perplexed when the instruction came through to assemble the

'Heyward version' from the odd bits and pieces that had been filmed. Most of Heyward's scenes had become redundant in light of the various rewrites, and simply hadn't been filmed, so Armstrong stood his ground and declined to become involved. Gerry Levy was then drafted in to help Peter Pitt put together a revised version.

Much to his surprise, Armstrong was invited to attend the formal screening in the company of Tenser, Heyward, Nicholson, Arkoff and Danny Skouras, the AIP European Director of Sales. It was an experience he is not liable to forget: 'The projector started up and what came on bore no resemblance to my film in any shape or form; you couldn't follow the plot; it was mess. There was no logic and without warning scenes would cut to stock footage of the Houses of Parliament and Big Ben, and of course poor Dennis in his wheelchair was just stuck in anywhere because none of his scenes fitted any more.' Needless to say Nicholson and Arkoff weren't impressed, not least because the footage they were now being shown didn't match the rushes they had already seen.

Armstrong found himself in the firing line: 'I appeared to be stuck in a political situation. As I understand it, Deke was in a very vulnerable position at the time career-wise with AIP. *De Sade*, which they had just filmed in Germany, had been a disaster and there had been a lot of political back-stabbing which I was unaware of until I became the fall guy. Heyward had jeopardised his position with AIP and saw my film as an effort to reassert himself.' Arkoff and Nicholson left the screening with Tenser and Heyward in tow. The following day at the Savoy the AIP executives held a meeting with Heyward, Tenser, Peter Pitt and Armstrong all in attendance. The decision was taken to allow Armstrong to re-cut his version and to shoot some additional scenes to cover the holes.

Armstrong was given no clue as to what had occurred prior to the meeting. 'I suppose,' he concludes, 'that tempers were raised and let's say, cross words spoken.' Even that wasn't an end to the drama; with both Avalon and Haworth no longer available, Armstrong was faced with the challenge of replacing the information lost from the original narrative without using the leading characters. The director wrote a number of revisions which he felt bridged the gaps, and handed these to Levy, who had taken over as the line producer; 'Gerry said thanks, and that he would have a look and let me know what they were going to do,' says Armstrong, and that was the last he heard.

Levy dumped the Armstrong rewrites, and under the name of Peter Marcus he proceeded to write his own scenes, which involved a romance between Gina Warwick and a new character played by George Sewell, who remembers the whole experi-

ence as being more than a little out of the ordinary: 'I got a call from Gerry Levy and we agreed to meet up to discuss a part, somewhere on the North Circular I think. He told me he had to fill out the running time on this film and would I help him by doing these inserts. He didn't say it outright but I got the impression that the original version was too strong, I don't know if that means too violent or explicit.' Levy's script included two additional killings and a musical ditty in the opening scene, as well as a revised closing exposition. The additional scenes were filmed at Grims Dyke House, with some location work done at sites in and around London, including Carnaby Street. Filming took place in February 1969, with Gerry Levy overseeing the new edit during March.

Armstrong was totally removed from the whole process; he had delivered a cut of the footage he had to hand and moved on to new projects. 'Out of the blue one morning I got a call from Tony inviting me to a screening of 'our' film,' Armstrong explains. 'I thought, 'oh no here we go again, but Tony told me not to judge it until I had seen it, but I went along with him expecting the worst. I sat there horrified with my hands over my eyes; I couldn't believe it. For the first fifteen minutes I wondered if there was going to be anything of mine in this thing.'

Lost somewhere along the way were the love scenes between Gary and Sylvia, the twisted sexual meanderings of the characters, the satire on the youth scene and the homosexual subplot. Armstrong had to shrug and accept the situation philosophically: 'About two thirds of it came from my footage. But it doesn't really resemble the movie I wanted to make. It caused a lot of pain at the time but you have to move on. I must say though, throughout, Tony was very supportive. We would have stand-up rows in his office but that was part of the filmmaking process. We were talking about other projects and whenever

above:
Artwork for what was re-titled **Horror House** for its US release. Armstrong's film made up part of a double bill with **The Crimson Cult**.

below:
Classic phallic imagery dominated the closing sequences of **The Haunted House of Horror**; Armstrong's homo-erotic subplot was an early victim of the script rewrites.

above:
Michael Gough in his meaningless cameo role in **Curse of the Crimson Altar**.

below:
Boris Karloff makes his point to Christopher Lee and Vernon Sewell.

we met, there was no animosity of any kind.' For his part, Tenser still hoped that Armstrong would continue to work with Tigon on other projects.

* * * *

While Armstrong was shooting in Southport, Tigon had their version of 'The Crimson Cult', now called *Curse of the Crimson Altar*, ready for trade screenings in London. At the same time, the film's star, Boris Karloff, was lying in the King Edward VII Hospital in Midhurst, Kent. Since filming for Tenser, Karloff had finished his scenes for the four Mexican films as well as making several television appearances. Karloff and his wife had been en route from Hollywood to London via New York when the actor caught a severe chill. By the time he arrived at Heathrow airport he was having difficulty breathing and was immediately rushed to the hospital. Despite being weak and exhausted, Karloff continued to work; he recorded stories for radio, gave interviews and even spoke about future movie projects. It would have been fitting if *Curse of the Crimson Altar* had opened to rapturous applause but it wasn't to be. Picked up by ABC, the film at least had the dignity of a circuit release but the reaction of the critics and the public was markedly indifferent.

CURSE OF THE CRIMSON ALTAR

'What Obscene Prayer of Human Sacrifice Can Satisfy the Devil-God?'
- US trade ads -

Synopsis

Robert Manning calls at Greymarsh Lodge, the ancestral home of the Morley family, to investigate the disappearance of his brother Peter, who like himself is an antique dealer. He arrives in the middle of a party and meets Eve, the niece of Greymarsh's owner J.D. Morley. Both Eve and Morley are polite and courteous but neither have any knowledge of Peter's current whereabouts. That evening happens to be the annual celebration of the burning of Lavinia, the Black Witch, and Manning accepts an invitation to stay for the fireworks party. Afterwards he meets the mysterious Professor Marsh, a local expert in the occult; Marsh explains that Lavinia cursed those who persecuted her and that many of their descendants had died in mysterious circumstances. That night Manning is haunted by dreams of black masses and witch trials. Warned by Elder, the butler, to leave and threatened by Marsh's chauffeur, Manning is convinced that Greymarsh is hiding a

COME FACE TO FACE WITH NAKED FEAR!
A madman's masquerade of vicious lusts and unspeakable cravings, of human sacrifice and hideous torture!

HIS LAST ROLE IS HIS FINEST HOUR OF EVIL!

BORIS KARLOFF
CHRISTOPHER LEE
THE CRIMSON CULT
COLOR BY MOVIELAB

STARRING MARK EDEN · BARBARA STEELE · MICHAEL GOUGH · VIRGINIA WETHERELL · RUPERT DAVIES
DIRECTED BY VERNON SEWELL · SCREENPLAY BY MERVYN HAISMAN AND HENRY LINCOLN · PRODUCED BY LOUIS M. HEYWARD
EXECUTIVE PRODUCER TONY TENSER ADDITIONAL MATERIAL BY GERRY LEVY A TIGON BRITISH-AMERICAN INTERNATIONAL PRODUCTION AN AMERICAN INTERNATIONAL RELEASE
©1970 American International Pictures, Inc.
AD MAT 406

left:
Incorrectly billed as Karloff's last role, the US release of **Curse of the Crimson Altar** was held up until after the actor's death.

secret in which his brother is somehow caught up. The police can't or won't interfere, and with only Eve to help him, Manning determines to confront the sinister Professor Marsh.

Critique

'I should be hard-pressed to defend The Crimson Cult on any grounds other than affection for the subject and some of the cast... Karloff himself, cadaverous and almost totally crippled, acts with a quiet lucidity of such great beauty that it is a refreshment merely to hear him speak old claptrap.'
- The New York Times, 12/11/70

'Professionally slick direction, a solid basis of logic in the development of plot, eerie music... and a strong cast who play it for real. There are virtues aplenty to satisfy the most fussy of horror addicts. The sick antics of the party guests add a gratuitous touch of obscenity.'
- The Daily Cinema, 10/11/68

'Let no-one be misled by the promise of whips, virgins, crimson altars and Barbara Steele: in spite of a deliciously bilious opening promising all manner of delights with Miss Steele... absolutely nothing materialises... this is one of the lamest and tamest horrors in a long time.'
- Monthly Film Bulletin, 01/69

'To list the clichés is a dispiriting occupation... It's a sad commentary that producers still insist on sticking to variations of existing formula, rather than attempting something new. This is a typical computer product.'
- Films and Filming, 02/69

Best known now for criminally wasting the talent of its three stars (Steele is restricted to a green-painted cameo as the witch in Manning's dreams), *Curse of the Crimson Atar* is probably a better film than it generally gets credit for, if only marginally so.

Vernon Sewell was adamant that the film was a 'lark' but only Karloff seems to catch on to the inherent fun, hamming his way through his role in a way that only he can get away with. He was, of course, too old and weak to play any sort of protagonist and it's hard to believe he represents any sort of a threat to Lee's sturdy villain. Lee, restricted to his library for most of the film, isn't too challenged by his material, expertly portraying the genial host and, when required, turning on the menace without too much difficulty. He lends the film considerable presence.

below:
Mark Eden and Christopher Lee. A small piece of useless trivia - the jacket that Lee is seen wearing throughout the film was not supplied by the wardrobe department; it was his own.

above:
British front of house for **Love in Our Time**. Note the 'Tony Tenser presents' credit, which was a throwback to the days of Compton and the only time it appeared on a film he actually produced.

below:
More of the sexual antics of 'real-life people' - actually a clever publicity stunt by Tigon.

In contrast, the younger cast members make little impact; Mark Eden carries out his leading man chores earnestly, but as *The Pleasure Girls* showed he is far better when playing deeply-flawed characters. Interestingly the film sets up Eden as an action hero, 'saving' Eve at the beginning, confronting Karloff's armed lout etc. but at the end he is totally dependant on the wheelchair-bound Karloff. One assumes there was a version of the script somewhere in which Eden rescues the girl - just in case. Virginia Wetherell struggles with her underwritten role and never really brings it to life. Neither is really at fault; the script completely fails in its attempt to integrate youthful exuberance with Gothic horror.

The sex and general kinkiness promised in the film's advertising never materialise on screen, at least not in the British print, which is a shame because this film really does need something to pep it up. The rewrites really took their toll; there are a large number of inconsistencies running through the narrative, these weaknesses being particularly apparent during the dénouement, which makes a nonsense of most of what has gone before. Levy retains the odd 'Lovecraftian' touch and the film isn't without its moments, particularly in the first half, during which Sewell handles the direction with quiet confidence. Also, John Coquillon's contribution is notable, as he managed to make the most of Grims Dyke's inherently gloomy corridors.

The critical reaction was a disappointment to Tigon, and confirmed what Tenser already suspected - *Curse of the Crimson Altar* wasn't going to be strong enough to topline its own bill. AIP reached much the same conclusion and shelved the film for the some time.[19] Tigon Pictures had however already identified a suitable partner, *Love in Our Time*. ABC had already negotiated a circuit release for Elkan Allan's film but remained unsure of exactly what to do with the film. A double-bill with *Curse of the Crimson Altar* seemed an ideal solution, but first there was the thorny problem of a classification row with the BBFC to deal with. *Love in Our Time* contained some explicit material and Trevelyan had insisted on an 'X' certificate. This suited Tigon, and the film's release was planned with *Curse of the Crimson Altar* making up the bill. The Viewing Committee of the Greater London Council took a somewhat different view however.

The BBFC was merely an advisory body, albeit an extremely influential one, and for some time local authorities had been taking their role as the statutory body responsible for the exhibition of new films very seriously, with the GLC being more active than most. The guardians of the nation's morality were self-appointed local pressure-groups, some of whom exercised their influence on democratically elected local authorities. As Tenser had proved with *Naked - As Nature Intended*, the grey area that existed between the role of the BBFC, and the statutory responsibility of the local authorities, could be exploited to a film distributor's advantage. In this regard the GLC in particular had been very supportive of the arts as a whole. *Love in Our Time* showed how easily the pendulum could swing the other way.

Ignoring the 'X' certificate awarded by the BBFC, the GLC's 'Viewing Committee' took the view that *Love in Our Time* promoted the views of the 'permissive society', presumably by showing that people who participated in anti-social activities such as wife swapping were both happy and well adjusted. *Love in Our Time* was banned outright within the London metropolitan area, a considerable blow to its potential box-office viability. Tigon's reaction was to canvass as many of the remaining 470 local authorities as they could, sending them press packs, details of the expert endorsements, and supportive comments from Trevelyan. Only the GLC remained unmoved; none of the other councils in the

UK supported an outright ban and *Love in Our Time* passed more or less unmolested, with only a handful of minor protests at local level. Despite the best efforts of the 'moral majority', *Love in Our Time* went on national release on the 15th of December.

LOVE IN OUR TIME

'The Most Talked About Film of Our Time!'
- British Trade ads -

Synopsis

Allan himself sets the mood, saying, 'Everyone agrees that our permissive society means more extra-marital sex, more teenage experiments, more liberal attitudes that make for freer human relations.' Amongst the delights on offer:
- Schoolgirl Jill, despite being underage, goes to bed with Michael on the first night they meet.
- John and Tara agree to affairs outside marriage and share the experiences with each other.
- Anne accepts her partner Ray's infidelities as part of their way of life but risks violence by going with other men herself.
- Sharon loses a bet with her fiancé Andrew that he won't sleep with her best friend.
- Andre and Yvonne explain that what makes their marriage so happy is wife-swapping.
- Jill and Keith, who have never gone all the way, proclaim that they won't do so until they are married.

Critique

'It alternates between moments of naive hilarity and stretches of excruciating tedium. By the time the final pair are wheeled on... one's feelings are divided between revulsion at the general air of prurient hypocrisy and irritation at the appalling standard of photography and construction.'
- Monthly Film Bulletin, 01/69

'It moves with a fluidity and pace that one would expect, except when the non-professional performers slow it down... the truly astounding thing about this film is the lack of self-consciousness of the participants.'
- The Daily Cinema, 12/68

'A degrading and self conscious embarrassment.'
- Films and Filming, 02/68

Unlike, say, *London in the Raw*, *Love in Our Time* benefits from reasonable production values and an experienced crew, but it still panders to the same voyeuristic desire to see what other people are up to. Allan directs with confidence and his narration is unobtrusive. Performances on the whole are

acceptable, if a little limp in some of the vignettes, but there really isn't too much for the moral majority to get upset about. After some initial reluctance to handle *Love in Our Time*, ABC tested the water with a scheduled series of pre-release screenings prior to the official opening and then when nothing terrible happened they opened the film to a full circuit release. Much to their surprise they found that the initial box-office in the provinces exceeded their earlier Tigon release, *Witchfinder General*! To capture the public's imagination Tigon repeated a tactic Tenser had first used to promote *Naked - As Nature Intended*, replacing the Front of House cards with a simple text message, in this case:

'Love in Our Time is something new in motion pictures, a group of true love stories, filmed with full colour production values, and acted out by the actual people who loved through them. Taken separately, each story is fascinating, unexpected, tragic or funny, happy or sad, taken together they add up to a vivid, intimate glimpse of what the title promises, love in our time.'

above:
The names of the principal actors who worked on **Love in Our Time** were deliberately left off of the publicity materials to help create the impression that they were real people, not actors.

below:
More fun and frolics from Elkan Allan. Claims that Tigon received over 1000 applications from people eager to appear in the film were greatly exaggerated.

above:
Difficulties concerning the censorship and distribution of **Love in Our Time** effectively finished off Tenser's plans to film a sequel to the film.

Not as eye-catching perhaps as *Naked*'s simple 'we regret the management will not allow us to show you scenes from this film,' but effective enough when displayed outside cinemas to help ensure that *Love in Our Time* played to reasonable houses everywhere in Britain, except for the capital of course. To cash-in on the controversy, Tigon asked New England Library to produce a paperback, which boasted eight fresh vignettes not filmed because of their 'immoral, perverted or simply obscene' nature.

Despite healthy returns from around the country - Glasgow for some reason reported extremely high figures - *Love in Our Time*, deprived of its the biggest market place, was exceptionally slow in covering its costs. As a result the intended sequel, 'He and She' - on the even more sensitive subject of homosexuality - suddenly looked like a considerable gamble. It was quietly dropped from the schedules. *Love in Our Time* finally managed to get its elusive London release when Tigon used Allan's movie to make up the lower half of a bill with *Female Animal* in 1972. By then the permissive society had moved on and *Love in Our Time* was no longer considered, by the GLC at least, to be a threat to the capital's morality.

right:
US lobby card for **Love in Our Time**.

Footnotes

1. Gilbert moved to Grims Dyke House in 1890 while he was still working in London, and finally retired there in 1896, by which time he had already written his most famous works. He did write four plays while staying at the house, though he preferred to spend his time well away from public attention - unlike his erstwhile partner Arthur Sullivan, who ended his days addicted to morphine and extravagant gambling. Gilbert suffered a heart attack and died while swimming in the lake at Grims Dyke in 1911. The house and its 29 acres, located only 10 miles from London, passed to Gilbert's widow and then through the hands of various owners including the Middlesex Cricket Club; by the time Tigon filmed there it had been all but abandoned. Needless to say, Tenser's publicity people made much of the alleged haunting by Gilbert's ghost - a nice story concocted specifically to promote their Boris Karloff movie. After its spell as a film location Grims Dyke was eventually renovated and enjoyed a successful renaissance as a 4-star hotel.

2. Christopher Lee told the authors of 'The Films of Christopher Lee', 'Boris was in wheelchair, virtually unable to talk. I shall never forget that film... He was already a sick man but his courage, sheer guts, and superb professionalism were literally boundless. I did this film simply to be with him before he left us.'

3. After taking the role of the creature in *The Curse of Frankenstein (1957)*, Lee had scored a huge personal success with Hammer's original *Dracula (1958)*. The films that followed, both in the UK and increasingly Europe, traded on his image as a horror star, and while he certainly added considerable presence most of these films made little use of his abilities. As far as the Americans were concerned, Lee and Hammer didn't score another major hit until *Dracula Has Risen from the Grave* in late 1968. At the time of making 'The Crimson Cult', AIP considered Lee to be a far less prominent marquee name than Karloff, or even Cushing. Over the next few years Lee's star would be strongly in the ascent and by the time he returned to Tigon in 1971, he was not only the pre-eminent post-War horror star, but also an international name in his own right.

4. The likeable British character actor, despite a varied career on the stage and in films, had struggled to shake off the image of television detective Maigret, due to his work in the BBC series of the same name. The role brought him fame and a Best Actor award in 1961, but hampered his desire for the diversity of roles he had he previously enjoyed. Davies struggled for a few years after the series was dropped before becoming a fixture in low-budget horrors, usually as a benign father figure. Interestingly, he came to acting having joined the concert party in a POW camp, Stalag Luft III, where in-between concerts he helped in the famous Wooden Horse escape. His last role was on the stage in Vienna in an English language version of 'Gaslight'. He died in 1976, leaving a wife and two sons.

5. With her long black hair, green eyes and prominent cheek bones, Barbara Steele was a natural fantasy cinema icon, but in fact she fell into it by chance and spent most of the rest of her career trying to get out. Born in Birkenhead in 1937, Steele trained at the London School of Dramatic Art before making her stage debut with Robert Morley, followed by spells in rep at Brighton and Glasgow. Stardom seemed to beckon when she signed a long-term contract with J. Arthur Rank as one of the last graduates of Rank's infamous Charm School. In fact the Company couldn't find much work for her except brief roles in *Bachelor of Hearts (1958)* and *The Thirty-Nine Steps (1959)*. Later, when her contract was sold to Fox, she moved to the States. Too strong-willed to fit into a studio system, Steele's sojourn in the States was a mixed success, and she subsequently found steadier work in Italy, starting with her unforgettable role in Mario Bava's *Black Sunday (1960)*, followed by such cult classics as *The Long Hair of Death (1964)*, and *Revenge of the Blood Beast (1965)* for Michael Reeves. Steele's cinematic work wasn't confined to crypts however; Federico Fellini put her in *8 1/2 (1963)*, she appeared in Volker Schlöndorff's *Young Törless (1966)* and a dozen years later Louis Malle cast her in *Pretty Baby (1978)*. James Poe, her husband, wrote her a part in *They Shoot Horses, Don't They? (1969)* but the studio cast Susannah York instead. If she had been granted the role it may have pushed her at last into the mainstream, but instead Steele continued to trade on her cult status with roles in the likes of *Caged Heat (1974)*, *Shivers (1975)*, and *Piranha (1978)*. Then, in the Eighties, she reinvented herself again, this time as an Executive Producer for Dan Curtis on his lavish mini-series *The Winds of War* and its sequel *War and Remembrance*. In the Nineties she came to terms with the image she had been trying to shake for 30 years, popping up happily at Horror Conventions and revelling in the 'Queen of Horror' moniker that had attached itself to her name. She also had a featured role in Curtis's deservedly short-lived revival of the TV series *Dark Shadows*. When she was interviewed for Video Watchdog magazine, Steele displayed no affinity for this film: 'I just flew in and did that to pay the rent.' However, she did remember Karloff with affection: 'I adored Boris Karloff. He had nobility, a sadness and humanity about his presence. His age and his charm and his dignity were completely fantastic.'

6. Karloff was quoted in Tigon's UK pressbook as saying, 'It's ridiculous working at my age, but I have been active all my life and feel marvellous. Even though I have got bronchitis, which incidentally I caught in California, not England, and an arthritic knee which I must have come about by carrying too many bodies up stairs.'

7. Menaham Golan was born Menahem Globus in Tiberias, in 1929. The son of a Polish immigrant, he grew up on a diet of Hollywood films and from an early age aspired to be a filmmaker. He served with the Israeli air force during the 1948 struggle for independence, taking a new surname from the infamous Golan Heights as a sign of patriotic fervour. Golan later came to the UK and enrolled at the Old Vic Theatre School on a stage management course, before successfully directing several plays in Israel. He still had movies on his mind though, and he eventually up-rooted his family and moved them to the USA, where he enrolled in the New York College Film Institute. Contacts in the industry led to film work for Roger Corman on movies like *The Young Racers (1963)*, which also counted Francis Ford Coppola and Robert Towne amongst its crew. He returned to the UK in the Sixties.

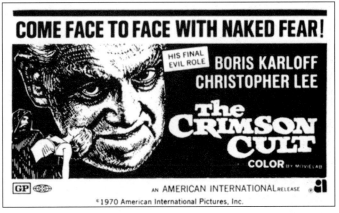

8. Wisdom was an unexpected box office draw in the Fifties and early Sixties, thanks to a series of Rank movies that capitalised on his trademark bumbling but loveable image. He was very much a British Jerry Lewis, loved by the public and generally ignored by the intelligentsia - one critic rather cruelly talked about his characters as possessing a 'bashfulness verging on mental deficiency'. Nevertheless, Wisdom enjoyed a long run of financially successful films and even as his audiences slowly dwindled, he remained a big star on television and in the West End. In the mid-Sixties he managed to transfer this success to Broadway in his one man show, 'Walking Happy', but the wider American market stubbornly failed to open up for him. Better known as a performer rather than a scriptwriter, Wisdom had in fact co-written several of his more successful films: *Follow a Star (1959)*, *The Bulldog Breed (1960)*, and *The Early Bird (1965)*. Throughout the Sixties he had established a rapport with his frequent director, the gentlemanly Robert Asher (the brother of Hammer cinematographer Jack).

9. Opened in 1866 at a cost of £60,000, the Palace Hotel occupied 20 acres of Southport sea-front and offered guests such delights as croquet lawns, bowling greens, archery fields and a 650ft promenade. It was somewhat isolated from the main town though, which contributed to a financial crisis and liquidation as early as 1871. Various efforts to revive its fortunes met with mixed success and over the years it alternated between operating as a hotel and hydropathic spa, a rest home for US servicemen, and in its later years as a 1000-room Conference Centre. Both Frank Sinatra and Clark Gable stayed there, and with its own railway station the Palace enjoyed a brief spell of popularity with fashionable Aintree race-goers. The building was abandoned in the 1960s before being demolished in 1969. Apart from the Tigon movies, one other movie was shot there; the bizarre *Ultus: The Man from the Dead (1915)*.

10. Stephen Weeks was something of a child prodigy, writing and directing television films for Southern Television while he was still at school! Passing on the opportunity to go to university, he joined J. Walter Thompson as a director of experimental cinema commercials, using this work as a base from which to launch himself into the world of feature film direction.

11. Compton had hopes that 'Beau Brigand' would make Nyasaland-born Allen a major star but it wasn't to be. In the past he had worked for

above:
Karloff's peripheral role was not reflected in the prominence of his billing or in AIP's artwork for **Curse of the Crimson Altar**. Sadly, even the actor's death did little to increase the film's box-office impact.

below:
Sexy goings on from **Love in Our Time**. Even an endorsement from a 'sex expert', Dr. Eustace Chesser (another trick from Tenser's Compton days) failed to convince the censor of the film's value as a documentary.

The BIG WINNER on ABC RELEASE

FROM TIGON

TONY TENSER PRESENTS

ELKAN ALLAN'S

LOVE IN OUR TIME

EASTMAN COLOUR

PLUS TONY TENSER PRESENTS

BORIS KARLOFF CHRISTOPHER LEE

CURSE OF THE CRIMSON ALTAR

A EASTMAN COLOUR
RELEASED BY TIGON PICTURES LTD

BOOK NOW FROM
TIGON PICTURES LIMITED
205 Wardour Street · London W1
Tel: 01-734 9743
Cables: TIGONPIX LONDON W1

above:
A very odd pairing! The two films had not been conceived as a double bill and the fact that they were ever considered as suitable partners once ready for release suggests an air of desperation.

Hitchcock on *Dial M for Murder (1954)* before going on to become a leading man in dozens of British movies, including *Never Takes Sweets from a Stranger (1960)*, and *Captain Clegg (1962)*. He had also taken the lead in the hit TV series *Crane*. Blessed with a resonant voice, he is most often recognised for his countless voiceovers, both in advertising and film dubbing (he did Leon Greene's voice in *The Devil Rides Out (1967)* and coincidentally is married to Sarah Lawson from the same film).

12. Suave, sophisticated and cynical, the 62-year-old Russian-born Sanders was a natural for handsome rakes even in his declining years. Hollywood had employed his slightly sinister manner in big-budget movies for two decades, his career reaching a pinnacle with an Oscar-winning performance in *All About Eve (1950)*. He will also be remembered for creating the original and best screen Saint. At the same time he became a firm favourite of the fan magazines and gossip columnists. A financially disastrous involvement with a Scottish meat company in the 1960's led to bankruptcy, and he was reduced to a series of 'here for the money' movies, amongst them *The Golden Head (1964)*, *One Step to Hell (1967)*, and Harry Alan Towers's *The Girl from Rio (1969)*.

13. Sanders himself could not have been more indifferent to the film, telling the press, 'I don't know what it was about. I never see any of my movies. All I know is there were some planes going over and parachutes fell out and there was a big mystery of some sort because there were no bodies. I played a General or something because I remember looking through a pair of binoculars and saying 'Good God!' and a lot of rubbish like that'.

14. Remembered only as a father/uncle figure from countless movies, Maurice Evans made his West End debut in 1929 at the age of 28. He was with the Sadlers Wells Company at the time of an acclaimed run that included 'Much Ado About Nothing' and 'Saint Joan,' before going on to Broadway and setting a record of 171 consecutive performances, which netted him the Actor of the Year award. He then had a similar success in the West End, in Hamlet, which was followed by another marathon - 131 performances of Macbeth. The televised broadcast of Macbeth won him an Emmy in 1961.

15. Born in Australia in 1909, Ashton made his movie debut working on *Tudor Rose (1936)* but he is best remembered as the make-up wizard responsible for most of the 'classic' Hammer monsters: *The Revenge of Frankenstein (1958)*, *The Curse of the Werewolf (1961)*, *The Gorgon (1964)*, and *The Reptile (1966)* are amongst his most celebrated achievements, but the list goes on. He left Hammer in the late Sixties to broaden his scope, and served on acclaimed films including *2001: A Space Odyssey (1968)*, *The Devils (1971)*, and *Star Wars (1977)*. Of course he would return to Tigon in the early Seventies for some more challenging work on *The Creeping Flesh*.

16. Born in Bolton in 1944, RADA graduate Michael Armstrong, originally trained as an actor, but after some West End work decided that he wanted to specialise more in writing and

directing. He first came to prominence of sorts with his 16mm short *The Initiate*, starring Ian Ogilvy and Simon Dee, which he followed with a couple of shorts using his friend and family as cast and crew; his most notable work during this time was *The Image*, featuring David Bowie. Directly after working for Tigon, he wrote and directed *Mark of the Devil (1969)*, a *Witchfinder General*-style epic starring Herbert Lom and Udo Kier, which was hugely controversial, and hence popular wherever it was screened. Unfortunately however, it was banned outright in Britain for decades due to its uncompromising juxtaposition of sex and violence. Disillusioned and frustrated by his experiences with Tigon and *Mark of the Devil*, Armstrong drifted away from directing and concentrated on writing, with occasional appearances in small budget exploitation movies, frequently made in association with Tudor Gates. Notable titles include *The Sex Thief (1973)*, *Eskimo Nell (1974)*, and *Adventures of a Private Eye (1977)*. *Eskimo Nell* is easily the best, and funniest, film of its type, with its scathing parody of Wardour Street in general and, allegedly Tony Tenser/Deke Heyward style producers in particular. After a spell working for TV shows like *The Professionals* and *Shoestring*, he emerged to write the unjustly neglected Pete Walker movie *House of the Long Shadows (1982)*. Armstrong also wrote and directed the Christopher Lee prologue to the video release of *The Phantom of the Opera (1925)*. In 1991 he produced Tudor Gates's play The Kidnap Game and in addition to his involvement in several theatre projects, he devotes his time to running the Armstrong Arts Academy.

17. Avalon had been a Fifties pin-up for pubescent teenagers, with a string of hits like Gingerbread and Venus to his name before transposing his talents to AIP's camp 'Beach Party' movies. Too short to be taken seriously as a leading man, he was adept at light comedy and held his own until the teen craze ran out of steam and his career faltered. Fabian, real name Fabiano Anthony Forte, came from the same teeny-bop background as Avalon, with hits including Hound Dog Man and Turn Me Loose. His film work was also restricted to drive-in fodder such as biker movies and beach flicks. His career evaporated in the mid-Sixties and he was consigned to making appearances on nostalgia revival shows and a notorious centre-spread for Playgirl magazine.

18. A former protégé of Otto Preminger, Haworth never achieved the stardom predicted for her, but she would go on to make several interesting contributions to the genre including *Tower of Evil (1971)* and *The Mutations (1973)*. She moved to the States in the Seventies and gave up acting completely until she was lured out of retirement for a part in the independent movie *Mergers and Acquisitions (2001)*.

19. The North American release would be held up for the best part of a year, during which time Karloff died. Still sporting its original title of *The Crimson Cult*, it was released on a double-bill with *The Haunted House of Horror*. AIP milked the late lamented star for all his worth with the ad-line, 'In his last and most diabolic role.' The film also boasted, 'Come face to face with naked fear on the altar of evil.'

'Far Out Sexploits in a Way Out Universe'

- (US poster, *Zeta One*)

On the 2nd of February 1969, the seemingly indestructible Boris Karloff died. He had been genuinely disappointed that he was unable to work on 'The Dark' the previous October, a reflection of his drive to keep busy. 'If I die, I'd rather be on the set,' he had said in January, and his wish very nearly came true. By that time much of the 'The Dark' had been re-shot and re-edited, and AIP were again expressing interest in the idea of exploiting Karloff's marquee value, so Gerry Levy devised a specially written prologue in the hope that the actor's health would recover sufficiently for him to take part. This was mere wishful thinking on everyone's part however, as, diagnosed a weak heart, arthritis and emphysema, he was clearly too ill to ever return to a film set.[1]

While the news hardly came as a shock to anyone who had met him in the last year of his life, Tenser was genuinely saddened by Karloff's passing: 'He was really under-rated, he never won an Oscar or got the credit he deserved. He was such a great man and a good friend to everyone, that when he died we took the front page of Today's Cinema, the main trade paper, and printed a picture of Boris with the heading, 'In Proud Memory of a Friend we have <u>ALL</u> Lost. Tony Tenser and all at Tigon.' The cover featured a still from *Curse of the Crimson Altar* but the film itself wasn't mentioned. Some weeks later Tenser even expressed a wish to build a lasting tribute to the star, proposing a new cinema in London's West End (which would have been his first venture into exhibition since leaving Compton), to be called The Karloff and committed to showing only horror movies. Permission had been obtained from Karloff himself some weeks before his death. A nice idea, but it fell by the wayside. 'I never got round to it,' Tenser says with some regret. 'Business was really taking off and I just didn't have the time to devote to it.'

If Karloff's death had been sad, it was followed by a genuine tragedy just a few days later. On the 11th of February, Michael Reeves died. Even during the filming of *Witchfinder General* Reeves hadn't been well, taking considerable quantities of prescribed medicines to counteract depression and anxiety. In late 1968 he had started pre-production for Deke Heyward on *The Oblong Box*, a conventional genre film intended, once again, as a vehicle for Vincent Price. Heyward became concerned

over Reeves's stability, and removed him from the project before shooting began. He was replaced by Gordon Hessler. Discussions had been on-going with both Tigon and AIP regarding a number of projects, but at the time of his death Reeves was working on nothing in particular. He had nothing to absorb his enormous energy and his mental state was at best fragile.

When his body was found in his London flat, there was a common assumption that he had taken his own life but those who were close to him dispute the suggestion. Nicky Henson, who had become a close friend says, 'Mike was taking a lot of pills, he had pills to get up, pills to go to bed, pills for everything - I remember on *Witchfinder* we had a pill-throwing-away-party! The night he died he went to bed, took his pills, woke up with a headache and took some more. Simple as that - a terrible accident.'

This view is shared by Tenser: 'Michael wouldn't do it deliberately, he had a nice girlfriend and he had money of his own, he came from a very wealthy family. He had been depressed and had various prescriptions but he had his whole future ahead of him and he knew that. He wouldn't have killed himself.' In fact, Reeves had been involved in a similar incident six months earlier, when he collapsed after taking five Nembutal capsules with alcohol and was found unconscious by his cleaning lady. At the inquest, Reeves's doctor expressed the view that he was trying to attract attention, going on to add that Reeves was a man prone to dramatic or theatrical actions, saying, 'these gestures were made to draw attention to himself because he felt he was

below:
Michael Reeves, Tony Tenser and Boris Karloff on the set of **The Sorcerers**. The director had contract offers from both Tigon and AIP at the time of his death.

above:
Some of the sexy
goings on from Tigon's
Zeta One. The girl
being manhandled is
Carol Hawkins.

below:
A suitably psychedelic
Tony Tenser shares a
moment with star Yutte
Stensgaard on the set
of **Zeta One**.

unable to cope.' It seems likely that Reeves was in a depressed state of mind but had no intention of inflicting any serious damage on himself. The Westminster Coroner recorded a verdict of accidental death.

Reeves's death didn't receive anything like the press attention given to Karloff. In a small obituary printed in CinemaTV Today, Tenser was quoted saying, 'He was a brilliant, young director of the calibre the industry can ill-afford to lose.' The irony of course is that Reeves had already caught the attention of Hollywood; apart from the AIP projects, John Coquillon recalled that Reeves had been sent an early draft of the script that was destined to become *Easy Rider*. Tragically, Reeves's early death has ensured that he is now remembered only for

his contribution to one genre when he clearly had the potential to have gone on to become one of the great cinema directors.

For a while, Tigon's world was over-shadowed by the deaths of Boris Karloff and Michael Reeves, but by the end of February the company had already shot their first film of 1969. Appropriately enough, for the year that marked the end of the psychedelic sixties, it was a very strange one indeed.

Tenser had been approached some months earlier by George Maynard - a film producer whose past credits were as varied as Michael Powell's *A Canterbury Tale (1944)*, and *The Strange World of Planet X (1958)* - with a script called *Zeta One*. A shrewd entrepreneur, Maynard looked on as studios such as Pinewood and Shepperton struggled to make money while wrestling with their fixed overheads and huge permanent payrolls. There was more and more demand to produce work for televi-sion, and the Pinewoods of the world couldn't reduce their prices far enough to attract the new generation of directors and producers who were supplying this market.

Maynard invested in the construction of a new complex, located in Camden and comprised of two small stages, cutting rooms etc., it was ideal for independent television, advertising and film producers who wanted state of the art facilities in the centre of London, at a fraction of the cost of hiring major studios. Even before building work had finished, Maynard was looking for a suitable project to launch the Camden Studios and had teamed up with a wannabe director called Michael Cort, who had approached him with his *Zeta One* script. Cort's film, which he described as 'a mixture of cartoon and live action', drew its inspira-tion from a bizarre photo-story comic strip, a sexy sci-fi fusion of Barbarella and Playboy's Little Annie Fanny that was running in the ultra-hip anti-establishment magazine Zeta.

The movers and shakers on Wardour Street weren't amused, and there were no takers until Maynard arrived at Tenser's offices. Comedy, sex, action and a host of scantily clad publicity hungry starlets - it seemed a natural for the ever-adventurous Tigon. The script, written by Cort in associ-ation with Alistair McKenzie, follows the activities of Britain's top secret agent, James Word, as he attempts to outwit thigh-booted, mini-skirt wearing alien vixens from the planet Angvia, who are bent on kidnap-ping nubile wenches from earth for reasons best known to themselves. To make matters worse, bondage-obsessed criminal master mind Major Bourdon and his henchman Swyne intend to exploit the situation to launch their own plans for world domina-tion. In one delirious package, Cort and McKenzie had appropriated elements of Bond, Barbarella and Modesty Blaise, to produce an intoxicating new brew! Surely only Tony Tenser could keep a straight face when telling the press that his next movie was, 'a space-age-strip-girlie-thriller!'

Budgetary limitations were never going to allow Cort to become the adult world's equivalent of Walt Disney and mix live actors with animation; it was a time-consuming and expensive process well beyond Tigon's reach. Therefore Cort pragmatically instructed art director Martin Gascoigne to recreate the look of the original strip with surreal sets and extravagant costumes, designed specifically to evoke a cartoon-like feel. It was an ambitious plan and to do it full justice the art department alone would have consumed a small fortune. Tigon, without the safety net of a production partner, had allocated around £60,000 for the entire production - or less than the cost of a single set on *2001: A Space Odyssey (1968)*.

Maynard and Cort were forced to compromise. Earthbound locations (filmed at Denham) substituted for alien landscapes, while the alien outfits themselves consisted of little more than glitter and pasties. Gascoigne did manage to improvise some futuristic sets but it was obvious, by the time the frankly kiddie-matinee standard constructions were squeezed into Camden's cramped facilities, that Cort would struggle to suggest anything even vaguely substantial. Problems also arose over the facilities at Camden Studios themselves, which comprised of two adjacent houses in Albert Street that had been converted into a pair of sound stages. Workmen were actually still on site even as the film geared up for shooting; dressing rooms and administra-

tive offices would remain only partly finished throughout the shoot, lending the set a chaotic air that frustrated both cast and crew.

Given the subject matter, Cort managed to assemble a surprisingly respectable cast for his debut feature. The leading role of Word went to Robin Hawdon, who had just finished duties on *When Dinosaurs Ruled the Earth (1969)*. Imogen Hassall, who had worked alongside Hawdon on the same film, was signed for the crucial role of Edwina Strain, a stripper used by Bourdon to infiltrate the Angvians. Though she hadn't made many films, Hassall, dubbed the 'countess of cleavage' by the salivating Sun newspaper, was very much a one-woman media event who guaranteed much needed press coverage for the film. When the animation sequences were dropped and the nudity element was beefed up, Hassall found herself being asked to show more flesh than she felt comfortable with, and promptly withdrew.[2] Unknown model Wendy Lingham was less squeamish and joined the cast just before shooting started.

Heading up the villains was British acting institution James Roberston Justice, better known from the popular series of 'Doctor' films in the Fifties and Sixties.[3] Originally, Justice was due to be aided and abetted by another actor better known for comedy roles, Frankie Howerd. Agreement had been reached with the actor on the delicate questions of billing and remuneration, and there is no doubt that the film would have been enlivened by Howerd's nudge-nudge brand of humour, but it wasn't to be. 'We had a scheduling problem,' says Tenser, 'which we could have probably worked around and certainly Frankie was keen but his agent used it to talk him out of it.' Howerd was replaced by another refugee from the *Carry On* series, Charles Hawtrey, who played the appropriately named Swyne.[4]

above:
Tony Tenser and James Robertson Justice on the set of **Zeta One**. The actor hated the experience and later refused to talk to the press or otherwise help publicise the film.

left:
It's tempting to think this was an attempt to save on the costume budget; an Angvian Amazon from **Zeta One**.

above:
An example of the enthusiastic British artwork produced to promote the release of **Zeta One**. The film would later be dubbed 'the worst British movie ever made!'

below:
The busty Angvians in one of Michael Cort's stylish and provocative but ultimately pointless sequences.

Even after Hassall bowed out, Cort could count himself lucky where his female cast was concerned. Respected actress Dawn Addams, who had worked for Chaplin and Lang, stayed fully-clothed but brought considerable dignity to the film, while Euro sex-kitten Anna Gael guaranteed some press attention.[5] Along for the ride were a crowd of starlets including the likes of Valerie Leon, Kirsten Betts, Carolanne Hawkins and Brigitte Skay.

Behind the camera, George Mills headed up the Tigon crew, working for Tenser as production manager for the last time - these production chores would later be assumed by Christopher Neame, the son of director Ronald Neame and an experienced production manager in his own right. Tenser and Maynard shared the producer chores.

'Our Word's as good as their Bond,' wise-cracked George Maynard to the Daily Cinema. Optimism was high as Cort took his crew onto the floor at Camden on the 19th of January 1969 to start the five-week shoot. In the same interview, Maynard accepted that the idea of a comic secret agent had been tried before but, he pointed out, 'rarely with enough humour. Some of them may be done light-heartedly enough but the hero is still very much the accomplished, triumphant hero. Ours is a complete idiot.'

To give the impression of more expansive sets, Cort was forced to re-shoot his interiors from different angles and during the constant redressing of the studio James Robertson Justice became increasingly disillusioned with the project. His bad mood wasn't helped by the half-finished changing-rooms and improvised canteen facilities. 'He really wasn't that interested, he was used to making big budget films at Pinewood and really didn't want to do it,' Tenser recalls. 'It was towards the end of his career and he kept forgetting his lines. Sitting at a table he would have the script written on his trouser leg, his lines would be all over the place because he couldn't remember them, or at least they wrote up the parts he didn't think he would remember.' When a reporter for the Daily Mirror was invited onto the set to prepare a feature on the film, Justice irritated the producers by refusing point blank to speak to him. Dawn Addams on the other hand was only too pleased to talk, dismissing the suggestion that the film was going too far by proclaiming, 'It's just a spoof.' Addams also commented on the alternative stronger scenes being shot for the European version: 'I understand that they are involved with torture and nude scenes, but I never took part in those so I don't know much about them. I hope nobody takes them seriously.' The European version showed the girls topless, while they wore nipple pasties when scenes were being shot for the British version. James Robertson Justice and Charles Hawtrey featured impassively in these shots, with the likes of Brigitte Skay and Carolanne Hawkins providing the glamour.

From the outset the filmmakers were fighting an uphill battle, something that Tenser now recognises: 'It could have been very good, certainly very funny but we simply didn't have enough money to do it properly and it showed when the film was pulled together.' By the time principal photography drew to a close, the cast and crew were sick of the claustrophobic atmosphere of Camden and anxious to move on to more dignified pursuits, but George Mills was already raising warning flags over the amount of film they actually had in the can.

By the time editor Jack Knight had assembled the first cut, Maynard and Tenser were forced to accept that they had miscalculated; Zeta One ran to a little over 60 minutes, reasonable perhaps for a support feature but hardly what Tenser expected. Worse still, in the effort to extend the running time as much as possible the plot, which was never entirely straight-forward, had gone from muddled to completely incomprehensible. 'Tony once said to me that if a film had a beginning, a middle and an end he could sell it to someone,' Christopher Neame recalls, 'Unfortunately with Zeta One we barely had a middle!'

Neame had joined Tigon as the company's resident production controller,

JAMES ROBERTSON JUSTICE
CHARLES HAWTREY
ROBIN HAWDON   ANNA GAEL

with BRIGITTE SKAY
and guest star DAWN ADDAMS

ZETA ONE
EASTMAN COLOUR   x

PRODUCED BY TIGON BRITISH FILM PRODUCTIONS
RELEASED BY TIGON PICTURES LTD.

and his first assignment was to make something usable out of Cort's footage. Neame remembers, 'Tony screened what he had for *Zeta One*, I think this was on my first or second day at Tigon. My first reaction was, 'oh my God what I have I let myself in for?'' Neame was given a small budget and a free hand to shoot a wrap-around sequence to spin the film out. 'I always seem to get credited with writing a beginning and end, probably because no-one else will admit it, 'Neame insists. 'I can say categorically it wasn't me, I am not sure who did but I did oversee the additional shooting.' It was Neame who brought in Vernon Sewell to shoot the book-ends involving the Word character recounting his adventures to his bosses' nubile secretary. Apart from extending the running time, the other aim of these sequences was to hopefully clarify some of the film's more obscure plot points! Perhaps appropriately the name of the actual writer of the sequences is lost in the mists of time. Sewell himself can shed no light: 'I can't remember anything about that film, ' he says with a broad smile, 'that's the advantage of being so old, your memory goes. Maybe it was Tony, who cares!'

Of the main cast, only Hawdon was available and there was no time to arrange a formal casting session so Maynard spoke to the agent Ronald Curtis, father of art designer on *The Sorcerers*, Tony Curtis. One of the actresses he proposed for the work was his daughter-in-law Yutte Stensgaard, later to become one of Hammer's most memorable vampires but at that stage still merely a promising, if beautiful, starlet with a few television credits to her name. Yutte may have been an open-minded Scandinavian, but she clearly wasn't fully convinced about the idea of a space-age-strip-girlie-thriller, as Tenser recalls: 'Yutte came to see me in my office, very upset, and said that she didn't realise that there was full frontal nudity and she couldn't do it. We had her under contract of course but I wouldn't have forced that sort of thing on her. We talked about it for a while and finally she agreed. It was for the briefest of shots though, hardly anything.'*6*

With the new scenes completed, there was still some re-shooting and re-dubbing required in order to try and straighten out the narrative of the main story. Even if he had been available, James Robertson Justice would have been loathe to return so Neame had to find a way of working around him. In conjunction with editor Dennis Lanning, he re-cut the movie, filming some inserts with a body double standing in for Justice and using a voice artist to re-dub his lines!

above:
Sexy British front of house still for **Zeta One** suggesting a **Barbarella** approach by director Michael Cort.

above:
Wisdom and Geeson
look like they are having
fun, but the film itself
struggled to find an
audience.

WHAT'S GOOD FOR THE GOOSE

*'What's Norman Doing That He Has
Never Done Before?'*
- UK Press Release -

Synopsis

When the manager of a City bank collapses at the office, his last request is for the branch's assistant manager, Bartlett, to replace him at the 'Banker's Conference' in Southport. With the manager's dying words - 'watch the expenses' - ringing in his ears, Bartlett leaves his dreary suburban life, his wife and children and sets off for Southport. On the way he picks up two teenage hitchhikers who introduce him to the delights of pop music and speeding. Bartlett forms a bond with one of the girls, Nikki. Some time later, they meet up by chance at a night club and Nikki suggests they go back to Bartlett's hotel; 'after all,' she coos, 'You want it don't you!' As Bartlett becomes more infatuated with Nikki and her free lifestyle, he becomes less inclined to play the corporate game.

Critique

'...a sad, bad failure. The story is tediously predictable and repetitious.'
- News of the World, 23/03/69

'It is in every way the most embarrassing, horrific and painful film I have seen in many a long year.'
- The Observer, 23/03/69

'Altogether repulsive.'
- Dylis Powell, The Sunday Times, 23/03/69

'...it's a vulgar, inept, graceless anecdote.'
- The Sunday Telegraph, 23/03/69

While the re-structuring of *Zeta One* was taking place, Tenser was pondering how to get the best from *What's Good for the Goose*. *Here We Go Round the Mulberry Bush* (1967) and *Prudence and the Pill* (1968) - both starring Judy Geeson - had featured prominently in the UK box-office charts for 1968, and Tenser was confident that Tigon could tap into the same market by emphasising their new film's adult content and youth orientated humour. As luck would have it Sally Geeson had in the meantime signed a contract with AIP to appear in *The Oblong Box*, and was already being hailed as the next big thing. In March 1969, a trade screening of the toned-down British version was arranged at the Sapphire preview theatre, next door to Hammer House in Wardour Street. The reaction was hardly enthusiastic but Tenser nevertheless managed to secure a wide circuit release through ABC, and *What's Good for the Goose* was unveiled to the nation on the 13th of April 1969.

above:
This shot was later
adapted for the British
quad poster, with
Geeson allowed to
protect her modesty
with a sheet held across
her breasts.

right:
Wisdom and Geeson on
location for **What's
Good for the Goose**,
on Southport pier.

above:
What's Good for the Goose was the film that effectively ended Norman Wisdom's film career. Given his fashion sense that may not have been such a bad thing.

'*Wisdom veering as always between pathos and manic comedy, is neither funny nor appealing in a piece that, quite honestly, made me feel rather ill.*'
- The Sun, 19/03/69

'*It is monumentally unfunny and rather nasty.*'
- The Daily Express, 21/03/69

Even playing a successful banker, Wisdom can't escape the perennial outsider/loser tag and *What's Good for the Goose* simply isn't the radical departure that the public were led to expect. Wisdom still hides behind the low-brow slapstick, silly voices and mugging; the 'new' Norman gets down to his Y-fronts with disturbing regularity but otherwise its more of the same old thing. The film itself suffers badly from the underwritten script; the satirical element consists of some establishing shots of regiments of bowler-hatted bankers and of course the revelation that middle-aged men are womanising drunks, snobs and hypocrites. Youths apparently all dress garishly, drink coca-cola unless someone else is buying, and spout banalities like, 'come on folks lets have a rave-up on the beach!' The script is hackneyed and insipid, and Golan's direction is as uninspired, as is Wisdom's performance. Only Sally Geeson, as the giggling Nikki, adds any life and effortlessly steals every scene; the film totally runs out of energy whenever she isn't in shot.

Tenser hoped that an Easter release would attract the holiday crowds and the Tigon sales team, pitching the film as a broadminded 'adult' comedy, relied heavily on Wisdom to sell the film. The UK poster was typical, featuring its star naked to the waist in bed with a coyly-smiling Sally Geeson - a sales drive completely undermined by the film's 'U' certificate.

The reception awaiting *What's Good for the Goose*, even in the provinces where audiences were generally deemed to be not particularly sophisticated, was best described as 'disappointing.' If the returns in the UK were patchy, in North America, where the title was inexplicably changed to *What's Good for the Gander*, it was even worse.[7] Wisdom's participation in the film was bordering on monopolistic - not only did he star, he also picked up credits for script and production, and warbled his way through Reg Tilsley's inane theme

below:
What's Good for the Goose was the first Tigon film to feature the principal actors in a nude sequence.

tune. Any hopes the actor still retained that the film would revive his screen career were quickly dashed; in fact the poor reception by both the critics and public all but killed his screen career.[8] Wisdom returned to the stage and television, where he was still considered a major star.

Sally Geeson fared slightly better. 'Deke' Heyward cast her in a couple of his horror movies and, although never quite making it as a star, she enjoyed a varied career over the next decade.[9] Menahem Golan of course went on to bigger, though not necessarily better, things when he founded the infamous Cannon group with his cousin, Yoram Globus.[10]

* * * *

Tenser sought to distract attention from *What's Good for the Goose* by setting up a trade screening of *Zeta One* in April 1969. The addition of the fresh sequences had brought the running time up to a more respectable 82 minutes, and although the film was still confusing, the new cut was some improvement. 'It wasn't my best film,' Tenser concedes wryly, 'but it wasn't altogether a bad film.' More importantly at least it was releasable and the film's chosen market certainly seemed interested. Cinema X ran a colour feature with several revealing stills, and Continental magazine - 'film reviews for the aware audience' - were impressed enough with Brigitte Skay's costume, or lack thereof, to run a cover feature.

below:
In a scene intended for the 'continental version' of **Zeta One**, 'Carry On' star Charles Hawtrey seems distracted while James Robertson Justice shows some passing interest in this unfortunate starlet's semi-naked body.

ZETA ONE

'It's Sexcitement in Time and Space'
- UK press release -

Synopsis

Over a light-hearted game of strip poker with his boss's secretary Ann, top secret agent James Word discusses his latest mission. Word had been instructed by his superior, 'W', to monitor the activities of arch-villain Major Bourdon who, together with his side-kick Swyne, had been trying to infiltrate the alien world of Angvia. Zeta, Queen of Angvia, has for some time been kidnapping earth women with the assistance of an army of Amazonian assassins, and turning them into Angvians. Edwina Strain, an undercover agent for Bourdon, gets kidnapped by the aliens and taken back to their planet. Zeta exposes the plot and dispatches her army to destroy Bourdon.

Critique

'...crude send up of the Bond films, overtly designed to appeal to insatiable voyeurs with kinky leanings... A parade of sub standard pin-ups in sado-masochistic array enlivened only by the vivacity and warm sensuality of Anna Gael.'
- The Daily Cinema, 17/04/69

'Some of the sequences are more than a little silly but generally speaking it is fairly entertaining nonsense on a small scale.'
- Kine Weekly, 18/04/70

Even with the inclusion of the new book-ending sequences it is hard to work out exactly what Cort had in mind. The film remains confusing and fragmented, comprising of little more than agent Word's energetic couplings intermingled with lightweight torture sequences and some far-out fashions. A more experienced director could possibly have made something out of it - one can image Val Guest, for example, at least injecting some fun - but Cort is simply out of his depth. In fairness the director wasn't helped by the performances of his leading players; a touch of self-deprecating humour would have done wonders, but no-one rose to the challenge. Dawn Addams at least has the decency to look embarrassed, but by far the worst offender is top-billed James Robertson Justice. Clearly indifferent to the whole farrago, he can't even bring himself to hold his eye line in-between mumbling his lines.

What the film lacks in wit it tries to make up for in sex, filling the screen with as many jiggling bosoms as possible in an effort to distract audiences from the thread-bare production values. The sets show some imagination but they fail to make up for the shortcomings of the film as a whole. A lively

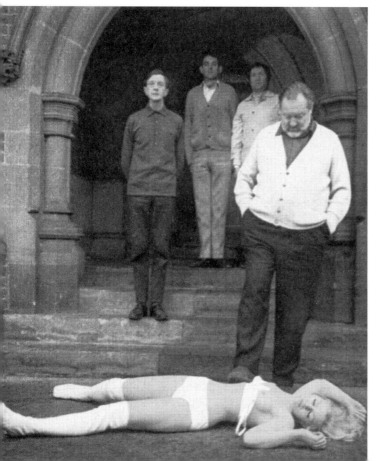

score by Johnny Hawksworth, best known for the theme tune to the animated children's series *Roobarb*, is wasted.

No sooner had the film surfaced than Tigon decided to put it on the shelf. Tenser accepted that neither *Zeta One* nor *What's Good for the Goose* had worked out: 'These were movies which I felt had sufficiently low budget to take a risk on. *Zeta One* turned out all right but not as good as I hoped and not really the way I wanted. They were something a bit out of the ordinary and I thought they would go well for the market we were looking at.' Tigon tinkered with the film off and on over the course of the next few months in an effort to try and get it into a releasable state, but Tenser had accepted that a circuit release was out of the question so the search was on to find an appropriate independent cinema to show the film, hopefully on an extended run. In the meantime Tenser showed that, provided certain components were right, there was no such thing as an unsaleable movie. *Zeta One*, taken out of circulation for the time being in its country of birth, was snapped up by the Americans and released variously as 'Alien Women' and 'The Love Factor.'[11]

What's Good for the Goose and *Zeta One* highlighted the risks associated with using inexperienced directors, a trait that had become something of a trademark for Tenser over the years. Other British companies, big and small, would hire first time directors but none as consistently as Tigon, and the policy had brought the likes of Michael Reeves and Stephen Weeks to the screen - though of course it had also resulted in some less auspicious efforts. Tenser remains characteristically modest about his preference for younger directors: 'I didn't hire these chaps because I was a saint or anything. There were sound financial reasons. It really is as simple as that. If they got something out of it all the better.'

*   *   *   *   *

Despite the disappointments of Tigon's two most recent productions, business was booming at the company, and the offices at 205 Wardour Street could no longer accommodate the growing army of sales, secretarial and creative staff. On the 25th of April, Tenser undertook his third move since leaving Compton, into 113/117 Wardour Street - Hammer House. Tigon Film Distributors took over the whole of the ground floor, which afforded them a much larger suite of offices and the opportunity to use the huge shop-front windows to display their lurid posters. Tenser and his administrative staff took over the third floor, where they were joined by the company's film production staff and the overseas distribution arm.

The second floor of the building was still the corporate head office of Hammer

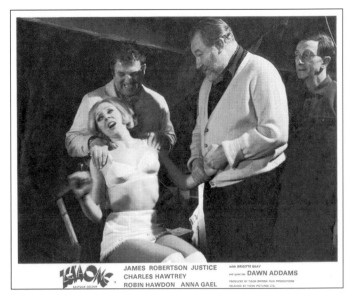

JAMES ROBERTSON JUSTICE
CHARLES HAWTREY
ROBIN HAWDON   ANNA GAEL
with BRIGITTE SKAY
and special star DAWN ADDAMS
PRODUCED BY TIGON BRITISH FILM PRODUCTIONS
RELEASED BY TIGON PICTURES LTD.

above:
Carolanne Hawkins (later Carol Hawkins) is tortured in the British print of **Zeta One**; the continental version had the same scene, but played topless.

Films, and housed the office of James Carreras himself. Leslie Grade, brother of industry titans Lew Grade and Bernard Delfont, occupied the top floor. Leslie Grade was a former partner in Delfont's Grade Organisation, later EMI, who had been Compton's principal rivals in their bid for British Lion. Ill-health had forced him to 'retire' to the world of talent agencies and Grade's office would become something of an oasis of calm for Tenser, away from the hurly-burly on the third floor. 'Leslie was a lovely man,' Tenser remembers, 'He would call me up for a coffee and we would have long chats about the industry, what he was up to what I was up to and so on. I think he just liked a chat.' The Grade family of course never did anything half-heartedly, and in between his friendly chats Leslie built up an agency representing such luminaries as Susan Hampshire, Dirk Bogarde and Paul Scofield.

Tigon's new windows were swiftly adorned with posters for 'The Dark', *What's Good for the Goose* and, still on national release, *Curse of the Crimson Altar* but the difficulties experienced on the Armstrong film had soiled the relationship between AIP and Tigon, so Tigon's 'forthcoming' board was noticeably lacking in terms of the promised co-productions. Tenser had wanted the two companies to collaborate on AIP's version of 'The Gold Bug', originally floated as an adventure/mystery project for Compton and now presented as a vehicle for Vincent Price. Nicholson and Arkoff were much less keen following the difficulties encountered during the making of 'The Dark' however and, with a number of English producers queuing up to get hold of Heyward's dollars, 'The Gold Bug' was quietly dropped. Price was sidelined into other projects and the option for AIP to co-produce more films under their agreement with Tigon was never exercised.[12]

below:
Robin Hawdon and Anna Gael in **Zeta One**.

above:
Sibylla Kay, in the title role of **Monique**, is visited on set by Tony Tenser and future wife Diane.

below:
Monique was the first British film to feature a *ménage a trois*. Actor David Sumner is sandwiched between Joan Alcorn (left) and Sibylla Kay (right).

AIP went on to develop a close relationship with Milton Subotsky and Max Rosenberg over at Amicus and also worked, for a short time, with Hammer. Without a regular production partner Tenser had to return to the tried and tested method of financing each film on a one-off basis. He blew the dust off an old project he had on hand, and decided that he would like the next Tigon production to be a murder mystery entitled 'The Maze'. His director of choice was Michael Armstrong, now rested after the rigours of 'The Dark' and keen to get back to work. Armstrong's own preference however was for a new synopsis he submitted called 'Kinky Death', a black comedy, which Tenser liked and had optioned. But before Tenser had a chance to commit, Armstrong accepted an offer to go to Germany in order to direct *Mark of the Devil*, a horror movie very much in the vein of *Witchfinder General*. The two men informally agreed to get to work on 'Kinky Death' after Armstrong had finished his German assignment.

Early in the spring of 1969, Tony Tenser received a script from Al Parker, an actors' agent, called 'North East Confidential'. Written by the actor John Bown, it was the story of a French au pair who, having come to work for an English couple, seduces first the wife, then the husband, then both together, naturally transforming their lives in the process. In March 1969, *The Killing of Sister George*, starring Beryl Reid and Susannah York, brought overt lesbianism into mainstream British cinema for the first time. The press worked itself into a frenzy over some very mild gay caresses and the impact on the box-office was predictably staggering. The British film industry had grown up considerably since the early days of *Naked - As Nature Intended* but one rule still applied - sex sells tickets.

'Sister George had been a huge hit because it had a 20-second lesbian kiss,' Christopher Neame explains, 'There was a feeling in Wardour Street, and probably still is, that if you double the length of the kiss you will double the box-office!' Tenser immediately saw the commercial possibilities of a *ménage a trois* and passed a copy of the hot new script to independent producer Michael Style asking if he would be interested in producing the film on behalf of Tigon. He readily agreed. (Incidentally, Style later founded Fantale Films along with Tudor Gates and Harry Fine - producer of *The Pleasure Girls*. Fantale were destined to be responsible for the likes of *The Vampire Lovers (1970)* and *Lust for a Vampire (1970)*.)

As an actor, John Bown had appeared mainly on the stage and also had some television experience. His directing career up to that point was limited to an eleven minute short called *North-West Confidential*; the title of Bown's new script was derived from this. Bown insisted that the deal with Tigon was conditional on him directing the film and the fledgling director tried to assuage the fears of the Tigon management by screening a copy of his short. Bown's plan wasn't entirely successful; neither Style nor Tenser was completely sold on the idea of allowing him to direct a feature film, but as always the investment wasn't huge so they knew they could afford to take a gamble.

Bown was very much on probation: 'At first it was a bit stressful, I knew Tony could have me off the film on two days notice. After a few days shooting, with good reports coming back from their production manager, they relaxed a bit.' One thing the producers didn't know was that Bown had written the script specifi-

above:
After the massive success of **The Killing of Sister George**, Tenser believed that the lesbianism in **Monique** was potential box-office dynamite.

left:
Bill (David Sumner) helps the au pair Monique (Sibylla Kay) with the Christmas decorations, in one of the more sedate scenes from John Bown's **Monique**.

cally for his wife Sibylla Kay, a trained actress who had also appeared in *North-West Confidential.*[13] 'We had all the little starlets of the day come in to to read for the film,' Bown recalls. 'All probably very beautiful middle-aged designers now, they all came through the door and did their bit. I just sent Sibylla in to Michael Style. I didn't say who she was, I think I might have said, 'this is the one for me - what do you think?' He obviously thought she had something - he took her for lunch!'

The script had been partly inspired by an au pair who had stayed with the Bown's some years earlier, and the family connection was strengthened when he cast his youngest daughter, Nicola, as one of the children of the household. The Bown's eldest daughter Maya had a small part in the playground scene. Even the family dog got in on the act! Also in the cast was David Sumner, a friend of the Bowns and a successful stage and television actor in his own right. Joan Alcorn was previously unknown but was cast after reading for the part. Tenser put forward Carol Hawkins (formerly Carolanne Hawkins) for the lead as he thought she had turned in good performances in *The Body Stealers* and *Zeta One*. She lost out to Kay but impressed Michael Style enough to secure a small role as 'girl in the pub.'

With a modest budget, even by Tigon's standards, of only £51,000 at his disposal and a five week shooting schedule, the fledgling director was expected to produce four and a half minutes of footage per day, quite a daunting task. In the early days of pre-production Bown found his producers exercising their prerogative. Tenser installed his new production manager Christopher Neame (George Mills having moved on to pastures new), and Michael Style insisted employing on the veteran cinematographer Moray Grant, Hammer's cameraman on such films as *Kiss of the Vampire (1963)* and *The Plague of the Zombies (1966)*. Both men were to play an important part in supporting the newcomer: 'Chris was beautiful, very experienced and did a good job. He understood that there were some scenes I would knock off very quickly, the straight-forward ones in order to meet the deadline. He then left me more time to shoot the scenes that really mattered. Moray Grant was terrific. I had no technical experience at all, I couldn't take a snapshot let alone talk about filters and lighting. I couldn't have done it without Moray.'

'North East Confidential' started shooting on the 16th of June at Isleworth studios in West London, later moving on to tackle location work in the Hounslow and Black Park areas. Bown managed to secure the use of Craven Cottage stadium for a night shoot which afforded Sibylla an unusual claim to fame: 'Fulham Football Club allowed us one night shooting at their ground. There is something special about the 'Cottage' and Sibylla is the only woman to have kept goal there!'

Of course, you couldn't have a sex film without sex. Filming the nude scenes was a little more daunting, as Kay recalls: 'I remember pacing the floor the night before, I was terribly worried. When it actually came to filming everybody was so professional and the fear just went. It was a closed set of course so even the producer wasn't allowed in. He was left panting at the door!' Bown remembers the humour on set: 'Michael Style pretended to be very put out

TIGON PRESENTS GEORGE SANDERS A TIGON-BRITISH SAGITTARIUS PRODUCTION
MAURICE EVANS PATRICK ALLEN HILARY DWYER
"THE BODY STEALERS" (A)
Introducing LORNA WILDE with Guest Stars ROBERT FLEMYNG and NEIL CONNERY
PRODUCED BY TONY TENSER DIRECTED BY GERRY LEVY EASTMAN COLOUR

above:
Allan Cuthbertson as the man from the Ministry engages in some overtime with his secretary, played by Sally Faulkner.

below:
Statuesque Lorna Wilde as the mysterious alien Lorna from **The Body Stealers**.

when we cleared the set. The crew who needed to be there stayed obviously and after we finished Michael came bursting in and shouted up to the lighting guy, 'what was it like, Charlie?' 'I don't know boss, I was too busy crawling around on all fives!'

Filming wrapped on time and within budget, but Bown's determination to treat sex with humour and as a normal part of family life caused difficulties both with Tigon and the censors. Generally speaking, Trevelyan was open to the idea of pushing back sexual boundaries and certainly the depiction of lesbianism wasn't something that held any great terrors for the BBFC secretary. *Therese and Isabelle*, starring Anna Gael, had been passed largely uncut in May 1969, Trevelyan being of the opinion that the two girls enjoyed a happy and fulfilling relationship, and the film did well on the UK art-house circuit. *The Killing of Sister George* represented the opposite side of the argument, at least as far as the BBFC was concerned. Trevelyan was less worried about the fleeting nudity and more by the theme of two sexually dominant middle-aged women competing to take advantage of an innocent, slightly simple, young girl. The brief lesbian clinch had been added as an afterthought by the film's director Robert Aldrich, whose interest was commercial rather than artistic. He argued strongly against the substantial cuts that were initially demanded, and Trevelyan accepted the director's arguments, eventually imposing only slight trims. The controversy guaranteed that *Sister George* made a far greater impression than would otherwise have been expected for what was, fundamentally, a rather stagy low budget film. Trevelyan resented the way that the director had used lesbianism to boost his box-office returns and was determined that he wasn't going to be caught out again. Bown was caught in the backlash and the effort to accommodate Trevelyan yet still meet the demands of a commercial film delayed the UK release of Bown's film for more than a year.

*　　*　　*　　*　　*

Trevelyan also imposed his will on 'Thin Air', or 'Invasion X' as it was now called. When Levy's cut was first submitted the censor awarded it an 'X' certificate. Tigon duly snipped most of Lorna Wilde's midnight skinny dip and a few seconds of Hilary Dwyer's energetic screaming, and the resubmitted film was passed as an 'A'. Tenser felt that the title still lacked a certain something, so he conjured up the suitably evocative *The Body Stealers*.[14]

The market for family movies was at its strongest by far during the summer months. The biggest Hollywood movies were traditionally released in late July and early August. Tenser argued that *The Body Stealers* would go down well with holiday-makers, but couldn't hold its own if put up against the mainstream blockbusters, so he decided to release the film in the early part of the summer when the competition was thinner on the ground. Tigon distributors already had the rights to a low-budget science-fiction thriller called *Mission Mars*, coincidentally also from a script by *The Body Stealers*' Mike St. Clair and starring one-time AIP contract player Nick Adams. Selling the double-bill offered Tigon an usual challenge. Adams, who had starred with Karloff in AIP's *Die, Monster, Die!* (1965), had died of a drug overdose only five days after Karloff had passed away. Wary that the actor's demise may spoil the holiday atmosphere, Tigon's publicity focused on his only part of any real note, in *Rebel Without a Cause* (1955), and simply ignored the fact that he was dead! There was, however, a much bigger problem looming.

Released as it was on the back of global fascination with the Apollo space programme, Stanley Kubrick's hugely influential *2001: A Space Odyssey* (1968), had upped the ante considerably in the arena of cinematic science-fiction. In Britain the tabloid build-up to the July moon shot had been elbowing everything else out of the headlines for months. Suddenly *The Body Stealers*, rooted in a Fifties-style alien invasion scenario, seemed quaintly old-fashioned. Ever resourceful however, Tigon opted to go with the flow and exercised some creative license, dubbing their double-bill 'the first ever great OUTER SPACE PROGRAMME'. Stretching the truth a little to emphasise the point, the poster for *The Body Stealers* was designed to 'suggest' Patrick Allen appeared in the role of an astronaut!

THE BODY STEALERS

'Out of Thin Air, Came a Terror
to Destroy the World!'
- UK Press Release -

Synopsis

Routine testing of experimental parachutes by the military is interrupted when the three 'paramen' mysteriously disappear. The only clue is an eerie sound that filled the air shortly before the soldiers disappeared. Some miles away at an air show, a free fall display team is the next victim of the mysterious attack. Jim Radford, the parachute designer, and General Armstrong, who had collaborated on the military tests, are instructed by the Government to conduct a thorough but discrete enquiry. They decide to bring in special investigator Bob Megan, formerly with the American Air Force and now a freelance trouble shooter.

Critique

'Any incidental tension is frittered away in the unintentional humour of scripting absurd-ities. Johnny Coquillon's often attractive photography is wasted on some very indiff-erent sets. And despite the efforts of Patrick Allen, George Sanders, and in particular Hilary Dwyer, disbelief is not suspended for one moment of the film's lengthy 90 minutes.'
- Films and Filming, 10/69

'Adequately exciting by fits and starts... Reliable undemanding capers for the school holidays.'
- The Daily Cinema, 13/06/69

above:
American admat for **The Body Stealers**. The film was also known as **Thin Air** and **Invasion of the Body Stealers**.

top left:
Hilary Dwyer, who made her debut in **Witchfinder General**, also gets lots to scream about in **The Body Stealers**. Sadly, despite appearances, the scene is a lot less interesting than it would appear.

below:
Robert Flemyng (centre) returned to Tigon for **The Body Stealers** along with George Sanders and Carl Rigg in uniform, and Hilary Dwyer, fretting over Patrick Allen.

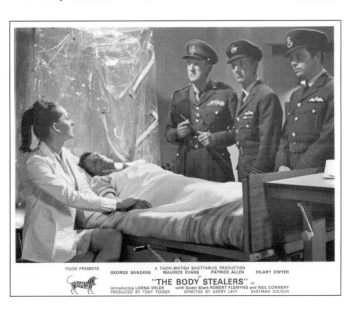

above:
Rare contact sheet showing star Patrick Allen on location during the making of **The Body Stealers**. Allen would later concede that he had no idea what his character was actually doing throughout the film.

Despite an energetic performance from Patrick Allen and some inspired screaming from Hilary Dwyer, *The Body Stealers* failed to impress anyone, Levy's flat direction simply making no impact on the insipid script. A simplistic plot and some truly awful acting from Neil Connery and Lorna Wilde define the film's standard and although things pick up when old ham Maurice Evans is on screen even he can't lift the lethargy at the core of the film. Tenser's policy of targeting the least discerning market ensured enough patrons for Tigon to post adequate if unspectacular returns.

* * * * *

During the summer, Tenser decided that Stephen Weeks's WWI short had been gathering dust for long enough, and finally covered his costs by securing a very short theatrical run for the film. Tenser recouped his investment due to the fixed price deal he signed, but *1917* didn't get anything like the degree of attention it deserved.[15]

1917

'Poor Willi, He Didn't Want to Die'
- British Press Book -

Synopsis

During the First World War, the German and British trenches were very close to each other - at their nearest point the respective armies are no more than a hundred yards apart. During a lull in the fighting a German corporal, Willi, weary of the war, considers deserting. In the British lines a young recruit full of youthful enthusiasm can't believe his luck when the hapless Willi wanders into his sights, and he realises he is about to kill his first German.

Critique

'Not a very original comment on the futility of war. There is some flair in the photography and the editing but a didactic piece like this essentially needs conviction and here only Timothy Bateson's Willi carries the necessary authority.'
- Monthly Film Bulletin, 03/70

Weeks's careful re-enactment of the grime and misery of the trenches was impressive enough. The young director managed to elicit some commendable performances from his cast. The running time was sufficiently economical to ensure that the low budget wasn't exposed; in fact Weeks's creative use of the resources he had at his disposal ensured that the film looked considerably more expensive than it was. Unfortunately, *1917* received very limited exposure due to critical and box-office indifference.

* * * * *

Back in the autumn of 1969, independent film producer Harry Alan Towers had returned to the UK looking for partners for his latest venture. Towers had a reputation as something of an adventurer and a maverick, and he had developed a unique style of financing and filming low-budget movies wherever and whenever the opportunity presented itself - be it in Spain, Israel, South Africa, Russia, Hong Kong or Ireland. Coming off a run of Spanish-made Fu Manchu films, Towers's latest proposal was for an updated adaptation of Anna Sewell's children's classic 'Black Beauty'.

Tigon of course wasn't his first port of call but Towers found that the doors of Wardour Street were pretty much closed to the idea of reviving the Sewell novel, which had already been filmed five times by Hollywood, most recently in 1946. Two years

right:
Two frames from a contact sheet showing Lorna Wilde, making her debut in **The Body Stealers**. She was a model and trained dancer rather than an actress but she had the sort of looks that were a godsend to Tigon's publicity men.

above:
Stephen Weeks's **1917** was a remarkable debut from a director who would struggle to realise his potential.

earlier he could have found interest at one of the many corporate offices of the Hollywood majors, who were then eagerly pouring money into everything with a British look or feel. By the end of 1969 however, the Americans had already started moving their investments out of the capital. Gaps began to appear in the production slates of all the major studios and British film producers, sensing there was a quick buck to be made, eagerly jumped in to fill the breach. The writing was already on the wall but the industry in the UK, blindly unaware of what was coming, optimistically forged ahead. Denied American money, the local producers retreated to those old standbys of low-budget filmmakers, sex and horror, and over the next few years the genres enjoyed something of a 'mini boom'.

Tigon had already successfully released Towers's previous effort, the unlikely *Sandy the Seal (1969)*, from a script by Towers himself. *Sandy*'s unexpected popularity had convinced Tenser that there was a profitable market for low-budget family films provided the release pattern was timed to coincide with the school holidays, so he jumped at the chance to partner Towers in the produc-tion, as well as securing the British release rights. With partial financing in place through Tigon, Towers was in a strong enough position to work on raising the remaining capital from his usual European sources. Over the next few months Towers would resume his travels in an effort to set up a multi-national deal involving money from both Germany and Spain.

Tenser pencilled in *Black Beauty* for shooting sometime during the autumn of 1970 and in the meantime concentrated on more immediate production plans. John Bown, still awaiting a UK release date for 'North East Confidential' (eventually re-titled *Monique*), proposed a road movie, 'Hey You!', which he described as 'a mixture of *The Graduate* and *Easy Rider*', but after a couple of exploratory meetings Tenser declined and Bown was free to take the project elsewhere. Tenser's preferred choice for the company's next project was an adaptation of Fanny Hill; he had asked Christopher Neame to engage a scriptwriter to bring John Cleland's

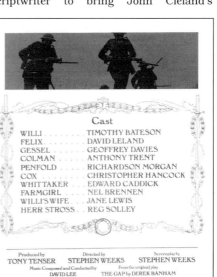

Cast

WILLI	TIMOTHY BATESON
FELIX	DAVID LELAND
GESSEL	GEOFFREY DAVIES
COLMAN	ANTHONY TRENT
PENFOLD	RICHARDSON MORGAN
COX	CHRISTOPHER HANCOCK
WHITTAKER	EDWARD CADDICK
FARMGIRL	NEL BRENNEN
WILLI'S WIFE	JANE LEWIS
HERR STROSS	REG SOLLEY

Produced by	Directed by	Screenplay by
TONY TENSER	STEPHEN WEEKS	STEPHEN WEEKS

Music Composed and Conducted by
DAVID LEE

From the original play
THE GAP by DEREK BANHAM

| RUNNING TIME : 34 MINS. | LENGTH : 3075 FT | CERT. X | IN TECHNICOLOR |

left:
The cast list and credits for **1917**. Tenser picked up a producer credit, though in fact his role on the film was limited to the signing of cheques.

notorious novel to the screen. Neame had other ideas however - he had already been approached by a new production company with what he thought was a far more interesting project: 'Leander films was Graham Harris and James Kelly, and they had a script called 'Young Man I Think You're Dying,' which I rather liked because it was different from the sort of stuff we were doing at Tigon, and I wanted to get away from the sex thing with *Zeta One* and *Monique*. Tony refused point blank to make it.'

Harris and Kelly were old friends who had met in the early Fifties when they were both jobbing editors. They formed Leander specifically to film a script by Kelly, who had picked up writing credits on *Doctor Blood's Coffin (1960)*, before moving into television with a number of scripts including the series *Our Man at St. Mark's*. He wanted more than anything to direct his own movies. Harris's ambition was to become a producer. His first foray into this arena took place when he signed on to produce what appeared to be a routine horror movie for Robert Hartford-Davis, called 'Doctors Wear Scarlet' and starring Peter Cushing. By the time the much-troubled production, eventually released as *Incense for the Damned*, or *Bloodsuckers*, finally wrapped, Hartford-Davis had taken his name from the credits and Harris had a hard-earned reputation as one of the most tenacious producers in Britain. Harris already had his fill of other

people's films and wanted more control over the day to day aspects of the job.

Armed with the first draft of a script called 'Young Man I Think You're Dying', Harris approached veteran actress Beryl Reid, then something of a *cause célèbre* thanks to the controversy surrounding *The Killing of Sister George (1968)*. At that stage the film was an anti-war drama centering on two rather eccentric middle-aged women. Having been offered a slew of films cashing in on *Sister George*'s notoriety, Reid was thrilled by the prospect of some real acting, and happily signed on.[16] With a star committed, Harris and Kelly took the film to Tigon as a package and offered it to Tenser as a joint production. 'I suppose if I was honest,' Neame admits, 'I just wanted to make a film with Beryl Reid. Tony insisted on Fanny Hill, which I would have made if we had the money to make it properly, but we didn't. In the end I said unless we made 'Young Man, I Think You're Dying,' I would resign. He thought about it for a bit and then, to my surprise, said okay make it.'

The seasonal downswing in production over the first quarter of the year meant that Tigon were able to agree extremely favourable terms at Pinewood Studios, home to the Rank Organisation, James Bond movies, and the lucrative Carry On series. In sharp contrast to Camden, Pinewood offered the biggest and best-equipped facilities in the UK, and the studio was available for a modest rental. Tenser committed to filming two projects at the studio starting early 1970, and Neame was told to make sure 'Young Man I Think You're Dying' was ready to go before the cameras, and also to find a suitable second feature. Despite the tight time-scales, Tenser was confident that Neame was up to the task: 'He was a very competent man, an excellent production controller in fact. I was thinking of him as a natural successor to me.' Neame confirmed to Pinewood that production on 'Young Man' would start at the end of February and that Tigon's second film under this agreement would begin at the beginning of April. He then started looking around for a suitable script.

By coincidence a letter addressed to Tenser at Hammer House arrived from a young scriptwriter called Robert Wynne-Simmons. The writer had entered the film industry straight from university, as a runner for Michael Winner of all people, but when Winner decided that Wynne-Simmons's services were no longer required, he sent speculative letters to as many production companies as he could identify. 'There must have been about one hundred letters sent out up to Christmas,' he recalls. 'The only reply I got was from Christopher Neame, asking if I had any script ideas.' Luckily he did have something in mind, though at the time it was little more than a few vague ideas and a title, "The Devil's Skin'.

below:
Tony Tenser and German distributor Dieter Menz visit Beryl Reid on the set of **The Beast in the Cellar**.

Footnotes

1. Karloff's last movies, *Isle of the Snake People*, *The Incredible Invasion*, *The Fear Chamber* and *House of Evil*, all for Filmica Azteca and financed through Columbia, were shot back-to-back in 1968. With only one functioning lung, Karloff's doctors would not allow him to work in the high altitude of Mexico so his scenes were shot in California. Other than Karloff's presence the films have no obvious worth and all of them were released posthumously on a piecemeal basis. Tigon's 1971 release *Cauldron of Blood*, filmed in Spain in 1967, is sometimes erroneously identified as being amongst this quartet.

2. A classically trained actress, Hassall's propensity to turn up at film premieres in low-cut tops distracted attention away from her limited abilities as an actress. Apart from some respectable stage credits and her loin cloth work for Hammer, she also appeared in Robert Hartford-Davis's *Incense for the Damned (1970)*, Freddie Francis's *Mumsy, Nanny, Sonny and Girly (1969)*, and *Carry On Loving (1970)*. Her career took a spectacular nosedive in the mid-Seventies and she committed suicide in 1980.

3. Scottish-born Justice began his professional life as a journalist and a naturalist before becoming an actor in the 1940s. Despite this late start, he assembled an impressive list of credits ranging from serious melodrama such as *Scott of the Antarctic (1948)* and *Moby Dick (1956)*, through action flicks like *The Guns of Navarone (1961)*, to unlikely appearances in the Brigitte Bardot movies *À coeur joie (1967)* and *Histoires extraordinaires (1968)*. His signature role was as Sir Lancelot Spratt, the bombastic patriarch in the *Doctor* series. He died in 1975.

4. Charles Hawtrey trained at the famous Italia Conti stage school and had made over thirty films before he signed on for *Carry On Sergeant* in 1958. Prior to that he had taken serious parts in films like *A Canterbury Tale (1944)*, as well as more light-hearted work in the likes of *Room to Let (1950)*. Openly homosexual and deeply insecure, he took to drinking heavily and soon his promiscuity and drunkenness became a problem for casting directors. In his later years practically his only source of income was the *Carry On*'s, where he was tolerated as an errant member of the family, but was consigned to increasingly smaller roles. Eventually they too had enough and he was dropped entirely from the series in the early 70s, after which he found film work impossible to come by. After a spell in provincial theatre milking what was left of his fame, he slipped quietly into retirement in 1978. A decade later his drinking denied him the use of both of his legs and, faced with the alternative of amputation or death within weeks, he instructed his doctors not to operate and died on the 27th of October 1988.

5. Hungarian Anna Gael, later Lady Weymouth, enjoyed a period of stardom in slightly tawdry Euro-dramas including *Therese and Isabelle (1968)*, where her willingness to disrobe made her something of a cult actress. She did make a number of English language films without any notable success, including *The Bridge at Remagen (1969)*, and *Sweeney 2 (1978)*. Her best British film was undoubtedly the bizarre but entertaining *Blue Blood (1973)*, filmed at her husband's stately home.

above:
British artwork for **The Body Stealers**. The film was to trail in the wake of **2001: A Space Odyssey** despite the best efforts of Tigon to suggest that they had a comparable product...

6. Stensgaard went on to make such films as *Scream and Scream Again (1969)* for Amicus/AIP, Vernon Sewell's *Burke and Hare (1971)* and of course Hammer's *Lust for a Vampire (1970)*. *Zeta One* - and in particular the nude scene - made a lasting impression on her; 30 years later she told Little Shoppe of Horrors magazine: 'I hate that film!'

7. In a curious footnote to *What's Good for the Goose*, when Foxtrot Films picked up the video rights in the mid-Eighties, they packaged the film with a drawing of Mary Millington lifted from Tigon's publicity materials for *Confessions from the David Galaxy Affair (1979)*. Despite the artistic license with Ms. Millington's exaggerated bosoms, the film wasn't a success. When Polygram acquired the rights in the Nineties they dropped the sex angle entirely and used a still from one of Wisdom's 1950s films. This re-issue met with no more success than the earlier release. In the US the video was promoted under the title 'Girl Trouble', also to no notable response.

8. After *What's Good for the Goose*, Wisdom all but gave up on films. Subsequent attempts to revitalise his career in 1970 with the TV series *Norman* flopped, though another series, *A Little Bit of Wisdom*, staggered to two series before being dropped. He paid the bills with pantomime and the odd personal appearance but didn't film again until 1992, when he made a cameo appearance in a British gangster movie, *Double X*. That same year, Wisdom was awarded a Lifetime Achievement Award by the British Academy of Dramatic Arts, followed three years later by an OBE. Wisdom, knighted in 2000, was a national institution long before he 'officially' retired in 2005 at the age of 90 and he remains a household name even if few people could identify any of his films. Interestingly, in 1970 Wisdom appeared in the Broadway version of Ray Cooney's sex farce 'Not Now Darling', later filmed by Tigon. Tenser and Wisdom did meet up again in the late Eighties when the comic was the guest of honour at The Clowns Association of Great Britain in Southport. Tenser, a resident of the town, presented the diminutive funnyman with a lifetime achievement award before a gala screening of his films including of course *What's Good for the Goose*

9. Always in the shadow of her more famous sister, Geeson had featured roles in *The Oblong Box (1969)* and *Cry of the Banshee (1970)*, both for

above:
Sally Geeson and
Norman Wisdom in
**What's Good for the
Goose**. The actress
was to receive the only
plaudits handed out to
the film and it launched
her career. By contrast
it would be over twenty
years before the actor
went back before film
cameras.

AIP, but considered herself more suited to comedy roles. In the Seventies she went into *Carry On* movies, as well as the long running *Bless This House* television series and the obligatory film spin-off. When the series ran its course Geeson retired from acting to devote herself to her family.

10. Golan and Globus, a.k.a. Cannon, were alternately portrayed as the saviours or villains of the British film industry. Taking over from the likes of Lew Grade and Lord Delfont, they established a major production company, complete with studio and distribution circuit, in the UK at a time when the rest of the industry was suffering a major recession. The partnership proceeded to flood the market with dozens of generally second-rate movies like *The Wicked Lady* (1983), *Hercules* (1983), and *Missing In Action* (1984). Along the way they produced the odd interesting effort: Pete Walker's *House of the Long Shadows* (1982) from a script by Michael Armstrong, Stephen Weeks's *Sword of the Valiant* (1983), and the remarkable *Lifeforce* (1985). None of the films were particularly successful - Cannon survived by constantly moving on to the next one before the receipts came in from the last. Needless to say it all caught up with them in the end and the whole empire collapsed. Golan, always the survivor, is still producing and directing films from his base in LA.

11. Tigon tried again with *Zeta One* in 1970 without any more success but the film enjoyed life far beyond its limited cinema release. It was resurrected by the Jezebel video label in the mid-1990's, prompting it to be dubbed by Loaded magazine as the 'worst British film ever made', but it proved a reliable top-shelf seller in the 'so bad its good' market. Interestingly, in the early part of the same decade no less a personage than Sir Clive Sinclair, inventor of the Sinclair C5, developed a series of small motorised bicycles which he christened the Zeta series, running to model numbers I, II and III!

12. 'Tigon's whole set-up was very loose. It had a smell of fun and games, of 'we're having good times'. But there was some in-fighting as well. They kept coming up with petty projects that really didn't serve our purpose; it was not really a place I wanted to be. Tenser disappeared from the scene not too long afterwards - he became something of a country squire!'
- Louis Heyward, Filmfax, issue 61.

13. Sibylla Kay was one of four sisters, born in 1936 to a German hotelier in the Baltic port of Riga. Following the outbreak of the Second World War, the family moved to Poland in 1940 before fleeing through Europe ahead of the advancing Red Army. After her schooling she moved to Paris and then, in 1960, to London. She toyed with a number of career options, including a stint as an air-hostess, before she decided on acting when she met and married struggling actor John Bown.

14. In the US, Sagittarius decided that *The Body Stealers* sounded too much like a horror film, and somewhat confusingly re-titled the film *Invasion of the Body*. Audience identification was so strong that the film was frequently labelled a re-issue or a remake of the Fifties classic *Invasion of the Body Snatchers*, and in some cases promoters played it under the original title of 'Thin Air.'

15. One of the few people who saw *1917* was actor Christopher Lee, who was impressed enough to recommend Weeks to the head of Amicus Films, Milton Subotsky. At the time Subotsky had written a script for a new version of the Jekyll & Hyde story and was struggling to understand the mechanics of a new 3-D process he had purchased for that film. Weeks was handed the poisoned chalice of his feature debut on the understanding that he shot it using the experimental process. The resulting film, *I, Monster* (1971) was a disappointment for everyone concerned. Weeks stayed at Amicus for a while, working on his 'Cawnpore' script but eventually moved on when he received backing from UA for a script called *Gawain and the Green Knight* (1972). Weeks had unhappy experiences on both films and in an effort to return to the type of creative freedom he enjoyed on *1917*, he resolved to write, direct and produce his next film, the remarkable *Ghost Story* (1974). Financed independently, Weeks took his entire cast and crew off to India to make one of the most under-rated films to come out of Britain in the Seventies. Denied a commercial release for *Ghost Story*, Weeks returned to documentaries and even tried Hollywood for a spell but again he experienced problems with the the the back office. He completed *Sword of the Valiant* (1983), the big budget remake of the Gawain story financed by Cannon, with a cast including Sean Connery, Peter Cushing and Ronald Lacey, but the film was ruined by a shocking performance from leading man Miles O'Keefe. Weeks was dogged by bad luck on another deeply personal project, *The Bengal Lancers*, when a completion fund fraud bankrupted the production after several weeks of filming. The subsequent lawsuits kept Weeks in the courts and away from filmmaking for over a decade. In the meantime he devoted himself to various conservation projects around his home in Wales. With the court actions now settled in his favour Weeks announced his intention of returning to filming.

16. Reid was, until her death from renal failure in 1996 aged 76, practically a British institution - in fact she is so familiar to the public that it is a surprise how few movies she actually made. Mainly a TV and theatre actress, Reid won a Tony in New York for the controversial *The Killing of Sister George* (1968), and a decade later a BAFTA for the BBC's *Smiley's People*. The high-point of her cinema work was undoubtedly Robert Aldrich's translation of the Sister George play, followed by *Entertaining Mr. Sloane* (1970), an adaptation of Joe Orton's stage play. Reid did make odd - sometimes very odd - cameo appearances in horror movies, including *Dr. Phibes Rises Again* (1972), *Psychomania* (1972), and one of her last film roles, Freddie Francis's *The Doctor and the Devils* (1985). A cantankerous and difficult woman at the best of times, her sometimes spiteful nature was regarded by her legion of fans as a loveable eccentricity, and the public's fascination with Reid survived her death. In 1997, the Daily Mail found her newsworthy enough to run a four-page story on how the bit-part actor Paul Stride, the main beneficiary of her will, had decided to sell off her cats, despite Reid's express instruction. Stride's argument was that they would be better looked after elsewhere and incredibly he was to suffer hate mail, harassment from the press and eventually death threats as a consequence.

opposite:
The original American
one-sheet poster for
Witchfinder General,
under the new title
given to it by distributors
AIP, reflecting their on-
going obsession with
the marquee value of
Edgar Allan Poe's
name. Note the shared
credit for the film's
writer Ronald Bassett
and Poe, whose only
connection to the film is
the fact that AIP used
his poem on this poster!

LEAVE THE CHILDREN HOME!
...and if YOU are SQUEAMISH STAY HOME WITH THEM !!!!!!!

A crawling shape intrude!
A blood-red thing that writhes
from out The scenic solitude!
It writhes!–it writhes!–
with mortal pangs
The mimes become its food,
And seraphs sob at vermin fangs
In human gore imbued.

EDGAR ALLAN POE

EDGAR ALLAN POE'S
THE CONQUEROR WORM

IN **COLOR** by PERFECT
FROM AMERICAN INTERNATIONAL

STARRING
VINCENT PRICE · IAN **OGILVY** · RUPERT **DAVIES** · AND INTRODUCING **DWYER**

EXECUTIVE PRODUCER · PRODUCED BY · DIRECTED BY · SCREENPLAY BY
TONY TENSER · **LOUIS M. HEYWARD** · **MICHAEL REEVES** · **MICHAEL REEVES & TOM BAKER**

BASED ON A BOOK ENTITLED
'WITCHFINDER GENERAL' BY
RONALD BASSETT AND THE
POEM BY EDGAR ALLAN POE

© 1968 American International Pictures

opposite top:
Hammer horror meets
Gainsborough melodrama
on the British quad for
The Black Torment.

opposite bottom:
John Turner throttles
Heather Sears on this
American lobby card for
The Black Torment.

above:
A British Pressbook for **Saturday Night Out**, giving
contemporary pop music group 'The Searchers' a
degree of prominence not reflected in the finished film.

left:
Pamela Green, showing off some of the spectacular
scenery on display in **Naked - As Nature Intended**!

below:
British admat for **Saturday Night Out**.

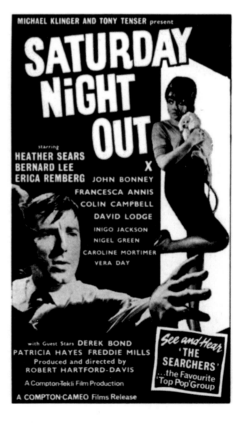

above: Spanish lobbycard for **Cul-de-Sac**.
below: British re-issue quad for **Repulsion**.

opposite top: Cover of the British pressbook for **Neither the Sea Nor the Sand**.
opposite bottom: Mary Kelly (Edina Ronay) and her last client, Jack the Ripper, in **A Study in Terror**.

Neither the Sea Nor the Sand

¡DEJE A LOS NIÑOS EN CASA...
Y SI USTED ES MIEDOSO
QUEDESE CON ELLOS!

CUANDO LAS BRUJAS ARDEN

VINCENT PRICE · IAN OGILVY
RUPERT DAVIES · HILARY DWYER

TONY TENSER · LOUIS M. HEYWARD

MICHAEL REEVES · MICHAEL REEVES & TOM BAKER

AMERICAN INTERNATIONAL
DISTRIBUIDA POR JO-EL, S.A. Monterrey 180 - México, D.F.

TRASPASA LO SOBRENATURAL EN EL MUNDO DE LOS MUERTOS

CUANDO LAS BRUJAS ARDEN

VINCENT PRICE · IAN OGILVY
RUPERT DAVIES · HILARY DWYER

VINCENT PRICE

IL GRANDE INQUISITORE

IAN OGILVY · RUPERT DAVIES · WILFRID BRAMBELL · PATRICK WYMARK · ROBERT RUSSEL ··· HILARY DWYER
diretto da: MICHAEL REEVES   prodotto da: TONY TENSER   EASTMANCOLOR

VINCENT PRICE

IL GRANDE INQUISITORE

IAN OGILVY · RUPERT DAVIES · WILFRID BRAMBELL · PATRICK WYMARK · ROBERT RUSSEL ··· HILARY DWYER
diretto da: MICHAEL REEVES   prodotto da: TONY TENSER   EASTMANCOLOR

TONY TENSER presents

VINCENT PRICE

IAN OGILVY RUPERT DAVIES
WILFRID BRAMBELL

WITCHFINDER GENERAL

WITH
PATRICK WYMARK
AS CROMWELL
ROBERT RUSSELL · NICKY HENSON
AND INTRODUCING
HILARY DWYER

Music by PAUL FERRIS · From the book by RONALD BASSETT · Directed by MICHAEL REEVES · Screenplay by TOM BAKER & MICHAEL REEVES · Photography JOHNNY COQUILLON
Producers ARNOLD MILLER · PHILIP WADDILOVE · LOUIS M. HEYWARD · Executive Producer TONY TENSER
RELEASED BY TIGON PICTURES LTD. · A TIGON BRITISH – AMERICAN INTERNATIONAL PRODUCTION   in EASTMAN COLOUR

above:
The British quad poster for Michael Reeves's last film,
Witchfinder General, emphasising spectacle and action.

right:
This Italian theatrical poster for the film showcases
Vincent Price as Matthew Hopkins, arguably his finest
ever screen creation.

opposite top:
Ian Oglivy and Vincent Price during the bloody climax of
Witchfinder General.

opposite centre left:
Mexican lobby card for **Witchfinder General**, borrowing
heavily from the US artwork.

opposite centre right:
This Mexican lobby card is taking a great deal of creative
license by introducing a werewolf to **Witchfinder General**!

opposite bottom left:
An Italian Fotobusta, emphasising the torture and
mayhem perpetrated by Matthew Hopkins (Vincent Price)
and John Stearne (Robert Russell).

opposite bottom right:
Another Italian Fotobusta for **Witchfinder General**.
The film's composer, Paul Ferris, can be seen in his
cameo appearance; he is the character in red, being
restrained.

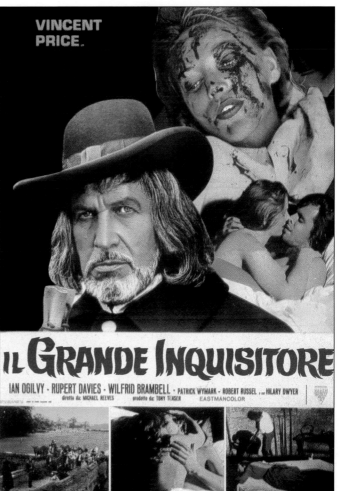

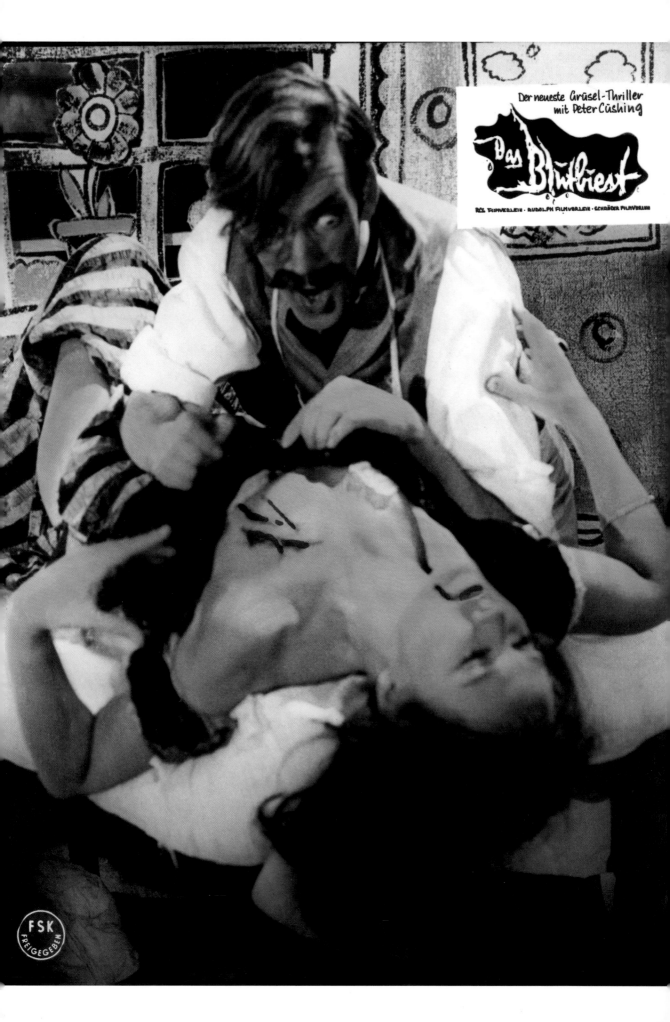

Der neueste Grusel-Thriller
mit Peter Cushing

Das Blutbiest

RCS FILMVERLEIH · RUDOLPH FILMVERLEIH · SCHRÖDER FILMVERLEIH

FSK
FREIGEGEBEN

above:
A British promotional flyer for Vernon Sewell's
The Blood Beast Terror.

opposite:
Wanda Ventham goes under the scalpel in the 'play within the
film' section of **The Blood Beast Terror**.

right:
More striking British artwork produced by Tigon in their
attempts to promote **The Blood Beast Terror**.

below:
Barbara Steele presides over one of **Curse of the Crimson
Altar**'s Satanic interludes. Sadly all such scenes appear to
have disappeared during editing. All we are left with are stills
such as this to show what might have been; the film as it
stands must be considered something of a missed opportunity.

above and below: Lurid Mexican lobby cards for **Curse of the Crimson Altar**.

opposite top and opposite bottom: British front of house stills for Tigon productions.

TONY TENSER PRESENTS

NORMAN WISDOM

in MENAHEM GOLAN'S

WHAT'S GOOD FOR THE GOOSE (A)

with TERENCE ALEXANDER   SARAH ATKINSON   SALLY BAZELY   DEREK FRANCIS
DAVID LODGE   PAUL WHITSUN-JONES   and introducing SALLY GEESON
RELEASED BY TIGON PICTURES LTD.   EASTMAN COLOUR

EASTMAN COLOUR   x

JAMES ROBERTSON JUSTICE   with BRIGITTE SKAY
CHARLES HAWTREY   and guest star **DAWN ADDAMS**
ROBIN HAWDON   ANNA GAEL   PRODUCED BY TIGON BRITISH FILM PRODUCTIONS
RELEASED BY TIGON PICTURES LTD.

above: The Devil makes a fleeting appearance during the climax of Piers Haggard's **Blood on Satan's Claw**.

below: A typically gaudy Mexican lobby card for **Blood on Satan's Claw**.

BERYL REID FLORA ROBSON
IN
THE BEAST IN THE CELLAR(X)
co-starring TESSA WYATT JOHN HAMILL T. P. McKENNA
Executive Producer TONY TENSER Producer GRAHAM HARRIS Director JAMES KELLY
A TIGON BRITISH PRODUCTION in association with LEANDER FILMS LTD.

RELEASED BY
TIGON PICTURES LTD.

above: Front of house still showing Beryl Reid, about to dispose of the evidence, in **The Beast in the Cellar**.

below: No Tenser film would be complete without a hint of bondage. Uschi Glas, as seen on the British lobby card for **Black Beauty**.

PARAMOUNT PICTURES
PRESENTS MARK LESTER · WALTER SLEZAK IN

"Black Beauty"

Based upon the Novel by ANNA SEWELL · Co-starring URSULA GLASS · PETER LEE LAWRENCE · JOHN NETTLETON
PATRICK MOWER · MARIA ROHM · Theme music composed by LIONEL BART · With additional music by JOHN CAMERON
Screenplay by WOLF MANKOWITZ · Executive producer TONY TENSER · Produced by PETER L. ANDREWS & MALCOLM B. HEYWORTH
Directed by JAMES HILL · A Tigon British/Chilton Film Production · In Color · A Paramount Picture

Raquel Welch shows how the West was won in Terry O'Neill's exclusive publicity shot, taken on the set of **Hannie Caulder**.

above: Lee and Cushing worked together on only one Tigon production, Freddie Francis's **The Creeping Flesh**. This is a British quad poster for the film.

below: Felicity Devonshire's dancing sequence, as featured in the opening credits of **The Magnificent 7 Deadly Sins**. This is the film's pressbook cover.

Chapter Eight

'Behind Its Forbidden Doors an Evil Secret Hides!'

- (US trade ads for *The Haunted House of Horror*)

If the Sixties represented a party for the British film industry then the Seventies was the morning after. By 1970 reality was making an unwelcome intrusion into the offices of the Wardour Street power brokers. The more astute businessmen, James Carreras amongst them, were already considering an exit strategy. Some still believed that the British could stave off the impending recession by simply increasing the number of their own productions, but this was a dangerous avoidance of the facts.

Hollywood's investment in the UK over the previous five years had been staggering: US majors such as MGM and United Artists had poured millions of dollars into mainstream filmmaking. Universal alone had sunk over $30m into British films in the three years up to 1969. Amongst the many films that had been made with US dollars were the likes of *Khartoum (1966)*, *Casino Royale (1967)*, and *2001: A Space Odyssey (1968)*. British-based actors, technicians and studios had never had it so good. During the same period, British films were finding it easier to penetrate the US market. While twenty years earlier UK producers needed to import an American star and/or contrive to set their films in the US before a wide release in America was feasible, in the late Sixties British films with British subjects were being freely distributed throughout North America. For Tenser it meant that films that would have otherwise struggled to find a distributor because of cast or subject matter, such as *What's Good for the Goose*, could reclaim at least part of their budget by selling the North American rights. Tenser however continued to budget his films on the basis that they needed to break even in the UK, thus freeing Tigon from dependence on overseas earnings. Good housekeeping ensured that by the end of their fourth year of operation, Tenser estimated that 70% of Tigon's films were making a profit, or at least breaking even. While Tigon continued to make movies that were relatively modest in terms of their ambition and scope, most producers operating out of London utilised American money to its full potential, so their productions swelled to undreamed-of proportions. It was only a question of time before the bubble burst.

The new decade saw US film companies with London offices accumulating huge losses on unwise investments such as *Half a Sixpence (1967)*, *Modesty Blaise (1966)*, and *The Charge of the Light Brigade (1968)*. The situation in Hollywood was equally depressing - of the major studios only Columbia and United Artists posted a profit in 1969 - and even for them returns were significantly down on previous years. Fox, MGM and Paramount were losing tens of millions worldwide. The predictable result was a dramatic reduction in the amount of American money coming into the UK, and the sudden cancellation of production schedules. In 1968, Fox, Paramount, United Artists and Universal had made 32 films in the UK between them. In 1970 this figure dropped to 5. The American public's love affair with all things British was also coming to an end too: *Bonnie and Clyde (1967)* was one of several landmark movies that re-introduced American cinema-goers to their own history.

opposite:
Spectacular Spanish poster artwork for Vernon Sewell's **Curse of the Crimson Altar**.

below:
Rare British admat. Filmed as **Young Man I Think You're Dying**, this film was briefly marketed as **The Cellar** before Tenser finally settled on the more exploitative **The Beast in the Cellar** title shortly before its release.

above:
Flora Robson and Beryl Reid as the Ballantyne sisters in **The Beast in the Cellar**. Both actresses believed they were making a drama with an anti-war theme!

below:
Anabel Littledale as a victim. Tenser insisted on re-shoots to make the attack sequences more exploitative.

Public statements of optimism from the Wardour Street moguls disguised the sense of pessimism that was engulfing the British industry, underscored by the continuing decline in cinema attendance - nearly two thirds of cinemas had closed since 1960. In the cafes of Soho the subjects dominating conversation were studio closures and wholesale redundancies, but at Tigon, Tenser's motto remained, 'if you stay on budget, you will stay in business'. As the industry pundits wrung their hands and battened down the hatches, Tigon was gearing up his production schedule. 'Young

Man I Think You're Dying' was ready to start shooting at Pinewood, to be followed provisionally by Robert Wynne-Simmons's still embyonic 'The Devil's Skin' project.

The central characters in James Kelly's 'Young Man I Think You're Dying' story were two slightly batty spinsters, Ellie and Joyce Ballantyne, living together, apparently alone, in an old secluded mansion. When squaddies start to disappear from the local army base, only to turn up shredded to pieces, the authorities start to suspect that the outwardly placid lifestyle of the sisters is hiding a terrible secret.

With Beryl Reid committed, Harris and Kelly set about finding a mature actress of sufficient stature to play alongside her in the crucial role of her slightly more stable sister, Joyce. Tigon set their sights on stage and screen veteran Flora Robson, but she was very reluctant until help arrived from an unlikely ally. 'She wasn't particularly keen on doing the part,' Christopher Neame says, 'and after we've met with her and discussed it, she was going home to where she lived in Brighton, and met Laurence Olivier on the train and she told him about the film. Olivier had said, 'really, in this terrible terrible business, it's better to be working than not working. So I think you should do it.' So the following day, her agent called up and said that Flora will do it.'[1]

The supporting cast was a mixture of youth and experience. Irish actor T.P. McKenna, with over a decade in films and television was joined by Tessa Wyatt, making only her second film (her debut the year before was in *I Can't... I Can't* directed by Piers Haggard). John Hamill, who took the lead, sandwiched his Tigon duties between *Trog (1970)* for Herman Cohen and *Tower of Evil (1971)* for Richard Gordon.[2] The pivotal role of Stephen Ballantyne, the sisters' guilty secret, went to Dafydd Havard, though he was to be unrecognisable under William T. Partleton's make-up.[3] Christopher Neame was promoted to Associate Producer, with Graham Harris taking over the reins as line producer. Desmond Dickinson, who had photographed *A Study in Terror*, worked alongside Harry Waxman on the photography.

To keep to his allocated shooting schedule of only four and a half weeks, Kelly had to drop most of the intended location work, limiting himself to two days so he could film the flashback sequences, which included some set-ups on the Bluebell Railway. The agreement with Pinewood precluded the idea of finding a 'Grims Dyke'-type environment for filming interiors, so the sets were all constructed at Pinewood. Shooting started later than planned, on the 24th of February, with the leading actresses proclaiming that they were embarking on an intense family drama with a strong anti-war theme. Interestingly, Tigon was also playing-down the horror element at this stage, Tenser pointing his publicity team in the direction of a more topical market. The Vietnam War was increasingly prominent, and headline writers on both sides of the Atlantic were

mesmerised as much by the high profile protests in the USA, as by conflict itself. The press releases coming out of Tigon throughout March clumsily attempted to focus on the script's anti-war stance.

*   *   *   *   *

If Tigon's press office was uncharateristically anaemic at this time, then Laurie Marsh was giving the City something meatier to get their teeth into. Since establishing himself within the Tigon set-up two years earlier, Marsh had stoked the financial engine that powered the company's expansion. For years Marsh had operated amongst the heavyweights in the City of London, controlling a series of mergers and acquisitions under the auspices of his Star Holdings property group. Marsh therefore had the contacts and the know-how to attract investors who

above:
A suitably horrified Beryl Reid; the actress later attacked Tigon in her autobiography, claiming, 'Flora and I were both disappointed that they'd slotted in some rather cheap effects...'

above:
One of **The Beast in the Cellar**'s more blatant inserts; 'we had a horror film so it has to be seen as a horror film,' commented Tony Tenser.

left:
From left to right: Flora Robson, Tessa Wyatt, John Hamill and Beryl Reid.

above:
Robson and Reid
visiting the Pinewood
backlot. **The Beast in
the Cellar** was the first
Tigon film shot at
Britain's premier studio.

below:
Anabel Littledale and
Peter Craze rolling in
the hay. Surprisingly for
a Tigon movie, **The
Beast in the Cellar** is
almost sex-free; this
light petting scene is
about as saucy as it
gets and again the
original scenes were
padded out with some
inserts.

would normally give the entertainment sector a wide berth. Having gradually become less and less of a silent partner, Marsh was now ready to step into the spotlight.

During early 1970, Tenser's Tigon Group was comprised of eight separate subsidiary companies. Most of the turnover was generated via the distribution arm Tigon Pictures Ltd and film production under Tigon British Films Ltd, but there were also largely inactive radio and television subsidiaries. Marsh was Chairman and major shareholder, whilst Tony Tenser, who still had a significant holding, was Managing Director and responsible for the day-to-day running of the company. Marsh's principal role was to define the Tigon business strategy, and it was clear to him that the company needed to expand across the full spectrum of the entertainment industry. Tigon, as one of the few profitable companies in the sector, was attracting interest from major players. As early as July 1969 the highly acquisitive Hemdale Group, owners of the Isleworth Studios where *Monique* was shot, had declared their desire to buy a major production company and although Hemdale's Managing Director, John Daly, declined to name any potential targets, Tigon undoubtedly featured prominently on his list. Formal overtures were made towards the end of autumn 1969 and Daly found Laurie Marsh to be very receptive.

Hemdale itself was not ostensibly a production company; it had been formed a little over two years earlier primarily to promote the interests of artists including founding partner David Hemmings and diverse talents such as Peter McEnery and child actors Mark Lester and Jack Wild. Under Daly's stewardship the company expanded into film production. They made a short film called *Simon Simon (1970)*, directed by comedian Graham Stark, and quickly built up an impressive production slate by acquiring the rights to a number of

mainstream projects. Tigon had in fact handled the UK distribution of *Simon Simon*, and Daly was already familiar with Tenser's film production work so the prospect of acquiring such a well-defined company was very appealing.

Negotiations between Daly and Marsh and their respective management teams began in earnest just as 'Young Man, I Think You're Dying' was going into pre-production, and in February 1970 the Hemdale Group announced the purchase of Tigon for the sum of £400,000. The deal gave Hemdale outright ownership of Tigon's parent company, Tigon Pictures Ltd, as well as its subsidiaries and all works-in-progress. Daly made it clear that while the Tigon name would be retained, this would be a short-term measure; the intention was to merge the whole Tigon operation into an enlarged group. City analysts estimated that the combined Hemdale/Tigon empire could boast an asset base in excess of £1.5m, quite a considerable amount for an independent company at the time. John Daly stayed on as Group MD, Laurie Marsh joined the Board of the Hemdale Group as a director, and Tony Tenser retained an executive role on the film production and distribution side. The new company's production strategy had not been worked out in any detail, but Daly confirmed that the broad plan was for Hemdale/Tigon to move away from the production and financing of exploitation films, and into a role as co-producers, with international partners, of projects with budgets of around £250,000. Wherever appropriate, the personnel needed to make the films would be drawn from Hemdale's stable of artistes.

The philosophy of the new Group was based on the old Hollywood model; generate their own film scripts in-house, and then finance the film externally while retaining the creative talent under contract. The company would own the production itself, make films using their own studio facilities and then release the product in their own cinemas. Daly was clear about his reasons for including Tigon in their plans: 'We have been looking around at a number of companies for some time now,' he told a press conference. 'Tigon was just right for a number of reasons. It wasn't too large, which was important as we very much wanted to keep control ourselves, it was making about four films a year and was using our studio at Isleworth anyway.' There was no clarification regarding what films the new team would make, as Tenser remarked at the time: 'It will really be a fusing on the production side. But as yet we haven't gone into great detail as to how the co-ordination will operate.'

For the cast and crew on the studio floor it was business as usual, albeit within a mildly schizophrenic environment. The first steps towards the winding down of the

Tigon name were already taking place, with Daly announcing that in going forward the new company would operate solely under the Hemdale banner, explaining that this would, 'give it a much wider channel through which to operate.' At Pinewood the daily call-sheets were still headed up with the Tigon logo, while press releases for public consumption listed 'Young Man I Think You're Dying', and later 'The Devil's Skin', as Hemdale films.

Hemdale was a far more mainstream operation than Tigon, and the new Board were probably not too impressed that two of their new assets could be comfortably described as softcore pornography. *Monique* was still being put together under the watchful eye of the censors, while *Zeta One* was ready to be shown again. Cort had returned to the cutting-rooms after the disastrous initial trade screening in an attempt to make something more out of the scant material at his disposal. On the 21st of March 1970 the latest cut, running some 82 minutes, was sheepishly shown to a selected audience of critics and potential buyers. Their reaction was underwhelming, and with no prospect of a circuit release *Zeta One* was shelved for the time being.

While Neame and Wynne-Simmons were developing the second movie to be shot on the Pinewood soundstages, they were approached by independent producers Peter Andrews and Malcolm Heyworth. The men, both still in their twenties, had formed a company called Chilton Films the previous year in order to produce a silent short, *The Undertakers*, starring Bernard Cribbins and Wilfrid Brambell. Andrews was a former editor who had moved into production some years earlier with a series of industrial shorts, travelogues and children's television shows under the banner of Victory Films. Heyworth had graduated from the London School of Film Technique in 1964 before founding his documentary film company 'Group '64', makers of short films such as *Life at the Top* featuring Harry H. Corbett. Tenser was impressed with both men. He remembers that they were very keen to make their feature film debut and that, 'they were very young of course but everyone was in those days. More important was that they knew their business and seemed very competent.'

Chilton signed a deal with Hemdale whereby they committed to take on the day-to-day production chores for the film as well investing a small financial stake; Hemdale agreed to contribute the bulk of the budget and took on the responsibility for UK distribution. All that was needed was a final script. Ideally Tenser was looking for a movie to occupy the top half of a double-bill and suggested a compendium film along the lines of Amicus's *Dr. Terror's House of Horrors (1964)* and *Torture Garden (1967)*, both of which had been reasonably

successful despite modest budgets. Neame explains Tenser's rationale: 'Tony wanted three short films because he had some idea that it could be crewed with less technicians if it was short films - which was actually true - with the idea that they could then be assembled together as one film or else marketed separately as support features.' Robert Wynne-Simmons didn't share Tenser's enthusiasm: 'I wasn't terribly keen to be frank but I thought it might be possible to do some stories with either a common theme or with recurring characters. I had written a number of short stories while at university. They were never published but I thought I could work them into a script.'

Wynne-Simmons really wanted to explore the idea of a primitive force of evil growing within a civilised society, having drawn partial inspiration from the horrific Manson cult murders of 1969. He also found a source of inspiration much closer to home: 'This was only few years after the Mary Bell child murders and there was something about Bell's attitude... she was only a child herself but she had such contempt, almost sneering I suppose, at her victims or at least their families. I wanted to capture that.' In Wynne-Simmons's first draft an ancient, primeval force was spreading like a virus through Victorian England, with the establishment too civilised to either accept what was happening, or defend themselves from gradual assimilation. Neame felt that the Victorian Gothic had been done to death and furthermore that the seventeenth century had proved quite conducive to this sort of treatment in *Witchfinder General*.

Wynne-Simmons reworked his synopsis, introducing a rural judge, who appeared in all three stories, fighting the evil manifestations that followed the

above:
Blood on Satan's Claw's grisly opening scene.

below:
Hammer leading man Barry (**Dracula Has Risen from the Grave**) Andrews and Charlotte Mitchell, after saving a witch - played by Michele Dotrice - from 'ducking' in **Blood on Satan's Claw**.

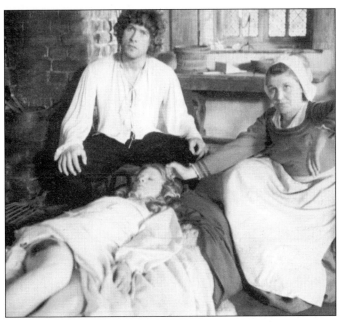

above:
The Devil comes in many disguises in **Blood on Satan's Claw**; this one takes the shape of actress and model Yvonne Paul, who later established the first agency for Page 3 girls, Yvonne Paul Management, and co-authored the book 'The Glamour Game', published in 1989.

below:
Linda Hayden was already a star thanks to schoolgirl sex epic **Baby Love**, produced by Michael Klinger.

he needed to be able to work fast and bring a film in on budget. So I got him into the office.' Haggard, then 31, remembers the interview well: 'Tony was looking for what he was he was always in that period, namely a lively action story, in the horror area with four or five very strong sequences involving sex, darkness and a bit of violence, but not too much. He understood what his audience was looking for. His gifts as a showman were very interesting to me because he was very different to people I had met and he was very charming in the way he explained everything to me, introducing this rather different world.' The director, who had one feature to his credit, was duly hired, while Neame handed the pre-production chores over to Heyworth and Andrews and promptly returned to his day job in Wardour Street.

unearthing of some bones found in a field by a peasant, but Tenser and Neame still had reservations: 'I wanted the Judge to be a more ambiguous character but it was felt that wouldn't work' the writer explains, 'and Tigon also insisted on a 'Book of Witches', to explain what was going on.' Tenser also suggested that various traditional witchcraft punishments such as ducking could be imported from *Witchfinder General*.

With an amended script and a new title - 'The Devil's Touch' - Christopher Neame drew up a short list of possible directors and presented it to the new producers and Tenser for consideration. The name that attracted Tenser's eye was Piers Haggard: 'Piers had done some television work so I went to the BBC and saw one of the episodes he had made. I thought that was good and I knew to work for the BBC

The first challenge facing the production team was to make sure that everything was ready for Tigon's scheduled start date. Moreover Haggard was expressing serious reservations about the format, convinced that a trilogy would be aesthetically unappealing as well as detrimental to the box-office potential of the film. Andrews and Heyworth convinced Tenser that a full feature could be made for the same money, and Wynne-Simmons was instructed to swiftly adapt his trilogy into a single narrative. Wynne-Simmons, working under considerable time pressure, did as he was asked, producing a single narrative that told of a farmer unearthing some animal bones, which turn out to be the dormant remains of a 'devil'. 'I was adamant that it was a 'devil' with a small 'd',' Wynne-Simmons

insists, 'I wanted a film about an ancient religion, not necessarily Satanism - I didn't want to be specific.' The evil contained in the remains soon infects the young of the village, in particularly the inappropriately named 'Angel', who quickly assumes the role of leader to her disaffected and gullible gang. What starts as mischief soon escalates into violence, and only the sombre 'Judge' has the knowledge and power to combat the growing menace. 'I was determined not to make a camp Hammer-style horror film,' Haggard remembers, 'I went to see a lot of horror movies and the best of the genre was where there was a strong human element like *Bride of Frankenstein (1935)*, where you feel for the characters and that's the direction Robert and I wanted to take the script.'

Crucial to the success of the film would be the performance of the younger members of the cast, in particular the person chosen to play 'Angel'. Haggard choose a protégé of Michael Klinger, teenager Linda Hayden, who had already starred in the controversial *Baby Love (1968)*, Klinger's first film as an independent producer.[4] The pouting, sensual Angel was a part that could have been custom-made for Hayden, already being hailed, by the press at least, as the screen's latest young temptress; Haggard was also confident of the starlet's ability to show a darker side: 'She was a very good actress but Tony wanted her because she

was something of a sex symbol at the time. I think she was 17 at the time but I have to say she was terrific and not bothered at all by the nudity, which was just part of the package.'

The supporting cast could all lay claim to an illustrious pedigree: Tamara Ustinov was the daughter of Peter; Michele Dotrice's father was noted actor Roy; and Simon Williams was the son of Hugh. The more experienced actor Anthony Ainley - himself part of a famous acting family - played the priest who is exposed, quite literally, to Angel's unabashed charms, and Barry Andrews was cast as Ralph, the unfortunate farmer. The crucial role of the Judge was more of a problem to fill. The first choice, Peter Cushing, declined; his wife was terminally ill and Cushing was winding down his film commitments to spend as much time as possible with her. Christopher Lee would have been ideal but he was by now a major star, and well beyond the reach of Tigon's budget. Despite persistent rumours to the contrary, Vincent Price was not considered, in fact Tenser dismisses the suggestion outright: 'He was the *Witchfinder General*, at least in my mind. So there was no way I would have put him forward for a role like this.' Instead, Tigon called on an actor who had already served Tenser in small but crucial parts in several of his most important films: Patrick Wymark. The veteran actor was a notorious drinker and

above:
Tony Tenser flanked by Barry Andrews and Patrick Wymark on location during the making of **Blood on Satan's Claw**. This was the veteran actor's last screen appearance. He died in October 1970.

above:
Linda Hayden as the inappropriately named Angel tempts Reverend Fallowfield (the late Anthony Ainley) in **Blood on Satan's Claw**.

below:
Barry Andrews as Ralph Gower faces his own temptations. The devil and his Angel can be glimpsed in the background. Writer Robert Wynne-Simmons insists his was a devil with a small 'd'...

was considered by some in the industry to be more trouble than he was worth. He had however been notably effective as Cromwell in his fleeting appearance in *Witchfinder General*, and before that he was excellent as the insidious landlord in *Repulsion*. Wymark would give the Judge a sense of moral ambiguity as well as iron resolution.

Haggard's crew was blessed by the appointment of Dick Bush from the BBC as cinematographer; he would later photograph the likes of *Twins of Evil (1971)* and *Dracula A.D. 1972 (1972)* before going on to work with Ken Russell and Blake Edwards. Marc Wilkinson, who worked extensively in the theatre as well as for Lindsay Anderson on *If.... (1968)*, was brought in to provide a suitably rustic and eerie soundtrack.

Insisting that he needed two weeks to rehearse his cast, Haggard pushed the first day of shooting back to the 14th of April, but even with this extra time to polish up their shooting script both director and writer accepted that the narrative had a number of loose ends. Some of the inconsistencies were resolved as the film was shot, which meant that the writer was on set throughout production, working with Haggard to hone the script as shooting progressed - Haggard in fact earned himself an 'additional material by...' credit for these last-minute amendments. Haggard also sought to exploit the new-found freedoms in the realms of censorship, seeking to push the barriers by juxtaposing teenage sex with violence - strictly forbidden under Trevelyan's previous informal codes.

In terms of style and setting the film was deliberately evocative of *Witchfinder General*; the director and writer wanted their countryside to look lived in. The costumes had to look like real clothes and not recent purchases from theatrical outfitters, and they worked hard to ensure the dialogue had the right period sound, even if the words and phases were modern. As Wynne-Simmons witnessed, the similarities didn't stop there: 'This was my first experience as a screenwriter on a film set but I remember quite vividly watching the make-up men preparing the 'Kensington Gore', the synthetic blood substitute. They made bucket after bucket of the stuff. In the end they were all lined up across the grass!'

One of Wynne-Simmons's stated intentions was to explore the balance between old and new religions, between nature and man. As Haggard entertained the press on the set at Pinewood he demonstrated his appreciation for the film's themes: 'It's rural mythology with the smell of the country earth and without any modish, urban confidence tricks. We're treating it as realistically as possible.' In tune with this philosophy studio work, ironically, was kept to a minimum as Haggard sought to exploit locations such as Bix Bottom in the Chiltern Hills, and Black Park at Pinewood. Art Director Arnold Chapkis lessened his workload when he discovered a ruined chapel and disused chalk pit within driving distance of Pinewood, both of which helped offset the cost of script re-writes. Amazingly, despite the difficulties, Haggard brought his film in at £82,000, only £7,000 over budget.

While Piers Haggard was still up to his knees in synthetic blood, the first cut of 'Young Man I Think You're Dying' was delivered to Wardour Street, where it was met with some disappointment by Tenser: 'There was too much dialogue, it was a very talky script. And there was simply too much talking instead of moving, but if the director wanted to do it that way it was hard to get him to change. We needed to edit a lot of the dialogue, which was a shame because both Beryl Reid and Flora Robson were brilliant, brilliant actresses.' In concentrating on his two leading actresses, Kelly had moved the focus of the film onto them, in the process sacrificing the suspense and drama of the film as a whole. Tenser, the master publicist, had nothing to work with: 'When there is a murder you have to see some blood or else why have a beast in the cellar? You aim your film at an audience. Something like *The Spy Who Shagged Me* was a big hit and some people loved it but it's not to everyone's taste - the producers managed to find their audience. In this case we had a horror film so it has to be seen to be a horror film. If you are making a woman's picture then you make a weepy, you don't make a western.' Kelly was dispatched back to the cutting rooms to construct a horror film.

* * * * *

Whilst Tenser was keeping himself busy on the day-to-day work, there was also a great deal of activity in the executive suites. Since the merger, corporate strategies were being conceived; plans were made throughout the spring of 1970 to bring the two companies together as one - or so it seemed to those outside of the Hemdale boardroom. The public show of unity was just that however - a show. The Board was comprised of a number of very strong

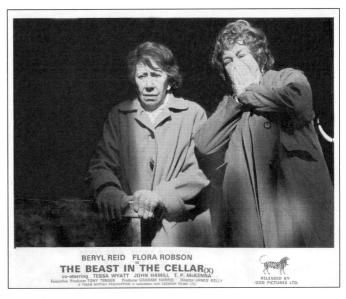

BERYL REID FLORA ROBSON
in
THE BEAST IN THE CELLAR(X)
co-starring TESSA WYATT JOHN HAMILL T. P. McKENNA
Executive Producer TONY TENSER Producer GRAHAM HARRIS Director JAMES KELLY
A TIGON BRITISH PRODUCTION in association with LEANDER FILMS LTD.
RELEASED BY
GON PICTURES LTD.

above: British front of house still for **The Beast in the Cellar**. The last-minute change of title from **The Cellar** meant that the first batch of stills had a sticker over the original title.

personalities, successful businessmen in their own right with very different ideas on how the business should be run; it wasn't long before rumours of disagreement were circulating through Wardour Street. By the summer the problems had became public knowledge. A full-blooded feud had erupted between Laurie Marsh and David Hemmings in one corner, and John Daly and fellow director, Derek Dawson, in the other. The 'big blow-up', as it was termed in one newspaper, centred on Hemmings and specifically his role as an executive member of the Board. Much was made of a quote, attributed to an unnamed source, expressing the Board's view that Hemmings was, 'spending too much time interfering with the business side when he should have been out making films.' Effectively, Hemmings had run up a debt during a period when, by choice, he had not been working.

At this point Tigon's day-to-day business was still being handled completely independently by a small group of people directly under the management of Tenser, who was responsible to Marsh. Neither Tenser nor the production team at Pinewood were directly involved in the dispute, however Laurie Marsh, who owned around 17% of the new company, found himself at odds with Daly and some of the co-directors over the future development plans. Marsh sided with Hemmings as the Board split into two camps, each vying for control of the whole company. No sooner had the rift been publicly acknowledged than Laurie Marsh resigned, followed by Hemdale Chairman Gerry Needleman, on the 7th of August. John Daly, on behalf of the Board, then issued writs against David Hemmings for repayment of some £43,000 outstanding and for breach of contract. As a result Hemmings, the star of such high profile films as *Blow-Up (1966)* and *Barbarella*

below: Some more family dramatics from the great Beryl Reid.

above:
British admat for **The Dark**, re-christened **The Haunted House of Horror** by the time of its release. The support feature, Lindsay Shontoff's **Clegg**, is often mistakenly thought to be a Tigon production.

below:
Frankie Avalon's death scene - a logical extension of director Armstrong's phallic imagery.

organised for the benefit of AIP. 'Tony told me not to judge it until I had seen the whole thing,' Armstrong recalls, 'but I waited, waited and waited, wondering if anything of my film would be in the print. By the time the lights came up my head was in my hands.'

Whatever the director's thoughts about his film may have been, Tenser considered it to be releasable, so he signed a deal with Lindsay Shontoff to use his 'X' certificate detective romp, *Clegg (1969)* as a co-feature. The publicity materials were duly commissioned and a release campaign for the double bill of 'The Dark' and *Clegg* was duly worked out. Even as the lurid posters were being hung in the Wardour Street shop-front, Tenser was having second thoughts: 'The selling of a film starts off with the title, and that's how to get the public into the cinema - after that it's down to the cinema manager. My job is giving them a title and promotion that captures the public's attention.' Tenser did not think that the title 'The Dark' was up to the task, so he considered a number of alternatives. The press advertisements were hastily withdrawn and new posters were designed. The final step in 'The Dark's' troubled journey from page to screen was complete in July 1970, when *The Haunted House of Horror* was released.

(1968), was designated a 'wholly owned asset' of the Group, and Hemdale gained exclusive rights to his earnings up to 1978.

While the Boardroom fracas played itself out above their heads, Tenser and his team devoted themselves to the bread and butter work of actually running a film production company. Delayed by the re-shoots and the re-editing, Gerry Levy finally delivered his cut of 'The Dark', complete with new sub-plot. In the meantime Michael Armstrong had already finished directing one feature film, the controversial *Mark of the Devil*, and was busy editing a short. With some trepidation he accepted an invitation from Tenser to attend a special screening of 'The Dark',

THE HAUNTED HOUSE OF HORROR

'A ghostly fiend lurks in an evil house to destroy its victims in an orgy of terror!'
- UK Press Release -

Synopsis

At a swinging London party, a group of bored teenagers decide they want a new experience so Richard (Julian Barnes) suggests they drive to an abandoned, supposedly haunted, house where he played as a child. After briefly exploring, their séance is disturbed by strange noises and they soon discover that a previously shut door is now open. A 'ghost hunt' is interrupted by a brutal murder, prompting the group to flee the scene. Afterwards they realise that the murderer must have been one of the gang and decide the only way to trap the killer is to revisit the scene of the crime.

Critique

'Ideas are all borrowed from other films, most notably 'The Haunted' and THAT Hitchcock movie.'
- Films and Filming, 08/70

'...this haunted house is more likely to induce sleep than nightmare.'
- Monthly Film Bulletin, 08/70

above:
The first of the two murders shot by director Armstrong. The film's second, almost bloodless, killing was actually directed by Gerry Levy.

left:
Pressbook cover promoting the delayed North American release for Tenser's last two AIP co-productions. The two companies went their separate ways after completion of **The Haunted House of Horror**.

'*...a sad mixture of haunted house and murder mystery clichés belonging to a different era.*'
- Cinefantastique, Fall 1970

Armstrong's story, stripped of all but a hint of its sexual tensions, was promoted as a somewhat melodramatic stalk-and-slash, and disappointed critics and viewers alike. Levy's sequences did little but add to the running time, and what remains of Armstrong's work was undermined by the poor editing. The scenes in the haunted house have some tension and Armstrong does well to create an atmosphere of menace in the cavernous Palace hotel, but the mood swiftly changes when any of the leading players open their mouths. The performances are generally poor - Julian Barnes and Frankie Avalon in particular struggle with their lightweight characterisations - although the murder sequences, with the exception of the George Sewell slaying, are well executed and for their day quite shocking.

Armstrong loathed the final film as well as its new catch-penny title, but Tenser at least felt he had a commercial package and despite the dismissive reviews *The Haunted House of Horror* opened to reasonable business in the UK. In the States, AIP sought to corner both the youth, and the more traditional horror, markets by pairing their two Tigon films under the banner: 'Terror and Torture Join Forces'. *Curse of the Crimson Altar*,

COME FACE TO FACE WITH NAKED FEAR!

BORIS KARLOFF
CHRISTOPHER LEE

HORROR HOUSE GP AND the CRIMSON CULT GP

COLOR by MOVIELAB

COLOR by MOVIELAB

AN AMERICAN INTERNATIONAL RELEASE

A TIGON BRITISH FILM PRODUCTION - AN AMERICAN INTERNATIONAL RELEASE

A TIGON BRITISH-AMERICAN INTERNATIONAL PRODUCTION

©1970 American International Pictures, Inc.

above:
US artwork for the AIP double bill. In contrast to promotional materials produced for **Witchfinder General** (aka **The Conqueror Worm** in America), the Tigon credit is given equal prominence with that of their US partners.

below:
Sibylla Kay and Joan Alcorn, 2/3 of the love triangle in **Monique**.

released as 'The Crimson Cult', formed the lower half of a double-bill with Armstrong's movie, now re-titled 'Horror House'. The films received much the same critical reaction as they had done in the UK, but the bill generated good returns and 'Horror House' managed to develop something of a cult following on the drive-in circuit.

*　*　*　*　*

While John Bown was completing the task of editing *Monique*, Michael Style asked the noted French musician Jacques Loussier whether he would like to write the film's soundtrack. Both Bown and Style took time off and flew to Paris to seal the deal with Loussier. The composer, whose only previous English language film credit was Jack Cardiff's *The Mercenaries (1968)*, agreed to provide a suitably continental score underpinning what Bown was confident would be a funny and intelligent adult comedy. The British Board of Film Censors didn't find the film amusing however, and Tenser was none too pleased either, for different reasons. 'Tony had expected an exploitation movie, which he didn't get, and he felt that the children slowed the film down too much,' Bown noted. Trevelyan also had problems with the presence of children in a sex film, even though there was no direct connection; Bown and Style were duly summoned to the BBFC's Soho Square head office to debate their cut. Trevelyan held firm and after some fairly major deletions, including the removal of nearly all the nudity, *Monique* was finally awarded its 'X' certificate on the 4th of June 1970.

By the time Bown's film received its UK press show a few weeks later it was already a major hit in North America. In the US, *The Killing of Sister George* had been a significant success, particularly in the East Coast cities, helped considerably by full-page adverts in magazines such as Playboy, which featured explicit stills of Coral Browne hovering over a naked Susannah York. Joe Levine, who had picked up the North American rights for Avco Embassy, stoked up anticipation for *Monique* with a similar campaign leading up to the official world premiere in Montreal. The public and press response was enthusiastic so, anxious to keep the ball rolling, Levine arranged the US premiere in New York,

flying over Sibylla Kay to attend in person. The scenes at the American premiere were something new for a Tigon movie: 'I arrived and they had all these television cameras outside,' Sibylla Kay recalls. 'There was a huge crowd and I arrived in a black limousine with four security police. When we got out of the car the crowd was massive, everybody surged forward and if the guards hadn't been there people would have taken bits of me, a finger or some skin!'

Although the reviews on the East Coast weren't particularly good, the box-office was solid, whereas in Los Angeles, where the critics were considerably kinder, the takings were down - perhaps cinema-goers on the West Coast were a little too jaded. In contrast to the North American hysteria, the British release, under the watchful eye of Trevelyan, was a low-key affair. *Monique* slipped quietly into the Cameo Poly in London's West End.

MONIQUE

'Bill & Jean have finally something in common... Monique!'
- UK press release -

Synopsis

Jean and Bill are a normal couple, living a drab but settled life in suburbia with their two children. Jean is particularly unsettled - she isn't happy with the sexual side of the relationship and she wants to go back to work. Things change when a French au pair, Monique, arrives to look after the children; young and vibrant, she attracts first David and then Jean, separately and then together in a ménage a trois. When Monique returns to France, she leaves Jean and Bill happy and fulfilled.

Critique

'Despite its naturalistic, almost prosaic approach Monique remains an unconvincingly sexual fairy tale... Its chief weakness lies in the over ambivalent title character - a mixture of shallow minded teenager and worldly wise sophisticate.'
- Monthly Film Bulletin, 05/70

'...avoids some of the broad sex overtones that characterise so many of the current X-rated films, but nevertheless socks its theme across. Sibylla Kay enacts the title role with a flourish and Bown's direction is fairly skilful.'
- Variety, 01/04/70

'...amuses in good taste with nary a leer or a false move. Sibylla, who never loses her sensual smile no matter what she is doing – and she does a lot - is particularly desirable, perfect for the part.'
- LA Citizen, 04/70

'Producers Tony Tenser and Michael Style, and director John Bown are to be congratulated.'
- New York Post, 08/03/70

Those critics who bothered to see the film found an amusing suburban fable, intelligently played and sensitively directed, but *Monique* struggled to find an audience in the UK, where it was released in its censored form. The film's London opening was a disappointment to John Bown: 'Tigon opened it in a tiny cinema off Charing Cross Road and predictably the audience were all men in dirty macs. Of course it's not that sort of film so after half an hour they all left to find something a little more to their tastes, leaving an empty cinema!' Tigon's publicity department didn't help, taking their lead from *Sister George* with some salacious promotions of their own: 'Does your marriage need Monique?' teased the posters over some 'three in bed' stills. The brazen advertising may have driven customers into that particular cinema but it only served to put off exhibitors in the provinces.

Despite the film's poor public reception, the sale to Avco Embassy ensured that Tenser made back his money on *Monique*, and subsequent sales to the European territories had secured a small profit. Tenser was certainly more than satisfied and encouraged Bown to develop a suitable follow up, reasoning that if the director could deliver on a film like *Monique*, he could do the same with a 'proper sex film.' Bown held out for his road movie 'Hey You!' but Tenser couldn't find any potential backers, so with

no common ground for future projects Bown and 'Hey You!' were allowed to go. The director ended up at Bernard Delfont's EMI for a while when they took an option on the script, but the film never materialised.[5] Michael Armstrong soon followed Bown out of the Hammer House door when he was released from his contract: 'There was nothing acrimonious, I liked Tony very much but I really didn't want to work that way. And after first Heyward and then *Mark of the Devil* I wasn't even sure I wanted to direct again.' Tenser remembers, 'we just didn't seem to have any projects in common.'

above:
Sibylla Kay, seen here in all her glory, was the wife of **Monique**'s writer/director John Bown; the couple's children and even their pet dog also appeared in the film.

below:
Too much for the UK censor - this shot was reserved for the European audiences.

above:
Sibylla Kay and David Sumner share a tender moment in **Monique**. Tenser ultimately was disappointed by the amount of nudity in the final cut, but it didn't prevent Tigon from selling the film as a sex movie.

* * * * *

Conciliatory talks between the former Board members of the Hemdale Group failed to broker an acceptable compromise. To the City pundits it looked like Marsh and Hemmings - who with their institutional backers controlled over fifty percent of the voting stock - were in a strong position. While Daly would not publicly voice his plans, Marsh announced his intention to call an extraordinary general meeting to oust the present Board and take control himself. He also hinted that he intended to resign his position in Star Holdings so he could devote his time entirely to a revamped Hemdale. Having ceased to exist as a corporate entity, the name Tigon was now only used to differentiate which parts of the new company had come from where. A new deal was slow in coming together, but when the expected announcement was made, it didn't come from Marsh, but John Daly. The proposal hinged on the Stock Exchange agreement to suspend Hemdale's quotation while the Board under Daly resigned. Daly would then lead a buy-out of Hemdale's interest in 14 of their 15 artists - the

exception being David Hemmings. Laurie Marsh would offset the loss of the stars and their earnings (a considerable asset to Hemdale, contributing two thirds of the Group's profit in 1969) by injecting some of his own property investments. Hemmings's contract with Hemdale would remain in place. The newly constituted Hemdale, under Marsh, would then consist of Tigon film production/distribution interests, Hemmings himself and such diverse interests as the studio and equipment hire ventures, a promotions company and two Golden Chef restaurants.

In August of that year the proposal was rejected outright, and relations hit a new low when the two leading protagonists, Daly and Hemmings, issued writs against each other. With no end to the row in sight, Marsh drafted a radical proposal suggesting the outright purchase of the former Tigon companies as an independent trading entity, effectively restoring Tigon to pre-Hemdale status. The plan was accepted, and in September 1970 Laurie Marsh formally purchased Tigon and its associated companies from Hemdale for the sum of £210,000. Marsh would be Chairman while Hemdale would retain, for the time being, 30% of the shares in the new company. Tony Tenser retained his position as Managing Director while David Haft, an American producer with strong connections in Hollywood, joined the Board to give the company a more international perspective. Hemdale disposed of their remaining Tigon shares in November 1970, severing the short lived and acrimonious marriage between the two companies.

The de-merger from Hemdale freed Tenser and Marsh to design their own production strategy. They had several low-budget horror movies awaiting release but Marsh wanted to push the company into bigger budget films, relying on David Haft's connections to attract Hollywood investment. The distribution side would still release double-bills of subtitled sex films with titles like *Inga - I Have Lust* and *Labyrinth of Sex*, imported at nominal cost from Sweden and Italy respectively, while the production arm would take a very different route, starting with the making of Tenser's first children's film, the long-planned Harry Alan Towers collaboration, *Black Beauty*.

* * * * *

The year 1970 was witness to a significant change to Tigon's most lucrative domestic market. The audience for British exploitation films had matured slowly over the last decade, causing John Trevelyan and the BBFC to come under increasing pressure from filmmakers to allow more nudity and violence in mainstream films. A firm opponent of unnecessary censorship throughout his professional life, Trevelyan had spoken about the failings of the existing classification criteria for a number of years but had always been reluctant to act. By the late Sixties the 'X' certificate, reserved for films that were not considered suitable for exhibition to persons under the age of sixteen, had become a blunt weapon and, outside of the private cinema clubs where business was booming, movies still had to be heavily censored before they were considered fit for this market.

Trevelyan's practice of pre-reading scripts - it was estimated that he was personally reading 80% of those submitted - to weed out the more undesirable elements gave him enormous influence over films shot in the UK. American films were of course governed by the infamous Production Code, which set down in detail what filmmakers could and couldn't show, ranging from the acceptable length of an on-screen kiss to guidelines regarding the depiction of 'characters of low morals.' The Code was enormously unpopular with the new breed of directors, so when films such as *Bonnie and Clyde (1967)* and *The Wild Bunch (1969)* were made, it was simply ignored. The old censorship order in the States effectively collapsed. Swamped by extreme American imports, Trevelyan was faced with cutting huge amounts of footage out of films to ensure they were suitable for exhibition to sixteen-year olds. Imposing outright bans on a large number of adult movies, or alternatively cutting them severely, would be a regressive step. Instead, he wanted to give filmmakers more freedom to express themselves. The BBFC's classification system was overhauled, and as of the 1st of July 1970 the ratings were:

U - Suitable for general exhibition.
A - Parents or guardians should be advised the film may contain scenes they might prefer children under the age of 14 not to see.
AA - Passed for exhibition only to persons of fourteen years and over.
X - Passed for exhibition only to persons of eighteen years and over.

The 'X' rating of course retained its 'forbidden fruit' image, and remained the natural home of the horror genre, despite the fact that most existing British horror movies would be comfortably accommodated within the new 'AA' classification. Trevelyan's new system fundamentally changed the market for 'X' certificate films, opening up the possibility that films containing sex and violence, previously the strict preserve of the independents, could now be screened on the national circuits. Paradoxically, this led to an unprecedented boom in private cinema clubs as pornographers became ever more extreme in their efforts to compete with the major distributors.

Within the horror genre, the likes of James Carreras now struggled to keep up with the trend for more graphic scenes and suddenly horror films increasingly mixed sex and violence in a way that had never even been considered before. A whole new sub-genre was created practically overnight. Any fears that Trevelyan might have reduced the size of the market for adult films proved completely groundless as in fact more and more filmmakers jumped on the bandwaggon, seeking to exploit the new freedom. Acting with the best of intentions, Trevelyan was ushering in cinema's 'permissive age'.

Sexploitation returned with a vengeance, led by a host of familiar names including Stanley Long, Derek Ford, Michael Armstrong and even Michael Klinger. In fact, within five years Klinger had produced the first 'sex' movie to top the UK box-office charts, *Confessions of a Window Cleaner (1974)*. Directors were also free to explore cinematic violence as never before: films like *The Devils (1971)*, *Straw Dogs (1971)*, and *A Clockwork Orange (1971)* were rushed into production, each one wilfully pushing the limits of the new censorship code. 'X' certificate films enjoyed something of a boom but the traditional markets for the low budget filmmakers - horror and sexploitation - became very crowded with mainstream filmmakers. Tigon, whose output had been more diverse than most, was particularly well placed to adapt, and true to form it moved in a direction that surprised the company's competitors.

above:
John Trevelyan, the Secretary of the British Board of Film Censors, whose personal friendship with Tenser would eventually lead to his appointment to the board of Tigon.

below:
Black Beauty was responsible for the unlikeliest of show-business combinations; Tony Tenser and Mark '**Oliver**' Lester.

KINE WEEKLY

above:
As a rule Tenser seldom used Kine Weekly covers after leaving Compton, as Tigon's advertising budgets didn't usually allow for such selective promotion.

right:
British promotional artwork for **Black Beauty**. Predictably, Anna Sewell fans protested about the Tigon treatment of their idol's book.

MARK LESTER   WALTER SLEZAK
in
BLACK BEAUTY

CO-STARRING

Ursula Glas
Peter Lee Lawrence
John Nettleton
Patrick Mower
Maria Rohm

MUSIC COMPOSED BY LIONEL BART
WITH ADDITIONAL MUSIC BY JOHN CAMERON
SCREENPLAY BY WOLF MANKOWITZ
EXECUTIVE PRODUCER TONY TENSER
PRODUCED BY PETER L. ANDREWS
& MALCOLM B. HEYWORTH
DIRECTED BY JAMES HILL

A TIGON-BRITISH-CHILTON FILM PRODUCTION
A TIGON RELEASE

Still the younger generation's favourite Best Seller in 1971

below:
UK lobby card for **Black Beauty**. The film's success led to Tenser's plans for a television series, which were later abandoned.

During the first few months of 1970, Harry Alan Towers had succeeded in his efforts to raise the remainder of the budget for *Black Beauty* from various sources in Germany and Spain. Tenser in the meantime had decided to split the risk as far as the UK end was concerned, and entered into a deal with Peter Andrews and Malcolm Heyworth's Chilton Productions Ltd to co-produce the movie. The risk all but disappeared entirely when the US giant Paramount bought the distribution rights to North America, giving Tigon the appealing prospect of a nationwide opening across the US.

Towers hired Wolf Mankowitz, whose previous work included *A Kid for Two Farthings (1955)* and *The Two Faces of Dr. Jekyll (1960)*, to write a script from Anna Sewell's out-of-copyright novel. Mankowitz decided to exercise his creative prerogative and freely adapted the story, adding several incidents and deleting characters. Although both Tenser and Towers were happy that the final script was true to the 'spirit' of the book, both underestimated how vociferous Sewell's admirers could be.[6] To be fair to Mankowitz a number of the changes were imposed on him due to the multi-national nature of the production, Towers had committed to film in Spain so the North West Frontier made an appearance but the remainder of the film, in episodic format, does stick fairly closely to the core of Sewell's book - the love between a child and his best friend, Beauty.

Tenser was determined to take no chances in this unfamiliar territory: 'It was important to get a director who had a feel for this sort of thing. It wasn't really the type of movie where we could use a new director and anyway we had partners to consider.' James Hill was duly signed up on the strength of his previous work, which included such films as *Born Free (1965)*, *An Elephant Called Slowly (1969)* and of course *A Study in Terror*. The additional budget allowed some flexibility in the choice of crew and, in keeping with the family theme, Lionel Bart was hired to write the score. The prolific composer had more than 2,500 songs to his credit. He worked on numerous stage musicals during his career but he is undoubtedly best known for the huge stage and film hit *Oliver! (1968)*. Appropriately enough Mark Lester, the juvenile lead from that film and still only thirteen years of age, was signed to play Beauty's first owner and childhood friend.

Holding up the British end of a multi-national cast was former Hammer leading man Patrick Mower as the roguish squire, altogether too free with both his evil cackle and his riding whip. As a concession to the film's originator, Towers's wife Maria Rohm, who made a career out of appearing in her husband's productions, was given a support role. German sensibilities were considered when the romantic lead went to Uschi Glas, the German-born actress who had carved a career in European movies. Hollywood veteran Walter Slezak, star of *Riffraff (1947)*, was persuaded out of semi-retirement in Switzerland to lend the film an air of Hollywood charm. Slezak took second-billing to Lester despite the fact that the latter only appears in the film's extended prologue sequence.

Having won their spurs on a low-budget horror, Heyworth and Andrews must have thought that making a children's classic would be something of a gentle romp - they were sadly mistaken. Dispensing with the expense of a studio shoot, the producers sought to take advantage of tax incentives by allowing Ireland to stand in for England.

Despite being granted access to some of the best stables and horse handlers in Europe, Hill was presented with a minor problem when he came to shoot the birth sequence. 'Finding a mare about to give birth was easy enough,' Tenser recalls, 'finding one having a black foal was a real problem. Jimmy had his camera set up for weeks before he got the right one.' In fact the second unit managed to capture five

left:
This looks more like a Tenser film! Aristocrat Patrick Mower as Sam Greene lashes out in **Black Beauty**. All the scenes featuring British stars Lester and Mower were shot in Ireland, though the story is actually set in England.

births before an appropriately coloured foal was found. The horse's colour also presented a unique problem for Tenser's make-up people: 'The film was set over a period of ten to fifteen years so we needed several horses, five altogether I think. Getting a black horse in Ireland was easy enough but getting the white blazon wasn't, so we had to paint it on. In Spain we couldn't get a black horse. We had to use a brown one and paint it up with water dye. Luckily this was one time that the weather was kind or it would have looked like its mascara was running.'

below:
The sultry German actress Uschi Glas, installed in the film as part of the complex multi-national finance package put together by Harry Alan Towers.

MARK LESTER · WALTER SLEZAK
in 'BLACK BEAUTY' u
Based on the novel by Anna Sewell
co-starring URSULA GLAS · PETER LEE LAWRENCE
JOHN NETTLETON · PATRICK MOWER
MARIA ROHM
Music composed by LIONEL BART with additional music by JOHN CAMERON
Screenplay by WOLF MANKOWITZ · Executive Producer TONY TENSER
Produced by PETER L. ANDREWS & MALCOLM B. HEYWORTH
Directed by JAMES HILL
A TIGON BRITISH-CHILTON FILM PRODUCTION   A TIGON RELEASE

above:
Proof that collaborating with Tigon need not lead to permanent harm; Mark Lester is now working happily as a chiropodist in the South of England.

Heyworth and Andrews had not arranged access to trained film horses, which added to their worries when Mark Lester admitted he couldn't actually ride; some hurried rescheduling allowed time for the young actor to take intensive lessons. Similar problems in Spain resulted in Maria Rohm falling off her horse while riding sidesaddle; she completed the film with several broken ribs. Despite the minor problems, Hill was an old hand with both animals and large-scale films. Sticking tightly to his schedule, he wrapped shooting in Spain and returned to the UK just before Christmas. Early in January he retired to the dubbing studios to 'anglicize' his multi-national cast.

Black Beauty had opened doors in Hollywood - in particular at Paramount - and Tenser had the perfect film to exploit the situation further. It came from an unlikely source, Patrick Curtis. In the years since making *The Sorcerers* Curtis had worked hard to establish himself as a major motion picture producer, embarking on a number of highly publicised films under the banner of Curtwel, all of course starring the company's only real asset, Raquel Welch, now Mrs Curtis. Unfortunately these movies failed to translate Ms Welch's staggering media popularity into box-office success; she remained a major movie actress without a major movie.[7] Curtis continued to work on his wife's behalf and in 1970 he persuaded MGM to bankroll *The Beloved*, purely on the basis that it starred Raquel.

After shooting wrapped in Europe, Curtis stopped over in London on his way back to Hollywood, and renewed his acquaintance with Tony Tenser. With, at best, a mixed track record as a producer Curtis wanted to branch out into directing. He offered Tigon two possible projects and suggested that he had access to the necessary finance to get them made, and distribution to get them shown in the States. Tenser was sufficiently intrigued to set up Curtis in a room at Tigon's Wardour Street head office while the two outlines were firmed up. Curtis's preferred choice was a re-vamp of the old Michael Reeves script, 'The Devil's Discord', previously optioned by both Compton and Tigon. Curtis planned to take the directorial reins himself on what was envisaged as a low-budget horror movie. Tenser however was far more attracted to Curtis's second proposal; not only was it more in keeping with Tigon's newly-found international image but it also fulfilled one of the producer's boyhood ambitions. 'I always wanted to make a cowboy film,' Tenser confesses. 'I had been watching Cowboys and Indians since I was a boy and as long as I could remember I wanted to make one. I needed to get it out of my system. When Patrick Curtis showed me this script called *Hannie Caulder*, I jumped at it.'

The script was a revenge drama from a story by Peter Cooper, set in the West of the 1870's and centred on a woman, Hannie, and her quest to kill the men who raped her and murdered her husband. Curtis assured Tenser that by shooting in Spain and using predominately European actors and crew he could bring the film in on a modest budget, however the two men differed on their thoughts regarding the leading lady. 'Originally we were going to make the film with another actress, an unknown, which suited our budget,' Tenser remembers. 'I was away somewhere on business and Patrick was in the office. He met Laurie Marsh and sold Laurie on the idea of Raquel Welch in the lead.' Of course, as executive producer Tenser could veto all casting decisions. Raquel herself did enough to convince him: 'I first met her when we made *The Sorcerers* and I thought she was beautiful, particularly in photographs. What sort of actress she was then, I don't know. But she went back to acting school after she had become a star, which was a brave thing to do, and became a very good actress. I agreed to cast her in the lead, which meant we now had a very much bigger film.'[8]

Casting Welch may have pushed up the budget but it had one huge advantage for Tigon, and Curtis wasn't slow to play it up to the gathered press at the Hammer House press launch: 'Finance has never been a problem,' he claimed. 'I have only to lift a phone, mention the subject and say that Raquel wants to do it - and I have the requisite financing from any one of five banks in London.' Producers are entitled to a little hyperbole, especially with the press, but in truth Curtis had in fact managed to convince none other than Barclays Bank, then dabbling in films as a source of venture capital investment, to underwrite part of Tigon's investment. The obvious attraction of Welch also secured the interest of the Bank of America, a more experienced player in movie finance, who came on board with a significant loan.

With credit agreements in place Tigon had covered 60% of the budget. Curtwel covered the remainder including, as was usual with co-productions, the salaries of the American cast and crew. As a gesture of goodwill neither Curtis nor Welch drew up-front salaries, both accepting a profit participation agreement. The budget could to some extent be off-set by tax incentives offered by the Spanish authorities to filmmakers working in Almeria, but the pressure would be very much on for Tigon until such time as a US distributor came on board.

An ebullient Patrick Curtis spoke enthusiastically to the trade-paper Kine Weekly about the future: 'I like the people at Tigon,' Curtis proclaimed from behind his desk at Hammer House. 'Tony Tenser, Laurie Marsh, David Haft - you can do business with them. No nonsense - a straight deal.' In fact Curtis went on: 'I'd rather have them run my company than me, and hopefully they would rather have me make their films.' The contracts for *Hannie Caulder* were signed in November 1970, by which time Tenser had dropped the idea of 'The Devil's Discord' once and for all, but had picked up an option on another Curtwel project, 'The Hooligan', to be filmed in Ireland in late 1971.

As well as being a personal milestone for Tenser, *Hannie Caulder* represented a significant step up for Tigon; for the first time the company was making a film with genuine Hollywood aspirations - a major motion picture with an international star. Like all good westerns, *Hannie Caulder* had some depth; not just a simple tale of good guys shooting bad guys, it was closer to a Jacobean revenge fable in a desert setting. As the titular Hannie, Raquel Welch's rancher's wife sets out for revenge against the three

hoodlums, adorned by a discretely draped poncho, and aided by a veteran gunslinger and a displaced English gunsmith.

The screenplay credit of Z.X. Jones hides an uneasy collaboration between veteran television writer Burt Kennedy and producer David Haft, the latter ensuring that the film contained the elements that, as Kennedy ruefully observed in his autobiography, could have caused the film to be subtitled 'A Titful of Dollars.' It was an uneasy alliance at best, with the hard-drinking, hard-living Kennedy - who had cut his teeth on shows like *The Virginian* and *Lawman*, and went on to write and direct such popular westerns as *The War Wagon (1967)* and *Support Your Local Sheriff! (1969)* - tolerating rather than accommodating what he saw as the producer's interference.

above:
Robert Culp, Christopher Lee and Raquel Welch help fulfill Tenser's lifelong ambition to make a Western, **Hannie Caulder**.

below:
Honouring a promise made on **Curse of the Crimson Altar**, Tenser cast Lee in a non-horror role as the family-loving gunsmith Bailey.

left:
Tenser chats to star Robert Culp during his visit to the Spanish location. **Hannie Caulder** was to become one of Tigon's most troubled productions.

above:
The film's star Raquel Welch in pensive mood. **Hannie Caulder** was effectively her second film for Tenser after she had been an uncredited 'gofer' on **The Sorcerers**.

times and hadn't worked for a while and Roger said she would be interested in anything I could give her. I thought about the Madame who helps Hannie out. It wasn't a big part but it took her out to Spain for a couple of days and gave her a bit of money. It also gave her one of the funniest scenes in the film and we got to put 'guest star Diana Dors' on the poster, which may have made some difference, I don't know.'[11]

Hannie Caulder provided Tenser with the opportunity to honour a promise he had made to Christopher Lee some years earlier: 'Christopher and I were talking on the set of *Crimson Altar* and he said, 'why don't you ever put me in any of your non-horror films?' I said as soon as I found something suitable I would. Patrick and I were running through the casting and we got to the part of the gunsmith, an Englishman surrounded by a posse of children. I said let's leave that for now, I think I know someone ideal for that one.' Christopher Lee jumped at the chance to play Bailey, one of the few times he had been cast in the role of a happy, well-adjusted family man. In fact, by 1971 Lee had largely passed through his 'graveyard period'; more than a decade after he had first played Dracula, the actor had outgrown the narrow range British producers pegged him into. In 1970, he played in *The Private Life of Sherlock Holmes* for Billy Wilder. It broke the mould and convinced the actor that he could be more daring in his choice of films. Although Lee would still occasionally appear in horror movies, these would be scattered amongst more mainstream outings. The character of Bailey was in fact originally conceived as an American, and it says much for Lee's developing screen persona that he was perfectly at home in the predominantly American cast.

The participation of Raquel and the subsequent increase in the scope of the picture meant that Tenser and Curtis needed to abandon the notion of casting European unknowns and opt instead for faces recognisable to an American audience. Kennedy was keen for Robert Culp to play the part of the gunslinger. The hugely successful TV actor had starred in the hit show *I Spy*, and was anxious to make the break into film stardom. Kennedy felt that Culp's easy charm would be a major hook to get American armchair viewers into the cinemas.[9]

Kennedy's trademark was broad humour in otherwise bleak situations, and to accentuate the comic elements of the script three of Hollywood's best known character actors were engaged: Jack Elam, Strother Martin and Ernest Borgnine brought to the production the experience of over 160 movie credits between them, including some of the best Westerns ever made.[10] At the British end the cast reflected similar depth of experience, though the casting process itself was a little unorthodox. 'A chap called Roger Black called on me,' Tenser confides. 'He was an agent representing Diana Dors, who I remembered very well from the Fifties as the 'blonde bombshell'. She had fallen on hard

On the 18th of January, Kennedy and his crew assembled on Spain's Almerian coast to begin principal photography. The director had in fact been in Spain since before Christmas, soaking up the atmosphere and fine-tuning the script. With the exception of a few interiors at Twickenham Studios, Curtis had scheduled the entire film to be shot over 10 weeks on a standing Western town set left over from the heyday of the 'spaghetti western' fad. The Italians had first hit on Spain as an exotic location during the sixties, and although production costs had rocketed since then, they were still running at around a quarter of the Hollywood equivalent. Spain did not just attract makers of Westerns - the country's generous tax allowances made it a sensible choice for major motion pictures such as David Lean's *Doctor Zhivago (1965)*. There were plenty of first-class hotels close to the set to accommodate cast and crew, as well as the visiting press men from London and around Europe who would be flown in from time to

time during the shoot. The studio facilities on the other hand were basic, at least by Hollywood standards, but adequate as Burt Kennedy recounted to Film Review: 'What you need when you are shooting a Western is basically a wind machine, a water truck and a camera.'

For Tony Tenser, *Hannie Caulder* could not have been further away from the tried and tested 'Tigon way of business'. It was an approach that he did not feel comfortable accommodating at first. 'When we were making budget films we had to save money wherever we could,' Tenser explains, 'and all the cast and crew would be asked to economise as much as possible, it was a recognised part of the British film industry. With Americans involved that changed and you can't cut corners. For example on something like *Witchfinder General*, which was our movie even though there was American money, we could ask the cast to share a car with the crew going to the location. On a Hollywood film you couldn't do that, they wouldn't stand for it. It made it very difficult for us to control the budget.'

With David Haft keeping an eye on the script and day-to-day production issues, Patrick Curtis appointed himself as controller of anything and everything that affected the film's star. It was Curtis who suggested hiring the celebrated photographer Terry O'Neill to take a series of shots of Raquel on location. Portrait shots of

Welch in her costume (what there was of it!) for *One Million Years B.C. (1966)* had made the front pages of newspapers across the globe, and had bought the film the type of saturation publicity that money simply can't buy. Curtis wanted to repeat the exercise by using shots of the highly photogenic Raquel, dressed only in the poncho she wore throughout the film, posing happily on set and with other members of the cast. The photos were accompanied by a short promotional 'making of' featurette, centred around Raquel of course, and while neither quite scaled the heights achieved by the doe-skin bikini, they nevertheless ensured a high profile for the movie. Kennedy was happy to get in on the game, telling the press that he was trying to play down the sex but admitting to Film Review, 'of course there are shots which are... well you know but they are down to a minimum.' In the same interview, conducted for the magazine's cover story, old-school director Kennedy confessed, 'The main problem I had in *Hannie Caulder* was to try and make the woman utterly believable. I mean, can you imagine a woman taking up a gun after three men?'

Kennedy may have had some reservations about the narrative but it was the uneasy relationship with the producers that began to create problems. Haft had very fixed ideas about how the film should look

above:
Great shot of Culp and Lee in character - though it is never explained in the film why Bailey is played as an Englishman.

right:
Billed only as 'the doctor', Howard Goorney removes the devil's skin - incidentally one of the earlier titles for the film - from alleged witch Margaret (Michele Dotrice) in **Blood on Satan's Claw**.

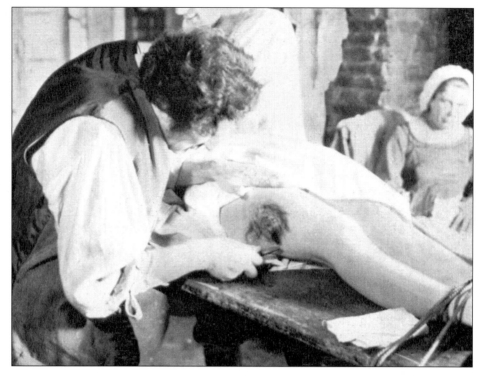

below:
Barry Andrews as Ralph during the film's climatic scenes of devilish revelry.

and Curtis, an ever-present figure on set, scrutinised and criticised every shot in which Welch appeared. Shooting slowed to a snail's pace as everyone clamoured to have their say. Less than two weeks into principal photography and Kennedy was, according to one telegram received at Hammer House, 'substantially' behind schedule. Tigon's production accountants in London calculated the spend rate and warned Tenser, to his great horror, that unless Kennedy picked up the pace or more money was found, the film would have to be shut down. Tenser immediately started calling for a number of changes. *Déjà vu*; if Tenser could have been on hand to rip out pages from the script he almost certainly would have done so. Instead he had to rely on Haft and Curtis. Appropriate instructions were duly given to the embattled director, who approached the revised shooting schedules with thinly disguised antagonism towards his producers.

On location, frustrations boiled over when Curtis took offence at some comments made by a Spanish extra and the resulting contretemps earned the producer a short stay in a Spanish jail. In London nerves were becoming equally frayed, and not just in the Tigon offices; there was unease within the financial institutions about the way the film was being made, as well as nervousness that the company had yet to find a US distributor. As the shoot staggered on Tenser resorted to drastic measures: 'I had them assemble a rough-cut of the scenes that had been shot so far, there was about thirty minutes I think. I took the stills and the publicity materials we had mocked up in London and set out to find additional backing. This was new for us but it wasn't an uncommon way of working in those days so no-one thought we were coming cap in hand or anything like that. The fact is though we didn't have enough money to finish the picture.' Much to everyone's relief Paramount came in with a decent offer and an agreement in principal to take the North American rights.

* * * * *

At the same time that Patrick Curtis was settling into his office at Tigon, the UK film industry was losing one of its most influential figures. In December 1970, John Trevelyan decided to end his twelve year reign as the Secretary of the British Board of Film Censors, by announcing his retirement. An intelligent and sensitive man, his tenure as Secretary had been distinguished by an enlightened approach not seen during the Board's previous half century. Trevelyan wanted to co-operate with filmmakers and reach an understanding rather than impose his opinions from on high; for the most part he successfully balanced the perceived need to protect the public from the excesses of filmmakers while also protecting filmmakers from the extremes of public opinion. The tightrope act won Trevelyan a great deal of respect in the film industry. Michael Armstrong, who crossed swords with Trevelyan on both *The Haunted House of Horror* and his subsequent feature *Mark of the Devil* remembers Trevelyan with affection: 'He was very kind to me. I used to go up and see him. If I was broke he would lend me some money, I'd smoke his Benson and Hedges, drink his whiskey and he would tell me about the bits he had cut out of films. He loved films and he loved the industry.' It was of course Trevelyan who had sent Armstrong along to see Tigon in the first place, and during his time at the BBFC he had been a good friend to Tenser, offering advice and guidance to his filmmakers, from Harrison Marks to Michael Reeves. Trevelyan's close personal relationship with Tenser and their mutual respect meant that it came as a surprise to no-one when Trevelyan agreed to join the board at Tigon, effective as of the 1st of August, specifically to use his network of contacts to identify new filmmakers and projects.

above:
Patrick Wymark's Judge finally acts. Wynne-Simmons's script emphasised the need for the forces of good to be just as ruthless as the enemy, with just a thin line dividing the methods used by the protagonists.

One of the last of the Tigon movies Trevelyan classified as censor was 'The Devil's Touch', which by the time he saw it had been renamed *Satan's Skin*. Of particular concern with this film was the juxtaposition of sex and violence, as well as the close association of both with children. Piers Haggard, like so many of Tenser's directors before him, trod the path to Soho Square to meet Trevelyan and plead his film's case. 'There is a moral question of whether the film is dangerous and I don't know the answer to that,' says Piers Haggard. 'I don't think so myself but I can see how people might argue otherwise. I suppose it is the censor's role to balance those considerations.'

Trevelyan was prepared to allow some compromise on the blood-letting but the sex scenes remained problematic. Not only did *Satan's Skin* include a graphic rape, but also the attempted seduction of a priest by the schoolgirl Angel Blake. The latter scene, shot over two days at Pinewood, was optically darkened to protect the sensibilities of the audience. Wynne-Simmons found some of his more intriguing suggestions received the same treatment:

below:
Barry Andrews holding out against the advances of Yvonne Paul in **Blood on Satan's Claw**. The actress also had a small part, appropriately enough, in the 'Lust' segment of **The Magnificent Seven Deadly Sins**.

left:
The film's controversial rape sequence. Wendy Padbury as Cathy Vespers is about to be inducted into the cult.

'There is a scene in the script, which we filmed, where I wanted to show Angel giving oral sex with the 'devil'. It was cut and darkened down but it's still there, just.' The rape scene had to be trimmed and at the suggestion of Trevelyan, re-framed and played out to a large extent on the faces of the watching children. Even so the effect remains unsettling, not least to its writer: 'The rape didn't really feature in my script - it is suggested but not really shown. I suppose by 1970 that was a rather old-fashioned approach. Anyway it was Piers who insisted in doing it that way. I found the whole thing rather disturbing and if anything the way it was re-cut made it even more unpleasant.'

Ultimately, Trevelyan asked for less than 10 seconds worth of cuts but the darkening of the print diluted the overall effectiveness of Haggard's movie. Trevelyan classified *Satan's Skin* with the new 'X' certificate, passed for exhibition to adults over the age of 18. Tigon Pictures planned a double-bill with Boris Karloff's creaky *Cauldron of Blood (1967)*, and following a trade show which produced a generally positive reaction, a tentative release schedule was planned. Unfortunately, public support didn't mirror the film's promise, so after a few disappointing initial play dates the film was duly pulled. Tenser

remained convinced it was an attractive film and felt that they had simply failed to find the right market. Haggard's movie was to be repackaged and re-titled.

As the winter came to an end and spring loomed, Tigon's focus switched to the Cannes film festival in May. Cannes, the event that had taken the likes of *Repulsion* and *The Blood Beast Terror* to obscure parts of the world, was as important as ever for Tenser, and the 1971 Festival proved to be the pinnacle of his career as a film producer. *Black Beauty* had been cut and scored and, in a sign of solidarity with the film's distributors, members of the press were shown the film at the prestigious Paramount Theatre in Wardour Street, though the film's 'official' world premiere took place at the Paris Cinema in Cannes, on the 25th of May 1971. Paramount had confirmed their purchase of the distribution rights to *Hannie Caulder*, and they were keen that it too - at least as a 'work in progress' - would be unveiled at the Festival.

In addition to handling the Paramount films, Tigon had returned to the Pinewood in April stages to start work on their latest comedy, from director Graham Stark. With a planned six-week shooting schedule, *The Magnificent Seven Deadly Sins* would actually be filming during the festival itself. By May Tenser could boast that Tigon had signed the contracts to deliver two more movies: another comedy, *For the Love of Ada* and a TV spin-off, *Doomwatch*. In a world removed from his exploitation roots the estimated budget for a Tony Tenser movie was now between £200,000 and £250,000 and, as *Hannie Caulder* illustrated, Tigon needed the protection of a financial partner if they were going to continue making movies at this level.

The 1971 Cannes festival also coincided with the completion of some important business deals that had been put together by Laurie Marsh. Since the de-merger with Hemdale the previous September, Marsh had committed himself totally to developing Tigon into a multi-faceted corporation. In March, a deal to merge Marsh's holding company Batavia Investments with Tigon Films Group was made public. Shares in Batavia were duly suspended while the details were worked out but essentially the proposal was a 'reverse buy-out', with Batavia purchasing outright the share capital of Tigon Films and then transforming itself into a re-launched Tigon Group. At the time, around 60% of Batavia was owned by a City syndicate. The valuation was pegged at around 35p, which gave the new company a capitalised value of around £1.9m. Marsh would be confirmed as Chairman and together with his family trusts would own around 42% of the Group, with Tenser - a significant but minority shareholder -

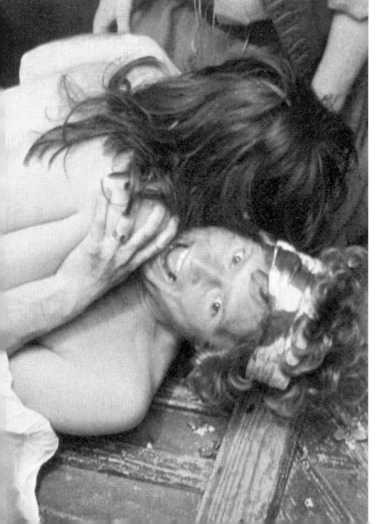

below:
Blood on Satan's Claw's rape scene, which is disturbing not so much for what is seen, but more for the way in which director Piers Haggard juxtaposed the beauty of nature with the violence and brutality of the cult.

retaining his position as Managing Director. Batavia Investments, which was incidentally listed on the Stock Exchange index as 'dealers and planters of rubber and tea', would cease to exist.

It was confidently predicted that the deal would net Marsh his second million. In anticipation of the deal, Tigon whetted the City's appetite by projecting a pre-tax profit of no less than £225,000 for the year to the 31st of January 1972, compared with £119,000 before tax for year to the 31st of January 1971. As if May 1971 was not already significant enough, Batavia's Annual General Meeting was scheduled to take place at the same time as the Cannes Festival, and would formally ratify the deal that would merge the two companies into one. The Tigon Films Group would then comprise of the film production and distribution companies as well as its subsidiaries: Minicini Ltd for cinema development and acquisition; Tigon Film Music; Tigon Properties; Tigon Management Agency; Tigon Television; Tigon Entertainment; and Tigon Audio-Visual.

Laurie Marsh carefully balanced his schedule, attending the crucial Board meeting in London where he witnessed the confirmation of his ambitious re-structure, before flying direct to Nice to attend a triumphant champagne reception on the 16th of May at the Carlton Hotel, Cannes. The format of the new Group was so well leaked in advance that the official launch was something of an anti-climax, and it was left to Tenser to tease the gathered press: 'We intend to make subjects for a price - going for a nominal profit on each one. By the law of averages one of them should come up big. We would like to make more films but we are not going to announce a programme and be hoist with our own petard.' To a round of applause he raised a press book for *The Magnificent Seven Deadly Sins* and announced: 'This is what we are making now and that's what counts.'

Laurie Marsh made it clear that his ambitions also lay in exhibition, confirming: 'We are in the process of constructing two cinemas but I will not and never have announced things until I will not and never have announced things until I have done them.' If anyone in the room had any doubts about the drive of Tigon's Chairman and largest shareholder, Marsh quickly moved to dispel them: 'I am over ambitious and unwarrantedly successful. I am not in movies for money or fame - I have some fame and more money already than I can ever spend. I am in it because I enjoy business.'

On the 30th of May 1971, *Black Beauty* became the first Tigon movie to be launched on the American market by a major US distributor. Simultaneously, it was released nationally in the UK through the Rank circuit.

above:
Uschi Glas with one of a number of horses used to play the title role in **Black Beauty**.

BLACK BEAUTY

'A timeless tale of love and courage'
- US trade ads -

Synopsis

At its birth Black Beauty is given to Joe, a penniless farmer's son, and the two develop a rare friendship and understanding, but when the farmer goes bankrupt the horse is taken by the local squire Sam Greene. Greene is only the first in a series of owners: a tinker, a circus owner, a soldier and a coalman, each of whom is more neglectful than the last. Finally, the aged and broken animal is bought by Anna Sewell and taken to her home for retired horses; there the old horse is reunited with Joe and his father.

Critique

'The characterisation is on a simple level but the horse behaves with dignity throughout. Children and other horses will probably enjoy it.'
- The Daily Express, 25/05/71

'What a mess they have made... mostly a bore for kids.'
- The People, 06/06/71

'...it's full of incident and colour, welcome provisions in the barren larder of family entertainment.'
- The Times, 28/05/71

above:
Mark Lester, aged 13, picking up above the title billing for appearing in the film's opening segment.

'Certainly it is quite a change to find a producer normally as grown up in approach as Tony Tenser sponsoring a melodrama as young and unsophisticated in mood as this one.'
- Daily Mail, 24/05/71

'More of a cartoon strip than a film of the book.'
- Kine Weekly, 03/04/71

'U'! 'U'! 'U'! for family entertainment,' declared the campaign ads for Hill's sentimental and simplistic version of the classic tale, and with a private screening already arranged for Princess Margaret and the Royal children, Tenser would have been forgiven for boasting, 'By Royal Appointment' under the Tigon logo. What the Royal patrons thought of the new version isn't recorded but Ms. Sewell's highly-charged followers, of whom there were many, were already sharpening their knives. The first sign of trouble came with a highly visible walk-out from a special RSPC screening - the headline in the Daily Mail screamed, 'Women Walk Out of Charity Film.' The paper went on to quote one young lady as saying: 'I know Black Beauty is a sad story but the cruelty and violence shown in the film are in excess of the original.' The man who had faced protests and bans over the likes of *Naked - As Nature Intended*, *Repulsion* and *Witchfinder General* was bemused by the reaction to his latest film. 'The film has a 'U' certificate,' Tenser told The Mail. 'Some people are disappointed that it does not keep to the original book, which is a bit wordy. Children like fast action, so we added scenes of a circus and the North West Frontier.' It was all good publicity of course, and Tigon happily added insult to injury by licensing their stills to Collins publishers to commit the ultimate blasphemy of reprinting the Sewell book with a dust cover illustrating the film.

Most of the film critics seemed more concerned with the over-simplistic episodic structure, but even the line producers found themselves tackling the charge of interfering with a classic, though it's hard to deny that Tigon at least stayed true to the book's basic anti-cruelty theme. Peter Andrews said, 'We had the task of retaining the spirit of the book, which is after all told in the first person, and yet giving it a strong story line. I believe we achieved this.' Andrews went on to hint at one of *Black Beauty*'s flaws: 'Maybe some people will say we've made an old fashioned picture. Well maybe we did, but it pulls at the heart strings and there's nothing wrong with that.' Curiously, given their earlier association with Tigon, Peter Andrews and Malcolm Heyworth stated in a joint press release: 'The trend now is towards sex, violence and sensationalism. We know that you are concerned about the lack of family entertainment in the cinemas today.' The two producers then went on the offensive against those who criticised the content of the film insisting: 'We deliberately set out to make a film that mum, dad and the kids could see and enjoy together, and today in cinema that's as rare as finding a diamond in the street.'

Released through the Rank circuit in the UK, Tigon took the unusual step of writing directly to 750 headmasters in the London and Home Counties, emphasising the 'good clean, wholesome' qualities of the film. They also stressed that the movie is, 'a captivating story - rich in entertainment and recommends itself to those concerned with the teaching of English literature.' The film hit cinema screens during the week of the bank holidays, and Tigon supplemented their press ads with promotional competitions in 'Woman's Own' and the 'Evening Standard.' This novel approach - for Tenser at least - succeeded, helping the film to achieve good box-office takings throughout the country, but *Black Beauty* was never going to smash any box-office records. After the holidays were over and the children were back at school attendances at the film dropped off markedly, and it quietly disappeared.

Paramount were sufficiently impressed with the UK response to schedule the film for a national US release on some three hundred screens in time for the Christmas holidays, but in a market where the literary source was much less well-known the film struggled and quickly vanished there too. In the age before video and endless television re-sales, the lack of longevity for the project compared with the durability of his horror films convinced Tenser that big-screen children's films represented too much of a high-risk market. Harry Alan Towers was less cynical, and having made a healthy profit from his pre-sales, the producer immediately announced a follow-up - Mark Lester starring in 'Treasure Island'.[12] Tenser declined to take a stake but had no regrets about his one and only children's film: 'A bloody good film, I liked it a lot. The ending where you see the old horse Ginger led off the knacker's yard brought tears to my eyes!'

Footnotes

1. Born in South Shields, Durham in 1902, Robson, a RADA graduate and a distinguished stage actress, was best known for playing Queen Elizabeth I in two movies: *Fire Over England (1937)* and *The Sea Hawk (1940)*. A spell in Hollywood brought Robson an Oscar nomination for *Saratoga Trunk (1945)* but her sturdy physique and sombre appearance restricted her to playing strong-willed housewives and domineering servants. She returned to England to pursue her theatrical career, interspersed with occasional interesting cinema outings including *Eye of the Devil (1966)* and *The Shuttered Room (1967)*. Never married, she died in July 1984. Her last film appearance was as a witch in *Clash of the Titans (1981)*.

2. John Hamill, like his contemporary Robin Askwith, could easily have become a leading man in horror movies or sex movies had the respective markets lasted a few years longer. Despite enjoying nothing like the success of Askwith, he found himself pigeon-holed into sexploitation after his horror movies, appearing in the likes of *The Over-Amorous Artist (1974)*, *Girls Come First (1975)* and *Hardcore (1977)*. When the UK industry staggered to its knees in the Eighties he moved out of acting completely, opening a furnishing business in London, but his propensity to disrobe and pose for cheesecake pictures ensured lasting popularity for him in the gay market.

3. William Partleton made his debut as a make-up artist at Gainsborough Studios with *Love Story (1944)* and worked on a number the Studio's better-known films including *The Wicked Lady (1945)*. Amongst the many highlights in his long career were: *A Night to Remember (1958)*, *Peeping Tom (1960)*, *Revenge (1971)*, and *The Wicker Man (1973)*. Perhaps his most unlikely credit was for his work on the silicates, the cheap but cheerful invaders in the enjoyable *Island of Terror (1966)*.

4. Born in Stanmore, Middlesex in 1953, Hayden signed on at the Aida Foster Stage School at the age of thirteen and had landed five leading roles before she was twenty. Michael Klinger took a shine to her early on when he picked her out of 300 girls who auditioned for the part of the underage sex kitten in *Baby Love (1968)*. After this film debut, he continued to be a guiding hand in the rest of her career. In 1973 he told Photoplay she 'has an extraordinary acting talent, sensitive and superbly intuitive'. At a time when British actresses fell either into the 'Jenny Agutter - English Rose' or 'Judy Geeson - Swinging Birds' categories, Hayden, along with Susan George, flaunted pubescent sex appeal. She made a couple of slightly tawdry shockers (for Klinger) before Hammer cast her as the corrupted innocent in one of the best of their later horrors, *Taste the Blood of Dracula (1970)*, then after her work for Tigon she reported back for duty in Klinger's *Something to Hide (1971)*. Predictably, the Wardour Street moguls couldn't really find anything for her to do, and as she matured she struggled to find decent roles. Short-lived controversy in the later banned *Exposé (1975)*, with Fiona Richmond and Udo Kier, brought back into the limelight but it didn't last. She paid the mortgage with Klinger's dire *Confessions of...* movies and the odd bit-part but she dropped out of acting altogether for a while.

When she returned she was still an attractive and capable mature actress but sadly by that stage she was relegated to roles in provincial theatre and West End farces.

5. With two children and a settled family life, the Bowns decided not to follow *Monique* to Hollywood; while John tried to set up other films Sibylla continued to act in the UK. They made one further film together as husband and wife - *Vampire Circus (1971)* - before Sibylla decided to give up on acting and trained as an international travel courier instead. John supplemented his work at the RSC with a recurring role on the *Doomwatch* TV series and a small part (as a policeman) in the 1972 Hammer feature *Fear in the Night*. Bown remains philosophical about his directing debut: 'I got two and a half percent of the net and I was being told by people that I would be buying a Rolls Royce out of it. In actual fact I never made any money. I think the last cheque I received was from John Henderson, who operated Tigon in Paris, and it was for eight quid! It comes in dribs and drabs from time to time but not so much as you would notice.' After a return to the sexploitation genre with *Confessions from the David Galaxy Affair (1979)*, John decided to devote his time to writing novels. Today the Bowns - now grandparents - are still married and still living in the same house where they conceived *Monique* over thirty years ago.

6. Yarmouth born Anna Sewell (1820-1878) was totally dependant on a horse and trap after being crippled in an accident as a child. Appalled by the unnecessary cruelty she witnessed, Anna became a crusader for horses' rights and succeeded in implementing several important improvements including the commission of horse troughs in the street. 'Black Beauty' was written specifically to draw attention to the cruelty and neglect of horses in England, and to date it has sold over six million copies and been translated into 17 different languages. Sewell herself did not live to see its worldwide success.

7. Three weeks after they met in a coffee bar in 1964, Curtis and Welch formed the partnership Curtwel to maximise their respective talents. Curtis, acting as her agent, masterminded a strategy of saturation press promotion for Raquel, which was particularly successful in Europe

above:
Uschi Glas as Marie Hackenschmidt is apparently about to meet her maker in James Hill's **Black Beauty**.

below:
Linda Hayden's Angel initiates the violation and murder of Cathy (Wendy Padbury) in **Blood on Satan's Claw**.

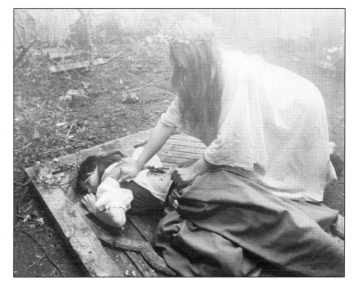

MARK LESTER WALTER SLEZAK
in
BLACK BEAUTY U

CO-STARRING
Ursula Glas
Peter Lee Lawrence
John Nettleton
Patrick Mower
Maria Rohm

above:
Black Beauty was not actually the first family film associated with Tigon, as the company had previously distributed **Sandy the Seal**, also from Harry Alan Towers.

photographed women in the world. She did display some excellent comic talent in Dick Lester's two 'Musketeers' movies, but Hollywood failed to capitalise. By the 1990's, after a long spell in Las Vegas with her cabaret act and a successful run on Broadway with 'Woman of the Year', she managed to reinvent herself as a 'new woman' with a phenomenally successful fitness and health video.

9. Culp made a number of mainstream films, including *Bob & Carol & Ted & Alice (1969)* and *The Great Scout and Cathouse Thursday (1976)* but never achieved anything like the success he had on television. He continued to work constantly as a television actor as well as a some-time director and writer of both regular series and one-off TV movies.

10. Best known of the trio was undoubtedly Ernest Borgnine, who had won a Best Supporting Oscar for *Marty (1955)* and who played heavies in such classics as *Bad Day at Black Rock (1955)*, *The Dirty Dozen (1967)* and *The Wild Bunch (1969)*. He enjoyed a prolific career and came very close to screen stardom late in life with films like *The Poseidon Adventure (1972)*. Wide-eyed Jack Elam had starred for Kennedy in *Support Your Local Sheriff!* and had lent demented presence to the likes *The Man from Laramie (1955)*, *Once Upon a Time in the West (1968)*, and *Rio Lobo (1970)*. Strother Martin made his name in the same television shows that established Kennedy and Sam Peckinpah, both life long friends: *Rawhide*, *Gunsmoke*, etc. He went on to essay roles in such memorable films as *Shenandoah (1965)*, *Butch Cassidy and the Sundance Kid (1969)*, and *The Wild Bunch (1969)*.

11. Diana Dors, the best-known British sex symbol of the Fifties, lived her life in the blaze of publicity, most of it engineered by her first husband Dennis Hamilton. Dors was a willing participant in Hamilton's headline-grabbing stunts, though in the long term it probably did her career more harm than good, and she never quite managed to shake off the 'showgirl on the make' tag. Curiously, Dors saw a lot of her relationship with Hamilton in the marriage of Welch and Curtis, telling a Daily Mail reporter who visited the set of *Hannie* that if she ever filmed her autobiography she would get Raquel to play her and Curtis to play Hamilton.

where by 1966 she had appeared on the cover of over 100 magazines. The couple's highly public marriage on St. Valentines Day 1967 was another publicity triumph for the fledgling producer, though his most famous stunt was posting Christmas cards featuring a shot if Ms. Welch in a revealing pose to 3000 movers and shakers in Hollywood. The couple began to drift apart at the end of the Sixties, and by the time *Hannie Caulder* started shooting they had already separated. They divorced in September 1971.

8. Former beauty queen Raquel was born Jo-Raquel Tegada, in Chicago, in 1940. The daughter of one of the US's most influential architects, on her mother's side she was descended from two US presidents, John Adams and John Quincy Adams, and she took her screen name from her childhood sweetheart and first husband, James Westley Welch, who she married in 1959. The couple had two children, Damon and LaTahn (Tahnee), before separating in 1964. Jobbing as a weather girl and TV bit-parter, Welch made her movie debut in *A House Is Not a Home (1964)*, followed by the Elvis movie *Roustabout (1964)*. In the years between *The Sorcerers* and *Hannie Caulder*, the actress became THE international sex symbol despite being reduced to the status of mere eye-candy in most of her movies. As she matured she made some interesting but largely unsuccessful films, including *The Beloved (1971)* and *The Wild Party (1975)*, but she remained one of the most

12. Despite his reputation as an exploitation giant, Towers also produced a number of family films. The out-of-copyright 'Treasure Island' struck him as being ripe for a remake with Lester in the Jim Hawkins role. Towers followed his usual pattern of announcing the film first and then finding the money, and by the time he had constructed one of his typically complex, multi-national finance deals, Hollywood had pinched the idea. Kirk Douglas already had his version in production - starring Mark Lester - by the time Towers got production under way. Undeterred, Towers went ahead and made his film, beating the Hollywood version to the screens after managing to reunite Walter Slezak and Maria Rohm with a script by Wolf Mankowitz; it also included contributions from genre vets John Hough (director) and Antonio Margheriti (writer), as well as featuring an appearance by Orson Welles as an unlikely Long John Silver.

Chapter Nine

'There Was a Notch on Her Gun for Every Man She Got'

- (British ads for *Hannie Caulder*)

The 'all new' Tigon that was launched at Cannes in 1971 had one last tenuous link with the company's previous owners, the Hemdale Group. In 1969 Hemdale had financed comedian Graham Stark's directorial debut, *Simon Simon*, an extended comic skit also written by Stark and starring a host of his personal friends including fellow comedians Peter Sellers and Eric Morecambe, as well as actors Michael Caine and David Hemmings. The end result was essentially a single gag stretched out over the half hour running time. It was, however, sufficiently fleshed out with star turns to generally over-shadow the main feature wherever it played. *Simon Simon* had been picked up by Tenser for a pittance, and it had managed to attract some creditable reviews so the idea of expanding the basic concept to a full length feature was too tempting to resist. Stark was duly invited along to Wardour Street to discuss a possible collaboration.

Graham Stark was better known as an actor, having featured in British comedies since the early Fifties. Taking the odd foray into serious dramatic roles in films such as *Sink the Bismarck!* (1960), he had also built an impressive array of television and radio credits. Stark was a close friend on Peter Sellers - he was the comic's best man and later his biographer - which, along with appearances on *The Goon Show*, led to recurring roles in the *Pink Panther* film series. He regarded Tenser's approach as an opportunity to broaden his horizons even further; by then Sellers had become a huge international star and Stark hoped to follow him to Hollywood as a director.

Stark's first thought was to film a series of comic takes on the Biblical deadly sins, running each together into one continuous narrative - essentially repeating the format from *Simon Simon*. Tenser liked the idea a lot and immediately coined the title *The Magnificent Seven Deadly Sins*; some days later however, he suggested to Stark there was a better way of approaching the subject. The prospect of collating short films as a cheap way to create features had first been considered at Tigon during the initial drafts of *Satan's Skin*; horror stories were ideally suited to the short format and Tenser reasoned that what was true of horror was equally true of comedy. On the

understanding that he could produce and direct the film, Stark agreed to format seven separate and self-contained stories within the overall remit of the Biblical sins - lust, greed, envy, sloth, pride, gluttony and avarice.

Stark first had to overcome the ticklish problem of the British trade union system though; he hadn't needed a union card to make *Simon Simon* because it was a short feature, but a full length film was a very different proposition for the highly active Association of Cinematograph Television and Allied Technicians. It speaks volumes for his standing amongst his fellow professionals that Stark could call on the likes of Ken Hughes, Peter Sellers and Stanley Kubrick to countersign his nomination for a union card, which to no-one's surprise was awarded without quibble.

below:
Promotional artwork for Graham Stark's celebration of British low-brow humour, **The Magnificent 7 Deadly Sins**.

right:
Leslie Phillips plays a
sheep in wolf's clothing
in the 'Gluttony'
segment of **The
Magnificent Seven
Deadly Sins**.

right:
Leslie Phillips plays a
sheep in wolf's clothing
in the 'Gluttony'
segment of **The
Magnificent Seven
Deadly Sins**.

Casting the film was a bit more complex; despite being, ostensibly, a mainstream movie, even if Stark had managed to persuade Sellers and Caine to appear, they couldn't have been accommodated within Tenser's relatively meagre £116,000 budget. Despite being denied a bona fide superstar Stark didn't do too badly, assembling an impressive range of comics including Bruce Forsyth, Harry Secombe, June Whitfield, Ian Carmichael, and Harry H. Corbett. Roy Hudd, who had provided the comic relief for *The Blood Beast Terror*, also appeared, as did three performers who would work together again for Tenser on the later *Not Now Darling*: Joan Sims, Julie Ege and Leslie Phillips.[1] The participation of the likes of Spike Milligan ensured a host of unbilled cameos from the likes of Ronnie Barker, Madeline Smith, and the ubiquitous David Lodge. Joan Collins was engaged to appear, again as a favour to Stark, but Tigon couldn't arrange for her to be released from her existing contract in time.

When he hired the likes of Michael Reeves and Stephen Weeks, Tenser had claimed he employed fledgling directors because they were cheap, but for once he conceded there was another motive: 'Graham Stark could get all the comedy actors and all the top writers of the day. They were all his friends and all happy to come and work for him.' The first-time director justified Tenser's faith by attracting an impressively illustrious list of writers to the project. Monty Python's Graham Chapman, John Esmonde and Bob Larbey (who went on to write *The Good Life*), Spike Milligan, and the legendary Galton and Simpson - Tony Hancock's writers - all signed on. Stark himself wrote the 'Lust' segment from a story by Marty Feldman. Working independently of each other, the writers very swiftly had the first draft of the script ready for Stark to assemble. Spike Milligan, allocated the 'Sloth' sequence, remembers that, 'really it was like writing a sketch for television. We were given a title and a free hand to come up with a synopsis. I had no idea how it was going to be fitted into the final film until I saw it.'

The loose, episodic format allowed Stark to pepper the film with in-jokes, amongst them Bob Guccione, the publisher of Penthouse magazine, who appeared as a 'photographer', and Stephen Lewis, cast more or less as his character 'Blakey' from *On the Buses*. The aforementioned Julie Ege supplied the glamour alongside starlet Anouska Hempel, model Sue Bond, and sexploitation star Felicity Devonshire, who posed for a number of salacious photographs to promote the film.

Stark started shooting at Pinewood on the 19th of April 1971. His cinematographer was Harvey Harrison, who had also shot *Simon Simon*, and the crew included production manager Jack Causey - later to work on *Doomwatch* - and Colin Corby, the clapper boy from *Saturday Night Out*, now promoted to camera operator. The film's continuity girl was veteran Renée Glynne, who had worked on many of the early Hammer movies, including *Four Sided Triangle (1953)* and *The Quatermass Xperiment (1955)*. Special effects were provided by Cliff Culley, who went on ply his cheap and cheerful trade on films like *Warlords of Atlantis (1978)* and *Arabian Adventure (1979)*.

Having an experienced crew at his disposal was an undoubted boon for Stark, as was seeing so many familiar faces in front of the camera. The director nevertheless put his tongue in his cheek when he told CinemaTV Today about his dread of the first day of shooting and how the film's format meant he was facing 'seven first days!' Renée Glynne remembers Stark on his first day on the set: 'If he was nervous he certainly didn't show it, quite the reverse actually - he was very much in control.' Filming was straightforward enough; the short format meant that location shooting had to be done in the immediate vicinity of the studio: 'Really it wasn't filmmaking at all,' Renée Glynne

below:
Former au pair turned
beauty queen Julie Ege
invites Leslie Phillips to
indulge in some
'Gluttony'.

below:
Former au pair turned
beauty queen Julie Ege
invites Leslie Phillips to
indulge in some
'Gluttony'.

above:
British promotional art
featuring the following
stars: Julie Samuel in
'Avarice'; Harry
Secombe in 'Envy'; Julie
Ege in 'Gluttony';
Harry H. Corbett and
uncredited co-star in
'Lust'; Ian Carmichael,
Robert Gillespie and
Alfie Bass in 'Pride';
Madeline Smith in
'Sloth'; Stephen Lewis
in 'Wrath'.

recalls, 'more like filming seven episodes of a television series rather than a film. There were a lot of wonderful people coming on for a few days at a time and we had a lot of fun.'

As a first time director, Stark was undoubtedly in the firing line and he felt under considerable pressure, especially when the film began to slip behind schedule. 'He had no need to worry,' Tenser reflects. 'We had to look at all our directors, especially the less experienced ones who perhaps would be less aware of the financial position. I was always as supportive as I could be and as it was I got on very well with Graham. I thought he did a very good job.' Tenser felt relaxed enough to leave the crew shooting *The Magnificent Seven Deadly Sins* while he left for his annual pilgrimage to Cannes. There was however one disagreement between the fledgling director and his producer, when Tenser suggested using animation to link the disparate stories together: 'I thought it would be a good idea to add something a little bit quirky and different. We featured Graham Stark himself, drawn as a caricature of a 1920s film director, providing a comic commentary on the screen action.' Stark was less convinced, feeling that it disrupted the flow of the film, but he reluctantly went along with the proposal. *The Magnificent Seven Deadly Sins* wrapped one week late, on the 1st of June 1971, but without going seriously over budget.

It was during the making of Stark's film that Tenser had an unfortunate reminder of his status as something of a public figure in the film industry. Television had grown up considerably since its early days mimicking the ethics and style of radio. When Tenser, perhaps naively, accepted an offer from the BBC to let a film crew into his offices to make a programme about the production of a typical feature film he found that the medium had developed an uncompromising journalistic approach. In the past Tenser had enjoyed a good relationship with the BBC, second only to his close association with the industry press, and this had resulted in some interesting on-set reports from Tigon films such as *Witchfinder General* and *Curse of the Crimson Altar*. This time round Tenser found the cameras were less interested in *The Magnificent Seven Deadly Sins*, and were instead focusing their attention much more closely on him.

'The BBC wanted to shoot a documentary around my day to day job as a film producer, featuring visits to the set, discussions with the director and so on,' Tenser explains. 'Desmond Wilcox was behind it for 'Panorama' I think, and I agreed to go along. It seemed an interesting idea and I thought it might do some good for the film. Everything went fine for the first couple of days; they filmed me at the office, at the studio and in a meeting at a restaurant. I don't know why but they then started asking a lot of personal

right:
Television's Harold
Steptoe, Harry H.
Corbett, fails to impress
Anouska Hempel in the
film's 'Lust' segment.

right:
Television's Harold
Steptoe, Harry H.
Corbett, fails to impress
Anouska Hempel in the
film's 'Lust' segment.

HARRY H. CORBETT in **THE MAGNIFICENT 7 DEADLY SINS** 'A'

Executive Producers Tony Tenser and Michael L. Green Produced and Directed by Graham Stark A TIGON BRITISH FILM PRODUCTION

This copyright material is leased and not sold and upon completion of the exhibition for which it has been leased should be returned to. Bovince Ltd., Ad-Sales Division, 276 Chase Road, Southgate, London N.14

questions. I don't know what they thought they would find but I had made it clear at the outset that this wasn't acceptable. They persisted, I asked them not to and they didn't stop. I said enough is enough and walked out.' The BBC scrapped the footage already shot and shelved the documentary. It was a salutary lesson for Tenser: 'It was a pity in a way. It would have been good publicity but they were just looking for a good story more than anything. I have never pushed myself forward, even in the early days at Compton I was always happy to be in the background and let others take the credit. I didn't need that kind of publicity and I didn't want it.'

*   *   *   *   *

below:
Flora Robson and Beryl
Reid as The Ballantyne
sisters, up to no good in
James Kelly's **The
Beast in the Cellar**.

BERYL REID   FLORA ROBSON
THE BEAST IN THE CELLAR (X)
co-starring TESSA WYATT   JOHN HAMILL   T. P. McKENNA
Executive Producer TONY TENSER   Producer GRAHAM HARRIS   Director JAMES KELLY
A TIGON BRITISH PRODUCTION in association with LEANDER FILMS LTD

RELEASED BY
TIGON PICTURES LTD.

After returning from Cannes, Laurie Marsh wasted little time before unveiling his ambitious plans for the Tigon Group. On the 4th of June 1970 he announced the acquisition of the Classic Cinema chain, which included 84 cinemas and private cinema clubs. With Marsh at the helm, the Tigon Group was staking a bold claim to a large slice of the exhibition business and the shareholders, Tenser and Marsh foremost amongst them, had good reason to feel pleased. Less than a year had passed since Tigon had been released from Hemdale's grasp, and in that time Marsh's Chairmanship had created the third largest entertainment group in the UK, behind Rank and EMI.

The Classic deal meant that Tigon had full control of its own production, distribution and exhibition facilities. The Classic Group itself was regarded as something of a sleeping giant in the industry, counting amongst its many assets: 20 bingo halls; a casino; a sauna; and around 100 other outlets including, curiously, two coffee bars and two sweet shops! The bricks and mortar value of the Classic chain amounted to £6.2m, with the biggest single asset by far being the showcase King's Road cinema, worth £540,000. The Classics had been on the market for more or less two years and the scale of the property assets alone had already attracted the interest of several potential buyers, including David Frost's highly acquisitive Paradine Group. In a typically audacious move Marsh had financed 50% of the deal through a fixed-interest loan and the remainder by share issue. To complete the integration Eric Rhodes, Managing Director of the Classic chain, joined the Tigon board.

At the obligatory press conference Marsh reflected on the deal with remarkable understatement: 'We needed an outlet to expand - and now we have got it.' An ebullient Tony Tenser underscored the company's new market position: 'We now have greater strength not only in ourselves but in the British film industry as a whole. We shall have more outlets for our films and therefore more money for production.' Marsh continued by confirming that this was only the first stage of his ambitious plan; Tigon would continue the expansion of their cinema exhibition arm, aiming to bring 200 new screens into service over the next two to three years.

*   *   *   *   *

Even before Marsh's announcement, Tigon were already making a big push for the mainstream market with the heavy promotion of *Black Beauty*, which had formed the mainstay of their Cannes campaign. Almost overlooked was James Kelly's 'Young Man I Think You're Dying', pulled down from the shelf just prior to the festival. Kelly had re-cut the film, reducing the dialogue and adding some inserts designed to bump up the body count. Tenser the showman introduced one last improvement: 'Young Man, I Think You're Dying is a good title and I liked it a lot, but let's face it you wouldn't walk across the street to see a horror film called that.' The title was duly changed to the less subtle but much more marketable *The Beast in the Cellar*. A trade show on the 28th of May was sparsely attended, but nevertheless a suitable slot was found in the company's summer release schedule.

BERYL REID   FLORA ROBSON
THE BEAST IN THE CELLAR(X)
co-starring TESSA WYATT   JOHN HAMILL   T. P. McKENNA
Executive Producer TONY TENSER   Producer GRAHAM HARRIS   Director JAMES KELLY
A TIGON BRITISH PRODUCTION in association with LEANDER FILMS LTD.

RELEASED BY
TIGON PICTURES LTD.

THE BEAST IN THE CELLAR

'And Much of Madness, And More of Sin,
And of Horror the Soul of the Plot.'
(Edgar Allan Poe)
- UK Trade Ads -

Synopsis

As the police investigate a series of brutal murders they are drawn to the home of two elderly sisters, living together in the otherwise apparently empty house. All the victims are servicemen from the local army base and there is no obvious connection between the sisters and the deaths. Following visits from a young nurse and a concerned soldier, the truth being hidden by the sisters emerges. The women had witnessed a frightening transformation in their father after he had served in the

above:
Incredibly, Flora Robson claimed that Laurence Olivier persuaded her to make **The Beast in the Cellar**. One wonders what the noted thespian made of the finished film.

below:
The Beast is on the prowl again, though actor Dafydd Havard in the title role was not glimpsed until the final third of the film.

above:
Dame Flora Robson in **The Beast in the Cellar**, a long way from her Oscar nomination for her work in **Saratoga Trunk**.

below:
Effective British front of house still complete with botched re-titling sticker.

army, and were unable to face the prospect of the same thing happening to their brother. When war broke out they sought to protect him from compulsory service by bricking him up in the cellar. Now, over twenty years later, they are still unable to release him for fear of prosecution. The brother however had already found his own way out.

Critique

'Very entertaining... two sisters living alone, probably, in an area in which savage, inhuman attacks are being made on soldiers from a nearby barracks. James Kelly's first-class script allows the tension to build up consistently and gives Flora Robson and Beryl Reid scope for genuine acting.'
- The Spectator, 17/07/71

'One of the most static and talkative horror films ever. Really it has the material of a reasonable 80-minutes television thriller... stretched to nearly twice its proper length.'
- The Times, 16/07/71

'The less explicable mystery is what induced two fine actresses like Beryl Reid and Flora Robson to get involved in this limp rubbish.'
- The Observer, 18/07/71

'The chemistry of quality, partially in James Kelly's script and direction, and largely in the two ladies performances, transforms the crude shocks into something approaching genuine compassion for the lives spent in the grip of memory (the ravages wrought by the 1914-18 War on a beloved father).'
- The Sunday Telegraph, 18/07/71

'...the sad sight of Flora Robson wasting her talents in a film that will probably finish up in somebody's collection of the greatest kitsch of all time.'
- The Guardian, 16/07/71

The two leading actresses were in uproar over the cutting of their best lines, hence neither found much time to express their views on the the film itself. Suffice to say neither Robson nor Reid are at their best here.[2] Pruning some of the dialogue hadn't helped. Where the inspiration should have been *What Ever Happened to Baby Jane?* *(1962)*, bristling with black humour and latent threat, instead the film is bogged down in a mire of stodgy dialogue. Tenser must have realised his film was in trouble when the entire first scene after the titles consisted of little more than two elderly actresses babbling on about celery. A performer such as Sheila Keith could deliver lines like, 'Father had his good days

BERYL REID FLORA ROBSON
in
THE BEAST IN THE CELLAR (X)
co-starring TESSA WYATT JOHN HAMILL T. P. McKENNA
Executive Producer TONY TENSER Producer GRAHAM HARRIS Director JAMES KELLY
A TIGON BRITISH PRODUCTION in association with LEANDER FILMS LTD.

RELEASED BY
TIGON PICTURES LTD.

- when he was just like before,' with some relish, but neither Robson nor Reid rose to the occasion.

The colourful and hopelessly unrepresentative trailers created the impression that the film was out-and-out 'Grand Guignol' but while the inserts provided the gore Tenser needed, the effect is undermined by clumsy editing. Kelly managed to build some tension with the murder of Christopher Chittell's squaddie, and his horror movie homework clearly shines through in the film's last ten minutes, when cliché builds on cliché as the 'beast' returns to its lair in a thunder storm. By then though it's too little too late, and Tenser knew it. Systematic of the desperation at Tigon was the publicity team's attempt to make a connection between *The Beast in the Cellar* and Edgar Allan Poe, whose short lived cinematic revival had been exhausted by 1971. What Kelly couldn't achieve in the cutting room, Tigon hoped they could at least suggest on the poster, a suitably lurid affair that depicted a decidedly 'wild' beast reaching out a bloodied claw. In reality though, the 'beast' was nothing more threatening than a little old man with very long finger nails.

While Kelly had been toiling away in the editing suite trying to make a saleable movie, Tigon had been unable to find a market for *Beast*'s stablemate, 'Satan's Skin'. Tenser reacted to this mini-crisis by trying his luck; he decided to market the pair together. To put some distance between the new double-bill and *Satan's Skin*'s earlier aborted release, Haggard's movie was re-christened *Blood on Satan's Claw*. The new title was formally registered at the Board of Trade on the 11th of June.[3]

BLOOD ON SATAN'S CLAW

'When the Devil's tomb is violated Satan returns from his empire of horror!'
- Mexican lobby cards -

Synopsis

A farmer, Ralph, unearths the remains of what seems to be an animal whilst working in a field. He reports the find to his mistress, Isobel Banham, and her houseguest, the Judge, but the remains disappear before they can investigate. Soon the local community falls victim to a series of mysterious incidents, most of which seem to revolve around the youths in the district; an evil is loose in the countryside. The Judge leaves the townspeople to their own devices, cautioning: 'You must let it grow.' A schoolgirl, Angel Blake, presides over a growing cult, initially afflicting the children of the village but later attracting various vagrants and down-and-outs. Angel incites her 'followers' to rape and murder. Various

Satanic rituals follow, as the undead spirit tries to 'reassemble' itself from the limbs and flesh removed from its followers. The Judge soon returns with a militia and a blessed sword to deal with the evil, tooth for tooth, and eye for eye.

Critique

'[Piers Haggard] tackles his first large screen assignment with panache and a genuine sense of period... It is good to record that the last film performance of Patrick Wymark was one of his best.'
- Films and Filming, 10/71

'...as silly as it is repulsive.'
- The Daily Express, 15/07/71

above:
A nice shot of Angel and her coven. Barry Andrews is about to become their latest victim.

left:
Guild Home Video cover features supporting actress Wendy Padbury on the cover. She was already well-known to British fantasy and horror fans due to her role as Zoe, one of the companions to Patrick Troughton's Doctor during the years 1968 and 1969 on BBC's long-running series **Doctor Who**. This rare tape features arguably the best print of the film available on any home video format, as it showcases a vibrantly colourful open-matte 'fullscreen' print of the film. Subsequent DVD releases have been cropped to fit the requirements of anamorphic widescreen presentation.

above:
Beautiful shot of Angel (Linda Hayden) and her master. A subsequent shot of more explicit affection was darkened to protect audience sensibilities.

below:
Striking German poster artwork for **Blood on Satan's Claw** captures the eroticism of the film at the price of the terror.

'This well made chiller convincingly suggests the atmosphere of fear in the tranquillity of a rural setting... It's a story that sets out to shock and it succeeds.'
- The Daily Mirror, 16/07/71

'...a rambling and episodic piece...nicely directed.'
- The Times, 16/07/71

'Linda Hayden makes a rather luscious young witch.'
- The Daily Mail, 17/07/71

'In the end, though, it doesn't frighten or convince, and the Somerset accents do nothing to help.'
- The Observer, 18/07/71

'...laughably crude.'
- The Financial Times, 16/07/71

'...it also comes very near to being a work of art, a minor triumph for the director Piers Haggard and also for Robert Wynne-Simmons, whose dialogue smoothly merges colloquial modern speech with archaism.'
- The Evening News, 17/07/71

'...a remarkably successful atmosphere of chilling, supernatural menace.'
- Kine Weekly, 23/07/71

Englands historischer Roman-Bestseller jetzt als großer sensationeller Farbfilm!

IN DEN KRALLEN DES HEXENJÄGERS

Regie: P. Haggard · Mit Patrick Wymark und Linda Hayden sowie Barry Andrews · Michele Dotrice · James Hayter u.a.
Eine TIGON BRITISH/CHILTON Farbfilm-Produktion im Verleih der CS

As a double-bill the two films actually represented fairly good value for money - for those who made the effort. *The Beast in the Cellar* wasn't the film that anyone involved had set out to make. Despite the best efforts of the editors it turned out to be a routine, uninspired thriller. However, even if was not considered true 'top of the bill' material, *Blood on Satan's Claw* was dark, downbeat and violent, and was something of a find for those who bothered to turn out to see it. The poverty of its budget is apparent too often but Haggard's direction was tight enough to ensure the lapses in logic didn't interfere with the film's growing sense of dread. Patrick Wymark, in his third film for Tenser, is a solid and commanding presence, and Haggard managed to elicit effective performances from the young cast, particularly the smouldering Linda Hayden.[4] The period setting is rendered with remarkable conviction, with just enough 'thou's and thee's' to add charm, while the eerie music compliments the unsettling atmosphere. On the downside, the best efforts of Haggard and Wynne-Simmons can't disguise the rush to restructure the film, resulting in a number of awkward loose ends.

Blood on Satan's Claw was a film slightly out of synch with the times, sadly appearing just as the market for period horror movies was starting to wane. Tigon secured a West End booking at the cavernous New Victoria, a 2,600 seater, but the booking lasted for just one week. After a poor take of £3,012, the films were unceremoniously replaced by *Carry On Henry (1970)*. Tigon moved the bill out into the provinces hoping, without success, to find a market amongst the holiday crowds.

* * * * *

Tenser never believed that Tigon could compete with Hollywood - they simply didn't have deep enough pockets. However both *Black Beauty* and the as yet unreleased *Hannie Caulder* proved that they could at least attract American money into international features. The shrewd David Haft had brought Hollywood contacts to Tigon and Tenser, in an effort to develop projects that would appeal specifically to the Americans, announced a new version of the classic novel 'The Last of the Mohicans.' The timing was not right however, as the Hollywood majors were rapidly becoming ever more insular in their outlook, preferring to keep their dollars in California rather than taking risks on trans-Atlantic adventures. Tigon's prospects of making further in-roads into the North American market finallly evaporated in June 1971 when Haft, who had been so key in delivering *Hannie Caulder*, resigned to form his own production company Bradford Broadway Productions.

The Raquel Welch movie caused problems for everyone involved. Kennedy had been working on a rough cut to show the backers, but following a dispute over his salary he walked out on the production and returned to New York. As the final cut of the movie was being assembled without his input, allegations of unpaid cast and crew salaries abounded and lawyers threatened to sue and counter sue. With Haft no longer on the scene, a very reluctant Kennedy was persuaded to return to London at the end of July 1971 to rubber stamp the final cut. This wasn't a philanthropic gesture but rather a part of his legal settlement: '...the only way I could stay out of court and get the money they owe me,' he sneered in his autobiography. The director went on to disown the film entirely.

The nature of Tigon's business had fundamentally changed. Tigon was now a public registered company, and a big one at that, with responsibilities to shareholders and of course regulatory obligations to the Stock Exchange authorities. The day-to-day running of the production and distribution business had become a full time job in itself and Tenser found his input at the filmmaking level diminishing to almost nothing. The days when he could stay with the cast and crew at the Palace Hotel were long gone. Tenser would still try, whenever possible, to spend some time on the studio floor but increasingly these would be swift impromptu visits. As the paperwork piled up Tenser increasingly relied on his production controller Christopher Neame, but soon after *The Beast in the Cellar* wrapped Tenser found himself without a right-hand man.

'Tony and I didn't fall out, I like him too much for that, but let's say we agreed to differ,' admits Neame. 'Hemdale when they were around had insisted that we use one of their artists for the soundtrack, they may have been releasing the album or something. I'm not sure. Anyway I hated it, I thought it was totally inappropriate and Tony wouldn't or couldn't change it. It was the last straw for me.' Neame resigned from Tigon and went back to work at Hammer. He and Tenser remained friends and even worked together again on later projects.

Neame was replaced by Peter Thompson, an experienced thirty-four year old production executive, whose undoubted production skills would prove to be a considerable asset to the company going forward. In May 1971, Thompson signed a three-year contract, assuming the title of Head of Production. A while later he took the opportunity of a CinemaTV interview to pay generous tribute to his new employers: 'I liked Laurie Marsh's ideas for expansion, Tony Tenser's ability for world selling and John Trevelyan's contacts. We have a sound economic base, and I shall personally go to locations to evaluate cost factors on individual projects before they are finally decided upon by the four of us.' As Managing Director Tenser still reviewed prospective projects; his input on casting and content was vital and of course he had the coveted power to green-light deals but increasingly Peter Thompson would assume control of the day-to-day production chores.

Thompson joined Tigon at a difficult time for the filmmaking in the UK. To fill the gap left by the withdrawal of American backing, British filmmakers invested increasingly in what was perceived to be the only remaining viable domestic market - horror movies. The result was predictable enough; a glut of movies with similar budgets and themes competing for the attentions of a dwindling audience. Without a guaranteed US release most of these films - good, bad and indifferent - withered away. Tigon's own *The Beast in the Cellar* and *Blood on Satan's Claw* had been among the first casualties. The knock-on effect was a major down-swing in the UK industry. Redundancies were threatened and studios cut back on expenditure at a time production costs were steadily rising.

The industry was also suffering a fresh onslaught from an old enemy, the small screen. Colour television, breaking one of cinema's last advantages over its previously monochromatic small screen rival, was taking off in the UK, and it accelerated the already declining cinema attendance numbers.

The vigorous Tigon management team however saw only opportunities in the summer of 1971. Rubbing shoulders with Laurie Marsh and Tony Tenser were recent arrivals including Eric Rhodes from the Classic chain and John Trevelyan, who formally joined Tigon in August. The diverse activities of the Group reflected its new status in the top flight: as well as the Classic cinemas, Tigon had a subsidiary that provided cinema services such as neon signs, seats etc. The Group could also boast a music publisher, property developers, and talent agencies. Closest to Tenser's heart were of course the distribution and production companies. As a film distributor (through Tigon Pictures Ltd) the Group was already handling *Black Beauty* and *Blood on Satan's Claw* / *The Beast in the Cellar*, as well as preparing for the release of *Hannie Caulder* and *The Magnificent Seven Deadly Sins*. Tigon British Film Productions Ltd had two films in pre-production, a third, 'The Chilian Club', in development from director Peter Collinson and the ink drying on a deal to film the science fiction novel 'Cold War in a Country Garden'.

On the 8th of October, CinemaTV Today picked up on the general air of optimism emanating from the Tigon offices and took the opportunity to reflect on the position of the Group relative to the rest of the UK industry. The magazine's editorial singled out the key Tigon Board members:

above:
Peter Thompson, who joined Tigon as Head of Production and went on to oversee many of their later projects.

above:
Tony Tenser in good mood as he eavesdrops on director Peter Sasdy during the filming of **Doomwatch**. Actors Shelagh Fraser and Ian Bannen appear to be somewhat less amused.

'Shrewd, confident men like Laurie Marsh, Tony Tenser and Eric Rhodes do not invest their time, their talent, and certainly not their money in a diminishing or unimportant industry.'

Dismissing any suggestion that the enlarged company would move away from film production, Tenser insisted: 'We will make commercial films with commercial budgets. That policy has not changed. I have always tried to make films not looking for the big profit but to bring in a reasonable return on the capital involved. Therefore most of our films break into the profit area. It almost eliminates the possibility of losing money on a film. At the same time it reduces the possibility of making a fortune on a film. In other words the accent in our involvement is on business rather than film.' Tigon's books from the time confirm that the average film production budget was between £100,000 and £150,000. Moreover, the sum of £100,000 had been allocated annually for the development of new projects, with a ceiling of £20,000 placed on the pre-production of any one project. However, an exception was made for one of John Trevelyan's pet projects, 'Cold War in a Country Garden,' a fantasy story about a man miniaturised to 1/4 of an inch. Tony Masters and Wally Veevers, two of the effects wizards from *2001: A Space Odyssey (1968)*, had already been engaged to solve the technical problems and with an estimated £1m budget Tenser was actively canvassing possible production partners in California.

With the company's film production plans looking promising, in the autumn of 1971 Tenser took the opportunity to promote Tigon's latest venture; opening cinemas with smaller screens, giving greater choice to the public by screening more films - predating the idea of multiplexes. Tigon had formed Minicinemas Ltd, and Tenser planned to open six of the new cinemas over the next twelve months: 'There is room for more cinemas,' he said at the time, 'many more - by making them smaller which is something I felt was right when I opened the Compton Cinema Club eleven years ago.'

*   *   *   *   *

The shrinking horror market had serious implications for Britain's low-budget filmmakers; if the old standby of horror couldn't make money what could? Not for the first time the answer came from James Carreras and Hammer Films. Hammer originally made its name not in horror movies, but in filmed adaptations of popular radio series, amongst them *The Adventures of P.C. 49 (1948)* and *Dick Barton Strikes Back (1949)*. No-one ever accused James Carreras of being dogmatic. With his horror and fantasy movies making less and less money, he looked around to see what else might be popular and bought the rights to the limp low-brow television series *On the Buses*, which he turned into an equally limp low-brow film. The summer release of Hammer's uninspired film version, with the same cast

above:
Inbreeding or contamination? Dr. Del Shaw (Ian Bannen) ponders the environmental issues raised by **Doomwatch**.

and the same situations as its television counterpart, was greeted by the industry as something akin to the 'Second Coming'. Despite a penny-pinching budget the film took a staggering £400,000 in its first four weeks on release, going on to become the biggest box-office hit of the year - much to the disgust of contemporary critics. Suddenly, adaptations of television series were the order of the day: *Steptoe and Son*, *Dad's Army*, and *Love Thy Neighbour* all found their way to the big screen. At Tigon, Tenser had already seen the writing on the wall. While *On the Buses* was still in production, he had signed the contracts on not one, but two television adaptations: *For the Love of Ada*, scheduled to shoot in early 1972, and *Doomwatch*, which was rushed through into principal photography with unseemly haste.

The television version of *Doomwatch* centred on actor John Paul, who had appeared in *The Blood Beast Terror*. He played Dr. Spencer Quist, a Quatermass type scientist, running the Department of Measurement of Scientific Work (codenamed 'Doomwatch'), environmental trouble-shooters invariably hampered by civil service bureaucracy and greedy corporations. Running for three seasons between 1970 and 1972, the series also concerned the exploits of Dr. John Ridge, played by Simon Oates, with occasional input from the likes of John Barron, Robert Powell and even John Bown. *Doomwatch* wasn't a huge hit on the small screen but was sufficiently popular to convince Tenser that a film version would

prove to be a sound investment. Keen to ensure that their movie wouldn't be branded as just another horror movie, Tigon were promoting *Doomwatch* as a thoughtful and provocative science fiction film, a worthy successor to the *Quatermass* films.

Clive Exton, who had previously written the screenplay for the 1970 thriller *10 Rillington Place*, was engaged to fashion a script from the characters and situations created by Kit Pedler and Gerry Davis for their BBC series *Doomwatch*. Exton wanted to retain as many characters as possible from the television series but appreciated the need to open the film out more, so while he wrote both Paul and Oates into the film, he introduced a new character, Dr. Del Shaw, believing that a more conventional leading man was needed. Tigon signed up Ian Bannen to play Shaw. The highly respected Scottish star of *The Hill (1965)* and *Too Late the Hero (1970)*, Bannen brought both intelligence and intensity to the character.

A stranger in a remote island community, Shaw initially fares badly in his encounters with the locals. His only solace in the hostile, close knit community comes in the shape of a local schoolteacher, Victoria. Exton suggested that Judy Geeson would be ideal for the role and Tenser wholeheartedly approved. The elder sister of Sally Geeson, Judy had been hailed as the 'next Julie Christie' and although some of her glamour had faded after she took roles in a few poor films, she was still considered a major star, at least in the UK.[5]

above:
Judy Geeson is startled by the grostesque appearance of Michael Brennan in **Doomwatch**.

below:
Adapted from the television series of the same name, **Doomwatch** was an attempt by Tigon to fashion a 'Quatermass' for the 1970s. The film's poor box-office killed off any plans for future instalments.

To supplement his leads, Tenser engaged George Sanders who, despite the downward spiral of his career, was still considered something of a 'name.' For Sanders the film represented a few pounds in the bank and yet another military role.*6* Geoffrey Keen was employed to represent the unacceptable face of corporate greed, one of the standard themes of the television series. Keen was no stranger to horror movies - he had been in Herman Cohen's *Berserk (1967)*, as well as *Taste the Blood of Dracula (1970)* - but would soon achieve his footnote in cinema history with a recurring role in the Bond series.

Tenser's somewhat unusual choice of director was Peter Sasdy, the Hungarian ex-pat whose previous work for Hammer had juxtaposed complex sexual tensions with violence.*7* Tenser awarded himself with a break from the office when he decided to line-produce the film himself - his first time as producer since *The Haunted House of Horror*. The film also saw the return of some other familiar faces: John Scott, composer from *A Study in Terror*; Derek Whitehurst, who had been second-unit director on *The Projected Man*; and of course Jack Causey, Tenser's production manager who had worked on *The Magnificent Seven Deadly Sins*. Sasdy naturally took the opportunity to bring some of his own people on board: cinematographer Ken Talbot, who had worked on *Countess Dracula (1970)*, *Hands of the Ripper (1971)* and *Nothing But the Night (1971)*, and production designer Colin Grimes, who had also worked on *Nothing But the Night*. Tom Smith was brought in to create the grotesque make-up that would become such a prominent feature of the film's publicity.

Shooting began in October 1971, on location at various sites around Cornwall including Polkerris and Falmouth. The interiors were filmed at Pinewood, with Tenser on hand throughout the shoot.

*   *   *   *   *

At the end of November 1971, Paramount opened *Black Beauty* in three hundred screens across the USA. Business was brisk and, although Tigon had no participation at the US box-office, there was considerable satisfaction with the film's performance. Tenser immediately saw the opportunity to continue Beauty's adventures on the small screen and, dusting off the long dormant Tigon Television subsidiary, he announced 'The Adventures of Black Beauty'; 39 half hour episodes to be filmed at Elstree under the guidance of Peter Thompson. Tenser was aiming the series well and truly at the family audience: 'We wanted it for children but with enough content to attract adults. Like a Hornby train set, which you buy for your son and end up playing with yourself. We very much wanted to move into television at the time; it would have been the next natural move for the company and *Black Beauty* seemed an excellent way to open the door.' Tenser's plans came to grief just a few days later when London Weekend Television announced a rival 'Black Beauty' project. LWT, with the weight of the independent broadcasting networks behind them, had the finance in place and contracts signed by the time Tigon contacted them to discuss a joint production. They were happy to trade on the success of the film but saw no need to involve Tenser: 'I would have liked to have done it with them but we couldn't reach an agreement with LWT over how to approach it. It would have been a good time for us to get into television just then but it wasn't to be.'

Despite the disappointment of the scuppered television series, the Tigon Group continued on something of a high; the share price, which during the summer had hovered at around 80p, now stood at 112p, a reflection of the City's confidence in the policies of Marsh and his Board. There was good reason for this confidence; *Hannie Caulder*, the first of the company's big international productions, was about to open with Laurie Marsh assuring everyone that the film's predicted success would dispel any doubts about Tigon's viability in the international market. The British premiere was set for late November, to be followed by a circuit release through Rank, and Tenser, leaving nothing to chance, engaged top marketing firm Davidson Dalling Associates to handle the promotion. This was the first time he had ever engaged an outside agency to sell a film. In addition to the obligatory paperback tie-in, Davidson Dalling managed to conjure up promotions involving Levi jeans and Hilton Poncho shawls. They also arranged for a single release of the main theme song, 'Life's Never Peaceful' by Bobby Hanna, through Philips Records. Meanwhile in London the obliging Ms. Welch, engaging in the compulsory press junkets, drove the papers into their usual frenzy.

above:
Mexican artwork for Burt Kennedy's British Western **Hannie Caulder**.

left:
Hannie (Raquel Welch) comforts her mentor Thomas Luther Price (Robert Culp) in **Hannie Caulder**.

opposite:
Raquel Welch is framed by Strother Martin, Jack Elam and Ernest Borgnine as the bumbling Clemens brothers in **Hannie Caulder**. The film's uncomfortable juxtapositioning of sexual violence and slapstick humour alienated the general public and critics alike.

below:
Robert Culp in action. **Hannie Caulder** was Tigon's first attempt at making a truly international big-budget movie and its failure to find a market was instrumental in Tigon's subsequent re-structure.

HANNIE CAULDER

'The First Lady Gun-Fighter!'
- Australian Trade Ads -

Synopsis

Left for dead in the burnt-out remains of her farm, Hannie Caulder swears revenge on the Clemens brothers, three thugs who murdered her husband and destroyed the farm after raping her. With nothing to her name - not even clothes - Hannie wanders into the desert wearing nothing but an ill-fitting poncho. A professional gunfighter, Thomas Luther Price, befriends Hannie and tries to dissuade her from confronting the Clemens brothers, but when she refuses he reluctantly agrees to help. Price introduces Hannie to Bailey, an English gunsmith, who fashions a lightweight pistol suitable for a woman's hand. Under Price's supervision she stars to train as a gun-fighter. Hannie gets her first taste of action when bandits attack Bailey's farm and together with Bailey and Price she has to find them off. She is sickened by the confrontation but isn't discouraged; if anything Hannie is even more determined to confront the Clemens clan.

Critique

'Raquel Welch... spends some time under a short blanket with no knickers like an advertisement for Western Women's Lib... Alas director Burt Kennedy isn't the man he was when he used to script for Budd Boetticher.'
- The Listener, 18/11/71

'Caulder herself is a vengeful creature impersonated by Raquel Welch, a singularly untalented creation of the gossip columns and publicity mills... there are at least 50 actresses who could have transformed Hannie Caulder into a characterisation worthy of the rest of the cast.'
- Village Voice, 06/07/72

'The mixture of sadistic enjoyment and holy homilies is not very pleasant.'
- The Sunday Telegraph, 14/11/71

'Hannie Caulder is quite an impressive Western. Exciting, well acted and I include Miss Welch.'
- The Daily Mirror, 19/11/71

'The truth is the film doesn't know where it's going or why. ...as Hannie she [Welch] makes a pretty dotty sex symbol and a very wooden actress.'
- The Guardian, 11/11/71

'Director Burt Kennedy seems to have been uncertain whether to treat the enterprise as a comedy or not, with the result that sometimes it is a comedy but mostly it is not.'
- The Daily Express, 11/11/71

By the time the film had completed its first week on release in London Tenser was, prematurely, proclaiming it a success and Patrick Curtis was hurrying to sign up Robert Culp as writer and director on his next film, 'Laurie Lee in the Movies' - which naturally would also star Raquel Welch. The reviews were mixed, as was public reaction. *Hannie Caulder* seemed to confuse its audience. Many viewers found the mixture of violence and slapstick jarring, and the attempt to show the leading lady in as sexy a light as possible did not sit well, following her gang rape at the beginning of the picture. The hurriedly re-written scenes and sloppy editing didn't help matters either.

To her credit, Raquel acquitted herself pretty well and certainly far better than most industry pundits had anticipated when the film had been announced the previous January. The supporting cast all performed well, with Robert Culp and Christopher Lee in particular bringing quiet dignity to their roles, offsetting the 'free for all' hamming of Messrs. Borgnine, Martin and Elam. Diana Dors may have felt a little discouraged when her already small cameo was cut down to a fleeting appearance, but her special billing nevertheless remained intact.

If the writers ever actually intended an in-depth analysis of the 'woman trying to be a man' theme, then clearly it had been abandoned somewhere along the line in favour of an all-out dash for the next gag or 'shoot-em up.' Borrowing liberally from some of the classics of the genre, Kennedy doesn't quite succeed in mixing the grim realism of the spaghetti westerns with the quality and depth of Hollywood, but *Hannie Caulder* was a notch above the standard set by most of its Almerian counterparts.

In the UK the market for Westerns had remained fairly static over the years and *Hannie Caulder* was reasonably well received. In the US where, with very few notable exceptions, the public's demand for cowboy films had all but evaporated. Cinema-goers couldn't see enough novelty in *Hannie Caulder* to turn out in force despite the energetic selling of the film's star. Tenser had succeeded in protecting Tigon's investment by pre-selling the film, not only to Paramount, but also to a number of other territories while the film was still in production. The showreel of work in progress and Terry O'Neill's provocative shots of Ms. Welch had proved particularly important in Europe where the actress was en-route to iconic status, but despite the enthusiasm of the buyers the film never caught the imagination of the public. The film's poor reception in the US meant that Tigon's short-lived flirtation with Hollywood effectively ended before it had really begun.

* * * * *

The next Tigon picture to be released was *The Magnificent Seven Deadly Sins*, a production much more in line with the company's core philosophy. This low-budget, home-grown film had an abundance of television talent on display and Tigon felt that they could more than compete in the spin-off market. Tigon's mutually rewarding relationship with ABC ensured that a circuit release would be forthcoming, but not until the New Year as ABC had bigger fish to fry during the Christmas holiday period. Tenser therefore secured a limited release in early December, hoping to generate maximum publicity ahead of their film's circuit release.

above:
Arthur Howard and Ronald Fraser plot their revenge in 'Wrath'.

opposite:
One of the shots that led director Burt Kennedy to dismiss **Hannie Caulder** film as 'a fistful of tits.'

below:
British artwork for Graham Stark's first and to date only attempt at feature film directing.

THE MAGNIFICENT SEVEN DEADLY SINS

'Hilarious Comedy! Glamorous Girls!
Hit Parade Music!'
- British Trade Ads -

Synopsis

Avarice: A down-trodden chauffeur is goaded into recovering a fifty pence piece from down a drain, and winds up falling in the sewer.

Envy: A hen-pecked amateur opera singer married to a pools winner tries a number of subterfuges to obtain the house of a middle-class couple, by hiding behind disguises ranging from a West Indian migrant to a red faced Welsh Water Conservancy Board officer.

Pride: Two drivers meet head on in a country lane and refuse to back up to allow each other to pass. One is rich and the other poor but they each refuse to admit they are wrong.

Sloth: A tramp is too lazy to move, even when confronted with disaster.

Lust: Ambrose dreams of seduction but spends his evening practising chat up lines in the mirror. His desperate efforts to pull girls at a tube station leave him threatened and insulted.

Gluttony: Dickie, an executive in a slimming biscuit company, prefers eating to the amorous attentions of his curvaceous vice president, Ingrid. Threatened with the sack, Ingrid offers to help him take his mind off food.

Wrath: A pair of pensioners who have their placid existence ruined by a bullying park keeper devise a series of wild murder schemes to rid themselves of the man.

Critique

'Seven self contained episodes from British comedy writers provide lots of laughs.'
- The Sunday Express, 05/12/71

'Most of the episodes labour a thin joke.'
- The Sunday Telegraph, 05/12/71

'I couldn't stop laughing at Ronald Fraser... but too many of the other episodes misfire.'
- News of the World, 05/12/71

'On the big screen they come across as inflated in their pretensions. I left the cinema feeling short changed.'
- The Observer, 05/12/71

'Like many disasters, great and small, this must have seemed like a good idea at the time.'
- The Daily Express, 02/12/71

below:
Game show host Bruce Forsyth in 'Avarice', proving that having the talent to present successful popular television entertainment is not necessarily enough to succeed on the big screen.

The poor reaction to *Deadly Sins* rather undermined Tigon's decision to rush it out prior to Christmas; certainly playing to empty cinemas didn't win any friends amongst the filmmakers. Spike Milligan summed it up: 'There was no promotion, no exploitation, no distribution, nobody even knew it was showing. It died on its feet.' Despite the heavily touted '23 Great British Comedy Stars', it simply lacked the clear brand identity of, for example, *On the Buses*. The hit-or-miss episodic format worked against the film's overall quality, some of the writers adapting to big screen writing better than others, and the final result was inconsistent; though sporadically very funny it was also occasionally very laboured. The performances were equally variable. Seasoned veterans such as Leslie Phillips coped easily with his familiar 'sheep in wolf's clothing' character and both Ian Carmichael and Harry H. Corbett slipped into well-recognised stereotypes. Others such as Bruce Forsyth were however clearly more suited to the small screen.

The film's reception was particularly disappointing to Graham Stark, who saw his hopes of a career as a director stumble. At Tigon the extent of the failure was rammed home when they reported better returns from one of their cheap imported films, *Kama Sutra (1970)*, released just prior to Stark's film. Every bit as salacious as it sounded, *Kama Sutra* made up a bill which included the long neglected *Zeta One* and played to respectable - if that's the word - business in London and throughout the UK.

*   *   *   *   *

1972 opened with mixed blessings for the Tigon Group in general and Tenser in particular. Everyone was putting on a brave face about *Hannie Caulder*, which was still on general release, but Tigon Pictures, having scored with *Kama Sutra*, was reporting more brisk business with another imported sexploitation gem, *Female Animal*, which opened in London with *Love in Our Time*. (A later re-release would see *Mini Weekend* being pulled off the shelf to make up the bill.)

On the 2nd of January, *The Magnificent Seven Deadly Sins* received its delayed national release through the ABC circuit, only to be greeted with general indifference despite, or perhaps even because of, the profusion of familiar faces. Harry H. Corbett for example was a huge star on television but the public didn't want to pay to see something that they could get for free on the small screen. *The Magnificent Seven Deadly Sins* highlighted a home truth for Messrs. Marsh and Tenser. Tigon had, until then, seemed immune to the vagaries of the industry - by carefully selecting projects Tenser had demonstrated that he could sell almost anything to anybody and as a result

the company's profits from film production had grown steadily year-on-year. If *The Magnificent Seven Deadly Sin* couldn't attract an audience in the UK, where almost every cast member was a household name, what chance would it have in the USA? [Without star names and an exploitable subject matter *The Magnificent Seven Deadly Sins* didn't find a US buyer until 1975, when it was finally picked up by the tiny Thaddeus Distribution Co. By that time Tigon were still trying to recoup their investment in the UK by re-issuing individual segments as support features for their adult movies.]

On the corporate side, Laurie Marsh continued with his policy of rapid growth and his announcement at the start of 1972 caused something of a stir in the City. January saw the formal confirmation of Tigon's purchase of the Essoldo chain of cinemas - some 56 sites spread across the country - for the sum of £4.3m. These cinemas were promptly subsumed into the existing Classic group, creating a formidable distribution network as well as a considerable bricks and mortar asset for the company's balance sheet. In less than a year, Marsh had taken the Tigon Group's asset base from £250,000 to more than £15m! The growing strength of Tigon did not escape the attention of the Group's landlord, Hammer's James Carreras, who by 1972 was actively looking for a way to disengage himself from film production.

Knighted in 1970 for his charitable works through the Variety Club, Sir James was the powerhouse behind Hammer Films, though he himself was never closely involved in the actual production of the movies. Carreras's knighthood was the crowning achievement of his career, and while he retained control of Hammer he had handed the day-to-day chores over to his son Michael. Hammer had shut down its distribution arm in the Fifties in order to concentrate on film production through a series of complex co-production and distribution deals. The real key to the company's success lay in collaboration with its US-based partners, which allowed their trademark horror movies access to the North American market. Hammer weren't immune to market

above:
Little seen Tigon release **Kama Sutra** (originally called **Kamasutra - Vollendung der Liebe**).

below:
Another scene from **Kama Sutra**, which incidentally features a brief appearance by **Mini Weekend** director Georges Robin.

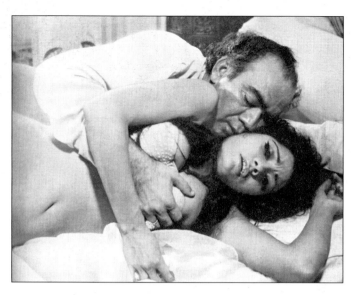

above:
Doing exactly what you would expect them to be doing in a film called **Kama Sutra**. The film was one of a number of increasingly explicit European sex films being imported into the UK at the time. This particular example came from West Germany.

conditions however, and despite the success of *On the Buses (1971)*, their films were gradually losing ground. Sir James decided to get out while the going was relatively good. Tenser was completely unaware of Carreras's intentions until he was somewhat informally approached: 'We rented the first and second floors at Hammer House and Jimmy had the third floor,' Tenser explains. 'There were two toilets, one on one floor for the gents and one on the second for the ladies. Come lunchtime all the men would go to wash their hands and have a leak or whatever and more often than not Jimmy and I would be leaking or washing and just chatting. He was getting on, I think he had got his knighthood by then which he had been hoping to get, and I think he wanted to move on. He did a lot for export; he was a very clever man, brilliant really and he did a good job with Hammer. He said, 'come in the office and talk to me after lunch.' So I went to talk to him and he told me that Hammer was for sale, was I interested? We chatted it over and it seemed to make sense. I would merge our two companies together under one name, Hammer, but I would make my films my way, which was a lot cheaper than Hammer's way. The people that he had were not used to working economically and we could do better.'

Sir James had already started negotiations with another potential buyer, Studio Film Laboratories, a film facilities company; their proposal involved Carreras taking control of a holding company and running the two Studio Film Labs and Hammer as independent subsidiaries. Hammer's Managing Director, Michael Carreras, had been aware of the Studio Facilities deal and, with ambitions of his own, was no doubt relieved when the talks stalled. Michael was not informed that Tigon had been approached or that Tenser had returned with what Sir James considered to be an attractive offer. Tigon's accountants valued Hammer at around £300,000, a figure which

covered all of the company's assets including: the back catalogue of films, or at least those films not owned elsewhere; the un-filmed rights and scripts they held; the lease to Hammer House; and the company Rolls Royce. Significantly, Hammer's existing production deals with various British distributors - a considerable asset - were not included at that stage. The purchase of their oldest rival fitted in with Laurie Marsh's strategy of continuing expansion, and with so many films already in pre-production Tenser was keen to merge Hammer's production people into his own organisation.

The proposal was agreed in principal between Sir James and Tenser: 'We went through the deal together and he said he would get some papers drawn up and take it from there. We tried to keep quiet about it, I don't know who leaked it out, but a week or so later he phoned me to come up. He said he hadn't realised he had a formal obligation to give first refusal to his son, Michael. He had spoken to Michael and he wanted to buy it.' Despite coming into the equation at a late stage Michael Carreras pulled a financial package together, submitted an offer (which was somewhat higher than the Tigon figure) and formally purchased the company from his father.

Tenser was initially disappointed but later realised that Tigon had actually had a narrow escape. Hammer's value on paper differed widely from their true worth; James Carreras had creatively represented the strength of his company to capture a buyer, knowing that the rights to their best-known films were all signed over to the distributors and financiers. The company's principal asset was the goodwill of the Hammer brand; the much-vaunted production deals were, it turned out, with Carreras personally and not the company. Without Carreras senior on board these deals weren't worth the paper they were written on and without them Hammer Films Ltd. was in fact worth only a fraction of the asking price. Beset by financial problems from the outset, Michael Carreras struggled on for a few years trying to make a go of it at Hammer but denied his father's network of contacts the company ground to a halt and slipped into receivership in 1978.

*   *   *   *   *

If Tenser was disappointed by the outcome of the Hammer deal, he was far too busy to dwell on it. With two of his productions on national release in the UK, Tenser embarked on a flurry of activity that would deliver five full length films in a little over two months.

The Royal Shakespeare Company had staged an adaptation of August Strindberg's 'Miss Julie' at The Other Place in Stratford during their 1971 season and the play's

director Robin Phillips was anxious to capture his production on celluloid in the form of a more of less straight translation from the stage.

If the RSC wasn't a name that one would immediately associated with Tony Tenser, then an alliance with the highly regarded Swedish playwright Strindberg seemed even more unlikely.[8] 'Miss Julie' had never been successfully transposed to the cinema screen in the English language, though the BBC had made a well received version in 1965. The last attempt to adapt the work cinematically was a Swedish version, made in 1951. Dramatising a single night 'below stairs', the story tells of a noblewoman's smouldering passion for a servant, as they spend an unsettling evening taunting and teasing each other. Whilst never scaling the heights of passion suggested, 'Miss Julie' was nevertheless considered something of a daring play in its time, and had been performed consistently since it was first staged a century earlier.

The RSC production had been a huge critical and popular hit. A number of film companies were approached but no real interest was shown. Phillips started to consider a televised 'play of the week' as his only viable option. The project attracted the interest of Sedgemoor, a company most well known for making television documentaries and light entertainment, who announced that they were willing to put up half the money if Phillips could find the remainder.

That's when Tigon stepped in, but Tenser's interest was based in pragmatism rather than aesthetics: 'We had bought some new cameras at the time, a technique known as 'multivista' which used television cameras and shot on tape. In a television studio there were four cameras on the floor and the director sits with a monitor, all four cameras are going at the same time and the director could see all the angles on his monitor. So television films could be edited more or less as they went along, which was fine for television. The big problem was transferring tape to celluloid for cinema screens, but now they had found a way to do it.'

The acquisitive Laurie Marsh had sanctioned the purchase of the whole system with the intention of using it to make Tigon movies and then selling the expertise to other film producers. A film of a stage play seemed an ideal opportunity to fully test the system. Tenser committed to fund the remaining half of *Miss Julie*'s modest £47,000 budget.

Robin Phillips was better known as an actor, having appeared in the BBC's costume epic *The Forsyte Saga* and on the cinema screen in the horror movie *Tales from the Crypt (1972)*. Although he was new to film direction Phillips had been directing on the stage since 1965, working on the likes of 'Timon of Athens' and 'Hamlet' for the RSC.[9] Wanting to make the most of the demanding new technology, Tigon wanted to install an experienced pair of hands at

above:
Passions begin to simmer downstairs in Tigon's production of the Royal Shakespeare Company play **Miss Julie**.

above:
Helen Mirren as the titular **Miss Julie** starts to taunt Donal McCann as Jean.

below:
Tony Tenser chatting with actress Susan Hampshire on the set of **Neither the Sea Nor the Sand**.

the helm, so the directing chores were shared with John Glenister, an experienced television cameraman who had been working his way up to director on TV series such as *Canterbury Tales* and *The Six Wives of Henry VIII*. Martin Schute of Sedgemoor line-produced the film, assisted on behalf of Tigon by the able Peter Thompson. Tenser took his customary executive producer credit. Glenister and Phillips worked directly from the version used by the RSC, itself a translation from the original Swedish text. They prefaced their script with a scene-setting quote from Strindberg and stayed fairly true to the original.[10]

Casting the film version was never going to be an issue for Tigon. Tenser retained his veto over the 'above the title' actors but he appreciated that *Miss Julie* was going to be sold on the strength of Strindberg's name and reputation, not that of the performers. There was no objection at Tigon when Phillips proposed casting entirely from the theatre. Key amongst the thespians recruited were Donal McCann and Heather Canning. McCann, who played Jean the servant, had a highly enviable reputation as a stage actor at Dublin's Abbey Theatre and some limited film experience (he had appeared in the comedy *Sinful Davey*). Heather Canning, a veteran of the RSC in both London and New York, was cast as Jean's fiancée, Christine. Canning had never made a film before, though she had worked on television. Her prior stage experience included the likes of 'All's Well That Ends Well' and 'The Revengers Tragedy'.

Helen Mirren was chosen for the title role. She was a relative newcomer, both to cinema and to the film's backer: 'I didn't know of Helen Mirren before she came in,' Tenser concedes. 'She wasn't very well known at the time but I could see she had talent. I knew she was going to be big.' Mirren in fact had already made half a dozen films including *Age of Consent (1969)* and *Savage Messiah (1972)* but her name had really been made at the RSC, where she was being hailed as a star performer.[11]

The requirements of the Multivista system meant that the majority of the film had to be shot in the studio on a single set, which perfectly suited the nature of the play. To open out the film a little, some second unit location work was incorporated, but essentially *Miss Julie* remained a filmed play and as such is proved to be a remarkably straightforward exercise. The rough cut, assembled and edited as the play was filmed, provided an excellent indication of how the final film would shape up; even without the music and final editing, Tenser was aware how remarkable his film looked almost as soon as principal shooting wrapped.

* * * * *

As the year drew to an end, Tenser was determined to continue his practice of exploiting the lower studio costs available during the winter months: 'The terms and conditions on offer were such that we got the very best deal for our films. Ultimately I would always try to get the very best facilities for the director at the very best price for me. We could get the largest studios and facilities for a very economical price.' No sooner had *Miss Julie* wrapped than Tigon entered what was by far its busiest ever period of film production. On the 17th of January, *Neither the Sea Nor the Sand*, which Tenser had

purchased the previous April, started filming at EMI-MGM Elstree. This marked the first time that Tenser arranged to have a film shot there. On the same day, *The Creeping Flesh* started its 16 week shoot at Shepperton, and within two weeks of that, principal photography on *For the Love of Ada* was under way.

Neither the Sea Nor the Sand was unusual for a Tigon movie in that it was an adaptation of a novel by a contemporary author; the only other comparable work for Tenser was *Witchfinder General*, though Tigon had acquired several options. Gordon Honeycombe's novel concerned the love between a lonely woman visiting Jersey and a local, introverted boy. They form a bond of such strength that it carries on beyond the grave. Reliant on atmosphere rather than action, Honeycombe's book had some of the trappings of the horror genre (for example a re-animated corpse, more than a hint of black magic, and a murder) but ultimately the book could only really be classified as a rather bizarre romance.

Curiously, the film rights had previously been picked up by Michael Carreras at Hammer, who was determined to take the company away from production line horrors. The project was offered to director Robert Young but when it proved impossible to raise the finance the idea was abandoned and Young was assigned to

more traditional Hammer fare in the shape of *Vampire Circus (1971)*.

With so many films in production at the same time Tigon's resources were at full stretch, so Tenser made a deal whereby the Portland Film Group - a relatively new player anxious to break into film financing - provided part of the budget. Even so the need to keep costs to a minimum was at the forefront of Tenser's mind when he set about finding a director. 'The BBC was a good recruiting ground for us,' Tenser explains. 'Piers Haggard came to us from television, as had Elkan Allan. The BBC in particular were doing some interesting

above:
Michael Petrovitch and Susan Hampshire in **Neither the Sea Nor the Sand**, the everyday story of love, death and love in death, adapted from the novel by newsreader Gordon Honeycombe.

below:
Trapped by the ocean, Michael Petrovitch's Hugh dies for the second time.

Susan Hampshire • **Frank Finlay** • *Neither the Sea Nor the Sand* (AA)
and introducing **Michael Petrovitch**
Eastman Colour   A Tigon Release
This copyright material is leased and not sold and upon completion of the exhibition for which it has been leased should be returned to Bovince Ltd., Ad-Sales Division, 276 Chase Road, Southgate, London N.14

right:
This front of house still shows Frank Finlay, who first worked for Tenser on **A Study in Terror**, as he starts to suspect that all is not right with his brother in **Neither the Sea Nor the Sand**.

Susan Hampshire · Frank Finlay · *Neither the Sea Nor the Sand*
Michael Petrovitch

Both Tenser and Peter Thompson had more than enough on their hands to keep them busy elsewhere, so as soon as the director and crew had been selected the production chores were handed over to Peter Fetterman and Jack Smith, whose biggest challenge would prove to be the casting of the film's leading lady. Honeycombe's script described Anna Robinson as a mature, world-weary woman who was mentally and physically strong but at the same time attractive. Names like Julie Christie and Diana Rigg had been considered but rejected because of the budget. Burnley then suggested an actress who was better known for her work at the BBC. Susan Hampshire had made a number of lightweight comedies like *Wonderful Life (1964)* and *Monte Carlo Or Bust (1969)*, but she had really come into her own when the BBC asked her to star as Fleur in their hugely successful *The Forsyte Saga*. Fetterman and Smith auditioned Hampshire and were convinced that she had the right looks and strength of character for such a demanding role.[14]

Burnley also found Michael Petrovitch, a theatre actor, who was cast opposite Hampshire in the role of Hugh, the doomed lover. Burnley felt that Petrovitch, who was half Yugoslavian on his father's side, brought the necessary melancholy air to the part. Taking on the role of the dour brother George was Frank Finlay, making a return visit to a Tenser set. In the years since he had played Lestrade in *A Study in Terror*, Finlay had appeared in mainstream films such as *The Molly Maguires (1969)* and *Cromwell (1970)*. Finlay had also scored considerable success with a BBC series, *Casanova*. He may have been afforded the relative luxury of Elstree studios but unfortunately for Burnley the film's script demanded a great deal of exterior work at a time of year not conducive to shooting outside. On the 17th of January he assembled his cast and crew for the first day's shooting on the wet and wind-swept Jersey coast.

productions and we watched a lot of their stuff.' Fred Burnley was approached directly after completing the Corporation's acclaimed *The Search for the Nile* drama/documentary. The 38-year old Englishman's previous cinema work had been as an editor on the likes of *The Bridge on the River Kwai (1957)*.[12]

Honeycombe was hired to adapt his own novel, though he had no previous scriptwriting experience, so Rosemary Davies was brought in to assist with the dialogue. Honeycombe was better known in fact as an ITN newscaster, through he had made the odd film and television appearance as an actor.[13] The remainder of the crew were new to Tigon, and indeed largely new to films. David Muir for example, the director of photography, had the likes of *Lust for a Vampire (1970)* and Freddie Francis's *Mumsy, Nanny, Sonny and Girly (1969)* to his credit, but very little else. Location manager Jilda Smith was an experienced production manager but this was her first work as a location manager, and with so much of the film shooting outside she proved to be a vital part of the production team.

below:
Bullet-headed Kenneth J. Warren attempts to rid Victorian London of another one of those busty doxies in Freddie Francis's **The Creeping Flesh**.

*   *   *   *   *

With so many films in production, it made most sense for Tenser to remain in Wardour Street and co-ordinate the production activity from here. One film which needed very little intervention was *The Creeping Flesh*, a package that had been brought to Tigon after the stars and director had already committed. *The Creeping Flesh* was a horror movie script so conventional as to be outright old-fashioned, which was in fact the precise intention of the film's producer Michael Redbourn, a freelance editor who had worked on Amicus's *Scream and Scream Again (1969)* and Herman Cohen's *Trog (1970)*. Redbourn, who had snatched up the rights over twelve months earlier, was determined to capture what he considered to be the best qualities of the classic Hammer/Amicus movies. Norman Priggen of World Film Services agreed to finance the film on the understanding that horror stalwarts Christopher Lee and Peter Cushing took the leads; Priggen also wanted Freddie Francis to direct.

From Tenser's perspective, Lee and Cushing made the film a 'bankable' proposition, at least in the UK where they were at that point thought of as being part of an elite group of stars whose mere presence could guarantee box-office receipts. Veteran cinematographer Freddie Francis had a reputation for quality work in the genre and more importantly, from Tigon's perspective, for delivering his films on time and within budget.[15] Tenser agreed to acquire the UK rights through Tigon in exchange for a financial stake. World Film Services would retain the overseas rights as well as owning the picture itself. Tenser of course took the executive producer credit but was content with the package as it stood, and called for no script or cast changes.

Cushing was given the major role of Emmanuel Hildern, a slightly potty scientist determined to win the coveted Richter prize for his research on some humanoid remains. Unusually for Cushing, Hildern is a weak, distracted man, whose failings, guilt and ambition lead to his destruction. Christopher Lee played the smaller role of James Hildern, the half-brother, and rival for the Richter prize. Despite the disparity between the two roles, Lee's status had by this time all but eclipsed that of his long-time friend, so he was assured both top billing and the larger pay packet.

The combination of Lee, Cushing and Francis was perfectly in keeping with Redbourn's vision for the film, and the Amicus ambiance was reinforced when he negotiated studio space at Milton Subotsky's favourite stomping ground, Shepperton. *The Creeping Flesh* was actually shot on the re-dressed sets from Amicus's *The House That Dripped Blood (1970)*, with some additional location work in the East End of London and Thorpe in Surrey.

Francis was particularly pleased to be working with Cushing and Lee on the film: 'Peter had that wonderful quality of making anything seem believable and you needed that on a film like this, he brought total conviction to everything he did. Christopher Lee of course is a marvellous actor and he and Peter were a tremendous partnership.' Tenser took the opportunity of a set visit to

above:
Obviously forgiven for making **The Blood Beast Terror**, Tony Tenser is greeted warmly on the set of **The Creeping Flesh** by star Peter Cushing.

below:
Alexandra Dane, who was given just one line in **The Creeping Flesh**. She graced many other British movies including **Corruption** and **The Ups and Downs of a Handyman**.

left:
Towering evil: Christopher Lee's James Hildern intimidates half-brother Emmanuel Hildern (Peter Cushing). **The Creeping Flesh** marked the only time the two actors appeared together in a Tigon film.

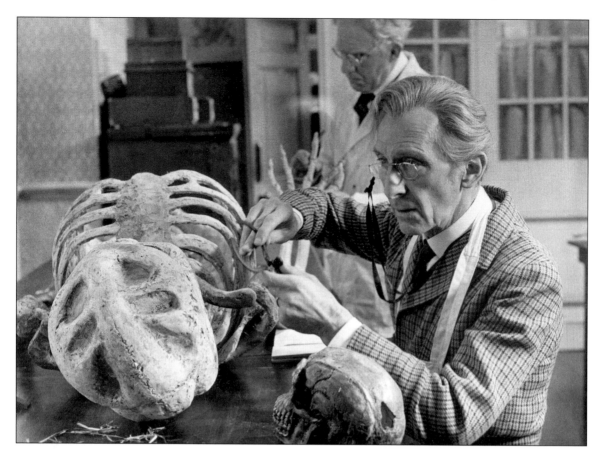

above:
Peter Cushing painstakingly piecing together the puzzle of The Evil One in **The Creeping Flesh**. Veteran actor George Benson is in the background.

right:
Unaware that water will revitalise The Evil One, Christopher Lee is about to pay the price for his greed.

Shepperton in order to renew his acquaintance with Peter Cushing, though the visit turned out to be tinged with sadness: 'Cushing had changed quite a lot, he had nursed his wife through a very long illness and when she died it had quite an impact on him. He was much quieter, withdrawn, and I think he had reached the point where he didn't want to make certain films or play certain parts.'[16]

Francis cast Lorna Heilbron in the pivotal role of Hildern's daughter. Glasgow-born Lorna was making her film debut though she had appeared in rep in Nottingham and in 'Play It Again Sam' with Dudley Moore. She would make only one other significant film, José Ramón Larraz's *Symptoms (1974)*. The remainder of the cast reinforced the general air of nostalgia on the set, as it included many jobbing actors from the Hammer/Amicus repertory company.[17] Francis was also instrumental in hiring the veteran character actor Michael Ripper, who had graced innumerable Hammer movies, for a cameo appearance.[18]

Francis also utilised many of his regular crew behind the camera: Norman Warwick photographed seven films for Francis including *Torture Garden (1967)*, *Tales from the Crypt (1972)* and *The Doctor and the Devils (1985)*. Warwick also did memorable work on *The Abominable Dr. Phibes (1971)* and *Dr. Jekyll & Sister Hyde (1971)* as well as non-genre movies including *The Italian Job (1969)* and

Confessions of a Window Cleaner (1974). Editor Oswald Hafenrichter worked with Francis on movies inclduing *The Skull (1965)*, *The Deadly Bees (1966)* and *Trog (1970)*. He got his break on *The Third Man (1949)* and also worked on the likes of *Cry of the Banshee (1970)* and *The Vault of Horror (1973)*. Designer George Provis had been

above:
German lobby card for **The Creeping Flesh**. Tigon owned only the UK rights; World Film Sales handled the overseas sales.

top left:
Lorna Heilbron's marvellous performance in **The Creeping Flesh** as the initially demure and then demented Penelope almost steals the film from her more established co-stars.

below:
Wilfred Pickles and Arthur English in a scene from Tigon's geriatric comedy **For the Love of Ada**, which is every bit as exciting as this shot suggests.

active in movies since the thirties, and his talents had graced Amicus and AIP efforts including *The Oblong Box (1969), Cry of the Banshee (1970),* and *Craze (1973),* along with cult favourites *Incense for the Damned (1970)* and *The Fiend (1971).* Roy Ashton was called in to create the special make-up effects. He was a well-regarded professional whose many genre credits included Francis's *Tales from the Crypt (1972).*

Surrounded by familiar faces, experienced veterans and sympathetic producers, Francis was in the perfect environment to create a happy and productive set. Apart from his brief visits, Tenser's direct involvement was not required. He was satisfied with the rushes he was shown as well as the reports from Redbourn, so Francis was left largely to his own devices.[19]

*   *   *   *   *

On the 31st of January, with *Neither the Sea Nor the Sand* in production at Elstree and *The Creeping Flesh* at Shepperton, Tigon finally entered the race to get TV sitcoms onto the screen in earnest, when they started shooting *For the Love of Ada.* The rights had been purchased the previous spring but it wasn't until the box-office bonanza sparked by the success of *On the Buses* that Tenser decided to force it into Tigon's crowded production schedule. The Thames television series wasn't exactly in the same league as *On the Buses* or *Steptoe and Son.* It lasted for 27 episodes that ran from April 1970 until September 1971, and told the story of Walter and Ada, two pensioners determined to find love and happiness together much to the disapproval of Ada's daughter, who feels they should live in a more dignified fashion. The series made household names of Irene Handl and Wilfred Pickles in the leads, and Jack Smethurst and Barbara Mitchell as the daughter and son-in-law.[20] Tenser's plan was simplicity itself; unlike *Doomwatch,* where the action had been opened out to appeal to a cinema audience, *For the Love of Ada* would be a straight transfer from television to screen. On television viewers had seen the couple finally marry, and the film would simply pick up with the couple settling into married life.

All of the leads from the television series were retained and Ronnie Baxter, who had been the series producer, was brought in to direct a script written by the regular series writers Vince Powell and Harry Driver. This was an impressive line-up of talent: Baxter would go on to produce such comic classics as *Rising Damp* and *Love Thy Neighbour,* and between them, Powell and Driver had a remarkable track record of writing and creating television comedy including hits such as *Bless This House, Nearest and Dearest, Love Thy Neighbour* and *Mind Your Language.* Music was supplied by Frank Barber, with minor pop star Gilbert O'Sullivan commissioned to write and perform 'What Could Be Nicer.' Jack Causey, Tenser's right hand man on *The Magnificent Seven Deadly Sins* and *Doomwatch,* fulfilled the role of production manager, with Alan Hume handing the photography and Peter Thompson taking on the production chores.

Tenser envisaged no need for a production partner and set a budget of slightly under £100,000. He did not anticipate any significant overseas interest but was not concerned as he believed that the film was a safe investment, even as a UK-only release. The series had ended in the autumn but a Christmas special broadcast on the 27th of December 1971 signalled the end of *For the Love of Ada* as a television sitcom. A month later the same cast assembled for the filming of the big-screen version.

*   *   *   *   *

above:
Adapted from the television series of the same name, **For the Love of Ada** also used the stars of the small screen series, Irene Handl and Wilfred Pickles.

At the end of January 1972 an overview of the industry revealed a remarkable statistic - out of the four features films being shot in the UK, three of them were being made by Tigon. Incredibly, at one point Tony Tenser was producing the only films being made on the Elstree and Shepperton lots, and he looked set to maintain this momentum throughout the rest of the year. Tenser had already taken on two new subjects: Douglas Hickox's 'Slag', and a co-production with old friend Herman Cohen called 'Infernal Idol.' These were in addition to 'The Chilian Club' and 'Cold War in a Country Garden' - both still very much regarded as 'go' projects. 'The Last of the Mohicans' on the other hand had failed to generate any interest and had been dropped from the schedules. A few weeks later Tenser was explaining his success to Kine Weekly: 'Tigon has made five 'nearly finished' films in two months. The only thing that stops films being made is money. If you look after the money and the people who put the money in, there will be an increase in the films being made. On these five films we spread the risk by getting other people to put money in too. The idea is to minimise our risk - and thereby everybody's risk. If someone brings a film to me, my first question - even before I read the script - is always, 'What are you going to put into it: your time, your money, your percentage?' If they are just there for a fat fee then Tigon won't take the picture.'

Despite Tenser's optimism, the reality for the film industry was extremely bleak. The cost of making a film had continued to rise at the same time that cinema attendances were declining, and the gap was widening to such an extent that it was considered exceptional for a medium budgeted film to recover its costs in the UK market alone. *On the Buses (1971)* was a notable exception - a low budget film that had recovered its budget several times over on a domestic, and limited overseas, release. The years that followed would throw up a number of other success stories, but these remained a tiny minority. Tigon were putting out an increasing number of films into a dwindling market. Plainly they were in danger of falling into the same trap that was catching out so many of their contemporaries.

Chairman Laurie Marsh remained confident in the Group's future. He insisted that Tigon was being transformed into a 'blue chip' company with a solid balance sheet. Amongst the more high profile assets that now constituted the new Tigon Group was the Sloane Square development on the Kings Road, mostly consisting of top fashion boutiques. Marsh's company Town Markets owned this development, which in turn was to become a wholly owned subsidiary of Tigon. The restructuring of Tigon and Marsh's own property assets had completely changed the complexion of the Group; film production, once Tigon's core activity, was buried beneath the mass of property assets. At the end of 1971, The Group's return on film production was down to just 15% of overall revenue, against 60% from exhibition at Tigon's cinemas, which now numbered in excess of 200.

On the 11th of March 1972 Laurie Marsh announced that the Group's profits forecast for the year 1971/72 amounted to £450,000. An impressive sum by any standards but as a public quoted company the Tigon Group of course had a duty to its shareholders and corporate investors in the City, and it was the commonly held view that the film industry was in free-fall. To ease City jitters that the company was over-committed to expensive and potentially risky film production, Marsh announced that Tigon's exposure to any individual film project would be limited to £60,000. This decision effectively limited Tenser's potential role in all but the cheapest of films to that of junior partner. Marsh had also made another announcement, one that would begin the slow process of dismantling Tigon as a filmmaking entity: 'Laurie Marsh wanted to rename the company,' Tenser relates. 'He felt that it would be better for the Stock Exchange, as Tigon had a certain image that was no longer relevant to the Group, so we changed the name to LMG, the Laurie Marsh Group.' The company records show that Marsh had been persuaded to change the name of the company by the Board, who voted 9-1 (Marsh was the one against) in favour of the change. It was a very clear signal that the company's priorities were being firmly realigned.

Spring 1972 was a deceptively productive time at Tigon's Wardour Street office. *Doomwatch* was shown to the trade, *For the Love of Ada* was editing at Elstree, *The Creeping Flesh* was being made at Shepperton, while *Neither the Sea Nor the Sand* was being dubbed at the Gate Recording Theatre in London. The posters for

IAN BANNEN · JUDY GEESON
also starring JOHN PAUL · SIMON OATES · JEAN TREND · JOBY BLANSHARD
DOOMWATCH (A)
Guest Star GEORGE SANDERS
with PERCY HERBERT · GEOFFREY KEEN · JOSEPH O'CONOR · SHELAGH FRASER
"Doomwatch" by KIT PEDLER and GERRY DAVIS Final Screenplay by CLIVE EXTON Music Composed and Conducted by JOHN SCOTT
Produced by TONY TENSER Directed by PETER SASDY · A TIGON BRITISH FILM PRODUCTION

each now adorned the walls at Tigon but the downscaling of the Group's film production unit had left Tenser with a peripheral role to play. This may have been acceptable if he was enjoying the challenge but as he says: 'I knew we were coming to the end of an era, an end to films which reigned back a little and didn't just throw everything at the screen. It was an end I suppose to my type of films.' While he was considering his future, Tenser's last film as a line producer, *Doomwatch*, complete since the start of the year, was being prepared for summer release.

DOOMWATCH

'A Chilling Story From Today's Headlines'
- British Press Release -

Synopsis

When an oil tanker runs aground off the coast of the small island of Balfe, Dr. Del Shaw (Ian Bannen) of Doomwatch goes to investigate the effects on the shore life. The locals he encounters are all suspicious and Shaw is alarmed by the almost Neanderthal features of some of the men on the island, and their aggressive nature. At the Doomwatch laboratory they discover abnormalities in the samples and request

more. These attempts to obtain more specimens lead to violence and encounters with the Ministry of Defence and a sinister multinational, Doran Chemicals.

Critique

'There is not much inspiration or use of the big screen possibilities about this reach-me-down bit of science fiction, and it's rather dismal to see the cinema limping along picking up scraps from TV. But I will own that Peter Sasdy's direction is workmanlike and passably entertaining.'
- The Evening News, 30/05/72

'...this one doesn't look too skimped. A tribute perhaps to Peter Sasdy's direction which, without actually setting Wardour Street on fire, at least has the virtues of narrative skill and a modicum of imagination.'
- The Guardian, 01/06/72

'Not for the first time I note Peter Sasdy is the director responsible for making a superior looking film out of a modest seeming project.'
- The Sunday Telegraph, 04/06/72

'I would like to say that it turns out as exciting on the big screen as the small but it doesn't, not by a long way.'
- The Sun, 03/06/72

above:
Final confrontation with the villagers in Peter Sasdy's **Doomwatch**.

below:
Michael Brennan as Tom Straker in make-up by Tom Smith, who would later work on **Star Wars: Episode VI - Return of the Jedi**.

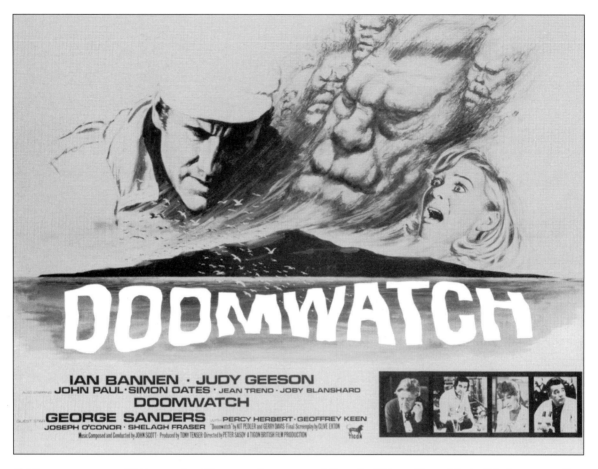

 IAN BANNEN · JUDY GEESON
JOHN PAUL · SIMON OATES · JEAN TREND · JOBY BLANSHARD
DOOMWATCH
GEORGE SANDERS ..... PERCY HERBERT · GEOFFREY KEEN
JOSEPH O'CONOR · SHELAGH FRASER 'Doomwatch' by KIT PEDLER and GERRY DAVIS Final Screenplay by CLIVE EXTON
Music Composed and Conducted by JOHN SCOTT · Produced by TONY TENSER Directed by PETER SASDY A TIGON BRITISH FILM PRODUCTION

above:
Cover of the British pressbook for **Doomwatch**.

below:
Gabrielle Drake gets to grips with Richard O'Sullivan in Val Guest's **Au Pair Girls**, which was released by Tigon. The company's plans to produce a sequel were cancelled when Tenser left.

'Creepy and exciting enough on a run of the mill horror film level... Quite a lark.'
- CinemaTV Today, 11/03/72

Doomwatch slipped into provincial cinemas without much in the way of fanfare in the early part of the summer. Sasdy's film had some fine moments, notably the performances of Bannen and Geeson, but it really didn't seem to know where it was going. The horror elements, downplayed in favour of the science fiction, would actually sit better with the overall air of menace and any value inherent in Tom Smith's extremely effective make-up is dissipated too cheaply. Sasdy is much better with more complex films; the plot here is too unremarkable, the characterisations too bland and the narrative too unchallenging for a director of his skill and verve. The lack of ambition shows; *Doomwatch* could be mistaken for a TV special and despite an attempt to open the film out there simply isn't enough quality and depth to fill the big screen. Tigon's problems were not limited to the film's lacklustre performance in the UK market, as strenuous efforts to find a US buyer had proved fruitless. *Doomwatch* joined *The Magnificent Seven Deadly Sins* on the shelf at Wardour Street after its first disappointing UK run.

The future of Tigon as a film production company was in the balance when Peter Thompson flew to Hollywood on the 24th of June to meet with American producer David

L. Wolper. The subject of their conversation was the completed script for 'Cold War in a Country Garden', which Tigon had been working on for some time and which Tenser was anxious to get into production. The company though were not prepared to undertake any more work on the project without securing a majority stake from a US investor and despite some enthusiastic noises emanating from Hollywood, no-one had yet confirmed. The discussions with Wolper were amicable but inconclusive and Thompson returned empty-handed.

Film production for Tigon reached its lowest point when, at the end of June, veteran film director/writer Val Guest announced he was to direct 'Glamour Incorporated' for Tigon at Twickenham. This was desiigned to be a follow-up to the Tigon-released sex comedy *Au Pair Girls (1972)*, also directed by Guest, and something of a minor hit. Guest had submitted the script for 'Glamour Incorporated' to Tigon and when he received what he perceived to be buying signals from Tenser, promptly said as much to the press. The failure to secure a backer for 'Cold War' as well as the disappointments of all their recent UK productions forced a re-think at Board level. Tigon issued a face-saving press release saying that they were discussing Guest's film but as yet hadn't committed. In fact they had already made the decision not to invest at the production stage, preferring instead to pick up the rights to the finished film. The writing was on the wall; exhibition through the Classic and Essoldo cinemas had become all-important to the Group. The property value of these sites constituted the most significant asset on the company's books, but in the City film production was viewed as 'venture capital' - high risk with a slow rate of return. The Board, despite Marsh's earlier assertion that he would restrict Tenser's commitment to a maximum of £60,000 per project, now revealed doubts about whether the Group should be involved in film production at all.

*   *   *   *   *

If ever Tigon needed a major hit with one of its own films it was now. *For the Love of Ada* had been shown to the trade on the 12th of August 1972, and was greeted by almost total derision from a cynical press. Tenser and the publicity team at Tigon put on a brave face and mused, in public at least, that *On the Buses* had been panned by every critic that saw it. Opting for a policy of all or nothing, Tigon Pictures decided to open their film in August, at the height of the holiday season, in the expectation that hordes of undiscriminating holiday makers would like nothing better than to visit some familiar territory.

FOR THE LOVE OF ADA

'I'm Sexy Sandra, I've Got Nothing On Underneath.'
- UK Press ads -

Synopsis

Ada was a widow, set in her ways, until she became friendly with the roguish Walter Bingley, the local gravedigger and the man who buried her husband. The two fell in love with each other and decided, despite their

age, to marry. Ada's daughter Ruth and her boorish husband Leslie live next door to the couple. They thoroughly disapprove of Walter and the effect he has on Ada, and make it clear that simply because the two pensioners are now married, it doesn't mean they have to like it. When Walter appears to have passed on comic chaos ensues.

above:
British seaside humour at its very worst - Jack Smethurst and Andrea Lawrence in Ronnie Baxter's **For the Love of Ada**.

Critique

'...is such a doleful little picture that it would not be worth mentioning, except as further evidence of the present strange state of play between films and television... so much stilted dialogue and in such lacklustre sets that the picture looks on the verge of collapse from sheer decrepitude.'
- The New Statesman, 18/08/72

'Designed for people for whom excitement might prove fatal, the film abounds in situations which have the relaxing effect of a warm bath.'
- The Daily Mirror, 11/08/72

left:
Pickles and Handl as the loving Bingleys in **For the Love of Ada**.

above:

For the Love of Ada was one of a rash of films based on British television series. Unusually this big screen outing actually provided an extension to the story rather than a re-tread. Most viewers at the time wondered why Tigon bothered.

'Hardly worth going on about except that it's the latest and worst of a long line of television spin-offs... but you really deserve better than this suffocating drivel.'
- The Guardian, 10/08/72

'A patronising entertainment designed seemingly for senile rather than merely senior citizens.'
- The Times, 18/08/72

'Honestly, I've had more fun cleaning out a blocked up drain.'
- The Daily Express, 18/08/72

The 'humour' in *For the Love of Ada* is summed up with one exchange of dialogue between Ada and Walter: 'I like my wife to look the way God made her.' 'You wouldn't object if I went about in my birthday suit then?' Cue double-takes and spluttering from the cast, and canned laughter from the studio audience. The sexual fumbling of Jack Smethurst and Barbara Mitchell, mistaken identities and stock comic characters make for extremely unrewarding viewing. Irene Handl may just have got away with it on the television, where sitcom's pander to the viewers' familiarity and affection for the eccentricities of the regular cast. Watching *For the Love of Ada* in the cinema on a wet August afternoon must have been a depressing experience. Not only was the script underwritten, but the demographics of the audience seem to have been completely ignored - if the average age of a cinema attendee was between 14 and 25, why would anyone want to make a film headlined by two pensioners?[21] Like *Doomwatch* before it, *For the Love of Ada* may well have found a place as a television film aimed at a specific target audience, but as a cinema experience it simply failed to find a market. Significantly, neither *Doomwatch* nor *For the Love of Ada* was sold to the US market.

Footnotes

1. Former Miss Norway Julie Ege was at one stage in the early Seventies a seemingly obligatory feature in any British film. Ege's main claim to fame came when James Carreras anointed her 'the sex symbol of the seventies', declaring, 'she has the same utterly feminine, earthly sexy quality as Raquel Welch.' As well as working for Hammer on *Creatures the World Forgot (1971)* and *The Legend of the 7 Golden Vampires (1974)*, she appeared in everything from *Up Pompeii (1971)* to *Craze (1973)*, to say nothing of countless appearances at premieres, on chat shows and even on vinyl when she had a single released. One Fleet Street wag estimated that between 1970 and 1972 Ege had generated an estimated 1660 column inches in British newspapers alone! Ege took it all in her stride with good-natured charm, saying, 'I was very willing if a photographer said, 'Can we have a picture? I'd say, of course. I believed in publicity.'

2. 'Flora and I were both disappointed that they'd slotted in some rather cheap effects afterwards - you have absolutely no control over this - which turned it into a much more bloodthirsty and horrible picture than either of us imagined.' Beryl Reid, 'So Much Love'.

3. A number of titles were considered, including the rather endearing 'The Ghouls Are Amongst Us' before Tenser settled on *Blood on Satan's Claw*. Neither Haggard nor Wynne-Simmons were involved in the re-titling.

4. Stout and slightly sinister, Wymark's background as the son of an art-shop dealer in Cleethorpes belies his screen image as a major powerbroker. A stage actor of considerable presence, Wymark worked with the RSC at both The Old Vic and Stratford-Upon-Avon, where he was nearly always cast as men in charge, though he was more than capable of displaying weakness. Sadly cinema did very little to exploit his considerable depth. Though he was well used by Polanski in *Repulsion*, his role as Cromwell in *Witchfinder* was necessarily brief. The pivotal role in *Blood on Satan's Claw* as The Judge was his best genre part but his film work also includes *The Secret of Blood Island (1964)*, *The Skull (1965)*, and *Where Eagles Dare (1968)*. Much like his contemporary Rupert Davies, he was cast in the lead of a popular TV series, *The Plane Makers*, and its sequel *The Power Game*, which brought him honours - Best Actor 1965 - and fame, but left him typecast and struggling for challenging parts for the rest of his life. Wymark died in Melbourne on the 20th of October 1970, at the age of 44, during a tour of the play 'Sleuth'.

5. Judy, and to some extent Sally, fitted in to the 'dolly-bird' mould that flourished in British cinema during the late Sixties. She appeared in endless inane but successful comedies and by the age of 23 was commanding a staggering £100,000 a film! When the fad for perky starlets died in the more sombre Seventies, Judy moved easily into more dramatic roles in film such as *10 Rillington Place (1970)* and *Fear in the Night (1972)*. She did not however appear in a particularly successful picture, and as her star faded she found herself reduced to taking on less and less worthy work, in the likes of *Percy's Progress (1974)* and *Carry On England (1976)*. Television success in *Danger UXB* and *Poldark* gave her financial security but an ill-fated move to Hollywood and an acrimonious divorce left her penniless and making ends meet by working in a shop. Ever the survivor, Geeson put her career back together again with guest spots on the likes of *MacGyver*, *Murder, She Wrote* and a recurring role on the sitcom *Mad About You*.

6. On the 25th of April 1972, George Sanders was found dead in a hotel room in the Spanish resort of Castell de Fels. A world-weary sense of detachment and obvious boredom became his trademark as the quality of his projects declined. His long and distinguished screen career ended with Don Sharp's *Psychomania (1972)*. Sanders took an overdose after writing his infamous suicide note, that read: 'Dear World, I am leaving because I am bored. I feel I have lived enough. I am leaving you with your worries in this sweet cesspool - Good Luck.' Sanders was 65. He had been married four times, once to Zsa Zsa Gabor in 1949 and then to her sister Magda in 1970.

7. Hungarian born Peter Sasdy started his directorial career on British television with shows like *Probation Officer* and *Journey to the Unknown*. The latter, for Hammer, led directly to *Taste the Blood of Dracula (1970)*, and a career in horror movies including *Countess Dracula (1970)*, *Hands of the Ripper (1971)*, *Nothing But the Night (1972)*, and *I Don't Want to Be Born (1975)*. Sasdy's films are not among the most popular and successful in the genre but he brought an intelligence and strong visual style to otherwise forgettable works.

8. August Strindberg was born in Stockholm in 1849 and is easily the best known Swedish playwright. He originally worked as a journalist after dropping out of University, and after struggling for a while his first published work, 'Master Olof,' was released in 1872. His predilection for attacking the complacent and pompous made him powerful enemies in the Church, press and public offices. Martial problems made him increasingly bitter and his hostility to women grew more pronounced, culminating in his novel 'Giftos'. An acrimonious divorce drove him to spend his final years in Paris, allegedly studying occultism and alchemy.

9. Phillips would direct only one other film, *The Wars (1983)*, an unsuccessful adaptation of the Timothy Findley novel. Phillips did however continue to enjoy success in the theatre, including a five year stint as Artistic Director of Canada's prestigious Stratford Festival.

10. Strindberg's preface is both an explanation and a warning: 'Miss Julie is a modern character - not that the half-woman, the man-hunter, has not existed in every age, but because now that she has been discovered she has stepped forward into the limelight and begun to make a noise.'

11. The daughter of a Southend traffic examiner, Convent educated Helen Mirren is generally recognised as one of the best theatre and film actresses of her generation. She has lifted the Best Actress at Cannes twice, for *Cal (1984)* and *The Madness of King George (1994)*, as well as picking up BAFTA and TV awards for her work on TV's *Prime Suspect*. Her extensive film work includes *Savage Messiah (1972)* for Ken Russell, Lindsay Anderson's *O Lucky Man! (1973)* and John Boorman's *Excalibur (1981)*. Known for her sex-appeal as much as her intelligence, Mirren could

quicken the pulse of the usually staid broadsheets, provoking the sort of headlines normally associated with tabloids:'I've been blonde and sexy looking since I was 14' - The Guardian, 04/09/69; 'Stratford's Very Own Sex Queen' - Sunday Times, 02/08/70. Married to American filmmaker Taylor Hackford, the director of *An Officer and a Gentleman (1982)*, she continues to be a forceful presence on stage, screen and increasingly television.

12. Burnley had obtained a first class honours degree at Oxford in philosophy, politics and economics, before he decided on a career in the film industry, starting as a trainee editor at Ealing in 1955. He moved to the BBC's drama department as a fully fledged director on well-received productions like *The Dream Divided* and *Down These Mean Streets a Man Must Go*. His work on *The Search for the Nile* won him a Television Critics Award in 1971 but sadly *Neither the Sea Nor the Sand* was his only film as a director. He died in 1975 aged only 42.

13. Honeycombe's acting career includes contributions to the likes of *The Medusa Touch (1978)*, *The Fourth Protocol (1987)*, and *Castaway (1986)*, all of which cast him as a newsreader. His writing career shows far more variety; as well as his fiction he has written the likes of 'Selfridges: The Story of a Store' and 'The Murders of the Black Museum 1870-1970'.

14. In 1965 Susan Hampshire told Film Review: 'It is my destiny to be a great movie star'. Sadly it wasn't. A contract with MGM landed her The *Three Lives of Thomasina (1963)* and *Night Must Fall (1964)* but her later appearances in *Monte Carlo Or Bust (1969)*, *Malpertuis (1971)*, and *Living Free (1972)* failed to bring her stardom. Hampshire did find herself extremely popular on British television serials like *The Forsyte Saga*, and *The First Churchills* in the Seventies, continuing to work through to *The Grand* in the Nineties. Her name has come to prominence over the years in other contexts too - she lost £500,000 as a Lloyds Name in the Eighties, and has appeared on TV spots promoting dyslexia awareness - a condition she has suffered from since childhood. She has been haunted by tragedy, having endured three miscarriages and the death of a day-old baby girl. These days Hampshire has one child, Christopher, from her marriage to the French film director Pierre Granier-Deferre, and is happily married to theatrical impresario Sir Eddie Kulukundis. She ventures out for the odd television or theatre part but is content to spend her time rearing chickens at the family home.

15. Starting his career as a clapper boy but excelling as a cinematographer, Freddie Francis had worked with the likes of Korda, Huston, Reed, and Welles by the time he won his first Oscar (for *Sons and Lovers*) in 1960. He also photographed such influential films as *The Innocents* and *Room at the Top*. His jump into directing came when Norman Priggen offered him *Two and Two Make Six (1962)*, quickly followed by such delights as *The Evil of Frankenstein (1964)*, *The Skull (1965)* and *Trog (1970)*. In between directing horror or thriller movies, Francis continued to practice his preferred craft, becoming a favoured cinematographer of David Lynch (*The Elephant Man (1980)*) and Martin Scorsese (*Cape Fear (1991)*). At a time when cinema was increasingly a young man's game the octogenarian Francis continued capture major awards; he

above:
This German lobby card shows one of Christopher Lee's attempts to isolate the cause of madness in **The Creeping Flesh**. David Bailie is the young doctor.

below:
Bailie and Lee ponder an earlier experiment. Note the billing of Lee above Cushing, despite the fact that he had a smaller part; by this time in his career Lee had eclipsed his old sparring partner in terms of box-office appeal.

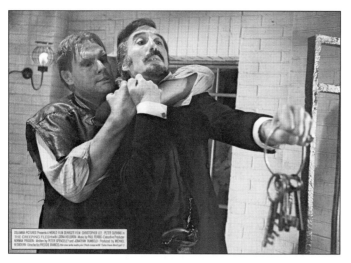

above:
American lobby card for
The Creeping Flesh.
The film was by far the
closest to the Hammer/
Amicus school that
Tigon ever produced,
which was ironic
because it therefore felt
like a re-tread of an era
that had already passed
before the film was
even released.

won his second Oscar for director of photography with *Glory (1989)*. This came on top of five British Society of Cinematographers awards, one American Society of Cinematographers award and a raft of BAFTA nominations gathered through the years. In 2000 Francis won the New York Critics Circle award for photographing David Lynch's *The Straight Story (1999)*. He retired from filmmaking after this triumph.

16. Peter Cushing's wife Helen died in January 1971 after a long battle with cancer. She had been Cushing's partner in every sense of the word and her death left him completely devastated. He dropped all his interests and pastimes and immersed himself in a punishing schedule of work. Between 1971 and 1972 Cushing acted in twelve films including *Twins of Evil (1971)* and *Tales from the Crypt (1972)*. He was never quite the same again; his face, always thin, grew painfully gaunt and he carried an air of sadness that permeated all of his roles. A deeply religious man for the remainder of his life, he viewed death as a release and his only wish was to be reunited with Helen. By contrast, Christopher Lee's career was reaching a peak in the early Seventies after he moved away from the superior, disinterested approach that had marred many of his less challenging appearances in the Sixties. He gradually broadening his range, taking roles in movies like *The Private Life of Sherlock Holmes (1970)*, *Hannie Caulder (1971)*, and *I, Monster (1971)*. Always a strong physical presence, by the time he came to make *The Creeping Flesh* he was being accepted as an actor of considerable depth as well, and he would continue to work over the next thirty plus years. The extent to which he had shed his 'graveyard' image was demonstrated in 1998 when he received universally enthusiastic reviews for his performance as Jinnah, the father of modern Pakistan, in the film of the same name. He returned to super-stardom with roles in the *Star Wars* and *Lord of the Rings* films.

17. The very experienced cast lent the film an air of quality but left the viewer with the over-riding feeling that they all deserved the chance to do more. Scottish-born Lamont had been an effective player in British movies for years; his best work had been for Hammer in *The Evil of Frankenstein (1964)* and *Quatermass and the Pit (1967)*. The always fidgety and contrite George Benson was the harassed Customs Official from *Dracula (1958)*. Here he is

given more screen time but he has less impact. Sadly this was his last film. He died in 1983. Despite his thuggish, bullet-headed appearance, Kenneth J. Warren was a noted gourmet cook and artist. He played memorably in *Circus of Horrors (1960)*, *Dr. Blood's Coffin (1960)*, and *Demons of the Mind (1971)*. Jenny Runacre made memorable appearances in *The Final Programme (1973)*, *The Duellists (1977)* and Hammer's last and least, *The Lady Vanishes (1979)*. She also made a memorable Queen Elizabeth in Jarman's shocking *Jubilee (1977)*. Minor parts were taken by Tony Wright and Marianne Stone, who had both appeared in *All Coppers Are... (1971)*. Wright generally made sexploitation movies such as *Clinic Xclusive (1971)* and *Can I Come Too? (1979)*. Stone, the wife of Peter Noble, had been in dozens of movies, from *Carry Ons* to the *Confessions of...* series.

18. Hugely popular, Michael Ripper became the best known of the regular company of character and bit-parters used by Hammer. He was born in 1913, and before coming to Hammer had been working as an actor and assistant director for both cinema and the stage. Tony Hinds took a shine to him in the late Fifties and cast him in many of the movies he produced. He typically appeared on screen as a barman, and frequently as comic relief. Not an actor of great range, he quickly became a firm favourite with the Hammer crowd and as much a recognisable feature of a Hammer movie as Peter Cushing or Christopher Lee. When Hinds left the Company in 1969, Ripper found himself out of sorts with Hammer's new image, and he drifted away from film work into the world of television. Over the years he did create some memorable characters for Hammer, notably in *The Mummy's Shroud (1967)*. He was always a jobbing actor, who had a professional if down to earth approach to all his roles and was modestly dismissive of his own genre contributions: 'Very often a man is forced to take a job that he does not particularly like. If it pays, you take it.' Michael Ripper died in 2000.

19. A week after *The Creeping Flesh* started shooting at Shepperton, it was joined on the backlot by Peter Newbrook's *The Asphyx*, starring Robert Powell and Robert Stephens. The latter had starred in *The Private Life of Sherlock Holmes*, which allowed Photoplay the opportunity to gather together Stephens, Cushing and Lee - all Sherlock Holmes - for an impromptu photo call.

20. Born in 1901, Irene Handl didn't make her film debut until 1937, in *Missing, Believed Married*. She went on to lend her considerable presence, and more or less the same character, to dozens of British films ranging from *Brief Encounter (1945)* to *The Great Rock 'n' Roll Swindle (1979)*. She died in 1987. Wilfred Pickles, three years younger than Handl, had been a huge star on the radio for a number of years and picked up an OBE in 1950 for his charity work. He only appeared in a couple of films - *Billy Liar (1963)* and *The Family Way (1966)* - but when he died in 1978 he left behind him an entertaining autobiography and several well-received volumes of poetry.

21. Amongst the aging cast there were two younger faces: Gareth Hunt, who for a time would grace *The New Avengers* as Gambit; and a four-year old Patsy Kensit, the archetypal rock chick who would also find time to make films such as *Absolute Beginners (1986)* and *Lethal Weapon 2 (1989)*.

Chapter Ten

'What Terrifying Craving Made Her Kill... and Kill... and Kill...?'

- (UK advertising slogan for *Frightmare*)

For the second time in its short existence Tigon was operating under two different names. Six months after the parent company had been renamed LMG, several films that had already been produced and registered with the Board of Trade under the name Tigon were still unreleased. Thus *Doomwatch*, completed the previous year, remained a Tigon British Film production, released by Tigon Pictures. However, *For the Love of Ada* - also a Tigon British Film - was released by LMG Film Distributors. Tenser's next film, *Not Now Darling*, was to be the first of a new breed, an LMG production.

Determined to exploit the Multivista camera system to the full, Tenser signed a deal with Ray Cooney to adapt his stage farce for the big screen. Sedgemoor, who had contributed to the still unreleased *Miss Julie*, came in with a financial stake while Ray Cooney took a production credit under the name of his own trading company, 'Not Now Films.' Cooney's farce had enjoyed a long and successful run in the West End. Like all of Cooney's best works it depended heavily on rapid-fire dialogue, constant movement and more importantly few if any set changes.[1]

The play revolves around a single gag: a successful West End furrier wants to give his mistress a fur as a gift but doesn't want either his wife or his mistress's husband to find out about it. Included in the mix are the usual stock characters that typically populate these marital farces, along with the obligatory half-dressed women and double entendres. Cooney's contract allowed him the option to direct the film,

below:
Writer-director-star Ray Cooney is taken to task by the semi-naked Julie Ege in **Not Now Darling**. Leslie Phillips, who was recreating his West End stage success in the same role, seems completely disinterested.

which he intended to do, but at Tigon's suggestion David Croft was brought in to assist him. As with the previous Multivista film, there was a concern that the system was just too difficult for inexperienced hands to cope with it unsupervised. Croft was a BAFTA award winner for sitcoms like *Dad's Army* and *Are You Being Served?* The rest of the production credits had an air of familiarity - apart from Tenser and Thompson from LMG, Martin Schute and Marvin Liebman represented Sedgemoor, Peter Thornton was hired to edit the footage on set, whilst veteran *Carry On* cinematographer Alan Hume handled the photography.

Casting the film was straightforward enough. Cooney's stage version had enjoyed a lengthy run in the West End and he insisted that the lead should go to the most successful of all his stage heroes, Leslie Phillips, the very embodiment of raffish charm.[2] Cooney hoped that *Not Now Darling* was going to be the first in a long series of films, adopting the 'Not Now...' prefix as a brand name; his model here was the now waning *Carry On* series and he was keen to incorporate as many elements as possible from those films into his new series. This approach extended beyond situations and jokes, to several of the cast members themselves. Barbara Windsor and Joan Sims, old hands at this sort of thing, duly joined Phillips in the cast list.

To play the role of the mistress, Cooney looked no further than Phillips's previous Tenser movie, *The Magnificent Seven Deadly Sins*. The object of the actor's

affections in that film was the voluptuous Julie Ege. Despite possessing limited acting ability, Julie still had the affections of a generally jaded British press. Simply by virtue of her presence, *Not Now Darling* was guaranteed serious column inches, thus generating the sort of publicity that *For the Love of Ada* had so desperately lacked.[3] Cooney filled out the supporting roles with familiar faces, opting for the likes of Bill Fraser, Jack Hulbert and Moira Lister, as well as the redoubtable Derren Nesbitt.[4] Graham Stark, another survivor of *The Magnificent Seven Deadly Sins*, featured as a randy workman in an unbilled cameo.

The idea of shooting the action entirely on one set using the Multivista cameras had been explored thoroughly on *Miss Julie*, but the cast and crew working on *Not Now Darling* nevertheless found it tough going.[5] Barbara Windsor was particularly unimpressed: 'It was such hard work, they didn't really know what they were doing. To be honest it was bit of a shambles.' Julie Ege on the other hand remembers the film with a great deal of affection: 'My English wasn't very good so that limited me a little - it was a very fast film lots of fast dialogue - but I loved working with Leslie Phillips, he was tremendous fun.'

By now Tenser was considering his position within the company and wasn't convinced he even wanted to continue working in the film industry. He still found time to visit the set however, where he discovered that whatever technological advances had been made, some things never change. 'Barbara Windsor came to

below:
Former Miss Norway Julie Ege taunting Messrs Phillips and Cooney in **Not Now Darling**. The film was predominantly shot on a single set using Tigon's Multivista process, and despite token efforts to open out the action it never looked like anything more than a filmed stage farce.

see me. I knew her of course from *A Study in Terror* and we had got on very well, anyway she was very worried about her nude scenes. I think she thought they were going to be stronger than they were. She was worried that she wasn't as young as she used to be but I told her not to worry, it really wasn't going to be that type of film.'[6] Of course this was now the Seventies, when even the 'Carry On's featured some nudity. *Not Now Darling*'s female leads were all required to strip down to their lacy underwear but the required glimpses of nudity were provided by Ms. Ege and the statuesque model Trudi Van Doorn.

With the Multivista process speeding up production, LMG estimated that they could save around 30% of their production costs and increase the amount of footage produced each day by as much as 100%. The company that had been expressing its reservations about being in the film production business at all suddenly saw its films not only as a profit making units in their own right, but also as big screen advertisements for their wholly-owned process. It didn't really surprise anyone when LMG snapped up the rights to 'Father Dear Father' - predictably an adaptation of the TV sitcom of the same name - and announced the film as their next intended Multivista project.

*　　*　　*　　*　　*

By the end of the summer of 1972 the British film industry was officially in crisis. Total investment in film production had amounted to less than £8.5m for the first quarter of the financial year, compared with just over £39m for the same period a year before. At a time when production is usually ramping up for the spring and summer there were only four films shooting - two at EMI/MGM and one each at Pinewood and Shepperton.[7] Isleworth and Ealing studios had closed completely and the remaining film studios scrambled to eke out a living, primarily by making television commercials. At LMG however, Laurie Marsh lit up the otherwise bleak landscape when he reported a post tax profit of £475k for year ended April 1972, a figure in line with forecasts. The news was well received by the Stock Exchange but the company's share price remained at 94p, down from 114p at the start of the year - reflecting investors' cautious views on the Group's continued involvement in filmmaking. Indeed, the company's accounts at the time revealed the sobering fact that film production was now responsible for slightly less than 3% of the Group's overall profits; this figure was vastly out of proportion with the capital investment involved. After careful consideration, balancing the performance of their

most recent films against the difficulties in obtaining American finance, the Board of LMG took Marsh's advice and decided to introduce an immediate 'no risk policy' in respect of its capital investments. Henceforth there would be no feature films made beyond their existing commitments. The filmmaking arm of LMG would effectively close.

Marsh conceded that the company 'may' still be involved with financing or producing films which use the Multivista system. LMG Film Productions (formerly Tigon British of course) was not actually wound down immediately; it remained teasingly in existence for some time but sadly remained inactive. The work of the

above:
Ms. Ege as Janie McMichael in a posed publicity still for **Not Now Darling**. Ege was being hailed at the time as The Sex Symbol of the Seventies.

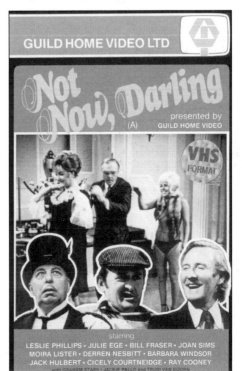

left:
The Guild Home Video release of **Not Now Darling**, showing Bill Fraser, Graham Stark and Leslie Phillips in the foreground. 'Carry On' stars Joan Sims and Barbara Windsor can be seen either side of Ray Cooney in the main picture.

above:
Mike Ewin, head of Tigon's distribution arm. By this time film distribution was outstripping production as a income source for the company, and would soon replace it completely.

below:
Rare British artwork for **Miss Julie**. Odd to think the only established playwrights filmed by Tigon were Strindberg and Cooney!

production company, such as it was, was assumed by Multivista under the control of Peter Thompson, who went on to oversee the completion of one remaining property, *Father Dear Father*, the last of the Sedgemoor co-productions.

'The idea is to phase myself out of the routine side of the business and lessen some of the stresses and strains,' Tony Tenser told CinemaTV Today, ending weeks of speculation regarding his future in a company that no longer made films. 'As this change takes place,' Tenser's press release continued, 'we will need a technical man to cope with the Multivista side and on the distribution side we have two very capable men in Eric Godwin and Mike Ewin.' The last sentence of the carefully worded press release well and truly showed the direction in which LMG were heading: 'We feel this reorganisation will be much more profitable to the company which has become more orientated towards cinema property.'

As is common practice in the world of 'boardroom reshuffles', Tenser indicated that he would continue to act as a 'consultant' to the Group but that his involvement would be wound down over a period of time. The consultancy announcement hid the fact that Tenser had already cleared his desk at Hammer House and

had, to all intents and purposes, removed himself from the running of the company he founded. Tenser bore no grudges to his successors at LMG: 'It was one of those things; the company was going in one direction and I was going in another. I was still a major shareholder, which was an important factor for a company like ours, so I agreed I would sell my shares off gradually over a period of time so as not to unsettle the market value.'[8] Tenser did have quite a few remaining attachments to LMG - the three completed films still awaiting release (*Miss Julie*, *The Creeping Flesh* and *Neither the Sea Nor the Sand*) and one that was still being edited (*Not Now Darling*). All four were, officially, 'Tony Tenser films.'

Miss Julie was the first of this quartet to be granted a release through LMG in selected Classic cinemas, during November 1972.

MISS JULIE

'Julie - the half-woman, the man hunter'
- UK Press Release -

Synopsis

Midsummer night, 1894. The daughter of the manor, Miss Julie, visits a party below stairs, in the servants' quarters. Julie is attracted to Jean, a footman, who unlike the others is worldly and intelligent, has travelled, speaks well, and doesn't kowtow to the aristocracy. Jean is engaged to Christine, a simple but honest and trusting servant at the house, but while she sleeps Jean and Julie sit in the kitchen, talking. They realise that their social positions make any relationship impossible. At first their conversation is antagonistic. As the evening progressed Jean and Julie discover they have much in common. They bare their souls to each other and by dawn they both want to break free of the class chains that bind them. The next day, as Christine wakes and goes off to church, Jean and Julie have their own decisions to make.

Critique

'...beautifully made version of August Strindberg's sensual tale. It is compelling entertainment.'
- The Daily Mirror, 10/11/72

'It is really no more than a photographed stage play.'
- The Daily Mail, 07/11/72

'...everything is okay except that there is no excitement, no sense of lust or degradation, and somehow Strindberg seems to have bolted.'
- Dilys Powell, The Sunday Times, 12/11/72

The
ROYAL SHAKESPEARE COMPANY
production of
Miss Julie
by AUGUST STRINDBERG
AA

Starring
HELEN MIRREN
DONAL McCANN
HEATHER CANNING

Directed by ROBIN PHILLIPS and JOHN GLENISTER
Produced by PETER J. THOMPSON and MARTIN C. SCHUTE
Executive Producers TONY TENSER and MARVIN LIEBMAN
Production Designed by DAPHNE DARE
Music Composed and Conducted by GORDON KEMBER
TECHNICOLOR
A Tigon British-Sedgemoor Production
A Tigon Release

LMG

FROM NOVEMBER 12th at
CLASSIC CURZON CHELSEA Tel: 01-352 7488
and
CLASSIC MAIDA VALE Tel: 01-624 6566

'...basically an impressive piece of work.'
- Barry Norman, The Times, 11/11/72

'The films of stage productions are seldom successful but this is a beautiful exception... the leading roles are superbly played by Helen Mirren, Donal McCann and Heather Canning.'
- The Daily Express, 10/11/72

In common with all of Tenser's movies, *Miss Julie* received decidedly mixed notices but for once the positive outweighed the negative. Certainly the mainstream critics appeared to have been impressed by what they perceived to be a RSC film rather than a Tigon production, but it was still to the company's considerable credit that they were prepared to sink money into such an apparently uncommercial venture.

Helen Mirren was naturally singled out for her powerful reading of the title role, effectively capturing the pent-up frustration and confusion of her character; *Miss Julie* would be worth a visit for Mirren alone. The work of the supporting players should not be undervalued - Donal McCann is quietly effective for example - but only Mirren displays genuine screen presence, and she alone eventually succeeded in making the transition from stage to screen stardom.

Predictably, there is rather too much dialogue for a cinema film - no-one could accuse Tigon this time of cutting the talking in favour of action - and this is a significant flaw. The second unit work, designed to open the film out, merely distracts rather than enhances. Only the party scene, where 'those below stairs' decide to let their hair down, offers any real life. The remainder looks exactly what it is - filmed theatre. As an adaptation of Strindberg it is as good as any in the English language, but as filmed entertainment it leaves a lot to be desired.

Miss Julie was a bold experiment at a time when British cinema was all but stagnant but it was never intended as a mass market film and that is arguably what Tigon should have been looking for. The new distribution team, now under the direction of Kamal Pasha, seemed to find *Miss Julie* something of an inconvenience and its bookings, even on the company's own circuits, were limited.

*   *   *   *   *

If *Miss Julie* clearly wasn't the mainstream vehicle to launch LMG into the market place it's just as hard to understand what made Marsh and Pasha think that *Neither the Sea Nor the Sand* fitted the bill. Certainly the Group had a lot more riding on the success of the Honeycombe film, as although production may have been brought to a halt, LMG's overall strategy was still dependent on a successful film distribution wing.

The trade papers hadn't wholeheartedly embraced the idea that LMG was withdrawing from film production; Tenser's continued enthusiasm during the early part of 1972 had been seen as something of a lifeline to the ailing industry. Moreover Tenser was thought of as one of them - an interesting position for the man who had been branded by the 'old school' as an outsider. Now it was Marsh who was on the defensive, as he fought against the perception that he was just a 'property man.' Marsh undoubtedly saw *Neither the Sea Nor the Sand* as an opportunity to redress the balance a little and get some positive publicity for the Group.

The film was billed prominently in the trades as the 'first LMG premiere' - neither *For the Love of Ada* or *Miss Julie* had been given a formal launch - and Kamal Pasha, a shrewd exhibitor in his own right, wanted to ensure that *Neither the Sea Nor the Sand* received a five star welcome. Pasha stage-managed an opening night gala on the 7th of December 1972, at the prestigious Carlton cinema in Haymarket, the very heart of London's West End. The film's leading players, Hampshire, Finlay and Petrovitch, all turned out, as did Gordon Honeycombe. Among the celebrities were the likes of Edward Woodward and *Avengers* girl Linda Thorson as well as the ubiquitous Graham Stark. The event harked back to the good old days of the Compton premieres, but there was too much missing

above:
Helen Mirren, the Royal Shakespeare Company's brightest star. In contrast to her image today, in 1972 the tabloids were focusing on her '36C-25-36' figure, and her propensity to show it off 'for art'.

below:
Avengers star Linda Thorson with Tigon's Chairman Laurie Marsh, who guided the company away from film production and made it into an entertainment/property conglomerate.

Susan Hampshire • **Frank Finlay** • *Neither the Sea Nor the Sand* (AA)

and introducing **Michael Petrovitch**

Eastman Colour   A Tigon Release

This copyright material is leased and not sold and upon completion of the exhibition for which it has been leased should be returned to Bovince Ltd., Ad-Sales Division, 276 Chase Road, Southgate, London N.14

above:
Anna (Susan Hampshire) loses Hugh (Michael Petrovitch) for the first time.

for it to directly compare; there were no 'A' list stars, no scantily clad showgirls or extravagant stunts to bring the London traffic to a halt, and there was no Tony Tenser. Nevertheless, the fact that LMG was taking all this trouble to launch a British-made film was a news story in itself, and the event was widely covered in the press.

NEITHER THE SEA NOR THE SAND

'...There Is Now Only Sea'
- UK Press Book -

Synopsis

During a winter break in Jersey, Anna Robinson meets a strange young man, Hugh Dabernon, who has an uncanny affinity with the sea and the rugged but beautiful coastline. The couple fall deeply in love but Hugh's elder brother George strongly resents Anna's presence on the island and her intrusion into their insular life. The couple escape from the claustrophobic atmosphere by taking a break in the North of Scotland where they can be alone, but tragedy strikes when Hugh collapses and dies. Anna refuses to accept Hugh's death and the strength of their love ensures that he, at least in body, lives on. When they return to Jersey however they discover the awful price that they must pay to be together.

Critique

'...can't seem to make up its mind whether it's a romance or out and out horror fodder.'
- The Guardian, 07/12/72

'...nor can I attempt to describe the ponderous inanity of this romantic, ghoulish nonsense.'
- The Daily Telegraph, 08/12/72

'More time on the script, more money on the filming might have solved the problem though I feel we needed a less creepy performance from Frank Finlay ...who tilts the romantic balance in favour of the gothic.'
- The Evening Standard, 07/12/72

'The dialogue is terrible, but I can't say I was bored.'
- The Observer, 10/12/72

'Must qualify as one of the worst films of the decade...'
- Time Out, 07/12/72

Despite the fixed smile of the film's star, Susan Hampshire, pictured on the arm of the beaming Laurie Marsh, and the back-slapping launch night party, Pasha's publicity team must have suspected that the glamour wasn't about to rub off on their film.

Burnley had set out to ensure that *Neither the Sea Nor the Sand* didn't pick up the tag of 'another Tigon horror movie', and

Tenser had supported this view, insisting soon after filming started that, 'It's a love story with a moral at the end but essentially it was about love being found and then lost.' By sticking closely to the tone of the novel and accepting Honeycombe's screenplay, Burnley delivered a Gothic romance story in the grandest tradition, replete with obligatory supernatural elements. The LMG publicity team picked up on this theme, and instead of falling back on the trademark hyperbole that normally accompanied Tony Tenser films, the decision was made to promote *Neither the Sea Nor the Sand* with lush artwork, which had more in common with *Doctor Zhivago (1965)* than traditional Tenser fare.

The result is rather a bore, reminiscent of one of the more impenetrable foreign films: full of ponderous silences and meaningful stares, bleak seascapes and dreary photography. This impression is reinforced by the central performances of both Susan Hampshire and Michael Petrovitch; even in the early scenes there is no apparent chemistry, either between the actors themselves or the characters they portray. Admittedly they are not helped by some leaden dialogue but Petrovitch in particular fails to generate any audience empathy, indeed given the outcome of the movie, one finds oneself asking with hindsight whether Petrovitch wasn't actually a zombie all along! The lumbering narrative is broken only by bouts of tastefully shot but passionless lovemaking (Hampshire had joined something of a recent trend at Tigon by refusing to appear nude).

The critics couldn't decide whether they had watched a horror story or a romance and the public were just as confused. On its first week on release *Neither the Sea Nor the Sand* took a paltry £1,969 in a theatre with 1,157 seats - by way of comparison the lacklustre thriller *Fear Is the Key*, which opened the same week, took £4,818 at the ABC Leicester Square, a theatre with only 581 seats.

above:
Neither the Sand Nor the Sea, which Time Out claimed was 'one of the worst films of the decade,' was hampered by a wooden performance from Petrovitch, who was even less animated alive than dead!

above:
Dead men don't ride bikes! Anna and Hugh in happier times.

left:
Anna starts to realise that there is a downside to living with a re-animated corpse - not least of which was his apparent refusal to change his clothes...

Susan Hampshire • Frank Finlay • *Neither the Sea Nor the Sand* (AA)
and introducing **Michael Petrovitch** Eastman Colour A Tigon Release
This copyright material is leased and not sold and upon completion of the exhibition for which it has been leased should be returned to Bovince Ltd., Ad-Sales Division, 276 Chase Road, Southgate, London N.14

above:
Susan Hamphire and
Michael Petrovitch in
one of the images that
confused the press; is
**Neither the Sea Nor
the Sand** a love story or
a horror film?

below:
Kamal Pasha, a
colleague and close
friend of Tenser's at
Tigon and later his
partner in Carnaby
Films.

*   *   *   *   *

Tony Tenser hadn't attended the premiere; he was busy building his latest business venture. He was financially secure and had absolutely no need to work at all, let alone in the high-stress environment of the British entertainment sector, but echoing the sentiment of 1966, he 'felt drawn back into the industry'. After exploring a number of options Tenser opted to push back the clock more than a decade by opening a new cinema club.

Private clubs were the one boom area remaining in the British film industry at the time. The format had progressed very little since the Compton Cinema Club days - they remained slightly tawdry 'mini-cinemas' devoted almost entirely to 'adult' films that were considered too strong for major circuit release. John Trevelyan's revision to the classification system at the start of the 1970s had opened the door to a large number of movies that previously would have been banned. Filmmakers seized the opportunity to compete with television by offering cinema-goers sights they could not yet hope to see on the small screen. The clubs in turn moved from softcore to much more explicit, usually imported, films.

By 1973 the momentum of the so-called permissive age seemed unstoppable. As the Seventies progressed films pushed the boundaries ever further until, inevitably, the middle classes reacted. Organised groups such as Mary Whitehouse's Festival of Light targeted both the high street cinemas and the private clubs in an effort to hold back the tide. Whitehouse's cronies believed that publicity was their main weapon, and when demonstrations and protests failed the middle class reactionaries increasingly resorted to high profile court actions in their attempts to curb the activities of the private clubs. Prosecutions were pursued under the

terms of the Obscene Publications Act, and charges of keeping a disorderly house were even cited in their increasingly exasperated attempts to close the clubs down. Needless to say, the publicity had the opposite effect and the early Seventies proved to be very much the golden age of the cinema club.

The Windmill, which had been transformed into a porno cinema, had briefly returned to Tigon's ownership as part of the Classic chain purchase. It was a prime piece of real estate but did not comfortably fit into the corporate image that the company wanted to project, so it was sold without ceremony to Paul Raymond.[9]

Raymond was an engaging opportunist - a daring publisher or a porn merchant, depending on which side of the fence you sat. The Raymond empire had been built on the success of a string of popular softcore porn magazines such as Club International, which had flourished during the permissive age and the attendant relaxation of publishing restrictions and censorship. Unlike many of his contemporaries, Raymond made a point of reinvesting his income into the industry and had made a considerable impact with his growing empire of adult shops and entertainment venues. The Windmill Theatre represented a return to an idea first mooted over a decade earlier. Tenser takes up the story: 'Paul Raymond bought it from us, I think he saw it as the flagship in his empire. I had known Paul Raymond for a while, he was based just around the corner in Soho and he said he was thinking of a cinema club as part of the set-up at the Windmill, in addition to the main cinema. So I told him I would come in as a partner and run it for him and he agreed to provide the finance to get it going. I brought in my old friend from Tigon, Kamal Pasha, and we ran this club together for a while and it was very successful. We then offered it to him as a going concern and Raymond bought us out. That was my second brush with a cinema club; it worked out very well for me.'

*   *   *   *   *

While Tenser was readying the Windmill cinema club to open its doors, the last movie to carry both the Tigon British production credit and the Tigon Pictures distributor brand was embarking on its initial circuit release. The market for horror films had been over-mined by so many for so long that a film like *The Creeping Flesh* could not hope for any sort of fanfare upon release. Even with the sensational Lee and Cushing partnership involved it wasn't considered any more than a routine programmer. *The Creeping Flesh* took the top half of a double-bill with Mario Bava's thriller *Blood Brides (1970)* - better known these days as *Hatchet for the Honeymoon* - and was unleashed in Britain during February 1973.

THE CREEPING FLESH

'More Frightening than Frankenstein!
More Dreaded than Dracula!'
- US Press Book -

Synopsis

Professor Emmanuel Hildern returns from an expedition to New Guinea with a humanoid skclcton which he discovers is the legendary 'Shish Kang' - The Evil One. Hildern is preoccupied by the belief that his work on the skeleton will win him the prestigious Richter prize, and neglects the needs of his daughter Penelope. Hildern's wife died in the lunatic asylum run by his half-brother, James, and when he detects the same symptoms of madness in Penelope he injects her with a serum derived from the Shish Kang remains. Far from curing her, the serum drives Penelope insane and she escapes in to the night. James, also a candidate for the Richter Prize, realises he has the opportunity to steal Emmanuel's research. Unfortunately his interfering results in the rejuvenation of the long dead skeleton and 'The Evil One' is free to walk the Earth once more.

Critique

'...you have too many threads in a very thick plot, too thick I think, though it is stylishly handled by Freddie Francis.'
- The Daily Telegraph, 02/03/73

'I thought Mr Cushing gave one of his best performances, and the screenplay... was on a higher level of invention than usual.'
- The Sunday Times, 04/03/73

'...both actors are so good it's a wicked waste. But the treatment is lumbering and uncertain, surprisingly from director Freddie Francis who usually knows his way around this type of shocker.'
- The Sunday Telegraph, 04/03/73

'...is directed with an unexpected sensitivity and sophistication. Peter Cushing's perform-ance as the mad Doctor has a sufficiently Boris Karloff quality of wisely controlled overacting to make the whole thing locate itself on the far side of self parody.'
- Village Voice, 08/03/73

above:
Peter Cushing confronts Shish Kang at the chilling climax of **The Creeping Flesh**. Cushing's instructions to himself were reportedly, 'Don't gabble. Don't overact. Don't be a conventional absent-minded professor.'

below:
Lorna Heilbron's scarlet woman, Penelope Hildern, starts to feel the effects of her father's serum. Her descent into madness was a highlight of the film.

right:
Another Victorian doxy; unusually for a horror film in 1972 (and a Tigon at that) **The Creeping Flesh** contained no nudity, even during the rape scene. The publicity department tried to make up for it with this type of publicity still.

right:
Another Victorian doxy; unusually for a horror film in 1972 (and a Tigon at that) **The Creeping Flesh** contained no nudity, even during the rape scene. The publicity department tried to make up for it with this type of publicity still.

The script by Peter Spenceley and Jonathan Rumbold is arguably one of the most literate and complex to be seen in an English horror movie but simply adding layer upon layer doesn't make the film any better to watch. The sexual undertones that run through the movie are merely hinted at and the intermingled themes of guilt, suppression and the nature of evil are all boldly introduced but never fully explored.

Francis's handling of the cast produced mixed results, as he appears to have given everyone more or less a free rein. Peter Cushing misjudged his performance by choosing to recreate the fussy and forgetful scientist from his earlier *Dr. Who* movies, becoming increasingly sniffling and piteous as the results of his own blundering bear dreadful fruit. Cushing's overacting totters close to the edge of hysteria and it is difficult not to find him irritating, which does nothing to bolster one's sympathy with his character. In contrast Christopher Lee is at the very peak of his physical powers here, and despite being given a far less well-defined role, he does far better with it. Whilst most of his early scenes serve no dramatic purpose - they are there only to establish how indifferent to human suffering he is - Lee creates a character of total and believable evil.[10] Lorna Heilbron's inexperience

below:
British front of house still showing the now insane Penelope.

That comfortable sense of familiarity that Redbourn had gone out of his way to recreate was to be *The Creeping Flesh*'s downfall; there just wasn't anything new in there. Francis was simply rehashing old tricks. It was as if *The Devils (1971)*, *A Clockwork Orange (1971)* and *Straw Dogs (1971)* had never happened.

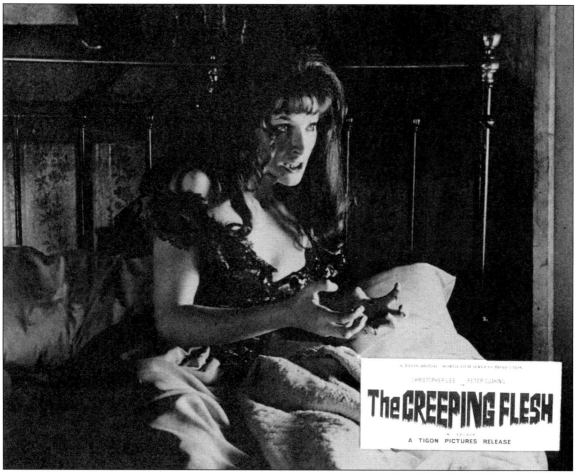

A TIGON BRITISH · WORLD FILM SERVICES PRODUCTION

CHRISTOPHER LEE · PETER CUSHING

The CREEPING FLESH

A TIGON PICTURES RELEASE

left:
Lorna Heilbron is dragged away to the asylum in a Victorian England recreated by Tigon in the image of Hammer and Amicus.

shows in the earlier scenes, where she depicts pent-up sexual frustration by recourse to girly pouting, but as her character sinks in to madness Heilbron demonstrates considerable presence.

Francis's great strength as a director is undoubtedly his visual sense, and he was on particular good form here - *The Creeping Flesh* has a stylish and sophisticated look. Paul Ferris's excellent score and Norman Warwick's photography contribute immensely to the overall air of quality but the LMG publicity machine of course demanded only four elements, and Redbourn was contractually obliged to deliver all of them: Cushing, Lee, a monster, and an 'X' certificate.

The monster in question, the immortal Shish Kang - The Evil One - doesn't actually get revived until the movie's last reel, and even then it doesn't appear to be much of a threat to anyone except of course Cushing's gibbering Hildern. The tagline for the UK release demonstrates the underselling and indifference that plagued the LMG films after Tenser left: 'Spine Chilling... Blood Curdling,' screamed the poster. It's hard to imagine that Tenser would have let his publicity managers display such a lack of imagination. *The Creeping Flesh* was released to a lukewarm reception in its home country and total disinterest elsewhere. The American release, a month earlier through Columbia, was notable for the complete indifference of the cinema-going public, prompting World Film Services to close the film quickly in order to allow a timely sale to US television.[11]

If *The Creeping Flesh* and *Neither the Sea Nor the Sand* had been disappointments to LMG distributors it didn't show. In May 1973 Laurie Marsh and entourage descended on the South of France for the Cannes Film Festival, determined to ensure that the Group was represented as a burgeoning distributor as well as a significant exhibitor. The catalogue of films however undermined the image LMG wanted to portray; as well as *Not Now Darling* and *For the Love of Ada*, both still without buyers, the Group also owned the rights to British exploitation films such as *The Sex Thief (1973)* and *The Flesh and Blood Show (1972)*, as well as imported softcore like *Naked Are the Cheaters (1970)* and *Frustrated Women (1971)*. Cannes also marked the first public airing for *Not Now Darling*.

below:
Barbara Windsor, who had expressed concerns about the degree of nudity in the film, seems happy enough to meet and greet Derren Nesbitt and Leslie Phillips sans clothes in **Not Now Darling**.

*   *   *   *   *

above:
British postcard humour at its most... British. Ray Cooney and Benny Hill girl Trudi Van Doorn (aka Geraldine Gardner) in **Not Now Darling**.

below:
Julie Ege in **Not Now Darling**'s requisite bath scene.

NOT NOW DARLING

'I Can Tell that Your Pants Have More than Ants...'
- UK Soundtrack -

Synopsis

Gilbert Bodley, the owner of an exclusive furriers, intends to give his prospective mistress, Janie, a gift of an expensive mink - without upsetting her husband, Harry. Gilbert intends to 'sell' the coat to Janie for a pittance and instructs his partner, Arnold, to arrange the sale. Things go wrong when Harry pretends he doesn't want the coat, and leaves. In reality he wants the coat for his mistress, Sue. Janie refuses to leave without it and strips naked in protest, throwing her clothes into the street below. Harry then returns with Sue to buy the coat and Arnold has to hide the naked Janie in the storeroom, while attending to the other customers, keeping the respective partners apart whilst coping with the arrival of Gilbert's wife.

Critique

'Neatly constructed farce... escapist fun with nudes and lots of naughty jokes.'
- CinemaTV Today, 25/08/73

'What an appalling waste of a remarkable cast. Leslie Phillips holds this threadbare piece together... rather tatty.'
- Radio Times, 30/08/73

'Silly cheapie with delusions of grandeur... a few witty moments but not enough to sustain a feature.'
- Motion Picture Guide, Review of 1975

'It's the kind of farce you don't dig too deeply into - just sit back and, if you are in the mood, roar your socks off at.'
- Cinema X, Vol.5 #7, 1973

'Even such experienced comic actors as Leslie Phillips and Joan Sims are unable, in the circumstances, to inject any pace into the proceedings.'
- Monthly Film Bulletin, April 1973

From the moment Trudi Van Doorn jiggles along a London street to tune of inane ditties by Cyril Ornadel and Norman Newell you know exactly what you have let yourself in for. Those opening shots, with their stock footage of marching guardsmen, are the closest the film comes to opening out, and like its predecessor *Miss Julie*, *Not Now Darling* remains firmly rooted in its theatrical origins.

Ray Cooney certainly tries his level best to inject pace and as a performer he is never still for a moment, mugging furiously and throwing his ungainly body around the set. As a director he displays the same energy and lack of discipline, packing in as many unnecessary close-ups and zooms as he can, to dizzying effect. As a ninety-seven minute advertisement for a production technique *Not Now Darling* may well be considered a success, as it goes flat out to demonstrate the full potential and versatility of the Multivista system. *Not Now Darling* in fact looks a lot more like a promotional film rather than a movie - all that is missing is a brief description of the product at the end and a list of recommended suppliers.

As a film, *Not Now Darling* is a misfire. The script is hackneyed in the extreme; the hurried exits, misunderstandings, mistaken identities, childish smut and seaside postcard humour have all been played out on the screen countless times before. Where *Not Now Darling* should have scored - through the strength of its cast - it fails miserably. Barbara Windsor and Joan Sims simply recreate their time-worn *Carry On* characterisations without enthusiasm, while Derren Nesbitt and Julie Ege both struggle to embellish their characters with any polish or humour. Ray Cooney is quite awful in the film's central role and it is left to Leslie Phillips, playing a part he could sleep walk through, to introduce something approaching wit to the proceedings.

Not Now Darling was met with resounding indifference at Cannes, and though it did manage to secure a buyer in the US, it never played more than a handful of dates.[12] In the UK, LMG were careful to place advertisements in the industry trade papers that focused on the viability of the Multivista system, rather than the merits of the film itself.[13] As a production company, Tigon/LMG had effectively ceased to exist with the abandonment of 'Cold War in a Country Garden' the previous summer. The fragmented and unsuccessful distribution of *Not Now Darling* meant it was the last LMG film that had Tenser's name attached to it.

LMG wasn't completely finished with film production; determined to capitalise on the early promise of the Multivista system, the company had already committed to a film version of the television series *Father Dear Father* - a big screen outing for the cast of the successful television sitcom, top-lined by Patrick Cargill. The film was put together through the subsidiary company LMG Film Services, which incidentally still featured John Trevelyan on its board and was marginally more successful than its LMG predecessor. With the decline of the Group's investment in films, Kamal Pasha, another link to the Tenser years, decided to leave. By then Marsh had decided to consolidate the company as a exhibitor and move its base away from the film industry per se.[14] In June 1973 LMG formally requested the Stock Exchange redefine the company's listing from the entertainment sector to property.[15]

*   *   *   *   *

Wardour Street was no longer the centre of a booming film and entertainment industry - the Sixties heyday was long gone. American companies still maintained representative offices, but these were sales outlets for handling their own products, not bases for meeting prospective filmmakers seeking finance. Likewise, the British companies had all but closed their doors; Rank and EMI would stagger on for a while yet but they were hardly in the market for new ideas, at least not in Britain. Lord Delfont's EMI tried to compete with Hollywood - without notable success - with a series of films shot overseas and Lew Grade, the last of the old style film moguls, was driven to the verge of bankruptcy by a series of well-publicised movie disasters. The old-style film industry collapsed into a cottage industry. Even Tigon's venerable competitors, Hammer and Amicus, eventually closed their doors to be replaced by a number of independent film producers scrambling for finance as best they could and setting up film production deals on a one-off basis.

Establishing the Windmill cinema club allowed Tenser to tread water for a while after leaving Tigon. After years managing his own production company it hardly represented a serious challenge. It was inevitable that he would be drawn back into film production sooner or later, saying simply that he 'missed the people and the fun.' Tenser was shrewd enough to realise that there was no appetite to make films the way he had done with Compton and Tigon, complete with the structure and associated overheads of a full-scale production/distribution company. Instead, Tenser fell back on his old tactics, and took a long hard look at the industry as it stood, what mistakes were being made and what opportunities existed. In May 1974 Tenser sat down with Kamal Pasha to discuss what he felt was a sure-fire gap in the market. At the end of that meeting the two friends formed Carnaby Films. They would set up in business as 'film brokers' who would buy, sell and package films while leaving the distribution to others.[16] A few days later Tenser was telling the press that the new company would be producing up to three

above:
Kim Butcher, right, as Debbie in **Frightmare**, the last film to carry Tony Tenser's credit.

below:
Keeping it in the family. After emerging from a mental institution for 'sickening crimes' Edmund Yates (Rupert Davies) relies on his daughter Jackie (Deborah Fairfax) to keep the family's dark secret in **Frightmare**.

above:
Care in the community... Edmund (Rupert Davies) and Jackie (Deborah Fairfax) conspire to keep Dorothy fed in **Frightmare**.

films a year - modest by the standards of Tigon or Compton but nonetheless ambitious for a new start-up in 1974.

The first client Carnaby Films dealt with was such an obvious name that it is something of a surprise that he and Tenser did not meet until 1974. Pete Walker was a 36 year old director-writer-producer whose films ran the full exploitation gamut from 8mm 'girlie' shorts in the early Sixties, via his feature debut *I Like Birds (1967)*, to thriller movies like *Die Screaming Marianne (1971)*.[17] Astute and independently wealthy, Walker financed his own films, retaining full creative control and therefore taking full blame or credit for his efforts. The earlier nudie exploitation work is pretty much interchangeable with that of any dozen similar filmmakers of the period but as he moved into the more sophisticated forms of thrillers and, eventually, out and out horrors, Walker developed a mature and uniquely unsettling eye for detail. 'I had known of Pete Walker of course, we had released one of his films (*The Flesh and Blood Show (1972)*),' Tenser recalls. 'but I don't think we had ever met. Somebody introduced us and he brought a script called, 'Covered in Blood'. I liked it. It was a well written horror movie and I thought it would make money, so I agreed to come in as a partner.'

'Covered in Blood', which was changed during shooting to 'Nightmare Farm', was a script by David McGillivray, the noted journalist and film critic who had first collaborated with Walker on *House of Whipcord (1974)*. *Whipcord* was a British version of that old exploitation standby, women in prison, which mixed some of Walker's favourite anti-Establishment themes with whippings and assorted sado-masochistic behaviour. Walker was impressed enough with his work to ask McGillivray to pen a suitable follow-up. In his serialised autobiographical essay in the Shock Xpress books, McGillivray recalls a lunch with Walker during the making of

House of Whipcord, which yielded the following diary entry: 'The story concerns an apparently innocent and charming girl who is in fact killing men for her mad cannibal mother to eat. It's outrageous enough to be another winner.' For Tenser the cannibal element was going to be key to selling the picture: 'You needed a hook to sell any film; we had used Venereal Disease in *That Kind of Girl* and we needed something that would get the attention of the press. Cannibalism was one of the last great taboos.' Walker and Tenser would undoubtedly have been aware that the subject had featured, albeit tangentially, in the 1972 British horror movie *Death Line*. What the filmmakers didn't know at the time was that an American director, Tobe Hooper, was fashioning a tale of mutilation and cannibalism that would become *The Texas Chain Saw Massacre (1974)*.

'Nightmare Farm' came to Carnaby Films with its leading player already cast. The remarkable Sheila Keith was a mild-mannered Scot who actually seemed more like a rather stern landlady than a horror movie icon. She had already starred in *House of Whipcord* and would go on to become a regular feature of Walker's movies over the course of the next decade. Playing opposite Keith, as her long-suffering husband, was Tenser veteran Rupert Davies. The gentle Davies's career had been in nosedive for some years. *Witchfinder General* and *Curse of the Crimson Altar* had offered something of a respite but by 1974 he was happy to take any work he was offered. Another name from the past in need of work was Leo Genn, who had made his mark playing unflappable officer types in countless British war films. Genn had already starred in *Die Screaming Marianne* for Walker, and would get special billing here as a doctor. The remainder of the cast was filled out by fresh young actors new to film. Behind the cameras however, Walker preferred the company of regular collaborators. Stanley Myers, who had scored *House of Whipcord*, would stay with Walker throughout the Seventies, as would sound engineer Tony Anscombe. Cameraman Peter Jessop had photographed *Tiffany Jones (1973)* and *Whipcord* for Walker, and production manager Robert Fennell had served on *Four Dimensions of Greta (1972)* and *The Flesh and Blood Show (1972)*.

Shooting started almost as soon as the contracts with Tenser were signed. The shoot took place, mainly on location, over a 25 day schedule. For once, the film's executive producer did not visit the set; Tenser chose instead to allow Walker a completely free hand: 'He made the film his way, there was absolutely no need for me to get involved. I did see the rushes but Peter got no interference from me except perhaps I would say tone this down a bit or that may cause a problem with the censor. Really I put money into it and had a look at the produc-

MIRACLE FILMS *present*
RUPERT DAVIES
SHEILA KEITH *in* **FRIGHTMARE**
COLOUR Cert **X**

tion but it's all Peter Walker's film, all his films are. A very competent and talented man.' Tenser did make one suggestion though, and a telling one at that: 'I didn't really like either title they had so I thought I could come up with something better, I suggested *Frightmare* and Peter agreed.'

As with all Pete Walker films, *Frightmare* was turned around extremely fast; shot in the late spring of 1974, Walker had his final print edited, scored and ready for cinemas by the early autumn. The finished film was considerably more polished than might have been expected given the speed of production and the size of the budget. Both Tenser and Walker were convinced that, if handled correctly, the film would do well on the major circuits. Ironically enough, Miracle Films picked up the UK rights to *Frightmare*; the independent distributor where Tenser had started his career twenty years earlier had trundled along in the intervening years, all the while releasing more or less the same type of product. *Frightmare* presented a problem for Miracle - they didn't quite know what to do with it - but they shared the view of the producers that they had an extremely exploitable subject. *Frightmare* was duly booked in to open at the London Pavillion just before Christmas 1974.

FRIGHTMARE

*'Worse Than Your Most
Shocking Nightmare!'*
- UK Press Release -

Synopsis

Fifteen years after being jailed for committing 'sickening murders', Dorothy and Edmund are living a solitary and apparently respectable life on a remote farm. Their daughters, Jackie and Debbie, live together but quarrel constantly; Debbie does not know that Jackie has been keeping Dorothy supplied with gruesome gifts. Dorothy though is not content with the 'special deliveries' and has been luring victims to the farm under the pretence of reading their fortunes. The two sisters soon find themselves embroiled in the consequences of their mother's insatiable hunger.

Critique

'Unnerving performances especially from Rupert Davies and Sheila Keith. Frighteningly well made by Peter Walker. It is also a moral obscenity and I loathed it.'
- The Daily Mail, 08/12/74

above:
The late great Sheila Keith as Dorothy in one of British horror's most disturbing and enduring images.

above:
Veteran actor Rupert Davies on the set of **Frightmare**, his last film appearance and his third for Tenser. His career never fully recovered from type-casting as Inspector Maigret in 1960, to the extent that when he died in 1976 the tabloids all ran headlines along the lines of 'Maigret is dead'.

'...*a peculiarly repellent little shocker.*'
- The Sunday Times, 08/12/74

'...*a thoroughly nasty film which, despite the obvious modest scale of the budget, is neatly and effectively made, like a well crafted gibbet.*'
- The Sunday Telegraph, 08/12/74

'...*disgusting, repulsive, nauseating rubbish.*'
- The Sun, 07/12/74

'*It's the ludicrous tale of a fortune telling madwoman... it contrives to be both ridiculous and nasty.*'
- The Guardian, 05/12/74

'*It's gory, brutal and very nasty at times. The film's only merit is the effective portrayal of mad menace by Sheila Keith.*'
- The Daily Mirror, 06/12/74

'What are Stars Like These Doing in Trash Like This?' screamed a headline in The Sun, before lamenting the decline from former star status of Messrs Davies and Genn. The journalist responsible went on to admit he hadn't actually seen the film but that didn't stop him shredding it![18] Setting aside the unnecessary hysteria, the reaction of serious film critics was not dissimilar, and most ignored the fact that *Frightmare* was a genuinely disturbing and scary film.

The script is a little shaky and in general the film demands a healthy suspen-sion of disbelief on behalf of its viewers; the idea for example that cannibalism is heredi-tary is a ludicrous plot device that should never have been allowed off the drawing board. Nevertheless the film manages to sustain tension throughout, thanks largely to the intelligent and thoughtful playing of Rupert Davies and Sheila Keith. Keith in particular is quite chilling; she appears to be on the brink of madness from the word go, and delivers easily her most unsettling performance for Walker. The sight of the grey-haired granny advancing with a powerdrill held high is so evocative that it was used extensively for the posters. The younger members of the cast are adequate but more or less forgettable, with the exception of Paul Greenwood as the psychi-atrist trying in vain to make sense of it all - he is quite awful.[19]

Walker's direction is assured and confident. He handles the shocks well and, though the film is gruesome and unsettling, it's not the gore-fest that punters were led to expect. Whereas on his earlier films Walker's limited budget was altogether too obvious, on *Frightmare* it was not allowed to intrude too much. The final film may still be a little raw and uneven but it was infinitely more professional that the press were suggesting. In the book 'Making Mischief', Walker recorded his satisfaction with the finished product, over twenty years later: '*Frightmare* is the only film I would look back on and say, 'Well that's the one.' If somebody said; 'oh you used to be a film director once show us one of your films, that's the one I would show.'

Frightmare opened at the worst possible time of year for a horror movie, the pre-Christmas period - traditionally a circuit release at this time was the kiss of death for anything except big budget family movies. The press hated it of course, burying the film with a barrage of vitriol, dispelling any lingering hopes Tenser had that 'all publicity is good publicity.' The film's cause was not helped by a particularly vicious IRA Christmas bombing campaign, which kept a lot of day-trippers out of the West End. After its slow opening *Frightmare* never gathered momentum and by the end of its London run, it had taken about half as much as *House of Whipcord*, despite being a far better film. This pattern was then repeated throughout the country.[20]

*   *   *   *   *

Walker shrugged off the disappointment of *Frightmare* but it convinced Tenser more than ever that the writing was on the wall for his breed of filmmaker: 'There wasn't a market for this type of operation,' Tenser admits, 'I thought we could make it work but *Frightmare* finished that idea. The industry by then had changed a lot. The films had to compete with tapes and what have you, and it had all gone a little too far, become too extreme. Making films had become so expensive and every film had to include sex and horror scenes; scenes where they had real guts and goodness what. I wouldn't have that in the Sixties, I certainly didn't want to do it in the Seventies. I'm not into all that, I'd had enough.'

Carnaby Films was closed down, and Pasha and Tenser parted company. But Tenser found moving on from the industry altogether quite difficult, and there were still loose ends that he felt the need to glance at from time to time. Soon after leaving LMG, he and Christopher Neame had met for lunch and, deciding that they would like to work together again, they formed Team Films to develop projects. 'Nothing much happened with the idea,' Tenser says, 'Chris was busy on a number things and then I was involved with Paul Raymond so we never really had proper go at it. It was shame really. I would have liked to make another film with Chris.'

Three years later Neame again called and showed him a script, for a film called *Emily*. 'I wanted to produce films and there was nothing being made except softcore sex,' Neame shrugs, 'I thought as long as I have to make a sex film I will make a stylish sex film so I went to see Tony and asked if would like to join me.' Tenser contributed some ideas to the film, including the alternative title of *The Awakening of Emily* but in the end he declined to take a partnership role in the

movie. 'I was out of it by then and pursuing other avenues,' Tenser says, 'I liked the script and I gave him some thoughts on it, whether he used them I don't know. I knew that Chris would do very well with it but it wasn't for me, I wasn't going back into films.' Neame's film, helped enormously by the scandal surrounding Koo Stark's amorous liasons with Prince Andrew, became a remarkable box-office success. Although Tenser took no direct credit, it was the last association he had with the film business.

In the New Year of 1978, Tony Tenser sold his home in Kent and, together with his wife Diane, moved to a house close to the site of the old Palace Hotel in Southport. Tenser may have turned his back on films but he put his boundless energies into other areas, notably property development. For the next twenty years he was to enjoy considerable success in this far less stressful but no less challenging environment.

Completely removed from the world of films, Tenser was staggered to be invited by the Manchester Society of Fantastic Films to attend screenings of some of his old movies at their annual festival in 1993 and then again in 1994. Until then he was genuinely unaware of the high regard his work had acquired over the years. 'The Manchester Film Festival was a real eye opener for me,' Tenser recalls, 'I had never been asked for my autograph before and suddenly these fans, and most of them weren't even born when I was making movies, were all over me. They knew far more about the films than I did and they had stills and press books that I hadn't seen for thirty years. It was a wonderful experience to know that so many people had an interest in my films but to be honest I was more than a little surprised.'

In 1998, aged 78, Tony Tenser finally decided enough was enough and retired officially from all his business interests. He now devotes himself, as he says, to 'keeping a low profile, to my family and golf.'

above:
Deborah Fairfax as Jackie during a tranquil moment in **Frightmare**, which was described by The Sun as 'disgusting, repulsive, nauseating rubbish.'

below:
Sheila Keith in **Frightmare**, going where no-one had gone before and tackling what Tenser described as, 'the last great taboo' - cannibalism!

Footnotes

1. *Not Now Darling* pales into insignificance when compared with Cooney's other hit, 'Run for Your Wife,' which has played in theatres off and on for over thirty years. Amongst his many other credits, Cooney directed the Garrick's 1965 production of 'Thark', which was Peter Cushing's last West End play. His exposure to film is limited - his best work is probably *What a Carve Up (1962)*, a lame horror spoof starring Sid James and Kenneth Connor.

2. Born in Tottenham, North London on the 20th of April 1924, Phillips trained at the Italia Conti School and made his film debut in 1936. Despite possessing a rather narrow range he has managed to amass a filmography of over 100 titles. His speciality was the slightly saucy, slightly roguish, old school type with a slight military air - not a million miles from the archetypal Terry-Thomas roles in fact. By the late Fifties he was a huge radio star. He managed to successfully translate this success onto the cinema screen, starring in the *Doctor* series as well as numerous *Carry On*s and, notably, a run of movies with Stanley Baxter and James Robertson Justice. Stage successes in the same vein included 'Boeing, Boeing' and 'On Monday Next'. He played in the hugely successful stage version of 'Not Now Darling' in London for 19 months and he even tried his hand at film production when his own company made the James Bond style thriller *Maroc 7 (1966)*, directed by Gerry O'Hara. When the bottom fell out of the market for postcard humour movies he struggled for a while before emerging as a distinguished and capable character actor in international movies like *Out of Africa (1985)*, *Empire of the Sun (1987)*, and *Scandal (1989)*. By the late 1990s his old movies were enjoying a revival and he could be seen in Shakespeare plays on the West End. Most recently,

he was awarded an OBE in 1998, was given a role in *Lara Croft: Tomb Raider (2001)* and is the voice of the Sorting Hat in the *Harry Potter* films.

3. Julie Ege justified her salary for Tenser in one afternoon when she posed for the front cover of the adult film magazine Cinema X, on the set of *Not Now Darling*. The accompanying six page spread created the impression for readers of that particular magazine that the film was going to be somewhat racier than its eventual 'A' certificate proved it to be.

4. Born in the dressing room of the Finsbury Park Empire, where his father was appearing, RADA trained Nesbitt worked with Peter Hall at Oxford Playhouse, though he is better known as the Nazi muscle in *Where Eagles Dare (1968)*. A regular on TV's *Special Branch*, he branched out into direction with the softcore sex epic *The Amorous Milkman (1974)* for his own company First Film Productions without notable success. He eventually found himself involved in more softcore sleaze, notably *The Playbirds (1978)* with Mary Millington, before moving into full time film production as Chief Executive of Touchdown Productions.

5. The Multivista technique had being evolving steadily and at that time comprised of 35mm Arriflex cameras with 1000ft magazines, and attached Plumbicon cameras. The sound was controlled remotely with a set of sound balancers sitting at a mixing console placed on the studio floor; effectively the post production sound synching was done at the same time as filming. The cameraman used a viewfinder in each camera and fed his pictures directly into a production control area where the director and editor mixed the shots as they came in - exactly as in a television studio.

6. Born in Shoreditch in 1936, Barbara Windsor (Barbara Ann Deeks) is another one of those actresses who, like Diana Dors and Beryl Reid, seem to have been around for so long that everybody thinks of them like a favourite if slightly disreputable aunt. She trained as a dancer and singer but after some modest stage work her busty 4'11" frame and raucous but girlish laugh seemed ideal for lowbrow comedy, so she fell into the *Carry On* niche that was to sustain her film career for 20 years. By the time that series ran dry Windsor was established as a good fun girl who didn't take herself too seriously. She made a good living out of pantomimes and personal appearances while the tabloids doted on endless tales of toy boy affairs (with one she ran her own pub!) and her marriage to alleged bank robber Ronnie Knight. As far as cinema was concerned, she was never thought of as much of an actress, and certainly seemed ill at ease away from light comedy - see *A Study in Terror (1965)* and Ken Russell's *The Boy Friend (1971)*. On the small screen though she displayed considerable dramatic potential when she settled down in 1996 as the 'tough as nails' landlady with a heart of gold on *EastEnders*.

7. The four were *Frankenstein and the Monster from Hell*, *Adolf Hitler: My Part in His Downfall*, *The 14*, and *Bequest to the Nation*. Only *Adolf Hitler...* went on to turn a profit.

8. Coincidentally, Tenser's old sparring partner at AIP, Deke Heyward, was moving on at the same time. On the 19th of September 1972 he resigned as vice-president in charge of European

below:
Christopher Lee and friend, Shish Kang, aka The Evil One on the set of **The Creeping Flesh**. Lee was soon to become an international star by way of **The Three Musketeers**; this new status put his services beyond the budgetary reach of most British horror movies.

Productions for American International Productions (England) Ltd. Heyward had been at AIP for nine years, most of that time spent in the UK making a remarkable series of pictures, ranging from the Tigon films through to *The Abominable Dr. Phibes (1971)* and *The Vampire Lovers (1970)*. He died in Los Angeles in 2002.

9. Raymond continued to develop his empire throughout the Eighties and Nineties. He opened the hugely successful Paul Raymond's Revue Bar, originally as an old-fashioned strip show and then, as tastes changed, a pole-dancing club. He was one of Britain's first porn entreprenuers to explore the viability of videotapes, with the massively popular *Electric Blue* series, which essentially reproduced Club International on tape, with the same cars-and-girls philosophy.

10. Christopher Lee's status in the horror genre was still considered bankable and filmmakers were keen to add his name to their cast list purely for marquee value. During the filming of *The Creeping Flesh*, Lee was excused from duties for one day to allow him to take a fleeting cameo in an apparently insignificant low-budget movie, which went on to score a considerable success in the US under the title of *Raw Meat*. Under its UK title, *Death Line* enjoyed cult status and influenced a number of filmmakers including Pete Walker..

11. By ensuring that the *The Creeping Flesh's* budget was kept to a minimum, World Film Services finally turned a small profit on residual sales such as television and, eventually, video. Tigon, or rather LMG, had a fixed time limit built into their contract with Priggen, and would draw revenue only for the first decade following release. For their part World Film Services was sufficiently impressed with the finished product to suggest a follow-up project for Francis; the film that would eventually become *Tales That Witness Madness (1973)*.

12. Cooney wasn't finished with 'Not Now', determined to create a successful series, he re-wrote and retitled an existing stage farce into *Not Now Comrade*, which was made two years later. Featuring Leslie Phillips, again as a caddish womaniser, the film also starred Carol Hawkins, Tenser's starlet from *The Body Stealers* and *Monique*. A far better and more polished film than *Not Now Darling*, the timing of *Not Now Comrade* was hopelessly wrong. Faced with a public that now wanted *Confessions of...* or *Adventures of...* movies, Cooney's series died a quiet death.

13. LMG Film Services, as the distribution and development arm was by now known, had in fact developed a sister product to Multivista - the Gemini system, which retained the same multi-camera technique but utilised 16mm, rather than 35mm, cameras. Aimed specifically at the television market, the system incorporated all the standard features - vision and sound mixing, instant playback, etc. LMG Film Services was conceived as a complete end-to-end production service, effectively offering everything that Tigon could offer as a production partner on a consultancy basis; hiring of production personnel, pre-production and packaging, securing script approvals and shooting permits, film processing and post production, insurance, and even music. The only thing that LMG Film Services wasn't selling was the creative expertise and, of course, financial backing.

MIRACLE FILMS present RUPERT DAVIES SHEILA KEITH in FRIGHTMARE COLOUR Cert X

14. Marsh remained a prominent figure in the film industry for some time, although he was not always popular. As the operator of the Classic chain of cinemas, still the third largest in the UK at the time, LMG had considerable profile in the industry. Marsh viewed his primary assets very differently from those who had been part of the industry for some time though. By 1973, the property market in the UK was as depressed as the rest of the commercial sector and LMG sought to offload the Classics - rumours that the chain was up for sale to the Price Freezer Group were treated with general dismay in the trade papers. David Lewin, the veteran columnist for CinemaTV Today, headed his editorial with: 'What's good for Laurie Marsh is not necessarily good for either the British film industry or for Britain.' Marsh was moved to defend his corporate policies in writing, stating: '...the comment that Rank and EMI open cinemas and that I close them is totally unfounded. I have always looked upon the cinema business as being property based - I see no reason to change this view.' In any event, that deal ran out of steam and Marsh held onto the Classics while rumours of buy-outs and deals continued over the course of the next few years. The group was finally merged into Lew Grade's multimedia empire, Associated Communications Corporation, in 1979, with Marsh taking a seat on the Board of the enlarged company.

15. As a blue chip property company, LMG obviously could not be associated with adult movies so the Tigon marque was hauled out and used over the next decade for movies like *Come Play with Me (1977)*, directed by one Harrison Marks, and its equally successful follow up *The Playbirds (1978)*, both of which featured the country's most popular sex starlet ever, Mary Millington.

16. Indian born Pasha had been Tenser's partner in the Windmill club, and the two men had been friends for over six years. Pasha , a chartered accountant by trade, joined Tigon in 1969 to run the company's books, taking up a Board appointment the same year. In 1971 he was appointed Financial Director for the Group and, after Tenser's departure in 1972, he took the post of Managing Director of Film Distribution, which was then consolidated into LMG Film Services. Reflecting his own Jewish origins, Tenser put his tongue in his cheek when he called their relationship, 'Lokshen and Curry'.

above:
Tenser's last bow. In Addition to the finance his major contribution was the film's memorable title.

MIRACLE FILMS *present*
RUPERT DAVIES
SHEILA KEITH *in* **FRIGHTMARE** X
COLOUR   Cert **X**

above:
The mild mannered Sheila Keith, already a horror icon in her second film for Pete Walker. She would go on to make three more: **House of Mortal Sin** which, like **House of Whipcord** and **Frightmare**, was scripted by David McGillivray, plus **The Comeback**, written by long-time Walker collaborator Murray Simth, and **House of the Long Shadows**, written by Michael Armstrong. Sheila Keith died on the 14th of October 2004, at the age of 84.

17. Walker's biography reads like it might have been the plot of a movie. The son of music hall comic Syd Walker, Peter was placed in an actor's orphanage in 1945 when his father died. It was there, and while he was at school, that Walker developed a love of all things cinematic. After a spell as a stand-up comic and some bit-part acting he talked his way into a job with Brighton Studios, a poverty row film company hiring third assistant directors. Walker then worked as a writer, actor and director, both in the US and England, gaining experience in everything from Michael Winner films to 8mm nudies. From there it was an easy jump into full blown sleaze features, but even then Walker was one step ahead. He had a huge hit with *Cool It Carol (1970)* starring Robin Askwith, and invested the profits in *Die Screaming Marianne (1971)*, which starred a young starlet called Susan George. From there Walker made the move into horror films, enjoying mixed success with the likes of *House of Whipcord (1974)*, *Schizo (1976)*, and *House of the Long Shadows (1982)*. Though he was always under attack from mainstream critics, Walker continued to enjoy popular success; his uncompromising camerawork and willingness to tackle the most extreme subjects made him ideal for the growing video market. But the blood and sex tended to overshadow a sound intelligence at work in his films allied to a natural love of tweaking the Establishment's nose; Walker's propensity to tackle issues which annoyed him head-on managed to turn otherwise routine horror films into social satires. When he retired from filmmaking in the Eighties, Walker poured his

natural energies into film exhibition, buying and running a successful independent cinema circuit, which specialised in renovating and restoring classic old cinemas under the Picturedrome Theatres banner.

18. The article went on to say: 'Today I am sorry to tell the Ban the Censor brigade that they are wasting their time. The job has already been done for them. If the disgusting, repulsive, nauseating rubbish that is *Frightmare* can arrive with an 'X' certificate then the censor can sell his porno-meter and go and look for another job.' We are then told that although the writer had not seen the film, a 'colleague' who had was apparently: '...broad minded and broad shouldered but could not stomach this drivel.' - The Sun, 07/12/74

19. The extreme press reaction was provoked by the presence of the two faded former stars, and it's amusing to consider what the headlines would have said if the film had been released a few years later when two of the cast, unknown in 1974, were huge television stars - Paul Greenwood of the sitcom *Rosie*, and Andrew Sachs, who played Manuel in *Fawlty Towers*.

20. *Frightmare* has enjoyed a prolonged shelf-life on video and DVD, partly due to the very same headlines that killed the cinema release. In the UK it is available under its original title, whilst in the US it has enjoyed a number of releases under a variety of titles including *Frightmare II* and *Once Upon a Frightmare*.

Films Produced by Tony Tenser

- (Appendix compiled by Francis Brewster and John Hamilton)

Unless otherwise indicated the distributor and running times refer only to the initial UK release.
For ease of reference, Tony Tenser's name is highlighted in bold wherever he granted himself an official credit.

1961   NAKED - AS NATURE INTENDED

Compass Films for Markten Film Productions Ltd.
Filmed at: On location in Cornwall and at the
Spielplatz Nudist Camp, St. Albans
BBFC: Certificate A, 24 November 1961
Distributed by: Compton-Cameo Films, November 1961
Running Time: 62 minutes
Colour

AKA: *As Nature Intended*, *Cornish Holiday* (working title)

Produced and Directed by: [George] Harrison Marks. Executive Producer: John Brason. Director of Photography: Roy Pointer. Camera Operator: Terry Maher. Editor: John Hann-Campbell, Commentary by: Gerald Holgate. Spoken by: Guy Kingsley Poynter. Stills: Douglas Webb [uncredited]. Sound: Derek Taylor [uncredited]. Make-Up: Gerry Fairbank [uncredited]. Hairdresser: Daphne Vollmer [uncredited]

cast: Pamela Green (Pamela), Bridget Leonard (Bridget), Angela Jones (Angela), Petrina Forsyth (Petrina), Jackie Salt (Jackie), Stuart Samuels

1963   THAT KIND OF GIRL

Michael Klinger and **Tony Tenser** present.
A Compton-Tekli Film
Filmed at: Shepperton Studios, 8/10/62, and on location in London
BBFC: Certificate X, 28 January 1963
Distributed by: Compton-Cameo Films, March 1963
Running Time: 78 minutes
B/W

AKA: *Teenage Tramp*

Directed by: Gerry O'Hara. Produced by: Robert Hartford-Davis. Assistant to Producer: Jack Taylor. Production Controller: Nat Miller. Production Manager: Ted Wallis. First Assistant Director: Tony Wallis. Screenplay: Jan Read. Director of Photography: Peter Newbrook. Camera Operator: Dennis Lewiston. Focus Puller: Hugh Davey. Stills Photography: Douglas Webb. Title animation: Doug Weymouth. Editor: Derek York. Assistant Editor: Raoul Sobel. Art Director: William Brodie. Wardrobe: Rene Coke. Make-up: Jill Carpenter. Music Scored and Directed by: Malcolm Mitchell. Sound Mixer: Peter Birch

cast: Margaret-Rose Keil (Eva), David Weston (Keith), Linda Marlowe (Janet), Peter Burton (Elliot Collier), Frank Jarvis (Max), Sylvia Kay (Mrs. Millar), David Davenport (Mr. Millar), Stephen Stocker (Nicolas), Charles Houston (Ted), Max Faulkner (Johnson), Patricia Mort (Barbara), Martin Wyldeck (Bates), John Wood (Doctor), Richard Bebb, Graeme Bruce, Alexandra Dane, Ann Gow, Betty Hardy, Peter Harrison, Audrey Muir, Larry Taylor, Julie Webb, Liz Zinn, Margot Travers

1963   THE YELLOW TEDDYBEARS

Michael Klinger and **Tony Tenser** present.
A Tekli Film Production
Filmed at: Shepperton Studios, 18/3/63
BBFC: Certificate X, 4 July 1963
Distributed by: Compton-Cameo Films, July 1963
(Premiere at Cinephone, Oxford Street 12/7/63)
Running Time: 85 minutes
B/W

AKA: *Gutter Girls*, *The Thrill Seekers*

Produced and Directed by: Robert Hartford-Davis. Associate Producer: Robert Sterne. Production Controller: Nat Miller. Original Screenplay by: Donald and Derek Ford. Director of Photography: Peter Newbrook. 1st Assistant Director: Ross McKenzie. Assistant Directors: Gordon Gilbert, Roger Simons. Stills: Laurie Turner. Make-up: Jimmy Evans. Hairdresser: Bobbie Smith. Wardrobe Mistress: Jackie Cummins. Grips: Bert Lott. Property Man: Sid Leggett. Camera Operator: Dennis Lewiston. Focus: Ronnie Fox-Rogers. Clappers/Loader: Colin Corby. Continuity: Phil Crocker. Sound Mixer: Bert Ross. Sound Recordist: Red Law. Boom Operator: Ken Reynolds. Editor: Teddy Darvas. Assistant Editors: John Poyner, David Woodward. Art Director: Bernard Sarron. Music Composed and Conducted by: Malcolm Mitchell. "A Lover and His Lass" sung by: The Wimbledon Girls Choir

cast: Jacqueline Ellis (Anne Mason), Annette Whiteley (Linda), Iain Gregory (Kinky), Douglas Sheldon (Mike Griffin), Georgina Patterson (Pat), Victor Brooks (George Donaghue), John Bonney (Paul), Anne Kettle (Sally), Jill Adams (June Wilson), Raymond Huntley (Harry Halburton), John Glyn Jones (Benny Wintle), Harriette Johns (Lady Gregg), Noel Dyson (Muriel Donaghue), Richard Bebb (Frank Lang), Ann Castle (Eileen Lang), Ruth Kettlewell (Mrs. Seymour), Hilary

Mason (Miss Fletch), Micheline Patton (Mrs. Broome), Norman Mitchell (Larry), Earle Green (Cliff), Shirley Cameron (Gloria), Lesley Dudley (Joan), Margaret Vieler (Marsha), Valli Newby (Kim), Lucette Miramar (Susie), Julie Martin (Liz), Bernadette Milnes (Sheila), Caron Gardner (Carol), Irene Richardson (Girl in Laboratory), Paula Gordon (Paula), Sheila Houston (A Teacher), The Embers (Musical Group)

1964 SATURDAY NIGHT OUT

Michael Klinger and **Tony Tenser** present.
A Compton Tekli Production
Filmed at: Shepperton Studios and on location in East London docks, 16/9-25/10/63
BBFC: Certificate X, 15 January 1964
Distributed by: Compton-Cameo Films, February 1964
Running Time: 96 minutes
B/W

Produced and Directed by: Robert Hartford-Davis. Associate Producer: Robert Sterne. Original Screenplay by: Donald and Derek Ford. Director of Photography: Peter Newbrook. First Assistant Director: Gordon Gilbert. Assistant Directors: Ray Frift, Barry Langley. Stills: Laurie Turner. Make-up: Jimmy Evans. Hairdresser: Joyce James. Wardrobe Master: Harry Haynes. Wardrobe Mistress: Tina Swanson. Grips: Tommy Miller. Property Master: Sid Leggett. Camera Operator: Dennis Lewiston. Focus: Ronnie Fox-Rogers. Clappers/Loader: Colin Corby. Continuity: June Faithful. Sound Mixer: Dickie Bird. Sound Supervisor: John Cox. Sound Recordist: Red Law. Boom Operator: Don Wortham. Editor: Alastair McIntyre. Dubbing Editors: John Poyner, Michael Hopkins. Assistant Editors: John Jeremy, David De Wilde. Titles designed by: Jim Baker, Robert Benson. Art Director: Peter Proud. Assistant Art Director: Ted Clements. Production Controller: Terry Glinwood. Music Composed and Conducted by: Robert Richards

cast: Heather Sears (Penny), John Bonney (Lee), Bernard Lee (George Hudson), Erika Remberg (Wanda), Colin Campbell (Jamey), Francesca Annis (Jean), Inigo Jackson (Harry), Vera Day (Arlene), Caroline Mortimer (Marlene), David Lodge (Arthur), Nigel Green (Paddy), Toni Gilpin (Margaret), Barbara Roscoe (Miss Bingo), Margaret Nolan (Julie), Martine Beswick (Barmaid), Patricia Hayes (Edie's Mother), Derek Bond (Paul),

Freddie Mills (Joe), The Searchers, David Burke (Manager), Shirley Cameron (Edie), Patsy Fagan (Barmaid), Gerry Gibson (Doorman), Barry Langford (Barman), Janet Milner (Waitress), Wendy Newton (Kathy), Jack Taylor (Landlord).

1964 LONDON IN THE RAW

A Searchlight Film
Filmed at: In and around London's West End
BBFC: Certificate X, 3 July 1964
Distributed by: Compton-Cameo Films, August 1964 (Premiere at The Jacey)
Running Time: 76 minutes
B/W
Written, Produced and Directed by: Arnold Louis Miller. Executive Producers: Michael Klinger and **Tony Tenser**. Director of Photography: Stanley A. Long. Editor: Stephen Cross. Research: Robert Gaddes. Narrator: David Gell

1964 THE BLACK TORMENT

Michael Klinger and **Tony Tenser** present.
A Compton-Tekli Production
Filmed at: Shepperton Studios and on location in Basingstoke and Northumberland, February 1964
BBFC: Certificate X, 11 June 1964
Distributed by: Compton-Cameo Films, October 1964 (Premiere at Rialto 15/10/64)
Running Time: 86 minutes
Colour

AKA: *The Estate of Insanity, Torment*

Produced and Directed by: Robert Hartford-Davis. Associate Producer: Robert Sterne. Original Screenplay by: Donald and Derek Ford. Director of Photography: Peter Newbrook. 1st Assistant Director: Ted Sturgis. Assistant Directors: Ray Frift, Roger Simons. Stills: Laurie Turner. Make-Up: George Partleton. Hairdresser: Joan White. Wardrobe Supervisor: Elsa Fennell. Grip: Ray Jones. Property Master: Sid Leggatt. Camera Operator: Dennis Lewiston. Focus: Ronnie Fox-Rogers. Clapper/Loader: Colin Corby. Continuity: Lee Turner. Sound Mixer: Bert Ross. Sound

MICHAEL KLINGER AND TONY TENSER present **The Black Torment** EASTMAN COLOUR
HEATHER SEARS JOHN TURNER ANN LYNN Co-Starring PETER ARNE NORMAN BIRD RAYMOND HUNTLEY ANNETTE WHITELEY
Produced and directed by ROBERT HARTFORD-DAVIS   A COMPTON Films Release

Supervisor: John Cox. Sound Recordist: John Aldred, Boom Operator: Peter Dukelow. Special Action and Sword Fight Arranged by: Peter Brace. Editor: Alastair McIntyre. Dubbing Editor: Peter Thornton. Assistant Editors: Karen Heward, Elizabeth Thoyts, Michael Hopkins. Art Director: Alan Harris. Assistant Art Director: John Siddall. Production Controller: Terry Glinwood. Costumes by: Bermans. Music Composed and Conducted by: Robert Richards

cast: Heather Sears (Lady Elizabeth), John Turner (Sir Richard Fordyke), Ann Lynn (Diane), Peter Arne (Seymour), Norman Bird (Harris), Raymond Huntley (Colonel Wentworth), Annette Whiteley (Mary), Francis de Wolff (Black John), Joseph Tomelty (Sir Giles), Patrick Troughton (Ostler), Roger Croucher (Apprentice), Charles Houston (Jenkins), Derek Newark (Coachman), Edina Ronay (Lucy Judd) [uncredited], Cathy McDonald (Kate) [uncredited]

Written and Directed by: Arnold Louis Miller. Produced by: Arnold Louis Miller and Stanley A. Long. Executive Producers: **Tony Tenser** and Michael Klinger. Narrator: David Gell. Editor: Stephen Cross. Music Composed and Arranged by: Basil Kirchin and Johnny Coleman. Orchestra Directed by: Basil Kirchin and Johnny Coleman. Assistant Cameramen: Don Lord, Keith Jones, Terry Winfield. Sound: Dudley Plummer, Edgar Vetter, Robert Allen, Derek Rolls. Electricians: Pax Electric. Production Secretaries: Sheila Miller, Patricia Preece. Research: Robert Gaddes, Phillip Steen. Director of Photography: Stanley A. Long

cast: MacDonald Hobley (Himself in T.V. Studio), Billy J. Kramer (Himself at Record Shop), Diana Noble (Herself at Churchills), Bobby Chandler (Himself at Churchills), Vicki Grey (Herself at Churchills), John Lee (Himself at Churchills), Ray Martine (Himself at Establishment Club)

1965   **PRIMITIVE LONDON**

Troubadour Films present. A Searchlight Film Production
Filmed at: On location in Soho and East End of London
BBFC: Certificate X, 18 March 1965
Distributed by: Compton-Cameo Films, May 1965
(Premiere at Windmill Theatre 25/3/65)
Running Time: 77 minutes
Colour

1965   **THE PLEASURE GIRLS**

Michael Klinger and **Tony Tenser** present.
A Compton Production. © Compton-Tekli Film Productions Ltd.
Filmed at: On location in West London and at Twickenham Studios
BBFC: Certificate X, 23 March 1965
Distributed by: Compton-Cameo Films, June 1965

(Premiere: Cinephone Cinema, Oxford Street, 27/5/65)
Running Time: 86 minutes
B/W

Written and Directed by: Gerry O'Hara. Producer: Harry Fine. Associate Producer: Robert Sterne. Production Controller: Terry Glinwood. Director of Photography: Michael Reed. Art Director: Peter James. Editor: Anthony Palk. Music composed and conducted by: Malcolm Lockyear. Theme Song 'The Pleasure Girls' composed by: Bob Barrett. Sung by: The Three Quarters. Assistant Director: Christopher Dryhurst. Camera Operator: Dennis Lewiston. Sound Mixer: John Mitchell. Continuity: Dee Vaughan. Casting: Irene Lamb. Stills: Laurie Turner. Sound Supervisor: Stephen Dalby. Sound Recordist: Gerry Humphreys. Make-Up: Ken MacKay. Hairdressers: Henry Montsash, Bobbie Smith. Props: Alf Pegley. Publicity: Dora Dobson. Wardrobe Mistress: Joyce Stoneman. Victor Josselyn 'Pleasure Girls' Clothes Designed by: Lee Landau

cast: Ian McShane (Keith Dexter), Francesca Annis (Sally), Klaus Kinski (Nikko Stalmar), Mark Eden (Prinny), Tony Tanner (Paddy), Suzanna Leigh (Dee), Rosemary Nicols (Marion), Anneke Wills (Angela), Colleen Fitzpatrick (Cobber), Julian Holloway, Hal Hamilton (Peter 'E'-Type), Jonathan Hansen (Ivor), Carol Cleveland (Ella), Tony Doonan (Reilly), Hugh Futcher (Pablo), David Graham (1st Gambler), David Cargill (2nd Gambler), Yvonne Antrobus (Hanger-on), Kate Binchy (Nurse), Peter Diamond (Rat-Face)

1965   **REPULSION**

Michael Klinger and **Tony Tenser** present.
A Compton Production. © Compton-Tekli Film Productions Ltd.
Filmed at: Twickenham Studios & on location in London
BBFC: Certificate X, 15 January 1965

Distributed by: Compton-Cameo Films, June 1965 (Premiere at Rialto 10/6/65)
Running Time: 105 minutes
B/W

Directed by: Roman Polanski. Produced by: Gene Gutowski. Associate Producers: Robert Sterne, Sam Waynberg. Original Screenplay by: Roman Polanski and Gerard Brach. Adaptation and Additional Dialogue by: David Stone. Music Composed and Conducted by: Chico Hamilton. Orchestrated by: Gabor Szabo. Director of Photography: Gilbert Taylor, Stanley A. Long [uncredited]. 1st Assistant Director: Ted Sturgis. Camera Operator: Alan Hall. Sound Mixer: Leslie Hammond. Continuity: Dee Vaughan. Stills: Laurie Turner. Sound Editor: Tom Priestley. Make-Up: Tom Smith. Hairdresser: Gladys Leakey. Sound Supervisor: Stephen Dalby. Sound Recordist: Gerry Humphreys. Assistant Editor: Karen Heward. Assistant Art Director: Frank Willson. Props: Alf Pegley. Art Director: Seamus Flannery. Editor: Alastair McIntyre. Production Controller: Terry Glinwood

cast: Catherine Deneuve (Carol), Ian Hendry (Michael), John Fraser (Colin), Patrick Wymark (Landlord), Yvonne Furneaux (Helen), Renee Houston (Miss Balch), Valerie Taylor (Madame Denise), James Villiers (John), Helen Fraser (Bridget), Hugh Futcher (Reggie), Monica Merlin (Mrs. Rendlesham), Imogen Graham (Manicurist), Mike Pratt (Workman), Roman Polanski (Spoons player) [uncredited], Wally Bosco (Old man) [uncredited], Hercules Bellville (Passerby on South Kensington Street) [uncredited]

1965   **A STUDY IN TERROR**

Michael Klinger and **Tony Tenser** present.
A Compton/Sir Nigel Films Production. © Compton-Tekli Film Productions Ltd. and Sir Nigel Films Ltd.
Filmed at: Shepperton Studios, May 1965 and on location at Osterley Park
BBFC: Certificate X, 25 October 1965
Distributed by: Compton-Cameo Films, November 1965 (Premiere at Leicester Square 4/11/65)
Running Time: 94 minutes
Colour

AKA: *Sherlock Holmes and the Vice Murders, Sherlock Holmes and the House of Ill Repute* [script titles]

Directed by: James Hill. Produced by: Henry E. Lester. Executive Producer: Herman Cohen. Associate Producer: Sam Waynberg. Production Supervisor: Robert Sterne. Film Editor: Henry Richardson. Production Designer: [Alex] Vetchinsky. Costumes by: Motley. Assistant Director: Barry Langley. Continuity: Gladys Goldsmith. Wardrobe: Laurel Staffel. Larry Stewart. Hairdresser: Gladys Leakey. Make-Up: Tom Smith. Casting: Maude Spector. Camera Operator: Norman Jones. Set Dresser: Helen Thomas. Special Effects: Wally Veevers. Sound Editor: Jim Roddan. Sound Mixer: H.L. Bird. Sound Supervisor: John Cox. Director of Photography: Desmond Dickinson. Music Composed and Conducted by: John Scott. Based on the characters created by: Sir Arthur Conan Doyle. Original Story and Screenplay by: Donald & Derek Ford cast: John Neville (Sherlock Holmes), Donald Houston (Doctor Watson), John Fraser (Lord Carfax), Anthony Quayle (Doctor Murray), Barbara Windsor (Annie Chapman), Adrienne Corri (Angela), Frank Finlay (Inspector Lestrade), Judi Dench (Sally), Charles Regnier (Joseph Beck), Cecil Parker (Prime Minister), Georgia Brown (Singer), Barry Jones (Duke of Shires), Robert Morley (Mycroft Holmes), Dudley Foster (Home Secretary), Peter Carsten (Max Steiner), Christiane Maybach (Polly Nichols), Kay Walsh (Cathy Eddowes), John Cairney (Michael Osborne), Edina Ronay (Mary Kelly), Avis Bunnage (Landlady), Barbara Leake (Mrs. Hudson), Patrick Newell (P.C. Benson), Norma Foster (Liz Stride), Terry Downes (Chunky), [uncredited: Jeremy Lloyd (Rupert), Corin Redgrave (Rupert's friend)]

1966   SECRETS OF A WINDMILL GIRL

Michael Klinger and **Tony Tenser** present.
A Searchlight Films Production. © Searchlight Films Ltd.
Filmed at: The Windmill Theatre, November 1964,
Twickenham Studios
BBFC: Certificate X, 22 April 1966
Distributed by: Compton-Cameo Films, May 1966
(Premiere at New Windmill Theatre 25/4/66)
Running Time: 86 minutes
Colour

Written & Directed by: Arnold Louis Miller. Produced by: Arnold Louis Miller and Stanley A. Long. Song: 'The Windmill Girls' sung by Valerie Mitchell. Camera Operator: Ron Bridger. Camera Assistants: Keith Jones, Don Lord. Lights: On the Spot. Make up: Bill D'Arcy. Assistant to the Producers: Phillip Steen. Editor: John Beaton. Sound: Peter Day, Derek Rye, Derek Rolls. Art Director: Tony Curtis. Production Secretaries: Sheila Miller, Patricia Preece. Special Choreography by: Peter Gordeno. Music Composed, Arranged & Conducted by: Malcolm Lockyer. Photography by: Stanley A. Long

cast: April Wilding (Linda Grey), Pauline Collins (Pat Lord), Renee Houston (Molly), Derek Bond (Ins. Thomas), Harry Fowler (Harry), Howard Marion Crawford (Richard), Peter Gordeno (Peter), Peter Swanwick (Len Mason), Martin Jarvis (Mike), Deidre O'Dea (Deidre), Pat Patterson (Pat), Jill Millard (Jill), Linda Page (Lynn), Dana Gillespie (Singer), Maurice Lane (Maurice), George Rutland (Dancer), Leon Cortez (Agent), Joan Hurley (Wife), Eddy Davis (Party Boy Friend), Laurence Beck (Sports Car Driver), Rey Anton & The Pro Form (Themselves), Corona School Children and the Boys and Girls of the Windmill, Sadie Eddon (Windmill Girl) [uncredited]

Directed by: Roman Polanski. Produced by: Gene Gutowski. Executive Producer: Sam Waynberg. Original Screenplay by: Roman Polanski and Gerard Brach. Translation: John Sutro. First Assistant Directors: Ted Sturgis, Roger Simons. Director of Photography: Gilbert Taylor. Camera Operators: Geoffrey Seaholme, Roy Ford. Sound Mixer: George Stephenson. Continuity: Dee Vaughn. Stills: Laurie Turner. Sound Editor: David Campling. Casting: Maude Spector. Make-Up: Alan Brownie. Hairdresser: Joyce James. Wardrobe: Bridget Sellers. Sound Supervisor: Stephen Dalby. Dubbing Mixer: Gerry Humphreys. Props: Alf Pegley. Special Effects: Bowie Films Ltd. Production Manager: Don Weeks. Production Controller: Terry Glinwood. Art Director: George Lack. Production Designer: Voytek. Editor: Alastair McIntyre. Production Supervisor: Robert Sterne. Music by: Komeda [Krzysztof Komeda]. Scenic Artist: Gilbert Wood [uncredited]

cast: Donald Pleasence (George), Francoise Dorleac (Teresa), Lionel Stander (Richard), Jack MacGowran (Albie), William Franklyn (Cecil), Robert Dorning (Philip Fairweather), Marie Kean (Marion Fairweather), Renee Houston (Christopher's Mother), Geoffrey Sumner (Christopher's Father), Iain Quarrier (Christopher), Jackie [Jacqueline] Bisset (Jacqueline), Trevor Delaney (Horace)

1966   CUL-DE-SAC

© Compton-Tekli Film Productions Limited
Filmed at: On location on Holy Island and at
Twickenham Studios 20/06/65
BBFC: Certificate X, 9 February 1966
Distributed by: Compton Films, June 1966 (Premiere at Cameo & Poly, Regent Street 2/6/66)
Running Time: 112 minutes
B/W

1966   THE PROJECTED MAN

Michael Klinger and **Tony Tenser** present.
A Compton Production.
© M.L.C. Productions Ltd.
Filmed at: Merton Park Studios, November 1965
BBFC: Certificate X, 23 March 1966
Distributed by: Compton Films, July 1966
Running Time: 90 minutes
Colour

Directed by: Ian Curteis, John Croydon [uncredited]. Produced by: John Croydon and Maurice Foster. Associate Producer: Pat Green. Screenplay by: John C. Cooper [John Croydon] and Peter Bryan. From an original story by Frank Quattrocchi. Director of Photography: Stanley Pavey. Art Director: Peter Mullins. 2nd Unit Photography: Brian Rhodes. Editor: Derek Holding. Assistant Directors: Derek Whitehurst, Tom Sachs. Camera Operator: Cece Cooney. Sound: S.G. Rider, Red Law. Continuity: Olga Brook. Dubbing Editor: Brian Blamey. Make-Up: Eric Carter. Hairdresser: Joan Carpenter. Wardrobe: Kathleen Moore. Special Effects: Flo Nordhoff, Robert Hedges, Mike Hope. Music Composed and Conducted by: Kenneth V. Jones. Played by: The Sinfonia Orchestra of London

cast: Bryant Haliday (Dr. Paul Steiner), Mary Peach (Dr. Patricia Hill), Norman Wooland (Dr. Blanchard), Ronald Allen (Dr. Chris Mitchel), Derek Farr (Inspector Davis), Tracey Crisp (Sheila Anderson), Derrick de Marney (Latham), Gerard Heinz (Dr. Lembach), Sam Kydd (Harry), Terry Scully (Steve), Norma West (Gloria), Frank Gatliff (Dr. Wilson), John Watson (Sergeant Martin), Alfred Joint (Security Man), Rosemary Donnelly (Girl), David Scheuer (Boy)

1967   MINI WEEKEND

A Tigon-Global Pictures Film
Filmed at: On location
BBFC: Certificate X, 21 April 1967
Distributed by: Tigon Pictures, May 1967
(Premiere at Jacey Cinema 11/5/67)
Running Time: 79 minutes
B/W

AKA: *The Tomcat*

Directed by: Georges Robin. Produced by: **Tony Tenser**. Executive Producer: Arnold Louis Miller. Screenplay by: Georges Robin and **Tony Tenser**. Director of Photography: Stanley A. Long. Editor: Roy Nevill. Art Director: Tony Curtis. Sound: Dudley Plummer Services

cast: Anthony Trent (Tom), Veronica Lang (Jenny), Anna Palk (Girl in Tiles Club and Cinema), Liza Rogers (Sandra), Connie Frazer (Tom's mother), Karen Leslie (Girl in pub), Nina Dwyer (Girl on bus), Valerie Stanton (girl in Barber's Shop), Eve Aubrey (Old hag), Vicky Hodge (1st dream sequence), Jane MacIntosh (Supermarket girl), Patti Bryant (Girl in café Sequence), Avril Gaynor (Girl in café Sequence), Rosalind Elliott (Girl in Tube sequence), Kathleen Southern (Girl in Tube sequence), Maria Hauffer (Girl in boutique sequence), Lucy Swain (Girl in boutique sequence)

1967   THE SORCERERS

A **Tony Tenser**-Curtwel-Global Production.
© **Tony Tenser Pictures Ltd.**
Filmed at: West London Studios, January 1967 and on location
BBFC: Certificate X, 8 May 1967

Distributed by: Tigon Pictures, June 1967 (Premiere at Carlton Theatre. Trade shown at Cannes, May 1967)
Running Time: 85 minutes
Colour

Directed by: Michael Reeves. Produced by: Patrick Curtis and **Tony Tenser**. Executive Producer: Arnold L. Miller. Assistant Director: Keith Wilkinson. Continuity: Doreen Soan. Production Secretary: Sheila Miller. Camera Operator: John Mantell. Camera Assistants: Don Lord, Gordon Thornton. Sound Mixer: Ken Osborne. Boom Operator: Mike Payne. Gaffer: Maurice Corcoran. Construction Manager: Jack Palmer. Make Up: Geoff Rodway. Art Director: Tony Curtis. Editing: David Woodward, Susan Michie. Director of Photography: Stanley A. Long. Music Composed & Conducted by: Paul Ferris. "Your Love" & "Sweet Nothing" sung by: Toni Daly. Played by: Lee Grant and the Capitols. Screenplay by: Michael Reeves and Tom Baker. From an idea by: John Burke

cast: Boris Karloff (Professor Monserrat), Catherine Lacey (Estelle), Elizabeth Ercy (Nicole), Ian Ogilvy (Mike), Victor Henry (Alan), Dani Sheridan (Laura), Alf Joint (Ron), Meier Tzelniker (Snack Bar Owner), Gerald Campion (Customer), Susan George (Audrey), Ivor Dean (Inspector Matalon), Peter Fraser (Detective), Martin Terry (Tobacconist), Bill Barnsley (Constable), Maureen Boothe, Arnold Louis Miller (Taxi Driver) [uncredited]

The Blood Beast Terror

1967   **THE BLOOD BEAST TERROR**

Tony Tenser presents. A Tigon-British Film Production. © Tigon British Films
Filmed at: Goldhawk Studios, Shepherds Bush, July 1967
BBFC: Certificate X, 1 January 1968
Distributed by: Tigon Pictures, February 1968
Running Time: 81 minutes
Colour

AKA: *The Vampire-Beast Craves Blood, Death's Head Vampire, Blood Beast from Hell*

Directed by: Vernon Sewell. Produced by: Arnold L. Miller. Executive Producer: **Tony Tenser**. Art Director: Wilfred Woods. Editor: Howard Lanning. Director of Photography: Stanley A. Long. Music Composed & Conducted by: Paul Ferris. Screenplay by: Peter Bryan. Production Manager: Ricky Coward. Assistant Director: George Pollard. Continuity: Eve Wilson. Production Secretary: Pat O'Donnell. Camera Operator: Norman Jones. Focus Puller: Jim Alloway. Sound Mixer: Alan Hogben. Boom Operator: Mike Tucker. Construction Manager: Len Harvey. Make-up Artist: Rosemarie McDonald Peattie. Dubbing Editor: Dennis Lanning. Set Dresser: Freda Pearson. Special Effects: Roger Dicken. Hairdresser: Henry Montsash. Wardrobe: Marie Feldwick

cast: Peter Cushing (Inspector Quennell), Robert Flemyng (Dr. Mallinger), Wanda Ventham (Clare), Vanessa Howard (Meg), David Griffin (William), Glynn Edwards (Sergeant Allan), William Wilde (Britewell), Kevin Stoney (Granger), John Paul (Warrender), Russell Napier (Landlord), Roy Hudd (Morgue Attendant), Leslie Anderson (Coachman), Simon Cain (Gardener), Robert Cawdron (Chief Constable), Kenneth Colley (James), Beryl Cooke (Housekeeper), Roy Evans (2nd Porter), Joan Ingram (Cook), David Lyell (2nd student), John Scott Martin (Snaflebum), William Maxwell (1st Porter), Mike Mundell (1st Student), Norman Pitt (Police Doctor), Malcolm Rogers (Dr. Elliott), Drew Russell (P.C. Smith), Honor Shepherd (Senior Housemaid), Robin Wentworth (Starkadder)

1968   **WITCHFINDER GENERAL**

A Tigon British - American International Production.
© Tigon British
Filmed at: On location in Bury St. Edmonds, Norfolk 17/09/67-13/11/67
BBFC: Certificate X, 26 April 1968
Distributed by: Tigon Pictures, May 1968
Running Time: 86 minutes
Colour

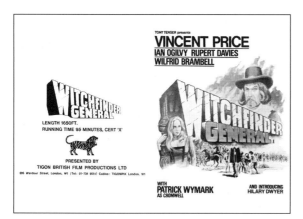

AKA: *Matthew Hopkins: Witchfinder General, The Conqueror Worm*

Directed by: Michael Reeves. Produced by: Louis M. Heyward, Philip Waddilove, Arnold Miller. Executive Producer: **Tony Tenser**. Art Director: Jim Morahan. Film Editor: Howard Lanning. Music Composed and Conducted by: Paul Ferris. Photographed by: John Coquillon. Screenplay by: Tom Baker and Michael Reeves. Additional Scenes by: Louis M. Heyward. From the novel by: Ronald Bassett. Assistant Directors: Ian Goddard, Ian Lawrence. Location Manager: Euan Pearson. Continuity: Lorna Selwyn. Production Secretary: Pat O'Donnell. Casting Director: Freddie Vale. Production Manager: Ricky Coward. Publicity: Jack Daw. Set Dresser: Jimmy James. Assistant Art Director: Peter Shields. Props: Sid Davies, Fred Harrison. Special Effects: Roger Dicken. Stills: Jack Dooley. Camera Operators: Brian Elvin, Gerry Anstice. Camera Assistants: Tony Breeze, Chris Reynolds. Grip: Feddie Williams. Construction Manager: Dennis Cantell. Dubbing Editor: Dennis Lanning. Sound Mixer: Hugh Strain. Sound Recordist: Paul Le Mare. Make-Up: Dore Hamilton. Hairdresser: Henry Montsash. Wardrobe: Jill Thomson. Gaffer: Laurie Shane. Assistant Editor: Marrion Curren

cast: Vincent Price (Matthew Hopkins), Ian Ogilvy (Richard Marshall), Rupert Davies (John Lowes), Hilary Dwyer (Sara), Robert Russell (John Stearne), Nicky Henson (Swallow), Tony Selby (Salter), Bernard Kay (Fisherman), Godfrey James (Webb), Michael Beint (Captain Gordon), John Treneman (Harcourt), Bill Maxwell (Gifford), Morris Jar [Paul Ferris] (Paul), Maggie Kimberly (Elizabeth), Peter Haigh (Lavenham Magistrate), Hira Talfrey (Hanged Woman), Ann Tirard (Old Woman), Peter Thomas (Farrier), Edward Palmer (Shepherd), David Webb (Jailer), Lee Peters (Sergeant), David Lyell (Footsoldier), Alf Joint (Sentry), Martin Terry (Hoxne Innkeeper), Jack Lynn (Brandeston Innkeeper), Beaufoy Milton (Priest), Dennis Thorne (Villager), Michael Segal (Villager), Toby Lennon (Old Man), Maggie Nolan (Girl at Inn), Sally Douglas (Girl at Inn), Donna Reading (Girl at Inn), Patrick Wymark (Cromwell), Wilfred [Wilfrid] Brambell (Master Loach), Philip Waddilove, Derek Ware, John Kidd, Susi Field

1968 CURSE OF THE CRIMSON ALTAR

Tony Tenser presents.
© Tigon British Film Productions Ltd.
Filmed at: Grims Dyke House December 1967-
January 1968
BBFC: Certificate X, 28 June 1968
Distributed by: Tigon Pictures, December 1968
Running Time: 87 minutes
Colour

AKA: *The Crimson Cult*

Director: Vernon Sewell. Producer: Louis M. 'Deke' Heyward. Executive Producer: **Tony Tenser**. Associate Producer: Gerry Levy. Art Director: Derek Barrington. Editor: Howard Lanning. Screenplay by: Mervyn Haisman and Henry Lincoln. From a story by: Jerry Sohl. Music Composed and Conducted by: Peter Knight. Director of Photography: Johnny Coquillon. Production Manager: Alex Carver-Hill. Assistant Director: Dennis Lewis. Continuity: Mary Spain. Production Secretary: Cynthia Palmer. Camera Operator: Peter Hendry. Focus Puller: Tony Breeze. Grips: Michael Beauchamp. Sound Mixer: Kevin Sutton. Dubbing Mixer: Hugh Strain. Dubbing Editor: Dennis Lanning. Construction Manager: Maurice Smith. Costume Designer: Michael Southgate. Editing Assistants: Marion Curren, Jonathan Morris. Property Master: John Poyner. Hairdresser: Ann Fordyce. Make-Up Artists: Pauline Worden, Elizabeth Blattner

Curse of the Crimson Altar

cast: Boris Karloff (Professor Marsh), Christopher Lee (Morley), Mark Eden (Robert Manning), Barbara Steele (Lavinia), Michael Gough (Elder), Virginia Wetherell (Eve), Rosemarie Reede (Esther), Derek Tansley (Judge), Michael Warren (Chauffeur), Ronald Pember (Petrol Attendant), Denys Peek (Peter Manning), Nicholas Head (Blacksmith), Nita Lorraine (Woman with whip), Carol Anne (1st Virgin), Jenny Shaw (2nd Virgin), Vivienne Carlton (Sacrifice Victim), Roger Avon (Sergeant Tyson), Paul McNeil (Party Guest), Christine Pryor (Party Girl), Kerry Dean (Party Girl), Stephanie Marrion (Party Girl), Rosalind Royale (Party Girl), Millicent Scott (Stripper at Party), Vicky Richards (Belly Dancer at Party), Tasma Bereton (Party Girl who is painted), Kevin Smith (Drunk at party), Lita Scott (Girl with Cockerel), Terry Raven (1st Driver in Car Chase), Douglas Mitchell (2nd Driver in Car Chase), Nova St. Claire (Girl in Car Chase), Rupert Davies (The Vicar)

1969 LOVE IN OUR TIME

Tigon British Film Productions
Filmed at: On location
BBFC: Certificate X, 7 November 1968
Distributed by: Tigon Pictures, December 1968
Running Time: 88 minutes
Colour

Directed by: Elkan Allan. Produced by: **Tony Tenser**. Production Manager: George Mills. Assistant Director: Keith Evans. Screenplay: Elkan Allan. Director of Photography: William Brayne. Music: Reg Tilsley. Sound: Iain Bruce. Narration: Elkan Allan

cast: Katie Allan, Ian Anderson, Declan Cuffe, Bill Cummings, Joanne Harding, Gino Meluazzi, Ann Michelle, Ann Rutter, Eddie Stacey

1969 WHAT'S GOOD FOR THE GOOSE

Tony Tenser presents.
© Tigon British Film Productions Ltd.
Filmed at: On location in Southport, July 1968
BBFC: Certificate A, 13 February 1969 (Re-classified 'U' after further cuts before release)
Distributed by: Tigon Pictures, April 1969
Running Time: 107 minutes
Colour

AKA: *Girl Trouble*

Directed by: Menahem Golan. Produced by: **Tony Tenser**. Associate Producer: Norman Wisdom. Director of Photography: William Brayne. Story and Screenplay by: Menahem Golan. Script by: Norman Wisdom. Dialogue by: Christopher Gilmore. Theme Song sung by: Norman Wisdom. Music and Lyrics by Reg Tilsley and Howard Blaikley. 'Blow Your Mind', 'Alexandra', 'Never Be Me', 'Eagle's Sun' Music and Lyrics by: The Pretty Things. Music Composed & Conducted by: Reg Tilsley. Editor: Dennis Lanning. Art Director: Hayden Pearce. Production Manager: George Mills. Assistant Director: George Gilbert. Continuity: Lorna Selwyn. Camera Operator: Leslie Young. Focus Puller: John

TONY TENSER PRESENTS
NORMAN WISDOM
in MENAHEM GOLAN'S
WHAT'S GOOD FOR THE GOOSE (A)
 with TERENCE ALEXANDER   SARAH ATKINSON   SALLY BAZELY   DEREK FRANCIS
DAVID LODGE   PAUL WHITSUN-JONES   and introducing SALLY GEESON
RELEASED BY TIGON PICTURES LTD.   EASTMAN COLOUR

Metcalfe. Dubbing Mixer: Hugh Strain. Sound Mixer: Alan Kane. Boom Operator: Peter Offer. Assistant Editor: Jonathan L. Morris. Grip: Dennis Lewis. Wardrobe: Glenda Slater. Make-Up: Barbara Daly

cast: Norman Wisdom (Timothy Bartlett), Sally Geeson (Nikki), Sarah Atkinson (Meg), Sally Bazely (Margaret), Stuart Nichol (Bank Manager), Derek Francis (Harrington), Terence Alexander (Frisby), Paul Whitsun-Jones (Clark), David Lodge (Porter), Karl Lanchbury (Pete), Hilary Pritchard (Cashier in Discotheque), H.H. Goldsmith (Policeman), Thelma Falls-Hand (Bank Clerk), The Pretty Things (Pop Group), George Meaton (Third Speaker), Duncan Taylor (Other Banker), Jonathan Cox (First Son), Patrick Goggin (Second Son), Sally Begley (Daughter)

1969   THE BODY STEALERS

Tony Tenser presents.
© Tigon British Film Productions Ltd.
Filmed at: On location & at Shepperton Studios, 22/7/68
BBFC: Certificate X, 4 March 1969 (Re-classified 'A' after cuts before release)
Distributed by: Tigon Pictures, June 1969
Running Time: 91 minutes
Colour

AKA: *Thin Air*

Directed by: Gerry Levy. Produced by: **Tony Tenser**. Production Manager: John Workman. Art Director: Wilfred Arnold. Editor: Howard Lanning. Music Composed and Conducted by: Reg Tilsley. Story and Script: Mike St. Clair. Revised Screenplay: Peter Marcus [Gerry Levy]. Photography by: Johnny Coquillon. 1st Assistant Director: Pat Morton. Continuity: Iris Karney. Camera Operator: Peter Hendry. Focus: Tony Breeze. Dubbing Mixer: Hugh Strain. Sound Mixer: Bob Peck. Make-up: Bunty Phillips, Roy Ashton. Hairdressers: Olga Angelinetta, Carol Beckett. Chief Electrician: Archie Dansie. Assistant Editor: Marion Curren

cast: Patrick Allen (Bob Megan), Hilary Dwyer (Julie Slade), Lorna Wilde (Lorna), Allan Cuthbertson (Hindesmith), Carl Rigg (Pilot Officer Briggs), Sally Faulkner (Joanna), Michael Culver (Lt. Bailes), Shelagh Fraser (Mrs. Thatcher), Neil Connery (Jim Radford), Robert Flemyng (Wing Commander Baldwin), George Sanders (General Armstrong), Maurice Evans (Dr. Matthews), Carolanne Hawkings [Hawkins] (Paula), Michael Graham (Pilot), Brian Harrison (Pilot), Dixon Adams (David), Derek Pollitt (Davies), Max Latimer (Guard Sergeant), Ralph Carrigan (M.P.), Johnny Wilde (Orderley), Dennis Chinnery (1st Control Officer), Michael Warren (Harry), Steve Kirby (Driver), Leslie Schofield (Gate Guard), Clifford Earl (Sgt. in Lab), Larry Dan (Jeep Driver), Arnold Peters (Mr. Smith), Michael Goldie (Despatch Driver), Wanda Moore (Secretary)

1969 **1917**

Tigon British Film Productions in association with
Cinetrend Motion
Filmed at: On location in Wales, September 1968
BBFC: Certificate X, 25 March 1969
Distributed by: Tigon Pictures, March 1970
Running Time: 34 minutes
Colour

AKA: *Nineteen Seventeen – The Gap*

Directed by: Stephen Weeks. Produced by: **Tony Tenser**. Screenplay by: Stephen Weeks. From the original play 'The Gap' by: Derek Banham. Director of Photography: Oluf Nissen. Editor: Roger Crook. Music Composed and Conducted by: David Lee. Sound: Alan Kane

cast: Timothy Bateson (Willi Falk), David Leland (Felix), Geoffrey Davies (Gessel), Anthony Trent (Colman), Richardson Morgan (Penfold), Christopher Hancock (Cox), Edward Caddick (Whittaker), Nel Brennen (Farmgirl), Jane Lewis (Willi's Wife), Reg Solley (Herr Stross)

1969 **THE HAUNTED HOUSE OF HORROR**

Tigon presents. A Tigon British - American
International Production.
© Tigon British Film Productions Limited
Filmed at: Birkdale Palace Hotel, Southport and Bank Hall, Bretherton, October 1968
BBFC: Certificate X, 11 July 1969
Distributed by: Tigon Pictures, July 1970
Running Time: 92 minutes
Colour

AKA: *The Dark, Horror House*

Directed by: Michael Armstrong. Produced by: **Tony Tenser**. Executive Producer: Louis M. Heyward [uncredited]. Director of Photography: Jack Atchelor. Screenplay by: Michael Armstrong. Additional Material by: Peter Marcus [Gerry Levy]. Music Composed and Conducted by: Reg Tilsley. "Responsibility" Words and Music by: Peter Marcus [Gerry Levy]. Art Director: Haydon Pearce. Editor: Peter Pitt. Production Manager: George Mills. Assistant Directors: Nick Caris Carter, Michael McKeag. Camera Operators: Jimmy Devis, Alan Boast. 2nd Unit Cameraman: Peter Hendry. Continuity: Lorna Selwyn. Sound Mixer: Alan Kane. Dubbing Editor: Howard Lanning. Make-Up: Cliff Sharp. Wardrobe: Kathleen Moore, Hilda Geerdts. Hairdressers: Carole Becket, Ross Carver. Wigs and Hairpieces supplied by: The House of Carmen. Set Decorator: Jack Holdon [uncredited]. Special Effects: Arthur Beavis [uncredited]

cast: Frankie Avalon (Chris), Jill Haworth (Sheila), Dennis Price (Inspector), George Sewell (Kellett), Gina Warwick (Sylvia), Richard O'Sullivan (Peter), Carol Dilworth (Dorothy), Julian Barnes (Richard), Veronica Doran (Madge), Robin Stewart (Henry), Jan Holden (Peggy), Clifford Earl (Police Sergeant), Robert Raglan (Bradley), Mark Wynter (Gary), Freddie Lees (Dave)

1969 **ZETA ONE**

© Tigon British Film Productions Ltd.
Filmed at: Camden Studios and on location at Denham, 20/1/69
BBFC: Certificate X, 5 March 1970
Distributed by: Tigon Pictures, April 1970
Running Time: 86 minutes
Colour

AKA: *The Love Factor, Alien Women*

Directed by: Michael Cort. Produced by: George Maynard. Executive Producer: **Tony Tenser**. Screenplay by: Michael Cort and Alistair McKenzie. Music Composed and Conducted by: Johnny Hawksworth. Costumes by: Collette du Plessis. Screenplay based on a story from 'ZETA' Magazine. Photography: Jack Atchelor. Production Managers: George Mills and Christopher Neame. Edited by: Jack T. Knight and Dennis Lanning. Art Director: Martin Gascoigne. Assistant Director: Michael McKeag. Camera Operators: Alan Boast. Geoff Glover. Sound Recordist: Alan Kane. Sound Editor: Roy Lafbery. Dubbing Mixer: Maurice Askew. Continuity: Lorna Selwyn. Make-Up: Bunty Phillips. Hairdressers: Pearl Tipaldi, Barbara Sutton. Wardrobe: Hilda Geerdts, Mary Gibson. Construction Manager: Alan Board, James Word's car by courtesy of Monteverdi Concessionaires Limited

cast: James Robertson Justice (Major Bourdon), Charles Hawtrey (Swyne), Robin Hawdon (James Word), Anna Gael (Clotho), Brigitte Skay (Lachesis), Dawn Addams (Zeta), Valerie Leon (Atropos), Lionel Murton ('W'), Yutte Stensgaard (Ann Olsen), Wendy Lingham (Ted), Rita Webb (Clippie), Carolanne Hawkins (Zara), Steve Kirby (Sleuth), Paul Baker (Bourdon's Assistant), Walter Sparrow (Stage Manager), Alan Haywood (Pilot), Anna Tunnard (Miss Johnson), Yolanda Del Mar (Striptease Artiste), Rose Howlett (Fat Lady), Nita Lorraine (Angvisa Girl), Trudi Nielson (Angvisa Girl), Olga Linden (Angvisa Girl), Vikki Richards (Angvisa Girl), Rina Brown (Angvisa Girl), Juliet Adams (Angvisa Girl), Gillian Aldham (Angvisa Girl), Kirsten Betts (Angvisa Girl), Hani Borelle (Angvisa Girl), Tasma Brereton (Angvisa Girl), Fay Browning (Angvisa Girl), Belinda Caren (Angvisa Girl), Yvonne Castelle (Angvisa Girl), Charleine (Angvisa Girl), Jenny Field (Angvisa Girl), Angie Grant (Angvisa Girl), Gilly Grant (Angvisa Girl), Caroline Johnson (Angvisa Girl), Helen Jones (Angvisa Girl), Sandra Kirwan (Angvisa Girl), Linda Lawson (Angvisa Girl), Jenny Le Fre (Angvisa Girl), Janet Pearce (Angvisa Girl), Angela Pitt (Angvisa Girl), Donna Reading (Angvisa Girl), Christine Rigg (Angvisa Girl), Birthe Sector (Angvisa Girl), Erika Simmonds (Angvisa Girl), Contessa Veronica (Angvisa Girl), Jennifer Watts (Angvisa Girl), Jeannette Wild (Angvisa Girl)

1969 **MONIQUE**

A Tigon British Film Production.
© Tigon British Film Productions Ltd.
Filmed at: On location and at Isleworth Studios, London

Monique

BBFC: Certificate X, 4 June 1970
Distributed by: Tigon Pictures, July 1970
Running Time: 88 minutes
Colour

Written and Directed by: John Bown. Produced by: Michael Style. Executive Producer: **Tony Tenser**. Music by the: Jacques Loussier Trio. Director of Photography: Moray Grant. Production Manager: Christopher Neame. Editor: Richard Sidwell. Art Director: Colin Southcott. Assistant Director: Michael McKeag. Camera Operator: Peter Hendry. Sound Recordist: Alan Kane. Dubbing Mixer: Maurice Askew. Sound Editor: Nestor Lovera. Continuity: Ann Edwards. Make-up: Elizabeth Blattner. Hair Stylist: Olive Mills. Wardrobe Mistress: Muriel Dickson. Construction Manager: Alan Board. Costumes by: Simon Massey. Paul Klee's "They're Biting" Copyright SPADEM Paris 1969

cast: Joan Alcorn (Jean), Sibylla Kay (Monique), David Sumner (Bill), Carolanne Hawkins (Girl), Howard Rawlinson (Richard), Davilia O'Connor (Babysitter), Nicola Bown (Susan), Jacob Fitz-Jones (Edward)

1970   THE BEAST IN THE CELLAR

A Tigon British Film Production in association with Leander Films Limited. © Tigon British Film Productions Ltd. and Leander Films Ltd.
Filmed at: Pinewood Studios, 23/2/70 and on location
BBFC: Certificate X, 10 July 1970
Distributed by: Tigon Pictures, July 1971
Running Time: 89 minutes
Colour

AKA: *The Cellar, Young Man I Think You're Dying* (shooting title)

Directed by: James Kelly. Produced by: Graham Harris. Associate Producer: Christopher Neame. Executive Producer: **Tony Tenser**. Original Screenplay by: James Kelly. Directors of Photography: Harry Waxman and Desmond Dickinson. Music by: Tony MacAuley. Conducted and arranged by: Lew Warburton. "She Works in a Woman's Way" written by Tony MacAuley & Barry Mason. Sung by Tony Burrows with the Edison Lighthouse. Art Director: Roger King. Assistant Director: Dominic Fulford. Camera Operator: Ronnie Maasz. Editor: Nicholas Napier-Bell. Sound

Mixer: Tony Dawe. Sound Editor: Colin Hobson. Dubbing Mixer: Ted Karnon. Casting Director: Weston Drury Jnr. Continuity: Annabel Davis-Goff. Make-up: W.T. Partleton. Hairdresser: Olga Angelinetta. Wardrobe Mistress: Mary Gibson. Unit Manager: Caroline Langley. Construction Manager: Ken Softley. Second Assistant Director: Paul Ibbetson. Production Secretary: Ann M. Paterson. Gaffer: Harry Woodley. Grip: Ted Underwood. Army manoeuvers were shot with the kind permission of The Queen's Own Hussars

cast: Beryl Reid (Ellie Ballantyne), Flora Robson (Joyce Ballantyne), Tessa Wyatt (Nurse Sutherland), John Hamill (Alan Marlow), T.P. McKenna (Det. Chief Sup. Paddick), David Dodimead (Dr. Spencer), Vernon Dobtcheff (Newsmith), John Kelland (Sgt. Young), Anthony Heaton (Anderson), Christopher Chittell (Baker), Peter Craze (Roy), Anabel Littledale (Gloria), Dafydd Havard (Stephen Ballantyne), Merlin Ward (Young Stephen), Elisabeth Choice (Young Joyce), Gail Lidstone (Young Ellie), Howard Rawlinson (Young Soldier), Roberta Tovey (Paper Girl), Robert Wilde (Soldier in N.A.A.F.I.), Reg Lever (Ambulance Man)

1970   BLOOD ON SATAN'S CLAW

A Tigon British/Chilton Film Production.
© Tigon British Film Productions Ltd. and Chilton Film and Television Enterprises Ltd.
Filmed at: Pinewood Studios, 14/4/70 and on location at Henley-on-Thames
BBFC: Certificate X, 21 September 1970
Distributed by: Tigon Pictures, July 1971
Running Time: 96 minutes
Colour

AKA: *Satan's Skin, The Devil's Touch*

Directed by: Piers Haggard. Produced by: Peter L. Andrews and Malcolm B. Heyworth. Executive Producer: **Tony Tenser**. Original Screenplay by: Robert Wynne-Simmons. With additional material by Piers Haggard. Director of Photography: Dick Bush. Music Composed and Conducted by: Marc Wilkinson. Art Director: Arnold Chapkis. Editor: Richard Best. Production Manager: Ron Jackson. Assistant Director: Stephen Christian. Camera Operator: Dudley Lovell. Sound Mixer: Tony Dawe. Sound Editor: Bill Trent. Dubbing Mixer: Ken Barker. Casting Director: Weston Drury Jnr. Set Dresser: Milly Burns. Continuity: Josie Fulford. Make-Up: Eddie Knight. Hairdresser: Olga Angelinetta. Wardrobe Mistress: Dulcie Midwinter. Focus Puller: Mike Rutter. Construction Manager: Ken Softley. Second Assistant Director: Bill Westley. Production Secretary: Caroline Langley. Gaffer: Harry Woodley. Grip: Reg Hall

cast: Patrick Wymark (The Judge), Linda Hayden (Angel Blake), Barry Andrews (Ralph Gower), Michele Dotrice (Margaret), James Hayter (Squire Middleton), Anthony Ainley (Reverend Fallowfield), Howard Goorney (The Doctor), Avice Landon (Isobel Banham), Charlotte Mitchell (Ellen), Wendy Padbury (Cathy Vespers), Tamara Ustinov (Rosalind Barton), Simon Williams (Peter Edmonton), Robin Davies (Mark Vespers), Milton Reid (Dog Handler) [uncredited], Yvonne Paul (Naked Temptress) [uncredited]

1971   BLACK BEAUTY

A Tigon British/Chilton Film Production.
© Tigon British Film Productions Ltd. and Chilton Film & Television Enterprises Ltd.
Filmed at: On location in Ireland, 1/7/70 and Spain
BBFC: Certificate U, 18 March 1971
Distributed by: Tigon Pictures, May 1971
(Premiere at The Paris Cinema, Cannes 24/5/71)
Running Time: 106 minutes
Colour

Directed by: James Hill. Produced by: Peter L. Andrews and Malcolm B. Heyworth. Executive Producer: **Tony Tenser**. Theme music by: Lionel Bart. Musical Director and additional music composed by: John Cameron. Art Director: Hazel Peiser. Editor: Ann Chegwidden. 2nd Unit Camerman: Patrick Carey. Production Manager: Ron Jackson. 1st Assistant Director: Stuart Freeman. Camera Operator: Godfrey Godar. Location Manager: Bill Westley. Sound Mixer: Paul Carr. Dubbing Editors: Chris Lancaster, Vernon Messenger. Continuity: Isobel Mula. Make-up: Stella Bowen. Hairdresser: Jeanette Freeman. Wardrobe: Eileen Long. Director of Photography: Chris Menges. Screenplay by: Wolf Mankowitz (Based upon the novel by Anna Sewell). Additional dialogue by: James Hill

cast: Mark Lester (Joe), Walter Slezak (Hackenschmidt), Peter Lee Lawrence (Gervaise), Ursula Glas [Uschi Glas] (Marie), Patrick Mower (Sam Greene), John Nettleton (Sir William), Maria Rohm (Anne), Eddie Golden (Evans), Clive Geraghty (Roger), Johnny Hoey (Muldoon), Patrick Gardiner (O'Flaherty), Brian McGrath (Mark Beauchamp), Ronan Smith (Farm Boy), John Franklyn (Coalman), Margaret Lacey (Anna Sewell), Fernando Bilbao (Mungo), Vicente Rola [Vicente Roca] (Flying Fred), Jose Niero [José Nieto] (Lorent), Eucilio Rodriguez (Horse Dealer), Daniel Martín (Lieutenant), Luis Induni (Sergeant), Ricardo Palacios (Russian General)

1971   HANNIE CAULDER

Tigon British Film Productions Limited presents.
A Tigon/Curtwel Production.
© Tigon British Film Productions Ltd.
Filmed at: On location in Almeria, Spain, 18/1/71.
Post Production Work at Twickenham Studios
BBFC: Certificate AA, 8 September 1971
Distributed by: Tigon Pictures, November 1971
Running Time: 85 minutes
Colour

Directed by: Burt Kennedy. Produced by: Patrick Curtis. Executive Producer: **S. Tony Tenser**. Director of Photography: Edward Scaife. Film Editor: Jim Connock. Art Director: Jose Alguero. Camera Operator: John Harris. Assistant Director: Julio Sempere. Continuity: Eva Del Castillo. Sound Mixer: Vernon Messenger. Sound Recordists: Wally Milner, Gerry Humphreys. Make-Up: John O'Gorman, Ricardo Vaquez Sese. Miss Welch's costumes by: Ray Agayan [Aghayan]. Hairdressers: Mary Bredin, Adela Del Pino. Wardrobe: Juan Antonio Parrage. Music Composed and Conducted by: Ken Thorne. Production Manager: Robert Goodstein. Production Accountant: Maurice Landsberger. Based on Characters Created by: Ian Quicke and Bob Richards. Original Story by: Peter Cooper. Screenplay by: Z.X. Jones [Burt Kennedy & David Haft]. Theme Song Sung by: Bobby Hanna. Lyrics by: Jack Fishman. Music by: Ken Thorne

cast: Raquel Welch (Hannie Caulder), Robert Culp (Thomas Luther Price), Ernest Borgnine (Emmett), Jack Elam (Frank), Strother Martin (Rufus), Christopher Lee (Bailey), Diana Dors (Madame), Stephen Boyd (The Preacher) [uncredited], Aldo Sambrell (Mexican soldier) [uncredited], Brian Lightburn (Sam Adams) [uncredited], Luis Barboo [uncredited]

1971 THE MAGNIFICENT SEVEN DEADLY SINS

© Tigon British Film Productions Ltd.
Filmed at: Pinewood, 19/4/71
BBFC: Certificate A, 11 October 1971
Distributed by: Tigon Pictures, December 1971
Running Time: 107 minutes
Colour

Produced and Directed by: Graham Stark. Executive Producers: **Tony Tenser** and Michael L. Green. "Avarice" written by: Bob Larbey & John Esmonde. "Envy" written by: Dave Freeman. "Gluttony" written by: Graham Chapman & Barry Cryer. "Lust" written by Graham Stark. From a story by: Marty Feldman. "Pride" by: Alan Simpson and Ray Galton. "Sloth" written by: Spike Milligan. "Wrath" written by: Barry Cryer and Graham Chapman. Director of Photography: Harvey Harrison Jnr. Production Manager: Jack Causey. Assistant Director: Derek Cracknell. Editors: Rod Nelson-Keys, Roy Piper. Art Director: Roger King. Camera Operator: Colin Corby. Location Manager: Jim Brennan. Sound Mixer: John Brommage. Dubbing

Editor: Pat Foster. Special Effects: Cliff Culley. Wardrobe: Roy Ponting. Continuity: Renee Glynne. Hairdresser: Gordon Bond. Make-Up: Geoffrey Rodway, Wally Schneiderman. Animation by: Bob Godfrey Films Limited. Music Composed and Conducted by: Roy Budd. "Envy, Greed an' Gluttony" (the Seven Deadly Sins theme) sung by: The Middle of the Road. Written by: Roy Budd and Jack Fishman

cast: Felicity Devonshire, "Avarice": Bruce Forsyth (Clayton), Paul Whitsun-Jones (Elsinore), Bernard Bresslaw (Mr. Violet), Joan Sims (Policewoman), Roy Hudd (Fisherman), Julie Samuel (Petrol Attendant), Cheryl Hall (Vanessa), Susanne Heath (Cloe), "Envy": Harry Secombe (Stanley), Geoffrey Bayldon (Vernon), June Whitfield (Mildred), Carmel Cryan (Vera), "Gluttony": Leslie Phillips (Dickie), Julie Ege (Ingrid), Patrick Newell (Doctor), Rosemarie Reed (Woman), Sarah Golding (Secretary), Bob Guccione (Photographer), Tina McDowell (Penthouse Pet), "Lust": Harry H. Corbett (Ambrose), Cheryl Kennedy (Greta), Bill Pertwee (Cockney Man), Mary Baxter (Charlady), Anouska Hempel (Blonde), Ken Earle (Boy Friend), Nicole Yerna (Thin Girl), Sue Bond (Girl with Glasses), Yvonne Paul (Receptionist), "Pride": Ian Carmichael (Mr. Ferris), Alfie Bass (Mr. Spooner), Audrey Nicholson (Mrs. Ferris), Sheila Burnette (Mrs. Spooner), Robert Gillespie (A.A. Man), Keith Smith (R.A.C. Man), Ivor Dean (Policeman), "Sloth": Spike Milligan (Tramp), Melvin Hayes (Porter), Ronnie Brody (Costermonger), Ronnie Barker, Peter Butterworth, Marty Feldman, Davy Kaye, David Lodge, Cardew Robinson, Madeline Smith, "Wrath": Ronald Fraser (George), Stephen Lewis (Jarvis), Arthur Howard (Kenneth)

1972   DOOMWATCH

© Tigon British Film Productions Ltd.
Filmed at: Pinewood Studios and on location in
Polkerris, Falmouth and in North Cornwall,
October 1971
BBFC: Certificate A, 17 February 1972
Distributed by: Tigon Pictures, March 1972
Running Time: 92 minutes
Colour

Directed by: Peter Sasdy. Produced by: **Tony
Tenser**. Director of Photography: Kenneth Talbot.
Production Manager: Jack Causey. Art Director:
Colin Grimes. Editor: Keith Palmer. Scientific
Advisor: Dr. Kit Pedler. Music Composed and
Conducted by: John Scott. Location Manager: Jim
Brennan. Assistant Director: Derek Whitehurst.
Sound Recordist: Ron Barron. Sound Editor:
Michael Hopkins. Camera Operator: Ron Maasz.
Continuity: Doreen Soan. Make-Up Supervisor: Tom
Smith. Hairdressing Supervisor: Ann McFadyen.
Wardrobe Master: John Hilling. Construction
Manager: Ken Softley. Dubbing Mixer: Ken Barker.
"Doomwatch" by: Kit Pedler & Gerry Davis. Final
Screenplay by: Clive Exton

cast: Ian Bannen (Dr. Shaw), Judy Geeson (Victoria
Brown), John Paul (Dr. Quist), Simon Oates (Dr.
Ridge), Jean Trend (Dr. Fay Chantry), Joby
Blanshard (Bradley), Percy Herbert (Hartwell),
Shelagh Fraser (Mrs. Straker), Geoffrey Keen (Sir
Henry Leyton), Joseph O'Conor (Vicar), Norman Bird
(Brewer), Constance Chapman (Miss Johnson),
Michael Brennan (Tom Straker), James Cosmo (Bob
Gillette), George Sanders (The Admiral), Cyril Cross
(George), Geoff L'Cise (Don), George Woodbridge
(Ferry Skipper), Jerome Willis (Lt. Com. Tavener),
Jeremy Child (David Broome), Brian Anthony (Brian
Murray), Rita Davies (Mrs. Murray), Walter Turner
(Mr. Murray), Paddy Ryan (Grandfather Murray),
Reg Lever (Sam), James Mellor (1st Man), Eamonn
Boyce (2nd Man), Paul Humpoletz (3rd Man), Pam
St. Clement (Young Woman), Katherine Parr (Middle-
aged woman)

1972   MISS JULIE

LMG Film-Sedgemoor Productions present.
A Tigon British-Sedgemoor Production.
© LMG Film-Sedgemoor Productions
Filmed at: Pinewood Studios
BBFC: Certificate AA, 8 August 1972
Distributed by: LMG Film Distributors, November
1972
Running Time: 105 minutes
Colour

AKA: *August Strindberg's "Miss Julie"*

Directed by: Robin Phillips, John Glenister.
Produced by: Peter J. Thompson, Martin C. Schute.
Executive Producers: **Tony Tenser**, Marvin
Liebman. Associate Producer: Norma Corney.
Filmed as directed for the stage by: Robin Phillips.
Translated by: Michael Meyer. Music Composed and

Conducted by: Gordon Kember. Production designed
by: Daphne Dare. Lighting Director: Ken Brown.
Assistant Director: Jim McCutcheon. Editors: Peter
Thornton, Roger Hoare. Assistants to the Directors:
Xenia Ager, Anne Rowe. Production Executive: Terry
Marcel. Assistants to the Producers: Michael
Rennison, Wendy Wilson. Production Manager:
Albert T. Tolley. Technical Supervisor: Vic Cornish.
Senior Camerman: Colin Callow. Sound Supervisor:
Doug Hopkins. Hairdresser: Maggie Whittle. Make-
Up: Bunty Phillips. Wardrobe Master: Roy Ponting

cast: Helen Mirren (Miss Julie), Donal McCann
(Jean), Heather Canning (Christine), From the Royal
Shakespeare Company: Mary Allen (House Servant),
Colin Edwynn (House Servant), Michael Egan
(House Servant), Ronald Forfar (House Servant),
Patrick Godfrey (House Servant), Valerie Minifie
(House Servant), Edward Phillips (House Servant),
Philip Sayer (House Servant), Holly Wilson (House
Servant)

1972   NEITHER THE SEA NOR THE SAND

LMG Film Productions Limited in association with
Portland Film Corporation present.
© LMG Film Productions Limited
Filmed at: On location in Jersey, 17/1/72
Completed at EMI-MGM Studios Borehamwood
BBFC: Certificate AA, 25 July 1972
Distributed by: LMG Film Distributors, December
1972 (Premiere at The Carlton, Haymarket,
7/12/72)
Running Time: 95 minutes
Colour

AKA: The Exorcism of Hugh

Directed by: Fred Burnley. Produced by: Jack Smith
and Peter Fetterman. Executive Producers: **Tony
Tenser** and Peter J. Thompson. Director of
Photography: David Muir. Film Editor: Norman
Wanstall. Art Director: Michael Bastow. Camera
Operator: John Crawfors. Production Manager: John
Peverall. Location Manager: Jilda Smith. Assistant
Director: Derek Whitehurst. Sound Recordist: Ron
Barron. Sound Editor: Mike Le Mare. Dubbing
Mixer: Maurice Askew. Continuity: Penny Daniels.
Focus Puller: Bob Smith. Stillsman: Norman
Gryspeerdt. Make-up: John O'Gorman. Hairdresser:
Pat McDermott. Wardrobe Mistress: Rita Wakely.
Production Accountant: Michael Brent. Production
Secretary: Beryl Harvey. Assistant Editor: Richard
Trevor. Supervising Electrician: Ted Hallows.
Chargehand Propertyman: Wally Hocking. Standby
Propertyman: Brian Lofthouse. Music composed and
conducted by: Nachum Heiman. Based on the novel
"Neither the Sea Nor the Sand" by: Gordon
Honeycombe. Screenplay by: Gordon Honeycombe.
Additional dialogue by: Rosemary Davies

cast: Susan Hampshire (Anna Robinson), Frank
Finlay (George Dabernon), Michael Petrovitch (Hugh
Dabernon), Michael Craze (Collie), Jack Lambert (Dr.
Irving), Betty Duncan (Mrs. MacKay), David Garth
(Mr. MacKay), Tony [Anthony] Booth (Delamare)

1972 THE CREEPING FLESH

An LMG World Film Services Production.
© World Film Services Limited
Filmed at: Shepperton Studios, 17/1/72
BBFC: Certificate X, 7 June 1972
Distributed by: Tigon Film Distributors, February 1973
Running Time: 92 minutes
Colour

Director: Freddie Francis. Producer: Michael Redbourn. Executive Producers: Norman Priggen, **Tony Tenser**. Production Supervisor: Geoffrey Haine. Art Director: George Provis. Editor: Oswald Hafenrichter. Assistant Director: Peter Saunders. Camera Operator: John Harris. Continuity: Pamela Davies. Sound Recordists: Norman Bolland, Nolan Roberts. Dubbing Editor: Colin Miller. Set Dresser: Peter James. Make-Up: Roy Ashton. Hairdresser: Barbara Ritchie. Wardrobe Supervisor: Bridget Sellers. Casting: Anne Donne. Music Composed and Conducted by: Paul Ferris. Director of Photography: Norman Warwick. An Original Screenplay by: Peter Spenceley and Jonathan Rumbold

cast: Christopher Lee (James Hildern), Peter Cushing (Emmanuel Hildern), Lorna Heilbron (Penelope), George Benson (Waterlow), Kenneth J. Warren (Lenny), Duncan Lamont (Inspector), Michael Ripper (Carter), Catherine Finn (Emily), Hedger Wallace (Doctor Perry), Harry Locke (Barman), Robert Swann (Young Aristocrat), David Bailie (Young Doctor), Maurice Bush (Karl), Tony Wright (Sailor), Marianne Stone (Female Assistant), Alexandra Dane (Whore), Jenny Runacre (Emmanuel's Wife), Larry Taylor (1st Warder), Martin Carroll (2nd Warder), Dan Meaden (Lunatic)

1972 FOR THE LOVE OF ADA

An LMG Film Production.
© Tigon British Film Productions Limited
Filmed at: EMI-MGM Elstree Studios and on location in London, 31/1/72
BBFC: Certificate A, 10 July 1972
Distributed by: LMG Film Distributors, August 1972
Running Time: 88 minutes
Colour

Director: Ronnie Baxter. Producer: Peter J. Thompson. Executive Producer: **Tony Tenser**. Production Designer: Bill Palmer. Editor: Anthony Palk. Production Manager: Jack Causey. Assistant Director: John K. Cooper. Art Director: Peter Williams. Camera Operator: Derek Browne. Sound Mixer: Leslie Hammond. Sound Editor: William Trent. Continuity: Doreen Soan.

Make-up: Ernest Gasser. Hairdresser: Joan Carpenter. Wardrobe Supervisor: John Hilling. Construction Manager: Jock Lyall. Director of Photography: Alan Hume. "What Could Be Nicer" written and sung by: Gilbert O'Sullivan. Music composed and arranged by: Frank Barber. Screenplay by: Harry Driver, Vince Powell.

cast: Irene Handl (Ada Bingley), Wilfred Pickles (Walter Bingley), Barbara Mitchell (Ruth Pollitt), Jack Smethurst (Leslie Pollitt), Arthur English (Arthur), Larry Martyn (Brian), Hilda Braid (Mrs. Armitage), Andria [Andrea] Lawrence (Sandra), David Collings (Mr. Johnson), Nancy Nevinson (Elsie Lockwood), Donald Bisset (Mr. Chapman), Duggie Brown (Duggie), Rose Power (First Mourner), Johnny Wade (Alan), John Boxer (Vicar), Arthur White (Hospital Porter), Norman Atkyns (Charlie Nugent), Gareth Hunt (Policeman), Veronica Doran (Carol), Rose Hill (Third Mourner), Winifred Sabine (Winnie), Jean Marlowe (Second Mourner), Brian Tully (Fourth Mourner), Joan Scott (Hospital Sister), Colin Cunningham (Colin), Winifred Braemar (Pensioner), Betty Hare (Pensioner), Cecily Hullett (Mrs. Skinner), Nicholas Ram (Anthony Pollitt), Patsy Kensit (Little Girl) [uncredited]

1972   **NOT NOW DARLING**

L.M.G./Sedgemoor Productions in association with Not Now Films Limited present. ©
L.M.G./Sedgemoor
Filmed at: EMI-MGM Elstree Studios
BBFC: Certificate AA, 8 December 1972 (later re-classified 'A' after cuts)
Distributed by: LMG Film Distributors, July 1973
Running Time: 93 minutes
Colour

Directed by: David Croft and Ray Cooney. Produced by: Peter J. Thompson and Martin C. Schute. Executive Producers: **Tony Tenser** and Marvin Liebman. Screenplay by: John Chapman. Based on the Stageplay by: Ray Cooney and John Chapman. Produced on the London stage by: Michael Codron. Production Manager: Brian Burgess. Assistant Director: Christopher Toyne. Production Assistant: Mary Ellis. Vision Mixer: Jennifer Menmuir. Chief Camera Operator: Andrew Tyler. Sound Editor: Jim Roddan. Sound Mixer: Don Warren. Make-up: Stella

Morris. Hairdressing: Colin Jamison. Wardrobe: Eileen Sullivan. Art Director: Michael Bastow. Editor: Peter Thornton. Production Executive: Robert Lynn. Lighting Director: John Rook. Music Composed and Conducted by: Cyril Ornadel. Lyrics for 'Not Now Darling' by: Norman Newell. Sung by: Vicki Brown. Director of Photography: Alan Hume [uncredited]

cast: Leslie Phillips (Gilbert Bodley), Julie Ege (Janie McMichael), Bill Fraser (Commissionaire), Moira Lister (Maude Bodley), Derren Nesbitt (Harry McMichael), Joan Sims (Miss Tipdale), Barbara Windsor (Sue Lawson), Jack Hulbert (Commander Frencham), Cicely Courtneidge (Mrs. Frencham), Ray Cooney (Arnold Crouch), Jackie Pallo (Mr. Lawson), Trudi van Doorn (Miss Whittington), Graham Stark (Window Cleaner) [uncredited], Peter Butterworth (Window Cleaner) [uncredited]

1974   **FRIGHTMARE**

Peter Walker (Heritage) Ltd.
Filmed at: On location in London and Haslemere
BBFC: Certificate X, 30 September 1974
Distributed by: Miracle Films, December 1974
Running Time: 86 minutes
Colour

AKA: *Covered in Blood*, *Nightmare Farm* (shooting titles)

Produced and Directed by: Pete Walker. Executive Producer: **Tony Tenser**. Music Composed and Conducted by: Stanley Myers. Screenplay by: David McGillivray. From an original story by: Pete Walker. Photographed by: Peter Jessop. Camera Operator: Peter Sinclair. Sound Recordist: Peter O'Connor. 1st Assistant Director: Brian Lawrence. 2nd Assistant Director: James Hamilton. Follow Focus: John Metcalfe. Boom Operator: Robert Edwards. Gaffer: Jim Davis. Production Secretary: Leigh Taylor. Dubbing Mixer: Tony Anscombe. Production Manager: Robert Fennell. Make-Up Supervision: George Partleton. Edited by: Robert Dearberg. Post Production Supervision: Matt McCarthy. Art Direction: Chris Burke

cast: Rupert Davies (Edmund Yates), Sheila Keith (Dorothy Yates), Deborah Fairfax (Jackie), Paul Greenwood (Graham), Kim Butcher (Debbie), Fiona Curzon (Merle), Jon Yule (Robin), Tricia [Trisha] Mortimer (Lillian), Pamela Farbrother (Delia), Edward Kalinski (Alec), Victor Winding (Detective Inspector), Anthony Hennessey (Detective Sergeant), Noel Johnson (The Judge), Michael Sharvell-Martin (Barman), Tommy Wright (Nightclub Manager), Andrew Sachs (Barry Nichols), Nicholas John (Pete), Jack Dagmar (Old Man), Leo Genn (Dr Lytell), Gerald Flood (Matthew Laurence), Sue Shaper (Female Guest), Martin Taylor (Male Guest) [uncredited], Bill Barnsley (Patrolman) [uncredited], L.W. Clarke (Patrolman) [uncredited], Donald Stratford (Actor) [uncredited], Beryl Nesbit (Actress) [uncredited], Jim Bowdell (Bike youth) [uncredited], Veronica Griffiths (1st Bike Girl) [uncredited], Deena Martyn (2nd Bike Girl) [uncredited], David McGillivray (Young Doctor) [uncredited], Pete Walker (Voice of Mr. Brunskill) [uncredited]

Censorship of Tony Tenser Productions: BBFC Cuts

- (Appendix compiled by Francis Brewster)

Tony Tenser's friendship and close working relationship with John Trevelyan, the secretary of the BBFC (British Board of Film Censors as it was then called, though it was later renamed the British Board of Film Classification) is well documented. Despite the fact that all of Tenser's 37 film productions were made under some form of guidance from Trevelyan (either as censor in residence, or as a business colleague after he left the BBFC), it is a sign of the censorious times in which Tenser worked that 24 of the 37 titles were still cut. This appendix reproduces the official BBFC records relating to the 24 films that required some sort of trimming before they were granted official BBFC sanction for theatrical release. These details are reproduced with the kind permission of the BBFC, who graciously allowed us access to their archives.

Naked As Nature Intended
Reel 5
Remove all shots of girls on beach when they are seen, front view, naked or virtually naked, full length.
Remove shot of Pamela posing on the edge of the water, with a filmy scarf in her hair.
Reel 6
Remove all shots of girls, both before and during the game with a ball, when they are seen naked frontview, full length.

That Kind of Girl
Reel 1
In striptease number, remove all shots in which girl's breast is visible.
Reel 3
Remove shot of boy kissing girl between breasts.
Remove shot of boy lying on top of girl on chaise longue.
Shorten scenes of boy and girl making love on bed, in particular concluding scene when he is naked.

The Yellow Teddybears
D.Reel 1(a)
The rhyme recited by Kinky must be either removed or replaced by something less censorable.
D.Reel 2(a)
Remove all shots where girls' bare bodies are practically seen through the window of the swimming-pool.
D.Reels 2(b) and 3(c)
Very considerably reduce the party scenes. The effect given should be no more than that there is a some drinking and leching.
D.Reel 4(a)
Reduce to a minimum the episode in which Livi's father finds her at the brothel.
Remove "He's a jockey - a ride for a ride" and "Get stuffed".

London in the Raw
Reel 1
In sequence in which prostitute entices man to her room, remove all shots in the room after the woman puts money in her blouse.
Remove whole sequence in which men watch women in static poses on a stage.
Reel 2
Shorten the sequence in which beatniks paint a half-naked model.
Shorten the sequence in the Paint Box Club, and in particular remove all close shots of the two models.
Reel 4
Remove entire sequence in Pink Elephant Club in which female impersonator appears.
Reel 5
In Venus Room, there must be a considerable reduction of shots of nude or semi-nude women. In particular close shots should be removed and also the final long shots of the woman on the stage.
In the montage at the end, remove all close shots of naked or semi-naked nude women and of the female impersonator.

The Black Torment
Reel 1
Remove all shots (in the pre-credit sequence) from the moment the man first stretches out his hand towards his victim.

Primitive London
Reel 1
Reduce to a minimum the episode of the birth of a baby, and remove all close shots of the baby covered in blood.
Reel 3
Remove the whole episode in which girls show off topless dresses and swimsuits.
Reel 4
Remove the end of the Casino de Paris strip-tease, stopping before the man removes the girl's bra and G-string. Remove the later shot of this stripped girl (see after the fan dance.)
Reel 5
Remove 'Screw one of their girls.'

Reel 6
Remove all but the beginning and the end of Jack the Ripper episode and all shots of the strangler of the six 'nudes,' including re-constructions and commentary.
Reel 7
Remove the whole dance of a girl in leopard-skin trousers and all shots of girls in cages.
Remove the whole strip of Lesley Glory.
Reel 8
Remove all shots of stripper when she is seen on a chair or rises from it.
Reel 9
Stop the Audrey Crane strip before she removes bra and G-string.
Remove the episode of a man and a woman going upstairs, of her entering the bedroom and starting to undress, and of the man's looking into a child's room.

The Pleasure Girls
Reel 2B
The love-scene between Prinny and Marion should stop after the first kiss on the bed, this scene should be removed when they are discussing the pregnancy and possible abortion, but the end of the love-scene should be removed.
Reel 3A
Darken the shot of Dee getting off the bed nearly naked, and remove the final shots of the couple on the bed.
Reel 4A
Remove shots of the nude model and of the girl when her scarf falls off her breast.
Reel 4B
Shorten the beating up of Nicolai.

A Study in Terror
Reel 1
Considerably shorten the episode in which a woman is murdered in a horse-trough; especially remove the first flurry of blood staining the water and reduce the shots that suggest repeated stabbing.
Considerably shorten the sight and sound of the struggle which ends in the death of the third prostitute (who wears a red dress and bonnet.)

Witchfinder General
Double Reel 2
Substantially reduce the spiking of Lowes in the back, and reduce his screams.
Remove the whole episode of a woman being hit and half-strangled in a cell; there should be no shot of her at all.
Double Reel 3
Reduce the ducking of the parson and two women.
Reduce to a minimum the burning of Elizabeth Clark, including shots of her being dragged to the gibbet: there should be only a distant shot of her in the flames.
Double Reel 5
Reduce the episode of Sara being tortured with a spike and screaming.
Substantially reduce the shots of Richard chopping up Matthew with an axe.

Curse of the Crimson Altar
Reel 1
Remove whole scene of the flagellation, including all shots of woman wielding a whip.

Love in Our Time
Double Reel 3
Remove all shots of John fondling Tina's bare breasts.
Double Reel 4
Remove all shots of man baring girl's breasts.
Remove all shots of girls' bare breasts when they are dressing.
Double Reel 5
Stop the bed-scene between couple before the girl gets off the bed, naked; resume when she is fully dresed.

What's Good for the Goose

Cuts for an 'A':
Reel 5
Remove shots of Nikki putting her hand inside Bartlett's shirt, and shots of his reaction to this.
Reel 6
The bedroom scene between Bartlett and Nikki must be reduced from the point where he comes out from behind a chair, with a towel over the lower half of his body.
Reel 9
Remove shots of Nikki in the bath, where her bare breasts are visible.
Reduce shots of half-naked hippies lying about a room and necking.
Reduce to a minimum the episode in which Bartlett finds Nikki in bed with a youth.

Cuts for a 'U':
Double Reel 2
Remove the whole incident of a man asking a hotel porter for the address of a woman and being given it.
Double Reel 5
Remove all shots of Bartlett and Nikki in bed together.
Remove all shots of Nikki in the bath when her breasts are visible.
Reduce the shots of half-naked hippies necking on the floor.
Remove the shots of Bartlett opening a bedroom door and seeing Nikki in bed with a youth.
Double Reel 6
Remove the shots of Bartlett taking off his towel and advancing on his wife who is in bed.

(NOTE: The original version of this film was cut for the 'A' Category in February 1969. The Production Company subsequently made a number of cuts with a view to securing a 'U' Certificate. The cuts listed above are additional to those made by the Company).

Zeta One
Reel 2
Remove sequences where James is seen in bed with two naked girls.
Reel 3
Remove all shots where naked girls are seen chained to the walls of the torture chamber.

Reels 3 and 4
Remove all shots of Zara being tortured and of her being strapped to the machine.
Reel 5
Remove the whole of the final sequence (i.e. of James being tended by girls in Angvia) after Ann and James are seen in bed together.

The Body Stealers
Reel 3
Remove shot of Lorna's naked breast as she removes her dress, and the ensuing medium close shot of her approaching the sea: (the longer shot as she enters the sea can be allowed).
Reel 4
Remove the whole of the love scene between Bob and Lorna from the point where he removes his shirt.

1917
Reel 2
Reduce shots and sounds of couple making love.

Monique
Double Reel 1
Considerably shorten the scene in which Jean and Bill make love.
Substantially reduce the scene in which Jean and Bill make love.
Double Reel 3
Substantially reduce the scene in which Bill makes love to Monique.
Double Reel 4
Substantially reduce the scene in which Bill makes love to Jean.
Double Reel 5
Reduce the shots of Jean and Monique naked together.
Remove all shots of the two girls making love, naked, with Bill watching them.

The Beast in the Cellar
Double Reel 2
Remove the shots of a man pulling off a girl's panties and of her undoing his trouser buttons; shorten the episode in which blood falls on to their bare bodies.

Blood on Satan's Claw
Double Reel 3
In the scene in which Cathy is raped and stabbed, remove the element of rape, and reduce the stabbing to a minimum.
Double Reel 5
Shorten the scene in which a naked girl writhes in front of a boy and he fingers a knife whilst looking at her.

For the Love of Ada
Reel 3
Remove all shots of the box in which the name "Durex" is visible, with accompanying dialogue.

Miss Julie
Reel 5
Remove the incident of Miss Julie removing her culotte and wiping her crotch with it.

Neither the Sea Nor the Sand
Reel 2
The love-making between Hugh and Anna must be removed, leaving only a shot of them lying on the bed afterwards, with the line: "Why can't all days be like this?"

The Creeping Flesh
Reel 7
Remove the shot of the dead sailor's body with its throat slashed by a broken bottle.

Not Now Darling
Reel 1
Remove shot of girl's breast popping out of her dress.
Remove complete sequence of Janie in bath showing her breasts and pubic hair.
Remove complete double-entendre dialogue spoken by Mrs. Frencham, reference her husband's car.
Remove dialogue: "Shall I take them down for you?" "Not now, later."
Reel 2
Remove dialogue: "Sometimes he pulls it out without any warning."
Reduce tits dialogue generally in this and other reels.
Reel 3
Remove shots of Janie standing bare-breasted on balcony and screaming.
Reel 4
Remove dialogue: "It's beginning to droop." "Put it in, couldn't get it out - not very good doing it backwards," etc.
Remove shot of Janie's bare breasts as she stands in closet as Arnold takes off her coat.
Reel 5
Remove dialogue: "From stuff to stuffing in one hour."
Reel 6
Remove shots of Janie standing bare-breasted on balcony and screaming.
Remove dialogue: "Where's my wife's tits?" "Opposite her blooming shoulder blades."
Remove close shots of Janie's bare bottom as Bodley checks the bottom of her dress.
Remove shot of girl's bare breasts after she has removed her bra.

Frightmare
Reel 3
In the sequence in which Dorothy kills a girl with a red hot poker, remove the shot of blood pouring from the girl's mouth.
Reel 4
Reduce the scene in which Dorothy kills a boy by stabbing him again and again in the face with a pitchfork to two blows.
Reel 5
Reduce the shot of Graham's bloody, dead face to a flash shot only.

COMPTON - CAMEO FILMS Present

ESTELLA BLAIN   AND   HAROLD KAY   IN

"ADULTERY AT NIGHT" A

COMPTON FILMS present

"GHOST of DRAGSTRIP HOLLOW" (A)

Featuring THE HOT-ROD GANG

Tony Tenser as a Film Distributor

- (Appendix compiled by Francis Brewster, Julian Grainger and John Hamilton)

In many ways Tenser's role as a distributor is more representative of his contribution to British cinema than as a producer, and this appendix is the first time this contribution has been documented. Ignoring the films that were shown in the Compton and other private cinema clubs run by Tony Tenser, these are the films distributed by the companies he ran. It is worth bearing in mind that Compton, Tigon and LMG all continued to distribute films after Tenser had left; Tigon in particular enjoyed considerable success up until the mid-1980s, virtually a decade after Tenser formally quit the film business. Indeed the company is still in existence today, managing rights to many of the films made and owned by Tenser. Many of the films listed were purchased while Tenser was still in charge, and some were not, but for the sake of completeness this appendix includes all the films released by the companies with which Tenser was associated, regardless of whether he was actively involved at the time of release. For details of Tenser's tenure at the companies please see the relevant chapters.

The date gives the year of release, not the year of production, which in the case of some of the more obscure foreign language movies can be markedly different. The first title is the British release title. A title following in parentheses is the original title. Titles in bold indicate a production credit for Tenser.

Apart from problems due to human error and inconsistent records, any filmography of 1960s exploitation movies is complicated by three factors:
- Firstly, a lot of these films were imported and therefore subject to many and varied title changes before they reached the screen.
- Secondly, the short term nature of the film distribution companies themselves means that rights to particular films changed hands with disturbing frequency, often before initial release had taken place. Compton in particular acquired the rights to a number of films which they never released, such as *The Rape of the Sabine Women* (*Il ratto delle sabine*), which was picked up by Regal, and *The Trip*, which was submitted to the BBFC but refused classification.
- Thirdly, and this is unique to Tenser, the ever present Compton Cinema Club and its voracious appetite for obscure titles complicates the issue. The Club was particularly active at seeking out and showing imported films which would have otherwise been denied a release in the UK. The films screened there ranged from Leslie Stevens's *Private Property* - the film that opened the Club - to the likes of Belinda Lee in *The Wild and the Wanton*, and *The Girls of Spider Island*, subtly billed as 'Six Girls, One Man, Marooned!' Other titles included *The Joyhouse of Yokohama*, *Nymphettes*, and Olle Hellbom's *Black Jackets*. Some better known films, such as Samuel Fuller's *Shock Corridor* and Roger Corman's *The Wild Angels*, were shown at the Compton Club and later, as tastes changed, awarded a certificate allowing wide distribution - frequently with distributors other than Compton.

COMPTON

1961 The Adventures of Remi (Sans famille) France, Italy André Michel
1961 The Captive (Vacances en enfer) France Jean Kerchbron
1961 A Taste of Love (Les grandes personnes) France, Italy Jean Valère
1961 The Day the Sky Fell In UK Barry Shawzin
1961 The Tower of Lust (La tour de Nesle) France, Italy Abel Gance
1961 One More River UK John Brason
1961 Stranger in the City UK Robert Hartford-Davis
1961 Assassins in the Sun (Assassinos) Brazil Carlos Hugo Christensen
1961 The Call Girl Business (Anonima cocottes) Italy, France Camillo Mastrocinque
1961 The Pavements of Paris (Le pavé de Paris) France, Italy Henri Decoin
1961 Ghost of Dragstrip Hollow USA William J. Hole Jr.
1961 Missile to the Moon USA Richard E. Cunha
1961 The Damned and the Daring (Les loups dans la bergerie) France Hervé Bromberger
1961 Paris Playgirls (Svenska flickor i Paris) Sweden Barbro Boman
1961 The Harlem Jazz Festival USA Joseph Kohn

1961 **Naked - As Nature Intended** UK George Harrison Marks
1961 Mam'selle Striptease (En effeuillant la marguerite) France Marc Allégret
1961 Blonde for Danger (Sois belle et tais-toi) France Marc Allégret
1962 Lola France, Italy Jacques Demy
1962 The Ninth Circle (Deviti krug) Yugoslavia France Stiglic
1962 A Day of Sin (La giornata balorda) Italy, France Mauro Bolognini
1962 Fires on the Plain (Nobi) Japan Kon Ichikawa
1962 Last Year in Marienbad (L'année dernière à Marienbad) France, Italy Alain Resnais
1962 Paris Vice Patrol (Brigade des moeurs) France Maurice Boutel
1962 The Light Across the Street (La lumière d'en face) France Georges Lacombe
1962 The Big Girl (Les frangines) France Jean Gourguet
1962 The Last Goal (Két félidö a pokolban) Hungary Zoltán Fábri
1962 Adultery At Night (Colère froide) France André Haguet
1962 The Girl with the Golden Eyes (La fille aux yeux d'or) France Jean-Gabriel Albicocco

1962 Dens of Evil (Dossier 1413) France Alfred Rode

1962 Girls Led Astray (Détournement de mineures) France Walter Kapps

1962 Girl on the Road (Les petits matins) France Jacqueline Audry

1962 The Wayward Girl (Ung flukt) Norway Edith Carlmar

1962 The Lonely One (Diferente) Spain Luis Maria Delgado

1962 Diary of a Nudist USA Doris Wishman

1962 Preludes to Ecstasy (Kuu on vaarallinen) Finland Toivo Särkkä

1962 Blood of the Warriors (La schiava di Roma) Italy Sergio Grieco

1962 My Bare Lady UK Arthur Knight

1962 The Nude Ones (Corsica) Switzerland Werner Kunz

1962 Women By Night (La donna di notte) Italy Mino Loy

1963 Vengeance of the Gladiators (Solo contro Roma) Italy Luciano Ricci

1963 The Wrestling Game UK Gerry Levy

1963 Chris Barber Bandstand UK Giorgio Gomelsky

1963 The White Slavers (La prostitution) France Maurice Boutel

1963 **That Kind of Girl** UK Gerry O'Hara

1963 Samson (Sansone) Italy Gianfranco Parolini

1963 Fury of the Wastelands (Cimborák) Hungary István Homoki-Nagy

1963 Goliath Against the Giants (Goliath contro i giganti) Italy, Spain Guido Malatesta

COMPTON—CAMEO FILMS presents

The Great New Double of Top Entertainment!

ROLAND CAREY in | FRANK LATIMORE in

'THE SWORD OF EL CID' (U) | 'THE SHADOW OF ZORRO' (U)

ALL COLOUR! ALL SCOPE!... FABULOUS!!

COMPTON—CAMEO FILMS LTD
60-62 OLD COMPTON STREET, LONDON, W 1.   Telephone: REGent 7521 (10 lines)
BRANCHES THROUGHOUT THE UNITED KINGDOM

1963 Fury of the Vikings (Gli invasori) Italy, France Mario Bava

1963 The Devil and the Ten Commandments (Le diable et les dix commandements) France, Italy Julien Duvivier

1963 Rome in Flames (Il crollo di Roma) Italy Antonio Margheriti

1963 Satan Leads the Dance (Et Satan conduit le bal) France Grisha M. Dabat

1963 The Girl with the Suitcase (La ragazza con la valigia) Italy, France Valerio Zurlini

1963 **The Yellow Teddybears** UK Robert Hartford-Davis

1963 Career Girl USA Harold David

1963 The Giants of Thessaly (I Giganti della Tessaglia) Italy, France Riccardo Freda

1963 Suleiman the Conqueror (Solimano, il conquistatore) Italy, Yugoslavia Mario Tota, Vatroslav Mimica

COMPTON—CAMEO FILMS presents ROSSANA PODESTA · GUY MADISON
BLOOD *of the* **WARRIORS** (A)
in EASTMAN COLOUR   TOTALSCOPE

1963 Operation Camel (Soldaterkammerater på vagt) Denmark Sven Methling Jr.

1963 The Terror of Dr. Hichcock (L'orribile segreto del Dr. Hichcock) Italy Riccardo Freda

1963 The Sword of El Cid (La spada del Cid) Italy, Spain Ferdinando Baldi, Miguel Iglesias

1963 The Shadow of Zorro (L'ombra di Zorro) Italy, Spain, France Joaquín Luis Romero Marchent

1963 Invasion of the Normans (I Normanni) Italy, France Giuseppe Vari

1964 The Big Risk (Classe tous risques) France, Italy Claude Sautet

1964 The Castle of Terror (La vergine di Norimberga) Italy Antonio Margheriti

1964 **Saturday Night Out** UK Robert Hartford-Davis

1964 The Spectre (Lo spettro) Italy Riccardo Freda

1964 Horror Italy, Spain Alberto De Martino

1964 Colossus of the Stone Age (Maciste contro i mostri) Italy Guido Malatesta

1964 Where Has Poor Mickey Gone? UK Gerry Levy

1964 I Married a Werewolf (Lycanthropus) Italy, Austria Paolo Heusch

1964 Monster from an Unknown World (Maciste nella terra dei Ciclopi) Italy Antonio Leonviola

1964 The Flying Scot (The Mailbag Robbery) UK Compton Bennett

1964 Ulysses Against Hercules (Ulisse contro Ercole) Italy, France Mario Caiano

1964 Five Guns West USA Roger Corman

1964 War of the Trojans (La leggenda di Enea) Italy, France Giorgio Rivalta

1964 The Chimney Sweeps UK Dudley Birch

1964 Blood of the Executioner (Il boia di Venezia) Italy Luigi Capuano

1964 **London in the Raw** UK Arnold Louis Miller

1964 The Demon (Il demonio) Italy, France Brunello Rondi

1964 **The Black Torment** UK Robert Hartford-Davis

1964 Trauma USA Robert M. Young

1964 The Cool World USA Shirley Clarke

1964 Nude Las Vegas (Bunny Yeager's Nude Las Vegas) USA Barry Mahon

1965 Hollywood Nudes Report USA Barry Mahon

1965 She Should Have Stayed in Bed USA Barry Mahon

1965 With Fire and Sword (Col ferro e col fuoco) Italy, France, Yugoslavia Fernando Cerchio

1965 Goliath, King of the Slaves (L'eroe di Babilonia) Italy, France Siro Marcellini

1965 Tiger of Terror (Sandokan alla riscossa) Italy, West Germany Luigi Capuano

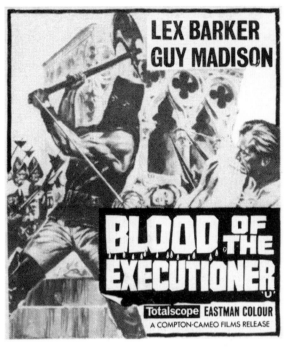

1965 **Primitive London** UK Arnold Louis Miller

1965 The Case of the 44's UK, Denmark Tom McGowan

1965 Runaway Killer (Runaway) New Zealand John O'Shea

1965 Nude in Charcoal USA Philip A. Melilla

1965 Ride and Kill (Cavalca e uccidi) Italy, Spain José Luis Borau

1965 Hercules Attacks! (Ercole contro Moloch) Italy, France Giorgio Ferroni

1965 The Magnificent Three (Tres hombres buenos) Spain, Italy Joaquín Luis Romero Marchent

1965 **The Pleasure Girls** UK Gerry O'Hara

1965 **Repulsion** UK Roman Polanski

1965 Go! Go! Go! World (Il pelo nel mondo) Italy Antonio Margheriti, Marco Vicario

1965 Duel at Rio Bravo (Desafío en Río Bravo) Spain, France, Italy Tulio Demicheli

1965 The Naked Hours (Le ore nude) Italy Marco Vicario

1965 **A Study in Terror** UK James Hill

1965 Midsummer Night in Sweden (Mittsommernacht in Schweden) Switzerland Werner Kunz

1965 Nudes on Tiger Reef USA Barry Mahon

1966 The Adventures of Scaramouche (La máscara de Scaramouche) Spain, Italy, France Antonio Isasi-Isasmendi

1966 Gunfight at High Noon (El sabor de la venganza) Spain, Italy Joaquín Luis Romero Marchent

1966 The Return of Sandokan (Sandokan contro il Leopardo di Sarawak) Italy, West Germany Luigi Capuano

1966 Damaged Goods (V.D.) USA Haile Chace

1966 **Secrets of a Windmill Girl** UK Arnold Louis Miller

1966 Mission Bloody Mary (Agente 077: missione Bloody Mary) Italy, Spain, France Sergio Grieco

1966 **Cul-de-Sac** UK Roman Polanski

1966 Seven Hours of Gunfire (Aventuras del Oeste) Spain, Italy, West Germany Joaquín Luis Romero Marchent

1966 Temple of the White Elephant (Sandok, il Maciste della giungla) Italy, France Umberto Lenzi
1966 Arrow of the Avenger (Goliath e la schiava ribelle) Italy, France Mario Caiano
1966 **The Projected Man** UK Ian Curteis
1966 Passport to Hell (Agente 3S3: passaporto per l'inferno) Italy, France, Spain Sergio Sollima
1966 I Am a Fugitive from a White Slave Gang (La traite des blanches) France, Italy Georges Combret
1966 Greenwich Village Story USA Jack O'Connell
1966 A Look at the Isle of Levant (Lockender Süden) Switzerland Werner Kunz
1967 From the Orient with Fury (Agente 077: dall'Oriente con furore) Italy, France, Spain Sergio Grieco
1967 Castle of Evil USA Francis D. Lyon
1967 Minnesota Clay Italy, Spain, France Sergio Corbucci
1967 Invasion of the Body Snatchers USA Don Siegel
1967 Circus of Horrors UK Sidney Hayers
1967 Pit and the Pendulum USA Roger Corman
1967 Horrors of the Black Museum UK Arthur Crabtree
1967 The Premature Burial USA Roger Corman
1967 Once Upon a Child UK John Morris
1967 Women of the Prehistoric Planet USA Arthur C. Pierce
1967 Monsters of the Night (The Navy Vs. the Night Monsters) USA Michael A. Hoey
1966 Brendan Behan's Dublin Ireland Norman Cohen

1967 So This Is God's Country? (America, paese di Dio) Italy Luigi Vanzi
1967 The Gospel According to St. Matthew (Il Vangelo secondo Matteo) Italy, France Pier Paolo Pasolini
1967 The Extravaganza of Golgotha Smuts UK Andrew Holmes
1968 I, a Woman (Jeg - en kvinde) Denmark, Sweden Mac Ahlberg
1968 Relax, Freddy (Slap af, Frede!) Denmark Erik Balling
1968 Strike First Freddy (Slå først, Frede) Denmark Erik Balling
1968 Fantomas Strikes Back (Fantômas se déchaîne) France, Italy André Hunebelle
1968 Marine Battleground (Toraoji annun haebyong) South Korea, USA Lee Man-hee
1968 Hell in the Pacific USA Ralph Shaker (producer)
1968 The Teacher Nansen (Timelærer Nansen) Denmark Kirsten Stenbæk
1968 Stay in the Marshland (Uppehåll i myrlandet) Sweden Jan Troell
1968 Warkill USA, Philippines Ferde Grofé Jr
1969 Nightmare (Nattmara) Sweden Arne Mattsson
1969 Seven from Texas (I sette del Texas) Italy, Spain Joaquín Luis Romero Marchent
1969 Two Gunmen (Los rurales de Texas) Spain, Italy Primo Zeglio
1969 The Fighting Legions (I diavoli di Spartivento) Italy, France Leopoldo Savona

TONY TENSER

1967 Twice Told Tales USA Sidney Salkow
1967 Lost Sex (Honno) Japan Kaneto Shindo
1967 Tower of London USA Roger Corman
1967 Carnival of Souls USA Herk Harvey
1967 G.G. Passion UK David Bailey
1967 The Devil's Hand USA William J. Hole Jr

LMG

1972 **For the Love of Ada** UK Ronnie Baxter
1972 You Can't Run Away from Sex (The Runaway) USA Bickford Otis Webber
1972 **Miss Julie** UK Robin Phillips, John Glenister
1972 **Neither the Sea Nor the Sand** UK Fred Burnley
1973 The Bubble USA Arch Oboler
1973 I Love You Rosa (Ani Ohev Otach Rosa) Israel Moshe Mizrahi
1972 The Legendary Champions USA Harry Chapin
1972 The World's Heavyweight Championship Fight (Cassius Clay Vs. Sonny Liston) USA
1973 **Not Now Darling** UK David Croft, Ray Cooney
1973 Sunlight on Cold Water (Un peu de soleil dans l'eau froide) France, Italy Jacques Deray
1973 The Sex Thief UK Martin Campbell
1973 Hellé France Roger Vadim
1973 Stork Australia Tim Burstall
1973 King, Queen, Knave (Herzbube) West Germany, USA Jerzy Skolimowski
1974 Jailbreak in Hamburg (Fluchtweg St. Pauli - Großalarm für die Davidswache) West Germany Wolfgang Staudte
1974 B.G. Remembers (Ben Gurion Zoher) Israel Simon Hesera
1974 The Stewardesses USA Alf Silliman Jr.
1974 The Girl from Hong Kong (Das Mädchen von Hongkong) West Germany, France Jürgen Roland
1974 The Black Hand (La mano nera) Italy Antonio Racioppi

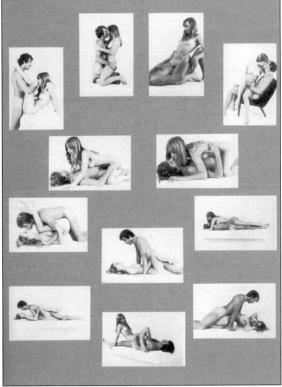

Love Variations

TIGON

1967 **Mini Weekend** UK Georges Robin
1967 Ride the Wind USA William Witney
1967 **The Sorcerers** UK Michael Reeves
1967 Giant Killer (Jack the Giant Killer) USA Nathan Juran
1968 Castle of the Living Dead (Il castello dei morti vivi) Italy, France Luciano Ricci, Lorenzo Sabatini
1968 Five Ashore in Singapore (Cinq gars pour Singapour) France, Italy Bernard Toublanc-Michel
1968 **The Blood Beast Terror** UK Vernon Sewell
1968 **Witchfinder General** UK Michael Reeves
1968 Terror-Creatures from the Grave (5 tombe per un medium) Italy, USA Massimo Pupillo
1968 **Curse of the Crimson Altar** UK Vernon Sewell
1968 **Love in Our Time** UK Elkan Allan
1969 **What's Good for the Goose** UK Menahem Golan
1969 **The Body Stealers** UK Gerry Levy
1969 Mission Mars USA Nicholas Webster
1969 Clegg UK Lindsay Shonteff
1969 **The Haunted House of Horror** UK Michael Armstrong
1970 Four Rode Out USA, Spain John Peyser
1970 Snow Treasure USA Irving Jacoby
1970 The Candy Man USA Herbert J. Leder
1970 Sandy the Seal UK Robert Lynn
1970 **1917** UK Stephen Weeks
1970 More Luxembourg, France Barbet Schroeder
1970 Kama Sutra (Kamasutra - Vollendung der Liebe) West Germany Kobi Jaeger
1970 **Zeta One** UK Michael Cort
1970 **Monique** UK John Bown
1970 The Last Day of the War (El ultimo dia de la guerra) Spain, Italy, USA Juan Antonio Bardem
1970 Britain at Expo '70 UK Martin Rolfe, Ken Goddard
1970 Simon Simon UK Graham Stark
1970 Labyrinth of Sex (Nel labirinto del sesso) Italy Alfonso Brescia
1970 Love Variations UK Terry Gould
1970 Inga - I Have Lust (Jag - en oskuld) Sweden, USA Joseph W. Sarno
1970 Permissive UK Lindsay Shonteff
1971 **Blood on Satan's Claw** (Satan's Skin) UK Piers Haggard
1971 Cauldron of Blood (El coleccionista de cadáveres) Spain, USA Santos Alcocer, Edward Mann
1971 **Black Beauty** UK, W.Germany, Spain James Hill
1971 **The Beast in the Cellar** UK James Kelly
1971 Sex, Love and Marriage UK Terry Gould
1971 **Hannie Caulder** UK Burt Kennedy
1971 Female Animal (La mujer del gato) Spain, Italy Juan Carlo Grinella
1971 **The Magnificent Seven Deadly Sins** UK Graham Stark
1972 Virgin Witch UK Ray Austin
1972 **Doomwatch** UK Peter Sasdy
1972 On Any Sunday USA Bruce Brown
1972 The Student Nurses USA Stephanie Rothman
1972 The Seduction of Inga (Någon att älska) Sweden, USA Joseph W. Sarno
1972 Au Pair Girls UK Val Guest
1972 The Longest Hunt (Spara, gringo, spara) Italy Bruno Corbucci
1972 The Flesh and Blood Show UK Pete Walker
1973 Sex in the Office (Erotic im Beruf) West Germany Ernst Hofbauer

PERMISSIVE
MAGGIE STRIDE   GAY SINGLETON   GILBERT WYNNE   FOREVER MORE
Music by FOREVER MORE   COMUS   TITUS GROAN
Produced by JACK SHULTON   Directed by LINDSAY SHONTEFF
RELEASED BY
TIGON PICTURES LTD.

1973 Nathalie After Love (Nathalie après l'amour) Belgium, France Boris Szulzinger
1973 **The Creeping Flesh** UK Freddie Francis
1973 Blood Brides (Un hacha para la luna de miel) Spain, Italy Mario Bava
1973 Frustrated Women (Frustration) France José Bénazéraf
1973 Dagmar's Hot Pants, Inc. (Dagmars Heta Trosor) USA, Sweden Vernon P. Becker
1973 The Wild Damned Girl (Barbara, mia kolasmeni fisi) Greece Pavlos Parashakis
1973 Born Black (Der Verlogene Akt) West Geramny, Italy Rolf von Sydow
1973 Swinging Wives (Der Neue Heisse Report - Was Männer Nicht Für Möglich Halten) West Germany Ernst Hofbauer
1973 The Nude Vampire (La vampire nue) France Jean Rollin
1974 The Love Keys (Rosy und der Herr aus Bonn) West Germany Rolf Theile
1974 A Very Special Stone UK Joe Mendoza
1974 The Magic of Diamonds UK Joe Mendoza
1974 Ballad of Bond Street UK Martin Benson (producer)
1974 The Naughty Stewardesses USA Al Adamson
1975 A Candle for the Devil (Una vela para el diablo) Spain Eugenio Martín
1975 Murder Inferno (Il boss) Italy Fernando Di Leo
1975 Carnal Contract (Contratto carnale) Italy, Ghana Giorgio Bontempi
1975 The Great McGonagall UK Joe McGrath
1975 All I Want Is You... And You... And You... UK Bob Kellett
1975 Last Chance (L'ultima chance) Italy Maurizio Lucidi
1975 Double Agent 73 USA Doris Wishman
1975 Naked Are the Cheaters (The Politicians) USA Derek Ashburne
1975 Submission (Pets) USA Raphael Nussbaum
1975 Confessions of a Sex Maniac UK Alan Birkinshaw
1975 One By One USA Claude DuBoc
1975 The Bit Player (Salut l'artiste) France, Italy Yves Robert
1975 Somebody's Stolen Our Russian Spy (O.K. Yevtushenko) UK José Luis Madrid
1975 The Bruce Lee Story (A Dragon Story) Taiwan, USA Shih Ti
1976 Intimate Games UK Tudor Gates
1976 Finishing School (Gefährlicher Sex Frühreifer Mädchen) West Germany Alois Brummer

1976 Sizzlers (Delinquent School Girls) USA Gregory Corarito
1977 Smash-Up Alley (43: The Petty Story) USA Edward Lakso
1977 Death Has Blue Eyes (To koritsi vomva) Greece Nico Mastorakis
1977 The Violation of Justine (Justine de Sade) France, Italy, Canada Claude Pierson
1977 When Girls Make Love (Schulmädchen-Report 9. Teil: Reifeprüfung vor dem Abitur) West Germany Walter Boos
1977 Innocent Girls Abroad (Die Jungen Ausreisserinnen) West Germany Walter Boos
1977 Look in on Sex (Schlüsselloch-Report) West Germany Walter Boos
1977 Come Play with Me UK George Harrison Marks
1977 Zebra Force USA Joe Tornatore
1977 When Girls Go to Bed (Jagd auf Jungfrauen) West Germany Jochen Wiedermann
1977 The Ups and Downs of Girls on Holiday (Sonne, Sylt und Kesse Krabben) West Germany Jerzy Macc
1977 When Sex Was a Knightly Affair (The Amorous Adventures of Don Quixote and Sancho Panza) USA Raphael Nussbaum
1977 Bed Neighbours (Les petits dessous des grands ensembles) France Christian Chevreuse
1977 Avarice (Episode from "The Magnificent Seven Deadly Sins") UK Graham Stark
1978 Blackboard Massacre (Massacre at Central High) USA Renee Daalder
1978 The Playbirds UK Willy Roe
1978 Oh! Calcutta! USA Jacques Levy
1978 Master of the Flying Guillotine (The One-Armed Boxer Vs. the Flying Guillotine) Hong Kong Jimmy Wang Yu
1978 Death Is Child's Play (¿Quien puede matar a un niño?) Spain Narciso Ibañez Serrador
1978 Landscape UK Peter Hall
1979 Confessions from the David Galaxy Affair UK Willy Roe
1979 Queen of the Blues UK Willy Roe
1979 Emanuelle Meets the Wife Swappers (Liebesmarkt) West Germany Hubert Frank
1979 Lust (Episode from "The Magnificent Seven Deadly Sins") UK Graham Stark
1979 Confessions of the Sex Slaves (Tänzerinnen für Tanger) Switzerland, France Erwin C. Dietrich
1979 Sexual Fantasies (I tvillingernes tegn) Denmark Werner Hedmann
1979 Massage Girls of B'Kok Hong Kong J. Armorn
1979 Kama Sutra Today (Together) USA Sean S. Cunningham
1980 More Danish Blue (Agent 69 Jensen - I skyttens tegn) Denmark Werner Hedmann
1980 The Violation of the Bitch (La visita del vicio) Spain José Ramón Larraz
1980 Rude Boy UK Jack Hazan, David Mingay
1980 Emanuelle Queen Bitch (Mavri Emmanouella) Greece, Cyprus Elia Milonakos
1980 Confessions of a Concubine (Yu T'ang Ch'un) Hong Kong Yang Chun
1980 Love Nest (Im Gasthaus zum Scharfen Hirschen) West Germany Hans Billian
1980 Teenager (Monique et Julie) France Alain Payet
1980 Girls After Midnight (Mädchen Nach Mitternacht) Switzerland Erwin C. Dietrich
1980 Erotic Encounters (I grossi bestioni) Italy, France Jean-Marie Pallardy

1980 Sex with the Stars UK Anwar Kawadri
1980 The Secret Policeman's Ball UK Roger Graef
1980 Desires Within Young Girls USA Richard Kanter
1980 The Alternative Miss World UK Richard Gayor
1980 Come Play with Me 2 (Die Nichten der Frau Oberst) Switzerland Erwin C. Dietrich
1981 Caligula's Hot Nights (Le calde notti di Caligola) Italy Roberto Bianchi Montero
1981 Midnight Blue (For Richer For Poorer) USA Gerard Damiano
1981 Erotic Confessions (Coming Attractions) USA Duncan Starr
1981 Ecstasy Girls (Small Town Girls) USA Tom Janovich
1981 Wrong Way USA Ray Williams
1981 Cherry, Harry & Raquel! USA Russ Meyer
1981 Vixen! USA Russ Meyer
1981 Up! USA Russ Meyer
1981 Emmanuelle in Soho UK David Hughes
1981 Come with Me My Love (Take Time To Smell the Flowers) USA Chris Caras
1981 Love Lust & Ecstasy (Erotiki ekstassi) Greece Elia Milonakos
1981 Love Camp (Der Todesgöttin des Liebescamps) West Germany Christian Anders
1981 Faster, Pussycat! Kill! Kill! USA Russ Meyer
1981 The Red Nights of the Gestapo (Le lunghe notti della Gestapo) Italy Fabio De Agostini
1981 I'm Coming Your Way (Orinoco prigioniere del sesso) Italy, Spain Edoardo Mulargia
1981 Finders Keepers, Lovers Weepers! USA Russ Meyer
1982 Warm Nights Hot Pleasures (Patricia - Einmal Himmel und Zurück) West Germany, Spain, Austria Hubert Frank

1981 Electric Blue the Movie UK Adam Cole (producer)
1982 Mary Millington's World Striptease Extravaganza UK Roy Deverell
1982 Sweet Sexy Savage (Sweet Savage) USA Virginia Ann Perry-Rhine
1982 Erotic Pleasure Girls (Invasion of the Love Drones) USA Jerome Hamlin
1982 Confessions of Lady Blue (Legend of Lady Blue) USA Antonio Fabritzi
1982 Lustful Desires (The Fur Trap) USA David Stitt
1983 Hellcat Mud Wrestlers UK Alan Hall, David Sullivan
1983 Ring of Desire USA Peter Balakoff
1983 Desires of a Nymphomaniac (La frigida y la viciosa) Spain Carlos Aured Alonso
1983 Female Foxy Boxers UK David Sullivan
1985 Sexy Feelings (Feelings) USA Kemal Horulu

Unfilmed Projects
- (Appendix compiled by John Hamilton)

At any given point every successful film company and film producer has a number of projects at various stages of development; in most cases few of these projects make it to the screen. In the case of the larger companies, options are picked up and lapse only to be picked up elsewhere, with smaller companies they generally vanish into the ether and exist only as intriguing 'what ifs'. All of the under noted projects were announced by Tenser during his spells at Compton/Tigon between the period 1963-1972.

COMPTON

1963

'*Theirs Is the Kingdom*'
(Robert Hartford-Davis to direct a large budget WW1 movie based around the battle of the Somme. Written by the Ford brothers.)

'*Bodicea*'
(Historic drama to be directed by Robert Hartford-Davis.)

1964

'*The Teenage Terror*'

'*The Face of Terror*'

'*Bed of Torment*'

'*The Shattered Room*'

'*The Day the Earth Caved In*'
(Science Fiction disaster movie.)

'*I Would Rather Stay Poor*'
Adaptation of James Hadley Chase book of same name.

'*The Loch Ness Monster*'
(Producer/Director Robert Hartford-Davis from a script by the Ford brothers based on an idea by Tony Tenser (later announced as 'The Legend of Loch Ness') and scheduled for spring 1965.)

1965

'*Treasure Island*'
(Adaptation of the Robert Louis Stevenson epic.)

'*Sherlock Holmes and the Trunk Murders*'
(Sequel to *A Study in Terror*. John Neville and Donald Houston pencilled in to repeat their roles.)

'*The Gold Bug*'
(Adaptation of the Edgar Allan Poe yarn.)

'*The Meter Man*'
(Adaptation of a stage play written and directed by C. Scott Forbes, later filmed as *The Penthouse (1967)*.)

'*Veronica*'
(Sex comedy.)

'*Luna Park Horror*'
(A horror thriller to be filmed in 3D entirely on location at Blackpool's pleasure beach.)

'*The Legend of Loch Ness*'
(A revised version of the earlier project with George Pal producing and directing on a budget of £500,000. To be shot on 70mm, Compton claimed to have sunk £25,000 on pre-production before it was scrapped.)

'*You'll Hang My Love*'
(Contemporary thriller.)

1966

'*Beau Brigand*'
(A French Foreign Legion yarn starring Patrick Allen, Sarah Lawson and Peter Cushing.)

'*Embryo*'
(Scientist grows a woman entirely from an embryo. Eventually filmed in the US starring Rock Hudson and Barbara Carrera.)

'*The Headsman*'
(Murder mystery with supernatural overtones.)

'*The Outcast*'
(*Repulsion*-esque thriller with a sane girl who is wrongly locked up in a lunatic asylum.)

'*Way Station Outer Space*'
(Science Fiction space opera.)

'*The Devil's Discord*'
(From director Michael Reeves and producer Harry Fine. Later optioned by Tigon.)

'*Crescendo*'
(From a script by Michael Reeves and Alfred Shaughnessy with Christopher Lee penned in to star. Finally re-worked by Jimmy Sangster and filmed in 1969 by Hammer.)

'*Blood Moon*'
(Later renamed 'Flame in the Blood' - a horror film written by Michael Reeves.)

above:
This wonderful rare full page advertisement, originally published in the Friday 8th of October, 1971 issue of Today's Cinema (incorporating Kine Weekly) shows otherwise unused promotional artwork for **Doomwatch** and **Neither the Sea Nor the Sand**, in addition to announcing the proposed filming of George Shipway's book 'The Chilian Club'.

above:

This full page advertisement, featuring two unmade Tigon projects, was also published in the Friday 8th of October, 1971 issue of Today's Cinema (incorporating Kine Weekly). Today's Cinema was a bi-weekly magazine (published on Tuesday and Friday each week), which incorporated Kine Weekly from the 1st of October 1971. On the 20th of November 1971 it moved to a weekly publishing schedule and was re-named CinemaTV Today.

'Alice in Wonderland'
(Big budget musical with actors and puppets. Featuring the Bolshoi Ballet.)

'The Magnificent Spy'
(A female James Bond style spy thriller with swimming champion Mary Rand as the all action heroine.)

TIGON

1967

'The Devil's Discord'
(Follow up to *The Sorcerers* with Curtis co-producing and Michael Reeves directing.)

'Trog, One Million Year Man'
(Script by Tony Tenser, alternatively announced as 'The Missing Link', 'The Million Year Old Man' or 'Trog - Billion Year Man'. Finally filmed as *Trog (1970)* by Herman Cohen.)

1968

'The Amorous Trooper'
(Follow up to *Witchfinder General* from the novel by Ronald Bassett. Reeves was provisionally slated to direct.)

'O'Hooligan's Mob'
(British gangster story involving the IRA. Reeves pencilled in to direct. Alternatively announced as 'Hooligans Mob'.)

'He and She'
(Elkan Allan's follow up to *Love in Our Time*.)

'Veronica'
(Sex film. Revised version of earlier Compton project. Budgeted at £50,000 and intended as a support feature for *I, A Woman*.]

'The Gold Bug'
(Title lifted from the Edgar Allan Poe tale, previously announced as a Compton film now co-financed by AIP. Robert Fuest pencilled to direct Vincent Price in lead.)

1969

'Kinky Death'
(A murder thriller from a synopsis by Michael Armstrong.)

'The Maze'
(A thriller to be directed by Michael Armstrong.)

'The Cawnpore Massacre'
(A big budget version of the infamous Indian Mutiny incident, from a script by Stephen Weeks, later optioned by Amicus but never filmed.)

'Kill Me Kindly'
(Big budget thriller intended for either Joan Crawford or Bette Davis.)

'Treasure Island'
(Proposed co-production with Harry Alan Towers, later filmed without Tigon and starring Orson Welles.)

1970

'Fanny Hill'
(Adaptation of the Eighteenth Century novel by John Cleland. Continental sex star Anna Gael, who appeared in *Zeta One*, was pencilled in for the title role.)

'Bury Me in My Boots'
(Formerly a Hemdale project from the book by Sally Trench. To be directed by Mai Zetterling with a budget set at £150,000.)

'Ritual'
(A thriller to star David Warner.)

'Afore Night Comes'
(A Peter Medak thriller to star Peter McEnery filming was scheduled for July 1970.)

'Hey You!'
(A British road movie written by John Bown later optioned by EMI but never filmed.)

'The Devil's Discord'
(A revised version of the earlier project, this time slated to be directed by Patrick Curtis.)

1971

'The Hooligan'
(Crime thriller to be co-produced by Patrick Curtis.)

'The Chilian Club'
(Adaptation of the novel to be directed by Peter Collinson on a budget of £150,000.)

'Cold War in a Country Garden'
(£1m budget special effects spectacular.)

'The Last of the Mohicans'
(New version of the James Fenimore Cooper classic.)

1972

'Slag'
(To star Glenda Jackson and be directed by Douglas Hickox.)

'Doomwatch 2'
(A sequel from the same team who produced the original, itself a spin-off from the television series.)

'Infernal Idol'
(A co-production with Herman Cohen, later filmed by Cohen as *Craze (1973)*.)

'Glamour Incorporated'
(To be directed by Val Guest as a follow-up to the Tigon release *Au Pair Girls (1972)*, also directed by Guest.)

Bibliography

- (Recommended further reading)

Books

Arkoff, Sam with Richard Trubo: *Flying Through Hollywood By the Seat of My Pants* - Birch Lane Press, USA 1992

Beck, Calvin Thomas: *Scream Queens. Heroines of the Horrors* - MacMillan Publishing, USA, 1978

Boëgler, Michel: *Peter Cushing. The Golden Horror Star* - Vintage Monsters, France 1998

Bojarski, Richard and Kenneth Beals: *The Films of Boris Karloff* - Citadel, USA 1974

Boot, Andy: *Fragments of Fear. An Illustrated History of British Horror Films* - Creation Books, UK 1996

Bouyxou, Jean-Pierre: *Pamela Green. Glamorous Elegance* - Gerard Noel Faneditions, France 1997

Briggs, Robin: *Witches and Neighbours* - Harper and Collins, UK, 1996

Brosnan, John: *The Horror People* - MacDonald and Janes, UK 1976

Brown, Paul J.: *Everything But the Nipple. Valerie Leon: A Pictorial Celebration* - Midnight Media, UK 1995

Butler, Ivan: *The Cinema of Roman Polanski* - AS Barnes, UK 1970

Chibnall, Steve: *Making Mischief. The Cult Films of Pete Walker* - FAB Press, UK 1998

Crawley,Tony: *Bébé. The Films of Brigitte Bardot* - LSP, UK 1975

Dacre, Richard: *Trouble in Store: Norman Wisdom, a Career in Comedy* - T.C. Farries & Co. UK, 1991

Deneuve, Catherine and Patrick Modiano: *Elle s'appelait Françoise* - Canal+ Editions, France 1996

Dixon, Wheeler Winston: *The Films of Freddie Francis* - Scarecrow, USA 1991

Dors, Diana: *Behind Closed Dors* - WH Allen, UK 1979

Dors, Diana: *Dors By Diana* - Futura, UK 1981

Fenton, Harvey (ed.): *Flesh & Blood Compendium* - FAB Press, UK 2003

Fenton, Harvey & Flint, David (eds.): *Ten Years of Terror. British Horror Films of the 1970s* - FAB Press, UK 2001

Foster, Harry: *New Birkdale. The Growth of a Lancashire Seaside Suburb 1850-1912* - Alan Sutton Publishing, UK 1995

Frank, Alan: *Horror Films* - Hamlyn, UK 1977

Gifford, Denis: *A Pictorial History of Horror Movies* - Hamlyn, UK 1975

Greaves, Tim: *Linda Hayden, Above and Beyond* - One Shot, UK 1995

Greaves, Tim: *Yutte Stensgaard, A Pictorial Souvenir* - One Shot, UK 1994

Greaves, Tim: *Yutte Stensgaard, Memories of a Vampire* - One Shot, UK 1995

Hardy, Phil (ed.): *The Aurum Film Encyclopedia Volume 3: Horror* - Aurum, UK 1985

Hardy, Phil: *The Encyclopedia of Western Movies* - Octopus, UK 1984

Hutchings, Peter: *Hammer and Beyond. The British Horror Film* - Manchester University Press, UK 1993

Jaworzyn, Stefan: *Shock Xpress 1* - Titan, UK 1994

Jaworzyn, Stefan: *Shock. The Essential Guide to Exploitation Cinema* - Titan, UK 1996

Johnson, Tom and Deborah Del Vecchio: *Hammer Films. An Exhaustive Filmography* - McFarland, USA 1996

Johnson, Tom and Deborah Del Vecchio: *Peter Cushing. The Gentle Man of Horror and His 91 Films* - McFarland, USA 1992

Kennedy, Burt: *Hollywood Trail Boss* - Boulevard Books, USA 1997

Kiernan, Thomas: *Repulsion. The Life and Times of Roman Polanski* - New English Library, UK 1982

Leaming Barbara: *Polanski. His Life and Films* - Hamish Hamilton UK, 1982

Lee, Christopher: *Tall Dark and Gruesome* - WH Allen, UK 1977

Lenne, Gérard: *Cela s'appelle l'horror. le cinéma fantastique anglais, 1955-1976* - France, Librairie Séguier, 1989

McFarlane, Brian: *An Autobiography of British Cinema* - Methuen, UK 1997

McGillivray, David: *Doing Rude Things* - Sun Tavern Fields, UK 1992

Meikle, Denis: *History of Horrors. The Rise and Fall of the House of Hammer* - Scarecrow, USA 1996

Miller, David: *The Peter Cushing Companion* - Reynolds and Hearn, UK 2000

Miller, Mark A.: *Christopher Lee and Peter Cushing and Horror Cinema. A Filmography of Their 22 Collaborations* - McFarland, USA 1994

Morley, Sheridan: *The Great Stage Stars* - Angus & Robertson, UK 1986

Murphy, Robert: *Sixties British Cinema* - BFI, UK 1992

Murray, John B.: *The Remarkable Michael Reeves* - Midnight Marquee Press, USA 2004

Neuhoff, Eric: *Catherine Deneuve* - Solar, France 1980

Newman, Kim: *Nightmare Movies* - Bloomsbury, UK 1988

Newman, Kim: *Wild West Movies* - Bloomsbury, UK 1990

Nollen, Scott Allen: *Boris Karloff. A Gentleman's Life* - Midnight Marquee Press, USA 1999

Paland, Jean-Marc: *Raquel Welch* - Artefact, France 1985

Pirie, David: *A Heritage of Horror. The English Gothic Cinema 1946-1972* - Gordon Fraser, UK 1973

Pohle, Robert W. Jr. and Douglas C. Hart: *Sherlock Holmes on the Screen* - AS Barnes & Co., USA 1977

Pohle, Robert W. Jr. and Douglas C. Hart: *The Films Of Christopher Lee* - Scarecrow, USA 1982

Polanski, Roman: *Roman By Polanski* - Heinemann, UK 1984

Price, Victoria: *Vincent Price. A Daughter's Biography* - St Martins Press, USA 1999.

Reid, Beryl: *So Much Love* - Hutchison & Co, UK 1984

Rigby, Jonathan: *English Gothic. A Century of Horror Cinema* - Reynolds and Hearn, UK 2000

Rigby, Jonathan: *Christopher Lee. The Authorised Screen History* - Reynolds and Hearn, UK 2001

Sachs, Bruce and Russell Wall: *Greasepaint and Gore. The Hammer Monsters of Roy Ashton* - Tomahawk Press, UK 1998

Svehla, Gary J. and Susan Svehla: *Vincent Price* - Midnight Marquee Press Inc, USA 1998

Trevelyan, John: *What the Censor Saw* - Michael Joseph Ltd., UK 1973

Vanderbeets, Richard: *George Sanders. An Exhausted Life* - Madison Books, USA 1990

Walker, Alexander: *Hollywood U.K. The British Film Industry in the Sixties* - Harrap, UK 1974

Walker, Alexander: *National Heroes. British Cinema in the Seventies and Eighties* - Harrap, UK 1985

Weinreb, Ben and Christopher Hibbert (eds.): *The London Encyclopedia* - Papermac, UK 1987

Williams, Lucy Chase: *The Complete Films of Vincent Price* - Citadel, USA 1995

Wilson, Colin and Robin Odell: *Jack the Ripper. Summing Up and Verdict* - Transworld Publishing, UK 1987

Wisdom, Norman: *Don't Laugh At Me* - Century Random House, UK 1992

Wright, Bruce Lanier: *Nightwalkers. Gothic Horror Movies: The Modern Era* - Taylor Publishing Co., USA 1995

Yule, Andrew: *Hollywood a Go-Go. An Account of the Cannon Phenomenon* - Sphere Books, UK 1987

Unpublished manuscript

Crowther, Andrew: *WS Gilbert. The World Turned Right Side Up*

Magazines and Periodicals

The following magazines or journals all contain articles or interviews relating specifically to the films produced by Tony Tenser or generally on British Films of the Sixties and Seventies:

Cinefantastique
Cinema X
CinemaTV Today
Classic Images
Club International
Continental Film Review
Daily Cinema, The
Darkside, The
Epi-Log
Fangoria
Fantasynopsis
Femme Fatales
Film Review
Films and Filming
Flesh & Blood
Hammer Horror
Imagi-Movies
Kine Weekly
Little Shoppe of Horrors
Mayfair
Monthly Film Bulletin
Parade
Photon
Photoplay
Premiere
Psychotronic Video
Rue Morgue
Samhain
Scarlet Street
Screen International
Sheila Keith File, The
Shivers
Shock Cinema
Starburst
Take
Variety
Video Watchdog
World of Horror
Zeta

Index

Index compiled by Francis Brewster

Page references in **bold** refer exclusively to illustrations, though pages referenced as text entries may also feature relevant illustrations.

Quality Books For Cult Connoisseurs from FAB Press

Beyond Terror
ISBN 0-9529260-6-7

Profondo Argento
ISBN 1-903254-23-X

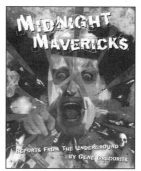

Midnight Mavericks
ISBN 1-903254-34-5

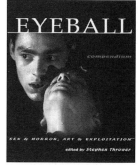

Eyeball Compendium
ISBN 1-903254-17-5

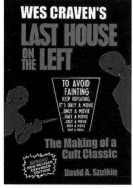

Last House on the Left
ISBN 1-903254-01-9

Book of the Dead
ISBN 1-903254-33-7

Iron Man
ISBN 1-903254-36-1

Agitator
ISBN 1-903254-21-3

Abel Ferrara
ISBN 1-903254-13-2

DVD Delirium vol.1
ISBN 1-903254-04-3

DVD Delirium vol.2
ISBN 1-903254-25-6

Motion Picture Purgatory
ISBN 1-903254-30-2

Donald Cammell
ISBN 1-903254-29-9

Shock! Horror!
ISBN 1-903254-32-9

The Gospel of Filth
ISBN 1-903254-38-8

Flesh & Blood
ISBN 1-903254-10-8

For further information about these books visit our online store, where we also have a fine selection of exploitation movie merchandise from all over the world!

www.fabpress.com